THE RIGHT TO DIE

A Two-Volume Anthology of Scholarly Articles

Series Editors

MELVIN I. UROFSKY
Virginia Commonwealth University

PHILIP E. UROFSKY
Washington, DC

A GARLAND SERIES

SERIES CONTENTS

VOLUME

1

DEFINITIONS AND MORAL PERSPECTIVES

DEATH, EUTHANASIA, SUICIDE, AND LIVING WILLS

Edited with introductions by

MELVIN I. UROFSKY
Virginia Commonwealth University

PHILIP E. UROFSKY
Washington, DC

GARLAND PUBLISHING, INC.
New York & London
1996

Library of Congress Cataloging-in-Publication Data

The right to die : a two-volume anthology of scholarly articles /
   edited with introductions by Melvin I. Urofsky and Philip E.
   Urofsky.
        p.   cm.
   Includes bibliographical references (p.   ).
   Contents: v. 1. Definitions and moral perspectives : death,
euthanasia, suicide, and living wills — v. 2. Who decides?
issues and case studies
   ISBN 0-8153-2208-9 (alk. paper)
   1. Right to die—Law and legislation—United States.
2. Euthanasia—United States.   3. Assisted suicide—United
States.   4. Right to die—Moral and ethical aspects.   5. Euthanasia—Moral and ethical aspects.   6. Assisted suicide—Moral and
ethical aspects.   I. Urofsky, Melvin I.   II. Urofsky, Philip E.
KF3827.E87R539   1996
344.73'04197—dc20
[347.3044197]   95-35829
                                                                      CIP

Printed on acid-free, 250-year-life paper
Manufactured in the United States of America

For Mimi Netter and
In memory of Howard Netter

Who taught us all a great deal
about life and death,
and especially love

CONTENTS

VOLUME 2

INTRODUCTION

Twenty years ago this collection would have been inconceivable, for a number of reasons. First of all, medical technology had not yet entered the breakthrough period in which it would be possible to keep people alive, seemingly indefinitely, using machines. Wonder drugs, heart transplants, arthroscopic surgery, kidney dialysis, and many other things now taken for granted were either in an experimental stage or had not yet been conceived. Serious accidents, advancing age, and disease caused death; doctors could do little to prevent it.

Many have benefited from new medicines and techniques, so that people who otherwise would have died young can now hope to live longer and more productive lives. Along with the benefits, however, there is a down side. Patients suffering from terminal injuries or illnesses or just the ravages of age can now be kept alive artificially. Many have lost consciousness or their mental facilities and are not functional or independent, but life-support systems or medication can keep their bodies going. Even when brain functions cease, machines can keep blood pumping through their bodies. At the other end of the spectrum, seriously deformed infants who would normally have died within hours or days can now be "saved," kept alive, although little can be done to repair physical defects or mental retardation.

To some people life—any life—is so precious that it should be saved or prolonged at all costs. Their beliefs are grounded in a reality that *demands* that life be saved. Life, they argue, is a gift—one that God gives and that, therefore, only God can take away. Theirs is a view that stretches back to the beginnings of organized religion.

There are other views, also with roots in antiquity, that are directed to the issue of the *quality* of life. This school believes that if the quality of life is so drastically and irrevocably deteriorated as to make life unbearable—because of illness, injury, or simply old age—then death is preferable. The Roman philosopher Seneca aptly summed up this belief when he wrote: "If I know that I must suffer without hope of relief I will depart not through fear of the pain itself but because it prevents all for which I would live."

The chasm between the two groups is often unbridgeable because each operates on a different assumption. When a philosophic debate becomes a question of public policy, the law becomes involved. The essays gathered here deal only tangentially with the moral debate; they are primarily concerned with legal questions connected to what has been termed "the right to die."

Law, as many first-year law students learn (often to their shock), is not the same as morality. In the best of all worlds, perhaps, secular law would parallel religious morality. Law, however, is concerned with the ordering of society, with providing rules that the majority of the population can live with, and with setting up boundaries of acceptable and unacceptable behavior. As conditions change and popular beliefs alter, the law must do the same or else law will become a straitjacket binding society.

The legal roots of the right-to-die issue are embedded in the common law, and, as early as the latter part of the nineteenth century, we can find American cases upholding a competent individual's right to refuse treatment, even if in so doing the person might die. The common law values personal autonomy.

The issue first caught widespread public attention with the 1975 case of Karen Ann Quinlan, a vivacious twenty-one-year-old woman who fell into a coma after what may have been a drug overdose. Karen never regained consciousness, and her parents, whose requests to terminate their daughter's life support were denied by the hospital, went to court to seek permission to discontinue life support. Fifteen years later, in a case involving another young woman, Nancy Beth Cruzon, the Supreme Court of the United States determined that there is a *constitutional* right to die, although that right may be partially limited by the state's interests in preserving life.

Today the debate continues on a number of fronts. A referendum allowing doctors to assist in suicide was proposed in several states. As the costs of health care spiral, discussions continue in both government and the private sector over how much society should spend to keep the elderly and the terminally ill alive. Although the law assumes that parents should control the medical care of their children, groups opposed to abortion have entered the fray in regard to who determines the level of care for newborns suffering from severe physical disabilities or mental retardation.

The key issue, which is explored in all of these articles, is *Who decides?* The law specifies that, in some circumstances, an individual may choose for himself or herself whether to live or die. Other circumstances, however, may require that a guardian assist in this decision. The legislature may also enact statutes permitting, or forbidding, doctors to assist their patients to die. If nothing else, the case of Dr. Jack Kevorkian has made all of us—private citizens as well as judges and legislators—think about what we as a society are prepared to do in regard to terminally ill patients.

These articles are not the last word on the subject, because the debate changes with every new medical advance and every change in the political climate. But the core question will continue to be the same: *Who decides?* That is what law is always about.

PART 1

DEFINING DEATH

Before discussing an individual's right to die, especially when that right is to be exercised for a comatose patient by others, it is important to define death itself. Until recently, the accepted medical and legal definition of death depended upon observable and clearly understood criteria that were accepted by society at large. Thus, although doctors were required to "declare" death and to sign the death certificate, the basis on which they did so—the cessation of spontaneous respiration and circulation—the person had stopped breathing and his heart had stopped pumping—was beyond dispute. Legal disputes focused not on the definition of death but on the time of death, an issue important mostly in homicides and inheritance disputes.

The development of machines that could keep a patient breathing and his heart pumping, together with the discovery of medicines and treatments that could cure previously mortal diseases, complicated the issue considerably. Although modern medicine now saved many lives that might otherwise have been lost, it also succeeded in prolonging the apparent life of those with no realistic hope of regaining consciousness. In response, doctors began to develop new definitions of death, often focusing on the absence of discernable brain activity. Now, instead of simply declaring the patient dead because she had stopped breathing and bleeding, the physician needed to take the affirmative step of turning off the machines, thus, to others' eyes, "killing" the patient by stopping her vital signs. In other cases, a patient might have lost all higher brain functions but still be breathing on his own—the so-called permanent vegetative state or irreversible coma. Were doctors required to maintain the "brain dead" body until it wore out or could they declare death based on the absence of higher brain activity?

As the medical community struggled to apply the old definition of death to these new circumstances, modern medicine complicated the task in another way. New techniques arose that enabled organs, including over time the heart, the liver, the kidneys, and the lungs, to be transplanted from one person to another. Obviously, except in extraordinary circumstances when a living person could donate a redundant organ, the organ to be transplanted had to be "harvested" from a recently dead body. Thus, doctors, perceived by themselves and by the public as the sustainers of life, now also were placed in the rather ghoulish position of waiting for the death of one person so that they might save the life of another.

This state of affairs created a situation in which the legal definition of death, tied to the traditional "vital signs", lagged behind the emerging medical definition based on the absence of higher brain activity, subjecting doctors to potential civil and criminal liability as they tried to navigate among the definitions. In 1968, the Harvard Medical School convened an Ad hoc Committee of the Harvard Medical School to Examine the Definition of Brain Death ("A Definition of Irreversible Coma"), made up of ten doctors, one lawyer, one theologian, and one philosopher. The Committee recommended that "irreversible coma," as measured by recognized medical standards, be adopted as a new criterion for death. The Committee justified the new definition on two grounds: (1) the burden on patients, their families, and hospitals of maintaining a patient whose heart continued to beat but whose brain was irreversibly damaged, and (2) the difficulty in obtaining organs for transplant in situations in which the "obsolete criteria for the definition of death" prevented the declaration of death of a person with no discernable central nervous activity. Of great significance for the debate on the right to die, the Harvard Committee emphatically declared that death was a purely medical determination that was solely within the purview of the attending physician. Thus, in determining whether a patient in an irreversible coma had died (and thus determining whether to shut off the life-support machines), the physician was not under obligation to consult with or to obtain the consent of the patient's family.

The Harvard Committee's definition stimulated the public and legal debate over who should define death and what standards should be used. Alexander Morgan Capron and Leon Kass ("A Statutory Definition of the Standards for Determining Human Death: An Appraisal and a Proposal") describe and join in this debate. They argue that the public is not willing to accept a definition crafted by the medical community, especially when the attending physician may be subject to a conflict of interest due to the need for transplant organs. To be generally accepted and enforceable, any new definition must be enacted by the people's representatives, the legislatures. Capron and Kass argue, however, that a legislatively enacted definition should set only general physiological standards, leaving it to generally accepted medical practices, as they exist at any particular time, to determine whether a patient has "died." Therefore, the legislature should decide, for instance, whether "brain death" as opposed to lack of vital signs is the appropriate definition of death but allow the medical profession to determine the most appropriate method of evaluating the presence or absence of vital signs or brain activity.

The debate over the definition of death continued throughout the 1970s. With increasing frequency, the issue of defining death was played out in the newspapers, the courts, and the legislatures. Although the debate continues, the President's Commission for the Study of Ethical Problems in Medicine and Biomedical and Behavioral Research ("The 'State of the Art' in Medicine" and "Who Ought to 'Redefine' Death?") summarized the emerging consensus in its 1981 report on "Defining Death." Reviewing the "state of the art" in medicine, the Commission recommended that death be determined by reviewing brain function. The Commission concluded that appropriately trained medical professionals, aided by state-of-the-art technology, have the ability to determine whether, in most cases, brain function (as opposed to mere cell activity) has ceased and is likely to restart. The Commission, however, argued that the new definition could not be imposed by judicial or medical fiat and had to be built on a public consensus. Thus, in contradiction to the Harvard Committee, the President's Commission advocated that the state legislatures, informed by public, medical, academic, and religious opinion, adopt a uniform definition.

As noted by Capron and Kass, the definition of death is only the beginning of the debate over the right to die. Both they and the Harvard Committee argue, in essence, that "death is death," and that once death has occurred, whether by traditional or modern measures, there should be no question but that life support should be terminated. Declaring that a patient is dead and thus terminating useless and wasteful treatment, they argue, is a separate issue from permitting a living patient to die by terminating the same treatment. The line, of course, is not always that clear, especially with comatose patients. These issues will be discussed in later parts.

Special Communication

A Definition of
Irreversible Coma

Report of the Ad Hoc Committee of the Harvard Medical School
to Examine the Definition of Brain Death

Our primary purpose is to define irreversible coma as a new criterion for death. There are two reasons why there is need for a definition: (1) Improvements in resuscitative and supportive measures have led to increased efforts to save those who are desperately injured. Sometimes these efforts have only partial success so that the result is an individual whose heart continues to beat but whose brain is irreversibly damaged. The burden is great on patients who suffer permanent loss of intellect, on their families, on the hospitals, and on those in need of hospital beds already occupied by these comatose patients. (2) Obsolete criteria for the definition of death can lead to controversy in obtaining organs for transplantation.

Irreversible coma has many causes, but *we are concerned here only with those comatose individuals who have no discernible central nervous system activity.* If the characteristics can be defined in satisfactory terms, translatable into action—and we believe this is possible—then several problems will either disappear or will become more readily soluble.

More than medical problems are present. There are moral, ethical, religious, and legal issues. Adequate definition here will prepare the way for better insight into all of these matters as well as for better law than is currently applicable.

The Ad Hoc Committee includes Henry K. Beecher, MD, *chairman;* Raymond D. Adams, MD; A. Clifford Barger, MD; William J. Curran, LLM, SMHyg; Derek Denny-Brown, MD; Dana L. Farnsworth, MD; Jordi Folch-Pi, MD; Everett I. Mendelsohn, PhD; John P. Merrill, MD; Joseph Murray, MD; Ralph Potter, ThD; Robert Schwab, MD; and William Sweet, MD.

Reprint requests to Massachusetts General Hospital, Boston 02114 (Dr. Henry K. Beecher).

Characteristics of Irreversible Coma

An organ, brain or other, that no longer functions and has no possibility of functioning again is for all practical purposes dead. Our first problem is to determine the characteristics of a *permanently* nonfunctioning brain.

A patient in this state appears to be in deep coma. The condition can be satisfactorily diagnosed by points 1, 2, and 3 to follow. The electroencephalogram (point 4) provides confirmatory data, and when available it should be utilized. In situations where for one reason or another electroencephalographic montioring is not available, the absence of cerebral function has to be determined by purely clinical signs, to be described, or by absence of circulation as judged by standstill of blood in the retinal vessels, or by absence of cardiac activity.

1. *Unreceptivity and Unresponsitivity.*—There is a total unawareness to externally applied stimuli and inner need and complete unresponsiveness—our definition of irreversible coma. Even the most intensely painful stimuli evoke no vocal or other response, not even a groan, withdrawal of a limb, or quickening of respiration.

2. *No Movements or Breathing.*—Observations covering a period of at least one hour by physicians is adequate to satisfy the criteria of no spontaneous muscular movements or spontaneous respiration or response to stimuli such as pain, touch, sound, or light. After the patient is on a mechanical respirator, the total absence of spontaneous breathing may be established by turning off the respirator for three minutes and observing whether there is any effort on the part of the subject to breathe

spontaneously. (The respirator may be turned off for this time provided that at the start of the trial period the patient's carbon dioxide tension is within the normal range, and provided also that the patient had been breathing room air for at least 10 minutes prior to the trial.)

3. *No reflexes.*—Irreversible coma with abolition of central nervous system activity is evidenced in part by the absence of elicitable reflexes. The pupil will be fixed and dilated and will not respond to a direct source of bright light. Since the establishment of a fixed, dilated pupil is clear-cut in clinical practice, there should be no uncertainty as to its presence. Ocular movement (to head turning and to irrigation of the ears with ice water) and blinking are absent. There is no evidence of postural activity (decerebrate or other). Swallowing, yawning, vocalization are in abeyance. Corneal and pharyngeal reflexes are absent.

As a rule the stretch of tendon reflexes cannot be elicited; ie, tapping the tendons of the biceps, triceps, and pronator muscles, quadriceps and gastrocnemius muscles with the reflex hammer elicits no contraction of the respective muscles. Plantar or noxious stimulation gives no response.

4. *Flat Electroencephalogram.*—Of great confirmatory value is the flat or isoelectric EEG. We must assume that the electrodes have been properly applied, that the apparatus is functioning normally, and that the personnel in charge is competent. We consider it prudent to have one channel of the apparatus used for an electrocardiogram. This channel will monitor the ECG so that, if it appears in the electroencephalographic leads because of high resistance, it can be readily identified. It also establishes the presence of the active heart in the absence of the EEG. We recommend that another channel be used for a noncephalic lead. This will pick up space-borne or vibration-borne artifacts and identify them. The simplest form of such a monitoring noncephalic electrode has two leads over the dorsum of the hand, preferably the right hand, so the ECG will be minimal or absent. Since one of the requirements of this state is that there be no muscle activity, these two dorsal hand electrodes will not be bothered by muscle artifact. The apparatus should be run at standard gains $10\mu v/$ mm, $50\mu v/5$ mm. Also it should be isoelectric at double this standard gain which is $5\mu v/mm$ or $25\mu v/5$ mm. At least ten full minutes of recording are desirable, but twice that would be better.

It is also suggested that the gains at some point be opened to their full amplitude for a brief period (5 to 100 seconds) to see what is going on. Usually in an intensive care unit artifacts will dominate the picture, but these are readily identifiable. There shall be no electroencephalographic response to noise or to pinch.

All of the above tests shall be repeated at least 24 hours later with no change.

The validity of such data as indications of irreversible cerebral damage depends on the exclusion of two conditions: hypothermia (temperature below 90 F [32.2 C] or central nervous system depressants, such as barbiturates.

Other Procedures

The patient's condition can be determined only by a physician. When the patient is hopelessly damaged as defined above, the family and all colleagues who have participated in major decisions concerning the patient, and all nurses involved, should be so informed. Death is to be declared and *then* the respirator turned off. The decision to do this and the responsibility for it are to be taken by the physician-in-charge, in consultation with one or more physicians who have been directly involved in the case. It is unsound and undesirable to force the family to make the decision.

Legal Commentary

The legal system of the United States is greatly in need of the kind of analysis and recommendations for medical procedures in cases of irreversible brain damage as described. At present, the law of the United States, in all 50 states and in the federal courts, treats the question of human death as a question of fact to be decided in every case. When any doubt exists, the courts seek medical expert testimony concerning the time of death of the particular individual involved. However, the law makes the assumption that the medical criteria for determining death are settled and not in doubt among physicians. Furthermore, the law assumes that the traditional method among physicians for determination of death is to ascertain the absence of all vital signs. To this extent, *Black's Law Dictionary* (fourth edition, 1951) defines death as

The cessation of life; the ceasing to exist; *defined by physicians* as a total stoppage of the circulation of the blood, and a cessation of the animal and vital functions consequent thereupon, such as respiration, pulsation, etc [italics added].

In the few modern court decisions involving a definition of death, the courts have used the concept of the total cessation of all vital signs. Two cases are worthy of examination. Both involved the issue of which one of two persons died first.

In *Thomas vs Anderson*, (96 Cal App 2d 371, 211 P 2d 478) a California District Court of Appeal in 1950 said, "In the instant case the question as to which of the two men died first was a question of fact for the determination of the trial court . . ."

The appellate court cited and quoted in full the definition of death from *Black's Law Dictionary* and concluded, ". . . death occurs precisely when life ceases and does not occur until the heart stops beating and respiration ends. Death is not a continuous event and is an event that takes place at a precise time."

The other case is *Smith vs Smith* (229 Ark, 579, 317 SW 2d 275) decided in 1958 by the Supreme Court of Arkansas. In this case the two people were husband and wife involved in an auto accident.

6

The husband was found dead at the scene of the accident. The wife was taken to the hospital unconscious. It is alleged that she "remained in coma due to brain injury" and died at the hospital 17 days later. The petitioner in court tried to argue that the two people died simultaneously. The judge writing the opinion said the petition contained a "quite unusual and unique allegation." It was quoted as follows:

That the said Hugh Smith and his wife, Lucy Coleman Smith, were in an automobile accident on the 19th day of April, 1957, said accident being instantly fatal to each of them at the same time, although the doctors maintained a vain hope of survival and made every effort to revive and resuscitate said Lucy Coleman Smith until May 6th, 1957, when it was finally determined by the attending physicians that their hope of resuscitation and possible restoration of human life to the said Lucy Coleman Smith was entirely vain, and

That as a matter of modern medical science, your petitioner alleges and states, and will offer the Court competent proof that the said Hugh Smith, deceased, and said Lucy Coleman Smith, deceased, lost their power to will at the same instant, and that their demise as earthly human beings occurred at the same time in said automobile accident, neither of them ever regaining any consciousness whatsoever.

The court dismissed the petition as a *matter of law.* The court quoted *Black's* definition of death and concluded,

Admittedly, this condition did not exist, and as a matter of fact, it would be too much of a strain of credulity for us to believe any evidence offered to the effect that Mrs. Smith was dead, scientifically or otherwise, unless the conditions set out in the definition existed.

Later in the opinion the court said, "Likewise, we take judicial notice that one breathing, though unconscious, is not dead."

"Judicial notice" of this definition of death means that the court did not consider that definition open to serious controversy; it considered the question as settled in responsible scientific and medical circles. The judge thus makes proof of uncontroverted facts unnecessary so as to prevent prolonging the trial with unnecessary proof and also to prevent fraud being committed upon the court by quasi "scientists" being called into court to controvert settled scientific principles at a price. Here, the Arkansas Supreme Court considered the definition of death to be a settled, scientific, biological fact. It refused to consider the plaintiff's offer of evidence that "modern medical science" might say otherwise. In simplified form, the above is the state of the law in the United States concerning the definition of death.

In this report, however, we suggest that responsible medical opinion is ready to adopt new criteria for pronouncing death to have occurred in an individual sustaining irreversible coma as a result of permanent brain damage. If this position is adopted by the medical community, it can form the basis for change in the current legal concept of death. No statutory change in the law should be necessary since the law treats this question essentially as one

of fact to be determined by physicians. The only circumstance in which it would be necessary that legislation be offered in the various states to define "death" by law would be in the event that great controversy were engendered surrounding the subject and physicians were unable to agree on the new medical criteria.

It is recommended as a part of these procedures that judgment of the existence of these criteria is solely a medical issue. It is suggested that the physician in charge of the patient consult with one or more other physicians directly involved in the case before the patient is declared dead on the basis of these criteria. In this way, the responsibility is shared over a wider range of medical opinion, thus providing an important degree of protection against later questions which might be raised about the particular case. It is further suggested that the decision to declare the person dead, and then to turn off the respirator, be made by physicians not involved in any later effort to transplant organs or tissue from the deceased individual. This is advisable in order to avoid any appearance of self-interest by the physicians involved.

It should be emphasized that we recommend the patient be declared dead before any effort is made to take him off a respirator, if he is then on a respirator. This declaration should not be delayed until he has been taken off the respirator and all artificially stimulated signs have ceased. The reason for this recommendation is that in our judgment it will provide a greater degree of legal protection to those involved. Otherwise, the physicians would be turning off the respirator on a person who is, under the present strict, technical application of law, still alive.

Comment

Irreversible coma can have various causes: cardiac arrest; asphyxia with respiratory arrest; massive brain damage; intracranial lesions, neoplastic or vascular. It can be produced by other encephalopathic states such as the metabolic derangements associated, for example, with uremia. Respiratory failure and impaired circulation underlie all of these conditions. They result in hypoxia and ischemia of the brain.

From ancient times down to the recent past it was clear that, when the respiration and heart stopped, the brain would die in a few minutes; so the obvious criterion of no heart beat as synonymous with death was sufficiently accurate. In those times the heart was considered to be the central organ of the body; it is not surprising that its failure marked the onset of death. This is no longer valid when modern resuscitative and supportive measures are used. These improved activities can now restore "life" as judged by the ancient standards of persistent respiration and continuing heart beat. This can be the case even when there is not the remotest possibility of an individual recovering consciousness following massive brain damage. In

7

other situations "life" can be maintained only by means of artificial respiration and electrical stimulation of the heart beat, or in temporarily by-passing the heart, or, in conjunction with these things, reducing with cold the body's oxygen requirement.

In an address, "The Prolongation of Life," (1957),[1] Pope Pius XII raised many questions; some conclusions stand out: (1) In a deeply unconscious individual vital functions may be maintained over a prolonged period only by extraordinary means. Verification of the moment of death can be determined, if at all, only by a physician. Some have suggested that the moment of death is the moment when irreparable and overwhelming brain damage occurs. Pius XII acknowledged that it is not "within the competence of the Church" to determine this. (2) It is incumbent on the physician to take all reasonable, ordinary means of restoring the spontaneous vital functions and consciousness, and to employ such extraordinary means as are available to him to this end. It is not obligatory, however, to continue to use extraordinary means indefinitely in hopeless cases. "But normally one is held to use only ordinary means—according to circumstances of persons, places, times, and cultures—that is to say, means that do not involve any grave burden for oneself or another." It is the church's view that a time comes when resuscitative efforts should stop and death be unopposed.

Summary

The neurological impairment to which the terms "brain death syndrome" and "irreversible coma" have become attached indicates diffuse disease. Function is abolished at cerebral, brain-stem, and often spinal levels. This should be evident in all cases from clinical examination alone. Cerebral, cortical, and thalamic involvement are indicated by a complete absence of receptivity of all forms of sensory stimulation and a lack of response to stimuli and to inner need. The term "coma" is used to designate this state of unreceptivity and unresponsitivity. But there is always coincident paralysis of brain-stem and basal ganglionic mechanisms as manifested by an abolition of all postural reflexes, including induced decerebrate postures; a complete paralysis of respiration; widely dilated, fixed pupils; paralysis of ocular movements; swallowing; phonation; face and tongue muscles. Involvement of spinal cord, which is less constant, is reflected usually in loss of tendon reflex and all flexor withdrawal or nocifensive reflexes. Of the brain-stem-spinal mechanisms which are conserved for a time, the vasomotor reflexes are the most persistent, and they are responsible in part for the paradoxical state of retained cardiovascular function, which is to some extent independent of nervous control, in the face of widespread disorder of cerebrum, brain stem, and spinal cord.

Neurological assessment gains in reliability if the aforementioned neurological signs persist over a period of time, with the additional safeguards that there is no accompanying hypothermia or evidence of drug intoxication. If either of the latter two conditions exist, interpretation of the neurological state should await the return of body temperature to normal level and elimination of the intoxicating agent. Under any other circumstances, repeated examinations over a period of 24 hours or longer should be required in order to obtain evidence of the irreversibility of the condition.

Reference

1. Pius XII: The Prolongation of Life, *Pope Speaks* 4:393-398 (No. 4) 1958.

8

A STATUTORY DEFINITION OF THE STANDARDS FOR DETERMINING HUMAN DEATH: AN APPRAISAL AND A PROPOSAL*

Alexander Morgan Capron†
Leon R. Kass‡

In recent years, there has been much discussion of the need to refine and update the criteria for determining that a human being has died.[1] In light of medicine's increasing ability to maintain certain signs of life artificially[2] and to make good use of organs from newly dead

* This Article grew out of discussions held by the Research Group (formerly Task Force) on Death and Dying of the Institute of Society, Ethics and the Life Sciences, a nonprofit organization engaged in interdisciplinary analysis of the issues generated by biomedical advances. The Research Group has been investigating various practical and philosophical problems in the "meaning" of death and the care of dying patients. Earlier drafts of the Article were discussed at meetings of the Research Group, and, although not the subject of formal approval by the group, the Article reflects the conclusions of the Research Group's members, who include Henry K. Beecher, M.D., Harvard University; Eric Cassell, M.D., Cornell University Medical College; Daniel Callahan, Ph.D., Institute of Society, Ethics and the Life Sciences; Renée C. Fox, Ph.D., University of Pennsylvania; Michael Horowitz, LL.B., New York, N.Y.; Hans Jonas, Ph.D., New School for Social Research; Irving Ladimer, S.J.D., American Arbitration Association; Marc Lappé, Ph.D., Institute of Society, Ethics and the Life Sciences; Robert Jay Lifton, M.D., Yale University; William F. May, Ph.D., Indiana University; Robert S. Morison, M.D., Cornell University; Paul Ramsey, Ph.D., Princeton University; Elisabeth Kübler-Ross, M.D., Chicago, Ill.; Alfred Sadler, M.D., Yale University; Blair Sadler, J.D., Yale University; Jane Schick, Ph.D., M.D., Cornell University Medical College; Robert Stevenson, Ph.D., Bionetics, Inc., Frederick, Md.; Robert Veatch, Ph.D., Institute of Society, Ethics and the Life Sciences. The work of the Research Group has been supported in part by a grant from the New York Foundation. The authors thank the members of the Research Group for their valuable suggestions and critical review of the manuscript and Sharmon Sollito, B.A., Institute of Society, Ethics and the Life Sciences, for her assistance in research.

† Assistant Professor of Law, University of Pennsylvania. B.A. 1966, Swarthmore College; LL.B. 1969, Yale University. Member, District of Columbia Bar.

‡ Executive Secretary, Committee on the Life Sciences and Social Policy, National Research Council—National Academy of Sciences. B.S. 1958, University of Chicago; M.D. 1962, University of Chicago; Ph.D. 1967, Harvard University.

[1] See, e.g., P. Ramsey, The Patient as Person 59-112 (1970); Louisell, *Transplantation: Existing Legal Constraints*, in Ethics in Medical Progress: With Special Reference to Transplantation 91-92 (G. Wolstenholme & M. O'Connor eds. 1966) [hereinafter cited as Medical Progress]; *Discussion* of Murray, *Organ Transplantation: The Practical Possibilities*, in id. 68 (comments of Dr. G. E. Schreiner), 71 (comments of Dr. M. F. A. Woodruff); Wasmuth & Stewart, *Medical and Legal Aspects of Human Organ Transplantation*, 14 Clev.-Mar. L. Rev. 442 (1965); Beecher, *Ethical Problems Created by the Hopelessly Unconscious Patient*, 278 New Eng. J. Med. 1425 (1968); Wasmuth, *The Concept of Death*, 30 Ohio St. L.J. 32 (1969); Note, *The Need for a Redefinition of "Death,"* 45 Chi.-Kent L. Rev. 202 (1969).

[2] A dramatic increase over the past twenty years in the use of extraordinary means of support such as artificial respirators for terminal patients is generally assumed by physicians, on the basis of observational and anecdotal evidence, but no quantitative studies of this phenomenon have been done. Telephone Interview with Dr. Claude L'Enfant, Director, Division of Lung Diseases, National Heart and Lung Institute, Bethesda, Md., Oct. 16, 1972. For this reason it is not possible to offer any detailed estimate of the impact that the proposed statute, *see* text accompanying note 86 *infra*, would have on the resources allocated to patient care.

9

bodies, new criteria of death have been proposed by medical authorities.[3] Several states have enacted or are considering legislation to establish a statutory "definition of death,"[4] at the prompting of some members of the medical profession who apparently feel that existing, judicially-framed standards might expose physicians, particularly transplant surgeons, to civil or criminal liability.[5] Although the leading statute in this area[6] appears to create more problems than it resolves,[7] some legislation may be needed for the protection of the public as well as the medical profession, and, in any event, many more states will probably be enacting such statutes in the near future.[8]

[3] *See, e.g.,* Ad Hoc Committee of the Harvard Medical School to Examine the Definition of Brain Death, *A Definition of Irreversible Coma,* 205 J.A.M.A. 337 (1968) [hereinafter cited as *Irreversible Coma*]; *Discussion* of Murray, *Organ Transplantation: The Practical Possibilities,* in MEDICAL PROGRESS, *supra* note 1, at 69-74 (remarks of Drs. G. P. J. Alexandre, R. Y. Calne, J. Hamburger, J. E. Murray, J. P. Revillard & G. E. Schreiner); *When Is a Patient Dead?,* 204 J.A.M.A. 1000 (1968) (editorial); *Updating the Definition of Death,* MED. WORLD NEWS, Apr. 28, 1967, at 47.

In an earlier article, our Research Group appraised the proposed new medical criteria for the determination of death and discussed some of the sources of public concern. Task Force on Death and Dying, Institute of Society, Ethics and the Life Sciences, *Refinements in Criteria for the Determination of Death: An Appraisal,* 221 J.A.M.A. 48 (1972) [hereinafter cited as *Refinements in Criteria*]. In discussing the procedures used to establish the new criteria, the article concluded:

> Clearly, these matters of decisionmaking and the role of law need further and widespread discussion. The acceptability of any new concept or criteria of death will depend at least as much on the acceptability of the procedure by which they are adopted as on their actual content.

Id. 53.

[4] KAN. STAT. ANN. § 77-202 (Supp. 1971); MARYLAND SESSIONS LAWS ch. 693 (1972). Bills are presently pending in Florida, H. 551, 2d Fla. Legis. (n.s.) (1971), Illinois, H. 1586, 77th Gen. Assemb., 1st Sess. (1971), and Wisconsin, S. 550, Biennial Sess. (1971).

Section IV of this Article argues that terms such as "defining death" and "definition of death" are extremely ambiguous, and that the ambiguity is an important cause of misunderstanding and confusion regarding the propriety of legislation in this area. Though it would be desirable not to use such terms, they are too well established in professional and public discourse on these matters to be eliminated. For convenience, and often deliberately to emphasize the problem of ambiguity, we occasionally use these terms in quotation marks. For an explanation of four different levels of specificity which may be intended when the term "definition of death" is employed, see notes 57-60 *infra* & accompanying text.

[5] *See, e.g.,* Taylor, *A Statutory Definition of Death in Kansas,* 215 J.A.M.A. 296 (1971) (letter to the editor), in which the principal draftsman of the Kansas statute states that the law was believed necessary to protect transplant surgeons against the risk of "a criminal charge, for the existence of a resuscitated heart in another body should be excellent evidence that the donor was not dead [under the "definition" of death then existing in Kansas] until the operator excised the heart." *Cf.* Kapoor, *Death & Problems of Transplant,* 38 MAN. B. NEWS 167, 177 (1971); Baker, *Liability and the Heart Transplant,* 6 HOUSTON L. REV. 85, 97-101 (1968). The specter of civil liability was raised in *Tucker v. Lower,* a recent action brought by the brother of a heart donor against the transplantation team at the Medical College of Virginia. *See* notes 42-50 *infra* & accompanying text.

[6] KAN. STAT. ANN. § 77-202 (Supp. 1971); see notes 74-88, 98-101 *infra* & accompanying text for a discussion of this statute.

[7] *See* notes 74-85 *infra* & accompanying text.

[8] In addition to the state medical societies, *see* Taylor, *supra* note 5, others have advocated a statutory definition of death. "Medical researchers and M.D.'s involved in transplants must break with their traditional reluctance to seek statutory changes in the definition of death or find themselves floundering in a morass of court suits in coming years." 15 DRUG RESEARCH REP., June 7, 1972, at 1. Moreover, once a statute is enacted

I. Background

Courts and physicians can no longer assume that determining whether and when a person has died is always a relatively simple matter. The development and use of sophisticated machinery to maintain artificially both respiration and circulation has introduced difficulties in making this determination in some instances. In such cases, the use of a cardiac pacemaker or a mechanical respirator renders doubtful the significance of the traditional "vital signs" of pulse, heartbeat, and respiratory movements as indicators of continuing life. Similarly, the ability of an organ recipient to go on living after his own heart has been removed and replaced by another's has further undermined the status of the beating heart as one of the most reliable—if not *the* most reliable—signs that a person is still alive. In addition, the need of transplant surgeons to obtain organs in good condition from cadavers has stimulated the search for tests that would permit the death of the organism as a whole to be declared before the constituent organs have suffered extensive deterioration. Consequently, new criteria for judging a person dead have been proposed and are gaining acceptance among physicians. The most prominent are those formulated in 1968 by the Harvard Medical School's Ad Hoc Committee to Examine the Definition of Brain Death, chaired by Dr. Henry K. Beecher.[9]

The Harvard Committee described in considerable detail three criteria of "irreversible coma": (1) "unreceptivity and unresponsivity" to "externally applied stimuli and inner need"; (2) absence of spontaneous muscular movements or spontaneous respiration; and (3) no elicitable reflexes.[10] In addition, a flat (isoelectric) electroencephalogram was held to be "of great confirmatory value" for the clinical diagnosis.[11] Although generally referred to as criteria for "cerebral

---

on a new subject in one state, there seem to be direct and indirect pressures for it to be viewed as a model for adoption in other states. *Cf. id.* 5, which notes that the Virginia statute allowing a medical examiner to provide a decedent's organs for transplantation is "the first of its kind in the nation" and terms it "a model for other states to emulate," when it is in fact poorly conceived and nearly incomprehensible.

[9] *See Irreversible Coma, supra* note 3. In addition to Dr. Beecher, the committee consisted of nine other physicians, an historian, a lawyer, and a theologian, all Harvard University faculty members. *Id.*

[10] *Id.* 337-38.

[11] The Harvard committee spelled out its central conclusions as follows:

An organ, brain or other, that no longer functions and has no possibility of functioning again is for all practical purposes dead. Our first problem is to determine the characteristics of a *permanently* nonfunctioning brain.

A patient in this state appears to be in deep coma. The condition can be satisfactorily diagnosed by points 1, 2, and 3 to follow. The electroencephalogram (point 4) provides confirmatory data, and when available it should be utilized. In situations where for one reason or another electroencephalographic monitoring is not available, the absence of cerebral function has to be determined by purely clinical signs, to be described, or by absence of circulation as judged by standstill of blood in the retinal vessels, or by absence of cardiac activity.

death" or "brain death," these criteria assess not only higher brain functions but brainstem and spinal cord activity and spontaneous respiration as well. The accumulating scientific evidence indicates that patients who meet the Harvard criteria will not recover and on autopsy will be found to have brains which are obviously destroyed,[12]

---

1. Unreceptivity and Unresponsivity.—There is a total unawareness to externally applied stimuli and inner need and complete unresponsiveness—our definition of irreversible coma. Even the most intensely painful stimuli evoke no vocal or other response, not even a groan, withdrawal of a limb, or quickening of respiration.

2. No Movements or Breathing.—Observations covering a period of at least one hour by physicians is [sic] adequate to satisfy the criteria of no spontaneous muscular movements or spontaneous respiration or response to stimuli such as pain, touch, sound, or light. After the patient is on a mechanical respirator, the total absence of spontaneous breathing may be established by turning off the respirator for three minutes and observing whether there is any effort on the part of the subject to breathe spontaneously. (The respirator may be turned off for this time provided that at the start of the trial period the patient's carbon dioxide tension is within the normal range, and provided also that the patient has been breathing room air for at least 10 minutes prior to the trial.)

3. No reflexes.—Irreversible coma with abolition of central nervous system activity is evidenced in part by the absence of elicitable reflexes. The pupil will be fixed and dilated and will not respond to a direct source of bright light. Since the establishment of a fixed, dilated pupil is clear-cut in clinical practice, there should be no uncertainty as to its presence. Ocular movement (to head turning and to irrigation of the ears with ice water) and blinking are absent. There is no evidence of postural activity (decerebrate or other). Swallowing, yawning, vocalization are in abeyance. Corneal and pharyngeal reflexes are absent.

As a rule the stretch of tendon reflexes cannot be elicited; i.e., tapping the tendons of the biceps, triceps, and pronator muscles, quadriceps and gastrocnemius muscles with the reflex hammer elicits no contraction of the respective muscles. Plantar or noxious stimulation gives no response.

4. Flat Electroencephalogram.—Of great confirmatory value is the flat or isoelectric EEG. We must assume that the electrodes have been properly applied, that the apparatus is functioning normally, and that the personnel in charge is competent. We consider it prudent to have one channel of the apparatus used for an electrocardiogram. This channel will monitor the ECG so that, if it appears in the electroencephalographic leads because of high resistance, it can be readily identified. It also establishes the presence of the active heart in the absence of the EEG. We recommend that another channel be used for a noncephalic lead. This will pick up space-borne or vibration-borne artifacts and identify them. The simplest form of such a monitoring noncephalic electrode has two leads over the dorsum of the hand, preferably the right hand, so the ECG will be minimal or absent. Since one of the requirements of this state is that there be no muscle activity, these two dorsal hand electrodes will not be bothered by muscle artifact. The apparatus should be run at standard gains $10\mu v/mm$, $50\mu v/5$ mm. Also it should be isoelectric at double this standard gain which is $5\mu v/mm$ or $25\mu v/5$ mm. At least ten full minutes of recording are desirable, but twice that would be better.

It is also suggested that the gains at some point be opened to their full amplitude for a brief period (5 to 100 seconds) to see what is going on. Usually in an intensive care unit artifacts will dominate the picture, but these are readily identifiable. There shall be no electroencephalographic response to noise or to pinch.

All of the above tests shall be repeated at least 24 hours later with no change.

The validity of such data as indications of irreversible cerebral damage depends on the exclusion of two conditions: hypothermia (temperature below 90 F. [32.2 C.]) or central nervous system depressants, such as barbiturates. *Irreversible Coma, supra* note 3, at 337-38.

[12] In the largest single study of patients with flat E.E.G.'s of twenty-four hours'

and supports the conclusion that these criteria may be useful for determining that death has occurred. The Harvard Committee's views were apparently well received in the medical community.[13] Not all physicians have been enthusiastic, however. Professor David Rutstein of the Harvard Medical School, for example, expressed concern over "this major ethical change [which] has occurred right before our eyes . . . with little public discussion of its significance."[14]

Not surprisingly, disquiet over the change in medical attitude and practice arose in lay as well as medical circles.[15] The prospect of physicians agreeing amongst themselves to change the rules by which life is measured in order to salvage a larger number of transplantable organs met with something short of universal approval.[16] Especially with increasing disenchantment over heart transplantation (the procedure in which the traditional criteria for determining death posed the most difficulties), some doubt arose whether it was wise to adopt measures which encouraged a medical "advance" that seemed to have gotten ahead of its own basic technology. Furthermore, many people —doctors included—found themselves with nagging if often unarticulated doubts about how to proceed in the situation, far more com-

---

duration, which involved 2639 comatose patients without anesthetic doses of c.n.s. depressants, not one recovered. Silverman, Masland, Saunders & Schwab, *Irreversible Coma Associated with Electrocerebral Silence*, 20 NEUROLOGY 525 (1970). In an unreported study on 128 individuals who fulfilled the Harvard clinical criteria, postmortem examinations showed their brains to be destroyed. Unpublished results of E. Richardson, reported in *Refinements in Criteria, supra* note 3, at 50-51.

[13] One member of the committee has observed that "since the publication of the report, the clinical recommendations have been accepted and followed on a worldwide basis in a most gratifying fashion." Curran, *Legal and Medical Death—Kansas Takes the First Step*, 284 NEW ENG. J. MED. 260 (1971). Dr. Beecher recently noted that legal doubts have prevented uniform acceptance of the Harvard Committee's views. "Almost every (doctor) on the East Coast has accepted irreversible brain damage as the criterion for death, whereas most West Coast physicians do not for fear of suits." Ross, *Death with Dignity*, The Washington Post, Aug. 9, 1972, at B-15, col. 1 (quoting Dr. Beecher); for a fuller account of the testimony, see *Hearings on Death with Dignity Before the Senate Special Comm. on Aging*, 92d Cong., 2d Sess. (1972).

[14] Rutstein, *The Ethical Design of Human Experiments*, 98 DAEDALUS 523, 526 (1969). Leaders of the Netherlands Red Cross Society's Organ Transplantation Committee argue that only "total absence of the brain's functional capacity" and not "irreversible coma" indicates that death has occurred and state the Dutch position that the Harvard criteria "are grounds for stopping treatment and letting the patient die," but not for declaring death. Rot & van Till, *Neocortical Death after Cardiac Arrest*, 2 LANCET 1099-100 (1971) (letter to the editor).

[15] *See, e.g.*, Arnold, Zimmerman & Martin, *Public Attitudes and the Diagnosis of Death*, 206 J.A.M.A. 1949 (1968) [hereinafter cited as Arnold]; Biörck, *When is Death?*, 1968 WIS. L. REV. 484, 490-91; N.Y. Times, Sept. 9, 1968, at 23, col. 1 (quoting Drs. F. C. Spencer & J. Hardy); *The Heart: Miracle in Cape Town*, NEWSWEEK, Dec. 18, 1967, at 86-87.

[16] [C]ertain actions by transplant surgeons in establishing time of death on death certificates and hospital records have shaken public confidence. Coroners have denounced them in the press for signing a death certificate in one county when the beating heart was removed a day later in a far-off city. The public wonders what the "item" was that was transplanted across the state line and later registered as a person in the operating room record.
Corday, *Life-Death in Human Transplantation*, 55 A.B.A.J. 629, 632 (1969).

mon than transplantation, in which a long-comatose patient shows every prospect of "living" indefinitely with artificial means of support.[17] As a result of this growing public and professional concern, elected officials,[18] with the encouragement of the medical community,[19] have urged public discussion and action to dispel the apprehension created by the new medical knowledge and to clarify and reformulate the law. Some commentators, however, have argued that public bodies and laymen in general have no role to play in this process of change.[20] Issue is therefore joined on at least two points: (1) ought the public to be involved in "defining" death? and (2) if so, how ought it to be involved—specifically, ought governmental action, in the form of legislation, be taken?[21]

II.   PUBLIC INVOLVEMENT OR PROFESSIONAL PREROGATIVE?

In considering the possible need for and the desirability of public involvement, the central question appears to be to what extent, if at all, the "defining" of death is a medical matter, properly left to physicians because it lies within their particular sphere of competence. The belief that the matter of "defining death" is wholly medical is frequently expressed, and not only by physicians.[22] Indeed, when a

---

17 [M]any people are now maintained in a sort of twilight state by the use of machines which do the work of their lungs or their heart while they are completely unconscious . . . . Many of these people will never resume an independent existence away from the machines . . . . One has to decide therefore when to switch off the machines, and this question arises quite independently of considerations about transplants.
Discussion of Murray, *Organ Transplantation: The Practical Possibilities*, in MEDICAL PROGRESS, *supra* note 1, at 71 (comments of Dr. M. F. A. Woodruff).

18 *See, e.g.*, Mondale, *Health Science and Society*, 117 CONG. REC. S3708 (daily ed. Mar. 24, 1971); H. Res. 2830, 2d Fla. Legis. (n.s.) (1971) (resolution introduced by Rep. Sackett, M.D., to create a commission to study death).

19 *See, e.g.*, Taylor, *supra* note 5, at 296; Arnold, *supra* note 15, at 1954; Corday, *Definition of Death: A Double Standard*, HOSPITAL TRIBUNE, May 4, 1970, at 8; Halley & Harvey, *On an Interdisciplinary Solution to the Legal-Medical Definitional Dilemma in Death*, 2 INDIANA LEGAL F. 219, 227 (1969).

20 *See, e.g.*, Kennedy, *The Kansas Statute on Death: An Appraisal*, 285 NEW ENG. J. MED. 946 (1971); *What and When is Death?*, 204 J.A.M.A. 539, 540 (1968) (editorial).

21 To some extent this formulation of the problem is, of course, unrealistic, since "public action" (*i.e.*, action by an official public body), in the form of a court decision, can come about at the instance of a private litigant regardless of any policy reasons in favor of public inaction. Although it may therefore be impossible to avoid creating "law" on the subject, there might still be no significant public involvement if the courts restricted themselves merely to endorsing conclusions reached by private groups, such as those representing physicians. Kennedy's support for judicial involvement in "defining" death seems to operate on that premise. *See* Kennedy, *supra* note 20, at 947. *See also* note 36 *infra* & accompanying text.

22 *See, e.g.*, Kennedy, *supra* note 20, at 947; Berman, *The Legal Problems of Organ Transplantation*, 13 VILL. L. REV. 751, 754 (1968); Sanders & Dukeminier, *Medical Advance and Legal Lag: Hemodialysis and Kidney Transplantation*, 15 U.C.L.A.L. REV. 357, 409 (1968) [hereinafter cited as Sanders]; NATIONAL CONFERENCE OF COMMISSIONERS ON UNIFORM STATE LAWS, HANDBOOK AND PROCEEDINGS OF THE ANNUAL CON-

question concerning the moment at which a person died has arisen in litigation, common law courts have generally regarded this as "a question of fact" for determination at trial on the basis (partially but not exclusively) of expert medical testimony.[23] Yet the standards which are applied in arriving at a conclusion, although based on medical knowledge, are established by the courts "as a matter of law."[24]

Thus while it is true that the application of particular criteria or tests to determine the death of an individual may call for the expertise of a physician, there are other aspects of formulating a "definition" of death that are not particularly within medical competence. To be sure, in practice, so long as the standards being employed are stable and congruent with community opinion about the phenomenon of death,

---

FERENCE 192 (1968); *cf.* Sadler, Sadler & Stason, *The Uniform Anatomical Gift Act: A Model for Reform,* 206 J.A.M.A. 2501 (1968). The ad hoc Harvard Committee, composed largely of physicians, came to the same conclusion. *See Irreversible Coma, supra* note 3, at 339.

[23] *See* Thomas v. Anderson, 96 Cal. App. 2d 371, 215 P.2d 478 (1950). In that appeal, the court was called upon to decide whether the trial judge had erred in holding inapplicable to the case a provision of the California Probate Code based on the Uniform Simultaneous Death Act which provided for the equal distribution of the property of two joint tenants "[w]here there is no sufficient evidence that [they] have died otherwise than simultaneously . . . ." The court cited the definition in *Black's Law Dictionary* that "death is the cessation of life; the ceasing to exist; defined by physicians as a total stoppage of the circulation of the blood, and a cessation of the animal and vital functions consequent thereon, such as respiration, pulsation, etc.," and went on to observe that "death occurs precisely when life ceases and does not occur until the heart stops beating and respiration ends. Death is not a continuing event and is an event that takes place at a precise time." *Id.* at 375, 215 P.2d at 482. It concluded that the "question of fact" as to which of the two deceased men died first had been correctly determined by the trial court in light of "sufficient evidence" given by nonmedical witnesses concerning the appearance of the men on the evening in question.

[24] Smith v. Smith, 229 Ark. 579, 587, 317 S.W.2d 275, 279 (1958) (quoting 41 AM. JUR. *Husbands and Wives* § 244 (1938)). The Smiths, a childless couple who by will had each left his or her estate to the other, were involved in an automobile accident. Mr. Smith apparently died immediately, but when assistance arrived Mrs. Smith was unconscious, and she remained so in the hospital for seventeen days. Thereafter, Mr. Smith's administrator petitioned for the construction of the wills, alleging:

> That as a matter of modern medical science, your petitioner . . . will offer the Court competent proof that the [Smiths] lost their power to will at the same instant, and that their demise as earthly human beings occurred at the same time in said automobile accident, neither of them ever regaining any consciousness whatsoever.

Id. at 582, 317 S.W.2d at 277. The Supreme Court of Arkansas upheld the trial court's dismissal of the petition as a matter of law on the ground that "it would be too much of a strain on credulity for us to believe any evidence offered to the effect that Mrs. Smith was dead, scientifically or otherwise, unless the conditions set out in the [*Black's Law Dictionary* (4th ed.)] definition existed." *Id.* at 586-87, 317 S.W.2d at 279. The court took "judicial notice that one breathing, though unconscious, is not dead," *id.* at 589, 317 S.W.2d at 281, and concluded that Mrs. Smith's death was therefore not simultaneous with her husband's.

Cf. In re Estate of Schmidt, 261 Cal. App. 2d 262, 67 Cal. Rptr. 847 (1968). *Schmidt*, like *Thomas* and *Smith*, involved an inheritorship issue under the Uniform Simultaneous Death Act. The court of appeals found that there was sufficient eyewitness testimony by laymen to support the trial court's conclusion that Mrs. Schmidt survived her husband by some minutes, and it found no fault in the use of the *Black's Law Dictionary* "definition of death" despite the argument that it "is an anachronism in view of the recent medical developments relating to heart transplants," since there was no evidence that the deceased were resuscitable. *Id.* at 273, 67 Cal. Rptr. at 854 (dictum).

most people are content to leave the matter in medical hands.[25] But the underlying extra-medical aspects of the "definition" become visible, as they have recently, when medicine departs (or appears to depart) from the common or traditional understanding of the concept of death. The formulation of a concept of death is neither simply a technical matter nor one susceptible of empirical verification. The idea of death is at least partly a philosophical question, related to such ideas as "organism," "human," and "living." Physicians *qua* physicians are not expert on these philosophical questions, nor are they expert on the question of which physiological functions decisively identify a "living, human organism." They, like other scientists, can suggest which "vital signs" have what significance for which human functions. They may, for example, show that a person in an irreversible coma exhibits "total unawareness to externally applied stimuli and inner need and complete unresponsiveness,"[26] and they may predict that when tests for this condition yield the same results over a twenty-four hour period there is only a very minute chance that the coma will ever be "reversed."[27] Yet the judgment that "total unawareness . . . and complete unresponsiveness" are the salient characteristics of death, or that a certain level of risk of error is acceptable, requires more than technical expertise and goes beyond medical authority, properly understood.

The proposed departure from the traditional standards for determining death not only calls attention to the extra-medical issues involved, but is itself a source of public confusion and concern. The confusion can perhaps be traced to the fact that the traditional signs of life (the beating heart and the expanding chest) are manifestly accessible to the senses of the layman, whereas some of the new criteria require sophisticated intervention to elicit latent signs of life such as brain reflexes. Furthermore, the new criteria may disturb the layman by suggesting that these visible and palpable traditional signs, still useful in most cases, may be deceiving him in cases where supportive machinery is being used. The anxiety may also be attributable to the apparent intention behind the "new definition," which is, at least in part, to facilitate other developments such as the transplantation of cadaver organs. Such confusion and anxiety about the standards for determining death can have far-reaching and distressing consequences for the patient's family, for the physician, for other patients, and for

---

[25] *See* Arnold, *supra* note 15, at 1950, in which the public's "nearly complete acceptance" of professional practice in this century until cardiac transplantation began is contrasted with the great concern manifested in the 19th century and earlier, before embalming became routine, largely because of the fear of premature burial.

[26] *Irreversible Coma, supra* note 3, at 337.

[27] *See* note 12 *supra.*

the community at large.[28] If the uncertainties surrounding the question of determining death are to be laid to rest, a clear and acceptable standard is needed. And if the formulation and adoption of this standard are not to be abdicated to the medical fraternity under an expanded view of its competence and authority, then the public and its representatives ought to be involved.[29] Even if the medical profession takes the lead—as indeed it has—in promoting new criteria of death, members of the public should at least have the opportunity to review, and either to affirm or reject the standards by which they are to be pronounced dead.

III. What Manner of Public Involvement?

There are a number of potential means for involving the public in this process of formulation and review, none of them perfect. The least ambitious or comprehensive is simply to encourage discussion of the issues by the lay press, civic groups, and the community at large. This public consideration might be directed or supported through the efforts of national organizations such as the American Medical Association, the National Institutes of Health, or the National Academy of Sciences.[30] A resolution calling for the establishment of an ad hoc body to evaluate public attitudes toward the changes wrought by biomedical advances has been sponsored by Senator Mondale since 1967 and was adopted by the Senate in December 1971.[31] Mondale's proposed National Advisory Commission on Health Science and Society,

---

[28] *See* Sanders, *supra* note 22, at 407-09; 3 M. Houts & I.H. Haut, Courtroom Medicine §§ 1.02(3)(a)-(g) (1971). As long as the legal standard is ambiguous, the possibility exists that the processes of criminal, as well as civil, justice will be impeded. *See, e.g.,* D. Meyers, The Human Body and the Law 116-18 (1970) (discussing an unreported British case, *Regina v. Potter,* in which a manslaughter defendant was convicted of common assault upon proof that surgeons had removed a kidney from the decedent while he was being maintained on a respirator and before he had been found to be "dead"); *Trial to Test M.D.'s Role in Death of Heart Donor,* A.M.A. News, Nov. 11, 1968, at 2 (man charged with manslaughter raised as defense surgeons' removal of victim's heart when he was kept alive by artificial means).

[29] Matte, *Law, Morals, and Medicine: A Method of Approach to Current Problems,* 13 J. For. Sci. 318, 331-32 (1968). *See also* note 19 *supra.*
    A theoretical risk of illegal conduct exists in the present state of the law. The law is apparently waiting for a social and theological consensus on this point [of "defining" death] . . . . The theologians, the philosophers and the physicians will have to formulate the judgment of propriety here before it is crystallized into a definite statutory rule.
Discussion of Louisell, *Transplantation: Existing Legal Constraints,* in Medical Progress, *supra* note 1, at 99 (comments of Prof. D. W. Louisell).

[30] For example, early in the debate over heart replacement the Board on Medicine of the National Academy issued a "Statement on Cardiac Transplantation," but addressed itself primarily to the need for caution in the spread of the operation to medical centers which were not suited to carrying it out scientifically. 18 News Report of the National Academy of Sciences 1 (Mar. 1968).

[31] S.J. Res. 75, 92d Cong., 1st Sess. (1971), in 117 Cong. Rec. S20,089-93 (daily ed. Dec. 2, 1971). *See also* note 18 *supra.* The joint resolution is now in the House Committee on Interstate Commerce.

under the direction of a board of fifteen members of the general public and professionals from "medicine, law, theology, biological science, physical science, social science, philosophy, humanities, health administration, government, and public affairs," would conduct "seminars and public hearings" as part of its two-year study.[32] As important as it is to ventilate the issues, studies and public discussions alone may not be adequate to the task. They cannot by themselves dispel the ambiguities which will continue to trouble decisionmakers and the public in determining whether an artificially-maintained, comatose "patient" is still alive.

A second alternative, reliance upon the judicial system, goes beyond ascertaining popular attitudes and could provide an authoritative opinion that might offer some guidance for decisionmakers. Reliance on judge-made law would, however, neither actively involve the public in the decisionmaking process nor lead to a prompt, clear, and general "definition." The courts, of course, cannot speak in the abstract prospectively, but must await litigation, which can involve considerable delay and expense, to the detriment of both the parties and society. A need to rely on the courts reflects an uncertainty in the law which is unfortunate in an area where private decisionmakers (physicians) must act quickly and irrevocably. An ambiguous legal standard endangers the rights—and in some cases the lives—of the participants. In such circumstances, a person's choice of one course over another may depend more on his willingness to test his views in court than on the relative merits of the courses of action.[33]

Once called upon to "redefine" death—for example, in a suit brought by a patient's relatives or, perhaps, by a revived "corpse" against the physician declaring death—the judiciary may be as well qualified to perform the task as any governmental body. If the issue could be resolved solely by a process of reasoning and of taking "judicial notice" of widely known and uncontroverted facts, a court could handle it without difficulty. If, on the other hand, technical expertise is required problems may arise. Courts operate within a limited compass —the facts and contentions of a particular case—and with limited expertise; they have neither the staff nor the authority to investigate

---

[32] S.J. Res. 75, 92d Cong., 1st Sess. (1971), in 117 Cong. Rec. S20,090 (daily ed. Dec. 2, 1971).

[33] For example, suppose that transplant surgeons were willing to employ a neurological definition of death, although most other physicians continued to use the "traditional" definition because of the unsettled nature of the law. If (*ex hypothesis*) those surgeons were less averse to the risks of testing their position in litigation, because of their temperament, training, values and commitments, or desire for success, their "courage" could lead to patients being declared dead prematurely according to the traditional standard.

or to conduct hearings in order to explore such issues as public opinion or the scientific merits of competing "definitions."[34] Consequently, a judge's decision may be merely a rubberstamping of the opinions expressed by the medical experts who appear before him.[35] Indeed, those who believe that the "definition of death" should be left in the hands of physicians favor the judicial route over the legislative on the assumption that, in the event of a law suit, the courts will approve "the consensus view of the medical profession"[36] in favor of the new standards. Leaving the task of articulating a new set of standards to the courts may prove unsatisfactory, however, if one believes, as suggested previously, that the formulation of such standards, as opposed to their application in particular cases, goes beyond the authority of the medical profession.[37]

Uncertainties in the law are, to be sure, inevitable at times and are often tolerated if they do not involve matters of general applicability or great moment. Yet the question of whether and when a person is dead plainly seems the sort of issue that cannot escape the need for legal clarity on these grounds. Therefore, it is not surprising that although they would be pleased simply to have the courts endorse their views, members of the medical profession are doubtful that the judicial mode of lawmaking offers them adequate protection in this area.[38] There is currently no way to be certain that a doctor would not be liable, criminally or civilly, if he ceased treatment of a person found to be dead according to the Harvard Committee's criteria but not according to the "complete cessation of all vital functions" test presently employed by the courts. Although such "definitions" were adopted in cases involving inheritors' rights and survivorship[39] rather than a doctor's liability for exercising his judgment about when a person has died, physicians have with good reason felt that this affords

---

[34] *See, e.g.,* Repouille v. United States, 165 F.2d 152, 153 (2d Cir. 1947) (L. Hand, J.), 154 (Frank, J., dissenting).

[35] Because of the adversary nature of the judicial process, testimony is usually restricted to the "two sides" of an issue and may not fairly represent the spectrum of opinion held by authorities in the field.

[36] Kennedy, *supra* note 20, at 947. Kennedy's reliance on a medical "consensus" has a number of weaknesses, which he himself seems to acknowledge: (1) there may be "a wide range of opinions" held by doctors, so that "there need not necessarily be only one view" on a subject which is supported by the medical community, in part because (2) the "usual ways" for these matters to be "discussed and debated" are not very clear or rigorous since (3) the "American medical profession is not all that well regulated" unlike its British counterpart and (4) is not organized to give "official approval" to a single position or (5) to give force to its decision, meaning (6) that "the task will be assumed by some other body, most probably the legislature." *Id.*

[37] *Cf.* Blocker v. United States, 288 F.2d 853, 860 (D.C. Cir. 1961) (en banc) (Burger, J., concurring in the result) (criticizing psychiatrists' attempt to alter legal definition of "mental disease").

[38] *See* note 19 *supra.*

[39] *See* notes 23-24 *supra; cf.* Gray v. Sawyer, 247 S.W.2d 496 (Ky. 1952).

them little assurance that the courts would not rely upon those cases as precedent.[40] On the contrary, it is reasonable to expect that the courts would seek precedent in these circumstances. Adherence to past decisions is valued because it increases the likelihood that an individual will be treated fairly and impartially; it also removes the need to relitigate every issue in every case. Most importantly, courts are not inclined to depart from existing rules because to do so may upset the societal assumption that one may take actions, and rely upon the actions of others, without fear that the ground rules will be changed retroactively.[41]

Considerations of precedent as well as other problems with relying on the judicial formulation of a new definition were made apparent in *Tucker v. Lower*,[42] the first case to present the question of the "definition of death" in the context of organ transplantation. Above all, this case demonstrates the uncertainty that is inherent in the process of litigation, which "was touch and go for the medical profession"[43] as well as the defendants. *Tucker* involved a $100,000 damage action against Drs. David Hume and Richard Lower and other defendant doctors on the Medical College of Virginia transplant team, brought by William E. Tucker, whose brother's heart was removed on May 25, 1968, in the world's seventeenth human heart transplant. The plaintiff claimed that the heart was taken without approval of the next of kin and that the operation was commenced before his brother had died. On the latter point, William Tucker offered evidence that his brother was admitted to the hospital with severe head injuries sustained in a fall and that after a neurological operation he was placed on a respirator. At the time he was taken to the operating room to have his organs removed "he maintained vital signs of life, that is, . . . normal body temperature, normal pulse, normal blood

---

[40] *See* Taylor, *supra* note 5, at 296. *But cf.* Kennedy, *supra* note 20, at 947.

[41] "[R]ules of law on which men rely in their business dealings should not be changed in the middle of the game . . ." Woods v. Lancet, 303 N.Y. 349, 354, 102 N.E.2d 691, 695 (1951). It must be admitted, however, that such principles usually find their most forceful articulation when the court is about to proceed on the counter-principle that when necessary the common law will change with the times to achieve justice. (In *Woods*, for example, the New York Court of Appeals overruled its prior decision in Drobner v. Peters, 232 N.Y. 220, 133 N.E. 567 (1921), in order to permit a child to sue for prenatal injuries.) Although in this country, at least, strict adherence to precedent has been less true on the civil side than on the criminal (where the courts hold closer to the doctrine of *nullum crimen sine lege* than do English courts), it is probably fair to state that judges are more likely to depart from precedent in order to *create* a new cause of action than they are to reject an existing standard and thereby destroy a cause; to adjust the "definition of death" to the perhaps changing views of the medical profession would be to derogate the rights of those litigants injured by declarations of death which departed from previously accepted standards.

[42] Tucker v. Lower, No. 2831 (Richmond, Va., L. & Eq. Ct., May 23, 1972).

[43] 15 DRUG RESEARCH REP., June 7, 1972, at 1.

pressure and normal rate of respiration."[44] Based on the neurologist's finding that the brother was dead from a neurological standpoint, the respirator was turned off and he was pronounced dead. The defendants moved to strike the plaintiff's evidence and for summary judgment in their favor, but the trial judge denied the motions.

> The function of This Court is to determine the state of the law on this or any other subject according to legal precedent and principle. The courts which have had occasion to rule upon the nature of death and its timing have all decided that death occurs at a precise time, and that it is defined as the cessation of life; the ceasing to exist; a total stoppage of the circulation of the blood, and a cessation of the animal and vital functions consequent thereto such as respiration and pulsation.[45]

The court adhered to "the legal concept of death" and rejected "the invitation offered by the defendants to employ a medical concept of neurological death in establishing a rule of law."[46] The court ruled that the jury would be allowed to assess damages if it concluded "that the decedent's life was terminated at a time earlier than it would ordinarily have ended had all reasonable medical efforts been continued to prolong his life."[47]

When he sent the case to the jurors, however, the judge permitted them to consider all possible causes of death, including injury to the brain as well as cessation of breathing or heartbeat, and a verdict was returned for the defendants. Unfortunately, the discrepancy between the initial ruling and the subsequent instructions to the jury did little to resolve the legal uncertainty. The plaintiff has announced that he plans to appeal to the Supreme Court of Virginia,[48] and the creation of a clear and binding rule will depend on the action of that court.[49]

In declining the defendants' suggestion that he adopt a standard

---

[44] Tucker v. Lower, No. 2831, at 4 (Richmond, Va., L. & Eq. Ct., May 23, 1972).

[45] *Id.* at 8 (citations omitted).

[46] *Id.*

> While it is recognized that none of the cases cited above involved transplants, to employ a different standard in this field would create chaos in other fields of the law and certainly it cannot be successfully argued that there should be one concept of death which applies to one type of litigation while an entirely different standard applies in other areas.

Id. at 8-9.

[47] *Id.* at 11.

[48] N Y Times, May 27, 1972, at 15, col. 5; *id.*, June 4, 1972, § 4, at 7, col. 1.

[49] As one medical journal, which favors legislative formulation of a "definition," said of the decision of the Richmond court: "It applies only to cases coming before that court and can be reversed on appeal or overriden by contrary decisions handed down in higher courts." 15 DRUG RESEARCH REP., June 7, 1972, at 1.

based on neurological signs, the judge stated that application for "such a radical change" in the law should be made "not to the courts but to the legislature wherein the basic concepts of our society relating to the preservation and extension of life could be examined and, if necessary, reevaluated."[50] A statutory "definition" of death would have notable advantages as an alternative to a judicial promulgation. Basically, the legislative process permits the public to play a more active role in decisionmaking and allows a wider range of information to enter into the framing of criteria for determining death. Moreover, by providing prospective guidance, statutory standards could dispel public and professional doubt, and could provide needed reassurance for physicians and patients' families, thereby reducing both the fear and the likelihood of litigation for malpractice (or even for homicide).

The legislative alternative also has a number of drawbacks, however. Foremost among these is the danger that a statute "defining" death may be badly drafted. It may be either too general or too specific, or it may be so poorly worded that it will leave physicians or laymen unsure of its intent. There is also the danger that the statutory language might seem to preclude future refinements that expanding medical knowledge would introduce into the tests and procedures for determining death. The problem of bad draftsmanship is compounded by the fact that a statute once enacted may be difficult to revise or repeal, leaving to the slow and uncertain process of litigation the clarification of its intent and meaning.[51] By contrast, although judges usually espouse the doctrine of stare decisis, flexibility over time is a hallmark of the common law. An additional practical problem is the possibility that the statutes enacted may reflect primarily the interests of powerful lobbying groups—for example, state medical societies or transplant surgeons. This possibility—similar to the danger of judicial "rubberstamping" of medical experts' opinions—may be avoided by legislatures' holding open and well-publicized hearings at which sociologists, lawyers, theologians, and representatives of various viewpoints are also called upon to testify.

Professor Ian Kennedy has suggested the further danger that a statutory "definition," rather than protecting the public may leave it vulnerable to physicians who through "liberal interpretation and clever argument" might take actions "just within the letter if not the spirit of the law."[52] Kennedy would rely instead on the medical profession's

---

[50] Tucker v. Lower, No. 2831, at 10 (Richmond, Va., L. & Eq. Ct., May 23, 1972).

[51] The general durability of statutes has the backhanded advantage, however, of emphasizing for the public as well as for legislators the importance of a thorough thrashing out of the issues in hearings and legislative debates.

[52] Kennedy, *supra* note 20, at 947.

22

generalized "consensus view"[53] of the proper "definition of death." It is, however, far from clear why physicians who would violate a statute are unlikely to depart from such an informal "consensus," which may or may not eventually be sanctioned by the courts. Legislation will not remove the need for reasoned interpretation—first by physicians and perhaps then by judges—but it can restrict the compass within which they make their choices to one which has been found acceptable by the public.

Finally, the legislative route may reduce the likelihood that conflicting "definitions" of death will be employed in different jurisdictions in this country. Theoretically, uniformity is also possible in judicial opinions, but it occurs infrequently. If the formulation and reception of the Uniform Anatomical Gift Act provide any precedent, the Commissioners on Uniform State Laws appear to be well situated to provide leadership in achieving an intelligent response to changes in medical procedure.[54]

In sum, then, official action, as opposed to mere discussion of the issues, is needed if the conflict between current medical practice and present law is to be eliminated. A reformulation of the standards for determining death should thus be undertaken by either courts or legislatures. There are strengths and weaknesses in both law-creating mechanisms, but on balance we believe that if legislators approach the issues with a critical and inquiring attitude, a statutory "definition" of death may be the best way to resolve the conflicting needs for definiteness and flexibility, for public involvement and scientific accuracy.[55] Moreover, since pressures for a legislative response to the problem appear to be mounting,[56] careful examination of the proper scope and content of such a statute seems to be called for.

---

[53] *Id.*

[54] Completed in July 1968 by the Commissioners on Uniform State Laws and approved by the American Bar Association in August of that year, the Uniform Anatomical Gift Act was adopted with only minor changes in 40 jurisdictions including the District of Columbia in 1969; by the end of 1971, the Act had been adopted in the remaining 11 states. For a detailed discussion of the national acceptance of the Act see Sadler, Sadler & Stason, *Transplantation and the Law: Progress Toward Uniformity*, 282 NEW ENG. J. MED. 717 (1970). *See also* Brickman, *Medico-Legal Problems with the Question of Death*, 5 CALIF. W.L. REV. 110, 122 (1968) (urging Commissioners to draft uniform act on "the procedures for determining death").

[55] This is, of course, not to say that a judge faced with a case to decide should hold back from engaging in the sort of analysis, or reaching the conclusions about a proper "definition," presented here. As Professor Clarence Morris once observed, the age-old argument that a legislature has a "superior opportunity" to frame general rules should not foreclose judicial reform of the law where the legislature has failed to act. A judge has, after all, "no reliable way of knowing" that legislative action will ever be forthcoming, and if he acts in a way the legislature finds erroneous, his mistake can be set right by statute. Morris, *Liability for Pain and Suffering*, 59 COLUM. L. REV. 476, 482 (1959).

[56] *See* note 8 *supra*. It would certainly be preferable for state legislatures and the Uniform Act Commissioners to begin work on laws now, rather than risking the enactment

IV. WHAT CAN AND SHOULD BE LEGISLATED?

Arguments both for and against the desirability of legislation "defining" death often fail to distinguish among the several different subjects that might be touched on by such legislation. As a result, a mistaken impression may exist that a single statutory model is, and must be, the object of debate. An appreciation of the multiple meanings of a "definition of death" may help to refine the deliberations.

Death, in the sense the term is of interest here, can be defined purely formally as the transition, however abrupt or gradual, between the state of being alive and the state of being dead.[57] There are at least four levels of "definitions" that would give substance to this formal notion; in principle, each could be the subject of legislation: (1) the basic concept or idea; (2) general physiological standards; (3) operational criteria; and (4) specific tests or procedures.[58]

The *basic concept* of death is fundamentally a philosophical matter. Examples of possible "definitions" of death at this level include "permanent cessation of the integrated functioning of the organism as a whole," "departure of the animating or vital principle," or "irreversible loss of personhood." These abstract definitions offer little concrete help in the practical task of determining whether a person has died, but they may very well influence how one goes about devising standards and criteria.

In setting forth the *general physiological standard(s)* for recognizing death, the definition moves to a level which is more medicotechnical, but not wholly so. Philosophical issues persist in the choice to define death in terms of organ systems, physiological functions, or recognizable human activities, capacities, and conditions. Examples of possible general standards include "irreversible cessation of spontaneous respiratory and/or circulatory functions," "irreversible loss of

---

of "emergency legislation hastily contrived in response to public pressure and emotional reaction to [a] particular medical calamity." Matte, *supra* note 29, at 332; *cf.* Woodside, *Organ Transplantation: The Doctor's Dilemma and the Lawyer's Responsibility*, 31 OHIO ST. L.J. 66, 96 (1970).

[57] For a debate on the underlying issues see Morison, *Death: Process or Event?*, 173 SCIENCE 694 (1970); Kass, *Death as an Event: A Commentary on Robert Morison*, 173 SCIENCE 698 (1971).

[58] To our knowledge, this delineation of four levels has not been made elsewhere in the existing literature on this subject. Therefore, the terms "concept," "standard," "criteria," and "tests and procedures" as used here bear no necessary connection to the ways in which others may use these same terms, and in fact we recognize that in some areas of discourse, the term "standards" is more, rather than less, operational and concrete than "criteria"—just the reverse of our ordering. Our terminology was selected so that the category we call "criteria" would correspond to the level of specificity at which the Ad Hoc Harvard Committee framed its proposals, which it called and which are widely referred to as the "new *criteria*" for determining death. We have attempted to be consistent in our use of these terms throughout this Article. Nevertheless, our major purpose here is not to achieve public acceptance of our terms, but to promote awareness of the four different levels of a "definition" of death to which the terms refer.

spontaneous brain functions," "irreversible loss of the ability to respond or communicate," or some combination of these.

Operational criteria further define what is meant by the general physiological standards. The absence of cardiac contraction and lack of movement of the blood are examples of traditional criteria for "cessation of spontaneous circulatory functions," whereas deep coma, the absence of reflexes, and the lack of spontaneous muscular movements and spontaneous respiration are among criteria proposed for "cessation of spontaneous brain functions" by the Harvard Committee.[59]

Fourth, there are the *specific tests and procedures* to see if the criteria are fulfilled. Pulse, heart beat, blood pressure, electrocardiogram, and examination of blood flow in the retinal vessels are among the specific tests of cardiac contraction and movement of the blood. Reaction to painful stimuli, appearance of the pupils and their responsiveness to light, and observation of movement and breathing over a specified time period are among specific tests of the "brain function" criteria enumerated above.

There appears to be general agreement that legislation should not seek to "define death" at either the most general or the most specific levels (the first and fourth). In the case of the former, differences of opinion would seem hard to resolve, and agreement, if it were possible, would provide little guidance for practice.[60] In the case of the latter, the specific tests and procedures must be kept open to changes in medical knowledge and technology. Thus, arguments concerning the advisability and desirability of a statutory definition of death are usually confined to the two levels we have called "standards" and "criteria," yet often without any apparent awareness of the distinction between them. The need for flexibility in the face of medical advance would appear to be a persuasive argument for not legislating any specific operational criteria. Moreover, these are almost exclusively technical matters, best left to the judgment of physicians. Thus, the kind of "definition" suitable for legislation would be a definition of the general physiological standard or standards. Such a definition, while not immutable, could be expected to be useful for a long period of time and would therefore not require frequent amendment.

There are other matters that could be comprehended in legislation "defining" death. The statute could specify who (and how many) shall make the determination. In the absence of a compelling reason to

---

[59] *See* notes 3, 10 *supra*.
[60] *Cf.* Robertson, *Criteria of Death*, 175 SCIENCE 581 (1972) (letter to the editor).

change past practices, this may continue to be set at "a physician,"[61] usually the doctor attending a dying patient or the one who happens to be at the scene of an accident. Moreover, the law ought probably to specify the "time of death." The statute may seek to fix the precise time when death may be said to have occurred, or it may merely seek to define a time that is clearly after "the precise moment," that is, a time when it is possible to say "the patient is dead," rather than "the patient has just now died." If the medical procedures used in determining that death has occurred call for verification of the findings after a fixed period of time (for example, the Harvard Committee's recommendation that the tests be repeated after twenty-four hours), the statute could in principle assign the "moment of death" to either the time when the criteria were first met or the time of verification. The former has been the practice with the traditional criteria for determining death.[62]

Finally, legislation could speak to what follows upon the determination. The statute could be permissive or prescriptive in determining various possible subsequent events, including especially the pronouncement and recording of the death, and the use of the body for burial or other purposes.[63] It is our view that these matters are best handled outside of a statute which has as its purpose to "define death."[64]

V. PRINCIPLES GOVERNING THE FORMULATION OF A STATUTE

In addition to carefully selecting the proper degree of specificity for legislation, there are a number of other principles we believe should guide the drafting of a statute "defining" death. First, the phenomenon of interest to physicians, legislators, and laymen alike is human death. Therefore, the statute should concern the death of a human being,

---

[61] *Cf.* UNIFORM ANATOMICAL GIFT ACT § 7(b).

[62] *See* note 99 *infra* & accompanying text.

[63] If . . . sound procedures for stating death are agreed to and carried out, then theologians and moralists and every other thoughtful person should agree with the physicians who hold that it is *then* permissible to maintain circulation of blood and supply of oxygen in the corpse of a donor to preserve an *organ* until it can be used in transplantation. Whether one gives the body over for decent burial, performs an autopsy, gives the cadaver for use in medical education, or uses it as a "vital organ bank" are all alike procedures governed by decent respect for the bodies of deceased men and specific regulations that ensure this. The ventilation and circulation of organs for transplant raises no question not already raised by these standard procedures. None are life-and-death matters. P. RAMSEY, THE PATIENT AS PERSON 72 (1970).

[64] Nevertheless, a statutory "definition" of death would most appropriately be codified with the provisions on the procedures to be followed to certify death, undertake post-mortem examinations, and so forth. For the reasons given below, the statute "defining" death ought not to be appended to the Uniform Anatomical Gift Act or other "special purpose" laws, however. *See* notes 65, 79-80 *infra* & accompanying text.

not the death of his cells, tissues or organs, and not the "death" or cessation of his role as a fully functioning member of his family or community. This point merits considerable emphasis. There may be a proper place for a statutory standard for deciding when to turn off a respirator which is ventilating a patient still clearly alive, or, for that matter, to cease giving any other form of therapy.[65] But it is crucial to distinguish this question of "when to allow to die?" from the question with which we are here concerned, namely, "when to declare dead?" Since very different issues and purposes are involved in these questions, confusing the one with the other clouds the analysis of both. The problem of determining when a person is dead is difficult enough without its being tied to the problem of whether physicians, or anyone else, may hasten the death of a terminally-ill patient, with or without his consent or that of his relatives, in order to minimize his suffering or to conserve scarce medical resources.[66] Although the same set of social and medical conditions may give rise to both problems, they must be kept separate if they are to be clearly understood.

Distinguishing the question "is he dead?" from the question "should he be allowed to die?" also assists in preserving continuity with tradition, a second important principle. By restricting itself to

---

[65] *See* Potter, *The Paradoxical Preservation of a Principle*, 13 VILL. L. REV. 784, 791 (1968):

> What type of questions are entailed in the debate concerning when a comatose patient should be declared dead? Medical questions and answers are only one element of the decisionmaking process. Medical skill may be used to establish that a patient has now entered and is likely to remain in a certain condition. But medical personnel along with the other members of the community must then ask: "What are we to do with patients in this condition?" The answer to that question does not flow directly from any medical knowledge. It is a question of social policy which must be decided by the entire community. Implementation of the communal policy may be left in the hands of physicians, but they act as agents of the communal conscience.

See generally Note, *Death with Dignity: A Recommendation for Statutory Change*, 22 U. FLA. L. REV. 368 (1970); Fletcher, *Legal Aspects of the Decision Not to Prolong Life*, 203 J.A.M.A. 65 (1968); Sharpe & Hargest, *Lifesaving Treatment for Unwilling Patients*, 36 FORDHAM L. REV. 695 (1968); Note, *The Dying Patient: A Qualified Right to Refuse Medical Treatment*, 7 J. FAM. L. 644 (1967); Elkinton, *The Dying Patient, The Doctor and the Law*, 13 VILL L. REV. 740 (1968); Biörck, *supra* note 15, at 488-90.

[66] The ease with which the two questions can become confused is demonstrated by the following "general definition of human death" proposed in Halley & Harvey, *Medical vs. Legal Definitions of Death*, 204 J.A.M.A. 423, 425 (1968):

> Death is irreversible cessation of *all* of the following: (1) total cerebral function, (2) spontaneous function of the respiratory system, and (3) spontaneous function of the circulatory system.

> Special circumstances may, however, justify the pronouncement of death when consultation consistent with established professional standards have been obtained and when valid consent to withhold or stop resuscitative measures has been given by the appropriate relative or legal guardian.

The authors seem to have realized the mistake in making the state of being dead (rather than the acceptance of imminent death) depend on the "consent" of a relative or guardian, and this aspect of the "definition of death" is absent from their subsequent writings. *See, e.g.*, Halley & Harvey, *Law-Medicine Comment: The Definitional Dilemma of Death*, 37 J. KAN. B. ASS'N 179, 185 (1968); *cf.* D. MEYERS, *supra* note 28, at 135-36 (criticizing Halley and Harvey's second definition for its internal inconsistency).

the "is he dead?" issue, a revised "definition" permits practices to move incrementally, not by replacing traditional cardiopulmonary standards for the determination of death but rather by supplementing them. These standards are, after all, still adequate in the majority of cases, and are the ones that both physicians and the public are in the habit of employing and relying on. The supplementary standards are needed primarily for those cases in which artificial means of support of comatose patients render the traditional standards unreliable.

Third, this incremental approach is useful for the additional and perhaps most central reason that any new means for judging death should be seen as just that and nothing more—a change in method dictated by advances in medical practice, but not an alteration of the meaning of "life" and "death." By indicating that the various standards for measuring death relate to a single phenomenon legislation can serve to reduce a primary source of public uneasiness on this subject.[67] Once it has been established that certain consequences —for example, burial, autopsy, transfer of property to the heirs, and so forth—follow from a determination of death, definite problems would arise if there were a number of "definitions" according to which some people could be said to be "more dead" than others.

There are, of course, many instances in which the law has established differing definitions of a term, each framed to serve a particular purpose. One wonders, however, whether it does not appear somewhat foolish for the law to offer a number of arbitrary definitions of a natural phenomenon such as death. Nevertheless, legislators might seek to identify a series of points during the process of dying, each of which might be labelled "death" for certain purposes. Yet so far as we know, no arguments have been presented for special purpose standards except in the area of organ transplantation. Such a separate "definition of death," aimed at increasing the supply of viable organs, would permit physicians to declare a patient dead before his condition met the generally applicable standards for determining death if his organs are of potential use in transplantation. The adoption of a special standard risks abuse and confusion, however. The status of prospective organ donor is an arbitrary one to which a person can be assigned by relatives[68] or physicians and is unrelated to anything about the extent to which his body's functioning has deteriorated. A special "definition" of death for transplantation purposes would thus need

---

[67] See notes 15, 16 supra. The way in which cardiopulmonary and brain functions relate to each other and to the phenomenon of death is explored in note 89 infra.

[68] UNIFORM ANATOMICAL GIFT ACT § 2(c). For example, if a special standard were adopted for determining death in potential organ donors, relatives of a dying patient with limited financial means might feel substantial pressure to give permission for his organs to be removed in order to bring to a speedier end the care given the patient.

to be surrounded by a set of procedural safeguards that would govern not only the method by which a person is to be declared dead but also those by which he is to be classified as an organ donor.[69] Even more troublesome is the confusion over the meaning of death that would probably be engendered by multiple "definitions."[70] Consequently, it would be highly desirable if a statute on death could avoid the problems with a special "definition." Should the statute happen to facilitate organ transplantation, either by making more organs available or by making prospective donors and transplant surgeons more secure in knowing what the law would permit, so much the better.[71]

If, however, more organs are needed for transplantation than can be legally obtained, the question whether the benefits conferred by transplantation justify the risks associated with a broader "definition" of death should be addressed directly[72] rather than by attempting to subsume it under the question "what is death?" Such a direct con-

---

[69] The Uniform Anatomical Gift Act, which establishes procedures for the donation of organs by an individual or his relatives, appears to operate on the premise that "death" will be determined by standards which are generally accepted and applied in the ordinary course of events; it does not undertake to "define" death. *But cf.* note 100 *infra.*

[70] For instance, suppose that Mr. Smith, a dying patient in University Hospital, is found to be immunologically well matched with Mr. Jones, a University Hospital patient awaiting a heart transplant. Under the special transplantation "definition" Smith is then declared dead, but just as the surgeons are about to remove Smith's heart, Jones suddenly dies. The doctors then decide that Smith is no longer needed as an organ donor. His condition does not meet the standards for declaring death in non-donors. Is Smith "dead" or "alive"?

[71] This would be the case if the generally applicable standards for determining death permit organs to be removed at a time when they are still useable for transplantation purposes. The "definition" suggested by the Article meets this objective, we believe.

[72] Much of the public's fear of premature excision arises from the failure to distinguish the general practitioner's and the transplant surgeon's meaning of the term 'death'. It would be desirable to distinguish the two formally, and use different terms. Hillman & Aldridge, *Towards a Legal Definition of Death*, 116 SOL. J. 323, 324 (1972) [hereinafter cited as Hillman]. These British medical-legal commentators suggest that "irreversible brain damage," which would include patients with no higher brain activity but continued spontaneous respiration, be recognized as a ground for removal of organs prior to ordinary death. They contemplate that certain "essential safeguards" be incorporated into a statute on "irreversible brain damage" to avoid abuse of this category. *Id.* 325.

Prior to the first heart transplant in France, a special "definition" was enacted to remove any uncertainty about the permissibility of removing a beating heart from a "dead" donor. In April 1968 the government decreed a "definition of clinical death" for use with organ donors, based on a flat electroencephalogram of ten minutes duration which was taken to show that an artificially maintained patient lacks "function in the higher nervous centers." D. MEYERS, *supra* note 28, at 113. Meyers seems to question this approach; he believes that the public must be shown

not just that the brain has been irreparably damaged, but also that the extent of this damage is absolutely inconsistent with continued maintenance of independent life in the individual. If electro-enphalograph testing can in fact show this, then it is a valuable definitional tool in ascertaining clinical death; but the medical profession as yet appears somewhat divided on its reliability. In such circumstances, the public cannot be expected to accept the evidence of an electro-encephalographic reading as part of a legislative definition of death.

Id. 135.

frontation with the issue could lead to a discussion about the standards and procedures under which organs might be taken from persons near death, or even those still quite alive, at their own option[73] or that of relatives, physicians, or representatives of the state. The major advantage of keeping the issues separate is not, of course, that this will facilitate transplantation, but that it will remove a present source of concern: it is unsettling to contemplate that as you lie slowly dying physicians are free to use a more "lenient" standard to declare you dead if they want to remove your organs for transplantation into other patients.

Fourth, the standards for determining death ought not only to relate to a single phenomenon but should also be applied uniformly to all persons. A person's wealth or his "social utility" as an organ donor should not affect the way in which the moment of his death is determined.

Finally, while there is a need for uniformity of application at any one time, the fact that changes in medical technology brought about the present need for "redefinition" argues that the new formulation should be flexible. As suggested in the previous section, such flexibility is most easily accomplished if the new "definition" confines itself to the general standards by which death is to be determined and leaves to the continuing exercise of judgment by physicians the establishment and application of appropriate criteria and specific tests for determining that the standards have been met.

VI. THE KANSAS STATUTE

The first attempt at a legislative resolution of the problems discussed here was made in 1970 when the State of Kansas adopted "An Act relating to and defining death."[74] The Kansas statute has

---

[73] *See, e.g.,* Blachly, *Can Organ Transplantation Provide an Altruistic-Expiatory Alternative to Suicide?,* 1 LIFE-THREATENING BEHAVIOR 6 (1971); Scribner, *Ethical Problems of Using Artificial Organs to Sustain Human Life,* 10 TRANS. AM. SOC. ARTIF. INTERNAL ORGANS 209, 211 (1964) (advocating legal guidelines to permit voluntary euthanasia for purpose of donating organs for transplantation).

[74] Law of Mar. 17, 1970, ch. 378, [1970] Kan. Laws 994 (codified at KAN. STAT. ANN. § 77-202 (Supp. 1971)). It provides in full:

A person will be considered medically and legally dead if, in the opinion of a physician, based on ordinary standards of medical practice, there is the absence of spontaneous respiratory and cardiac function and, because of the disease or condition which caused, directly or indirectly, these functions to cease, or because of the passage of time since these functions ceased, attempts at resuscitation are considered hopeless; and, in this event, death will have occurred at the time these functions ceased; or

A person will be considered medically and legally dead if, in the opinion of a physician, based on ordinary standards of medical practice, there is the absence of spontaneous brain function; and if based on ordinary standards of medical practice, during reasonable attempts to either maintain or restore spontaneous circulatory or respiratory function in the absence of aforesaid brain

received a good deal of attention; similar legislation was enacted in the spring of 1972 in Maryland and is presently under consideration in a number of other jurisdictions.[75] The Kansas legislation, which was drafted in response to developments in organ transplantation and medical support of dying patients, provides "alternative definitions of death,"[76] set forth in two paragraphs. Under the first, a person is considered "medically and legally dead" if a physician determines "there is the absence of spontaneous respiratory and cardiac function and . . . attempts at resuscitation are considered hopeless."[77] In the second "definition," death turns on the absence of spontaneous brain function if during "reasonable attempts" either to "maintain or restore spontaneous circulatory or respiratory function," it appears that "further attempts at resuscitation or supportive maintenance will not succeed."[78] The purpose of the latter "definition" is made clear by the final sentence of the second paragraph:

> Death is to be pronounced before artificial means of supporting respiratory and circulatory function are terminated and *before any vital organ is removed for the purpose of transplantation.*[79]

The primary fault with this legislation is that it appears to be based on, or at least gives voice to, the misconception that there are two separate phenomena of death. This dichotomy is particularly unfortunate because it seems to have been inspired by a desire to establish a special definition for organ transplantation, a definition which physicians would not, however, have to apply, in the drafts-

---

function, it appears that further attempts at resuscitation or supportive maintenance will not succeed, death will have occurred at the time when these conditions first coincide. Death is to be pronounced before artificial means of supporting respiratory and circulatory function are terminated and before any vital organ is removed for purposes of transplantation.

These alternative definitions of death are to be utilized for all purposes in this state, including the trials of civil and criminal cases, any laws to the contrary notwithstanding.

[75] *See* note 4 *supra.* In the Maryland law, which is nearly identical to its Kansas progenitor, the phrase "in the opinion of a physician" was deleted from the first paragraph, and the phrase "and because of a known disease or condition" was added to the second paragraph following "ordinary standards of medical practice." MARYLAND SESSIONS LAWS ch. 693 (1972). Interestingly, Kansas and Maryland were also among the first states to adopt the Uniform Anatomical Gift Act in 1968, even prior to its official revision and approval by the National Conference of Commissioners on Uniform State Laws.

[76] Note 74 *supra.*

[77] *Id.* In using the term "hopeless," the Kansas legislature apparently intended to indicate that the "absence of spontaneous respiratory and cardiac function" must be irreversible before death is pronounced. In addition to being rather roundabout, this formulation is also confusing in that it might be taken to address the "when to allow to die?" question as well as the "is he dead?" question. *See* note 85 *infra* & accompanying text.

[78] Note 74 *supra.*

[79] *Id.* (emphasis added).

man's words, "to prove the irrelevant deaths of most persons."[80] Although there is nothing in the Act itself to indicate that physicians will be less concerned with safeguarding the health of potential organ donors, the purposes for which the Act was passed are not hard to decipher, and they do little to inspire the average patient with confidence that his welfare (including his not being prematurely declared dead) is of as great concern to medicine and the State of Kansas as is the facilitation of organ transplantation.[81] As Professor Kennedy cogently observes, "public disquiet [over transplantation] is in no way allayed by the existence in legislative form of what appear to be alternative definitions of death."[82] One hopes that the form the statute takes does not reflect a conclusion on the part of the Kansas legislature that death occurs at two distinct points during the process of dying.[83] Yet this inference can be derived from the Act, leaving open the prospect "that X at a certain stage in the process of dying can be pronounced dead, whereas Y, having arrived at the same point, is not said to be dead."[84]

The Kansas statute appears also to have attempted more than the "definition" of death, or rather, to have tried to resolve related questions by erroneously treating them as matters of "definition." One supporter of the statute praises it, we think mistakenly, for this reason: "Intentionally, the statute extends to these questions: When can a physician avoid attempting resuscitation? When can he terminate resuscitative efforts? When can he discontinue artificial main-

---

[80] Taylor, *supra* note 5, at 296.

[81] *Cf.* Kass, *A Caveat on Transplants*, The Washington Post, Jan. 14, 1968, § B, at 1, col. 1; *Discussion* of Murray, *Organ Transplantation: The Practical Possibilities*, in MEDICAL PROGRESS, *supra* note 1, at 67 (comments of Dr. T. E. Starzl): "[T]he new risk is introduced [by the use of cadaver organs] that the terminal care of such potential donors may be adversely influenced by the events which are expected to follow after death, which might conceivably remove whatever small chance there might have been for survival."

[82] Kennedy, *supra* note 20, at 947.

[83] General use of the term "resuscitation" might suggest the existence of a common notion that a person can die once, be revived (given life again), and then die again at a later time—in other words, that death can occur at two or more distinct points in time. But resuscitation only restores life "from *apparent* death or unconsciousness." WEBSTER'S THIRD NEW INTERNATIONAL DICTIONARY 1937 (1966) (emphasis added). The proposed statute, text accompanying note 88 *infra*, takes account of the possibility of resuscitation by providing that death occurs only when there has been an *irreversible* cessation of the relevant vital bodily functions. *Cf.* 3 M. HOUTS & I.H. HAUT, COURT-ROOM MEDICINE § 1.01 (3)(d) (1971):

> The ability to resuscitate patients after apparent death, coupled with observations that in many cases the restoration was not to a state of consciousness, understanding and intellectual functioning, but merely to a decerebrate, vegetative existence, and with advances in neurology that have brought greater, though far from complete, understanding of the functions of the nervous system, has drawn attention to the role of the nervous system in maintaining life.

[84] Kennedy, *supra* note 20, at 948.

tenance?"[85] To be sure, "when the patient is dead" is one obvious answer to these questions, but by no means the only one. As indicated above, we believe that the question "when is the patient dead?" needs to be distinguished and treated separately from the questions "when may the doctor turn off the respirator?" or "when may a patient —dying yet still alive—be allowed to die?"

VII. A STATUTORY PROPOSAL

As an alternative to the Kansas statute we propose the following:

> A person will be considered dead if in the announced opinion of a physician, based on ordinary standards of medical practice, he has experienced an irreversible cessation of spontaneous respiratory and circulatory functions. In the event that artificial means of support preclude a determination that these functions have ceased, a person will be considered dead if in the announced opinion of a physician, based on ordinary standards of medical practice, he has experienced an irreversible cessation of spontaneous brain functions. Death will have occurred at the time when the relevant functions ceased.

This proposed statute provides a "definition" of death confined to the level of *general physiological standards*, and it has been drafted in accord with the five principles set forth above in section V. First, the proposal speaks in terms of the *death* of a *person*. The determination that a person has died is to be based on an evaluation of certain vital bodily functions, the permanent absence of which indicates that he is no longer a living human being. By concentrating on the death of a human being as a whole, the statute rightly disregards the fact that some cells or organs may continue to "live" after this point,[86] just as others may have ceased functioning long before the determination of death. This statute would leave for resolution by other means the question of when the absence or deterioration of certain capacities, such as the ability to communicate, or functions, such as the cerebral, indicates that a person may or should be allowed to die without further medical intervention.

Second, the proposed legislation is predicated upon the single phenomenon of death. Moreover, it applies uniformly to all persons,[87]

---

[85] Mills, *The Kansas Death Statute: Bold and Innovative*, 285 NEW ENG. J. MED. 968 (1971).

[86] *Cf.* F. MOORE, TRANSPLANT 27-36 (1972).

[87] Differences in the exact mode of diagnosing death will naturally occur as a result of differing circumstances under which the physician's examination is made. Thus, the techniques employed with an automobile accident victim lying on the roadside at

by specifying the circumstances under which each of the standards is to be used rather than leaving this to the unguided discretion of physicians. Unlike the Kansas law, the model statute does not leave to arbitrary decision a choice between two apparently equal yet different "alternative definitions of death."[88] Rather, its second standard is applicable only when "artificial means of support preclude" use of the first. It does not establish a separate kind of death, called "brain death." In other words, the proposed law would provide two standards gauged by different functions, for measuring different manifestations of the same phenomenon. If cardiac and pulmonary functions have ceased, brain functions cannot continue; if there is no brain activity and respiration has to be maintained artificially, the same state (*i.e.*, death) exists.[89] Some people might prefer a single standard, one based either on cardiopulmonary or brain functions. This would have the advantage of removing the last trace of the "two

---

night may be less sophisticated than those used with a patient who has been receiving treatment in a well-equipped hospital.

[88] KAN. STAT. ANN. § 77-202 (Supp. 1971).

[89] [L]ife is supported by the smooth and integrated function of three principal systems: circulatory, respiratory and nervous . . . . So long as the integrated function of these three systems continues, the individual lives. If any one of them ceases to function, failure of the other two will shortly follow, and the organism dies. In any case it is *anoxia*, or deprivation of oxygen, that is the ultimate cause of death of cells: in central nervous system failure, because the impulses which maintain respiration cease; in cardiac failure, because oxygenated blood is not moved to the cells; and in respiratory failure, because the blood, although circulating, is not releasing carbon dioxide nor replenishing oxygen in the lungs. Although other organs, such as the liver and kidneys, perform functions essential to life, their failure does not *per se* result in immediate death; it results, rather, in the eventual failure of one of the three systems described, and is thus only an indirect cause of death.

3 M. HOUTS & I.H. HAUT, COURTROOM MEDICINE § 1.01(2)(a) (1971).

It has long been known that, even when a patient loses consciousness and becomes areflexive, he may recover if heartbeat and breathing continue, but if they do not there is no hope of recovery. Thus, death came to be equated with the absence of these two "vital signs," although what was being detected was really the permanent cessation of the integrated functioning of the circulatory, respiratory, and nervous systems. In recent years, the traditional concept of death has been departed from, or at least severely strained, in the case of persons who were dead according to the rationale underlying the traditional standards in that they had experienced a period of anoxia long enough to destroy their brain functions, but in whom respiration and circulation were artificially re-created. By recognizing that such artificial means of support may preclude reliance on the traditional standards of circulation and respiration, the statute proposed here merely permits the logic behind the long-existing understanding (*i.e.*, integrated trisystemic functioning) to be served; it does not create any "new" type of death. Practically, of course, it accomplishes this end by articulating the "new" standard of "irreversible cessation of spontaneous brain functions," as another means of measuring the existing understanding. Dr. Jean Hamburger has observed, "After the guillotine has cut off a criminal's head, it is possible now to keep the heart and lungs going on for days. Do you think that such a person is dead or alive?" *Discussion* of Louisell, *Transplantation: Existing Legal Constraints*, in MEDICAL PROGRESS, *supra* note 1, at 100. The purpose of the "new" standard is to make it clear that the answer to Hamburger's question is unequivocally that the person is dead. *Cf.* Gray v. Sawyer, 247 S.W.2d 496 (Ky. 1952) (newly discovered evidence that blood was gushing from decedent's decapitated body is significant proof that she was still alive following an accident); Biörck, *supra* note 15, at 485; Note, *supra* note 1, at 206.

deaths" image, which any reference to alternative standards may still leave. Respiratory and circulatory indicators, once the only touchstone, are no longer adequate in some situations. It would be possible, however, to adopt the alternative, namely that death is *always* to be established by assessing spontaneous brain functions. Reliance only on brain activity, however, would represent a sharp and unnecessary break with tradition. Departing from continuity with tradition is not only theoretically unfortunate in that it violates another principle of good legislation suggested previously, but also practically very difficult, since most physicians customarily employ cardiopulmonary tests for death and would be slow to change, especially when the old tests are easier to perform,[90] more accessible and acceptable to the lay public, and perfectly adequate for determining death in most instances.

Finally, by adopting standards for death in terms of the cessation of certain vital bodily functions but not in terms of the specific criteria or tests by which these functions are to be measured, the statute does not prevent physicians from adapting their procedures to changes in medical technology.[91]

A basic substantive issue remains: what are the merits of the proposed standards? For ordinary situations, the appropriateness of the traditional standard, "an irreversible cessation of spontaneous respiratory and circulatory functions,"[92] does not require elaboration. Indeed, examination by a physician may be more a formal than a real requirement in determining that most people have died. In addition

---

[90] The clinical signs of irreversible loss of brain functions are probably not a great deal more difficult to elicit than the traditional signs of death are to detect, although the former are less accessible since they require active intervention to be educed and are not susceptible of mere observation. Aside from the taking of an electroencephalogram, the tests involved (such as tickling the cornea, irrigating the ear with ice water, and tapping the tendons with a reflex hammer) are fairly simple, but unlike the customary tests (such as listening for heartbeat with a stethoscope, seeing if a mirror held by the nose and mouth is clouded by breathing, and measuring pulse), they require equipment which a physician may be less likely to have at hand.

[91] For example, it remains to be determined whether an electroencephalographic reading is necessary for an accurate diagnosis, as many now hold, or whether it should be regarded as having only "confirmatory value," as urged by the Harvard Committee. *See* note 11 *supra*.

[92] This language, taken from the proposed statute, is intended as a succinct summary of the standard now employed in ordinary circumstances. Of course, the requirement that the cessation of these functions be *irreversible* cannot be emphasized too strongly. A physician may be needed to make this determination in some cases—and to apply the means necessary to reverse a temporary cessation caused by a heart attack or the like. But laymen are also aware of the significance of the requirement as is indicated by the common practice of giving "first aid," in the form of artificial respiration, to restore breathing in victims of mishaps, particularly drowning, electric shock, and poisoning.
Two British commentators suggest that legislation "defining" death also prescribe the resuscitative efforts required to be made before death may be declared. Hillman, *supra* note 72, at 325. We believe it is enough to demand "irreversibility," as a consequence of which whatever attempts at resuscitation are established by current standards of good medical practice would be compelled.

to any obvious injuries, elementary signs of death such as absence of heartbeat and breathing, cold skin, fixed pupils, and so forth, are usually sufficient to indicate even to a layman that the accident victim, the elderly person who passes away quietly in the night, or the patient stricken with a sudden infarct has died.[93] The difficulties arise when modern medicine intervenes to sustain a patient's respiration and circulation. As we noted in discussing the Harvard Committee's conclusions, the indicators of brain damage appear reliable, in that studies have shown that patients who fit the Harvard criteria have suffered such extensive damage that they do not recover.[94] Of course, the task of the neurosurgeon or physician is simplified in the common case where an accident victim has suffered such gross, apparent injuries to the head that it is not necessary to apply the Harvard criteria in order to establish cessation of brain functioning.

The statutory standard, "irreversible cessation of spontaneous brain functions," is intended to encompass both higher brain activities and those of the brainstem. There must, of course, also be no spontaneous respiration; the second standard is applied only when breathing is being artificially maintained. The major emphasis placed on brain functioning, although generally consistent with the common view of what makes man distinctive as a living creature, brings to the fore a basic issue: What aspects of brain function should be decisive? The question has been reframed by some clinicians in light of their experience with patients who have undergone what they term "neocortical death" (that is, complete destruction of higher brain capacity, demonstrated by a flat E.E.G.). "Once neocortical death has been unequivocally established and the possibility of any recovery of consciousness and intellectual activity [is] thereby excluded, . . . al-

---

[93] The statute provides that the determination of death depends on "the announced opinion of a physician." This raises two distinct sorts of questions. First, which physician's opinion is decisive? As previously observed, text accompanying note 64 *supra*, under "ordinary standards of medical practice" the physician declaring death would be the patient's own attending physician; this is particularly true of a patient who is receiving cardiopulmonary support in a hospital. Since, however, circumstances such as an automobile accident may arise in which death will have to be determined by a physician who had not previously attended the decedent, it was thought best to cast the language in terms of "a physician."

Second, questions may arise concerning the determination of death by nonphysicians. In an emergency, laymen may sometimes have to decide whether death has occurred, and to act on that determination, as in deciding whether to attempt to rescue someone who may or may not have already died. The proposed statute does nothing to change that practice or to alter any liability that might result under such circumstances, but merely specifies that an official determination must rest on "the opinion of a physician." This is consistent with existing state laws on the procedures by which death is "certified." These provisions, as well as ordinary medical practices, make it unnecessary to spell out in the model statute the exact manner in which the physician's opinion should be recorded or certified in the medical files or official documents.

[94] *See* note 12 *supra* & accompanying text.

though [the] patient breathes spontaneously, is he or she alive?"[95] While patients with irreversible brain damage from cardiac arrest seldom survive more than a few days, cases have recently been reported of survival for up to two and one-quarter years.[96] Nevertheless, though existence in this state falls far short of a full human life, the very fact of spontaneous respiration, as well as coordinated movements and reflex activities at the brainstem and spinal cord levels, would exclude these patients from the scope of the statutory standards.[97] The condition of "neocortical death" may well be a proper justification for interrupting all forms of treatment and allowing these patients to die, but this moral and legal problem cannot and should not be settled by "defining" these people "dead."

The legislation suggested here departs from the Kansas statute in its basic approach to the problem of "defining" death: the proposed statute does not set about to establish a special category of "brain death" to be used by transplanters. Further, there are a number of particular points of difference between them. For example, the proposed statute does not speak of persons being "medically and legally dead," thus avoiding redundancy and, more importantly, the mistaken implication that the "medical" and "legal" definitions could differ.[98]

---

[95] Brierley, Adams, Graham & Simpsom, *Neocortical Death After Cardiac Arrest*, 2 LANCET 560, 565 (1971) [hereinafter cited as Brierley]. In addition to a flat (isoelectric) electroencephalogram, a "neuropathological examination of a biopsy specimen . . . from the posterior half of a cerebral hemisphere" provides further confirmation. *Id.* The editors of a leading medical journal question "whether a state of cortical death can be diagnosed clinically." Editorial, *Death of a Human Being*, 2 LANCET 590 (1971). *Cf.* note 14 *supra*.

[96] Brierley and his colleagues report two cases of their own in which the patients each survived in a comatose condition for five months after suffering cardiac arrest before dying of pulmonary complications. They also mention two unreported cases of a Doctor Lewis, in one of which the patient survived for $2\frac{1}{4}$ years. Brierley, *supra* note 95, at 565.

[97] The exclusion of patients without neocortical function from the category of death may appear somewhat arbitrary in light of our disinclination to engage in a philosophical discussion of the basic concepts of human "life" and "death." *See* text accompanying notes 57-60 *supra*. Were the "definition" contained in the proposed statute a departure from what has traditionally been meant by "death," such a conceptual discussion would clearly be in order. But, as this Article has tried to demonstrate, our intention has been more modest: to provide a clear restatement of the traditional understanding in terms which are useful in light of modern medical capabilities and practices. *See* note 89 *supra*.

A philosophical examination of the essential attributes of being "human" might lead one to conclude that persons who, for example, lack the mental capacity to communicate in any meaningful way, should be regarded as "not human" or "dead." It would nevertheless probably be necessary and prudent to treat the determination of that kind of "death" under special procedures until such time as medicine is able routinely to diagnose the extent and irreversibility of the loss of the "central human capacities" (however defined) with the same degree of assurance now possible in determining that death has occurred. Consequently, even at the conceptual level, we are inclined to think that it is best to distinguish the question "is he dead?" from such questions as "should he be allowed to die?" and "should his death be actively promoted?"

[98] The use of the word "legally" (as in "a person will be considered legally dead") in a law defining death is redundant. Besides, if there were a distinction between a

Also, the proposed legislation does not include the provision that "death is to be pronounced before" the machine is turned off or any organs removed. Such a *modus operandi*, which was incorporated by Kansas from the Harvard Committee's report, may be advisable for physicians on public relations grounds, but it has no place in a statute "defining" death. The proposed statute already provides that "Death will have occurred at the time when the relevant functions ceased."[99] If supportive aids, or organs, are withdrawn after this time, such acts cannot be implicated as having caused death. The manner in which, or exact time at which, the physician should articulate his finding is a matter best left to the exigencies of the situation, to local medical customs or hospital rules, or to statutes on the procedures for certifying death or on transplantation if the latter is the procedure which raises the greatest concern of medical impropriety. The real safeguard against doctors killing patients is not to be found in a statute "defining" death. Rather, it inheres in physicians' ethical and religious beliefs, which are also embodied in the fundamental professional ethic of *primum non nocere* and are reinforced by homicide and "wrongful death" laws and the rules governing medical negligence applicable in license revocation proceedings or in private actions for damages.

The proposed statute shares with the Kansas legislation two features of which Professor Kennedy is critical. First, it does not require that two physicians participate in determining death, as recommended by most groups which set forth suggestions about transplantation. The reasons for the absence of such a provision should be obvious. Since the statute deals with death in general and not with death in relation to transplantation, there is no reason for it to establish a general rule which is required only in that unusual situation. If particular dangers lurk in the transplantation setting, they should be dealt with in legislation on that subject, such as the Uniform Anatomical

---

"medical" and a "legal" standard of death, a statute could only legislate the legal standard. Consequently, the adjectives "medical" and "legal" are unnecessary as well as potentially misleading. *Cf.* Halley & Harvey, *Medical vs. Legal Definition of Death*, 204 J.A.M.A. 423 (1968).

[99] It is necessary to state a standard for judging *when* death occurred for disputes, typically concerning inheritance or rights of survivorship, in which the exact time of death is a decisive factor. The proposed statute, in accordance with existing practice, *see* text accompanying note 62 *supra*, fixes the time of death as the point at which the person actually dies, not the point at which the diagnosis is confirmed. This approach conforms to the commonsense understanding that both a man who dies in a coal mine and cannot be found for 24 hours and one who dies in a hospital where the practice is to require confirmation of the diagnosis by repeating the tests after 24 hours have been dead for a day before their deaths can be pronounced with certainty. The statutory phrase "relevant functions" refers to whichever functions are being measured: cardiopulmonary functions in the usual case, or brain functions where the others are obscured by the artificial means being employed.

Gift Act.[100] If all current means of determining "irreversible cessation of spontaneous brain functions" are inherently so questionable that they should be double-checked by a second (or third, fourth, etc.) physician to be trustworthy, or if a certain means of measuring brain function requires as a technical matter the cooperation of two, or twenty, physicians, then the participation of the requisite number of experts would be part of the "ordinary standards of medical practice" that circumscribe the proper, non-negligent use of such procedures. It would be unfortunate, however, to introduce such a requirement into legislation which sets forth the general standards for determining who is dead, especially when it is done in such a way as to differentiate between one standard and another.

Kennedy's second objection, that a death statute ought to provide "for the separation and insulation of the physician (or physicians) attending the patient donor and certifying death, from the recipient of any organ that may be salvaged from the cadaver," is likewise unnecessary.[101] As was noted previously, language that relates only to transplantation has no place in a statute on the determination of death.

VIII. CONCLUSION

Changes in medical knowledge and procedures have created an apparent need for a clear and acceptable revision of the standards for determining that a person has died. Some commentators have argued that the formulation of such standards should be left to physicians. The reasons for rejecting this argument seem compelling: the "definition of death" is not merely a matter for technical expertise, the uncertainty of the present law is unhealthy for society and physicians alike, there is a great potential for mischief and harm through the possibility of conflict between the standards applied by some physicians and those assumed to be applicable by the community at

---

[100] In fact, § 7(b) of the Uniform Anatomical Gift Act calls only for one physician: "The time of death [of a donor] shall be determined by a physician who attends the donor at his death, or, if none, the physician who certifies the death."

In *Tucker v. Lower* (*see* notes 42-50 *supra* & accompanying text) the defendants argued that this provision amounted to a "definition" of death (death is when a physician says you're dead), although Virginia had not adopted the Act until 1970, two years after the transplantation of the plantiff's brother's heart. The court rejected this argument since "neither the decedent nor anyone acting on his behalf had made a gift of any part of his body" and the Act was therefore inapplicable. The reasons for rejecting the defendant's suggestion seem to us to go deeper; they have been presented throughout this Article and are summarized in the concluding section.

[101] Kennedy, *supra* note 20, at 949. Again, § 7(b) of the Uniform Anatomical Gift Act covers this point adequately: "The physician [who declares death] shall not participate in the procedures for removing or transplanting a part."

large and its legal system, and patients and their relatives are made uneasy by physicians apparently being free to shift around the meaning of death without any societal guidance. Accordingly, we conclude the public has a legitimate role to play in the formulation and adoption of such standards. This Article has proposed a model statute which bases a determination of death primarily on the traditional standard of final respiratory and circulatory cessation; where the artificial maintenance of these functions precludes the use of such a standard, the statute authorizes that death be determined on the basis of irreversible cessation of spontaneous brain functions. We believe the legislation proposed would dispel public confusion and concern and protect physicians and patients, while avoiding the creation of "two types of death," for which the statute on this subject first adopted in Kansas has been justly criticized. The proposal is offered not as the ultimate solution to the problem, but as a catalyst for what we hope will be a robust and well-informed public debate over a new "definition." Finally, the proposed statute leaves for future resolution the even more difficult problems concerning the conditions and procedures under which a decision may be reached to cease treating a terminal patient who does not meet the standards set forth in the statutory "definition of death."

The "State of the Art" in Medicine

Until the past few decades, comatose patients fairly rapidly either improved or died. If no other complication supervened and the patient did not improve, death followed from starvation and dehydration within days; pneumonia, apnea, or effects of the original disease typically brought on death even more quickly. Before such techniques as intravenous hydration, nasogastric feeding, bladder catheterization and respirators, no patient continued for long in deep coma.

With the aid of modern medicine, some comatose patients can be kept from a rapid death. Many, however, become permanently and totally unresponsive. In other words, their appearance resembles that of the dead as traditionally perceived: they no longer respond to their environment by sensate and intellectual activity. But their appearance also differs from that traditionally associated with the dead because mechanical support generates breathing, heartbeat, and the associated physical characteristics (e.g., warm, moist skin) of life.

The ever more sophisticated capabilities developed by biomedical practitioners during the past quarter century to support or supplant certain vital functions have thus created new problems in diagnosing death. If these diagnostic problems were the only consequence of medicine's new capabilities, those who developed and employed them might well be criticized for having opened a Pandora's Box of troubles for physicians and for society. But, as witnesses told the Commission, in a portion of the cases the armamentarium of resuscitative medicine brings comatose patients back from the brink of death by supporting their breathing and blood flow during a period of acute need.

Since the witnesses and existing medical literature lacked information on the relative proportion of comatose,

41

respirator-assisted patients who survive versus those who die (as determined by either brain-based or heart/lung-based tests), the Commission sponsored a small study. This study was not intended to generate definitive data on the incidence of such outcomes but rather to provide a rough estimate of the extent of the various outcomes. The study examined the experience over a period ranging from two months to one year at seven hospitals serving major metropolitan areas. (A full description of the study and its results appears in Appendix B.) At the four acute care centers from which such data were available, 2-4 cases of irreversible loss of all brain functions arose each month, a figure consistent with other data.[1] These figures convey a useful, if limited, perspective on the frequency with which the medicolegal dilemma of determining death in comatose, respirator-assisted cases arises at such hospitals.

The social and legal as well as medical consequences attached to a determination of death make it imperative that the diagnosis be incontrovertible. One must be certain that the functions of the entire brain are irreversibly lost and that respiration and circulation are, therefore, solely artifacts of mechanical intervention. Indeed, though suspicious that their interventions may be doing nothing more than masking what would otherwise manifestly be death by the traditional measures, physicians are concerned about doing anything—such as removing a respirator—that would hinder the recovery of a patient whose loss of brain functioning might be only partial or reversible.[2]

Development of the Concept of "Brain Death"

The concept of "brain death" and efforts to refine criteria to identify that condition have been developing during the last two decades, concomitant with the spread of life support systems in clinical medicine. In 1959, several French neurophysiologists published results of research they had conducted on patients in extremely deep coma receiving respirator assistance, a condition they termed "coma dépassé."[3] Multiple tests showed these patients

---

[1] Ake Grenvik, David J. Powner, James V. Snyder, Michael S. Jastremski, Ralph A. Babcock and Michael G. Loughhead, "Cessation of Therapy in Terminal Illness and Brain Death," 6 *Critical Care Med.* 284 (1978).

[2] Accordingly, in the procedures for diagnosing death set forth by the Commission's medical consultants in Appendix F *infra*, the test for apnea involves elevating the level of circulating oxygen before turning off the respirator and allowing the level of carbon dioxide to rise as a stimulus for spontaneous respiration. The high level of oxygen protects the brain cells (if any remain active) from further damage.

[3] P. Mollaret and M. Goulon, "Le Coma Dépassé," 101 *Rev. Neurol.* 3 (1959).

lacked reflexes and electrophysiologic activity. The investigators concluded that the patients had suffered permanent loss of brain functions—they were, in other words, "beyond coma." Postmortem examinations of those patients revealed extensive destruction (necrosis and autolysis) of the brain—a phenomenon that has since been called the "respirator brain."[4]

With the advent of transplant surgery employing cadaver donors—first with kidney transplantation in the 1950's and later, and still more dramatically, with heart transplantation in the 1960's—interest in "brain death" took on a new urgency.[5] For such transplants to be successful, a viable, intact organ is needed. The suitability of organs for transplantation diminishes rapidly once the donor's respiration and circulation stop. The most desirable organ donors are otherwise healthy individuals who have died following traumatic head injuries and whose breathing and blood flow are being artifically maintained. Yet even with proper care, the organs of these potential donors will deteriorate. Thus, it became important for physicians to be able to determine when the brains of mechanically-supported patients irretrievably ceased functioning.

Yet, the need for viable organs to transplant does not account fully for the interest in diagnosing irreversible loss of brain functions. The Commission's study illustrates this point; of 36 comatose patients who were declared dead on the basis of irreversible loss of brain functions, only six were organ donors. Other studies also report that organs are procured in only a small percentage of cases in which brain-based criteria might be applied.[6] Thus, medical con-

---

[4]A. Earl Walker, E. L. Diamond and John Moseley, "The Neuropathological Findings in Irreversible Coma; A Critique of the Respirator Brain," 34 *J. Neuropath. Exp. Neurol.* 295 (1975); John I. Moseley, Gaetano F. Molinari and A. Earl Walker, "Respirator Brain: Report of a Survey and Review of Current Concepts," 100 *Arch. Pathol. Lab. Med.* 61 (1976).

[5]*See, e.g.,* Renée C. Fox and Judith P. Swazey, *The Courage to Fail: A Social View of Organ Transplantation and Dialysis,* University of Chicago Press, Chicago, (1978); Francis D. Moore, *Give and Take: The Biology of Tissue Transplantation,* W.B. Sanders, Co., Philadelphia, Pa. (1964).

[6]*See e.g.,* Howard H. Kaufman, John D. Hutchton, Megan M. McBride, Carolyn A. Beardsley and Barry D. Kahan, "Kidney Donation: Needs and Possibilities," 5 *Neurosurg.* 237 (1979); K. J. Bart, "The Prevalance of Cadaveric Organs for Transplantation" in S.W. Sell, U.P. Perry and M.M. Vincent (eds.) *Proceedings of the 1977 Annual Meeting of American Association Tissue Banks,* American Association of Tissue Banks, Rockville, Md. (1977) at 124–130; A. Earl Walker, "The Neurosurgeon's Responsibility for Organ Procurement," 44 *J. Neurosurg.* 1 (1976).

cern over the determination of death rests much less with
any wish to facilitate organ transplantation than with the

 the need both to render ap-
propriate care to patients
and to replace artificial
support with more fitting
and respectful behavior
when a patient has become
a dead body. Another in-
centive to update the criteria for determining death
stems from the increasing
realization that the dedica-
tion of scarce and expen-
sive intensive care facilities to bodies without brain
functions may not only
prolong the uncertainty
and suffering of grieving
families but also preclude
access to the facilities for
patients with reversible
conditions.[7]

The Emergence of a Medical Consensus

Medical concern over making the proper diagnosis in
respirator-supported patients led to the development of criteria which reliably establish permanent loss of brain functions. A landmark in this process was the publication in
1968 of a report by an *ad hoc* committee of the Harvard
Medical School which became known as the "Harvard criteria."[8] The Committee's report described .the following
characteristics of a permanently nonfunctioning brain, a
condition it referred to as "irreversible coma":

---

[7]B.D. Colen, "Medical Examiner's Solution to Life and Death
Problem," January 28, 1978, *Wash Post* §A at 8, col. 1, describing
the attempts of Dr. Ron Wright, deputy chief medical examiner for
Dade County Florida, to have medical interventions ceased for
bodies declared dead on the basis of brain-oriented criteria.
(Florida did not enact a statute on the subject until 1980.) "Wright
was able to get a judge to hold a special Sunday morning hearing
at the hospital—with reporters and photographers in attend-
ance—at which he successfully argued that the family was being
forced to pay $2,000 a day to keep a dead body in the intensive
care unit." Patricia H. Butcher, "Management of the Relatives of
Patients with Brain.Death" in Ronald V. Trubuhovich (ed). *Management of Acute Intracranial Disasters*, Little, Brown and Company, Boston, Mass. (1979) at 327.

[8]Ad Hoc Committee of the Harvard Medical School to Examine
the Definition of Brain Death, "A Definition of Irreversible Coma,"
205 *J.A.M.A.* 337 (1968).

1. *Unreceptivity and unresponsitivity.* The patient shows a total unawareness to externally applied stimuli and inner need, and complete unresponsiveness, even when intensely painful stimuli are applied.

2. *No movements or breathing.* All spontaneous muscular movement, spontaneous respiration, and response to stimuli such as pain, touch, sound or light are absent.

3. *No reflexes.* Among the indications of absent reflexes are: fixed, dilated, pupils; lack of eye movement even when the head is turned or ice water is placed in the ear; lack of response to noxious stimuli; and generally, unelicitable tendon reflexes.

In addition to these three criteria, a flat electroencephalogram (EEG), which shows that there is no discernible electrical activity in the cerebral cortex, was recommended as a confirmatory test, when available. All tests were to be repeated at least 24 hours later without showing change. Drug intoxication (e.g., barbiturates) and hypothermia (body temperature below 90°F), which can cause a *reversible* loss of brain functions, also had to be excluded before the criteria could be used.

The "Harvard criteria" have been found to be quite reliable. Indeed, no case has yet been found that met these criteria and regained any brain functions despite continuation of respirator support. Criticisms of the criteria have been of five kinds. First, the phrase "irreversible coma" is misleading as applied to the cases at hand. "Coma" is a condition of a living person, and a body without any brain functions is dead and thus *beyond* any coma. Second, the writers of these criteria did not realize that the spinal cord reflexes actually persist or return quite commonly after the brain has completely and permanently ceased functioning. Third, "unreceptivity" is not amenable to testing in an unresponsive body without consciousness. Next, the need adequately to test brainstem reflexes, especially apnea, and to exclude drug and metabolic intoxication as possible causes of the coma, are not made sufficiently explicit and precise. Finally, although all individuals that meet "Harvard criteria" are dead (irreversible cessation of all functions of the entire brain), there are many other individuals who are dead but do not maintain circulation long enough to have a 24-hour observation period. Various other criteria have been proposed since 1968 that attempt to ameliorate these deficiencies.[9]

---

[9]David J. Powner, James V. Snyder, and Ake Grenvik, "Brain Death Certification: A Review," 5 *Crit. Care Med.* 230 (1977); Julius Korein, "Brain Death," in J. Cottrell and H. Turndorf (eds.) *Anesthesia and Neurosurgery* (1980) at 282; Peter McL. Black, "Brain Death" 299 *N.E.J.M.* 338 & 393 (1978).

As the Harvard Committee noted, permanent loss of brain functions can also be confirmed by absence of circulation to the brain. The brain necessarily ceases functioning after a short period without intracranial circulation, unless it is protected by hypothermia or drug induced depression of neuronal metabolism. In recent years, several procedures have been developed to test for absence of intracranial blood flow, including radioisotope cerebral angiography by bolus or static imaging and four vessel intracranial contrast angiography.[10]

Clinical research has emphasized the development of procedures that can be performed reliably at a patient's bedside, so as to interfere as little as possible with treatment and not to risk harming the patient when recovery may still be possible. The aim of the tests is to reduce mistaken diagnoses that a patient is still alive, without incurring risks of erroneous diagnoses that a patient lacks all brain functioning when such functions actually remain or could recur. This is achieved by establishing first that all brain functions have ceased and then ascertaining that the cessation is irreversible. To do this, the cause of coma must be established and this may require, in addition to history and physical examination, such tests as computerized axial tomography, electroencephalography and echoencephalography.[11] The cause of the cessation of functions must be sufficient to explain the individual's clinical status and must be demonstrated to be permanent during a period of observation.[12]

---

[10]See, e.g., Julius Korein (ed.), Brain Death: Interrelated Medical and Social Issues, 315 Ann. N.Y. Acad. Sci. 62–214 (1978); Julius Korein, Phillip Braunstein, Ajax George, Melvin Wichter, Irving Kricheff, Abraham Lieberman and John Pearson, "Brain Death: I. Angiographic Correlation with the Radioisotopic Bolus Technique for Evaluation of Critical Deficit of Cerebral Blood Flow," 2 Ann. Neurol. 206 (1977); Andrew J.K. Smith and A. Earl Walker, "Cerebral Blood Flow and Brain Metabolism as Indicators of Cerebral Death: A Review," 133 Johns Hopkins Med. J. 107 (1973); Julius M. Goodman and Larry I. Heck, "Confirmation of Brain Death by Bedside Isotope Angiography," 238 J.A.M.A. 966 (1977).

[11]See, e.g., Gian Emilio Chatrian, "Electrophysiologic Evaluation of Brain Death: A Critical Appraisal," in M. J. Aminoff (ed.) Electrodiagnosis in Clinical Neurology, Churchill Livingstone, New York (1980); Donald R. Bennett, Julius Korein, John R. Hughes, Jerome K. Merlis and Cary Suter, Atlas of Electroencephalography in Coma and Cerebral Death, Raven Press, New York (1976); Fred Plum and Jerome B. Posner, op. cit.; Stuart A. Schneck, "Brain Death and Prolonged State of Impaired Responsiveness," 58 Denver L. J. 609, 612–613 (1981).

[12]See, e.g., U.S. Department of Health and Human Services, The NINCDS Collaborative Study of Brain Death, N.I.H. Publication No. 81–2286, U.S. Government Printing Office (1980), reported in,

The studies that document the adequacy of criteria have followed one of two general formats. Some define a group of subjects who have met the proposed criteria and demonstrate that in all such cases the heart soon stopped beating despite intensive therapy.[13] Other studies identify a group of subjects who met the proposed criteria and demonstrate widespread brain necrosis at autopsy, providing the body has remained on a respirator for sufficient time for necrosis to occur.[14] All the studies focus on patients with deep coma including absence of spontaneous breathing (apnea); in addition, some require known and sufficient cause for the absence of brain functions, isoelectric electroencephalogram, dilated pupils, or absent circulation shown by angiography. The published criteria for determining cessation of brain functions have been uniformly successful in diagnosing death. The differences among criteria often arise from differing assessments of the technical skill and instrumentation available to the physician. Experts now generally agree that careful clinical assessment (including identification of a cause of the damage to the brain which is sufficient to explain the clinical findings) is the *sine qua non* of a diagnosis.

The role of confirmatory tests such as electroencephalography or circulation tests beyond such bedside judgments in establishing either the cessation of brain functions or the irreversibility of such cessation has been the subject cf considerable discussion.[15] For example, the Conference of Royal Colleges and Faculties in Britain focused on the function of the brainstem alone to diagnose death.[16] Since the brainstem's retricular activating formation is essential to generating consciousness and its transmittal of motor and sensation impulses is essential to these functions, loss of brainstem functions precludes discernable functioning of the cerebral hemispheres. In addition, the brainstem is the locus of homeostatic control, cranial nerve reflexes, and control of respiration. Thus, if the brainstem

---

"An Appraisal of the Criteria of Cerebral Death. A Summary Statement. A Collaborative Study," 237 *J.A.M.A.* 982 (1977); Peter McL. Black, *op. cit;* Pamela F. Prior, "Brain Death" 1980(i) *Lancet* 1142.

[13]See, *e.g.,* Bryan Jennett, John Gleave and Peter Wilson, "Brain Death in Three Neurosurgical Units" 282 *Brit. Med. J.* 533 (1981).

[14]See, *e.g.,* U.S. Department of Health and Human Services, *The NINCDS Collaborative Study of Brain Death, op. cit.*

[15]Peter McL. Black, *op. cit.*

[16]Conference of Royal Colleges and Faculties of the United Kingdom, "Memorandum on the Diagnosis of Death" (January 1979), *in* Working Party of the United Kingdom Health Departments, *The Removal of Cadaveric Organs for Transplantation: A Code of Practice* (1979) at 32–36.

completely lacks functions, the brain as a whole cannot function. American physicians, however, judge the reliability of brainstem testing to be incomplete. Therefore they endorse the appropriate use of cerebral blood flow testing or electroencephalography in order to confirm the completeness of injury and the irreversibility of conditions that have led to cessation of brain functions.[17] The published data support the reliability of both approaches.

The prevailing British viewpoint on the neurologic diagnosis of death is closer to a *prognostic* approach (that a "point of no return"[18] has been reached in the process of dying), while the American approach is more *diagnostic* in seeking to determine that all functions of the brain have irreversibly ceased at the time of the declaration of death. Also, the British diagnose brain death almost entirely where irremediable structural injury has occurred while the American concept has encompassed all etiologies that may lead to irreversible loss of brain functions in respirator-maintained patients.

The British criteria resemble the American, however, in holding that death has been established when "all functions of the brain have permanently and irreversibly ceased."[19] In measuring *functions*, physicians are not concerned with mere *activity* in cells or groups of cells if such activity (metabolic, electrical, etc.) is not manifested in some way that has significance for the organism as a whole. The same is true of the cells of the heart and lungs; they too may continue to have metabolic and electrical activity after

---

[17] See Appendix F, *infra*; Peter McL. Black *op. cit*; Julius Korein, "Brain Death" *op. cit.*

[18] Conference of Royal Colleges and Faculties, *op. cit.* at 35. "Medicine and the Media," 281 *Brit. Med. J* 1064 (1980). *See also* A. Mohandas and Shelley Chou, "Brain death: A Clinical and pathological study," 35 *J. Neurosurg.* 211, 215 (1971) (authors of so-called "Minnesota criteria" hold that "the state of irreversible damage to the brain-stem ... is the point of no return"). The more typical contrast between the American and British approaches is illustrated by the criteria employed at the University of Pittsburgh School of Medicine where "brain death" is defined as the "irreversible cessation of all brain function," as demonstrated by coma of established cause, absence of movements and brain stem reflexes, and an isoelectric EEG. David J. Powner and Ake Grenvik, "Triage in Patient Care: From Expected Recovery to Brain Death," 8 *Heart & Lung* 1103 (1979). The British rely instead on another observation, confirmed by the University of Pittsburgh, that "*prognosis* appears to be *similarly hopeless* for those patients who have clinical findings consistent with brain death but who have a nonisoelectric EEG." *Id.* at 1107 (emphasis added) (cited by British neurologist Christopher Pallis in lecture at Conference on Brain Death, Boston, Mass., April 4, 1981).

[19] Conference of Royal Colleges and Faculties, *op. cit.* at 36.

death has been diagnosed by cardiopulmonary standards.[20] Tests that measure cellular activity are thus relevant to the determination of death only when they forecast whether missing functions may reappear.

Translating Medical Knowledge into Policy

Knowledgeable physicians agree that, when used in appropriate combinations, available procedures for diagnosing death by brain criteria are at least as accurate as the customary cardiopulmonary tests. Indeed, medical experts testified to the Commission that the risk of mistake in a competently performed examination was infinitesimal. Plainly, the results depend on the personal knowledge, judgment and care of the physicians who apply them. Expert witnesses before the Commission pointed out that many physicians (including some neurologists and neurosurgeons) are not sufficiently familiar with the criteria (much less the detailed tests) by which the cessation of total brain functions is assessed. As one step toward professional education, a group of physicians, working with the encouragement of the Commission, has developed a summary of currently accepted medical practices. (The statement appears as Appendix F to this Report.) Such criteria—particularly as they relate to diagnosing death on neurological grounds will be continually revised by the biomedical community in light of clinical experience and new scientific knowledge.

At present, the accepted norm is that the tests will be employed by a physician who has specialized knowledge of

---

[20] See also pp. 75–76 infra.

their use. Consultation with another appropriately trained physician is typically undertaken to confirm a brain-based diagnosis in an artificially supported individual before any decisions are made on whether to discontinue support.

Particular care must be exercised to establish the cause of the patient's condition and especially to rule out conditions (such as drug intoxication or treatable brain lesions) that can give the misleading appearance that brain functions have stopped irreversibly. (Research is currently underway to test whether hypothermia and large doses of barbiturates might be used to reduce brain injury after trauma or surgery. This will complicate the diagnosis of death in these patients.)

The Commission concludes that reliable means of diagnosis are essential for determinations of death and that the medical community has developed such means. Insistence that determinations of death accord with "accepted medical standards" would thus, in the opinion of the Commission, bring to bear all the usual stimuli for assuring accuracy in medical diagnosis: the testing of practices through biomedical research and the dissemination of the results of such research; the continuing education of physicians and other health care personnel; the conscientious application of professional skills and knowledge; and the encouragement of due care provided by professional standards and by state civil and criminal laws. In the Commission's view, it is not necessary—indeed, it would be a mistake—to enshrine any particular medical criteria, or any requirements for procedure or review, as part of a statute.

Who Ought to "Redefine" Death?

4

The developments in medical technology that permit maintenance of respiration and circulation have engendered broad social concern over unnecessary or inappropriate use of that technology. This, in turn, has provoked the call for new standards by which to determine that death has occurred. To respond, we must ask two questions: What sort of standards, and by whom devised and promulgated? The first question is easier to answer than the second.

As described in the preceding chapter and elaborated in Appendix F, the medical profession has generally accepted the new brain-based critieria as one means for diagnosing death. Yet medical criteria alone cannot meet the public concern, which arose not only because of advances that complicated the decisions of physicians, but also because the public perceived a departure from long-accepted social standards for differentiating life and death. This departure seemed to have momentous implications for many social practices and institutions. Criminal prosecution, inheritance, taxation, treatment of the cadaver, and mourning are all affected by the way society draws the dividing line between life and death.[1]

That the definition of death can touch social life so profoundly, explains why the need for law is perceived. Legal standards for determining when death occurs evolved over the years. They sanctioned the "all bodily functions" view traditionally accepted by the public and practiced by physicians. Any newly formulated standard should attain equal recognition by the public and physicians before being adopted. One must turn, then, to the second question: Who ought to devise and announce the law "defining" death?

[1] See, e.g., Harold L. Hirsh, "Brain Death" 12 *Med. Tri. Tech. Q.* 377, 391 (1975); Kathleen Price, "Defining Death and Dying: A Bibliographic Overview," 71 *L. Library J.* 49, 59–63 (1978).

The Scope of Medical Authority

Traditionally, great deference has been paid to medical expertise in the making of diagnoses of death. As long as the standards employed by the profession were stable and basically congruent with opinion in the community at large, there was little reason for public scrutiny. The law simply reflected the common opinion about death and largely let the physicians—once their techniques and skills had risen to the necessary level of reliability—formulate and apply the tests to measure vital human functions. Yet the movement toward ever more sophisticated medical science, which produced treatments that interfered with the efficacy of the accepted tests, led medicine to new tests that were less comprehensible to the public. This made clear that a choice about the "definition" of death was at issue, a choice that ought to involve people beyond the biomedical community.

Furthermore, even the customary deference of the common law—which regarded the moment of a person's death as a "question of fact" for determination at trial largely on the basis of expert testimony[2] should not obscure the public choices that have been, and must be, made. For despite that deference, the standards applied to give legal effect to the testimony about death (medical as well as lay) were established by the courts "as a matter of law."[3]

Biomedical knowledge ought to continue to inform public policy in revising the legal standards concerning death. Physicians have taken the lead in reconsidering the criteria used in diagnosis. They now know what evidence is needed to attest the cessation of brain functions to be complete and irreversible. Furthermore, they can explain what this irreversible cessation means for various human capabilities and biological activities. But, in the end, the society as a whole must judge that these technical standards and the opinions they reflect conform to the society's settled values and accepted conceptions of human existence and personal rights.[4] This judgment will be most clearly ex-

---

[2] See, e.g., Thomas v. Anderson, 96 Cal. App. 2d 371, 375, 215 P.2d 478, 482 (1950).

[3] See, e.g., Smith v. Smith, 229 Ark. 579, 587, 317 S.W.2d 275, 279 (1958); In re Estate of Schmidt, 261 Cal. App. 2d 262, 273, 67 Cal. Rptr. 847, 854 (1968).

[4] In light of the challenges that have been mounted to any professional prerogative in establishing the standards for determining that a human being has died, it may seem surprising that the traditional role of physicians in applying the standards has not been challenged. The difference in the tasks probably explains the lack of controversy in the latter situation. Application of an agreed-upon standard is a matter for technical expertise, and it is not doubted that competent physicans (among others) possess the necessary proficiency in diagnosis.

pressed through the medium of the law of the land.

Judicial Revision of the Common Law

The medical profession itself has come to recognize the need for official action on the definition of death.[5] Litigation involving physicians as defendants or as key witnesses has been largely responsible for this recognition. These cases made it clear that, surface appearances notwithstanding, the standards by which death is declared are not left to medical discretion alone. There may have been no *statutes* on death, but the "common law", which is to be found in the decisions of judges in prior cases, had established a legal standard.

It might appear simplest to change the common law on death—if change is needed—the same way it was made. Confronted with new biomedical developments—in the form of respirators that make comatose patients without brain functions appear "alive" and tests that show that they are really "dead"—judges might be expected to bring the judicially established standards into line. Predictably, however, while some courts adhered to existing law, others cautiously moved away from it.[6] No clear pattern emerged. This is one of several reasons for doubting that judicial revision of the common law presents a promising route to death policy reform, although it does not counsel against appropriate rulings by judges as cases are presented in which the need to "update" the "definition" arises.

A judge's unwillingness to alter the common law on death does not necessarily mean that the judge adheres unthinkingly to tradition or unreasonably resists new knowledge. Anglo-American jurisprudence is based on precedents. It places great value on evenhandedness among litigants and on assuring everyone that the rules by which they conduct themselves will "not be changed in the middle of the game.[7] Allowing judges to decide every rule of law anew in every case would jeopardize the impartiality of the judicial process and place an impossible burden on the courts.

Nonetheless, precedents must be rethought; such rethinking may occasionally lead to bold statements of new rules of law, rather than the incremental (indeed, often imperceptible) modifications favored in judge-made law. Some judges have made sweeping changes regarding the "redefinition" of death (these are discussed in detail in

---

[5]Frank J. Veith, Jack M. Fein, Moses D. Tendler, Robert M. Veatch, Marc A. Kleiman and George Kalkines, "Brain Death: II. A Status Report of the Legal Considerations" 238 *J.A.M.A.* 1744 (1977).

[6]The judicial rulings on the "definition" of death appear in Appendix D.

[7]Woods v. Lancet, 303 N.Y. 349, 354, 102 N.E. 2d 691, 695 (1951).

Chapter Five). More can be expected over time. Additional reasons militate, however, against relying on common law revision as the primary route to revising the standards for declaring that a person has died.

First, the judicial route would extend the period of uncertainty. This could be unfortunate since the application of some standards could cause unwarranted prolongation of treatment (for bodies that have died) while the application of others could cause premature termination of useful treatment (for patients still alive by "whole brain" criteria). A period of legal uncertainty arises because courts cannot simply "declare" law whenever they decide to do so; revision of the common law awaits litigation in which the parties contend over a particular rule of law in the context of a factual dispute. The parties usually identify the issues, articulate the scope and nature of the dispute, provide the legal reasoning and expert testimony, and propose outcomes. The parties to a dispute may present differing views of an issue without presenting *all* views or even the true polar positions. A judge may not know enough about a field to recognize the need for expert witnesses to supplement the litigants' positions. Anglo-American courts have neither authority nor personnel to conduct independent investigations.

Furthermore, even when courts rule on cases, they do not always "make law." The outcome of a jury trial, for example, is the verdict, usually a simple conclusion to an often complex and secret process. Unless appeal is taken to a higher court, that part of the trial process which *is* public—namely, the judge's rulings on evidence and instructions to the jury—will not emerge in a form that would give them value as a precedent. In most states the appellate process has multiple levels; proceeding through the court system to the highest court involves much time and expense. Only the latter court can promulgate law binding on all the lower courts in the jurisdiction. Finally, even when a case has been decided by the highest court, the "holding" which the case establishes is, strictly speaking, limited to the facts of that case. Courts sometimes state their conclusions in broad terms, of course. But the "obiter dicta"—that is, the court's comments incidental rather than necessary to its decision—are often disregarded. Moreover, the standard declared in a homicide case involving the victim's having been disconnected from the respirator that the defense maintains was keeping him "alive" might be disregarded in a later inheritance case involving the time of death.[8] Also, if the facts of two cases—even those in the same field of law—are sufficiently distinguishable, the ruling of one might not be applied in the second.

Beyond differences in the resulting rules supposedly rooted in the particular (and perhaps peculiar) facts of each case, other variations are likely to arise from the difficulties judges have in stating their conclusions about a specialized field that is probably unfamiliar to them. Further, judges may be quite tempted to "improve" on the decisions of courts that have dealt previously with the subject. Thus, although general rules may emerge from judicial decisions, they emerge slowly and somewhat roughly—despite the pains taken.

In some areas of the law, piecemeal modification of rules is rightly seen as a great strength of the common law. A federal system, such as that of the United States, magnifies this process by greatly increasing the number of appellate courts ruling on an issue in a "binding" fashion. As desirable as this step-by-step process may seem, a persistent diversity of standards on a matter as fundamental as the "definition" of death does not seem desirable. There is nothing to applaud in the prospect that small, and perhaps inadvertent, differences in the opinions of the highest courts in two neighboring states might make a "live" patient "dead" as the ambulance carrying him or her crosses their border.

Legislative Reform

Judicial revision of the common law is too dilatory to dispel public confusion and professionals' doubts. Its tardiness and conservatism may fail to capture the movement of public values, frustrating the norms of participation and pluralism that are important in our society.

Legislative modification—the adoption of a statute to supplement or supplant the common law on death—could include public hearings through which members of the general public would both become more familiar with the issue

---

[8] See Chapter 5, n.42 and accompanying text, and Appendix D at 137 –38. *infra.*

and have their views taken into account in the framing of policy. Legislators, acting directly through legislative committees or with the aid of special purpose study commissions, can investigate both public views and the full range of expert opinion. The views of many groups—representing patients, religious bodies, professional groups, and the general public—should be heard on the "definition" of death. The legislative process easily accomodates the full range of views, unlike the more closed and formal judicial process. (The Commission, in considering the statute recommended in this Report, was likewise able to hear a wide range of professional and lay opinion.)

Legislative reform also has its risks, one of the most prominent being poor drafting. This is a particular danger when issues appear highly technical, uninteresting to legislators, and unlikely to generate passionate feelings. None of these factors should characterize the process of "defining" death, accurately assessed. Though the question has technical aspects, the task of the legislature is not to do the work of physicians in developing medical criteria for diagnosis but to establish the general standards to which society will give legal significance. Similarly, although the attention of the legislature is not likely to be focused on the task of "defining" death the way it is on issues involving economic and political matters that provoke powerful interest groups, there is no question that the subject is one of basic importance to any society: who is alive and who is dead? Finally, the subject is most likely to engender passion when misunderstood, particularly when it becomes confused with the distinct but related question of terminating treatment of respirator-supported patients who still have brain functions although they may not be conscious. With a little care, discussion can be confined to the topic at hand—the recognition of a new formulation of the standards for determining death—standards on which there appears to be general professional and public consensus.

A statute on death ought to guide physicians and others in decision-making about respirator-maintained patients; it ought also to educate those who must make legal and policy decisions. "Legislation will not remove the need for reasoned interpretation—first by physicians and perhaps then by judges—but it can restrict the compass within which they make their choices to one which has been found acceptable by the public."[9] Furthermore, if legislators are guided by a single model bill the likelihood of statutory law that is uniform in language and intent is greatly increased.

---

[9] Alexander M. Capron and Leon R. Kass, "A Statutory Definition of the Standards for Determining Human Death: An Appraisal and a Proposal," 121 *U. Pa. L. Rev.* 87, 101 (1972).

In sum, while the Commission believes that courts should update the standards for declaring death as the issue arises in litigation, it does not think the formulation of new standards should have to await judicial decision. Besides the uncertainty engendered, litigation (civil or criminal) involves time, expense and psychological trauma; it would be unfortunate for society to have to rely on retrospective determination of the basic rules concerning such a fundamental problem as the "definition" of death. The legislative alternative may have drawbacks; still the Commission concludes that (subject to the guidance provided in the next chapter) it is the better course.

The Federal Role

The articulation of standards for determining that a human being has died has traditionally been a matter for state rather than federal law. Necessarily, this allocation of law-making responsibility gives rise to the possibility of variations among the laws of the several states. In the field of concern here, just such variation has come about over the past decade, as some states have made statutory or judicial changes in their "definition" of death and others have not.

For reasons set forth more fully in the next chapter, the Commission believes that uniformity on this matter is a desirable goal. One would expect the same basic rule about who is dead, and who is not, to apply everywhere in the United States. Moreover, since certainty and clarity are highly valuable in this area, uniformity of statutory language would be preferable lest differences in words seem to open the door to differences in substance.

The federal government could respond to the harm that is risked by diversity in the states' legal rules for determining death by passing a statute intended to preempt the field. The Commission believes that such action would be premature, before seeing whether the states all adopt the Uniform Determination of Death Act and secure uniformity that way. Until this is tried, there is no justification for disturbing the traditional allocation of state and federal responsibilities on this subject.

The federal government may have two constructive (and non-coercive) roles to play in defining death, however. First, the federal government can usefully bring together experts and representatives of different streams of thought on the matter, seek to clarify the issues at stake, and facilitate cooperative formulation of a statute and medical criteria. The Commission has attempted to perform precisely this role through its hearings, its participation in law reform efforts, its encouragement of medical groups to examine the reliability of criteria for diagnosing death, and its publication and distribution of this Report.

Second, the federal government should "define death" for matters under direct federal jurisdiction. When legal disputes arise in such places—for example, military installations (including military hospitals), Indian reservations, and other federal preserves[10]—governing law may be either that of the state within which the place is located or special federal law applicable to such places.

Federal law arises in some instances from Congressional enactment and in others from the decisions of federal judges, who have on occasion created a "federal common law" rule different from existing state law.[11] A federal judge faced with an issue turning on the "definition" of

---

[10]U.S. CONST. Art. 1, § 8, cl. 17, "The Congress shall have Power. . . . To exercise exclusive Legislation in all Cases whatsoever. . . over all Places purchased by the Consent of the Legislature of the State in which the Same shall be, for the Erection of Forts, Magazines, Aresenals, dock-Yards, and other needful Buildings," U.S. CONST, Art. 4, § 3, cl. 2, "The Congress shall have Power to dispose of and make all needful Rules and Regulations respecting the Territory or other Property belonging to the United States,"; 18 U.S.C. 7 (statute defining special maritime and territorial jurisdiction of the United States for the purpose of federal criminal law.)

[11]The "international rule" of Chicago, Rock Island & Pacific Ry. v. McGlinn, 114 U.S. 542 (1885), under which the rules of state law existing at the time the federal enclave was acquired continue to apply until the federal government imposes a new rule has been

death applicable in a federal preserve would probably rely upon the standard for determining death in force in the state where the federal land was located. If that state has failed to update its legal standard to reflect the developments discussed in this Report, the Commission believes that it would be appropriate for the court to take account of the material discussed in this Report and to employ a legal standard that includes irreversible cessation of total brain functions as well as irreversible cessation of heart and lung functions. To promote uniformity, the court ought to establish the more inclusive standard as a matter of federal common law.

It would be both simpler and more certain, however, were the federal rule to follow the route the Commission has endorsed for state law, namely the adoption of a statute. Accordingly, the Commission recommends that the Congress adopt the Uniform Determinationn of Death Act proposed in this Report as the governing rule in instances falling within federal jurisdiction. (The statute should be enacted as a definitional provision of general application, probably as an amendment to Title 1 of the United States Code.)

The Commission believes that federal adoption of the statute recommended herein for use in only these matters already under direct federal jurisdiction would be salutary in its own right. Furthermore, without in any way coercing the States, federal adoption would offer useful encouragement to the States to place this matter on their legislative agendas.

---

substantially weakened by Howard v. Commissioners, 344 U.S. 624 (1953) and its progeny, which accept coexisting state authority over federal enclaves provided that state law does not interfere with federal jurisdiction. Some relief from the problems faced by individuals who reside on federally owned land which "are especially acute where the litigation arises from acts occurring upon the enclave itself," Richard T. Altieri, "Federal Enclaves: The Impact of Exclusive Legislative Jurisdiction upon Civil Litigation," 72 *Military L. Rev.* 55 (1976), is provided by federal statutes making state law governing, for example, wrongful death, 16 U.S.C. 457 (1970), and criminal law, 18 U.S.C., 14 (1970), applicable to federal enclaves. *See generally* U.S. Attorney General, *Report of the Interdepartmental Committee for the Study of Jurisdiction over Federal Areas Within the States* (1957); Note, "The Federal Common Law," 82 *Harv. L. Rev.* 1512 (1969).

EUTHANASIA

In its original Greek, the term "euthanasia" refers to allowing a person to die a "good death," whether that meant with dignity, without pain, or with honor. In modern times, the term took on more sinister connotations, referring to the eugenics movements of the early twentieth century and the Nazi policies of the mid-twentieth century. In the right-to-die debate, the term has been used in both senses as proponents seek a "good death" and opponents warn of social engineering and discrimination against aged and disabled members of society.

The term euthanasia is also subject to numerous subdivisions, such as those between voluntary and involuntary euthanasia and between passive and active euthanasia. Each of these terms may then be combined as in voluntary passive euthanasia, voluntary active euthanasia, and so on. Although most courts uphold the right of a competent patient to decline treatment and thus to die (*i.e.*, voluntary passive euthanasia), the issue is not a closed one. David Schanker ("Of Suicide Machines, Euthanasia Legislation, and the Health Care Crisis") argues, for instance, that the current acceptance of voluntary euthanasia, active or passive, masks the failure of health care systems to address the needs of the terminally ill, the elderly, and the indigent. Schanker is concerned that informing a terminally ill patient of his right to die essentially sends a message that it is time to die, and he is concerned that the "health care crisis" in the United States may create incentives for health-care professionals to urge euthanasia upon the "medically indigent."[1] Apart from the socioeconomic aspects of euthanasia, Schanker suggests that the medical profession has failed in its "management" of death and that much of the attractiveness of euthanasia may be due to the public's legitimate fear "of pain, of dying alone, and of the tyranny of medical technology." Thus, in warning of the flaws of euthanasia, Schanker both invokes the fear of social engineering masquerading as beneficent euthanasia and suggests that so-called "voluntary" euthanasia may not be truly voluntary.

In contrast, Dana Hirsch ("Euthanasia: Is It Murder or Mercy Killing? A Comparison of the Criminal Laws in the United States, the Netherlands, and Switzerland") advocates permitting more, rather than less, euthanasia. Hirsch focuses on the distinction between voluntary "active" euthanasia, something akin to suicide (addressed in a later section) where a person, or those acting on his or her behalf, affirmatively ends life in some manner, and voluntary "passive" euthanasia, where no affirmative actions are taken to extend a dying patient's life. The grey area, of course, is when the patient's life is already being artificially maintained: is it active or passive euthanasia to remove the life support and allow the patient to die? In practice, voluntary passive euthanasia is routinely accepted while active euthanasia of any kind, or at least that which requires the active assistance of a third party, is often criminalized. Hirsch argues, however, that voluntary active euthanasia should be permitted and that the law, instead of punishing it as murder, should treat it differently and more leniently. She suggests, as alternatives to the current American treatment (exemplified by the Michigan authorities' attempts to prosecute Dr. Kevorkian), the more permissive approaches adopted in the Netherlands, where physician-assisted suicide is permitted in limited circumstances, and in Switzerland, where "mercy killings" are given a different classification than murder and are subject to lesser penalties.

Euthanasia has become, in modern times, an ugly word. It is, however, an appropriate one in the right-to-die context, for both its connotations. Quality of life and a good death are important, and a fully competent and informed adult should be allowed to choose death when life, current or future, becomes unbearable. Regardless of whether euthanasia is active or passive, voluntary or involuntary, the fact remains that someone is either being killed or allowed to die. If we are making quality-of-life judgments, or ratifying the quality-of-life judgments of the disabled and the ill, we must do so openly and honestly and not force our views on the person who must make the decision. Euthanasia in modern times must be a "good death" and not a coerced one.

NOTES

1. For similar views, see Jennifer Zima's article in Part 4 on assisted suicide and Mary Johnson's article in Part 10 on voluntary active euthanasia.

Of Suicide Machines, Euthanasia Legislation, and the Health Care Crisis

DAVID R. SCHANKER[*]

Helping another person to die is presently against the law. You may think this is a stupid, unreasonable ban but we live in a society under the rule of law so we have to be careful about what we do.[1]

The moment had come. With a nod from Janet I turned on the ECG and said, "Now." Janet hit the Mercitron's switch with the outer edge of her palm. In about ten seconds her eyelids began to flicker and droop. She looked up at me and said, "Thank you, thank you." I replied at once as her eyelids closed, "Have a nice trip."[2]

INTRODUCTION

On June 4, 1990, a bizarre event in a trailer park in a suburb of Detroit, Michigan, brought national attention to the issue of euthanasia. In the back of a rusted Volkswagen van, retired pathologist Dr. Jack Kevorkian assisted Janet Adkins to take her own life using a "suicide machine" he had invented.[3] Adkins, a victim of Alzheimer's disease, had only to touch a hair-trigger switch to begin the intravenous self-administration of a coma-inducing drug, followed by a lethal dose of potassium chloride.[4] While much of the medical community condemned Kevorkian, public opinion supported Adkins's right to control her own fate,[5] and the incident helped move euthanasia from a fringe belief to a mainstream concern.[6] Since Adkins's death, a series of events has kept the issue before the public,[7] and if euthanasia advocates have their way,

---

* J.D. Candidate, 1993, Indiana University School of Law–Bloomington; M.F.A., Columbia University, 1987; B.F.A., New York University, 1979. I wish to thank Professor Roger Dworkin for his guidance and comments on drafts of this Note.

1. DEREK HUMPHRY, FINAL EXIT 29 (1991).

2. JACK KEVORKIAN, PRESCRIPTION: MEDICIDE 230 (1991).

3. Lisa Belkin, *Doctor Tells of First Death Using His Suicide Device*, N.Y. TIMES, June 6, 1990, at A1.

4. *Id.* at B6.

5. Tamar Lewin, *Doctor Cleared of Murdering Woman with Suicide Machine*, N.Y. TIMES, Dec. 14, 1990, at B8.

6. Timothy Egan, *Washington Voters Weigh If There Is a Right to Die*, N.Y. TIMES, Oct. 14, 1991, at A1.

7. In July, 1991, a grand jury in Rochester, New York, refused to indict a physician who admitted helping a leukemia patient commit suicide. Lawrence K. Altman, *Jury Declines to Indict a Doctor Who Said He Aided in a Suicide*, N.Y. TIMES, July 27, 1991, at A1; *see infra* notes 77-83 and accompanying text. In August, 1991, *Final Exit*, a do-it-yourself suicide manual by Hemlock Society founder Derek Humphry reached *The New York Times* bestseller list, where it stayed for 18 weeks. *Best Sellers*, N.Y.

voluntary euthanasia will be legalized, irrevocably altering the way death occurs in our society and the fundamental relationship of human beings to death and dying.

Euthanasia proponents contend that allowing a patient to request medical assistance in dying is "the ultimate extension of patients' rights."[8] Opponents maintain that medicine should remain a profession dedicated to healing—"[i]ts tools should not be used to kill people."[9] Legal euthanasia represents a momentous departure from medical tradition, and it presents a host of problematic legal, moral, ethical, and medical issues.

The rapid advance of biotechnology over the past three decades has revolutionized the process of dying, and many terminally ill patients and their families have found themselves helplessly confronted with a death agonizingly

---

TIMES, Jan. 26, 1992, § 7 (Book Review) at 22. In September, 1991, the Dutch government released the first comprehensive study of the practice of euthanasia in the Netherlands. Marlise Simons, *Dutch Survey Casts New Light on Patients Who Choose to Die*, N.Y. TIMES, Sept. 11, 1991, at C12. In October, 1991, Kevorkian assisted the suicides of Sherry Miller, 43, a victim of multiple sclerosis, and Marjorie Wantz, 58, who had papilloma virus; neither woman was terminally ill. *Suicide Victims Were Adamant, Lawyers Claim*, L.A. TIMES, Oct. 28, 1991, at A17. In November, 1991, an "Initiative for Death With Dignity" went before the voters in Washington State, who rejected the opportunity to make Washington the first state in the union to allow doctors actively to end the life of a terminally ill patient upon request. Egan, *supra* note 6. Designated "Initiative 119," the measure was put on the ballot after 233,000 signatures were gathered by a coalition of pro-euthanasia groups. *Id.* On May 15, 1992, Kevorkian assisted the suicide of Susan Williams, 52, a multiple sclerosis victim. Al Koski, *Dr. Death Strikes Again*, UPI, May 15, 1992, *available in* LEXIS, Nexis Library, Wire Service File. On July 21, 1992, Kevorkian was acquitted of the October 1991 suicides. Al Koski, *Judge Frees 'Dr. Death' of Murder Charges*, UPI, July 21, 1992, *available in* LEXIS, Nexis Library, Wire Service File [hereinafter Koski, *Acquittal*]. On September 26, 1992, Kevorkian assisted the suicide of Lois Hawes, 52, a cancer victim. Robert Ourlian & Elizabeth Atkins, *Supporters of 'Dr. Death' See New Era in Assisted Suicides*, Gannett News Service, Sept. 28, 1992, *available in* LEXIS, Nexis Library, News Service File. On October 6, 1992, the Michigan House of Representatives Subcommittee on Death and Dying approved a bill to allow physician-assisted suicide. Joyce Price, *Michigan Committee Approves Assisted-Suicide Bill*, WASH. TIMES, Oct. 8, 1992, at A5. On November 3, 1992, California voters rejected Proposition 161, a measure to legalize voluntary active euthanasia in that state. George de Lama, *States Take Pulse on Morality*, CHI. TRIB., Nov. 5, 1992, § 1, at 7. On November 23, 1992, Kevorkian assisted the suicide of Catherine Andreyev, 46, a breast cancer victim. Al Koski, *Kevorkian Helps Sixth Woman Commit Suicide*, UPI, Nov. 23, 1992, *available in* LEXIS, Nexis Library, Wire Service File. On December 15, 1992, Kevorkian assisted the suicides of Marguerite Tate, a 70-year-old victim of heart disease, emphysema, and arthritis, and Marcella Lawrence, a 67-year-old victim of amyotrophic lateral sclerosis, just hours before Michigan Governor John Engler signed legislation banning assisted suicide for two years beginning March 30, 1993, while a commission studies the issue. *Two More Suicides Before Governor OKs Ban*, CHI. TRIB., Dec. 16, 1992, § 1, at 6; *see infra* notes 72-73 and accompanying text. In the weeks before the ban was to take effect, Kevorkian stepped up his pace, assisting the suicides of four men and three women, ages ranging from 41 to 82. Tom Morganthau, *Dr. Kevorkian's Death Wish*, NEWSWEEK, Mar. 8, 1993, at 46. In response, the Michigan legislature moved the ban's effective date up to February 25, 1993. *Id.*

8. Egan, *supra* note 6 (quoting Dr. Linda Gromko, a Seattle family physician and euthanasia advocate).

9. *Id.* (quoting the American Medical Society's ethics committee).

protracted through the intervention of life-sustaining medical devices. From the New Jersey Supreme Court's *Quinlan*[10] decision in 1976 through the United States Supreme Court decision in *Cruzan*[11] in 1990, the judicial system has struggled to define the limits of patient autonomy.[12] Most states now recognize that patients have the right to refuse medical treatment, including artificially supplied nutrition and hydration, either themselves, if competent, or through the use of advance directives.[13] Opinion polls indicate

---

10. *In re* Quinlan, 355 A.2d 647 (N.J.), *cert. denied,* 429 U.S. 922 (1976).

11. Cruzan v. Director, Mo. Dep't of Health, 497 U.S. 261 (1990).

12. Courts have defined the limits of patient autonomy by balancing self-determination interests against state interests in the preservation of life. In *In re Quinlan,* the New Jersey Supreme Court held that the federal constitutional right to privacy encompassed "a patient's decision to decline medical treatment under certain circumstances . . . ." *In re* Quinlan, 355 A.2d at 663. In Superintendent of Belchertown State School v. Saikewicz, 370 N.E.2d 417 (Mass. 1977), the Supreme Judicial Court of Massachusetts held that incompetent persons retain the same rights as competent persons "because the value of human dignity extends to both," and balanced those rights against countervailing state interests. *Id.* at 427. In the first federal case to confront these issues, Gray v. Romeo, 697 F. Supp. 580 (D.R.I. 1988), the court distinguished suicide from self-determination, finding that suicide is "deliberately ending a life by artificial means," while self-determination is "allowing nature to take its course." *Id.* at 589 (citations omitted). In its 1990 *Cruzan* decision, the United States Supreme Court assumed, for purposes of its decision, that "the United States Constitution would grant a competent person a constitutionally protected right to refuse lifesaving hydration and nutrition." *Cruzan,* 497 U.S. at 279.

Of the several cases dealing with the right of competent patients to refuse life-saving treatment, most early cases involved Jehovah's Witnesses' refusal of blood transfusions. *See* Martha A. Matthews, Comment, *Suicidal Competence and the Patient's Right to Refuse Lifesaving Treatment,* 75 CAL. L. REV. 707, 716-18 (1987). Since 1973, however, competent patients have been permitted to refuse a breast biopsy, *In re* Yetter, 41 Northampton County Rptr. 67, 62 Pa. D. & C.2d 619 (1973), refuse amputation of a gangrenous limb, *In re* Quackenbush, 383 A.2d 785 (Morris County Ct., N.J. 1978); Lane v. Candura, 376 N.E.2d 1232 (Mass. Ct. App. 1978), refuse dialysis, *In re* Lydia E. Hall Hospital, 455 N.Y.S.2d 706 (Sup. Ct. 1982), and demand the removal of a respirator, Satz v. Perlmutter, 362 So.2d 160 (Fla. Dist. Ct. App. 1978). Two California cases, Bartling v. Superior Court (Glendale Adventist Medical Center), 209 Cal. Rptr. 220 (Cal. Ct. App. 1984), and Bouvia v. Superior Court (Glenchar), 225 Cal. Rptr. 297 (Cal. Ct. App. 1986), allowed the refusal of treatment by individuals who were not considered terminally ill. In *Bartling,* the court held that competent patients have the right to decide whether to submit to medical treatment, balancing that right against the state interests enunciated in *Saikewicz. Bartling,* 209 Cal. Rptr. at 224. The *Bouvia* court, in deciding to allow a 28-year-old quadriplegic woman with cerebral palsy and degenerative arthritis to compel the removal of a nasogastric feeding tube, denied a state interest in preserving the life of an individual in Bouvia's condition:

> We do not believe it is the policy of this State that all and every life must be preserved against the will of the sufferer. It is incongruous, if not monstrous, for medical practitioners to assert their right to preserve a life that someone else must live, or, more accurately, endure for "15 to 20 years."

Bouvia, 225 Cal. Rptr. at 305.

13. An advance directive is a document that allows an individual to specify the kind of care he or she wishes to receive (or not to receive) in the event of incompetency. Advance directives generally take two forms: living wills and durable powers of attorney. Living wills permit patients to request that medical interventions that would prolong the dying process not be administered. PRESIDENT'S COMMISSION FOR THE STUDY OF ETHICAL PROBLEMS IN MEDICINE AND BIOMEDICAL AND BEHAVIOR RESEARCH, DECIDING TO FOREGO LIFE-SUSTAINING TREATMENT 139 (1983). Durable power of attorney

widespread support for extending patient autonomy to permit voluntary euthanasia,[14] and while physicians' associations, including the American Medical Association, oppose euthanasia, many doctors support the administration of euthanasia in exceptional circumstances.[15] In the Netherlands, despite its statutory illegality, euthanasia was practiced routinely under judicial guidelines for nearly twenty years, until the Dutch Parliament codified a set of guidelines in February 1993, virtually immunizing physicians from prosecution.[16] Many American physicians believe that active euthanasia is already performed on a regular basis in hospitals throughout the United States.[17]

The spread of AIDS, the suffering of patients with advanced cancer, and the desire of many Americans to wrest control of their medical destinies from the health care establishment may be important factors in public support for legal euthanasia. Moreover, euthanasia is emerging as a significant public policy issue at a time when health care policy making is in turmoil. Issues of resource allocation, the care of the medically indigent, and the care of the terminally ill are facets of a health care crisis of dire proportions. The recent surge of interest in euthanasia may also be symptomatic of many Americans' lack of faith in our ability to solve the seemingly intractable dilemmas in our health care system.

This Note examines the question of whether the law should accommodate a mechanism by which physicians may actively end the life of a terminally ill

---

statutes permit individuals to appoint a surrogate to make health care decisions should the individual become incompetent. *Id.* at 145. The Patient Self-Determination Act, which went into effect on December 1, 1991, was intended to bring about greater awareness of advance directives. Omnibus Budget Reconciliation Act of 1990, Pub. L. No. 101-508 (1990), §§ 4206(a), 4751(a) (Patient Self-Determination Act). Hospitals and nursing homes participating in Medicare or Medicaid are now required to inform all adult patients of their rights under state law to make decisions concerning their care, including the right to accept or refuse treatment. *Id.*

    14. An April, 1990, Roper poll asked: "When a person has a painful and distressing terminal disease, do you think doctors should or should not be allowed by law to end the patient's life if there is no hope of recovery and the patient requests it?" The results: Yes, 64%; No, 24%; Don't know, 13%. Don C. Shaw, *Reflection, in* ACTIVE EUTHANASIA, RELIGION, AND THE PUBLIC DEBATE 98 (Ron Hamel ed., 1991) [hereinafter ACTIVE EUTHANASIA]. Polls taken in Washington State during the campaign for Initiative 119 and in California during the campaign for Proposition 161 showed wide margins of support for the measures until the last days before voting took place. Peter Steinfels, *Beliefs*, N.Y. TIMES, Nov. 9, 1991, at 11; *California: Proposition 166 on the Defensive*, HEALTH LINE, Oct. 13, 1992. The last-minute change of heart in both states may be attributed to the effective and ubiquitous anti-euthanasia advertising campaigns by a coalition of Catholic and pro-life groups and medical associations. de Lama, *supra* note 7; Egan, *supra* note 6.

    15. Robert Moss, *Reflection, in* ACTIVE EUTHANASIA, *supra* note 14, at 95-97.

    16. William Drozdiak, *Dutch Remove Barrier to Doctors Carrying Out Euthanasia*, WASH. POST, Feb. 10, 1993, at A23. *See infra* notes 84-124 and accompanying text.

    17. Richard A. Knox, *Dutch Study Reports Euthanasia Practiced Widely but Cautiously*, BOSTON GLOBE, Sept. 13, 1991, at 1; *see also infra* note 39 and accompanying text.

patient through voluntary euthanasia. Much of the recent dialogue concerning euthanasia has centered on whether euthanasia is ever morally justifiable.[18] In this Note, I set aside the moral and ethical dimensions of the debate and deal primarily with the likely consequences attending the various schemes for legal voluntary euthanasia in our society and present health care system.

Part I of this Note surveys current arguments for and against the legalization of euthanasia. Part II examines the way courts in the United States and the Netherlands have dealt with voluntary euthanasia and analyzes proposals for statutory reform. Part III presents an argument that the law should not accommodate voluntary euthanasia until systemic problems in our health care institutions are resolved and our management of death and dying is reformed.

I. BACKGROUND: THE EUTHANASIA DEBATE

To the ancient Greeks, the term *eu thanatos* meant "good or easy death," in the sense of dying peacefully and with a psychologically balanced state of mind.[19] Today, euthanasia is commonly understood to refer to the intentional medical inducement of death.

Arguments in favor of legal euthanasia stress autonomy and mercy as values served by voluntary euthanasia. The autonomy argument holds that a patient's power to request that a physician end his life is the ultimate extension of self-determination, based on the established right of privacy and right to refuse treatment.[20] The mercy argument holds that if a terminal patient prefers

---

18. For a detailed analysis of the moral aspects of euthanasia from a pro-euthanasia point of view, see JAMES RACHELS, THE END OF LIFE (1986). The opposing moral arguments are well expressed in Arthur J. Dyck, *An Alternative to the Ethic of Euthanasia, in* ETHICAL ISSUES IN DEATH AND DYING 281 (Robert F. Weir ed., 1977).

19. Edwin R. DuBose, *A Brief Historical Perspective, in* ACTIVE EUTHANASIA, *supra* note 14, at 18.

20. *See supra* note 12. *See generally* Steven J. Wolhandler, Note, *Voluntary Active Euthanasia for the Terminally Ill and the Constitutional Right to Privacy*, 69 CORNELL L. REV. 363 (1984); Note, *Physician-Assisted Suicide and the Right to Die with Assistance*, 105 HARV. L. REV. 2021 (1992). The concept of patient autonomy, when framed in terms of rights, is ultimately unhelpful in formulating euthanasia policy. Even fundamental libertarianism derived from John Stuart Mill and the contractual libertarian theory of Hobbes and Locke recognize that government may interfere in the sphere of private action when societal interests are implicated. *See generally* John S. Mill, *On Liberty, in* PREFACES TO LIBERTY: SELECTED WRITINGS OF JOHN STUART MILL 239 (Bernard Wishy ed., 1959) (1859); THOMAS HOBBES, LEVIATHAN (Cambridge Univ. Press 1991) (1651); JOHN LOCKE, TWO TREATISES OF CIVIL GOVERNMENT (Peter Laslett ed., student ed. 1988) (1698). Suicide, assisted suicide, and voluntary euthanasia are activities which may be described on a continuum of autonomy: suicide is a solitary, self-referential act; assisted suicide requires advice or assistance with the act; voluntary euthanasia needs the completion of the act by another. Suicide is more likely than are assisted suicide and voluntary euthanasia to satisfy libertarian criteria for a liberty which deserves no interference, but, as Mill asserts, "No person is an entirely isolated being; it is impossible for a person to do anything seriously or

death to lingering on in torment, it is not immoral to help the patient die sooner.[21] At the same time, the values of autonomy and mercy can each be extrapolated to situations which do not involve the other. Autonomy may be extended to allow euthanasia where the patient is not in pain but wishes to die for other reasons: a deterioration in quality of life, the loss of dignity, or the wish not to burden his family financially with a prolonged hospital or nursing home stay. The value of mercy may be extended to allow euthanasia for patients who are incompetent to make informed decisions regarding their care—such as Alzheimer's patients, the senile, children, or the retarded—yet who suffer intense and intractable pain. Proposed euthanasia legislation is generally intended to permit the narrow range of cases embodying both the expression of autonomy and the merciful alleviation of suffering.[22]

Arguments against legalization of euthanasia comprise three major themes: the sanctity of human life, the slippery slope, and the danger of abuse.[23] The sanctity of life argument emphasizes the inviolability of our cultural prohibition against killing.[24] Slippery slope arguments envision the legalization of voluntary euthanasia as inexorably leading to forms of involuntary euthanasia and an attendant devaluation of human life.[25] Danger of abuse arguments envision the coercion of patients by their families, doctors, or health care workers to request euthanasia, and the disregard of euthanasia guidelines by physicians and institutions.[26] The arguments presented in Part III of this Note fall roughly into this last category, examining the potential effects of allowing the practice of euthanasia in our health care system.

---

permanently hurtful to himself without mischief reaching at least to his near connections, and often far beyond them." Mill, *supra*, at 326.

21. RACHELS, *supra* note 18, at 154. Rachels develops the mercy argument using utilitarian principles: "Any action is morally right if it serves to increase the amount of happiness in the world or to decrease the amount of misery." *Id.*

22. *See infra* notes 125-73 and accompanying text.

23. *See* Tom L. Beauchamp & Seymour Perlin, *Euthanasia and Natural Death, in* ETHICAL ISSUES IN DEATH AND DYING 217-18 (Tom L. Beauchamp & Seymour Perlin èds., 1978) [hereinafter ETHICAL ISSUES].

24. *See* C. Everett Koop, *The Challenge of Definition*, 19 HASTINGS CENTER REP. (Special Supp.), Jan.-Feb. 1989, at 2.

25. Yale Kamisar and Glanville Williams debated "slippery slope" and "wedge" (Williams's term) arguments on euthanasia in an exchange of articles in the late 1950s. Kamisar wrote an article, Yale Kamisar, *Some Non-Religious Views Against "Mercy Killing" Legislation*, 42 MINN. L. REV. 969 (1958) [hereinafter Kamisar, *Non-Religious Views*], in response to Williams's book *The Sanctity of Life and the Criminal Law.* GLANVILLE WILLIAMS, THE SANCTITY OF LIFE AND THE CRIMINAL LAW (1957). Williams replied with an article of his own. Glanville Williams, *"Mercy Killing" Legislation—A Rejoinder to the Non-Religious Objections*, 43 MINN. L. REV. 134 (1959). In 1991, Kamisar revisited the debate. Yale Kamisar, *When Is There a Constitutional "Right to Die"? When Is There No Constitutional "Right to Live"?*, 25 GA. L. REV. 1203 (1991) [hereinafter Kamisar, *Right to Die?*].

26. Beauchamp & Perlin, *supra* note 23, at 218.

At the core of the euthanasia debate, however, is the distinction between active and passive euthanasia, that is, between "killing" and "letting die."[27] Active euthanasia is the administration of any means intended to produce death, such as the deliberate injection of a lethal dose of morphine. Passive euthanasia is the withdrawal of life-sustaining care, such as artificially supplied nutrition and hydration or a respirator.

Passive euthanasia has been legally sanctioned since *In re Quinlan*,[28] in which the New Jersey Supreme Court permitted a respirator to be removed in order to allow an incompetent patient to die. No statutory change was necessary to immunize physicians from legal responsibility for withdrawal of treatment.[29] Legalizing active euthanasia, on the other hand, is likely to necessitate a statutory change because the act of killing a patient, regardless of the circumstances, is currently considered murder.[30] Even if a physician were merely to supply a patient with lethal drugs for the patient's self-administration, as Dr. Kevorkian did, the physician would, in most states, be violating laws against assisted suicide.[31]

---

27. Six identifiable major forms of euthanasia were delineated from a medical perspective by Dr. George Lundberg, editor of the *Journal of the American Medical Association*: (1) *passive*, where a physician may choose not to treat a life-threatening condition in a noncomatose patient; (2) *semipassive*, where a physician may withhold medical treatment, such as nutrition or fluids, from a person in a coma; (3) *semiactive*, where a physician may disconnect a ventilator from a patient who is in a stable, vegetative state and has no hope of regaining consciousness; (4) *accidental ("double effect")*, where a physician may administer a narcotic to relieve pain and the narcotic may incidentally depress respiration sufficiently to cause death; (5) *suicidal*, where a physician may provide a patient with lethal drugs which the patient may choose to take; and (6) *active*, where a physician may administer a lethal overdose of morphine or potassium in a patient with, for example, advanced AIDS. George D. Lundberg, *'It's Over, Debbie' and the Euthanasia Debate*, 259 JAMA 2142, 2143 (1988).

28. 355 A.2d 647 (N.J.), *cert. denied*, 429 U.S. 922 (1976).

29. In 1983, two California doctors were convicted of murder and conspiracy to commit murder for removing a respirator and withdrawing artificially supplied nutrition and hydration from a comatose patient at the family's request. Barber v. Superior Court, 195 Cal. Rptr. 484, 486-87 (Cal. Ct. App. 1983). On appeal, the court ruled for the first time that nutrition and hydration constituted a medical procedure, and stated that physicians are under no duty to continue treatment when there is no hope of recovery. *Id.* at 493.

30. *See infra* notes 41-43 and accompanying text. It is possible, however, that if a constitutional "right to die" is established for patients, homicide statutes could not be constitutionally applied to physicians who kill patients in furtherance of that right. A case has yet to be reported in which a physician uses a constitutional argument as a defense to homicide (or assisting a suicide) in voluntary euthanasia.

31. Currently, 31 states and Puerto Rico have statutes criminalizing assisted suicide: Alaska, ALASKA STAT. § 11.41.120(a)(2) (1989); Arizona, ARIZ. REV. STAT. ANN. § 13-1103(A)(3) (1989); Arkansas, ARK. CODE ANN. § 5-10-104(a)(2) (Michie 1987); California, CAL. PENAL CODE § 401 (West 1988); Colorado, COLO. REV. STAT. § 18-3-104(1)(b) (1978); Connecticut, CONN. GEN. STAT. ANN. § 53a-56(a)(2) (West 1985); Delaware, DEL. CODE ANN. tit. 11, § 645 (1987); Florida, FLA. STAT. ANN. § 782.08 (West 1992); Hawaii, HAWAII REV. STAT. § 707-702(1)(b) (1985); Illinois, ILL. ANN. STAT. ch. 38, para. 12-31 (Smith-Hurd 1992); Indiana, IND. CODE ANN. § 35-42-1-2 (Burns 1985); Kansas, KAN. STAT. ANN. § 21-3406 (1988); Maine, ME. REV. STAT. ANN. tit. 17-A, §§ 201, 204 (1983);

Euthanasia proponents assert that the distinction between active and passive euthanasia is arbitrary and morally irrelevant.[32] Opponents uphold the active/passive distinction as the most appropriate place to draw the line on how far society can safely go in allowing any form of euthanasia.[33] Efforts to legalize active voluntary euthanasia have relied on the premise that the active/passive distinction is irrelevant—in other words, since the lethal injection or the withdrawal of treatment both result in the patient's death, the lethal injection should also be allowed.[34] The active/passive distinction is closely related to the categorical differences of acts of commission and omission, of withholding and withdrawing treatment, and of the direct and indirect causation of death.[35] Perhaps the strongest argument for its maintenance is that it preserves the historical role of physicians as healers and comforters, not as agents of death.[36] The fact remains that the active/passive distinction is the prevailing legal boundary which physicians must observe with respect to their patients' right to die.

II. EUTHANASIA AND THE LAW

Euthanasia has been addressed in courts and legislatures in the United States sporadically during the twentieth century. Its treatment suggests public

---

Michigan, Act of Dec. 15, 1992, 1992 Mich. Pub. Acts 270 (creating Michigan commission on death and dying and prohibiting certain acts pertaining to suicide assistance); Minnesota, MINN. STAT. ANN. § 609.215 (West 1987); Mississippi, MISS. CODE ANN. § 97-3-49 (1973); Missouri, MO. REV. STAT. § 565.023 (1992); Montana, MONT. CODE ANN. § 45-5-105 (1991); Nebraska, NEB. REV. STAT. § 28-307 (1989); New Hampshire, N.H. REV. STAT. ANN. § 630:4 (1986); New Jersey, N.J. STAT. ANN. § 2C:11-6 (West 1982); New Mexico, N.M. STAT. ANN. § 30-2-4 (Michie 1984); New York, N.Y. PENAL LAW § 120.30 (McKinney 1987); North Dakota, N.D. CENT. CODE § 12.1-16-04 (1991); Oklahoma, OKLA. STAT. ANN. tit. 21, §§ 813-818 (West 1983); Oregon, OR. REV. STAT. § 163.125(1)(b) (1990); Pennsylvania, 18 PA. CONS. STAT. ANN. § 2505 (1983); Puerto Rico, P.R. LAWS ANN. tit. 33, § 4009 (1984); South Dakota, S.D. CODIFIED LAWS ANN. § 22-16-37 (1988); Texas, TEX. PENAL CODE ANN. § 22.08 (West 1989); Washington, WASH. REV. CODE ANN. § 9A.36.060 (West 1988); and Wisconsin, WIS. STAT. ANN. § 940.12 (West 1982).

32. RACHELS, *supra* note 18, at 108. James Rachels, Glanville Williams, and Joseph Fletcher, among others, have argued against the active/passive distinction. *See id.*; WILLIAMS, *supra* note 25; JOSEPH FLETCHER, MORALS AND MEDICINE (1954).

33. TOM L. BEAUCHAMP & JAMES F. CHILDRESS, PRINCIPLES OF BIOMEDICAL ETHICS 146-47 (3d ed. 1989). Yale Kamisar, Tom Beauchamp, and Daniel Maguire have argued in favor of maintaining the distinction. *See generally* DANIEL MAGUIRE, DEATH BY CHOICE 97-103 (1987); Tom L. Beauchamp, *A Reply to Rachels on Active and Passive Euthanasia, in* ETHICAL ISSUES, *supra* note 23, at 246; Kamisar, *Non-Religious Views, supra* note 25; Kamisar, *Right to Die?, supra* note 25.

34. James Rachels, *Active and Passive Euthanasia, in* ETHICAL ISSUES, *supra* note 23, at 245.

35. BEAUCHAMP & CHILDRESS, *supra* note 33, at 134-47.

36. Daniel Callahan, *Can We Return Death to Disease?*, 19 HASTINGS CENTER REP. (Special Supp.), Jan.-Feb. 1989, at 4, 6.

sympathy for the principle of euthanasia and judicial and legislative reluctance to grant euthanasia the protection of the law. In court cases of mercy killings or assisted suicides by physicians, courts have generally either acquitted or failed to indict the physician,[37] but no precedent has been set explicitly granting judicial approbation to either euthanasia or assisted suicide.

In the Netherlands, euthanasia has held a unique quasi-legal status for nearly two decades. Despite its statutory illegality, courts have, in a series of mercy killing acquittals, promulgated guidelines for physicians in the practice of euthanasia. The result has been its de facto legalization.

Section A of this Part surveys euthanasia in the courts, beginning with instances of physicians charged with mercy killing in the United States. This section then examines the development of guidelines governing the practice of euthanasia in the Netherlands and discusses arguments against adoption of an analogous system in the United States. Section B of Part II analyzes several statutory proposals for the legalization of euthanasia that have been made in the United States and Great Britain since 1906.

A. Judicial Responses to Euthanasia

1. The United States

Active euthanasia is illegal in the United States. Physicians who cause the death of a patient or assist in a patient's suicide may be prosecuted under homicide statutes, which exist in every state, or laws prohibiting assistance to suicide, which currently exist in thirty-one states.[38] Despite the reputed practice of active euthanasia by physicians,[39] few indictments have been returned, and very few cases have been brought to trial. The greatest number of mercy killing cases have involved the killing of a spouse, parent, or child

---

37. Two exceptions are Dr. Joseph Hassman of New Jersey and Dr. Donald Caraccio of Michigan. *See infra* note 41.

38. *See supra* note 31.

39. Some commentators believe the frequency of euthanasia in the U.S. to be fairly close to that of the Netherlands (about three percent of all deaths), though the practice is much more covert here. Knox, *supra* note 17. Dr. Jan van Eys of the University of Texas Medical Center, a Dutch native who has served on U.S. panels debating euthanasia, said, "I wouldn't be surprised if the U.S. had that incidence already." *Id.*

by a nonphysician,[40] and, until recently, most have occurred without the consent of the victim.[41]

The first widely publicized mercy killing case involving a physician took place in New Hampshire in 1949. Dr. Herman Sander, a general practitioner, injected air into the vein of a comatose cancer patient who was on the verge of death. Dr. Sander dictated a description of his actions into the hospital record, and was arrested two weeks later when the hospital's records librarian reported the incident to her superiors. After an outpouring of support from the general public (and condemnation from religious groups),[42] a jury trial was held and Dr. Sander was acquitted.[43]

In 1973, Dr. Vincent Montemarano, chief surgical resident at the Nassau County Medical Center in New York, was indicted for murder after giving a fifty-seven-year-old throat cancer victim a fatal injection of potassium chloride.[44] The victim, who had only days to live, died within five minutes of the injection. After deliberating for fifty-five minutes, the jury returned a not guilty verdict.[45]

---

40. In 1938, a Nassau County, New York, grand jury refused to indict Harry C. Johnson, who had asphyxiated his cancer-stricken wife. Kamisar, *Non-Religious Views, supra* note 25, at 971 n.11. In 1950, Carol Ann Paight was acquitted on grounds of temporary insanity in the shooting death of her father, who had just been diagnosed with cancer. *Id.* at 1020 & n.173. In 1939, Louis Greenfield was acquitted in New York of chloroforming his son, an "incurable imbecile," to death. *Id.* at 1021 n.180. The Greenfield case inspired Louis Repouille, a resident alien, to administer chloroform to his own imbecilic son, who was blind and bedridden since infancy. Repouille was found guilty of manslaughter and freed on a suspended sentence, but years later was denied naturalization because he had not exhibited "good moral character." The Second Circuit Court of Appeals, in a now famous opinion by Judge Learned Hand, held that "only a minority of virtuous persons would deem the practice morally justifiable, while it remains in private hands, even when the provocation is as overwhelming as it was in this instance." Repouille v. United States, 165 F.2d 152, 153 (2d Cir. 1947).

41. Of the eleven physicians who have been charged in connection with the killing of a patient or an ill or incapacitated member of the physician's family, none has been imprisoned. In Colorado in 1935, Dr. Harold Blazer killed his daughter, a victim of cerebral spinal meningitis, using chloroform, and was acquitted at trial. In New York in 1985, Dr. John Kraai killed a friend and patient who suffered from Alzheimer's disease and gangrene of the foot; Dr. Kraai subsequently killed himself three weeks after his arrest. In 1986 in New Jersey, Dr. Joseph Hassman injected his mother-in-law, an Alzheimer's victim, with a lethal dose of Demerol; he was found guilty and sentenced to two years' probation, fined $10,000, and ordered to perform 400 hours of community service. In 1987 in Ft. Myers, Florida, Dr. Peter Rosier was acquitted after a botched attempt at ending the life of his cancer-stricken wife (the mercy killing was successfully completed by the wife's stepfather). In Michigan in 1989, Dr. Donald Caraccio pleaded guilty to the murder, by lethal injection, of a comatose 74-year-old woman; he received five years probation with community service. DEREK HUMPHRY, EUTHANASIA 129-35 (1991).

42. O. RUTH RUSSELL, FREEDOM TO DIE 104-06 (rev. ed. 1977).

43. At trial, the defendant asserted that the patient was already dead when he injected the air. It was also revealed that the patient's family was split over the doctor's actions. The husband and one brother sided with the doctor; another brother felt the patient's fate belonged to "the will of God." Kamisar, *Non-Religious Views, supra* note 25, at n.172 (quoting *40 cc of Air*, TIME, Jan. 9, 1950, at 13).

44. RUSSELL, *supra* note 42, at 197.

45. HUMPHRY, *supra* note 41, at 130.

The June, 1990, suicide of Janet Adkins generated worldwide interest as the first use of the notorious "suicide machine" invented by longtime euthanasia advocate Dr. Jack Kevorkian.[46] Kevorkian, who had publicized his device (dubbed the "Mercitron") in the national media since 1989, was contacted by Adkins, who asked his help in ending her life. Adkins, who was fifty-four, said that she had made her decision to die nearly a year earlier, when she was first diagnosed with Alzheimer's disease.[47] At the time of her death, the disease had progressed to the point where Adkins had begun to lose her memory and could no longer play the piano and flute, but she was well enough to play tennis with her son and to enjoy a last romantic weekend with her husband.[48]

Dr. Kevorkian's suicide machine was a sophisticated extrapolation on the concept of a physician leaving a lethal dose of medication by a patient's bedside. It consisted of an intravenous tube connected to three bottles, one containing harmless saline solution, one containing thiopental, and one containing potassium chloride. After Kevorkian inserted the intravenous tube into Adkins's arm and began the saline solution, she pressed a button which switched the line to the thiopental, which caused her to lose consciousness. A minute later, a timing device switched the line to the potassium chloride, which stopped her heart and caused death within minutes.[49] By activating the fatal device, Adkins had, in effect, taken her own life.

Kevorkian's device was designed to take advantage of the then-existing gap in Michigan law regarding assisted suicide, which had been uncertain since the 1984 Michigan Supreme Court refused to consider an appeal from the Michigan court of appeals in *People v. Campbell*.[50] In that case, the defendant, who was charged with murder in a suicide death, appealed from the denial of a motion to dismiss on the ground that providing a weapon to an individual who subsequently uses it to commit suicide does not constitute

---

46. Belkin, *supra* note 3. Kevorkian, 67, has been considered "something of an eccentric" since his days as a resident at the hospital at the University of Michigan, where he was forced to leave when officials heard of his proposal to make death row prisoners permanently unconscious for medical experimentation. Isabel Wilkerson, *Physician Fulfills a Goal: Aiding a Person in Suicide*, N.Y. TIMES, June 7, 1990, at D22. A self-described "outcast," Kevorkian claims not to have held a job since 1982 because his "renegade ideas" have frightened hospitals from hiring him—"I don't apply anymore," he said. *Id.* Derek Humphry has called Kevorkian "the loose cannon of the euthanasia movement." Jane Gross, *Voters Turn Down Mercy Killing Idea*, N.Y. TIMES, Nov. 7, 1991, at B16.

47. Belkin, *supra* note 3.

48. Albert W. Alschuler, *Reflection*, in ACTIVE EUTHANASIA, *supra* note 14, at 107.

49. Belkin, *supra* note 3.

50. 342 N.W.2d 519 (Mich. 1984), *appeal denied from* 335 N.W.2d 27 (Mich. Ct. App. 1983).

murder.[51] The court of appeals agreed, reversing the trial court, and stated that "[w]hile we find the conduct of the defendant morally reprehensible, we do not find it to be criminal under the present state of the law."[52] In doing so, the court rejected the prosecution's reliance on a 1920 case, *People v. Roberts*,[53] in which the defendant had placed a potion of paris green, a highly poisonous pigment containing arsenic trioxide, within the reach of his wife, who had terminal multiple sclerosis and who had requested her husband to help her die. Roberts was charged and convicted of first degree murder. The *Roberts* court treated issues of homicide only, and did not discuss the incident as a suicide.[54] In contrast, the *Campbell* court held, "the term suicide excludes by definition a homicide. Simply put, the defendant here did not kill another person."[55] The court further explicitly invited the legislature to adopt legislation regarding assisted suicide.[56]

Nearly six months after Janet Adkins's death, Kevorkian was arrested and charged with first degree murder.[57] The prosecutor cited *Roberts*, which was never explicitly overturned, and called Kevorkian "the legal and primary cause" of Adkins's death, asserting that Kevorkian could not "avoid culpability by the clever use of a switch."[58] Kevorkian's attorneys invoked *Campbell*.[59] Ten days later, after a two day preliminary hearing, Judge Gerald McNulty of the Oakland County District Court dismissed the murder

---

51. Steven Paul Campbell was charged in the October 4, 1980, suicide of Kevin Patrick Basnaw. According to testimony, two weeks earlier Campbell had caught Basnaw in bed with Campbell's wife. On the night of the suicide, Campbell and Basnaw were drinking heavily at Basnaw's home. Late in the evening Basnaw began talking about committing suicide, and said he did not have a gun. At first, Campbell refused to allow Basnaw to borrow or buy one of his guns, but later changed his mind and drove with Basnaw to Campbell's parents' home to get a gun. They returned to Basnaw's home with a gun and five shells, and Basnaw told his girlfriend to leave with Campbell because he was going to kill himself. Basnaw put the shells and the gun on the kitchen table and began to write a suicide note. Campbell and Basnaw's girlfriend left at approximately 3:00 a.m. The next morning, Basnaw was found dead at the kitchen table with the gun in his hand. People v. Campbell, 335 N.W.2d 27, 28-29 (Mich. Ct. App. 1983).

52. *Id.* at 31.

53. 178 N.W. 690 (Mich. 1920).

54. *Campbell*, 335 N.W.2d at 29.

55. *Id.* at 30.

56. *Id.* at 31. The Michigan legislature has since taken action on both sides of the issue. In October, 1992, the Michigan House of Representatives Subcommittee on Death and Dying approved a bill to permit physician-assisted suicide and sent it to the House Judiciary Committee for debate. Price, *supra* note 7; *see infra* notes 161-70 and accompanying text. On December 15, 1992, an anti-euthanasia bill was signed into law by Michigan Governor John Engler. *Two More Assisted Suicides Before Governor OKs Ban*, *supra* note 7; *see infra* notes 72-73 and accompanying text.

57. Isabel Wilkerson, *Inventor of Suicide Machine Arrested on Murder Charge*, N.Y. TIMES, Dec. 4, 1990, at A1.

58. *Id.*

59. *Id.*

charges, finding no probable cause that Kevorkian had committed murder.[60] Stating that it was Mrs. Adkins, not Kevorkian, who had caused her death, he called upon the state legislature to address the issue of assisted suicide.[61]

On October 23, 1991, nearly seventeen months after Adkins's death, Kevorkian assisted two other women to commit suicide in Michigan.[62] One was a forty-three-year-old victim of multiple sclerosis; the other woman, fifty-eight, suffered from papilloma virus, a painful pelvic condition.[63] Neither woman was in danger of imminent death.[64] Kevorkian used a newly designed version of his suicide machine in one death; the other was accomplished using a carbon monoxide tank and mask.[65] On November 20, 1991, the Michigan Medical Association suspended Kevorkian's license to practice medicine in that state.[66] On January 6, 1992, an Oakland County grand jury opened an investigation into Kevorkian's role in the suicides; an indictment was returned and on February 21, 1992, Kevorkian was ordered to stand trial for murder. While awaiting trial, on May 15, 1992, Kevorkian assisted the suicide of Susan Williams, a fifty-two-year-old victim of multiple sclerosis.[67] Prosecutors had not yet filed charges in that case when, on July 21, 1992, Oakland County Circuit Judge David Breck dismissed the charges in the October, 1991,

---

60. Tamar Lewin, *Doctor Cleared of Murdering Woman with Suicide Machine*, N.Y. TIMES, Dec. 14, 1990, at B6.

61. *Id.* Although charges were dropped against Kevorkian, he remained barred by judicial order issued four days after Adkins's death from using his suicide device again. *Id.* Two months after Adkins's suicide, Bertram and Virginia Harper and their daughter flew to Michigan from California, where assisted suicide is a felony, to exploit the legal vacuum Kevorkian had publicized. In a suburban Detroit motel room, Virginia Harper, who suffered from liver cancer, took an overdose of sleeping pills and fastened a plastic bag over her head. After Virginia became unconscious, Bertram fastened the bag more securely around her neck; this fact was seized upon by prosecutors who hoped to show that Bertram caused her death. Bertram Harper was charged with first degree murder, but a jury acquitted him nine months later, finding that the sedatives taken by Virginia's own hand were the primary cause of death. *Man Who Helped Wife Commit Suicide is Acquitted of Murder*, CHI. TRIB., May 11, 1991, at C2.

62. *Doctor Assists in Two More Suicides in Michigan*, N.Y. TIMES, Oct. 24, 1991, at A1.

63. *Id.*

64. *Suicide Victims Were Adamant, Lawyers Claim, supra* note 7.

65. *Doctor Assists in Two More Suicides in Michigan, supra* note 62. Carbon monoxide gas became Kevorkian's exclusive method after his medical license was suspended and it was no longer possible for him to obtain potassium chloride. David Margolick, *Doctor Who Helps Suicides Has Made the Bizarre Banal*, N.Y. TIMES, Feb. 22, 1993, at A1. To begin the flow of gas, the individual tugs a string attached to a clip on the plastic tube running from the carbon monoxide canister to the mask. Death occurs within minutes. *Id.*

66. *In Wake of 3 Suicides, Dr. Kevorkian Loses Michigan License*, CHI. TRIB., Nov. 21, 1991, at C16.

67. *Kevorkian Provided the Gas for Woman's Suicide*, N.Y. TIMES, May 17, 1992, at A21.

suicides, explicitly rejecting *Roberts*[68] and holding that "because physician-assisted suicide is not a crime, defendant was wrongly bound over."[69]

On September 26, 1992, Kevorkian assisted the suicide of Lois Hawes, a fifty-two-year-old cancer victim, again employing carbon monoxide.[70] Chastened by the two previous dismissals, Oakland County prosecutor Richard Thompson said that he would not prosecute again without action by the legislature or appellate courts.[71]

On November 24, 1992, the Michigan House of Representatives acted, passing a provisional anti-euthanasia measure that outlawed assisted suicide for two years beginning March 30, 1993, while a newly created commission on death and dying studies the problem and develops recommendations for legislation.[72] The measure, which makes assisted suicide a felony punishable by up to four years imprisonment and a $2,000 fine, was quickly passed by the Senate, then signed by Michigan's governor on December 15, 1992, a day on which Kevorkian aided two additional suicides.[73]

During the next two months, Kevorkian aided the suicides of seven other individuals, prompting the Michigan legislature to move the effective date of the ban to February 25, 1993.[74] On March 1, 1993, the American Civil Liberties Union of Michigan filed suit on behalf of two terminally ill cancer patients and seven local doctors, challenging the law as an unconstitutional violation of the right to privacy and asking for a preliminary injunction to stop enforcement of the law.[75] Kevorkian, who is not a party to the suit, said

---

68. People v. Roberts, 178 N.W. 690 (1920); *see supra* notes 53-54 and accompanying text.

69. Koski, *Acquittal, supra* note 7.

70. Ourlian & Atkins, *supra* note 7.

71. *Id.*

72. Act of Dec. 15, 1992, 1992 Mich. Pub. Acts 270 (creating Michigan commission on death and dying and prohibiting certain acts pertaining to suicide assistance).

73. Michael Abramowitz, *Kevorkian Aids in 2 More Suicides; Michigan Governor Signs Bill Making Practice a Felony*, WASH. POST, Dec. 16, 1992, at A2; *see supra* note 7.

74. Act of Feb. 25, 1993, 1993 Mich. Pub. Acts 3 (amending 1992 Mich. Pub. Acts 270 to take effect Feb. 25, 1993).

75. Carol J. Castaneda, *Aided-Suicide Ban Faces Challenge*, USA TODAY, Mar. 1, 1993, at 6A. According to attorney and law professor Robert Sedler, who is litigating the case for the American Civil Liberties Union of Michigan, the ACLU's challenge relies on due process liberty interests of the kind protected in Planned Parenthood v. Casey, 112 S. Ct. 2791 (1992), and the line of reproductive rights cases articulating the constitutional right to privacy. Telephone interview with the author, Mar. 9, 1993. Sedler emphasized that the suit "has nothing to do with euthanasia" and is not intended to free Kevorkian's hand; rather, the challenge has been brought to preserve the privacy of the doctor-patient relationship, including the freedom of doctors to prescribe barbiturates and other pain-killing drugs which may have the effect of hastening death and to instruct patients on the proper dosage if a lethal effect is desired. *Id.*

that he would not assist any additional suicides until a decision is rendered in the preliminary injunction hearing.[76]

Another physician, Dr. Timothy Quill, attracted the attention of prosecutors when he published an article in the *New England Journal of Medicine* in March, 1991, describing his role in enabling a forty-five-year-old leukemia victim to end her life.[77] Dr. Quill, a professor at the University of Rochester Medical School, had been the patient's physician for many years.[78] He supported her adamant decision to forego chemotherapy and prescribed, at her request, enough barbiturates to kill her. The patient did not use the barbiturates until several months later, when her condition had deteriorated considerably. Dr. Quill was not present at her suicide.[79] Nonetheless, prosecutors in Rochester, New York, where the incident took place, searched death records to find a case which matched the one described in Quill's article.[80] The victim was identified and her body found at a local college, where it was being used as an instructional cadaver.[81] The prosecutors requested an indictment under the New York statute criminalizing assisting suicide,[82] but after three days of hearings a grand jury failed to indict him. Following that decision, both the New York State Medical Society and the New York State Health Department declined to initiate disciplinary proceedings.[83]

Physician involvement in patient suicide remains an offense in most states, though the degree to which prosecutors, juries, and courts will tolerate the practice depends on the circumstances of the suicide. The willingness of prosecutors to enforce assisted suicide statutes may face further tests if more physicians come forward with tales of euthanasia and assisted suicide. Public sympathy for physicians who aid their terminally ill patients in dying would also be tested. While it is likely that Dr. Kevorkian could have been

---

76. Castaneda, *supra* note 75.

77. Timothy E. Quill, *Death and Dignity*, 324 NEW ENG. J. MED. 691 (1991). Dr. Quill decided to write his article after reading an anonymous account of a mercy killing by a physician published in 1988 in the *Journal of the American Medical Association* (*JAMA*). Robert Steinbrook, *Support Grows for Euthanasia*, L.A. TIMES, Apr. 19, 1991, at A1. The article, *It's Over, Debbie*, described the administration of a lethal injection of morphine to a dying, pain-racked cancer patient whom the doctor had never before met. Name Withheld By Request, *It's Over, Debbie*, 259 JAMA 272 (1988). The article sparked heated debate, and letters to *JAMA* from physicians ran four to one against the mercy killing. Lundberg, *supra* note 27, at 2142.

78. Altman, *supra* note 7.

79. Quill, *supra* note 77, at 693.

80. Altman, *supra* note 7.

81. *Id.*

82. N.Y. PENAL LAW § 120.30 (McKinney 1987) ("A person is guilty of promoting a suicide attempt when he intentionally causes or aids another person to attempt suicide.").

83. Altman, *supra* note 7.

successfully prosecuted under New York's statute, the circumstances under which Dr. Quill enabled his patient to die are likely to be tolerated in most parts of the country.

2. The Netherlands

Active voluntary euthanasia has been practiced openly in the Netherlands since 1973,[84] when, for the first time, a Dutch physician was charged with participating in a mercy killing under Article 293 of the *Netherlands Penal Code*.[85] In that case, which was heard by the lower court in Leeuwarden, the physician acceded to repeated requests for death by her seventy-eight-year-old mother, who was wheelchair-bound, incontinent, and partially deaf.[86] The physician was found guilty and given a suspended sentence, but the court set forth four conditions under which euthanasia would be acceptable: (1) the patient's condition is incurable; (2) the patient's suffering is unbearable; (3) the patient requests euthanasia in writing; and (4) a physician performs the euthanasia.[87] Also in 1973, the Royal Dutch Medical Association (KNMG) issued a statement asserting that circumstances exist under which euthanasia is justifiable, but that it should remain illegal.[88]

The Leeuwarden decision and the KNMG statement set the stage for a series of court decisions during the 1970s and early 1980s which developed the existing guidelines into three necessary conditions for the acceptable practice

---

84. The judicial decisions which led to the decriminalization of euthanasia in the Netherlands must be viewed in the context of the Dutch civil law system, which differs from the United States' common law system in several crucial respects. Judges in the Netherlands are appointed for life by the Queen, and their independence is constitutionally guaranteed. There is no form of trial by jury. The judge's task is to interpret the law and apply it to the case before him. There is no precedent law, except for the rulings of the Supreme Court, which does not have the power of judicial review of the other branches of government—Crown and Parliament. The rigidity of the system, as regards criminal law, is compensated for by placing discretion in the Public Prosecutor's Office, which may drop criminal cases if doing so serves the public interest. Euthanasia cases, because of their controversial nature, are given special treatment and may be referred to the Minister of Justice. The Public Prosecutor's Office also has the discretion to involve the Office of Medical Inspectors, which controls the quality of health care, so as to insulate euthanasia cases whenever possible from the criminal law. Eugene Sutorius, How Euthanasia Was Legalized in Holland, Address at Hemlock Society Convention 9-11 (Feb. 9, 1985) (transcript on file with the *Indiana Law Journal*).

85. Article 293, enacted in 1886, states: "He who robs another of life at his express and serious wish is punished with a prison sentence of at most twelve years or a fine of the fifth category." CARLOS F. GOMEZ, REGULATING DEATH 19 (1991). A fine of the fifth category may reach 100,000 guilders (approximately $50,000 at 1991 exchange rates). *Id.* at 147 n.1. Article 294 provides criminal sanctions for incitement or assistance to suicide, including a prison term of up to three years and a fine. *Id.* at 19.

86. Nederlandse Jurisprudentie 1973:183; *see* GOMEZ, *supra* note 85, at 28.

87. *Id.* at 30.

88. M.A.M. de Wachter, *Active Euthanasia in the Netherlands,* 262 JAMA 3316, 3317 (1989).

of active euthanasia: (1) the patient must request euthanasia freely, without solicitation or family pressure; (2) the patient must experience his condition as unbearable; and (3) the physician must consult a colleague to confirm the prognosis and diagnosis, to verify the medical performance of euthanasia, and to ensure all legal requirements are met.[89] Courts generally applied these standards, though judges were free to apply, and did apply, other standards, including "the presence of an incurable disease" or that "unnecessary suffering" not be inflicted on others.[90] In 1981, however, the boundaries of toleration of euthanasia were unsettled when the Rotterdam district court convicted a nonphysician of assisting in a suicide, and in the process promulgated a new set of euthanasia guidelines.[91] The variation in criteria signalled physicians that although Article 293 would not be strictly interpreted, there was no assurance that they would not be prosecuted.[92] If unfortunate enough to encounter a zealous prosecutor or unsympathetic judge, a physician could be charged and convicted of a felony under Article 293.[93]

The Supreme Court of the Netherlands clarified much of the ambiguity in its 1984 ruling on the euthanasia conviction of a physician from Purmerand, Dr. Schoonheim.[94] In 1976, at age eighty-nine, Maria Barendregt, a "vital, mentally strong person,"[95] was forced by infirmities to move into a "living-center," where she came under the care of Dr. Schoonheim. In 1980, she signed a euthanasia declaration, and in 1981, after fracturing her hip in a fall, declared that she would not submit to an operation unless assured that she would not live through it. Dr. Schoonheim declined to operate, and over the following months, Maria became bedridden, catheterized, and totally dependent on the nursing staff. Her requests to be helped to die increased in urgency until, in the last week of her life, she could no longer speak or drink. After a few days, there was a slight remission, and she was able to speak, at which time Maria begged her son to ensure that she receive euthanasia. She repeated her request to Dr. Schoonheim, who ultimately agreed. Later that week, after saying goodbye to her son and daughter-in-law, Maria again confirmed her wish to die: "If it can be done please do it at once doctor;

---

89. *Id.*
90. *Id.*
91. GOMEZ, *supra* note 85, at 32-33.
92. *Id.* at 34.
93. *Id.*
94. Nederlandse Jurisprudentie 1984:106.
95. Sutorius, *supra* note 84, at 3.

quickly, not one night more."[96] Dr. Schoonheim then gave Maria three injections to end her life.[97]

After Dr. Schoonheim obeyed the law by reporting his actions to the municipal medical examiner and the police, he was charged under Article 293 and brought to trial. His defense was that a conflict of loyalties—to the law and to his patient—had caused him to act under *force majeure*.[98] He said he had weighed the "conflicting duties and interests" of the case and acted in accordance with professional standards of medical ethics.[99]

The court acquitted Schoonheim, finding that no crime had been committed. The prosecutor appealed to the Amsterdam Court of Appeals, which reversed the district court on the grounds that Article 293 had clearly been violated. The court of appeals further asserted that the physician had not proved "unbearable suffering" on the patient's part and therefore could not demonstrate that the patient's suffering had left him no reasonable alternative.[100]

The Netherlands Supreme Court, in what became a landmark decision, reversed the Amsterdam Court of Appeals. The Court agreed that Article 293 had been violated, but criticized the appellate court for not investigating further into the specific circumstances under which the physician had acted. Was the patient's suffering (mental or physical) expected to worsen? Was it foreseeable that the patient would no longer be able to live in a dignified way? Were there still alternative ways to alleviate the patient's suffering?[101] Because the Supreme Court could only consider questions of law, it referred the case to the Court of Appeals of the Hague, and instructed that court to consider whether euthanasia, as practiced in this case, would be justified by *force majeure* from a medical perspective.[102]

The Court of Appeals of the Hague fulfilled its mandate by requesting that the KNMG present an opinion. The KNMG's response was to affirm that there were situations of necessity in medicine in which physicians and patients might be under such duress that euthanasia would be justifiable. Therefore, the legality of euthanasia need not be questioned; the defense of necessity, for

---

96. *Id.* at 5.
97. *Id.*
98. The defense of *force majeure* has become standard in Dutch euthanasia cases, and stands for the idea that the patient's extreme and enduring pain forces the physician to do something outside normal practice. The concept of *force majeure* has historically been used to excuse defendants who broke the law under coercion. GOMEZ, *supra* note 85, at 150 n.26 (quoting personal interview with Sutorius).
99. Sutorius, *supra* note 84, at 6.
100. GOMEZ, *supra* note 85, at 35-36.
101. Sutorius, *supra* note 84, at 13.
102. GOMEZ, *supra* note 85, at 36.

which the physician would bear the burden of proof, would justify acquit-tal.[103]

After the Supreme Court decision, policies and guidelines to govern the administration of euthanasia were developed by several institutions, including the KNMG, the University of Utrecht, and the health care services directors of Amsterdam and Rotterdam. Generally, such guidelines dictate procedures for consultation with the family and hospital authorities after a patient has requested euthanasia—setting timetables, documentation, and the actual performance of the euthanasia.[104] The Amsterdam policy also specifically sets forth procedures for post-mortem review, addressing the issue of the physician's liability.[105]

In September, 1991, the first long-term study of the practice of euthanasia in the Netherlands, commissioned by the Dutch government, was released.[106] Researchers from four Dutch universities studied individuals who requested euthanasia or suicide assistance from 1986 to 1989,[107] with results that surprised both sides of the debate.[108] The study found that about three percent of all Dutch deaths—about 3,900 out of 129,000 deaths annually—are caused by euthanasia, though thirty-five percent of all deaths involve the withdrawal of care or the administration of potentially life-shortening painkillers.[109] These figures were far lower than predicted, lending credence to the view that euthanasia can be controlled. At the same time, the official study's figures contrasted with those of the Ministry of Justice, which showed

---

103. *Id.* at 37-38.

104. de Wachter, *supra* note 88, at 3318-19.

105. According to the Amsterdam policy, the following steps must be taken: (1) the coroner, who must be contacted before a death certificate can be written, examines the reasons for the euthanasia and whether it was performed with professional care; (2) the coroner reports to the district attorney; (3) the police question the physician and investigate the circumstances of the euthanasia (the family is not questioned unless something unusual is uncovered); (4) the district attorney decides whether an autopsy is necessary; (5) the district attorney consults with the public health inspector; (6) the district attorney submits a final report to the appropriate attorney general; (7) all five attorneys general and the secretary general of the Ministry of Justice discuss the case and decide whether to prosecute or to dismiss the case. *Id.* at 3319.

106. Simons, *supra* note 7.

107. *Id.* The researchers reviewed 7,000 deaths, interviewed 405 physicians, and arranged for 322 doctors to keep track of all deaths in their practices over a six-month period. Knox, *supra* note 17.

108. Knox, *supra* note 17.

109. *Id.* The study also revealed: In nearly two-thirds of the cases, the patients were estimated to have two weeks or less to live when they asked to die. In eighty-three percent of the cases, the patients first broached the subject of euthanasia, while in ten percent the physician first raised it. Doctors more readily applied euthanasia when patients had just days to live; if life expectancy was three months or more, doctors preferred to assist the patient in taking his own life. Simons, *supra* note 7.

only 454 cases officially reported in 1990,[110] indicating that physicians are largely ignoring the existing guidelines.[111]

On February 9, 1993, after lengthy and contentious debate, the Dutch Parliament approved (by a vote of 91 to 48 in the lower house) legislation that codifies and strengthens the existing guidelines.[112] Scheduled to take effect in 1994, the new law stops short of legalizing euthanasia, which is still punishable under Article 293, but effectively immunizes from prosecution physicians who follow a detailed set of rules.[113] Among other requirements, these rules specify that the patient must voluntarily request euthanasia repeatedly over a period of time, be mentally competent, and have a terminal disease accompanied by unbearable physical or mental suffering.[114] The physician must consult a colleague experienced in euthanasia and submit a documented report stating the patient's medical history and the circumstances of the euthanasia.[115]

Two critics of Dutch euthanasia, the American physician Carlos Gomez, author of the first detailed American study of the Dutch system of euthanasia,[116] and Richard Fenigsen, a Dutch cardiologist,[117] argue that not only are abuses inevitable and ongoing, but endemic to the practice of euthanasia.

Based on his analysis of twenty-six cases of euthanasia that took place between 1985 and 1988, Dr. Gomez charges that the regulatory framework governing euthanasia is a sham. In the vast majority of cases, self-reporting by physicians does not occur, and even in instances where the district attorney is notified, physicians are rarely brought to court.[118] The requirement that physicians consult with another doctor is vague, and does not specify the

---

110. *Dutch Study Brings Euthanasia Taboo Out into the Open*, Reuters Library Report, Sept. 13, 1991, *available in* LEXIS, Nexis Library, Wires File.

111. *Id.* Dutch proponents of euthanasia have been split over whether statutory legalization of euthanasia would improve adherence to guidelines and accountability. Pieter V. Admiraal, a Delft oncologist and practitioner of euthanasia, says, "It wouldn't change much." Eugene Sutorius, the leading defense attorney for physicians in euthanasia cases, worries that legalization will make euthanasia "mechanical" and remove responsibility from doctors. Klazien Sybrandy, founder of the Information Center for Voluntary Euthanasia, contends that the ambiguous legal status of euthanasia gives prosecutors such discretion that physicians are discouraged from reporting. She argues that formal legalization would encourage openness and reduce the potential for abuse. John Horgan, *Death with Dignity: The Dutch Explore the Limits of a Patient's Right to Die*, SCI. AM., March 1991, at 17, 20.

112. Drozdiak, *supra* note 16.

113. Marlise Simons, *Dutch Parliament Approves Law Permitting Euthanasia*, N.Y. TIMES, Feb. 10, 1993, at A5.

114. *Id.*

115. *Id.*

116. *See* GOMEZ, *supra* note 85.

117. *See* Richard Fenigsen, *A Case Against Dutch Euthanasia*, HASTINGS CENTER REP. (Special Supp.), Jan.-Feb. 1989, at 22.

118. GOMEZ, *supra* note 85, at 130.

other physician's public function and accountability. As a result, doctors who do seek outside review before performing euthanasia do so to fulfill the legal formality, not as a test of their clinical assessment.[119]

Dr. Fenigsen paints an even more frightening picture of the practice of euthanasia, presenting a litany of abuses that he claims occur routinely: sloppy diagnosis, misrepresentation of the family's wishes, hasty evaluation of the patient's wishes, coercion of one spouse by the other, and coercion and intimidation of patients by doctors and nurses.[120] He claims that involuntary active euthanasia has been widely performed on adults and children,[121] and that Holland has created a culture of propaganda in favor of death, applying praise to the request to die, terming it "brave," "wise," and "progressive."[122] Fenigsen reports that severely handicapped adults live in fear and uncertainty, and that the practice of euthanasia has brought about an "ominous" change in society, sending a message to the weak and dependent that "we wouldn't mind getting rid of you."[123]

According to Dr. Gomez, the chaotic, extralegal state of affairs that existed in the Netherlands derived from an unresolvable tension in public policy between favoring greater autonomy and the unwillingness to dispense with legal prohibitions against killing, no matter how well-intentioned.[124] The new Dutch law, despite retaining criminal penalties for assisting suicide, may be an attempt to ameliorate that tension. While the Netherlands model of legal euthanasia may be too idiosyncratic in its development to transplant to the United States, the same unresolvable tension exists in our society, as evidenced by the ongoing euthanasia debate and the near misses of Washington State's Initiative 119 and California's Proposition 161.

---

119. *Id.*
120. Fenigsen, *supra* note 117, at 22.
121. Two cases illustrate what Fenigsen considers to be the dangerously tolerant attitude of the Dutch medical profession. In 1985, a physician was arrested under suspicion of having performed involuntary euthanasia on twenty patients at the *De Terp* nursing home in the Hague. *Id.* at 25. He was convicted of three killings, but the charges were dismissed by a higher court after an intensive lobbying effort on the physician's behalf by the Royal Dutch Medical Association (KNMG) and other groups. *Id.* Likewise, four nurses who admitted having secretly killed several unconscious patients won a dismissal of all charges and an emotional televised thank you from the victims' parents. *Id.*
122. *Id.* at 24.
123. *Id.* at 26.
124. GOMEZ, *supra* note 85, at 131-32.

B. Legislative Responses to Euthanasia

The first modern proposal for euthanasia legislation, made in the Ohio legislature in 1906, provided that when an adult of sound mind had been fatally hurt or was terminally ill, his physician would be permitted to ask him in the presence of three witnesses if he wished to die.[125] If the answer was yes, three other physicians were required to confirm the original prognosis before the individual could be put to death.[126] The bill was defeated by a vote of twenty-three to seventy-nine.[127]

In the 1930s, Great Britain and the United States witnessed a burst of pro-euthanasia activity, including the founding of euthanasia societies on both sides of the Atlantic. In 1936, a "Voluntary Euthanasia Bill" was introduced into the House of Lords.[128] The bill permitted adult patients suffering from an incurable and fatal illness to request euthanasia by signing a form in the presence of two witnesses. This form, accompanied by medical certificates, was then to be submitted to a "euthanasia referee" appointed by the Minister of Health. The euthanasia referee was required to interview the patient, and if satisfied that the patient sincerely desired death, he would issue a certificate. The patient's application, the medical certificates, and the referee's certificate would then go to a special court, which had the right to question the referee, the physicians, and family members. If the court was satisfied, it would issue two certificates, one to the patient and one to the physician, allowing death to be administered in the presence of an official witness.[129] These cumbersome safeguards were intended by promoters of the bill to mollify the opposition,[130] but the effect was just the opposite—it was complained that the safeguards created too much formality, destroying the doctor-patient relationship.[131] Yale Kamisar has theorized that the stringency of these safeguards was calculated with the expectation of pushing through a second and less restrictive bill as soon as the first had sufficiently "educated" public opinion.[132]

---

125. RUSSELL, *supra* note 42, at 61.
126. *Id.*
127. *Id.*
128. JONATHAN GOULD & LORD CRAIGMYLE, YOUR DEATH WARRANT? 29 (1971).
129. *Id.* at 29-30.
130. WILLIAMS, *supra* note 25, at 334.
131. *Id.*
132. Kamisar, *Non-Religious Views, supra* note 25, at 1015. Kamisar supports this contention with a quote from Lord Chorley during a 1950 House of Lords debate on another euthanasia measure:
> Another objection is that the bill does not go far enough, because it applies only to adults and does not apply to children who come into the world deaf, dumb and crippled, and who have a much better cause than those for whom the Bill provides. That may be so,

In the United States, a bill similar to the British bill was introduced and rejected in the Nebraska legislature in 1937.[133] A year later, the Euthanasia Society of America was formed in New York, where a bill based on the British model was introduced and defeated in 1939.[134] In 1947, a similar bill was again introduced in the New York legislature and rejected.[135] By that time, reports of the Nazi practice of euthanasia and medical experimentation on human subjects were widespread, and offered support for the notion that euthanasia, once legalized, could not be effectively controlled.[136]

The next significant effort to pass a euthanasia bill did not take place until 1969, when the House of Lords debated a revised version of the 1936 bill. The 1969 bill attempted to relax some of the formal procedures of the earlier bill by permitting a patient to make a "declaration in advance" requesting the administration of euthanasia in the event of an "irremediable condition," defined as a serious physical illness or impairment reasonably thought to be incurable and "expected to cause him severe distress or render him incapable of rational existence."[137] The bill required two physicians to verify the patient's condition and two witnesses to the declaration, and it contained a series of provisions that have become standard in subsequent legislative proposals: the declaration may be revoked at any time by destruction or cancellation; no physician or nurse is under any legal duty to participate in euthanasia; no physician or nurse shall be found guilty of an offense in connection with authorized euthanasia; and no insurance policy in force for twelve months shall be vitiated by the administration of euthanasia to the

---

but we must go step by step.
Id. at 1016 (quoting 169 H.L. Deb. 551, 559 (1950)).
    133. GOULD & CRAIGMYLE, *supra* note 128, at 30.
    134. RUSSELL, *supra* note 42, at 74.
    135. *Id.* at 95-96.
    136. German Jews were at first excluded from euthanasia under the Nazis; it was originally considered that "the blessing of euthanasia should be granted only to [true] Germans." Kamisar, *Non-Religious Views, supra* note 25, at 1033 (quoting defendant Viktor Brack, Chief Administrative Officer in Hitler's private chancellory, testifying at the Nuremberg Medical Trial, 1 Trials of War Criminals Before the Nuremberg Military Tribunal Under Control Council Law No. 10, 877-80 (1950)).
    An examination of euthanasia in Nazi Germany by Dr. Leo Alexander describes propaganda efforts to facilitate acceptance of euthanasia. In a high school textbook, for example, a mathematics problem compared the cost of caring for the disabled with the cost of building new housing units or marriage-allowance loans for newly married couples. Leo Alexander, *Medical Science Under Dictatorship, in* DEATH, DYING AND EUTHANASIA 571, 572 (Dennis J. Horan & David Mall eds., 1977). Alexander also describes the resistance of Dutch physicians to the imposition of euthanasia by the Nazis. One hundred Dutch physicians were sent to concentration camps to force the profession's compliance, but "not a single euthanasia or nontherapeutic sterilization was recommended or participated in by any Dutch physician." *Id.* at 586.
    137. GOULD & CRAIGMYLE, *supra* note 128, at 139.

insured.[138] The bill was ultimately defeated, forty to sixty-one, after a lengthy debate.[139] Among the objections to the bill was that the declaration, once renewed, was valid for life unless canceled or destroyed—no provision had been made for revocation by a new declaration. Also, unlike the 1936 bill and most subsequent proposals, the bill allowed euthanasia to be performed on incompetent patients who had previously signed a declaration. Further, the "irremediable" condition required by the bill was so vaguely defined that it could apply to the loss of a limb, and it was never specified that the illness be fatal.[140]

The 1969 English bill was the first directive-type statute to be proposed, and it provided the model for bills introduced in legislatures in Idaho, Oregon, and Montana between 1969 and 1974.[141] After the 1976 *Quinlan*[142] decision, the development and proliferation of living wills statutes largely preempted the euthanasia debate until the 1980s, when the Hemlock Society and its founder, Derek Humphry, began their national campaign of euthanasia advocacy.[143] In 1988, a group called Americans Against Human Suffering attempted to place a euthanasia initiative on the California ballot, but failed to gather enough signatures.[144] Then, in 1991, Washington Citizens for Death with Dignity, in coalition with other advocacy groups, placed an "Initiative for Death with Dignity" on the Washington ballot.[145] Designated "Initiative 119," the Washington measure came closer to enactment than any previous euthanasia proposal, winning forty-six percent of the popular vote.[146]

Initiative 119 was a proposal to amend Washington's Natural Death Act,[147] a living wills statute, to accommodate voluntary euthanasia, or

---

138. *Id.* at 139-41.

139. *Id.* at 63.

140. *Id.* at 33-35.

141. RUSSELL, *supra* note 42, at 192-94.

142. *In re* Quinlan, 335 A.2d 647 (N.J.), *cert. denied*, 429 U.S. 922 (1976).

143. HUMPHRY, *supra* note 41, at 107-08.

144. Allan Parachini, *The California Humane and Dignified Death Initiative*, 19 HASTINGS CENTER REP. (Special Supp.), Jan.-Feb. 1989, at 10.

145. Michael McCarthy, *Euthanasia on the Ballot; Voters in Washington State May Endorse Right to Die*, WASH. POST, Aug. 20, 1991, at Z12. Washington is one of 26 states allowing the adoption of statutory reform by direct election through initiatives. Two states allow initiatives only for constitutional amendment. Julian N. Eule, *Judicial Review of Direct Democracy*, 99 YALE L.J. 1503, 1510 (1990).

146. Jane Gross, *Voters Turn Down Legal Euthanasia*, N.Y. TIMES, Nov. 7, 1991, at A10. With 99% of the vote tabulated, there were 701,440 votes against the initiative (54%), 606,039 in favor (46%). *Id.*

147. WASH. REV. CODE §§ 70.122.010-.905 (1990). Initiative 119 also included two proposals relating to passive euthanasia. The first categorized "artificially administered nutrition and hydration" as a "life-sustaining procedure," allowing its withdrawal if requested in a living will. The second included "irreversible coma" and "persistent vegetative state" in the definition of "terminal conditions," allowing life-sustaining procedures to be withdrawn or withheld from patients in those conditions.

"physician aid-in-dying" as it was called in the initiative. Only competent patients with six months or less to live (in the written opinion of two examining physicians) would be eligible for aid-in-dying, which must be requested solely by the patient in the presence of two disinterested witnesses.[148] An aid-in-dying directive could only be executed at the time euthanasia was requested, not in advance.[149] In addition, no physician would be compelled to provide aid-in-dying; physicians who object to the practice would be obliged only to make a good faith effort to transfer the patient to a physician who would perform the service.[150] Other provisions were designed to allow the patient to revoke the directive at any time, to ensure that life insurance is not impaired, and to provide criminal penalties for interference with a directive or the revocation of a directive.[151]

Initiative 119 was carefully drafted to permit voluntary euthanasia for a narrow range of cases with a moderate degree of bureaucratic oversight. The restriction of euthanasia to competent patients would prevent its use by (or on) victims of Alzheimer's disease, the senile, the mentally ill, or children. Comatose patients and patients in a persistent vegetative state would also be ineligible; advance directives by such patients would only allow the withdrawal of life-sustaining treatment.

California's Proposition 161, the "California Death with Dignity Act,"[152] on the ballot in 1992, was a revision of the 1988 bill proposed in that state.[153] Although it was designed to improve upon the procedural safeguards in the Washington initiative, its provisions created new possibilities for abuse. For example, the Washington measure failed to provide for any waiting time or cooling-off period between execution of the aid-in-dying directive and the administration of euthanasia. The California bill attempted to remedy this problem by requiring the directive to be executed and witnessed in advance.[154] However, under the California bill, the directive could have been executed years before death, and no witness was required for the final request for death or at the time of death.[155] Also, while the Washington measure made no special provision for nursing home patients, the California bill

---

Initiative for Death with Dignity § 2 (Washington Committee for Death with Dignity 1991) [hereinafter Initiative 119], amending WASH. REV. CODE § 70.122.020(4), (7) (1990).

148. Initiative 119, *supra* note 147, §§ 2, 3.

149. *Id.* § 10, amending WASH. REV. CODE § 70.122.100 (1990).

150. *Id.* § 6(2), amending WASH. REV. CODE § 70.122.060(2) (1990).

151. *Id.* §§ 4(1), 7(2), 9, amending WASH. REV. CODE §§ 70.122.040(1), .070(2), and .090 (1990).

152. The California Death with Dignity Act (Californians Against Human Suffering 1992) [hereinafter Proposition 161].

153. *See supra* note 144 and accompanying text.

154. Proposition 161 § 2525.3.

155. *Id.* §§ 2525.2(i), 2525.7.

required that in such cases a patient advocate or ombudsman designated by the state Department of Aging be a witness to the directive.[156] However, the state official need only be present when the directive is signed, not when it is carried out.[157] The California measure was also flawed by its failure to contain a requirement that the patient be experiencing a certain level of pain and suffering before the directive could be made. Finally, its definition of "terminal condition" was so vague as to include serious, but not immediately life-threatening illnesses, like diabetes.[158]

In 1992, euthanasia bills were also introduced in the state legislatures of Iowa, Maine, Michigan, and New Hampshire. The Iowa[159] and Maine[160] bills closely track Proposition 161. The Michigan bill[161] contains a number of innovative safeguards. First, the directive must be certified within seven days of execution by a psychologist or psychiatrist, attesting that the patient is of sound mind and not suffering from depression.[162] Second, the attending physician must have attended the patient for at least six months.[163] Third, the patient must be determined to be suffering from both a terminal illness and physical pain so great that its elimination would render the patient unconscious.[164] Fourth, sixty days must pass between the execution of the directive and the euthanasia,[165] and the patient must request euthanasia at least twice, with seven days between each request.[166] Fifth, each request must be videotaped and witnessed by two individuals, and the performance of euthanasia must also be videotaped.[167] Finally, the decision of the attending physician to administer euthanasia must be reviewed and approved by at least two members of a three-member committee appointed by the county medical examiner or the administrator of the health facility where the patient is dying.[168] This complex and unwieldy procedure was criticized by both pro- and anti-euthanasia forces.[169] Kevorkian commented, "You don't have a law

---

156. *Id.* § 2525.4.
157. *Id.*
158. *Id.* § 2525.2(j).
159. Assistance-in-Dying Act, Iowa Senate, Sen. File 2066 (1992).
160. An Act Regarding the Terminally Ill, Maine Senate, 2nd Sess., S.P. 885, Legislative Doc. No. 2257 (1992).
161. Death with Dignity Act of 1992, H.R. 5415, 86th Leg., Reg. Sess., Mich. (1992).
162. *Id.* § 3(4).
163. *Id.* § 4(b).
164. *Id.* § 4(c).
165. *Id.* § 4(d).
166. *Id.* § 4(e), (e)(ii).
167. *Id.* § 4(e)(iii), (k).
168. *Id.* § 4(h).
169. Price, *supra* note 7.

telling doctors how to perform gallbladder operations or any other surgeries."[170]

The New Hampshire measure[171] takes a unique approach. Upon request by a patient determined to be terminally ill by two physicians, the attending physician may prescribe a lethal dose of medication that the patient may self-administer at the time and place and in the manner of his choosing.[172] Before acceding to the patient's request, the physician must consult with an institutional or state ethics committee, which will review the case.[173]

Despite their attempts to strike an adequate balance between respect for patient autonomy and societal safeguards, each of these four legislative efforts, like Initiative 119 and Proposition 161, is still susceptible of abuse, and raises the question, again, of whether euthanasia legislation is a fundamentally unsound idea. On the one hand, it is possible to imagine a safe and compassionate administration of euthanasia, with physicians and families working together to create a supportive and loving environment in which to make the crucial decision about the appropriateness of euthanasia. This ideal may have been accomplished in some cases in the Netherlands, as well as in the case of Dr. Quill, where the physician's longstanding relationship with the patient provided a foundation for his decision to accede to her request for assistance with suicide. On the other hand, it is equally possible, and perhaps closer to reality, to imagine deathbed scenes fraught with anxiety, conflict, and mistrust. As ethicist Leon Kass hypothesized:

> Imagine the scene: you are old, poor, in failing health, and alone in the world; you are brought to the city hospital with fractured ribs and pneumonia. The nurse or intern enters late at night with a syringe full of yellow stuff for your intravenous drip. How soundly will you sleep? It will not matter that your doctor has never yet put anyone to death; that he is legally entitled to do so will make a world of difference.[174]

The realities of terminal care and dying in our present health care system constitute the strongest argument against legalizing euthanasia. A system which fails to care adequately for the living must not be empowered with a license to kill.

---

170. *Id.* (quoting Dr. Jack Kevorkian).

171. Death with Dignity Act, H.R. 1275, 152d Leg., Reg. Sess., N.H. (1992). [House Bill 92-2332 (1992)].

172. *Id.* § 137-K:3(I).

173. *Id.* § 137-K:4.

174. *Euthanasia: Final Exit, Final Excuse*, FIRST THINGS, Dec. 1991, at 4, 8 (quoting Leon Kass in an editorial).

III. EUTHANASIA AND THE HEALTH CARE CRISIS

In formulating public policy on euthanasia, the benefits of legalization must be balanced against the harms legalization may entail. Public policy is not created in a vacuum; arguments for euthanasia that rely on autonomy or mercy are persuasive when applied to specific cases, but a public policy to lift the general prohibition on euthanasia must take societal consequences into account. If legalized, euthanasia would be practiced within a health care system that is reaching a critical state: rising costs in all areas of the industry and the care of the uninsured and underinsured have placed onerous burdens on hospitals, employers, and federal and state governments. An examination of euthanasia through the lens of the health care dilemma moves the debate from the context of issues of autonomy and mercy into the sphere of externalities—systemic pressures and the quotidian realities of the health care industry. If euthanasia is to be seriously considered as an addition to the canon of medical procedures to be performed within that system, it must be assessed in the context of our health care institutions.

This Part examines what the legalization of voluntary euthanasia might mean in the context of our health care system. The first section argues that our present health care system is incapable of safely accommodating euthanasia. The second section argues that reform of the management of death in health care institutions would preempt the need for legal euthanasia.

A. The Cost Factor

A presumption in favor of treatment remains strong in the practice of medicine. Traditionally, health care professionals have tended to regard the cost of treatment as irrelevant to their obligation to act for the good of their patients.[175] Today, however, the rising cost of health care has forced the federal and state governments, private insurers, and employers to set limits on health care coverage.[176] Thirty-four to thirty-seven million Americans are without medical insurance, including entire families with full-time job holders.[177] Medical indigence is a "silent, largely invisible epidemic,"[178] spreading quickly—the number of Americans with private coverage of hospital

---

175. THE HASTINGS CENTER, GUIDELINES ON THE TERMINATION OF LIFE-SUSTAINING TREATMENT AND THE CARE OF THE DYING 123 (1987).

176. *Id.*

177. Edwin Chen, *Medical Care Reform May Be Reaching Turning Point*, L.A. TIMES, July 21, 1991 (Sunday final ed.), at A1.

178. Emily Friedman, *The Torturer's Horse*, 261 JAMA 1481, 1481-82 (1991).

costs continues to decrease at the rate of one million per year.[179] In 1989, hospitals provided $11.1 billion in uncompensated care. Among the costliest afflictions were those that often stem from poverty: AIDS, drug abuse, and problem pregnancies.[180]

The financial survival of health care institutions now depends directly on controlling costs generated by individual patient care decisions.[181] Cost containment already affects patient decision making, particularly when health insurance benefits fail to keep pace with the cost of treatment. Patients are sometimes forced to forego beneficial treatments they wish to receive.[182] For the twenty-six million poor, disabled, and elderly Americans who receive health care through Medicaid,[183] the "unrealistically low" provider reimbursement levels mean limited access to treatment.[184] For the uninsured, receiving access to any form of health care is problematic. More and more hospitals are faced with the choice of caring for all the uninsured and going under financially, or turning at least some of them away.[185] The cost of care of the uninsured has become a significant factor in the increase in the cost of care for everyone,[186] and as cost containment measures are implemented in Medicaid and private health insurance programs, the quality of care declines.[187]

The medically indigent are most at risk of abuse in a scheme of legal euthanasia. The uninsured poor, who include the very elderly, AIDS patients, the homeless, and the mentally ill,[188] receive not only diminished access to health care providers, but fewer services once entry to the health care system is achieved.[189] The uninsured usually receive no more than last-minute interventions in emergency departments, and the availability of non-emergency care for indigents continues to erode.[190]

---

179. *Id.*

180. Emily Friedman, *The Uninsured: From Dilemma to Crisis*, 265 JAMA 2491, 2491 (1991).

181. OFFICE OF TECHNOLOGY ASSESSMENT, U.S. CONGRESS, INSTITUTIONAL PROTOCOLS FOR DECISIONS ABOUT LIFE-SUSTAINING TREATMENTS 4 (1988).

182. *Id.*

183. Gail R. Wilensky, *From the Health Care Financing Administration*, 265 JAMA 2461, 2461 (1991).

184. James S. Todd et al., *Health Access America—Strengthening the U.S. Health Care System*, 265 JAMA 2503, 2504 (1991).

185. Friedman, *supra* note 180, at 2494.

186. *Id.*

187. OFFICE OF TECHNOLOGY ASSESSMENT, U.S. CONGRESS, LIFE-SUSTAINING TECHNOLOGIES AND THE ELDERLY 18 (1987) [hereinafter OTA].

188. Friedman, *supra* note 178, at 1481.

189. Mark B. Wenneker et al., *The Association of Payer with Utilization of Cardiac Procedures in Massachusetts*, 264 JAMA 1255, 1255 (1990).

190. Friedman, *supra* note 178, at 1481.

For indigent patients, particularly those without family members willing to challenge health care providers to maintain a reasonable standard of care, the option of euthanasia is fraught with danger. An institution providing an indigent patient with care would be called upon to resist substantial incentives to encourage the patient to avail himself of euthanasia, including financial savings and the release of resources to insured patients. The same incentives already exist for institutions to influence the decision to withhold or withdraw treatment from a terminally ill indigent patient. The possible statistical correlation between insurance status and withholding or withdrawal of treatment should be studied. The changing policies of health care institutions in response to the Patient Self-Determination Act and the likely increase in execution of advance directives by inpatients may shed light on this question, and consequently illuminate the potential for abuse under legal euthanasia.

Even under circumstances of non-indigence, when a patient is dying or terminally ill, family members, physicians, and nurses are under great physical and psychological stresses.[191] Family members are dealing with anticipatory grief, financial burdens, and excessive demands on their time, and involvement in treatment decisions is likely to be filled with anxiety and guilt.[192] Health care professionals must deal with the emotional burdens of the ill patient and the grieving family, and with constant reminders of their own mortality.[193] As cost containment becomes a factor in the decision whether or not to offer specific life-saving treatment, this already tense environment is likely to become charged with a sense of futility and hopelessness.

If voluntary euthanasia is legalized before the financial stresses in our health care system are reasonably ameliorated, the potential for abuse is great. As ethicist Tom Beauchamp warns, "[T]he aged will be even more neglectable and neglected than they now are, . . . [and] doctors would have appreciably reduced fears of actively injecting fatal doses whenever it seemed to them propitious to do so . . . ."[194] Pressures on terminally ill patients to "get it over with" and spare their loved ones expense and misery will be exerted by families and caregivers, and such subtle (or unsubtle) coercion would hardly be discouraged by hospitals stretching tight budgets. If one takes into account the fact that more than 10,000 American adults remain in nursing homes and hospitals in vegetative comas at the public expense of $350 million per

---

191. OTA, *supra* note 187, at 25.
192. *Id.*
193. *Id.*
194. Tom L. Beauchamp, *A Reply to Rachels on Active and Passive Euthanasia, in* ETHICAL ISSUES, *supra* note 23, at 253.

year,[195] the potential utility of euthanasia as a cost containment device becomes clear.

Comparison with health care in the Netherlands reveals the inadvisability of transplanting euthanasia to the United States. According to Teresa Takken, a Catholic nun and ethicist from the University of Utrecht, Holland's comprehensive health care and welfare system probably keeps requests for euthanasia at a minimum and makes abuses unlikely.[196] But, she insists, "We have no business even talking about euthanasia here [in the United States] until we have health care for all, . . . and even housing for all."[197] Ethicist Corrine Bayley agrees that economic considerations could corrupt decisions involving euthanasia in the United States, and adds that American physicians generally have much shorter term and less trusting relationships with their patients than Dutch physicians, and so are less equipped to cope with requests for euthanasia.[198] Dr. Carlos Gomez, who argues that significant abuses have taken place in the Netherlands, fears that "euthanasia will be used, as it sometimes is in Holland, as a tool of social and economic control . . . . Poor people, especially in this country where we deny medical services to many of them, are the most vulnerable to be euthanized."[199]

Moreover, sanctioning physicians to kill patients may rob the health care establishment of the impetus to make serious movement toward reform of the care of the terminally ill, and may serve as a pressure valve, enabling the system to avoid the financial and ethical dilemmas now crying out to be addressed.

B. The Care of the Dying

The power of medicine to extend life under circumstances of technological dependency, pain, incompetency, and coma is widely feared.[200] Treatment in hospitals has become increasingly fragmented, and people who two decades ago might have died quietly at home or in the company of a trusted family doctor today die surrounded by machines and teams of specialists they hardly know.[201] Yet, concurrent with the development of life-sustaining technology

---

195. Shaw, *supra* note 14, at 97-98.
196. Horgan, *supra* note 111, at 20.
197. *Id.*
198. *Id.*
199. Egan, *supra* note 6.
200. Callahan, *supra* note 36, at 4.
201. Elisabeth Rosenthal, *In Matters of Life and Death, the Dying Take Control*, N.Y. TIMES, Aug. 18, 1991, § 4, at 1. In an intensive care unit, a cancer patient's general practitioner is a bystander to the oncologist, infectious disease specialist, kidney consultant, and a rotating team of intensive care doctors. *Id.*

has been the growth of awareness that the management of death in health care institutions must be reformed. The general acceptance by the medical profession of the concept of patient autonomy and of the participation of patients and their families in health care decision making is one positive development.

Another significant development has been the growth of the hospice movement and the proliferation of hospice programs throughout the country.[202] The hospice concept, which can be realized in a patient's home or in institutions, was created to remedy the sense of isolation, depersonalization, and loss of control that dying patients suffer in hospitals, surrounded by medical technology.[203] When a patient begins hospice care, all extraordinary or life-sustaining measures are discontinued, and the focus of treatment is on palliative care only—comfort and symptom control.[204] Hospice is intended to meet the physical, social, psychological, and spiritual needs of both the dying patient and family,[205] and provides a caring response to many patients' fears of pain, of dying alone, and of the tyranny of medical technology.[206]

Voluntary euthanasia, on the other hand, may provide not release from medical technology, but a "deceptively easy technological 'quick fix' . . . the ultimate triumph of technical virtuosity over humane medicine,"[207] as it may be a symptom of our cultural avoidance of the responsibility to come to terms with death and dying.[208] As Dr. Elisabeth Kubler-Ross wrote more than twenty years ago, the further that science advances, "the more we seem to fear and deny the reality of death."[209] Physicians and nurses often become neglectful of patients once they have been diagnosed as terminal and may separate themselves mentally and physically from the dying patient.[210] Hospitals, which are primarily focused on preserving life, curing, diagnosis, and treating illness, tend to conceal death.[211] If the option of ending a

---

202. *See* Vande Cox, *The Hospice Concept: Dying as a Part of Living*, NURSING HOMES AND SENIOR CITIZEN CARE, July-Aug. 1988, at 29, 29.

203. *Id.* at 29-30.

204. *See id.* at 30. The hospice patient, however, "retains the option to reinstate treatment at any phase of his illness." *Id.* at 32.

205. *Id.* at 31.

206. *See* ELISABETH KUBLER-ROSS, TO LIVE UNTIL WE SAY GOOD-BYE 138-40 (1978).

207. James F. Bresnahan, *Reflection, in* ACTIVE EUTHANASIA, *supra* note 14, at 83, 85.

208. *Id.*

209. ELISABETH KUBLER-ROSS, ON DEATH AND DYING 6-7 (1969).

210. Cox, *supra* note 202, at 29-30.

211. *Id.*

terminally ill person's life early is available to physicians and hospitals, the quality of care given to such patients is unlikely to improve.[212]

If care of the dying were more humanely managed, there would be little need for euthanasia.[213] In a 1989 article in the *New England Journal of Medicine*, twelve physicians set forth views concerning treatment of hopelessly ill patients.[214] The article gained notoriety through the endorsement of physician-assisted suicide by ten of the twelve physicians,[215] but the article also addressed the inadequacies of current modes of care for the dying and proposed a number of feasible and cost-effective reforms. Among these proposals were the initiation of timely discussions with patients about dying, the solicitation and execution of advance directives, the facilitation of dying at home, the development of hospice care, the discouragement of intensive care units for dying patients, the formulation by physicians of flexible and adjustable programs of care, the training of physicians in care of the dying, and the aggressive use of painkillers, even if death is thereby hastened.[216]

Many of these reforms are already, to varying degrees, in practice in many parts of the country. Doctors are far more likely now than ever before to honor patients' wishes to forego aggressive treatment; the hospice movement uses sophisticated technology to keep terminal patients pain free and comfortable; and physicians are becoming more comfortable with administering increased morphine doses to control pain.[217] There is still much to be accomplished. Radical changes in the care of the terminally ill are needed, and should be an integral part of any health care reform package to come out of the United States Congress.

CONCLUSION

Voluntary euthanasia may ultimately be viewed as a backlash against a medical profession that failed to address the needs of the terminally ill, or it may be an idea whose time has come. Over the coming decades, the elderly population will increase dramatically, and if the spread of AIDS and social

---

212. Stephen Sapp, *Reflection*, in ACTIVE EUTHANASIA, *supra* note 14, at 88, 90.

213. Ronald E. Cranford, *Reflection*, in ACTIVE EUTHANASIA, *supra* note 14, at 80, 81.

214. Sidney H. Wanzer et al., *The Physician's Responsibility Toward Hopelessly Ill Patients*, 320 NEW ENG. J. MED. 844 (1989).

215. *Id.* at 848. The acceptance of assisted suicide under certain conditions by the ten physicians is couched in terms that would limit the procedure to exceptional cases: "If care is administered properly at the end of life, only the rare patient should be so distressed that he or she desires to commit suicide." *Id.* at 847.

216. *Id.* at 844-49.

217. Rosenthal, *supra* note 201, at 1-2.

ills associated with poverty continues unabated, our health care system will be burdened far beyond its present capacity. If reforms are not undertaken to ensure access to adequate health care for all Americans and to provide for more compassionate policies and strategies in the care of the dying, voluntary euthanasia may one day be seen, for the terminally ill and their families, as presumptively correct—the only way out of a hellish situation.

Even in the absence of legal voluntary euthanasia, some physicians will continue to assist patients to end their lives. In certain cases, such assistance may be justified, just as mercy killing may, under extreme circumstances, be so morally justified as to warrant acquittal in court. Yet to authorize euthanasia legislatively would be to create social policy based on the exceptional situation. Hard cases do indeed make bad law. Passing legislation to permit the few justifiable cases of euthanasia, at the expense of potentially opening the door to widespread abuses, is bad law and irresponsible social policy.

Euthanasia: Is It Murder or Mercy Killing? A Comparison of the Criminal Laws in the United States, the Netherlands and Switzerland

I. INTRODUCTION

With the advent of modern medical technology and progressive medical treatments, such as "miracle drugs," life support systems, artificial organs and organ transplants, the human race now has the novel ability to prolong life and to postpone death.[1] However, prolonged suffering is often a negative consequence of this improved ability to prolong life,[2] as evidenced by the many Americans who are held hostage by the excruciating and intolerable pain that accompanies death from degenerative and incurable diseases.[3] This severe pain has caused many people to plead with their doctors, families and loved ones to release them from their suffering in any manner possible, including death.[4] Because of the frequency of patients' requests for an end to their suffering, and because many such requests have been granted by doctors, friends and loved ones, the courts are now struggling with the difficult issue of whether or not a person has the right to die, with assistance if necessary.

The purpose of this Comment is to examine the current status of the right to die in the United States, focusing particularly on active

---

1. Hitts, *Life Expectancy Rises 3 Years to 74 for Men, 86 for Women*, Wash. Post, May 31, 1983, at A2, col. 1, *cited in* O'Brien, *Facilitating Euthanatic, Rational Suicide: Help Me Go Gentle into That Good Night*, 31 St. Louis U.L.J. 655, 655 (1987).
2. *In re* Farrell, 108 N.J. 335, 340, 529 A.2d 404, 406 (1987). The court stated:
While medical advances have made it possible to forestall and cure certain illnesses previously considered fatal, they also have prolonged the slow deterioration and death of some patients. Sophisticated life-sustaining medical technology has made it possible to hold some people on the threshold of death for an indeterminate period of time.
Id.
3. *See* D. HUMPHREY & A. WICKETT, THE RIGHT TO DIE (1986). The authors state that "[i]nfectious diseases, once life-threatening, have become reversible, while degenerative and chronic diseases have become the predominant cause of death." *Id.* at 189.
4. *Merciless Jury; Pressures for Commutation*, TIME, May 27, 1985, at 66. This article concerned a recent case in Florida where a 75-year-old man, Roswell Gilbert, was convicted of first-degree murder for shooting his wife. Gilbert asserted that his wife had repeatedly asked him to kill her to relieve her suffering. *Id.*

voluntary euthanasia. This Comment will compare the legality of euthanasia in the United States, the Netherlands and Switzerland by examining the criminal laws of each of these countries. Next, the future of United States law will be analyzed to determine the likelihood of legalized euthanasia in the United States. Finally, some suggestions for legal reform will be proffered.

II. DEFINITIONS AND DISTINCTIONS

Before analyzing the current status of the law, it is first necessary to explain the meaning and implications of euthanasia and clarify some important distinctions that arise when the right to die is considered. The word "euthanasia" is derived from the Greek words *eu*, which means good, and *thantos*, which means death.[5] However, from this etymology, the term has acquired a broader, more complex meaning. Today, "euthanasia" encompasses any action that helps one achieve a painless death.[6]

The *Medical Dictionary for Lawyers* defines euthanasia as "[a]n act or practice, which is advocated by many, of putting persons to death painlessly who are suffering from incurable and malignant diseases, as an act of mercy."[7] While most commentators suggest that euthanasia is motivated by kindness and a desire to end the intense suffering of another,[8] not all individuals view euthanasia in such a positive manner. For example, some commentators think euthanasia is a euphemism for murder,[9] while others object to euthanasia because it is contrary to the Hippocratic Oath,[10] or because it violates

---

5. M. HEIFETZ, THE RIGHT TO DIE 99 (1975).

6. D. Humphrey, *The Case for Rational Suicide*, 17 SUICIDE AND LIFE-THREATENING BEHAVIOR 355 (1987).

7. MEDICAL DICTIONARY FOR LAWYERS 287 (3d ed. 1960).

8. *See, e.g.*, Kohl, *Voluntary Beneficent Euthanasia*, in BENEFICENT EUTHANASIA 130-40 (M. Kohl ed. 1975). Kohl argues that the dominant motive of a person performing euthanasia is a desire to help the intended recipient. He defines euthanasia as "the inducement of a relatively painless and quick death, the intention and actual consequences of which are the *kindest possible treatment* of an unfortunate individual in the actual circumstances." *Id.* at 134.

9. D. HORAN, EUTHANASIA AND BRAIN DEATH: ETHICAL AND LEGAL CONSIDERATIONS 11 (1977). The author quotes Percy Foreman who states that "euthanasia is a highfalutin word for murder." *Id.*

10. The Hippocratic Oath, taken by all doctors, provides in pertinent part: "I will give no deadly medicine to anyone if asked, nor suggest any such counsel." *Reprinted in* Levisohn, *Voluntary Mercy Deaths: Socio-Legal Aspects of Euthanasia*, 8 J. FORENSIC MED. 57, 60 (1961).

their religious and moral beliefs.[11]

There are differences between the terms involuntary and voluntary euthanasia and active and passive euthanasia. The courts have taken these distinctions into account when assessing the criminal liability of the actor engaging in euthanasia. The rationale for recognizing these distinctions becomes evident upon an examination of the definitions of these terms. Involuntary euthanasia occurs when an individual, other than the patient, decides to discontinue treatment or to terminate an incompetent or a competent unconsenting person's life.[12] In contrast, voluntary euthanasia occurs when the patient himself decides to terminate treatment or to end his life.[13] Thus, involuntary euthanasia and voluntary euthanasia differ in that the former occurs without the patient's consent, while the latter occurs with the patient's consent.

It is the nature of the third party's actions that distinguishes active euthanasia from passive euthanasia.[14] With active euthanasia, a physician administers treatment which induces a painless death,[15] while with passive euthanasia,[16] the physician withdraws or withholds treatment or nourishment.[17] Thus, involuntary and voluntary eutha-

---

11. In Judeo-Christian religions, man is specifically prohibited from taking the life of another, regardless of the circumstances. The command is "thou shalt not kill." Exodus 20:13. Members of these religions believe that the right over life and death belongs exclusively to God and that society has no right to intervene. For a discussion of religious views of euthanasia, see Sherwin, *Jewish Views of Euthanasia*, in BENEFICENT EUTHANASIA 3-10 (M. Kohl ed. 1975); Maguire, *A Catholic View of Mercy Killing*, in BENEFICENT EUTHANASIA 34-42 (M. Kohl ed. 1975).

12. Comment, *Voluntary Active Euthanasia for the Terminally Ill and the Constitutional Right to Privacy*, 69 CORNELL L. REV. 363, 365-66 (1984).

13. *Id.* at 366.

14. *See* Sherlock, *For Everything There Is a Season: The Right to Die in the United States*, 1982 B.Y.U. L. REV. 545, 550.

15. In most instances, doctors induce a painless death with a lethal injection of drugs or an injection of air into the patient's bloodstream. For a discussion of the methods and drug doses used in performing euthanasia and auto-euthanasia, see generally D. HUMPHREY, LET ME DIE BEFORE I WAKE (1988).

16. Sherlock, *supra* note 14, at 550.

17. *See generally* Admiraal, *Euthanasia in the Netherlands—Justifiable Euthanasia*, 3 ISSUES L. & MED. 361 (1988). Passive euthanasia is defined as "the discontinuance of life sustaining means or treatment as a result of which the patient dies after a shorter or longer period." *Id.* at 368-69. Examples of passive euthanasia include "[s]topping existing [life support] medications such as antibiotics, cytotoxins, antiarrythmia's [heart regulating medications], medications for increasing blood pressure, diuretics, cortico-steroids, or insulin." *Id.* at 369. Other examples include "[s]topping existing nonmedication treatments such as kidney dialysis, blood transfusions, intravenous or tube feeding, reanimation, physiotherapy, or antidecubitis treatment." *Id.*

nasia may either be active or passive.

Although this Comment will briefly discuss all four types of euthanasia, it will focus mainly on active voluntary euthanasia. This form of euthanasia is commonly called "mercy killing" because the person administering the fatal treatment is motivated by an altruistic desire to alleviate the patient's suffering and to fulfill the patient's last, and perhaps most personal, wish. Thus, for the purposes of this Comment, the terms voluntary active euthanasia and "mercy killing" will be used synonymously.

III.   THE CURRENT STATE OF THE LAW IN THE UNITED STATES

A.   Active and Passive Involuntary Euthanasia

With involuntary euthanasia, the active/passive distinction is immaterial in assessing the actor's criminal liability. Since involuntary euthanasia is the taking of a person's life against his will or without his express consent, it constitutes homicide, regardless of whether it is active or passive.[18]

The legal prohibition against involuntary euthanasia stems from the theory of informed consent and the right of self-determination. Under these two doctrines, "[e]very human being of adult years and sound mind has a right to determine what should be done with his own body."[19] Therefore, without the patient's consent, or the consent of a relative or guardian, a physician may not engage in involuntary euthanasia.[20] Involuntary euthanasia involves a doctor acting without such requisite consent, thereby violating a patient's right of self-determination, privacy and life.[21] Thus, the courts do not, and should never, sanction involuntary euthanasia.

B.   Passive Voluntary Euthanasia

As previously mentioned, in cases involving involuntary euthanasia, the active/passive distinction is immaterial when assessing criminal liability, since both active and passive involuntary euthanasia are illegal in the United States. In contrast, in cases involving voluntary

---

18.   Comment, *The Right to Die—A Current Look*, 30 LOY. L. REV. 139, 142 n.18 (1984).

19.   *See* Schloendorff v. Soc'y of N.Y. Hosp., 211 N.Y. 125, 105 N.E.2d 92 (1914), *rev'd on other grounds*, 2 N.Y.2d 656, 163 N.Y.S.2d 3, 143 N.E.2d 3 (1957). The court stated that "[t]he patient's right to an informed consent makes no sense without a right to an informed refusal." *Id*. at 129, 105 N.E.2d at 114.

20.   Comment, *Euthanasia: A Comparison of the Criminal Laws of Germany, Switzerland and the United States*, 4 B. C. INT'L & COMP. L. REV. 533, 538-39 (1983).

21.   Comment, *supra* note 18, at 142.

euthanasia, the active/passive distinction is crucial when assessing the criminal liability of the actor. Most jurisdictions in the United States permit voluntary passive euthanasia, which is commonly characterized as the right to withdraw or refuse medical treatment.[22] However,

---

22. The following states have held that a patient has the right to withdraw or refuse medical treatment: Arizona, *see* Rasmussen v. Fleming, 154 Ariz. 200, 741 P.2d 667 (1987) (holding that there is a constitutional and common-law right to refuse treatment which may be exercised on an incompetent patient's behalf); California, *see* Bouvia v. Superior Court, 179 Cal. App. 3d 1127, 225 Cal. Rptr. 297 (1986) (holding that a mentally competent patient has a right to refuse medical treatment); Connecticut, *see* Foody v. Manchester Memorial Hosp., 40 Conn. Supp. 127, 482 A.2d 713 (Super. Ct. 1984) (holding that parents of a comatose patient had the right to discontinue the use of life-sustaining systems and that compliance with this right would not subject the physicians or the hospital to civil or criminal liability); Delaware, *see In re* Severns, 425 A.2d 156 (Del. 1980) (holding that an individual's right, expressed through a guardian, to decline to be kept alive as a veritable vegetable overcomes the interest of the state in the preservation of life); District of Columbia, *see* Tune v. Walter Reed Army Hosp., 602 F. Supp. 1452 (D.D.C. 1985) (holding that a competent adult has the right to determine whether his life should be prolonged by artificial means, such as life support systems); Florida, *see* Satz v. Perlmutter, 362 So. 2d 160 (Fla. Dist. Ct. App. 1978), *aff'd*, 379 So. 2d 359 (Fla. 1980) (holding that a competent individual has the right to refuse medical treatment); Georgia, *see In re* L. H. R., 253 Ga. 439, 321 S.E.2d 716 (1984) (holding that in the case of an incompetent patient who is terminally ill, in a chronic vegetative state, and with no reasonable possibility of regaining cognitive function, a family member or legal guardian may decide, on the patient's behalf, to terminate life-support systems without prior judicial approval); Illinois, *see In re* Estate of Longeway, 133 Ill. 2d 33, 549 N.E.2d 292, *reh'g denied*, 58 U.S.L.W. 2306 (1989) (holding that the common-law right to refuse medical treatment includes the right to withdraw artificial nutrition and hydration); Indiana, *see* Kumple v. Bloomington Hosp., 422 N.E.2d 1309 (Ind. 1981) (holding that the constitutional right of privacy includes a patient's right to refuse medical treatment); Maine, *see In re* Gardner, 534 A.2d 947 (Me. 1987) (holding that an individual's personal right to refuse life-sustaining treatment is firmly anchored in the common-law doctrine of informed consent, which requires the patient's informed consent to the administration of any medical care); Maryland, *see* Mercy Hosp., Inc. v. Jackson, 62 Md. App. 409, 488 A.2d 1130 (Ct. Spec. App. 1985) (holding that an individual has a right of informed consent to medical treatment and the corollary right to refuse medical treatment); Massachusetts, *see* Superintendent of Belchertown v. Saikewicz, 373 Mass. 728, 370 N.E.2d 417 (1977) (holding that a terminally ill person has a general right to refuse medical treatment and such general right extends to the case of a mentally incompetent patient); Minnesota, *see In re* Torres, 357 N.W.2d 332 (Minn. 1984) (holding that if an incompetent patient's best interests are no longer served by continuance of life-support systems, the court may empower the guardian to order their removal); Mississippi, *see* Brown v. Mississippi, 478 So. 2d 1033 (Miss. 1985) (holding that an individual's rights to free exercise of religion and privacy were broad enough to allow him to refuse medical treatment, such as a blood transfusion); New Jersey, *see In re* Farrell, 108 N.J. 335, 529 A.2d 404 (1987) (holding that any person who, in good faith reliance on procedures established by the state supreme court, withdrew life-sustaining treatment at the request of informed and competent patient who had undergone a required independent medical examination would incur no civil or criminal liability); *In re* Conroy, 188 N.J. Super. 523, 457 A.2d 1232 (1983) (holding that the nasogastric tube should be removed from an 84-year-old patient who is suffering from severe organic brain syndrome and a variety of other ailments, even though removal will almost certainly lead to the patient's death by starvation and dehydration); *In re* Quinlan, 70 N.J. 10, 355 A.2d 647,

voluntary active euthanasia has not received the same treatment by the courts.[23]

With voluntary euthanasia, the actor's liability will depend upon whether the action taken was "active" or "passive." However, this is an artificial distinction. There is little, if any, difference between killing someone through suffocation or starvation (which are considered "passive" acts because they involve "pulling the plug" or disengaging a nasogastric tube) and killing someone with a fatal injection (which is considered "active"). To stop or withdraw treatment, with the intention of relieving the patient's suffering through death, is no different than giving a fatal injection, since both actions ultimately achieve the same result—the patient's death.[24]

The distinction between active and passive euthanasia is illusory. For example, many commentators and legal scholars assert that this distinction simply does not make sense.[25] It is merely an artificial line that the courts have drawn for their own administrative convenience. As a prominent oncologist stated, "the difference between [voluntary active] euthanasia [that is killing or participating in a suicide] and letting the patient die by omitting life-sustaining treatment is a moral quibble."[26] In other words, it is logically inconsistent to impose no legal penalty on a doctor who removes life support equipment, but to

---

cert. denied, 429 U.S. 922 (1976) (holding that the right to refuse medical treatment may be asserted by a guardian on the patient's behalf and that life-support systems may be withdrawn without civil or criminal liability on the part of any participant, whether guardian, physician, hospital or others); New York, *see* Delio v. Westchester County Medical Center, 129 A.D.2d 1, 516 N.Y.S.2d 677 (N.Y. App. Div. 1987) (holding that a patient has a common-law right to refuse medical treatment in the form of nutrition and hydration by artificial means); Ohio, *see* Leach v. Shapiro, 13 Ohio App. 3d 393, 469 N.E.2d 1047 (1984) (holding that a patient has the right to refuse medical treatment, and that this refusal may not be overcome by the doctrine of implied consent); Pennsylvania, *see In re* Jane Doe, 16 Phila. 229 (Pa. Ct. Com. Pl. 1987) (holding that life-sustaining medical treatment may be withdrawn at the request of a competent person); Washington, *see In re* Guardianship of Hamlin, 102 Wash. 2d 810, 689 P.2d 1372 (1984) (holding that in the case of an incompetent patient, life-support systems may be withdrawn without prior judicial approval, if the members of the patient's immediate family (guardian if no family), treating physician and the prognosis committee all agree that the patient's best interests would be served by the withdrawal of life-sustaining treatment).

23. Active euthanasia is universally classified as murder, even when performed at the victim's request or with the victim's consent. Sherlock, *supra* note 14, at 553.

24. Potts, *Looking for the Exit Door: Killing and Caring in Modern Medicine,* Hous. L. Rev. 493, 500 (1988).

25. For a general discussion of the irrelevancy of the active/passive distinction, see O'Brien, *supra* note 1, at 663; Sherlock, *supra* note 14, at 550; Comment, *supra* note 12 at 368.

26. O'Brien, *supra* note 1, at 663.

impose legal penalties on one who helps implement a patient's decision to end his life.[27]

1. Sources of the Right To Refuse or Withdraw Medical Treatment

The right to refuse or withdraw medical treatment is based upon three sources—the constitutional right of religious freedom, the common-law right of bodily self-determination, and the constitutional right to privacy.[28]

Most courts have held that a person has a right to refuse medical treatment, based upon his or her religious convictions, where the individual's right of religious freedom outweighs the state's interest in preserving life.[29] For example, in the case of *In re Brooks' Estate*,[30] the Illinois Supreme Court held that the patient, a Jehovah's Witness, could not be forced to have a blood transfusion contrary to her religious beliefs. The court stated that the U.S. Constitution protects an individual's absolute right to exercise his or her religious beliefs. The government may only limit this right where the exercise of the right presents a clear and present danger to the public health, welfare or morals.[31] Since there was no clear and present danger in *In re Brooks' Estate*, the court held that the transfusions should not be administered against the patient's will.[32]

However, in *Application of President & Directors of Georgetown College, Inc.*,[33] the District of Columbia Circuit Court ordered that the patient, a Jehovah's Witness, be administered blood transfusions, despite her objections to the treatment. The court held that the compelling state interests present in this case—the possibility that the patient's seven year old daughter would become a ward of the state as well as the state's interest in preserving life—and the potential civil

---

27. Comment, *supra* note 12, at 369.

28. Comment, *supra* note 18, at 145.

29. In determining whether a person may refuse medical treatment based upon his or her religious convictions, a court will balance the individual's right to religious freedom against the state's interest. *See generally* D. MEYERS, MEDICO-LEGAL IMPLICATIONS OF DEATH & DYING (1981); Sullivan, *The Dying Person—His Plight and His Right*, 8 NEW ENG. L. REV. 197, 205-209 (1973).

30. *In re* Brooks' Estate, 32 Ill. 2d 361, 205 N.E.2d 435 (1965).

31. *Id.* at 372, 205 N.E.2d at 441.

32. *Id.* at 373, 205 N.E.2d at 441-42. The court stated that "[n]o overt or affirmative act of appellants offers any clear and present danger to society—we have only a governmental agency compelling conduct offensive to appellant's religious principles." *Id.*

33. Application of President & Directors of Georgetown College, Inc., 331 F.2d 1000 (D.C. Cir. 1964).

and criminal liability of the physician and hospital outweighed the patient's constitutional right of religious freedom.[34]

A second proposition upon which the refusal or withdrawal of medical treatment is justified is the common-law right of bodily self-determination and the doctrine of informed consent. Self-determination means that an individual has a right to control what is done with his or her body. The United States Supreme Court has stated that "no right is held more sacred, or is more carefully guarded by the common law, than the right of every individual to the possession and control of his own person, free from all restraint or interference of others, unless by clear and unquestionable authority of law."[35]

The doctrine of informed consent was developed to protect the right of self-determination.[36] Under this doctrine, "no medical procedure may be performed without a patient's consent, obtained after explanation of the nature of the treatment, substantial risks, and alternative therapies."[37] Taken together, the right of bodily self-determination and the doctrine of informed consent require that a patient must consent before he or she is subjected to invasive medical treatments.

A patient's right to bodily self-determination only has meaning if a patient's right to informed refusal is also recognized.[38] Thus, one may not be forced to submit to medical treatment to which he or she does not consent. This concept was recognized by the California appellate court in the case of *Bouvia v. Superior Court*:[39]

> a person of adult years and in sound mind has the right, in the exercise of control over his own body, to determine whether or not to submit to lawful medical treatment. It follows that such patient has the right to refuse *any* medical treatment, even that which may save or prolong her life.[40]

The court incorporated the right of bodily self-determination into the constitutional right of privacy developed in *Griswold v. Con-*

---

34. *Id.* at 1008-09. By contrast, these interests were not present in the *Brooks'* case, as the patient had no minor children and had executed documents releasing both the doctor and hospital from any civil liability which might result from a failure on the part of either to administer the transfusions. *In re* Brooks' Estate, 32 Ill. 2d at 372, 205 N.E.2d at 442.

35. *In re* Conroy, 98 N.J. 321, 346, 486 A.2d 1209, 1221 (1985).

36. Cantor, *A Patient's Decision To Decline Life-Saving Medical Treatment: Bodily Integrity Versus the Preservation of Life*, 26 RUTGERS L. REV. 228, 237 (1973).

37. *In re* Conroy, 98 N.J. at 346, 486 A.2d at 1222.

38. *Id.* at 347, 486 A.2d at 1222.

39. Bouvia v. Superior Court, 179 Cal. App. 3d 1127, 225 Cal. Rptr. 297 (1986).

40. *Id.* at 1137, 225 Cal. Rptr. at 300 (citation omitted).

necticut.[41] The defendants in *Griswold* had disseminated information, instruction, and medical advice to married couples regarding contraception.[42] Subsequently, they were convicted under a Connecticut statute which prohibited the aiding or counseling of others regarding the use of contraceptives.[43] On appeal to the United States Supreme Court, the defendants challenged the constitutionality of both the Connecticut statute and another statute which prohibited the use of contraceptives.[44] The Court held that "the First Amendment has a penumbra where privacy is protected from governmental intrusion."[45] Based on this finding, the Court concluded that a married person's right to use contraceptives fell within this penumbra.[46] Accordingly, the two challenged statutes were struck down as unconstitutional.[47]

In *Roe v. Wade,* the Court expanded the right to privacy which it had recognized in *Griswold.*[48] In *Roe,* the Court held that a Texas law prohibiting all abortions, except those necessary to save the life of the mother, violated the due process clause of the fourteenth amendment.[49] The Court stated, "th[e] right of privacy . . . is broad enough to encompass a woman's decision whether or not to terminate her pregnancy."[50]

The right to privacy is also broad enough to encompass a patient's decision to be free from unwanted medical care. Several recent court opinions have recognized that the right to refuse or withdraw medical treatment is also a fundamental and unabridgable component of the right to privacy.[51] For example, in *Bouvia v. Superior Court,*

---

41. Griswold v. Connecticut, 381 U.S. 479 (1965).

42. *Id.* at 480.

43. *Id.*

44. *Id.*

45. *Id.* at 483.

46. Griswold v. Connecticut, 381 U.S. 479, 485 (1965).

47. *Id.*

48. Roe v. Wade, 410 U.S. 113 (1973).

49. *Id.* at 163-64.

50. *Id.* at 153-54. Although the Court stated that a woman has a right to an abortion, the Court held that this right is not absolute:

> [M]ost of these courts have agreed that the right of privacy, however based, is broad enough to cover the abortion decision; that the right, nonetheless, is not absolute and is subject to some limitations; and that at some point the state interests as to the protection of health, medical standards, and prenatal life, become dominant. We agree with this approach.

Id. at 155.

51. Bouvia v. Superior Court, 179 Cal. App. 3d 1127, 1137, 225 Cal. Rptr. 297, 301 (1986). In *Bouvia,* the court stated that "[t]he right of a competent adult patient to refuse medical treatment is a constitutionally guaranteed right which must not be abridged." *Id.* at 1141, 225 Cal. Rptr. at 304.

the California Court of Appeals ordered that Elizabeth Bouvia's naso-gastric tube be removed.[52] The doctors had inserted the tube in Bouvia's stomach without her consent, thereby keeping her alive through involuntary, forced feeding. In reaching its conclusion, the court stated that "[t]he right to refuse medical treatment is basic and fundamental. It is recognized as a part of the right of privacy protected by both the state and federal constitution."[53] Furthermore, in *In re Farrell*, the New Jersey Supreme Court stated that, "[w]hile we held that a patient's right to refuse medical treatment even at the risk of personal injury or death is primarily protected by the common law, we recognized that it is also protected by the federal and state constitutional right of privacy."[54] Therefore, most courts recognize that the right to refuse or withdraw medical treatment is firmly grounded in the constitutional right to freedom of religion, the common law right of self-determination and the right to privacy.

2. Consent in the Case of the Incompetent Patient

When a patient is incompetent, a surrogate decision-maker may exercise the patient's right to refuse medical treatment.[55] In the case of an incompetent patient, the courts use three tests to determine whether medical treatment will be withdrawn: (1) the subjective test; (2) the limited-objective test; and (3) the pure-objective test.[56]

Under the subjective test, the decision-maker determines what the particular patient would have chosen to do, had he or she been competent.[57] This is not an objective standard; the question is not what a reasonable person would have done under these circum-

---

52. *Id.* at 1146, 225 Cal. Rptr. at 307.

53. *Id.* at 1137, 225 Cal. Rptr. at 301. The right to refuse medical treatment was also recognized as being basic and fundamental by the courts in Bartling v. Superior Court, 163 Cal. App. 3d 186, 209 Cal. Rptr. 220 (1984); Barber v. Superior Court, 147 Cal. App. 3d 1006, 195 Cal. Rptr. 484 (1983); *In re* Quinlan, 70 N.J. 10, 355 A.2d 647, *cert. denied*, 429 U.S. 922 (1976).

54. *In re* Farrell, 108 N.J. 335, 341, 529 A.2d 404, 410 (1987).

55. *See In re* Quinlan, 70 N.J. 10, 355 A.2d 647, *cert. denied*, 429 U.S. 922 (1976). The right of an incompetent to decide whether to discontinue the use of the mechanical respirator which maintained her vital processes was a valuable incident to her right to privacy and may be asserted on her behalf by her guardian) *Id.* at 20-21, 355 A.2d at 664; *In re* Conroy, 98 N.J. 321, 486 A.2d 1209 (1985) (a surrogate decision-maker has the right to direct the withdrawal or withholding of life-sustaining treatment for an incompetent patient under certain circumstances if certain procedures are followed) *Id.* at 342, 486 A.2d at 1231.

56. *Conroy*, 98 N.J. at 360-67, 486 A.2d at 1229-32.

57. *Id.* at 360, 486 A.2d at 1229.

stances, but what this particular patient would have done.[58] The following evidence may be used in discerning whether the patient would have chosen to withdraw or withhold treatment, if he or she had been competent to make the decision: evidence of oral directives previously given by the patient to family members or friends; evidence of proxies or powers of attorney authorizing a particular person to make the decision on the patient's behalf; evidence of religious beliefs; and evidence of the patient's pattern of conduct with respect to prior decisions about his or her medical care.[59] Thus, under this test, treatment may only be withdrawn or withheld if there is clear evidence that the patient would have chosen this course of action had he or she been competent to make the decision.

Under the limited-objective test, a guardian may refuse treatment on a patient's behalf when there is "some trustworthy evidence that the patient would have refused treatment, and the decision-maker is satisfied . . . that the burdens of the patient's continued life with the treatment outweigh the benefits of that life for him."[60] Medical evidence is essential in order to establish that the burdens of treatment (i.e. the pain and suffering) outweigh the benefits of treatment.[61] Thus, this test allows termination of an incompetent patient's treatment if two conditions are met. First, it must be clear that the treatment in question would merely prolong the patient's suffering. Second, there must be some "trustworthy" evidence that the patient would have wanted the treatment terminated, had he or she been competent to make the decision. Facts capable of satisfying the second part of this test include all evidence that is acceptable to satisfy the subjective test. However, the "some trustworthy evidence" standard is a lower standard of proof than that required under the subjective test.[62] Thus, evidence that is too tenuous to satisfy the subjective test might nevertheless be sufficient to satisfy this part of the limited-objective test.[63]

---

58. *Id.*

59. *Id.* at 361-65, 486 A.2d at 1229-31.

60. *In re* Conroy, 98 N.J. 321, 365, 486 A.2d 1209, 1232 (1985).

61. *Id.*

62. Silving, *Euthanasia: A Study in Comparative Criminal Law*, 103 U. Pa. L. Rev. 350, 378 (1954).

63. *Conroy*, 98 N.J. at 366, 486 A.2d at 1232. The court stated, "[e]vidence that, taken as a whole, would be too vague, casual, or remote to constitute the clear proof of the patient's subjective intent that is necessary to satisfy the subjective test—for example, informally expressed reactions to other people's medical conditions and treatment—might be sufficient to satisfy this prong of the limited-objective test." *Id.*

In the absence of any evidence regarding what the patient would have done had he or she been competent to make the decision, treatment may still be withdrawn or withheld from an incompetent patient if the pure-objective test is satisfied.[64] The pure-objective test provides that:

> the net burdens of the patient's life with the treatment should clearly and markedly outweigh the benefits that the patient derives from life. Further, the recurring, unavoidable and severe pain of the patient's life with the treatment should be such that the effect of administering life-sustaining treatment would be inhumane.[65]

However, the treatment may not be withheld if there is any evidence suggesting that the patient would have chosen to accept the treatment, had he or she been competent to make the decision.[66]

In summary, the right to refuse or withdraw medical treatment has been explicitly recognized by most state courts.[67] Additionally, many state legislatures have passed Natural Death Acts that facilitate the exercise of this right.[68] For instance, Section 7186 of the California Health and Safety Code provides that "adult persons have the

---

64. *Id.* at 366, 486 A.2d at 1232.
65. *In re* Conroy, 98 N.J. 321, 366, 486 A.2d 1209, 1232 (1985).
66. *Id.*
67. *See supra* note 22.
68. Currently, thirty-eight states, including the District of Columbia, have enacted some type of living will statute. *See* ALA. CODE §§ 22-8A-1 to -10 (1975); ALASKA STAT. §§ 18.12.010-12.100 (1986); ARIZ. REV. STAT. ANN. §§ 36-3201 to -3210 (1986); ARK. STAT. ANN. §§ 20-17-201 to -218 (Supp. 1989); CAL. HEALTH & SAFETY CODE §§ 7185-7195 (West Supp. 1990); COLO. REV. STAT. §§ 15-18-101 to -113 (1987 & Supp. 1989); CONN. GEN. STAT. ANN. §§ 19a-570 to -575 (West Supp. 1989); DEL. CODE. ANN. tit. 16, §§ 2501-2508 (1983); D.C. CODE. ANN. §§ 6-2401 to -2430 (1982); FLA. STAT. ANN. §§ 765.01-.15 (West 1986); GA. CODE ANN. §§ 31-32-1 to -12 (Harrison 1985); HAW. REV. STAT. §§ 327 D-1 to -27 (Supp. 1987); IDAHO CODE §§ 39-4501 to -4509 (1985 & Supp. 1989); ILL. ANN. STAT. ch. 110½, paras. 701-710 (Smith-Hurd Supp. 1989); IND. CODE ANN. §§ 16-8-11-1 to -22 (Burns 1990); IOWA CODE ANN. §§ 144A.1 to .11 (West 1989); KAN. STAT. ANN. §§ 65-28,101 to 28,122 (1985); LA. REV. STAT. ANN. §§ 40:1299.58.1 to .10 (West Supp. 1990); ME. REV. STAT. ANN. tit. 22, §§ 2921-2931 (Supp. 1988); MD. HEALTH-GEN. CODE ANN. §§ 5-601 to -614 (1990); MISS. CODE ANN. §§ 41-41-101 to -121 (Supp. 1989); MO. ANN. STAT. §§ 459.010 to .055 (Vernon Supp. 1990); N.H. REV. STAT. ANN. §§ 137-H:1 to H:16 (Supp. 1990); N.J. STAT. ANN. §§ 52:9Y-1 to -6 (West 1986); N.M. STAT. ANN. §§ 24-7-1 to -10 (1986); N.C. GEN. STAT. §§ 90-320 to -323 (1985); OKLA. STAT. ANN. tit. 63, §§ 3101-3111 (West Supp. 1990); OR. REV. STAT. §§ 97.050 to .090 (1987); S.C. CODE ANN. §§ 44-77-10 to -160 (Law. Co-op. Supp. 1989); TENN. CODE ANN. §§ 32-11-101 to -110 (Supp. 1986); TEX. HEALTH & SAFETY CODE ANN. § 4590h-1 (Vernon Supp. 1990); UTAH CODE ANN. §§ 75-2-1101 to -1118 (Supp. 1989); VT. STAT. ANN. tit. 18, §§ 5251-5262 (1987); VA. CODE ANN. §§ 541-2981 to -2992 (1988 & Supp. 1989); WASH. REV. CODE ANN. §§ 70.122.010 to .905 (Supp. 1989); W. VA. CODE §§ 16-30-1 to -10 (1985); WIS. STAT. ANN. §§ 154.01 to .15 (West 1989); WYO. STAT. §§ 35-22-101 to -109 (1988).

fundamental right to control the decisions relating to the rendering of their own medical care, including the decision to have life-sustaining procedures withheld or withdrawn in instances of a terminal condition."[69]

C. Active Voluntary Euthanasia

Currently, United States criminal law classifies mercy killing as murder.[70] For example, the California Penal Code provides that "murder is the unlawful killing of a human being with malice aforethought."[71] It is first degree murder if the killing is "willful, deliberate, and premeditated."[72] The consent of the victim does not vitiate the crime.[73] Similarly, the fact that the patient is in a terminal condition[74] or that the actor was motivated to act out of mercy or compassion will not excuse or lessen the crime.[75]

In *People v. Conley*,[76] the court stated that "one who commits euthanasia bears no ill will toward his victim and believes his act is morally justified, but he nonetheless acts with malice if he is able to comprehend that society prohibits his act regardless of his personal belief."[77] Thus, when a person ends the life of another person, regardless of whether the victim is a loved one or a consenting patient, the

---

69. CAL. HEALTH & SAFETY CODE § 7186 (West Supp. 1988).

70. *See* F. WHARTON, WHARTON'S CRIMINAL LAW §§ 137-170 (14th ed. 1979); Foreman, *The Physician's Criminal Liability for the Practice of Euthanasia*, 27 BAYLOR L. REV. 54, 54 (1975).

71. CAL. PENAL CODE § 187(a) (West Supp. 1988).

72. *Id.* § 189.

73. R. PERKINS, CRIMINAL LAW 1075 (3d ed. 1982). *See also* Turner v. State, 119 Tenn. 663, 671, 108 S.W. 1139, 1141 (1908). The court held that "[m]urder is no less murder because the homicide is committed at the desire of the victim. He who kills another upon his desire or command is, in the judgment of the law, as much a murderer as if he had done it merely of his own head." *Id.*

74. Garbesi, *The Law of Assisted Suicide*, 3 ISSUES L. & MED. 93, 94 (1987). Professor Garbesi states that "[t]he fact that death may have been imminent at any rate is immaterial. The crime lies in causing death to occur earlier than otherwise would have been the case." *Id.*

75. People v. Conley, 64 Cal. 2d 310, 411 P.2d 911, 49 Cal. Rptr. 815 (1966); People v. Mangano, 375 Ill. 72, 30 N.E.2d 428 (1940); State v. Ehlers, 98 N.J.L. 236, 119 A. 15 (1922); Turner v. State, 119 Tenn. 663, 108 S.W. 1139 (1908). For example, in State v. Ehlers, the court stated,

> the state has a deep interest and concern in the preservation of the life of each of its citizens, and . . . does not either commit or permit any individual, no matter how kindly the motive, either the right or the privilege of destroying such a life, except in punishment for a crime and in the manner prescribed by law.

98 N.J.L. at 241, 119 A. at 17.

76. People v. Conley, 64 Cal. 2d 310, 411 P.2d 911, 49 Cal. Rptr. 815 (1966).

77. *Id.* at 322, 411 P.2d at 918, 49 Cal. Rptr. at 822.

act is done intentionally and, therefore, constitutes first degree murder.[78]

Despite the statutory prohibitions against active voluntary euthanasia, the courts have not been consistent when deciding cases involving mercy killings. The defendants are usually charged with some type of homicide, but the actual verdicts range from first degree murder to outright acquittal.[79] Two cases exemplify the disparate outcomes in euthanasia cases. First is the case of *People v. Roberts*.[80] In this case, the victim had multiple sclerosis and was suffering from excruciating pain. She had unsuccessfully attempted suicide by ingesting carbolic acid. Following this attempt, her husband succumbed to her urgent and repeated requests and placed poisoned water on a chair within her reach. The woman drank the poisoned water and subsequently died.[81] The husband was convicted of first degree murder, despite his altruistic motives.[82]

The outcome in *Roberts* is in sharp contrast with the result in the case of Dr. Hermann Sander. Dr. Sander was acquitted in the death of his terminally ill, cancer-stricken patient, despite evidence that clearly indicated that he had injected a lethal dose of air into his pa-

---

78. Silving, *supra* note 62, at 352.

79. Note, *The Right of the Terminally Ill to Die, with Assistance If Necessary*, 8 CRIM. JUST. J. 403, 414 n.74 (1986). According to Gilbreath, an analysis of the verdicts in the 48 reported mercy killings between 1930 and 1960 reveals the following disparate resolutions:

Type of sentence/final outcome of case	# of people
Mercy killer committed suicide	17
Manslaughter/second-degree murder	11
First-degree murder	
life sentence	4
death sentence	1
Temporarily insane	
Acquitted and freed	6
Not indicted	1
Committed to mental institution	3
Acquitted outright	3
Dismissed by judge	1
Died while under indictment	1

Id. at 416.

80. People v. Roberts, 211 Mich. 187, 178 N.W. 690 (1920).

81. *Id.* at 192, 178 N.W. at 691.

82. *Id.* at 199, 178 N.W. at 694. The court stated that,

We are of the opinion that, when defendant mixed the paris green with water and placed it within reach of his wife to enable her to put an end to her suffering by putting an end to her life, he was guilty of murder by means of poison within the meaning of the statute, even though she requested him to do so.

Id. at 197, 178 N.W. at 693.

tient's veins.[83] Thus, these two divergent cases demonstrate the desperate need for either a federal statute or a Supreme Court ruling to remedy the lack of uniform adjudication by the courts in this area.

Generally, the actual practice of criminal law does not coincide with strict legal theory.[84] Cases such as *People v. Roberts*[85] are the exception, rather than the rule. It is more common for persons performing euthanasia to not be prosecuted.[86] The reasons for this are two-fold. First, the decedent's relatives ordinarily do not cooperate with the prosecutor since they consented to the euthanasia.[87] Second, juries are often unwilling to return guilty verdicts against defendants who killed out of mercy or kindness.[88] It is time that legal theory changed to comport with actual societal practice. The Netherlands and Switzerland may serve as useful models for implementing changes in the United States' euthanasia law.

IV.   The Current State of the Law in the Netherlands

Holland has come close to legalizing the practice of euthanasia.[89] Although Article 293 of the Dutch Criminal Code expressly provides for a twelve-year prison sentence for any person who "takes the life of another at his or her explicit and serious request,"[90] thousands of cases of euthanasia occur annually in the Netherlands without criminal prosecutions.[91] The doctors who practice euthanasia are rarely, if ever, prosecuted.[92] For example, Dr. Pieter V. Admiraal, an anesthesiologist at a hospital in Delft, has openly performed euthanasia over

---

83.   N.Y. Times, Feb. 8, 1950, at 1, col. 2. For other examples of the inconsistent court rulings in mercy killing cases, see Note, *supra* note 79, at 414 n.74.

84.   Levin & Levin, *DNR: An Objectionable Form of Euthanasia*, 49 U. Cin. L. Rev. 567, 575 (1980).

85.   People v. Roberts, 211 Mich. 187, 178 N.W. 690 (1920).

86.   For example, in March 1988, Marty James appeared on national television announcing that he had assisted two people, who were suffering from AIDS, in ending their lives. While the television revelation sparked a criminal investigation, no charges were ever filed. Braun, *Deliver Them from Death*, L.A. Times, Aug. 28, 1988, at 1, col. 1.

87.   Levin & Levin, *supra* note 84.

88.   *Id.*

89.   Potts, *supra* note 24, at 495.

90.   Clines, *Dutch Quietly in Lead in Euthanasia Requests*, N.Y. Times, Oct. 31, 1986, at 4, col. 3.

91.   Estimates of the number of euthanasia cases per year in the Netherlands vary considerably. One source suggests that between 6 and 12 thousand cases of euthanasia occur annually in the Netherlands. Dessaur & Rutenfrans, *The Present Day Practice of Euthanasia*, 3 Issues L. & Med. 399, 402 (1988). Other sources suggest that the number may be as high as 20 thousand. *60 Minutes: The Last Right?* (CBS television broadcast, Aug. 21, 1988).

92.   Potts, *supra* note 24, at 495.

one hundred times in the past ten years; however, he has been prosecuted only once.[93] Furthermore, he was acquitted of the charges even though he admitted to giving his patient a fatal injection.[94]

Additionally, in 1984, the Supreme Court of the Netherlands decided a case in which it held that mercy killing was privileged conduct in certain circumstances.[95] The case involved a ninety-four-year-old woman, named Maria, who had poor eyesight, poor hearing, suffered from dizzy spells and had difficulty moving. Although she had urged her doctor to end her life, he had not granted her request. Several months later Maria fell and broke her hip. By this time, her hearing and sight had rapidly deteriorated and she was barely able to speak. She was totally dependent on the nursing staff with regard to bathing and personal hygiene. She could no longer eat or drink and had lost consciousness for a period of time. After several urgent requests from Maria and her family members, the doctor finally relented and agreed to end Maria's suffering. She died in her sleep from an injection administered by her doctor. The doctor was later prosecuted but was acquitted at the trial court level. However, the intermediate appellate court overturned the acquittal and found the doctor guilty. The intermediate appellate court's decision was then overturned by the Supreme Court which held that mercy killing is not punishable if it is carried out in the context of an emergency situation and results from the physician's careful consideration of his conflicting duties and responsibilities.[96]

Since 1973, Dutch courts have ruled that active voluntary euthanasia is not a punishable offense under certain conditions.[97] These conditions are:

(1) euthanasia may be practiced only by a doctor;
(2) there must be evidence of a verbal or written decision by the deceased that he wanted his life terminated;
(3) that decision must have been made without coercion and must have been of a lasting, settled nature;
(4) alternatives must have been considered, with the deceased having been informed of the particulars of his situation and the

---

93. *60 Minutes: The Last Right?* (CBS television broadcast, Aug. 21, 1988).
94. *Id.*
95. Garbesi, *supra* note 74, at 108.
96. Vervoorn, *Voluntary Euthanasia in the Netherlands: Recent Developments*, 6 BIOETHICS NEWS 19, 20 (1987).
97. *Id.* at 19.

alternatives open to him while he was still in a state to consider those alternatives and actually did so;

(5)   the case must have involved severe or unbearable physical or mental suffering of a lasting nature, for the relief of which there was no reasonable alternative available;

(6)   there must be evidence that careful decision-making took place, including consultation with another medical practitioner.[98]

Therefore, as long as doctors follow the guidelines delineated above, they will not be punished for performing euthanasia.

Several groups within the Netherlands' government have actively campaigned to change the penal laws, which criminalize euthanasia, to coincide with current case law, which allows euthanasia to be performed if certain conditions exist.[99] For example, in 1984, Mrs. Wessel-Tunistra introduced a bill to legalize the practice of euthanasia. Although the bill did not pass, it was not the end of the euthanasia debate in the Netherlands.[100] In 1985, a State Commission on Euthanasia presented its findings to the Queen and stated its position that a doctor who takes the life of a patient, at the patient's request, should not be punished, provided that certain conditions have been met.[101] On January 20, 1986, a draft bill on euthanasia was sent by L.C. Brinkman, Minister of Well-Being, Public Health and Culture, to the President of the Lower Chamber.[102] Additionally, in March 1987, the Royal Netherlands Society for the Promotion of Medicine and the Dutch Nurses' Union issued a joint statement which advocated euthanasia and set forth what the "normal" conduct of nurses and doctors should be at the bedside of a patient desiring to end his suffering.[103] Furthermore, in January 1987, the Royal Netherlands Society for the Promotion of Pharmacy issued a pamphlet which contained a list of the drugs and the appropriate mixtures that could be used by a doctor

---

98.   *Id.* The last requirement, that there must be evidence that careful decision-making took place, was set aside in a 1985 case in which the court ruled that consultation with a second doctor was not necessary. The court reasoned that it was unnecessary to consult a second doctor before performing euthanasia, because a second doctor would not be as well informed as the treating doctor about the circumstances of the particular patient. *Id.*

99.   *Id.*

100.   Schepens, *Euthanasia: Our Own Future?*, 3 ISSUES L. & MED. 371, 375 (1988).

101.   Driesse, Van der Kolk, Van Nunen-Forger & de Marees van Swinderen, *Euthanasia and the Law in the Netherlands*, 3 ISSUES L. & MED. 385, 395 (1988). These conditions are: the patient must be in a hopeless condition with no hope of recovery; the request for euthanasia must be voluntary; and the termination of life must take place within the framework of careful medical practice. *Id.*

102.   Schepens, *supra* note 100, at 375.

103.   *Id.* at 378.

to perform euthanasia.[104] Finally, a member of the Dutch Parliament proposed a bill to amend the Criminal Code to make it consistent with the current case law. However, no action has been taken on this bill as of the writing of this Comment.[105]

Therefore, even though the penal statutes remain on the books, the Netherlands' courts have in effect made euthanasia a non-punishable offense.[106] Euthanasia in the Netherlands is a common practice, accepted by the general public,[107] physicians, nurses, hospital boards, politicians and the courts.[108] It is merely a matter of time before euthanasia will also be accepted by the Netherlands' legislature.

V. THE LAW IN SWITZERLAND

A. The Element of Motive

In the United States, an actor's motive is immaterial in assessing his culpability for a crime.[109] A compassionate motive will not exonerate one who commits murder[110] and will not alter the fact that an intent to end a human life existed. "If the proved facts established that the defendant in fact did the killing willfully, that is with intent to kill . . . and as the result of premeditation and deliberation . . . there is murder in the first degree, no matter what the defendant's motive may have been."[111] Hence, an individual who kills another out of empathy or compassion will be accorded the same treatment as one who commits a cold-blooded murder.[112]

---

104. *Id.*

105. Garbesi, *supra* note 74, at 111. I have spoken with Professor Garbesi, General Counsel for the Hemlock Society, and the Dutch Embassy who have confirmed that no action has been taken on the bill to amend the criminal code to remove euthanasia from the category of first-degree murder.

106. *Id.* at 109-10.

107. Vervoorn, *supra* note 96, at 20.

108. Schepens, *supra* note 100, at 378.

109. Comment, *supra* note 20, at 547.

110. *See supra* note 75. *See also* W. LA FAVE & A. SCOTT, CRIMINAL LAW 204 (1972). The authors state that motive is immaterial in determining the culpability of the actor. "The most laudable motive is no defense [to a criminal act]." *Id.*

111. State v. Ehlers, 98 N.J.L. 236, 238, 119 A. 15, 17 (1922).

112. The fact that euthanasia is not accorded a more lenient treatment than murder is illustrated by the following two cases. Ronald Fisher Elam brutally murdered Debbie Ann Scott by shooting her in the head as he drove by her car on the freeway. Elam was convicted of first-degree murder and sentenced to 27 years. Ramos, *Man Sentenced for Killing Woman in Passing Truck*, L.A. Times, May 10, 1988, at 1, col. 1. He will be eligible for parole in 13½ years. *Id.* at 4, col. 2. *See also* Gilbert v. State, 487 So. 2d 1185 (Fla. Dist. Ct. App. 1986). Roswell and Emily Gilbert had been married for 51 years. They had a wonderful relationship and were in the habit of lunching together every day. Emily suffered from osteoporosis and

By contrast, under the Swiss Penal Code, the actor's motive is the essential factor in determining the actor's culpability.[113] The motive which caused the actor to commit the crime is relevant in determining the actor's dangerousness and in predicting whether or not he will repeat the crime.[114] The theory is that one who kills to gain a reward or a financial benefit will do so again, while one who kills out of mercy or compassion is unlikely to repeat the act.[115]

A Swiss judge will also consider a defendant's motive in the grading and the sentencing of an offense.[116] Article 63 of the Swiss Penal Code provides that, "[t]he judge will determine the penalty according to the culpability of the offense, taking into account *the motives*, prior offenses and the personal circumstances surrounding the latter."[117] Accordingly, a defendant who has a highly reprehensible motive will be guilty of murder, while a defendant who has a more benign motive will be guilty of a lesser crime. Furthermore, if the actor is motivated by a desire to comply with a patient's request to be relieved from his suffering through death, the actor will be guilty of a completely separate crime, called "homicide upon request."[118]

In Switzerland, the actor's motive is relevant in determining the length and severity of the criminal sentence.[119] This is reflected in article 64 of the Swiss Penal Code which provides that "[t]he judge will be able to lighten the sentence . . . when the offender [has] acted, by yielding to *honorable motives*."[120] Thus, one who kills another out of compassion—an "honorable" motive—will receive a lighter sentence than one who kills out of anger or greed.

The Swiss Penal Code mandates that the judge consider motive

Alzheimer's Disease. She was suffering from intense pain and was often confused. On March 3, Emily was hospitalized. Emily did not want to stay at the hospital, so Roswell took her home. On March 4, Emily was in intense pain. Roswell gave her four pain pills, which had been prescribed by Emily's doctor. When these were ineffective she said, "Please, somebody help me. Please, somebody help me." *Id.* at 1187. In an effort to relieve Emily's suffering and respond to her pleas, Roswell shot Emily. She died instantaneously. *Id.* at 1188. Despite Roswell's compassionate motive, he was convicted of first-degree murder and sentenced to serve a minimum of 25 years in prison. *Id.* at 1187. Thus, it is possible that Mr. Elam, a vicious criminal, acting with an evil motive, will be released 11 1/2 years before Mr. Gilbert, a peaceful citizen, acting with an altruistic motive.

113.   Comment, *supra* note 20, at 547.
114.   Silving, *supra* note 62, at 361.
115.   *Id.* at 362.
116.   Sw. STGB art. 63 (1982).
117.   *Id.* (emphasis added).
118.   *Id.* art. 114.
119.   *Id.* art. 64.
120.   *Id.* (emphasis added).

when determining a defendant's sentence.[121] Thus, a Swiss judge must reduce the sentence if a defendant has a compassionate motive.[122] By contrast, a judge in the United States need not consider motive when determining a defendant's sentence. Therefore, it is conceivable that a mercy killer, who acted out of compassion and love, could receive a harsher sentence than one who committed a cold-blooded murder.[123] It is flagrantly unfair to treat one who acts with a benevolent motive the same as, or more severely than, someone who acts with a malignant and sinister motive. Therefore, it is time to change the laws of the United States to remedy this gross injustice.

Under the Swiss system, a defendant will be guilty of one crime with a given punishment if his motive is altruistic, while he will be guilty of an entirely different crime, with a greater punishment, if his motive is malevolent.[124] Thus, one who commits euthanasia and, thereby, acts with an "honorable motive," will either be acquitted or will receive a reduced sentence.[125]

B. Homicide Upon Request

In the United States, one who kills another in response to the decedent's request is guilty of murder.[126] The fact that the victim desired to be killed or asked to be killed is not a defense and, therefore, will not mitigate the defendant's sentence.[127] By contrast, in Switzerland, one who commits a homicide at the decedent's request will receive a mitigated sentence.[128]

The governing belief in Switzerland is that although killing is always reprehensible, it is less reprehensible when performed at the decedent's request.[129] Therefore, the Swiss legislature has created a separate crime called "homicide upon request" which is punished less

---

121. Comment, *supra* note 20, at 548.
122. *Id.*
123. For an example of a judge imposing a harsh sentence on a defendant who acted with an altruistic motive, see Gilbert v. State, 487 So. 2d 1185 (1986), discussed *supra* note 114.
124. Comment, *supra* note 20, at 548.
125. *Id.* at 553. The author states that
> [i]n some cases, the motives may be so benevolent that total exculpation of the actor is warranted. A physician who has acted with a benevolent motive in terminating the life of an individual lacks the malice which is a major element in the exigency to punish a person for homicide.

Id.
126. CAL. PENAL CODE § 187(a) (West Supp. 1988).
127. *See* Garbesi, *supra* note 74.
128. *Id.*
129. Silving, *supra* note 62, at 378.

severely than murder.[130] Article 114 of the Swiss Penal Code provides that "[h]e who kills another upon the latter's earnest and urgent request will be punished by imprisonment."[131] Although the statute mandates imprisonment, a benevolent motive will mitigate this punishment considerably.[132] Thus, the statute incorporates the equitable principle that "justice requires that killing a consenting person . . . should not be punished as severely as killing a person against his will."[133]

In order to qualify as a "homicide upon request," the victim's request must be both "earnest and urgent."[134] An earnest request is one that is serious and sincere, not one that is made in jest. Also, for a request to be considered "earnest," the victim must understand the nature and the consequences of the type of request he is making. Thus, someone who has a diminished capacity, because he is mentally ill, drunk or in the heat of passion, may not be capable of making an "earnest" request.[135] A request will be deemed "urgent" if it is repeated several times by the victim.[136]

Thus, the Swiss legislature has ameliorated the problem of euthanasia in two ways. First, a defendant's motive will be taken into account when determining a defendant's sentence.[137] Hence, one who kills with a benevolent motive will receive a mitigated sentence. Second, "homicide upon request" is a separate crime, carrying a lighter sentence than murder.[138]

VI. CONCLUSION

While both the Dutch parliament and the Swiss legislature have attempted to deal with the growing problem of euthanasia in creative ways, the United States legislature has not. Instead, the United States has chosen to ignore the problem. As a result, euthanasia occurs covertly, subject to the dangers of abuse.[139] Furthermore, neither the

---

130. Sw. STGB art. 114 (1982).

131. *Id.*

132. Comment, *supra* note 20, at 554.

133. Silving, *supra* note 62, at 378.

134. Sw. STGB art. 114 (1982).

135. Silving, *supra* note 62, at 384.

136. Comment, *supra* note 20, at 555.

137. Sw. STGB arts. 63-64 (1982).

138. *Id.* art. 114.

139. For example, in an euthanasia survey conducted in California by the Hemlock Society, a national group that advocates euthanasia, 79 physicians claimed that they deliberately took the lives of terminal patients who asked to die. Of the 79 physicians who said they had

Supreme Court[140] nor Congress has considered the legality of euthanasia. Hence, the area is left to the states which results in inconsistent and conflicting decisions.[141] Therefore, it is time that either Congress or the Supreme Court dealt with the issue so that euthanasia can be practiced overtly, subject to both governmental control and proper safeguards. Federal action will also ensure that euthanasia cases are uniformly decided from state to state.

The distinction between active and passive euthanasia is artificial and without merit. It is illogical to permit a doctor to withdraw life support systems without incurring a penalty, while imposing a penalty on a doctor who helps implement a patient's desire to end his suffering. An individual has a right to determine what is done to his or her body. Accordingly, an individual has a right to choose death over a life of pain and suffering, as long as the decision to die is competent, well-informed and made after careful thought and deliberation.

> To require that a person be kept alive against his will and to deny his pleas for a merciful release after the dignity, beauty, promise and meaning of life have vanished, when he can only linger on in stages of agony or decay, is cruel and barbarous. The imposition of

---

performed active euthanasia, 15 had done so once, 35 had done so two or three times, and 29 had done so on more than three occassions. Derek Humphrey, the Hemlock Society's director, states that the study is significant because "it's an indicator that active euthanasia is going on covertly in hospitals now." Parchini, *Euthanasia: New Findings in the Hemlock Poll*, L.A. Times, Feb. 25, 1988, at 1, col. 3.

140. Currently, in the case of Cruzan v. Missouri Dept. of Health, the Supreme Court is considering whether a person has a right to refuse unwanted medical care. Cruzan v. Harmon, 760 S.W.2d 408 (1988), *cert. granted*, 109 S. Ct. 3240 (1989). Since a severe car crash in 1983, Nancy Beth Cuza has remained in a vegetative state, with no chance of recovery. She is unconscious and being fed through a tube. Her parents wish to remove the tube, but are being blocked by the state of Missouri. Thus, they have appealed to the Supreme Court.

It is unclear how the Court will rule on this issue. The Court's conservative members expressed doubts that the Constitution expressly gives an individual a right to be free from unwanted medical care. Thus, a broadly written decision could overturn those state court rulings, such as the *Quinlan* case and the *Bouvia* case, which have found such a right. On the other hand, Justice Sandra Day O'Connor, the fifth and pivotal vote of the conservative majority, seems to be leaning towards a more narrow ruling which would balance the state's interest in preserving life against the wishes of the individual or the individual's guardian. The Supreme Court will most likely issue its opinion in the spring of 1990. Savage, *Justices Grapple with 1st "Right-to-Die" Case*, L.A. Times, Dec. 7, 1989, at 32, col. 1. However, even if the Supreme Court does issue a broad ruling regarding whether a person has the right to die through passive measures (i.e. whether one has a right to terminate or refuse medical treatment), the question of whether one has a right to die through active measures remains unanswered.

141. *See supra* note 79 and accompanying text.

unnecessary suffering is an evil that should be avoided by civilized society.[142]

The Dutch and Swiss approaches may serve as useful models to the United States for implementing changes in the United States euthanasia laws. Specifically, the United States should follow Switzerland's example and consider the actor's motive and the victim's wishes when determining the penalty for one who commits euthanasia.[143] An individual who helps implement a patient's decision to die should be accorded more lenient treatment than one who performs premeditated murder. Thus, the harsh rule on murder should be modified so that courts may consider the compassionate motives of one who commits euthanasia. However, in formulating any laws regarding euthanasia, the legislature must be careful to impose sufficient safeguards so that a euthanasia defense will not be abused. "Specifically, there is a danger that homicidal charlatans will perform euthanasia on demurring subjects and later elude prosecutions by falsely claiming that they merely facilitated a rational suicide."[144] The time is ripe for Congress to promulgate laws regarding the right to die or for the Supreme Court to rule on the legality of active euthanasia.

Dana Elizabeth Hirsch

---

142. Comment, *A Right to Choose Death*, 13 CUMB. L. REV. 117, 135 (1982).

143. This attitude is best exemplified by Judge Letts' opinion in *Gilbert v. State* where he stated:

> Finally, this court notices that this aged defendant has been a peaceful, law-abiding and respected citizen up until this time. No one has suggested that he will again kill someone or enter upon a criminal career. However, the absolute rigidity of the statutory mandatory minimum sentences do not take into account any mitigating circumstances. Whether such sentences should somehow be moderated so as to allow . . . distinctions to be made in sentencing between different kinds of wrongdoers . . . are all questions which, under our system, must be decided by the legislature.

Gilbert v. State, 487 So. 2d 1185, 1192 (1986).

144. O'Brien, *supra* note 1, at 665.

SUICIDE

Suicide, the voluntary taking of one's own life for whatever reason, has a varied history. Accepted in some early societies and rejected in others, it was condemned by the Catholic church and the civil authorities in the Middle Ages. Although most civil and criminal penalties applicable to suicides and their families were repealed in the nineteenth century, until recently society continued to attach a stigma to suicide and considered the desire to commit suicide as evidence of mental illness. Recently, however, several organized groups and philosophers argued that suicide, both within and outside the health care context, may be a rational and justifiable response to some circumstances and should be, if not encouraged, at least permitted.

Professor Manuel Valesquez ("Defining Suicide") argues that we must first define suicide in a nonjudgmental fashion before deciding whether suicide is permissible. He rejects several common definitions on the grounds that they are overly inclusive or exclusive and incorporate moral judgments that predetermine the issue. In his view, the moral content of an act that results in the actor's death is determined by the underlying intent and causation. Thus, any definition must be general, leaving the moral judgment in abeyance until one can evaluate the specific situations under which the act took place.

Joseph Fletcher ("In Defense of Suicide"), the dean of situational ethics, similarly argues that suicide has no moral content in and of itself. Thus, a person's choice to commit suicide may not be condemned without first examining the surrounding circumstances. Starting from the premises that "no action is intrinsically wrong" and that the morality of an act is dependent upon whether the action maximizes human well-being, he concludes that quality of life is more valuable than life itself. Thus, a poor, painful, or burdensome quality of life may justify a person's decision to commit suicide. Only that person, however, is able to weigh the value of his life against other concerns, whether they be personal, medical, or social, and therefore, the state should neither condemn or mandate suicide in any particular situation.

Stacy Mojica and Dan Murrell ("The Right to Choose: When Should Death Be in the Individual's Hands?") approach the issue from the point of view of sanctions and incentives. After reviewing the historical criminalization of suicide, they argue that the few remaining suicide laws should be eliminated and that society should develop non-penal methods of reducing the incidence of suicide. When, however, a mentally healthy and properly counseled adult chooses suicide, society should not intervene to prevent him from exercising his right to do so.

To some degree, these articles are ahead of public opinion in that they appear to approve of suicide in a wide range of circumstances. Their analysis, however, can be applied, with some chance of consensus, to the more limited issue of an individual's choice to terminate treatment. If, as they argue, suicide is not intrinsically wrong, then the question is whether it is wrong for a terminally ill patient or for someone who is suffering from excruciating pain. If a person is capable of rational thought and decision making, is it right to deny that person the right to end his or her life in dignity and without pain? The more difficult issue is whether society may set limits on when that choice is permissible. Fletcher's analysis, for instance, would not permit suicide when an individual's suicide is not in the best interests of society (i.e., when the harm to others or to society of permitting a particular person's suicide outweighs the benefits to the person). Mojica and Murrell, however, set no limits on their proposed right, except that the person must be rational and properly counseled.

Defining Suicide

Manuel G. Velasquez, Ph.D.*

A growing number of courts are authorizing the withdrawal or withholding of nutrition and hydration from patients with non-terminal conditions.[1] The complex issues raised by these rulings and the legal and ethical implications involved have aroused concern and generated intense debate. Some of these court decisions have been interpreted by some as authorizations of suicide.[2] Others, however, have maintained that these cases need not be construed as suicide.[3] These debates have raised the question: *What is suicide?*

Traditionally, the law applied the term suicide to cases in which an individual purposely set in motion a death-producing agent with the specific intent of effecting his or her own destruction.[4] In *Super-*

*Director, Santa Clara University Center for Applied Ethics; Associate Professor, Philosophy Dept., University of Santa Clara; B.A., Gonzaga University, 1967; M.A., Gonzaga University, 1968; Ph.D., University of California at Berkeley, 1975.

[1]*See, e.g.,* Bouvia v. Superior Court (Glenchur), 225 Cal. Rptr. 297 (Cal. App. 2 Dist. 1986); Corbett v. D'Alessandro, 487 So. 2d 368 (Fla. App. 2 Dist. 1986); In re Jobes, 510 A. 2d 133 (N.J. Super. Ct. Ch. Div. 1986); Brophy v. New England Sinai Hospital, Inc., 497 N.E. 2d 626 (Mass. 1986); In re Conroy, 486 A. 2d 1209 (N.J. 1985).

[2]*See, e.g.,* Dyck, *A Commentary on Brophy v. New England Sinai Hospital,* 2 BIOLAW U:172–74 (1986); Note, *Elizabeth Bouvia v. County of Riverside: Riverside General Hospital,* 1–2 BIOETHICS REP. 460–61 (1984); Kane, *Keeping Elizabeth Bouvia Alive for the Public Good,* 15 HASTINGS CENTER REP. 5–8 (Dec. 1985); Annas, *When Suicide Prevention Becomes Brutality: The Case of Elizabeth Bouvia,* 14 HASTINGS CENTER REP. 20–21, 46 (April 1984).

[3]*See, e.g., Brophy,* 497 N.E. 2d at 626, 638; *Conroy,* 486 A. 2d at 1209–10; O'Rourke, *The A.M.A. Statement on Tube Feeding: An Ethical Analysis,* 155 AMERICA 321–23, 331 (1986); Annas, *Elizabeth Bouvia: Who Should Prevail?,* 15 HASTINGS CENTER REP. 50 (April 1985).

[4]Byrn, *Compulsory Lifesaving Treatment for the Competent Adult,* in DEATH, DYING, AND EUTHANASIA 721 (D. J. Horon & D. Mall eds. 1980).

intendent of Belchertown State School v. Saikewicz, it was the presence of specific intent and the element of active causation which was used to distinguish suicide from the refusal of medical treatment.[5]

In other cases, however, the courts appear to have relied upon a different notion of suicide; a death resulting from the knowledge that one's act or failure to act will produce death has been deemed equivalent to suicide, and the law's traditional requirement of specific intent to die having been dismissed.[6] Indeed, examining the nature of intention in order to determine whether a refusal of treatment could be construed as suicide was referred to by the court as "quibbling."[7] Similarly, the weight accorded to the agent's role in causation as a factor distinguishing suicide from the refusal of life-sustaining treatment has varied from case to case.[8]

Apart from the consideration of the two elements of intention and causation, the common law has required that, for an act to be classified as suicide, it must be "committed by a person of years of discretion and of sound mind."[9] But, again, the concurrence of opinion in this regard is not evident. It was precisely the absence of sound mind that was used to distinguish suicide as "irrational self-destruction" from the "rational decision" to refuse life-sustaining treatment in *Saikewicz*.[10] And, although the courts did not confine suicide to irrational acts in *In re Yetter*, the patient's decision to forego treatment, which entailed a presumed right to die, was regarded as an irrational and unwise, foolish, or ridiculous, albeit competent, decision.[11] In accordance with these rulings, then, suicide is at one and the same time an act of sound mind, an irrational act, and an irrational, but competent, act.

These cases illustrate a general lack of societal consensus about what constitutes suicide. The need for such a consensus is evident since the decision to label an act "suicide" may have significant legal implications. In California, for example, an individual who deliberately aids, advises, or encourages an act of suicide is guilty of a felony.[12]

---

[5]Superintendent of Belchertown State School v. Saikewicz, 370 N.E. 2d 417, 426 n. 11 (Mass. 1977).

[6]*See, e.g.,* John F. Kennedy Memorial Hospital v. Heston, 279 A. 2d 670, 672–73 (N.J. 1971).

[7]Application of the President and Directors of Georgetown College, Inc., 331 F. 2d 1000, 1008–09 (D.C. Cir. 1964).

[8]*See, e.g., Saikewicz*, 370 N.E. 2d at 417, 426 n. 11; *Kennedy Memorial Hospital*, 279 A. 2d at 670, 672–73; Note, *supra* note 2, at 460–61; *Brophy*, 497 N.E. 2d at 638.

[9]Byrn, *supra* note 4, at 721–22.

[10]*Saikewicz*, 370 N.E. 2d at 417, 426 n. 11.

[11]*In re* Yetter, 62 Pa. D. & C. 2d 619, 623–24 (C.P. Northampton County Ct. 1973).

[12]CAL. PENAL CODE §401 (West 1985).

For a physician to facilitate an act which has been labelled "suicide" can constitute a violation of his or her professional code of ethics, calling into question the physician's role as preserver of life. Furthermore, in some cases, an individual's request for assistance to carry out an act labelled "suicide" has raised issues for public policy regarding public assistance in and financing of suicide.[13]

By 1986, at least thirty-five states had passed living will statutes.[14] These statutes enable individuals to issue advance directives for their health care should their condition ever render them unable to actively direct it. Some of these statutes explicitly state that the implementation of a living will does not constitute suicide. However, how suicide is defined may determine if, in fact, honoring the choices of formerly competent patients can be construed as suicide.

Perhaps greater than the implications of "a" definition of suicide are those which may follow from the absence of a definition. In *Bouvia v. County of Riverside*, the court stated:

> During the hearing, Plaintiff's decision to end her life has been called various things: the right of self-determination, the right of privacy, the right to determine the quality of one's life, the right to control one's own life and body, the right to be left alone, the right to determine one's own future, the right to be protected from force feeding, the right to escape a useless body, freedom of choice, the acceptance of death, self-starvation, self-destruction, suicide, voluntary euthanasia, and finally, the right to die with dignity.[15]

Granted, the distinctions between and among some of these terms may be purely semantic. However, when dealing with complex issues of such ethical, legal, and social import, it becomes mandatory to determine if, in fact, these are matters of semantics and, if not, how to distinguish between them. Precision and accuracy in our choices of terms and in the meanings ascribed to them is critical.

Historical Perspective

According to the Oxford English Dictionary, the word "suicide" is derived from the Latin word *"suicidium,"* meaning "to kill oneself," and was first used in 1651. Prior to the seventeenth century, the English terms for suicide included self-homicide, self-destruction, self-slaughter, and self-murder. These terms, in contrast to other terms of Semitic Indo-European origin, describe suicide as a kind of killing,

---

[13]Kane, *supra* note 2.
[14]Areen, *Death and Dying*, 1 Biolaw 278 (1986).
[15]Note, *supra* note 2, at 459.

rather than a mode of dying. In ancient Greece, for example, phrases used to convey the concept of suicide included "to grasp death," "to die voluntarily," and "to die by one's own hand." Daubes, in his review of the linguistic history of suicide, suggests that whether suicide was described linguistically as a kind of killing or as a kind of dying was, in part, dependent on the historical and cultural context within which the term appeared and reflected the prevailing attitudes toward suicide.[16]

The influence of social attitudes toward suicide extends beyond its influence on the choice of terms used to denote it. The meaning imported to the term is also nuanced by prevailing attitudes toward suicide. Consequently, a first step toward defining suicide would seem to require attention to contemporary attitudes toward suicide, which, in turn, necessitates an examination of the historical context from which they arose.

Public policy is one of the means through which a society translates its values and applies them to human conduct. In the United States today, public policy condemns suicide.[17] It has been suggested that the condemnation of suicide which has characterized many Western societies can be traced to taboos associated with shedding blood and to an instinctive "fear of the ghost" in "primitive" cultures.[18]

In ancient Greece, taboos inspired by popular superstitions often entailed the denial of burial rites and the desecration of the corpse. A condemnation of suicide is evident in the writings of early Greek philosophers, including Plato and Aristotle, who condemned suicide as an offense against the gods or the state. By contrast, later philosophers, the Roman Stoics in particular, tended to condone suicide as a lawful and rational exercise of individual freedom and even wise in the cases of old age, disease, or dishonor.

It was this later Stoic attitude, favorable to judicious self-destruction, that prevailed within the early Roman Empire. The popular superstitious and religious practices against the corpse tended to

---

[16]Daube, *The Linguistics of Suicide,* 1 PHIL. & PUBLIC AFFAIRS 387–437 (1972).

[17]Although suicide is no longer punished as a felony in the United States, attempted suicide is often a basis for state intervention. *See* N. ST. JOHN-STEVAS, LIFE, DEATH AND THE LAW 232–46 (1961); Engelhardt & Malloy, *Suicide and Assisting Suicide: A Critique of Legal Sanctions,* 3 BIOETHICS REP. 762–96 (1984); Brenner, *Undue Influence in the Criminal Law: A Proposed Analysis of the Criminal Offense of "Causing Suicide,"* 47 ALB. L. REV. 64–66 (1982).

[18]*See* H. FEDDEN, SUICIDE: A SOCIAL AND HISTORICAL STUDY 27–48 (1980); Alvarez, *The Background,* in SUICIDE: THE PHILOSOPHICAL ISSUES 10–12 (M. P. Battin & D. J. Mayo eds. 1981); Mair, *Suicide,* in 11 ENCYCLOPEDIA OF RELIGION AND ETHICS 30–31 (J. Hastings ed. 1928); Farberow, *Cultural History,* 1-2 BIOETHICS REP. 690–91 (1984).

decrease, and, with few exceptions, suicide was not prohibited under Roman law.[19]

The toleration of suicide that characterized the Roman Empire continued well into the third century. However, with the break-up of the Empire, opposition to suicide reemerged. The reason for this renewed opposition to suicide is difficult to identify.[20] One hypothesis is that the elite, whose reasoned arguments had prevailed over the popular condemnation of suicide, grew fewer in number and less influential as Rome declined. As a result, the antisuicide attitudes still prevalent among the uneducated resurfaced. These attitudes were reinforced by the requirements of the feudal economy: the nobleman's fear of losing his serf to an early death may have played a major role in establishing antisuicide legislation during this period.[21]

The Church legitimated the popular attitude. Writing in the fourth century, Augustine of Hippo pronounced suicide as the worst of sins, establishing the Church's, thus society's, antisuicide stance which prevailed, virtually unchallenged, for approximately one thousand years. During this time, popular, often barbarous, measures against suicide increased and laws punishing suicide were established by the Church and the state.

The centuries marked by the Renaissance and the Protestant Reformation revealed little change in society's attitude toward suicide. Church and civil law remained unaltered in their prohibitions of suicide. However, by the end of the seventeenth century, the enforcement of these laws had begun to lapse, reflecting a change in popular opinion that may be traced to a growing toleration toward suicide within the educated class. The Renaissance revival of classical learning brought a rediscovery of the Stoic acceptance of suicide and an emphasis on self-determination in decisions about life and death. With the Reformation, which entailed a new respect for personal inquiry, a weakening of the scholar's allegiance to the Church, and a critical examination of long-held premises, the parameters of philosophical discussion were redefined. Society's absolute condemnation of suicide was called into question.

With the increasing secularization of philosophical thought in the eighteenth century, arguments opposing the absolute condemnation of suicide multiplied and mitigated the view of suicide as inherently sinful or criminal. Likewise, popular attitudes revealed an increasing toleration of suicide; the divergence between the laws

---

[19] FEDDEN, *supra* note 18, at 85–95.

[20] *See* Alvarez, *supra* note 18, at 24–29; Rosen, *History*, in A HANDBOOK FOR THE STUDY OF SUICIDE 12 (S. Perlin ed. 1975).

[21] FEDDEN, *supra* note 18, at 111–12; Farberow, *supra* note 18, at 694–95.

against suicide and the enforcement of those laws grew wider, and in some places, penalties against suicide altogether disappeared.

By the end of the nineteenth century, most of the laws penalizing suicide had disappeared. The final impetus for the change in public policy was the elevated status accorded to scientific inquiry leading to the "discovery" that suicide was a disease. The field of medicine, psychiatry in particular, provided the theoretical framework for linking suicide to mental illness. Another theory of suicide also emerged during this century, proposed by Emile Durkeim. Durkeim maintained that suicide was not a result of individual psychopathology, but was a product of social forces impacting on the individual, indicative of a diseased civilization.[22]

Throughout the first half of the twentieth century, variations of these theories established the confines within which the subject of suicide was discussed. Once suicide came to be viewed as a product of individual psychopathology or socioeconomic conditions, rather than a rational, deliberate, voluntary act of the individual, philosophical discussion of the morality of suicide was neither relevant nor appropriate. The theories also influenced public policy. Classifying suicide as a symptom of a *disordered* individual or a *disordered* society served to preserve the deviant character of the act and accordingly, it became something to be treated and prevented. Legal sanctions against attempted suicide now took the form of coerced treatment and observation, the law assuming the presence of irrationality or mental incompetence.

Within the past few decades, assumptions about the nature of suicide and the attitudes toward suicide based on those assumptions have been challenged by a variety of factors, including the development of medical technology to prolong and sustain lives, increased concern with patient autonomy and the right to self-determination, and a change in attitudes toward death and dying. These factors have combined to create a climate conducive to a concept of suicide as a rational, freely chosen, deliberate act in place of the view of it as a deviant, irrational act symptomatic of mental illness. No longer confined to the once-prevalent medical model, philosophical discussion of the rationality of suicide, the morality of suicide, and the right to suicide has once again emerged.

Current Philosophical Debate

Not surprisingly, then, a large number of philosophers have once again begun to address the problem of defining suicide and to discuss

---

[22]Rosen, *supra* note 20, at 19–26.

its morality.[23] The definitions that appear in the literature they have produced range from broad definitions of suicide to narrow definitions. Broad definitions allow any act of self-destruction to count as suicide, as long as the act meets a very few minimal conditions. Broad definitions do not exclude much. Narrow definitions, on the other hand, place several additional restrictions on what counts as suicide. Because narrow definitions place several conditions on what counts as suicide, they restrict the term to a smaller range of candidates.

The most well-known broad definitions of suicide are those that are inspired by the work of Emile Durkeim. Durkeim defined suicide as any act that brings about the agent's own death, provided *only* that the agent knew the act would bring about his death. A suicide, he writes, is any "death resulting directly or indirectly from a positive or negative act of the victim himself, which he knows will produce this result."[24] Thus, the only crucial requirement for suicide is knowledge of the result. Any self-destructive act counts as suicide so long as the agent had knowledge that the act would be self-destructive.

Richard Brandt, a contemporary philosopher, has also urged a broad definition of suicide, claiming that an act of suicide is "doing something which results in one's death, either from the intention of ending one's life or the intention to bring about some other state of affairs (such as relief from pain) which one thinks it certain or highly probable can be achieved only by means of death or [an act that] will produce death."[25] According to Brandt, any intentional act that one *believes* will *probably* result in one's death is an act of suicide. For Brandt, then, any intentional self-destructive act counts as suicide so long as the agent had certain *beliefs* about the *probability* that the act would be self-destructive.

These broad definitions seem to identify an important necessary condition of suicide. If a person kills herself but does so accidentally or without knowing that she was killing herself, we would not say that the person committed suicide. Suicide requires that one know or believe that one's death will result from one's act.

But the problem with these broad definitions is that they let in too much. Suicide would seem to require more than the mere knowledge or belief that one's act is self-destructive. A soldier who throws himself on a live grenade for the sole purpose of saving his compan-

---

[23]For a review of the literature, *see* Mayo, *Contemporary Philosophical Literature on Suicide: A Review*, in Suicide and Ethics (M. P. Battin & R. W. Maris eds. 1983).

[24]E. Durkheim, Suicide: A Study in Sociology 44 (1951).

[25]Brandt, *The Morality and Rationality of Suicide*, in A Handbook for the Study of Suicide 117 (S. Perlin ed. 1975).

ions, for example, may know or believe that he will die as a result. But most would not say that the soldier committed an act of suicide. Rather, the soldier has performed a heroic act. Similarly, the act of the early Christian who steadfastly refuses to worship an idol, knowing that his refusal will lead to his death, should not be construed as suicide. His act was an act of martyrdom, not suicide. Yet, both the hero and the martyr acted with the knowledge and belief that his act would result in death.

These broad definitions also fail to make a distinction between suicide and "suicidal behavior".[26] The person who smokes too much or drives too fast, the terrorist, the underground resistance fighter, or anyone who willingly takes great risks may do so with the knowledge or belief that those acts will result in death. But if that person dies, we do not call it suicide. At most, we would call it suicidal behavior. The person may have believed that this behavior would eventually bring about death, but the motives for engaging in such behavior outweighed the fear.

The inadequacies of these broad definitions are obvious. Why, then, have such definitions been advanced? There appear to be two main reasons behind the formulation of broad definitions of suicide. First, the aim of Durkeim and other empirical researchers has been to characterize suicide in an empirically ascertainable way. If, like Durkeim, one intends to study the frequency of suicide, one must characterize suicide in a way that allows it to be easily identified by empirical means. The broad definitions, insofar as they abstract from intentions and other conditions that are not empirically ascertainable, provide a basis for empirical study.

The second reason for offering broad definitions is that philosophers like Brandt are interested in determining whether suicide is morally acceptable, and if so, under what conditions it is acceptable. Thus, they have set as few conditions as possible on what counts as suicide so as not to prejudge the issue. In particular, they have attempted to characterize suicide in such a way that suicide, by definition, would not be immoral. They have sought to avoid building into their definition of suicide a judgment about its morality.

This concern for a morally neutral definition of suicide is legitimate; the term suicide itself has pejorative connotations and perhaps it should be reserved for describing morally reprehensible acts of self-destruction. Some people, in fact, argue that heroes who kill themselves to save others should not be said to have committed suicide because their acts are morally admirable. Underlying such arguments

---

[26]*See* E. Kluge, The Practice of Death 103 (1975).

is the assumption that morally admirable acts should not be counted as suicides.[27] According to this view, suicide is by definition an immoral act. If so, it is pointless to discuss the morality of suicide since the question is settled by definitional fiat. To avoid this prejudging of the issue, philosophers like Brandt have looked to morally neutral definitions which import few conditions into their characterization of suicide.

But whatever the motivation, as we have already seen, these broad definitions of suicide, in fact, fail. Let us turn, therefore, to some of the narrower definitions that have emerged in the literature to see how successful they are. Narrow definitions, as we mentioned, impose additional conditions on what is to count as suicide, and thereby exclude more candidates.

Joseph Margolis, in his well-known discussion of suicide, is sensitive to the intuition that self-inflicted death to save others should not be described as suicide. He, therefore, characterizes suicide in a manner designed to exclude self-destructive acts that are carried out for an altruistic purpose. In fact, his definition of suicide excludes self-destructive acts that are carried out for *any* ulterior purpose. According to Margolis, suicide is "the deliberate taking of one's life in order simply to end it, not instrumentally for any ulterior purpose."[28] Margolis' definition, like Brandt's, is meant to be morally neutral. Nevertheless, Margolis' definition relies on the moral judgment that a self-destructive act that is self-sacrificial or altruistically motivated should not be counted as suicide. Such acts are not morally blameworthy and should be excluded from the category of suicide with its pejorative connotations.

A similar moral premise seems to underlie another narrow definition recently advanced by Tom Beauchamp. Beauchamp notes that, when a person is forced or coerced into taking his life, it commonly is not classified as suicide. For example, Beauchamp argues, many do not say that Socrates committed suicide when he was forced to drink the hemlock in prison.[29] Consequently, Beauchamp's characterization of suicide is designed to exclude death by coercion. Although Beauchamp is unclear on this point, his reason for excluding deaths

[27]*See, e.g.*, Lesser, *Suicide and Self-Murder*, 55 Phil. 255–57 (1980); Edwards, *Hunger Strike: Protest or Suicide?*, 6 America 458 (1981); Donnelly, *Suicide and Rationality*, in Language, Metaphysics, and Death 93–101 (J. Donnelly ed. 1978).

[28]J. Margolis, Negativities: The Limits of Life 26 (1975).

[29]The question of whether Socrates should be said to have committed suicide has been extensively discussed. *See* Frey, *Did Socrates Commit Suicide?*, 53 Phil. 106–108 (1978); Smith, *Did Socrates Kill Himself Intentionally?*, 55 Phil. 253–54 (1980); Walton, *"Socrates" Alleged Suicide*, 14 J. Value Inquiry 287–99 (1980).

by coercion seems to be that such deaths are not blameworthy and so should not count as suicides.

Beauchamp also notes that, when a person's death is the result of a terminal disease that the person fails to treat, it also commonly is not classified as suicide. Take, for example, a person who is suffering from cancer who refuses to undergo any treatment, knowing death will result. Such is classified as a death from natural causes and not as suicide. Beauchamp's characterization of suicide excludes death that results from a condition, such as a disease, that the agent did not arrange as a means of death. Here, again, what seems to be operating is the moral intuition that, since it is not blameworthy to permit one's death from natural causes, such a death should not be counted as suicide. At any rate, Beauchamp's somewhat complicated definition of suicide is as follows: "An act is a suicide if a person brings about his or her own death [1] in circumstances where others do not coerce him or her to the action, [2] except in those cases where death is caused by conditions not specifically arranged by the agent for the purpose of bringing about his or her own death."[30] The first condition excludes death by coercion, while the second excludes death from an untreated terminal disease or mortal injury.

There is yet a third narrow definition of suicide that is influenced by the desire to exclude deaths that are not morally blameworthy. This third definition takes into account the fact that many self-destructive people are not rational because they are undergoing severe psychological disturbances. Germain Grisez and Joseph Boyle, Jr., have suggested that, when a nonrational person brings about his death, the death is not to be counted as suicide.[31] Apparently underlying this approach, again, is the idea that self-destructive acts should be counted as suicides only if they are morally blameworthy. Since the acts of a nonrational person are not morally blameworthy, they should not be counted as suicide.

Each of these narrow definitions, unfortunately, fails to provide an adequate characterization of suicide. By excluding what is not morally blameworthy, they exclude too much. Consider first, Margolis' view that killing oneself for an altruistic purpose is not suicide. Clearly this view is mistaken. If a man kills himself so that his impoverished family can collect the insurance, many would say that he committed suicide. The fact that he has a further purpose in taking his life does not mean that his act is not suicide. Second, consider Beauchamp's view that death resulting from coercion is not suicide. This claim, too,

---

[30]Beauchamp, *Suicide,* in Matters of Life and Death 77 (T. Regan ed. 1980).

[31]G. Grisez & J. Boyle, Life and Death with Liberty and Justice 407–12 (1979).

seems mistaken. A person who is coerced into self-destruction by the threat of blackmail will be said to have committed suicide.

Or, consider Beauchamp's view that, when a person's death is caused by some condition not specifically arranged for that purpose, the death is not a suicide. Imagine a skier who is racing down a mountain and has decided to commit suicide. Ahead, the skier sees an avalanche. If he stops, he can avoid the avalanche, but, instead, the skier seizes the chance and continues skiing down into the path of the avalanche. It seems appropriate to describe the skier as having committed suicide. Yet, because the avalanche was not "arranged" by the agent for the purpose of committing suicide, Beauchamp's definition would refuse to count it as suicide. Lastly, consider the view of Grisez that a nonrational person cannot commit suicide. If Grisez were right, then it would sound contradictory to describe some suicides as irrational suicides or as nonrational suicides. But, in fact, when persons who are mentally ill intentionally kill themselves, many say that they committed suicide. Nonrational suicides are still suicides.

Each of these narrow characterizations of suicide, then, are failures. Nevertheless, the attempts are instructive. Each characterization alerts us to some important questions that an adequate definition of suicide must address. First, why is it that some altruistically motivated self-killings are not counted as suicides? The soldier who throws himself on a grenade to save his companions is not said to have committed suicide. Second, why is it that some coerced self-killings are not counted as suicides? Most would agree that Socrates, who was forced to drink the hemlock, did not commit suicide. Third, why is it that the person who dies as a result of refusing to treat a deadly disease usually is not said to have committed suicide? And fourth, why is it that there is a reluctance to classify nonrational self-killing as suicide?

One might be tempted to try to answer these questions by simply pointing to a feature common to all of them: each refers to a class of self-killings which is not morally blameworthy. Thus, suicide could be defined as intentional self-killing that is morally blameworthy. There are three reasons for not pursuing this suggestion. First, such a definition would preclude discussion of the question whether suicide is ever morally permissible. Suicide, by definition, would be a morally blameworthy act. Second, such a definition would be wrong. Some acts of self-destruction are clearly acts of suicide, yet, one can argue that they are not morally blameworthy. For example, the persons who are mentally ill, who are not responsible for their actions, would not be said to have committed suicide should they kill themselves. Or, consider the example of the sick explorer whose illness is slowing down the rest of his party so that they are all in danger of dying since the others refuse to leave him behind. To save their lives, the sick explorer shoots himself, allowing them to hurry on without him and thus save their lives. He clearly committed suicide. But his act of suicide, one can argue, was heroic and not morally blameworthy. Thus, it would be a mistake to define suicide as the morally blameworthy act of killing oneself. Third, and most importantly, the cases that Margolis, Beauchamp, Grisez, and others want to exclude from the category of suicide should be excluded *not* because they are not blameworthy. Rather, they should be excluded because of the kind of *agency* or mental state that each case involves.

How, then, is suicide to be defined? The author proposes a characterization of suicide that answers the questions that have been raised. The proposed definition has two main components similar to the two main elements of the traditional legal definition of suicide: the element of intention and that of causation. This two-part definition will allow us to deal with many of those problems that the narrow definitions have tried to address, while incorporating the factors that the broad definitions emphasized. Suicide, then, can be characterized best as follows:

> Suicide is the act of bringing about a person's death, provided that: 1) death is brought about by that person's own acts or omissions, and 2) those acts or omissions are (a) intentionally carried out (b) for the purpose of bringing about death (c) by those concretely particular means that actually brought death about.

Let me explain now the rationale for advancing this definition. First, it provides a morally neutral definition of suicide. Given this definition, suicide might turn out to be an immoral or a moral act. In this respect the definition achieves one of the aims of the broad definitions: moral neutrality.

Second, the definition is designed to retain the idea that the person who commits suicide had to know or believe that his act would result in his death. This is part of what is meant by saying that the act that brings about death must be carried out for that purpose intentionally. Intention implies knowledge or belief that one's acts will have the intended effects.

Third, the definition is intended to capture the kernel of truth in the notion that a person who is forced to self-destruction, or a person who dies from a disease, usually is not considered to have committed suicide. As the definition makes clear, suicide requires that death be brought about by the person's own acts. To the extent, therefore, that a death is felt to have resulted from something other than the person's own agency, the death would not be classified as suicide. When one person forces another to act, the real agency is attributed to the person who exerts the force. For this reason, therefore, when a person's self-killing is perceived as being the result of force or coercion, the self-killing is attributed to an agency other than the person and, therefore, the act is not classified as suicide. For a similar reason, when a death is perceived as being the result of a disease, it is not seen as suicide because the death is attributed to the agency of the disease and not of the person. Suicide requires that persons be seen as the agents of their own death.

Fourth, the definition is intended to explain why there is sometimes a reluctance to classify the self-inflicted death of a person who is mentally disturbed as suicide. To the extent that an act is felt to have been caused by a mental affliction and to the extent that a person is felt not to be in control of himself or herself, to that extent there is reluctance to attribute genuine agency to that person. From this reluctance stems the reluctance to classify a person's self-inflicted death as suicide when the person is mentally ill. But that reluctance is only partial, there is also an intuition that even the acts of a person who is mentally ill are his own acts. To the extent that this intuition prevails, the self-inflicted death of a person who is mentally ill may be classified as suicide.

Fifth, the definition is intended to explain why some altruistically motivated self-killings may not be classified as suicides, while others are. When persons act or fail to act, knowing that their act or failure to act will result in death, they may or may not be aiming at death by their actions or omissions. The definition of suicide requires that one's actions be carried out for the purpose of bringing about death either as an end or as a means. The soldier who throws himself on the live grenade to save his companions, for example, is not aiming at death. That is, he does not intentionally jump on the grenade for the purpose of bringing about his death, but rather for the purpose of saving his companions. This is clear if one considers that, if he lives and his companions are saved, then he would have achieved his purpose without dying. For this reason, his act is not counted as suicide. On the other hand, consider the man who kills himself so his family can enjoy the proceeds from his life insurance. Clearly, he intentionally carries out his actions for the purpose of bringing about death. He is aiming at his death, albeit as a means to another end: if he lives, he would have failed in his purpose since, without his death, no inheritance will be forthcoming.

Sixth, the definition is also intended to deal with a little knot of technical problems that are raised by what are called "deviant causal chains."[32] Consider the man who intends to kill himself by running out into a street of speeding cars. As he runs out into the street, however, he steps into the path of a bullet from the gun of a boy shooting at tin cans in an empty lot across the street. Here death is brought about by the man's own acts which were carried out for the purpose of bringing about his death, but the death did not occur quite by those means he intended it to occur. For that reason, we do not classify the death as suicide, but as accidental. Death was the result of (what philosophers call) a "deviant causal chain," and not by the intended means. If a person's death is to count as suicide, then, the particular concrete means that actually bring the death about must be those by which one was intentionally acting to bring death about. This match between actual means and intended means does not have to be exact: the means that actually bring death about need merely be reasonably close to the intended means. For example, if a person intends to kill himself with a shot in the head, but nervously shakes the gun so much that the person shoots himself in the heart instead, then, this is close enough to what the person intended to qualify the death as suicide.

Finally, the definition is intended to retain and explain some of the ambiguities that our concept of suicide carries with it. Sometimes, there is an uncertainty as to whether something should be called suicide. The definition identifies several sources of uncertainty. That uncertainty may be related to the inability to identify the agent of death. Thus, there is an uncertainty about element 1. Sometimes it is unclear whether the person's actions are intentional or accidental. Thus, there is an uncertainty about element 2(a). Sometimes it is difficult to discern the person's purpose for carrying out the act that resulted in death, thus there is an uncertainty about element 2(b). Finally, there may be uncertainty about whether the particular concrete means that actually brought death about were those by which death was intentionally being brought about. We are then unsure about element 2(c).

Given the proposed definition, it may appear that assisted suicide is a contradiction in terms. If one is assisted in killing oneself, then one's death seemingly is not brought about by one's own acts and so it does not appear to qualify as suicide. This appearance, however, is mistaken.

People can bring about their own deaths in many different ways. One way is by getting others to do their bidding. In assisted suicide, a person brings about death by getting others to act. Thus, an assisted

---

[32]These problems are broadly discussed but not adequately resolved in Tolhurst, *Suicide, Self-Sacrifice and Coercion,* 21 S. J. PHILOSOPHY 109–22 (1983).

suicide is indeed a death that is brought about by that person's own acts. The death is brought about by the person's own acts of bidding others to kill or to help kill.

Thus, this definition is perfectly adequate to serve as the basis for a discussion of assisted suicide, as indeed it was designed to be. But the definition is intended to do more than serve as a mere dictionary definition of a term. It is also intended to suggest how other pertinent concepts might relate to suicide in general and to assisted suicide in particular.

In Defense of Suicide[*]

Joseph Fletcher

Most of us know that anthropologists have found every imaginable attitude toward suicide in both savage and civilized societies. Anthropologists, however, like psychiatrists and sociologists, are able only to provide us with data; in their scientific capacity they cannot jump the gap between what is and what ought to be. To suppose that tabulating moral sentiments described from observation settles an ethical question is what is called the naturalistic fallacy — confusing what is with what ought to be. Whether we ought to be free to end our lives or not is a question of philosophy, of ethics in particular. If a psychiatrist, for example, asserts or implies that people ought not to choose naughtness or oblivionate themselves (to use Herman Melville's neologisms), that scientist is wearing a philosopher's hat. *Ought* is not in the scientific lexicon.

In spite of the defiant immortalists who look forward to resurrection by cryonics or by outwitting cell death biochemically (such as Alan Harrington, who stated, "Death is an imposition on the human race, and no longer acceptable"), we know perfectly well that aging is a fatal disease and we all are its victims. The ethical question is whether we may ever rightly take any rational human initiative in death and dying or are, instead, obliged in conscience to look upon life and death fatalistically, as something that just has to happen to us willy-nilly.

We have pretty well settled the life-control issue with our contraceptive practices and policies; now we must look just as closely at the death-control problem. If we may initiate life, may we not terminate it? Were Ernest Hemingway and his father before him wrong to shoot themselves? Ethically? Psychologically?

The Ethical Question

Speaking as we are from the vantage point of moral philosophy, we must begin with the postulate that no action is intrinsically

[*]Translated from "In Verteidigung des Suizids," initially published in *Suizid und Euthanasie*, ed. Albin Eser (Stuttgart: Enke, 1976).

38

right or wrong, that nothing is inherently good or evil. Right and wrong, good and evil, desirable and undesirable – all are ethical terms and all are predicates, not properties. The moral "value" of any human act is always contingent, depending on the shape of the action in the situation – *Sitz im Leben* or *Situationsethik*. The variables and factors in each set of circumstances are the determinants of what ought to be done – not prefabricated generalizations or prescriptive rules. Clinical analysis and flexibility are indispensable. No "law" of conduct is always obliging; what we ought to do is whatever maximizes human well-being.

It is essential to grasp the difference between moral values and behavioral norms. Only in this way will we understand why our values are a priori while our actions should be flexibly selective and not legalistic or rule-bound. We might say that our opinions about what is good is subjective and visceral; our judgments about what we ought to do about what we feel is good are more objective and cerebral.

There simply is no way to "prove" our values by logic; they are established by a mixture of conditioning, choice, and commitment. As Ludwig Wittgenstein saw the problem, "This is a terrible business – just terrible. You can at best stammer when you talk of it."

On the other hand, when acting as moral agents, tailoring our deeds to fit our values and ideals, we have to use logic and critical reason, especially when we have to decide which value gets priority in cases of competing values. For example, if truth telling has a high-order value but conflicts with a therapeutic goal, telling the truth might sometimes be the wrong thing to do.

To suppose that we would always be obliged to follow any rule of conduct is only tenable on a metaphysical basis or because of an alleged revelation of eternal absolutes. Such universals are what the Greeks called the *proton pseudon*, the basic error of conventional (that is, unexamined) moralism. Most Christian and many Jewish moralists use starting points of this kind. Without such a supernatural support, however, any attempt to assign intrinsic moral value to anything – truth, chastity, property, health, or even life itself – is an abysmal ethical mistake.

Stepping for a moment into another context, we can clarify

39

the point at stake by quoting a question-and-answer column in a religious magazine: "*Q*. My wife is sterile but wants her 'marital rights.' I have a contagious venereal disease. May I wear a prophylactic sheath? *A*. No. Even though she could not conceive and you would infect her, contraceptive intercourse is an intrinsically evil act." The situation makes no difference. The end sought makes no difference. The good consequences make no difference. Nothing makes any difference. The act itself is wrong. This is the essence of "intrinsic" morality.

The typical moral theologian, for example, whose ethics prohibit suicide as such, would condemn a captured soldier's committing suicide to avoid betraying his comrades under torture — because suicide is held to be an evil act in itself, like Kant's *Ding-an-sich*, a defiance of the will of God. An empirical or clinical ethic, being without that kind of dogmatic sanction, would have to agree that suicide can be right sometimes, wrong sometimes.

A slight variant on saying "suicide is not right" is saying "we have no right" to end our lives by choice. People are always mixing human "rights" and right conduct together. In a humanistic ethics, when suicide helps human beings it is right. That is, we have a right to do it. What makes it right is human need. Human rights are not self-validating, not intrinsically valid. It is need that validates rights, not the other way around. When rights are asserted over or cut across human needs, we are faced with a set of superhuman moral principles that often can be callous and cruel contradictions of a humane morality.

Some History

William Shakespeare put the ethical question this way: "Then is it sin / To rush into the secret house of death / Ere death dare come to us?" *Anthony and Cleopatra* IV, XV:80–82. Cassio, though a good Catholic, thought Othello's suicide was noble. In *Romeo and Juliet* the priest did not condemn the self-conclusion chosen by the young lovers. Shakespeare never expressed the kind of moralistic horror we find in Dante, who put suicides in the Seventh Circle of Hell, lower than murderers and heretics. As a matter of fact, few

40

cultures or traditions have condemned suicide out of whole cloth, indiscriminately.

Suicide poses an ethical issue that is ultimately a matter of values and how we reason about them. The story of what various people have thought and done about suicide does not settle the problem of what is right and good about it. Even so, the pages of history tell us things that help us to put the ethics of elective death in perspective, and we will look at the record in capsule.

Europe, Asia, Africa, America – all tell much the same story. Suicide is seen as absurd and tragic, noble and mean, brave and cowardly, sane and silly; every way of judging it has been taken. Some of the religious and the superstitious have condemned it wholesale; others have even praised it. For example, the Koran holds that suicide interferes with kismet, Allah's control of life and destiny, making it therefore much more to be condemned than homicide. Cardinal Richelieu expressed a similar idea. Some cultures, on the other hand, have honored suicides; the American Indians endured genocide at the hands of the Christian conquistadors Cortez and Pizarro even while their Spanish priests were condemning the Indians' selective suicide.

The Japanese honor the rite of seppuku, or hara-kiri, and the Hindu's honor suttee. Buddhist monks who used self-immolation to protest Thieu's dictatorship in South Vietnam are another example.

The Buddhist admiration for kamikaze is more complicated ethically because suicidal practices of that order combine killing oneself with killing others. Something like banzai is to be seen in the suicidal commando tactics of Palestinian guerrillas and in the "living bomb" gestures of Viet Cong terrorists. The supposed difference between committing suicide in banzai and volunteering to fly in the Luftwaffe or the RAF during the Battle of Britain poses an interesting analysis problem – speaking ethically, not psychiatrically.

More primitive peoples often believed that a suicide's soul or ghost would wander around without a resting place, haunting the living. To prevent this, medieval Christians buried a suicide with a stake through the heart and dug the grave at a crossroads instead of in "hallowed" (blessed) ground to keep it from poisoning the soil. The Baganda people used a similar defense strategy, as the storied

41

missionary Livingstone discovered when he stayed among them. The Alabama Indians threw the bodies of suicides into a river; people in Dahomey threw them where they would become carrion. As often as culture groups made suicide taboo, however, others respected it or even revered it. In North American the Zuni frowned on it, but the Navajo and the Hopi did not; in the Pacific suicide was condemned in the Andaman Islands, praised in the Fijis.

The Bible never condemned suicide, although in later times the rabbinical Talmud did and the Christian church followed suit. Samson, Saul, Abimilech, Achitophel — their stories are told without censure. The term *suicide* itself only appeared in the seventeenth century. Not until the sixth century was the act proscribed; until that time, in the absence of biblical authority, condemnation of suicide had to be inferred from the sixth of the Ten Commandments, "Thou shalt not kill."

The Greeks were more judicious and therefore more selectively in favor of suicide than the Jews, and so were the Romans. Both the Stoics and the Epicureans approved it in principle. Zeno approved and so did Cleanthes. Seneca actually committed suicide, to forestall the murderous Nero's fun and games, and his wife Paulina joined him. On the other hand, the Pythagoreans, opponents of Hippocratic medicine, having their special knowledge of the god's decrees, opposed suicide because of what Islam later called kismet. (After all, if one "knows" what a transcendental and ultimate will forbids, one would be prudent not to do it.)

Plato allowed euthanasia, as Aristotle did, but in the manner of suicide, not in the manner of "letting a patient go." Homer and Euripides thought well of Jocasta committing suicide after she learned that her new husband Oedipus was her own son — which was, perhaps, an excessive and irrational reaction, but humanly understandable because of the strength of the incest taboo. The Romans, as we all know, allowed the *liber mori* for a great many reasons; they denied it only to criminals, soldiers, and slaves — for obvious military and economic reasons. Justinian's *Digest* spelled out the subject judiciously.

Christian Europe started moving from pagan Rome's compassionate regard for the dignity of free persons to the savagery of an indiscriminating condemnation of all suicide in the Middle Ages only

42

after the Greco-Roman civilization had been ended by the Barbarian-Teutonic hordes. Once the classical philosophy was buried, the Catholic-medieval synthesis was able to take over, and one of its first major elements was an absolute taboo on suicide. In the manorial system nearly everybody was enfeoffed to somebody else; hence suicide was, in effect, a soldier's or a slave's unlawful escape from somebody's possession. It was fundamentally "subversive" of property rights.

The Christian moralists never put it that way, of course. Instead, they said that human life is a divine monopoly: "Our lives are God's." To take one's own life, therefore, is to invade Jesus Christ's property rights because he has saved us "and we are therefore his." This mystical theology was the bottom layer of the moral and canonical prohibition. It led some theologians to say that Judas Iscariot's suicide in remorse and despair was even more wicked than his earlier betrayal of Jesus and Jesus' consequent crucifixion.

A False Turning Point

St. Augustine marked the turning point in the hardening process. He was the first to make the prohibition absolute. None of the later antisuicide moralists improved on him; even Aquinas added only "It is unnatural," thus buttressing the theology with a religious metaphysics of "natural law."

We can outline Augustine's objections to any and all suicide in four propositions: (1) If we are innocent, we may not kill the innocent; if we are guilty, we may not take justice into our own hands. (2) The sixth commandment of the Decalogue forbids it, *non occides*; suicide is homicide; it is a felony, *felo de se*. (3) Our duty is to bear suffering with fortitude; to escape is to evade our role as soldiers of Christ. (4) Suicide is the worst sin; it precludes repentance; to do it in a state of grace (after one is saved, or cleansed of sin by Christ's blood) means one dies out of grace (unsaved, eternally lost or rejected). Augustine allowed an occasional exception for martyrs who had God's express directive or "guidance" to kill themselves; they were said to be acting as innocently as those who sin *ex ignorantia inculnata* (in invincible ignorance). This is the argument Augustine used to answer the Donatists, a Christian sect that pointed

43

out that dying baptized in a state of grace, by one's own hand, was better than living long enough to fall back into sin, losing one's chance to have eternal life in heaven.

At the end of the Holy Roman hegemony, people began to reason again. By 1561 Thomas More (the "man for all seasons" who died for conscience' sake) had allowed suicide in his *Utopia*, even though Sir Thomas Browne frowned on it in his *Religio Medici* (1642). Montaigne backed More, and so it went. The great classic *coup de grâce* to the moral prohibition of suicide came with David Hume's essay *On Suicide* (1777), in which he reasoned that if suicide is wrong it must be because it offends God, one's neighbor, or one's self, and then showed how this would not always be true. Hume was joined by Voltaire, Rousseau, Montesquieu, and d'Halbach.

The conventional wisdom after nearly a thousand years of prohibition continued unchanged, as attempted suicides were hanged from the public gibbet. In Christian France, as in animist Dahomey, the bodies of the executed were thrown on garbage dumps. The properties of suicides were confiscated in England until 1870, and prison was the legal penalty for attempts until 1961.

At last, in the Suicide Act of 1961, England stopped making it a crime for a person, whether well or ill, to end his life or attempt to do so. There are only a few places left in the world where the courts are still trying to catch up to that kind of moral "sanity." Courts of law today are seldom as unethical about suicide as the conventional moralists continue to be.

Always and everywhere we find cultural variety and difference all along the spectrum of ethical opinion — from blanket prohibition to selective justification. In a very sane and discriminating fashion most communities, both savage and civilized, have believed that disposing of one's own life is like disposing of one's own property, that is, a personal election.

It is on this last ground that most governments in the West have been opposed to suicide. They have followed Aristotle and Plato, who contended pragmatically that except for grave reasons suicide seriously deprived the community of soldiers to defend it and workers to do its labor of head and hand. How weighty this objection is now, in an age of overpopulation, cybernated warfare,

44

and automated industry, is an open question. In any case, the "right" to die is not right if and when it invades the well-being of others. On the other hand, when it is truly and only a personal choice, it is right. To deny this is to deny the integrity of persons, to reduce them to being only functions or appendages of systems of lords and seigneurs, or church and state.

Types of Suicides

Just as facts cannot tell us which things to value (although they may help) or how to rank them as priorities, neither can typologies. This caution applies, for example, to Emile Durkheim's famous classification of suicides into egoistic and altruistic, which is close to what we have come to mean in more recent days by "inner directed" and "other directed" — in the language of Riesman's *Lonely Crowd*.

Strong self-sustaining personalities are able (have the "ego strength") to defy cultural disapproval when or if a balance of pro-life and pro-death factors seems to weigh against going on living. As Albert Camus said, "Judging whether life is or is not worth living amounts to answering the fundamental question of philosophy." To drive home his point that philosophy is not merely impersonal abstraction, he added drily, "I have never seen anyone die for the ontological argument." There are times, although we may hope not often, when people find that the flame is no longer worth the candle. History and literature abound with instances.

Similarly, on the altruistic side, there are times when sacrificial love and loyalty may call on us for a tragic decision, to choose death for the sake of a wider good than self. The decision is made pragmatically, to promote the greater good or the lesser evil. An example is Captain Oates in the Antarctic snafu, who eliminated himself to speed up the escape of his companions; other instances are disabled grandparents pushing off on ice floes to relieve hungry Eskimos and brave men staying on the sinking *Titanic* or dropping off from overloaded lifeboats.

Durkheim had a third type of suicides, the anomic — those who suffer anomie, who have come to despair for either subjective

45

reasons (including psychogenic illness) or objective reasons (maybe unemployability or outright social rejection). They reach a point where they cannot "care less." Demoralized, unnerved, disoriented, they throw in their remaining chips. One recalls Jeb Magruder telling the Senate Watergate committee, by way of self-excuse, that he had lost his "ethical compass." Suicide out of anomie or being normless, just as in cases when it is done out of ego strength or for loyalty reasons, may be rationally well-founded and prudent or may not. Suicides of all kinds, in any typology, can be wise or foolish.

This is perhaps the point at which to challenge directly and flatly the widespread assumption that "suicides are sick people, out of their gourds." This canard has lodged itself deeply even in the mental attitudes of physicians. It has managed to become the "conventional wisdom" of psychiatric medicine, partly, no doubt, because psychiatrists deal so much with false suicides whose verbal or nonverbal threats or "attempts" are signals of emotional or mental distress. Nevertheless, for all its persistence, the idea is basically silly.

Like universalized or absolutized moral norms, this one, too, is undiscriminating — a frequent diagnosis turned into a universalized stereotype. Some suicides are suffering from what Freud first called misplaced aggression and later thought to be diseased superego, but not all are. To say *all* is to be playing with universalized characterizations, and universals of any kind are fantasies, not empirical realities. (The hypocrisy of the courts has done a lot to encourage the dogma that suicides are unhinged.) The fact is that suicide sometimes can be psychiatrically discredited or sometimes can be ethically approved, depending on the case.

Those suicides who tell us about the fears and doubts that go through their minds are the "attempteds," not the successful and thorough ones, and the result is a marked bias or skew to the speculations and theories of therapists. Even more speculative are the ideas of writers who have lively imaginations (Thomas Mann, Boris Pasternak), especially when imagination is combined with a grasp of psychological jargon. Real suicides rarely leave any record and even more rarely explain themselves in any reflective detail; there are only a few exceptions like Arthur Schopenhauer, who thought suicide through but did not do it, and Sylvia Plath, who did. We only have to read Lael Wertenbaker's *Death of a Man* (1957), the

46

story of her husband's noble and sane decision to cheat Big C, to get a more realistic appreciation of what suicide can be.

Suicide Today

In recent years the ethical issue about human initiatives in death and dying has been posed most poignantly for the common run of those in medical care, in the treatment of the terminally ill. Resuscitative techniques now compel them to decide when to stop preserving and supporting life; people no longer just die. What is called negative euthanasia, letting the patient die without any further struggle against it, is a daily event in hospitals. About 200,000 legally unenforceable "living wills" have been recorded, appealing to doctors, families, pastors, and lawyers to stop treatment at some balance point of pro-life, pro-death assessment.

What is called positive euthanasia — doing something to shorten or end life deliberately — is the form in which suicide is the question — as a voluntary, direct choice of death.

For a long time the Christian moralists have distinguished between negative or indirectly willed suicide, like not taking a place in one of the *Titanic's* lifeboats, and positive or directly willed suicide, like jumping out of a lifeboat to make room for a fellow victim of a shipwreck. The moralists mean that we may choose to allow an evil by acts of omission but not to do an evil by acts of commission. The moralists contend that since all suicide is evil we may only "allow" it; we may not "do" it. The moralists do not mean that death is evil, only that dying is evil if it is done freely and directly by personal choice. Choosing to die is self-murder, just as a physician or friend helping you die at your earnest request would be guilty of murder.

Is it not ridiculous, however, to say that given the desirability of escape from this mortal coil or a tragic "crunch" in which one elects to give one's life for another value, all acts of omission to that end are licit, yet all acts of commission to the same end are wrong? Taboo thinking such as "all suicide is wrong" enlists false reasoning and invites inhumane consequences. The end or goal or purpose in both direct (positive) and indirect (negative) euthanasia is precisely the same — the end of the patient's life, release from pointless misery and dehumanizing loss of functions. The logic here is inexorable.

47

As Kant said, if we will the end we will the means, and if the means required is inordinate or disproportionate we give up the end. The old maxim of some religious thinkers was *finis sanctificat media*. Human acts of any kind, including suicide, depend for their ethical status on the proportion of good between the end sought and the means needed to accomplish it. Only if the means were inappropriate or too costly would the end have to be foregone. It follows that suicide is probably sometimes a fitting act and well worth doing.

How can it be right for a person to go over the cliff's edge helplessly blindfolded, while we stand by doing nothing to prevent it, but wrong if that person removes the blindfold and steps off with eyes open? It is naïve or obtuse to contend that if we choose to die slowly, forlornly, willy-nilly, by a natural disintegration from something like cancer or starvation, we have no complicity in our death and the death is not suicide; but if we deliberately our "quietus make with a bare bodkin," it is suicide. Every person's fight with death is lost before it begins. What makes the struggle worthwhile, therefore, cannot lie in the outcome. It lies in the dignity with which the fight is waged and the way it finds an end.

The summary principle is limpid clear: Not to do anything is a decision to act every bit as much as deciding to *do* what we would accomplish by "not" acting.

Consideration of suicide for social reasons (Durkheim's altruistic type) can easily lead to a philosophical debate about ethical egoism or self-interest *versus* social integration and utilitarian concern for the greatest good of the greatest number. Whether we limit our obligation to others to the parameters of enlightened self-interest or, more altruistically, of social solidarism, it still follows that we may be called to suicide for heroic or for sacrificial reasons. The fact that sometimes suicide subjects are unconsciously wanting to die anyway (Menninger 1938) is psychiatrically important but ethically irrelevant — unless, of course, we slide into the semantic swamp and assert that all who sacrifice their lives — parents, soldiers, police officers, researchers, explorers, or whoever — are sick.

More problematic and subtle than suicide for medical or social reasons are what we may call the personal cases. The ethical principle here is the integrity of persons and respect for their freedom.

48

Sometimes suicides act for profoundly personal, deeply private reasons. Often enough other people, even those close to the suicides, cannot add things up in the same way to justify the election of death. If there is no clear and countervailing injustice involved, however, surely the values of self-determination and liberty weigh in the suicide's favor. Social, physical, esthetic, and mental deficiencies, when combined, could weigh against the worth of a person's life. And who is to be the accountant or assessor if not the one whose death it is?

Conclusion

It appears that a basic issue is whether quality of life is more valuable than life *qua* life. And defense of suicide has to opt for quality, not quantity. The sacralists, those who invest life with a sacred entelechy of some kind, consequently make all direct control over life taboo. (We see this in the abortion debate as well as in the question of suicide.)

This question, whether we may act on a quality-of-life ethic or must go on with the medieval sanctity-of-life ethic, runs through nearly every problem in the field of biomedical policy — genetics, transplants, the determination of death, allocation of scarce treatment resources, management of the dying patient, human experimentation, fetal research, nearly everything.

Quality concern requires us to reorder values; those who promptly and dogmatically put being alive as the first-order value need to reappraise their ethics. One's life is a value to be perceived in relation to other values. At best it is only *primus inter pares*. Without life other things are of no value to us, but by the same token without other things life may be of no value to us. In *The Tyranny of Survival* Daniel Callahan puts it succinctly: "Unlike other animals, human beings are consciously able to kill themselves by suicide; some people choose to die." They want more than "mere survival," he thinks. "Models which work with ants do not work well when extrapolated to human beings."

The reason for this, we can add, is that human beings, unlike purely instinctual creatures, do not regard life as an end in itself. Life, to be up to human standards, has to integrate a number of

49

other values to make it worth our while. Human beings can choose to die not only for reasons of love and loyalty but just because life happens to be too sour or bare. In Sean O'Casey's words, a time may come when laughter is no longer a weapon against evil.

The ethical problem, how to make value choices, comes down, as we have seen, to whether we reason with or without absolutes of right and wrong. Bayet back in 1922 had his own way of putting it in *Le Suicide et la Morale*. He said there are two kinds of approaches: an ethic of a priori rules and taboos or universal prohibitions or, alternatively, a *"morale nuancee,"* an ethic rooted in variables and discrimination, that judges acts by their consequences, a posteriori. This essay is built on moral nuances.

Socrates and Karl Jaspers, 2,300 years apart, thought that the business of philosophy is to prepare us for death. Religionists, in their own way, have taken hold of that task; they have coped by a denial maneuver and a counterassertion of eternal life. Philosophers have ignored the problem for the most part. A good start was made with Epictetus' dictum: "When I am, death is not. When death is, I am not. Therefore we can never have anything to do with death. Why fear it?" Or take, in present-day terms, Camus' opening remark in his absurd essay *The Myth of Sisyphus*, that there is "but one truly serious philosophical problem, and that is suicide."

We have a striking paradigm for the ethics of suicide. In his *Notebooks 1914–16* Wittgenstein says that suicide is the "elementary sin" — blandly assuming, in tyro fashion, that survival is the highest good, even though it is individually impossible and corporately improbable that experience will bear this assumption out. Only on that unacknowledged premise was he able to say that "if anything is not allowed then suicide is not allowed." But then his superb mind forced him to ask, in conclusion, "Or is even suicide in itself neither good nor evil?" There, in a phrase, is the whole point ethically. Nothing in itself is either good or evil, neither life nor death. Quality is always extrinsic and contingent.

The full circle is being drawn. In classical times suicide was a tragic option, for human dignity's sake. Then for centuries it was a sin. Then it became a crime. Then a sickness. Soon it will become a choice again. Suicide is the signature of freedom.

50

THE RIGHT TO CHOOSE—WHEN SHOULD DEATH BE IN THE INDIVIDUAL'S HANDS?

STACY L. MOJICA*
DAN S. MURRELL**

To most people, the prospect of death is a frightening reality. Each person, throughout the course of his or her life, will be forced to deal with the deaths of relatives, friends, and acquaintances. While death, like taxes, is certain,[1] the majority of people in our society prefer not to deal with the ethical, moral, and legal issues surrounding the subject. When death results from suicide, the idea becomes even more disconcerting. Not only are we reminded of the certainty of its occurrence, we are also faced with the suggestion of despair incomprehensible to the senses. This Article will examine the history of suicide; the views on suicide in other cultures and the United States; the legal treatment of suicide in the criminal law, including the treatment of assisted suicides; and, finally, examine some of the ethical dilemmas raised by this issue.

I. HISTORICAL TREATMENT OF SUICIDE

Reports of suicide go back to biblical times. There are six cases of suicide reported in the bible, and numerous historical writings chronicle the suicides of famous leaders.[2] The Bible does not condemn or prohibit suicide, and the incidents chronicled speak in general terms,

---

* B.S., Mankato State University; J.D./M.B.A., Memphis State University.

** Professor of Law, Memphis State University; B.A., J.D., University of Mississippi; LL.M, George Washington University.

1. Benjamin Franklin, in a letter to Jean Baptiste Le Roy dated November 13, 1779, coined the phrase oft repeated by politicians that "in this world nothing is certain but death or taxes," *reprinted in* M. MCNAMARA, 2000 FAMOUS LEGAL QUOTATIONS 106 (1967).

2. A HANDBOOK FOR THE STUDY OF SUICIDE 4-26 (S. Perlin ed. 1975) [hereinafter HANDBOOK]. Four of the reported cases are in the Old Testament. STENGEL, SUICIDE AND ATTEMPTED SUICIDE 68 (1st Aronson ed. 1974).

for there was no specific word used for suicide.[3] Among the Greeks, Romans, and other ancient cultures, a number of forms of suicide arose, including institutional, honor, and ritual suicides.[4] Except in those cases where the act was committed to sanctify or uphold religious convictions, suicide was generally disfavored.[5] Even in those societies that viewed it with disfavor, however, suicide was often tolerated, and some who committed suicide were deemed to be martyrs.[6]

The number of suicides continued to increase until the views of the Christian church began to have an impact on the legal and social attitudes toward suicide.[7] In some cultures, penalties were imposed against those who committed suicide in an attempt to deter others from doing so.[8] During the Middle Ages, suicide was condemned by the Roman Empire, and the Church declared that suicide was "tantamount to murder" and, therefore, was a sin.[9] In Europe and England, suicide was dealt with on the basis of custom rather than legal authority until the middle of the fourteenth century,[10] at which time it was declared to be a felony. Prior to and after the declaration that suicide was a felony, forfeiture of goods and/or land was imposed in England

---

3. HANDBOOK, *supra* note 2, at 4. *See also* SUICIDE IN DIFFERENT CULTURES 1 (N. Farberow ed. 1975) [hereinafter Farberow]; Larremore, *Suicide and the Law*, 17 HARV. L. REV. 331 (1903).

4. HANDBOOK, *supra* note 2, at 5-6.

5. *Id.* at 5.

6. *Id.* at 10.

7. *Id.* Suicide was viewed with antagonism and hostility by the Church and society as a whole except in the cases of voluntary martyrdom, as a way to preserve chastity, and as a form of religious humility. Farberow, *supra* note 3, at 6-7.

8. HANDBOOK, *supra* note 2, at 11. Some examples of the penalties imposed are: chopping off the hand with which the act was committed, refusal of an honorable burial, and carrying the deceased to the grave naked. *Id.*

9. *Id.* at 12. Christians believed that those who committed suicide were destined to live for eternity in hell absent mitigating circumstances that indicate that the deceased lacked the capacity for rational thought. *Id.* at 15, 17-18. The Jewish orthodoxy was opposed to suicide, but recognized a number of exculpable justifications for suicide, including honor, atonement, preservation of chastity, and escape from torture or religious persecution. *Id. See also* Farberow, *supra* note 3, at 4. For almost nine hundred years, from the fourth to the thirteenth centuries, suicide was almost unknown in Europe due to the great influence of the Catholic Church. *Id.* at 6. The attitude held by the Church toward suicide continues to be one of condemnation. STENGEL, *supra* note 2, at 69.

10. HANDBOOK, *supra* note 2, at 13.

until the nineteenth century.[11] It was also common practice to disfigure or otherwise punish the corpse of the successful suicide and to refuse burial in consecrated ground.[12]

It appears from the literature of the seventeenth and eighteenth centuries that England was generally perceived as a "land of melancholy and suicide."[13] This supports the theory that the strict views against suicide that prevailed in the English common-law and, consequently, in the common-law of this country, resulted from a perceived necessity to combat this general societal malaise. Beginning in the late eighteenth century, these strict views began to change, reflecting the trend among commentators of that period to view suicide as a medical and social phenomenon.[14] Suicide was looked on more as a disgrace rather than a sin, and was excusable if it resulted from an infirmity of the mind.[15]

During the 1800's, clinicians, physicians, and other medical investigators began to collect statistics on suicide in order to explain the causes of suicide.[16] The results of these studies were in agreement with the conclusion arrived at by Emile Durkheim in 1897 that in a society that is well integrated socially, economically, and politically, suicide rates will be low.[17] Legal changes also began to occur during this period, including the abolishment or lessening of criminal penalties.[18] The Church continues to view suicide as a sin; however, attitudes are more lenient, showing a tendency to equate suicide with a mental disorder.[19] Attempted suicide remains a crime in many Middle European countries, Japan, and the Soviet Union, but statutes in England and the United States making suicide a crime have recently been abolished.[20]

---

11. *Id.* During the Roman period, forfeiture and confiscation of estates was the usual punishment for suicide by a soldier or slave. Farberow, *supra* note 3, at 6. *See also infra* discussion at notes 81-86.

12. HANDBOOK, *supra* note 2, at 13-14. Common practices included burying the body at a crossroad at night with a stake through the heart, dragging the body through the street by the feet followed by disposal of the body in the sewer or the town dump, and treating the corpse in the same manner as those who were executed for murder. *Id. See also* Farberow, *supra* note 3, at 7; STENGEL, *supra* note 2, at 69.

13. HANDBOOK, *supra* note 2, at 19-20.

14. *Id.* at 20-22.

15. *Id.* at 22. *See also* Farberow, *supra* note 3, at 11.

16. HANDBOOK, *supra* note 2, at 24-26. *See also* Farberow, *supra* note 3, at 11-12.

17. E. DURKHEIM, SUICIDE (1897) (cited in HANDBOOK, *supra* note 2, at 26).

18. Farberow, *supra* note 3, at 12.

19. *Id.*

20. *Id.* at 12-13.

II. VIEWS ON SUICIDE IN OTHER CULTURES

A. JAPAN

Japan has one of the highest suicide rates in the world, and, while the rates in other countries tend to increase with population age, there is a peak in the rate among Japanese youths along with a corresponding peak in the rate among the elderly.[21] The rate among women in Japan is equal to that of men, unlike all other countries.[22] Other interesting differences concerning suicides in Japan include the fact that most occur at night, that the relationship between social or economic status to the suicide rate is inverse, and that the suicide rate is rising while the homicide rate is falling.[23] Suicides in Japan can be classified by a number of important distinguishing characteristics, including the method of, and the motivation behind the act. Common methods include: 1) *Dokuyaku Jisatsu*—the use of poison or sleeping pills to ensure a normal appearance after death;[24] 2) *Jusui Jisatsu*—drowning of the self to seek the "Pure Land"; 3) *Tooshin Jisatsu* or *Minage*—leaping from a height in order to merge with nature;[25] and 4) *Hara-kiri* or *Seppuku*—ritual self-disembowelment as a show of bravery and honor.[26] Similar uniqueness of thought concerning suicide is found in the motives for suicide, which include: 1) *Junshi*—suicide of the wife and servants following the death of the master in order for their spirits to continue service in the afterlife;[27] 2) *Gisei-shi*—as sacrifices to appease the gods or for war, as in the *kamikaze* pilots of World War II; 3) *Funshi* or *Munenbara*—to signify indignation or mortification based on resentment, hatred, or bitterness toward superiors; 4) *Kashitsu-shi* or *Sokotsu-bara*—paying for a mistake with death in order to achieve redemption; and 5) *Kanshi* or *Kangenshi*—in order to reproach a superior.[28]

---

21. *Id.* at 255-56.

22. *Id.* at 256. The rate among males versus the rate among females is higher in every other country.

23. Farberow, *supra* note 3, at 257. The reverse is true in Western countries, where most suicides occur during the day and economic status is generally not related to the suicide rates. *Id.*

24. The Japanese are particularly sensitive to the avoidance of "ugliness" in death. *Id.* at 258.

25. The leaping is normally done from a natural height, such as a waterfall or volcano. *Id.*

26. *Id.* at 258-59. Compulsory *hara-kiri* was made illegal in 1868. However, voluntary *hara-kiri* continued to be highly regarded but is not practiced in modern day Japan. STENGEL, *supra* note 2, at 67.

27. Forced suicides of this nature were banned in 659 A.D., but voluntary acts of this nature have been reported as recently as this century. Farberow, *supra* note 3, at 259.

28. *Id.* at 259-60.

Suicide pacts, called *shinju*, are also common in Japan, and are divided into two types: *jyoshi* (love pact) and *oyako* (parent-child). The first type is generally extolled as a way to enforce society's constrained code of behavior, and it includes cases of murder-suicide.[29] The second type is viewed as "a merciful deed" because it does not force the children to live as orphans.[30] The acceptance of these acts, along with the general disregard of suicide as a social problem, springs from the basic Japanese philosophy that life on earth is temporary, but filled with suffering and misery, and that real life begins at death.[31] It is believed that the attitude among the Japanese toward suicide is changing, but the process is slow even in the face of rapid cultural changes.[32]

B. *TAIWAN (CHINA)*

In ancient China, slaves were forced to commit suicide following the death of their master in order to ensure his prosperity in the afterworld.[33] This characterizes one of the recurring motives for suicide in China. Other motives include family loyalty, pressures from politics or war, and losing face or shame.[34] Suicides committed for these reasons are accepted; but when the motive is unhappiness or mental illness, the Chinese react with fear.[35] Buddhists believe that those who commit suicide remain in hell for eternity and are condemned to forego future reincarnation.[36] This belief, combined with the Confucian education that stresses the doctrines of family duty and rejects self-destructive behavior, creates a general societal attitude toward suicide as an act of weakness and shame.[37] However, suicide is not a crime in Taiwan. Suicide rates in Taiwan have been among the highest worldwide, but show signs of decreasing.[38] The highest rates occur

---

29. *Id.* at 260. In approximately one out of eight cases, one person forces the other to commit suicide or kills the other person. *Id.*

30. *Id.*

31. *Id.* at 270-73. The Japanese tend to view life as negative and death as a positive step in the event of failure. *Id.* at 271.

32. Farberow, *supra* note 3, at 273, 276-77.

33. *Id.* at 240-41.

34. *Id.* at 241-42. Many women have committed suicide in performance of *tseng*, or suicide out of loyalty to a deceased spouse. *Id.* at 242.

35. *Id.* at 246.

36. *Id.* The Buddhists believe that suicide results from a lack of tolerance for the stress of human life, and should be pitied, but is nonetheless to be sanctioned. *Id.* at 247.

37. Farberow, *supra* note 3, at 247-48. The Chinese do not condemn suicide, but rather deem it to be foolish and cowardly. *Id.* at 248.

38. *Id.* at 248-49.

among young females of the lower classes, and the reasons for suicides generally revolve around family issues such as frustrated love affairs.[39]

C. *INDIA*

Suicide is generally viewed with fear, shame, and censure in India. Attempted suicide is a crime, and the survivors are viewed as tainted members of society.[40] Historically, women committed a form of suicide called *sati* in which women burned themselves over the funeral pyre of their deceased husbands.[41] *Sallekhana*—suicide by starvation—is accepted under some religious views, and has been used as a threat for political reasons.[42] The primary motives for suicide in India center around the marital and family relationship, two areas with special cultural significance. Impotence, sterility, and infidelity account for a large proportion of the suicides.[43] Poverty and unemployment are also major factors in the suicide rate.[44]

D. *ISRAEL (JEWISH)*

Under ancient Jewish law, those who committed suicide were deemed to be wicked and were denied sacred burial.[45] The prevailing attitude remains one of unacceptability. Current legal provisions derive from English law. Suicide has never been a crime in Israel, although it was a crime in England until 1961.[46] Attempted suicide was a misdemeanor punishable by up to three years in prison until the law was changed in 1966.[47] Suicide pacts and assisting suicide are still

---

39. *Id.* at 251-52.

40. *Id.* at 234.

41. *Id.* at 233. For a more complete discussion of the practice of *sati, see generally* Stein, *Burning Widows, Burning Brides: The Perils of Daughterhood in India,* 16 PAC. AFF. 465 (1988). *Sati* was strictly regulated beginning in the early nineteenth century to meet with the requirements spelled out in sacred writings and to ensure voluntariness on the part of the women. *Id.* at 470. These regulations did not, however, reduce the number of *satis,* as had been hoped. *Id.* Consequently, the practice of *sati* was officially outlawed in 1892. Farberow, *supra* note 3, at 233.

42. Farberow, *supra* note 3, at 234, 237.

43. *Id.* at 235-36.

44. *Id.* at 237.

45. *Id.* If at all possible, the law prescribed that the act should be deemed to result from murder rather than suicide, and suicide caused by madness or fear was to be treated as a natural death. *Id.*

46. *Id.* at 218.

47. Farberow, *supra* note 3, at 218. There were no prosecutions for attempted suicide from 1948, the year in which Israel became an independent state, until 1966 when the statute was repealed. *Id.*

illegal, and are treated as murder punishable by life imprisonment.[48] The Jewish suicide rate is below that of the United States, but higher than the rates in Norway and the Netherlands.[49] The rate among females is above average, and more married people commit suicide than those who are single or divorced.[50]

E. *ITALY*

In Italy, suicide is regarded as a grievous sin, a view which stems from the ability of the Catholic Church to influence societal views.[51] As a result, it is common practice to report suicide as death from another cause. Therefore, the reported rate of suicide in Italy, which is very low, is likely understated.[52] It is illegal to aid or encourage suicide, and citizens are expected to use all possible efforts to stop attempted suicides.[53] Suicide, for the purpose of saving honor, *suicidio per motivi di onore*, is viewed with less disfavor, but is generally decreasing in frequency.[54]

F. *NORWAY*

Initially, suicide was viewed in Norway as the act of a weak man.[55] Following the adoption of Christianity, suicide was regarded as a sin, and it was commonly believed that the soul of the person who committed suicide would never rest.[56] Suicide was deemed to be a dishonorable homicide, punishable by forfeiture of property and refusal of burial in the church unless the act resulted from a mental infirmity.[57] These penalties were gradually rejected and, since 1902, only aiding suicide has been considered a punishable offense.[58] Norwegians continue to view those who attempt or commit suicide as weak, and many view suicide as a sin.[59] The suicide rate in Norway

---

48. *Id.*

49. *Id.* at 216.

50. *Id.* Widows and widowers, however, have a relatively high suicide rate. *Id.*

51. *Id.* at 179, 182.

52. Farberow, *supra* note 3, at 179, 182. It is possible, however, that this attitude of strong discouragement could result in rates that are much lower than in those countries where suicide is treated with more tolerance. Also, the emphasis on family in the Italian culture, with a corresponding strengthening of support systems, could reduce the incidence of suicide.

53. *Id.* at 180.

54. *Id.* at 182-83.

55. *Id.* at 78.

56. *Id.*

57. Farberow, *supra* note 3, at 78.

58. *Id.* at 78-79.

59. *Id.*

has remained relatively stable, with the highest rates occurring among persons between the ages of fifty and fifty-nine.[60] The suicide rate in Norway is one-third the rate of Sweden and Denmark; however, these rates may be explained in part by the fact that reports of death by suicide in Norway are misreported.[61] It is interesting to note that social welfare programs are relatively advanced in the Scandinavian countries, creating a form of economic security, which may be one reason for the stable suicide rates in those countries.[62]

G. SWEDEN

The suicide rate in Sweden has traditionally been high, but this rate may be overstated, when compared to the reported rates of other countries, due to differences in certification methods.[63] The Swedish culture is based on the Protestant work ethic, and is characterized by increasing materialism and secularism.[64] There is an absence of denouncement of suicides, possibly due to Sweden's longstanding attitude of pacifism as evidenced by its international neutrality.[65] Social programs are widely available and are utilized mainly by the country's large middle class.

H. FINLAND

Finland was part of Sweden until 1809, and during that period the suicide rate was quite low.[66] Rates increased steadily in the twentieth century, and are currently nearing that of Sweden. The first laws concerning suicide declared the act to be a crime against the state. Attempted suicide was made criminal in the eighteenth century, punishable by fine or imprisonment.[67] With the lessening of the power of the church in the early part of this century came a reduction in the penalties for suicide and, although no true causal connection between

---

60. *Id.* at 80. The suicide rate among children under the age of fifteen is very low, and the rate among older teenagers has remained stable throughout this century. *Id.* at 81.

61. *Id.* at 83-85. It has also been noted that Sweden has the world's most reliable suicide statistics; the population as a whole is older (the group most likely to commit suicide), Swedish society views suicide with more tolerance, and the birth rate is lower. *Id.* at 85-86.

62. Farberow, *supra* note 3, at 93.

63. *Id.* at 116, 131. The suicide rate in Sweden is higher than that in the United States, as are the rates in Austria, Finland and Hungary. HANDBOOK, *supra* note 2, at 197.

64. Farberow, *supra* note 3, at 131.

65. *Id.*

66. *Id.* at 96.

67. *Id.* at 97.

the two has been shown, an increase in the suicide rates.[68] Finns generally disdain persons with mental disorders, and view those who seek treatment with shame.[69] A large majority of those who commit suicide are men, especially elderly men.[70]

I. THE NETHERLANDS

The Netherlands has a well developed mental health program, one of the best in Europe, and this factor is viewed as one of the reasons for the country's low suicide rate.[71] Other factors which contribute to the low rate include the historical emphasis on religious faith that precludes an idolization of martyrs, the tradition of urban lifestyle that resulted in only minor changes in lifestyles as the sizes of cities increased, curiosity about others leading to increased social interaction, and an attitude toward honest realism.[72] Suicide and suicide attempts are not illegal, but criminal penalties are imposed on those who take another person's life at his or her request, or provide assistance or the means for a successful suicide.[73] Both the Protestant and Catholic Churches disfavor suicide, but do not adjudge a person as a sinner on this basis—the ultimate judgment comes from the victim or the survivors.[74] It is interesting to note that the suicide rate, which had remained steady for many years, began to rise starting in the 1970's.[75] At the same time, many of the traditional values and ideals in society had begun to change, including a decrease in the influence of the church.[76] Since 1984, voluntary euthanasia has been legally "sanctioned," and an estimated 2,000 persons per year choose this method to end their lives.[77]

---

68. *Id.* While over ninety percent of the population belongs to the church, present attitudes toward religion show a marked amount of indifference. *Id.* at 109.

69. Farberow, *supra* note 3, at 97. Like suicide, psychiatric treatment is generally treated as a secret. *Id.*

70. *Id.* Roughly three-quarters of the suicides are committed by men. *Id.*

71. *Id.* at 165. The rate is about one-third that of Germany, the Netherland's largest neighbor, and about one-half that of Belgium, which borders the country to the south. *Id.*

72. *Id.* at 166-69.

73. *Id.* at 170.

74. Farberow, *supra* note 3, at 170. The church believes that suicide is a sin, but the question of whether the victim will be denied entry into heaven is solely between the victim and God. *Id.*

75. *Id.* at 176.

76. *Id.*

77. *Janet Adkins: The Torchbearer*, 39 HEMLOCK Q. 1 (July 1990). One author has suggested that the number of euthanasia cases in the Netherlands is as high as 5,000 to 8,000 each year. Angell, *Editorial on Euthanasia*, 319 NEW ENG. J. MED. No. 20 (Nov. 17, 1988).

III. VIEWS ON SUICIDE AT ENGLISH COMMON LAW

English common law embodied the attitude of the church concerning the sinful and wicked nature of suicide, asserting that suicide was a crime against not only God, but also the king.[78] Initially, suicide was viewed as merely a confession of guilt for another crime.[79] The English considered suicide, or *felo de se*,[80] to be an immoral crime akin to murder and a felony,[81] punishable by harsh treatment including mutilation of the body, burial at a crossroads with a stake through the heart, and forfeiture of property to the Crown.[82] These penalties were imposed in hopes of deterring suicides.[83] Forfeiture of land was only imposed when the suicide was committed to avoid punishment for another crime or out of anger.[84] Only a person's chattels were forfeited if the act was committed to ease the pain of disease or to

---

"[E]uthanasia officially remains a crime, punishable by up to 12 years in prison, but it is practiced fairly commonly and openly . . . protected by a body of case law and strong public support." *Id.* See also Zucker & Annarino, *Department of Law and Ethics*, 11 DEATH STUD. 67 (1987).

78. Larremore, *supra* note 3, at 332 (citing 4 W. BLACKSTONE, COMMENTARIES, ch. 14, at 189).

79. Mikell, *Is Suicide Murder?*, 3 COLUM. L. REV. 379 (1903).

80. Numerous cases in this country use the terms *felo de se* and *malum in se* when referring to suicide. *See, e.g.*, McMahan v. State, 168 Ala. 70, 74, 53 So. 89, 91 (1910); State v. Campbell, 217 Iowa 848, 850, 251 N.W. 717, 718 (1933); May v. Pennell, 101 Me. 516, 518, 64 A. 885, 886 (1906); Commonwealth v. Bowen, 13 Mass. 356, 357 (1816); Commonwealth v. Mink, 123 Mass. 422, 426 (1877); State v. Willis, 255 N.C. 473, 475, 121 S.E.2d 854, 855 (1961); State v. Levelle, 34 S.C. 120, 13 S.E. 319 (1891). *Felo de se* was used at common law to mean "the felon himself," *see* R. PERKINS, CRIMINAL LAW 65 (1957) (cited in Brenner, *Undue Influence in the Criminal Law: A Proposed Analysis of the Criminal Offense of "Causing Suicide,"* 47 ALB. L. REV. 62, 64 n.13 (1982)), but is now synonymous for the act of suicide. BLACK'S LAW DICTIONARY 555 (5th ed. 1979). *Malum in se* is defined as "[a] wrong in itself . . . inherently and essentially evil . . . [and] immoral in its nature. . . ." *Id.* at 865. Thus, it appears that courts in this country originally adhered to the English common law view that suicide is in the nature of an immoral and infamous act.

81. It is likely that suicide was considered to be a form of murder rather than a separate and distinct offense, although it is not entirely clear if this was the case. *See* W. LAFAVE & A. SCOTT, JR., CRIMINAL LAW § 7.8, at 649 (2d ed. 1986). *See* Mikell, *supra* note 79, at 388-90 (citing two early English cases, one holding that the crime committed was treason rather than murder, the other holding that attempted suicide is an attempt to commit a felony, not an attempt to commit murder, but concluding that suicide was murder under English common law).

82. *See* Note, *Criminal Aspects of Suicide in the United States*, 7 N.C. CENT. L. REV. 156, 156-57 (1976) [hereinafter *Criminal Aspects*]; *see also* Brenner, *supra* note 80, at 64; Larremore, *supra* note 3, at 332. No other forms of punishment were imposed on either the deceased or the survivors. *Pennell*, 101 Me. at 518, 64 A. at 886.

83. There is no evidence that the imposition of penalties actually had any deterrent effect, which is one of the main reasons that the law against suicide was repealed in 1961. STENGEL, *supra* note 2, at 71-72.

84. Brenner, *supra* note 80, at 64. Forfeiture was imposed for "cheating the law out of its punishment," and to compensate the king for the loss of his subject, breaching the peace, and

escape the ravages of old age.[85] Ignominious interment was formally abolished by statute in 1824[86] and forfeiture of property was ended by the Forfeiture Act of 1870.[87]

Attempts to commit suicide were treated as misdemeanors, although there is no evidence of an act by Parliament to make it a statutory offense.[88] One who persuaded a person to commit suicide was guilty of second degree murder as a principal if present at the time of the act, but was not punished at common law if not present at the time of the act.[89] This latter principle was changed in 1857 by the case of *Regina v. Ledington*.[90] In *Ledington*, the Court of Criminal Appeals held that the defendant, who was not present at the time of the suicide, was nevertheless guilty of manslaughter because one who persuades another to commit suicide is an accessory to the crime of murder.[91] The survivor of a suicide pact could be held to be guilty of murder.[92] In 1961, legislation was passed in England abolishing the crime of suicide.[93]

---

setting a bad example for the rest of the population. *Id.* at 64-65, 64 n.15 (citing Hales v. Petit, 75 Eng. Rep. 387 (C.B. 1565)).

85. *Id.* at 64-65. Forfeiture was avoided completely if the victim was adjudged to be insane at the time of commission of the act. *Id.*

86. *See* Comment, *The Punishment of Suicide—A Need for Change*, 14 VILL. L. REV. 463, 465 (1969) [hereinafter *Punishment*], *see also Criminal Aspects, supra* note 82, at 157; State v. Willis, 255 N.C. 473, 476, 121 S.E.2d 854, 855 (1961).

87. *Punishment, supra* note 86, at 465.

88. May v. Pennell, 101 Me. 516, 519-20, 64 A. 885, 886-87 (1906); Commonwealth v. Mink, 123 Mass. 422, 425 (1877). It is likely that the misdemeanor charged was actually an attempt to commit a felony, not distinguishable from any other attempted crimes, rather than a separate misdemeanor. *Pennell*, 101 Me. at 520, 64 A. at 887.

89. *Mink*, 123 Mass. at 425 (citing numerous early English cases). Presence at the time of the suicide was a determinative factor under common law because the person giving aid or encouragement, if not present at the time of the criminal act, was tried as an accessory. Under English common law, the accessory could not be tried for the crime until after the principle had been tried; therefore, because a successful suicide could not be tried, the accessory also could not be tried. Mikell, *supra* note 79, at 387. *See also* Larremore, *supra* note 3, at 335.

90. 9 Car. & P. 79 (1857) (cited in Mikell, *supra* note 79, at 387).

91. Mikell, *supra* note 79, at 387. A statute was passed during the early part of Queen Victoria's reign providing that those who assist another in the commission of suicide could be convicted as an accessory or a principal in the second degree. Larremore, *supra* note 3, at 335.

92. Mikell, *supra* note 79, at 388 (citing Regina v. Allison, 8 Car. & P. 418 (1838)); *Mink*, 123 Mass. at 425.

93. The Suicide Act of 1961, 9 & 10 Eliz. 2 ch. 60, § 1 (cited in *Punishment, supra* note 86, at 465 n.19). Under the Act, aiding or procuring a suicide or attempted suicide is punishable as manslaughter. *Id.* at § 2.

IV. SUICIDE AND ATTEMPTED SUICIDE IN THE UNITED STATES

A. HISTORY

In the United States, as in England, suicide was considered to be a common law crime and required a specific intent to die by one's own hand.[94] Most states, however, failed to pursue those who committed suicide because forfeiture of property was forbidden under the Constitution, and therefore, the deceased could not be punished.[95] In many of the states that adopted penal codes as a complete replacement of the common law crimes, suicide was not included in the offenses that constitute murder, nor was it specifically mentioned elsewhere.[96]

Some courts have held that suicide is illegal or criminal, even in the absence of specific supporting statutory authority or the availability of punishment.[97] In one interesting case, the Indiana Supreme Court held that "self-destruction" or suicide, while not criminal, was "against the law of God and man."[98]

The Supreme Court of North Carolina in *State v. Willis*,[99] while recognizing that the common law regarding suicide had been repealed

---

94. D. MEYERS, MEDICO-LEGAL IMPLICATIONS OF DEATH AND DYING § 7:11, at 132 (1981). Some states, such as Iowa, Indiana, and Texas, do not recognize any common law crimes. *See* Prudential Ins. Co. v. Rice, 222 Ind. 231, 52 N.E.2d 624 (1944); State v. Campbell, 217 Iowa 848, 251 N.W. 717 (1933); Grace v. State, 44 Tex. Crim. 193, 69 S.W. 529 (1902).

95. *Criminal Aspects, supra* note 82, at 157. Some state constitutions specifically provide that suicide does not work a forfeiture of the estate of the deceased. *See, e.g.,* COLO. CONST. art II, § 9; DEL CONST. art I, § 15; KY. CONST. Bill of Rights § 21; MO. CONST. Bill of Rights, art I, § 30; TEX. CONST. art I, § 21; VT. CONST. ch. II, § 65. Some states have enacted statutes that abolish forfeiture of property in the case of suicide. NEV. REV. STAT. ANN § 212.010 (Michie 1986); N.Y. CIV. RIGHTS LAW § 79-b (McKinney 1981); TEX. PROB. CODE ANN. § 41 (Vernon 1980); VA. CODE ANN. § 55-4 (1950); WASH. REV. CODE ANN. § 9.92.110 (1988); W. VA. CODE § 61-11-4 (1989).

96. *Criminal Aspects, supra* note 82, at 158. North Carolina specifically adopted a statute that abolished the common law crime of suicide. N.C. GEN. STAT. § 14-17.1 (1986). The states that continued to recognize the common law have had to wrestle with the issue of whether to follow the lead of those states that specifically exempted suicide from the ranks of felonies or remain loyal to the English approach. Most persisted in holding that suicide was *malum in se*, or inherently immoral, but did not consider it to be a crime. Burnett v. State, 204 Ill. 208, 68 N.E. 505 (1903); Hundert v. Commercial Traveler's Mut. Acc. Ass'n, 244 A.D. 459, 279 N.Y.S. 555 (1935). *But see* Southern Health Ins. Co. v. Wynn, 29 Ala. App. 207, 194 So. 421 (1940); Commonwealth v. Mink, 123 Mass. 422 (1877); State v. Carney, 69 N.J.L. 478, 55 A. 44 (1903); State v. Levelle, 34 S.C. 120, 13 S.E. 319 (1891). This dilemma should have been resolved after the enactment of the Suicide Act of 1961 abrogating suicide as a crime in England. Suicide Act of 1961, 9 & 10 Eliz. 2, ch. 60. *See* discussion of the effects of this Act in Engelhardt & Malloy, *Suicide and Assisting Suicide: A Critique of Legal Sanctions*, 36 SW. U.L. REV. 1003, 1027-29 (1982).

97. *Punishment, supra* note 86, at 465.

98. Wallace v. State, 232 Ind. 700, 116 N.E.2d 100 (1953).

99. 255 N.C. 473, 121 S.E.2d 854 (1961).

by the state constitution and statutes, held that only the punishment and possibly the degree of the offense had been abrogated.[100] Suicide retained its criminal character, and was declared to be a misdemeanor punishable by fine or imprisonment in the county jail.[101] The court also stated that those who aided or abetted another in the commission of a suicide, or those who accidently killed another while attempting suicide or survived a suicide pact, could be held to be guilty as an accessory to self-murder, and criminal penalties could therefore be imposed.[102] The North Carolina Legislature, however, abolished the crimes of suicide and attempted suicide in 1973.[103]

In 1904, the Kentucky Court of Appeals in *Commonwealth v. Hicks*[104] construed the state murder statute to include suicide as an offense, on the ground that suicide was murder at common law.[105] Consequently, the defendant, who was charged with being an accessory to self-murder, was subject to the same punishment as for the crime of murder in the first degree.[106] In *Commonwealth v. Mink*,[107] the Massachusetts Supreme Judicial Court declared that the repeal of the act that made suicide a crime and the failure of the legislature to enact a statute providing for punishment for attempted suicide did not change the character of suicide to a lawful or non-criminal act.[108] The court acknowledged that suicide was not "technically a felony in this [state]," but stated that the commission of a suicide was nevertheless criminal and unlawful as *malum in se*.[109]

---

100. *Id.* at 476, 121 S.E.2d at 856. The relevant statute provides that only those crimes that were felonies at common law or are punishable by death or imprisonment are felonies, and all others are misdemeanors. The statutory requirements have remained the same under the present statute. N.C. GEN. STAT. § 4.1 (1986).

101. *Willis*, 255 N.C. at 477, 121 S.E.2d at 856-57.

102. *Id.*

103. N.C. GEN. STAT. ch. 14, § 17.1 (1986).

104. 118 Ky. 637, 82 S.W. 265 (1904).

105. *Id.*

106. *Id.* at 639, 82 S.W. at 266-67. The statute imposed the penalty of death or life imprisonment for "willful murder." KY. STAT. § 1149 (1903) (cited in *Hicks*, 118 Ky. at 638, 82 S.W. at 266). *Hicks* was cited with approval in Dugan v. Commonwealth, 333 S.W.2d 755, 756 (Ky. 1960), in which the court stated that an attempt to commit suicide would be deemed "a voluntary and intentional wrongful act." *Id.*

107. 123 Mass. 422 (1877).

108. *Id.* at 428-29.

109. *Id.* at 429. The court further stated that suicide attempts are also unlawful and criminal. Therefore, the accidental killing of another during a suicide attempt was grounds for a finding of guilt for murder. *Id.* This is consistent with the earlier Massachusetts cases, including Commonwealth v. Bowen, 13 Mass. 356 (1816), the first recorded case dealing with assisting or counseling a person to commit suicide. Although it was not explicitly stated in *Bowen* that suicide is a crime, the court did hold that the "act of advising to the commission of a *crime* is of

Suicide was declared to be *malum in se* and a felony by the South Carolina Supreme Court in *State v. Levelle.*[110] The court based its decision on the fact that the statute establishing the reporting method to be used by the coroner in cases of suicide uses the term "feloniously."[111] In *Southern Life & Health Ins. Co. v. Wynn,*[112] the Court of Appeals of Alabama adopted the common law view that suicide is a voluntary act of criminal self-destruction with felonious intent.[113] While there have been no suicide prosecutions in Alabama or South Carolina, nor any cases upholding the statements in *Wynn* or *Levelle,* at least two commentators have stated that suicide is still a crime in Alabama and South Carolina.[114]

Prior to 1971, there was some confusion in New Jersey concerning the criminal or non-criminal nature of suicide. In 1901, the Court of Errors and Appeals in *Campbell v. Supreme Conclave Improved Order Heptasophs*[115] held that neither suicide nor attempted suicide were criminal on the ground that the state constitution, enacted in

---

itself unlawful." *Id.* at 358. Because the defendant was charged with aiding a suicide, the underlying act, the suicide, was implicitly declared to be criminal. The holding in *Mink* is also consistent with the court's previous determination in Commonwealth v. Dennis, 105 Mass. 162 (1870). The court in *Dennis* held that an attempt to commit suicide was not punishable in the absence of a statute providing for modes of punishment, even though the underlying offense, the suicide, was prohibited by law. *Id.* Two later cases cited *Mink* with approval, stating that suicide is a criminal offense. Fernald's Case, 240 Mass. 547, 134 N.E. 347 (1922); Hughes v. New England Newspaper Pub. Co., 312 Mass. 178, 43 N.E.2d 657 (1942). In the latest Massachusetts case involving a suicide, the issue of whether the act was a crime was not addressed because the case was decided on other grounds, but the court implied that defendant's conduct in taunting his wife to shoot herself was in the nature of wanton and reckless disregard for life, rather than assisting a suicide. Persampieri v. Commonwealth, 343 Mass. 19, 175 N.E.2d 387 (1961). The court in Brophy v. New England Sinai Hosp., Inc., 398 Mass. 417, 497 N.E.2d 626 (1986), however, in recognizing a right to refuse medical treatment in some instances, stated in a footnote that "[o]f course, the law does not permit suicide." *Id.* at 430 n.29, 497 N.E.2d at 635 n.29.

110. 34 S.C. 120, 13 S.E. 319 (1890).

111. *Id.* at 131, 13 S.E. at 321. This decision was followed almost two decades later by the court's ruling in State v. Jones, 86 S.C. 17, 67 S.E. 160 (1910) upholding the trial court's instruction to the jury that a person who persuades another to commit suicide and whose acts rise to the level of participation in the act is guilty of murder. This naturally implies that suicide is itself a crime, because guilt would necessarily be premised on participation in a criminal act.

112. 29 Ala. App. 207, 194 So. 421 (1940).

113. *Id.* at 208, 194 So. 421 at 424. The court stated that it must be shown that the act was voluntary and made with "felonious intent" in order to be deemed a suicide. *Id.* What is meant by felonious intent is not entirely clear from the opinion.

114. D. MEYERS, *supra* note 94, § 7:11, at 133; *Criminal Aspects, supra* note 82, at 157. The Alabama Court of Appeals in Penn Mutual Life Ins. Co. v. Cobbs, 23 Ala. App. 205, 123 So. 94 (1929) implied that suicide was still to be considered a crime, stating that a showing of felonious intent is involved in cases concerning suicide. *But see* McCorkle v. State, 446 So. 2d 684 (Ala. Crim. App. 1984), in which the court stated that there is no legal duty to live imposed by statute in Alabama, and that there is no provision in the criminal code prohibiting suicide.

115. 66 N.J.L. 274, 49 A. 550 (1901).

1796, abolished the punishment of forfeiture for suicides. Two years later, however, the Supreme Court of New Jersey in *State v. Carney*[116] held that attempted suicide was a misdemeanor. The court in *Carney*, without explicitly overruling *Campbell*, stated that while the state constitution abolished forfeiture, this did not affect the criminal nature of the act.[117] The holding in *Carney*, that attempted suicide is a misdemeanor, was upheld in a number of subsequent cases.[118] In 1957, the New Jersey Legislature adopted a statute specifically declaring attempted suicide to be illegal.[119] In 1971, however, the New Jersey Legislature reversed its position by repealing the 1957 law.[120]

B. CURRENT STATISTICS AND VIEWPOINTS ON EUTHANASIA

According to statistics compiled by the Hemlock Society,[121] incidences of all forms of euthanasia occurring in only the last eleven years, which includes murder/suicide, double suicide, mercy killing, assisted suicide, and autoeuthanasia, constitute more than 85% of all reported incidences of euthanasia.[122] Ninety-seven percent of all murder/suicides, almost 90% of double suicides, 71% of assisted suicides, and 72% of all mercy killings have occurred since 1980.[123] Between 1920 and 1989 there were 293 reported cases of euthanasia, and 115 reported cases of mercy killing.[124] It appears at first glance that this indicates an alarming rise in the incidence of euthanasia; however, it must be recognized that these statistics measure only those cases that were reported. With the heightened attention on this area, it is likely that the increase is due at least in part to more stringent reporting of

---

116. 69 N.J.L. 478, 55 A. 44 (1903).

117. *Id.* at 479, 55 A. at 45. The court based its decision on section 215 of the then existing Crimes Act, which stated that all offenses indictable at common law were misdemeanors unless specifically provided otherwise by statute. The fact that no punishment was available for successful suicides did not deter the court from its holding, nor did the fact that the offense was not indictable.

118. *See* Potts v. Allied Chemical & Dye Corp., 48 N.J. Super. 554, 138 A.2d 574 (1958); Green v. Simpson & Brown Constr. Co., 24 N.J. Super. 422, 94 A.2d 693 (1953); Jochim v. Montrose Chemical Co., 3 N.J. 5, 68 A.2d 628 (1949); State v. LaFayette, 15 N.J. Misc. 115, 188 A. 918 (1937).

119. N.J. STAT. ANN. § 2A-170-25-6 (West 1957) (cited in *Criminal Aspects, supra* note 82, at 158 n.14).

120. N.J. STAT. ANN. § 2A-85-5.1 (West 1971).

121. For more information concerning the Hemlock Society, see *infra* notes 220-21 and accompanying text.

122. HEMLOCK SOCIETY, CASES OF EUTHANASIA, MURDER AND ASSISTED SUICIDE (1987) (updated on Dec. 6, 1990).

123. *Id.*

124. *Id.*

such cases. It is also arguable that this escalation is due to an increased awareness of euthanasia resulting from efforts on the part of organizations such as the Hemlock Society, and an increase in the number of persons whose lives have been prolonged, sometimes against their wishes, by the advent of new medical technology.

In a 1988 poll conducted by the Roper Organization of New York,[125] 58% of those surveyed stated that physicians should be allowed to assist a terminally ill patient to commit suicide without the threat of legal sanctions.[126] When broken down into demographic subgroups,[127] only one of the subgroups, blacks, did not have a group majority in favor of legalizing physician-assisted suicide.[128] These results are virtually identical to the results of the same poll taken two years earlier, which found that 62% were in favor of allowing physicians to aid the terminally ill in committing suicide.[129] In addition, 72% of those polled felt that doctors should be bound by patients' requests regarding the termination of life support, as evidenced by a living will.[130]

The medical profession's attitude toward this issue also appears to be moving in the direction of recognizing the need to defer to the patient's wishes—including the desire to end life. The majority of doctors responding to a recent survey favored euthanasia in some form for terminally ill patients.[131] In 1988, the Center for Health Ethics and Policy at the University of Colorado conducted a survey regarding views on euthanasia, and received answers from over 2,000 physicians. The results indicated that 60% had patients for which euthanasia was

---

125. Surveys of 1,982 American adults were included in the results. THE ROPER ORGANIZA-TION, ATTITUDES TOWARD ACTIVE VOLUNTARY EUTHANASIA (1988) [hereinafter ROPER POLL].

126. *Id.*

127. The subgroups were based on religion, sex, race, income level, occupation, geographic location, education, political affiliation, political philosophy, union membership, and the presence of children in the household. *Id.*

128. *Id.*

129. *Id.*

130. ROPER POLL. In a survey of 10,545 individuals in Colorado following a two-year program on "hard choices in medical care," 83% believed that doctors should follow patients' wishes with regard to the termination of treatment, 62% preferred death to the sustaining of life by artificial means, and 85% expressed the desire to end their life rather than be in a permanent, unconscious state. *Colorado Votes for Quality of Life*, 35 HEMLOCK Q. 4 (Apr. 1989). Other polls indicate that 80% of Americans do not oppose passive euthanasia (allowing a person to die) and 60% favor active euthanasia (taking some action to hasten death). *Q. and A. on the Hemlock Society*, 34 HEMLOCK Q. 4, 5 (Jan. 1989) [hereinafter *Q. and A.*].

131. *Doctors' Views on Dying are Changing*, 35 HEMLOCK Q. 3 (Apr. 1989).

justified if it were legal.[132] A panel of doctors recently concluded that
it was within the scope of professional ethics for physicians to assist
the terminally ill to commit suicide by prescribing drugs for that purpose.[133] The Hippocratic Oath forbids abortion and euthanasia; however, only 6% of medical schools in this country use the classic form
of this oath.[134]

C.   CURRENT LEGAL STATUS OF SUICIDE AND ATTEMPTING SUICIDE

Attempted suicide, which was a misdemeanor at common law, is
no longer a crime in any state in this country.[135] In New Jersey,
attempted suicide was at one time a disorderly persons offense, but
that provision was repealed in 1972.[136] While suicide is not a crime in
any state, some states have a provision stating that certain practices,
including mercy killing and suicide, are not condoned.[137] A majority
of states have enacted provisions, ordinarily as part of a natural death
act, that declare that the withholding or withdrawal of life sustaining

---

132. *Id.* The survey also indicated that approximately 60% favored the legalizing of euthanasia but, of those, 50% would not practice it themselves. *Id..*

133. Haney, *Doctors Ethically Can Aid Suicide of Terminally Ill, Panel Decides*, The Orego-
nian, Mar. 30, 1989. The report is published in the New England Journal of Medicine dated
March 30, 1989.

134. *Medicine Divided on Its Oaths*, 39 HEMLOCK Q. 2 (July 1990). Forty-two percent of
medical schools use a modified version of the Hippocratic Oath, 28% use the Declaration of
Geneva, which was written in 1948 by the World Medical Association, and others use an oath
authored by Dr. Louis Lasagna. *Id.* Dr. Lasagna's oath recognizes that "it may also be within
my power to take a life." *Id.*

135. *Q. and A., supra* note 130. The last states with statutes making attempted suicide a
crime have repealed those statutes in the last decade. OKLA. STAT. ANN. tit. 21, § 812 (West
1976) (repealed 1976); TEX. REV. CIV. STAT. ANN. art 609 (Vernon 1962) (repealed 1962);
WASH. REV. CODE § 9:80:220 (1975) (repealed 1975). In a comment to its murder statute, however, the Alabama legislature stated that, while aiding suicide was specifically left out of the
criminal code, decisions concerning prosecutions of "exceptional cases" for murder or manslaughter would be left to the discretion of the grand jury. ALA. CODE § 13A-6-3 (1975), and
comments. This could be read to include prosecutions for attempted suicide. The Kansas Judicial Council of 1968, in a comment to section 21-3406 of the Kansas Criminal Code, stated that
"suicide is not now a crime in Kansas." KAN. CRIM. CODE ANN. § 21-3406 (Vernon 1988).
The advisory committee comment to section 609.125 of the Minnesota Code also states that
suicide and attempted suicide are no longer crimes in Minnesota. MINN. STAT. ANN. § 609.125
(West 1987).

136. N.J. STAT. ANN. § 2A:170-25.6 (West 1972) (repealed 1972).

137. Most of the codes, rather than specifically naming suicide, refer to affirmative acts or
omissions to end life except to permit nature to take its course. CAL. CIV. CODE § 2443 (West
Supp. 1990); FLA. STAT. ANN. § 765.11(1) (West 1986); LA. REV. STAT. ANN.
§ 40:1299.58.10(A) (West Supp. 1990); MINN. STAT. ANN. § 145B.14 (West 1990); MO. REV.
STAT. § 459.055(5) (Vernon Supp. 1990); OR. REV. STAT. §§ 127.570, 127.645 (Supp. 1990);
UTAH CODE ANN. § 75-2-1118 (1953); WIS. STAT. ANN. § 154.11 (West 1989).

procedures does not constitute suicide.[138] South Dakota has a statute that places a duty on police officers to report any known attempted suicides to the state's attorney.[139] Many states have provisions authorizing the use of force to prevent suicides.[140] In addition, a few states have provided that involuntary committal to an institution of persons who attempt suicide is permitted if it is reasonably probable that the person will make another attempt.[141] One state, Tennessee, has a provision allowing police officers to arrest, without a warrant, persons attempting suicide.[142]

In some cases, persons who attempted suicide were prosecuted for murder or manslaughter when a third party was killed while trying to stop the attempt. In the first of such cases, *Commonwealth v. Mink*,[143] the court held the defendant guilty of manslaughter for the death of her fiance. The deceased was killed in a struggle with the defendant

---

138. ALA. CODE § 22-8A-9 (1975); ALASKA STAT. § 18.12.080 (1986); ARIZ. REV. STAT. ANN. § 36-3208 (1986); ARK. STAT. ANN. § 20-17-210 (Supp. 1989); CAL. HEALTH & SAFETY CODE § 7192 (West Supp. 1990); COLO. REV. STAT. § 15-18-111 (1987); DEL. CODE ANN. tit. 16, § 2507 (1974); FLA. STAT. ANN. § 765.11 (West 1986); GA. CODE ANN. § 31-32-9 (1985); HAW. REV. STAT. § 327D-14 (1985); IND. CODE ANN. § 16-8-11-18 (Burns 1990); IOWA CODE ANN. § 144 A.11 (West 1989); LA. REV. STAT. ANN. § 40:1299.58.10 (West Supp. 1990); ME. REV. STAT. ANN. tit. 22, § 2929 (1964); MD. HEALTH-GEN. CODE ANN. § 5-613 (1990); NEV. REV. STAT. ANN. § 449.650 (Michie 1986); N.M. STAT. ANN. § 24-7-8 (1953); N.C. GEN. STAT. § 90-321 (1990); TENN. CODE ANN. 32-11-110 (1984); TEX. HEALTH & SAFETY CODE ANN. § 672.017 (Vernon 1991); UTAH CODE ANN. § 75-2-1116 (1953); VT. STAT. ANN. tit. 18, § 5260 (1987); VA. CODE ANN. § 54.1-2991 (1950); WASH. REV. CODE ANN. § 70.122.070 (1975); W. VA. CODE § 16-30-8 (1985); WIS. STAT. ANN. § 154.11 (West 1989).

139. S.D. CODIFIED LAWS ANN. § 22-16-40 (1988). The purpose of this provision is unclear because suicide and attempted suicide are not crimes in South Dakota.

140. ALA. CODE § 13A-3-24 (1975) (reasonable physical force); ALASKA STAT. § 11.81.430 (1989) (nondeadly force); ARIZ. REV. STAT. ANN. § 13-403 (1989) (physical force); ARK. STAT. ANN. § 5-2-605 (1987) (nondeadly force); COLO. REV. STAT. § 18-1-703 (1986) (reasonable and appropriate physical force); CONN. GEN. STAT. ANN. § 53a-18 (West Supp. 1990) (reasonable physical force); DEL. CODE ANN. tit. 11, § 467 (1974) (force); HAW. REV. STAT. § 703-308 (1985) (force); KY. REV. STAT. ANN. § 503.100 (Baldwin 1985) (physical force); ME. REV. STAT. ANN. tit. 17A, § 106 (1964) (reasonably necessary force); MO. ANN. STAT. § 563.061 (Vernon 1979) (physical force); NEB. REV. STAT. § 28-1412 (1943) (physical force); N.J. STAT. ANN. § 2C:3-7(e) (West 1982) (force); N.Y. PENAL LAW § 35.10 (McKinney 1987) (reasonably necessary physical force); OR. REV. STAT. § 161.205 (1983) (reasonably necessary physical force); 18 PA. CONS. STAT. ANN. § 508 (Purdon 1983) (force); TENN. CODE ANN. § 39-11-613 (1984) (nondeadly force); TEX. PENAL CODE ANN. § 9.34 (Vernon 1974) (nondeadly force); WIS. STAT. ANN. § 939.48 (West 1982) (reasonably necessary force).

141. ARK. STAT. ANN. § 20-47-207 (Supp. 1989); HAW. REV. STAT. § 334-59 (1985); N.H. REV. STAT. ANN. § 135-C:27 (1990); N.M. STAT. ANN. § 43-1-10 (1953); N.Y. MENTAL HYG. LAW §§ 9.37, 9.39, 9.41 (1988 & Supp. 1990); 50 PA. CONS. STAT. ANN. § 7301 (Purdon Supp. 1990); R.I. GEN. LAWS § 40.1-5.3-4 (1956); WIS. STAT. ANN. §§ 51.15, 51.20 (West Supp. 1990).

142. TENN. CODE ANN. § 40-7-103(5) (Supp. 1990).

143. 123 Mass. 422 (1877).

during an attempt by the defendant to commit suicide. The court based its ruling on the fact that suicide was a crime; therefore, a death arising out of that unlawful act would be considered criminal homicide.[144] The court, while not reversing the verdict of manslaughter, stated that it considered the jury instruction too lenient, evidencing a belief that the act of committing suicide was sufficiently legally malicious to warrant a conviction for murder.[145]

In *State v. Levelle*,[146] the defendant was convicted for the murder of his wife, who was killed while trying to stop his suicide attempt. The court stated that the law implies that a person committing an unlawful act[147] is presumed to have intended the natural or probable consequences of that act, and is responsible for those consequences; therefore, a jury instruction charging that a death resulting from an attempt to stop a suicide would constitute murder was proper.[148] In *Dugan v. Commonwealth*,[149] the Kentucky Court of Appeals cited *Mink* and *Levelle* with approval, stating that "the accidental killing of another person, in the course of an attempt to commit suicide, is a criminal homicide amounting at least to involuntary manslaughter."[150]

The Iowa Supreme Court, however, in *State v. Campbell*,[151] reversed the defendant's conviction for murder on the ground that, because suicide is not unlawful in Iowa, the death of a third party

---

144. *Id.* at 428. The court further stated that the deceased had a right and a duty to prevent the suicide, and the accidental shooting arising from the exercise of that right or duty constituted manslaughter. *Id.* at 429.

145. *Id.*

146. 34 S.C. 120, 13 S.E. 319 (1891).

147. The court recognized the unlawful character of suicide, stating that the use of the term "feloniously" in a statute referring to suicide evidenced legislative intent to retain the felony nature of suicide. *Id.* at 130-31, 13 S.E. at 321. *See also* Wallace v. State, 232 Ind. 700, 116 N.E.2d 100 (1953) (self-destruction, while not necessarily criminal, "is against the law of God and man").

148. 34 S.C. 130-31, 13 S.E. at 321.

149. 333 S.W.2d 755 (Ky. 1960). At the time of this decision, the court of appeals was the highest court in Kentucky.

150. *Id.* at 756. *See also* People v. Chrisholtz, 55 Misc. 2d 309, 285 N.Y.S.2d 231 (N.Y. Sup. Ct. 1967). The court in *Chrisholtz* denied defendant's motion for dismissal of a second degree manslaughter indictment. The defendant claimed that the deceased's death was purely accidental, the result of an attempt to stop the defendant from committing suicide and, therefore, legally insufficient to sustain a conviction. Stating that suicide is a "grave public wrong" which had previously been characterized as an illegal act and *malum in se*, although not punishable as a crime, the court held that this evidence would warrant a conviction by a trial jury. *Id.* at 313, 285 N.Y.S.2d at 233 (citing Shipman v. Protected Home Circle, 174 N.Y. 398, 406, 67 N.E. 83, 85 (1903)).

151. 217 Iowa 848, 251 N.W. 717 (1933).

while trying to stop a suicide attempt was not sufficient to constitute murder, in the absence of evidence of malice aforethought and the other elements of the offense of murder.[152] The court did not rule out the possibility of a manslaughter conviction for reckless use of a weapon on the same facts, but made its decision solely on the error assigned in the case.[153]

In some states, survivors of suicide pacts have been held to be guilty of manslaughter or murder when the other party to the pact dies.[154] In *Turner v. State*,[155] the Tennessee Supreme Court upheld the defendant's first degree murder conviction. The defendant claimed to have killed the deceased in furtherance of a suicide pact and with the victim's consent. The court stated that consent of the victim does not reduce the degree of the crime, and that the existence of a joint agreement to commit suicide did not negate the culpability for murder.[156] In *McMahan v. State*,[157] the defendant alleged that the trial judge erred in instructing the jury that the survivor of a death compact or agreement would be guilty of murder. The Alabama Supreme Court upheld the conviction, citing with approval a criminal law treatise that stated that the survivor is guilty of murder under the doctrine of unlawful combination.[158] In *State v. Willis*,[159] the North Carolina Supreme Court upheld a criminal indictment charging the defendant with attempting suicide. While not faced with a suicide pact situation, the court cited *Turner* and *McMahan* with approval, stating that when only one of the two who agree to kill themselves dies, the other party is subject to prosecution for murder.[160]

In the two most recent cases involving suicide pacts, both courts held that the survivor could not be held guilty of murder. The California Supreme Court in *In re Joseph G*,[161] after discussing the difference between genuine suicide pacts and murder/suicides, held that the

---

152. *Id.* at 851, 251 N.W. at 719.

153. *Id.*

154. In England, the survivor of a suicide pact is deemed to be guilty of manslaughter regardless of the nature of the pact. Homicide Act of 1957 ch. 11, § 4.

155. 119 Tenn. 663, 108 S.W. 1139 (1908).

156. *Id.* at 665, 108 S.W. at 1141. The court stated that all of the elements of murder were present in the case, including malice, deliberation and premeditation. *Id.* Malice was found in the "actual and deliberate intention to take the life of [the victim]." *Id.*

157. 168 Ala. 70, 53 So. 89 (1910).

158. *Id.* at 72, 53 So. at 91 (citing McCLAIN ON CRIMINAL LAW § 290). The court necessarily had to find that suicide was felonious in nature in order to uphold the conviction, as it stated that the act of suicide must be *felo de se* for the contributor to be guilty. *Id.*

159. 255 N.C. 473, 121 S.E.2d 854 (1961).

160. *Id.* at 476, 121 S.E.2d at 857.

161. 34 Cal. 3d 429, 667 P.2d 1176, 194 Cal. Rptr. 163 (1983).

defendant, a minor, could not be found guilty of a crime other than aiding and abetting a suicide. The court stated that in a murder/suicide, one person kills the other prior to killing himself, while in a genuine suicide pact, each person kills himself either by separate means or simultaneously with a common instrumentality.[162] In the former, the active participation in the death of the victim would constitute action sufficient for a finding of murder.[163] The court held, however, that suicides pursuant to an agreement or pact do not give rise to culpability for murder, as this would result in punishment for attempted suicide.[164]

In addition, the potential for fraudulent allegations of suicide in order to escape liability for murder is greater in murder/suicide cases, which justifies the imposition of more severe penalties.[165] In *State v. Sage*,[166] the Ohio Supreme Court held that the survivor of a suicide pact was not guilty of any crime under Ohio law, stating that "[t]he assertion that death was the result of a mutual suicide pact is a complete defense to any crime by the survivor."[167] The court based its conclusion on the fact that suicide, attempted suicide, and aiding and abetting a suicide are not crimes in Ohio.[168]

D. CURRENT LEGAL STATUS OF AIDING OR ASSISTING A SUICIDE

A number of states have enacted statutes prohibiting the aiding or abetting of a suicide.[169] The provisions vary in their terms and penalties. Nine states include the offense within the crime of manslaughter, requiring intentional, purposeful or knowing assistance of the suicide.[170] Seventeen other states recognize a separate crime of aiding,

---

162. *Id.* at 434, 667 P.2d at 1180, 194 Cal. Rptr. at 167.

163. *Id.*

164. *Id.*

165. *Id.* at 435, 667 P.2d at 1182, 194 Cal. Rptr. at 167.

166. 31 Ohio St. 3d 173, 510 N.E.2d 343 (1987).

167. *Id.* at 177, 510 N.E.2d at 347.

168. *Id.* The court referred to the decision in *Joseph G*, distinguishing the result on the basis that California had a statute making aiding and abetting a suicide a crime. *Id.*

169. It is still a crime in England to aid or assist another in committing or attempting suicide. *See supra* note 93.

170. ALASKA STAT. § 11.41.120(a)(2) (1982) (class A felony); ARIZ. REV. STAT. ANN. § 13-1103(A)(3) (1989) (class 3 felony); ARK. STAT. ANN. § 5-10-104(a)(2) (1987) (class C felony); COLO. REV. STAT. § 18-3-104(1)(b) (1986) (class 4 felony); CONN. GEN. STAT. ANN. § 53a-56(a)(2) (West 1975) (class C felony); FLA. STAT. § 782.08 (1976) (second degree felony); HAW. REV. STAT. § 707-702(1)(b) (1985) (class B felony); MO. ANN. STAT. § 565.023.1(2) (Vernon Supp. 1984) (class B felony); OR. REV. STAT. § 163.125(1)(b) (1985) (class B felony).

assisting or procuring a suicide.[171] Of those states, some create a separate provision for aiding or assisting an attempted suicide, which usually results in a lesser penalty than when the suicide was successful.[172] In New York, a person who aids or assists another in attempting suicide is guilty of the offense of procuring a suicide, but if the attempt is successful, the person is guilty of second degree murder.[173] Still other statutes provide for penalties even when the conduct of assisting or encouraging suicide does not result in an attempt or a successful suicide.[174] South Dakota has repealed its statute that made aiding an attempted suicide a crime.[175] North Dakota has repealed all provisions concerning suicide.[176] The use of coercion or duress to cause another to commit suicide is a crime in some states.[177] In the absence

---

171. CAL. PENAL § 401 (West 1988) (felony); DEL. CODE ANN. tit. 11, § 645 (1974) (class F felony); IND. CODE ANN. § 35-42-1-2 (Burns 1985) (class B felony); KAN. CRIM. CODE ANN. § 21-3406 (Vernon 1988) (class E felony); ME. REV. STAT. ANN. tit. 17-A, § 204 (1964) (class D crime); MINN. STAT. ANN. § 609.125 (West 1987) (penalty of up to fifteen years imprisonment, or fine of up to $30,000, or both); MISS. CODE ANN. § 97-3-49 (1972) (penalty of up to ten years imprisonment in the penitentiary, or fine up to $1,000 and imprisonment in the county jail for up to one year; NEB. REV. STAT. 28-307 (1989) (CLASS IV FELONY); N.H. REV. STAT. ANN. § 630:4 (1986) (class B felony); N.J. STAT. ANN. § 2C:11-6 (West 1982) (crime of the second degree); N.Y. PENAL LAW § 120.30 (Consol. 1987) (class E felony only for aiding attempted suicides); OKLA. STAT. ANN. tit., 21, §§ 813-815, 817-818 (West 1990) (punishable by not less than seven years in the penitentiary if the suicide is successful; and by imprisonment in the penitentiary for not more than two years, or a fine of not more than $1,000, or both if the attempt is unsuccessful); 18 PA. CONS. STAT. ANN. § 2505 (Purdon 1983) (second degree felony if suicide successful, second degree misdemeanor if the attempt is unsuccessful); S.D. CODIFIED LAWS ANN. § 22-16-37 (1991) (class 6 felony); TEX. PENAL CODE ANN. § 22.08 (Vernon 1989) (class C misdemeanor unless conduct causes serious bodily injury, then third degree felony); WASH. REV. CODE ANN. § 9A.36.060 (1990) (class C felony); WIS. STAT. ANN. § 940.12 (West 1982) (class D felony). In Oklahoma and South Dakota, the incapacity of the person who attempted or committed suicide is not a defense in a prosecution for aiding suicide or attempted suicide. OKLA. STAT. ANN. tit. 21, § 816 (West 1990); S.D. CODIFIED LAWS ANN. § 22-16-39 (1991).

172. MINN. STAT. ANN. § 609.125(2) (West 1987); OKLA. STAT. ANN. tit. 21, §§ 815, 818 (West 1983); 18 PA. CONS. STAT. ANN. § 2505 (1983).

173. N.Y. PENAL LAW § 125.25(1)(b) (Consol. 1987). If the person's conduct rises to the level of coercion or duress, the crime becomes one of murder.

174. N.H. REV. STAT. ANN. § 630:4(II) (1990) (misdemeanor); N.J. STAT. ANN. § 2C:11-6 (West 1982) (fourth degree crime). Montana has a similar statute, which provides for a penalty for the offense of aiding or soliciting a suicide only where the suicide does not occur. MONT. CODE ANN. § 45-5-105 (1989). The provision is unclear concerning whether a person who aids or solicits a successful suicide is guilty of a crime. It would be inconsistent to impose a penalty only for an attempt or solicitation that does not lead to an attempt or a suicide; therefore, it appears that a person aiding or soliciting a suicide that results in a successful attempt could be prosecuted for manslaughter or murder, even in the absence of specific language to that effect in those statutes.

175. S.D. CODIFIED LAWS ANN. § 22-16-38 (repealed 1968).

176. N.D. CENT. CODE § 3303.04 (repealed 1975).

177. ALASKA STAT. § 11.41.100 (1989); CONN. GEN. STAT. ANN. § 53a-54a (West 1983); DEL. CODE ANN. tit. 11, § 636 (1974); ILL. REV. STAT. ch. 38, para. 12-31 (1990) (class 2

of coercion or duress, however, the act of aiding or assisting suicide is an affirmative defense to murder in New York and Oregon.[178]

Commonwealth v. Bowen[179] appears to be the first reported case concerning the solicitation of a suicide. In *Bowen*, the court held that it was not necessary to prove that the counsel given by the accused induced the deceased to commit suicide, but rather, that the act of advising suicide was unlawful due to the criminal nature of suicide.[180] The court did state, however, that if the deceased had a previous inclination to commit suicide, and the accused had merely discussed it with him, this would not rise to the level of counseling or inducing.[181]

In *Grace v. State*,[182] the Texas Court of Criminal Appeals held that merely providing the means for a suicide, even where the accused knew of the victim's intent to commit suicide, does not rise to the level of murder so long as there is no active participation in the actual suicidal act.[183] The person committing suicide is innocent of any crime; therefore, the person furnishing the means did not violate the law in the absence of a specific statute to that effect.[184] The decision in *Grace* was followed six years later in *Sanders v. State*,[185] wherein the court stated that the administering or giving of poison to another in furtherance of a suicide does not constitute murder.[186] The *Sanders* decision was overruled by the criminal appellate court in *Aven v. State*[187] to the extent that it excluded the act of administering the means of the suicide from criminal liability. The court in *Aven* held that mere preparation of poison and placing it within the reach of a potential suicide does not constitute murder or manslaughter in the absence of a specific provision in the criminal code.[188]

The court in *Aven* made the distinction between administering and merely providing the means in furtherance of a suicide which was

---

felony); IND. CODE ANN. § 35-42-1-2 (Burns 1989) (class B felony); ME. REV. STAT. ANN. tit. 17-A, § 201 (1964); N.Y. PENAL LAW § 120.35 (Consol. 1987) (punishable as attempted murder); 18 PA. CONS. STAT. ANN. § 2505(a) (Purdon 1983).

178. N.Y. PENAL LAW § 125.27(2)(b) (Consol. 1987); OR. REV. STAT. § 163.117 (1983).

179. 13 Mass. 356 (1816). It should be noted that the text of this case is as reported in a pamphlet published by a man who attended the trial. The official reporter was not present at the trial. *Id.* note, at 361.

180. *Id.* at 359.

181. *Id.* at 360.

182. 44 Tex. Crim. 193, 69 S.W. 529 (1902).

183. *Id.* at 195, 69 S.W. at 530.

184. *Id.*

185. 54 Tex. Crim. 101, 112 S.W. 68 (1908).

186. *Id.* at 102, 112 S.W. at 69.

187. 102 Tex. Crim. 478, 277 S.W. 1080 (1925).

188. *Id.* at 480-82, 277 S.W. at 1081-83.

in direct contradiction to the principle announced in *Blackburn v. State*[189] by the Ohio Supreme Court. In *Blackburn*, the act of taking poison at the direction of the accused was held to constitute the act of administering.[190] The court further stated that "it is immaterial whether the party taking the poison took it willingly . . . or was overcome by force, or overreached by fraud."[191] The intent of the deceased to commit suicide did not change the nature of the act of administration as constituting murder, even where the administering was done in furtherance of a suicide pact.[192]

Following these decisions, and prior to the adoption of statutes concerning aiding and abetting, the level of conduct that gave rise to criminal liability for inciting a suicide continued to be a matter of debate. In *State v. Jones*,[193] the South Carolina Supreme Court upheld a jury instruction that the incitement to commit suicide must be a producing cause of the act in order for the accused to be guilty of murder, and the question of whether the counseling or persuasion was sufficient participation was for the jury.[194] In *Commonwealth v. Hicks*,[195] the court held that providing morphine to a person who had expressed the intent to commit suicide did not rise to the level of activity sufficient to punish the provider as an accessory. In *Hicks*, the Kentucky Court of Appeals based its decision on the findings of the trial judge that the accused believed that the deceased was joking at the time he stated he was going to kill himself.[196]

In *Burnett v. People*,[197] the Illinois Supreme Court held that mere knowledge of the deceased's intent to commit suicide and assent to that intent was insufficient to constitute murder, but that evidence of any level of inducement would sustain a murder conviction.[198] The Michigan Supreme Court, in *People v. Roberts*,[199] upheld the defendant's murder conviction based on his mixing of poison and placement

---

189. 23 Ohio St. 146 (1872).

190. *Id.* at 163.

191. *Id.* at 162-63.

192. *Id.* at 163. For a discussion on the criminal liability of the survivor of a suicide pact, *see supra* notes 154-64.

193. 86 S.C. 17, 67 S.E. 160 (1910).

194. *Id.* at 21-22, 67 S.E. at 162.

195. 118 Ky. 637, 82 S.W. 265 (1904). The defendant was tried as an accessory because, at that time, suicide was considered a crime in Kentucky, and no statute existed that made aiding and abetting suicide a crime. *Id.* at 640, 82 S.W. at 266.

196. *Id.* at 640, 82 S.W. at 267.

197. 204 Ill. 208, 68 N.E. 505 (1903).

198. *Id.* at 218-20, 68 N.E. at 511.

199. 211 Mich. 187, 178 N.W. 690 (1920).

of it within the reach of his bedridden wife. The court found that the mixing of the poison with water and making it available constituted the act of administering poison, and was therefore, murder within the meaning of the statute criminalizing the administering of poison.[200] The fact that the poison was placed at the request of the deceased had no bearing on the guilt or innocence of the defendant.[201]

In 1983, the Michigan Court of Appeals in *People v. Campbell*,[202] stated that it is "extremely doubtful" that aiding or soliciting a suicide was a crime at common law, and that suicide, by definition, excludes homicide. The court held that the act of providing a gun and bullets to a person who had expressed the intent to commit suicide, while "morally reprehensible," was not a crime under the existing law of Michigan, and invited the legislature to adopt a provision regarding inciting suicides as had been proposed.[203] In so ruling, the court found that *Roberts* was no longer the law in Michigan.[204] The statement by the court in *Campbell*, that aiding suicide was not a common law crime, was supported by the Iowa Supreme Court in *State v. Marti*.[205] In *Marti*, the court upheld the trial court's ruling that, because suicide is not a crime, aiding and abetting suicide cannot be punished as criminal.[206]

The lack of a statute making aiding or soliciting suicide a crime did not stop two courts from imposing criminal liability on other grounds for acts that would ordinarily fall within such a statute. In *Persampieri v. Commonwealth*,[207] the Supreme Judicial Court of Massachusetts held that the defendant's conduct in mocking his wife's failed suicide attempts, and daring her to try again "could be found to

---

200. *Id.* at 193, 178 N.W. at 693.
201. *Id.*
202. 124 Mich. App. 333, 335 N.W.2d 27 (1983).
203. *Id.* at 337-38, 335 N.W.2d at 29-30.
204. *Id.*
205. 290 N.W.2d 570 (Iowa 1980).
206. *Id.* at 579. In August of 1990, a California man and his wife, who was terminally ill with cancer, traveled to Michigan so that he could aid her in committing suicide. The couple chose Michigan on the basis of the lack of a statute banning assisted suicides, a fact known to them from the coverage of the Kevorkian case. For a discussion of the Kevorkian case, *see infra* notes 213-17 and accompanying text. The man tied a plastic bag to his wife's head, resulting in her asphyxiation death, then called the police. The man has been charged with murder in the death on the ground that, while assisting suicide is not banned by statute in Michigan, no one has the right to aid in this "self-destruction." *Murder Trial Is Ordered for Man Who Helped Wife Commit Suicide*, N.Y. Times, Sep. 8, 1990, § 1, at 10. Prosecutors also cited the need to discourage the view that Michigan is a "haven for . . . suicides." *Second Assisted-Suicide Case Spurs Concern in Michigan*, LA. Times, Aug. 24, 1990, pt. P, at 2; Byland, *Man Charged With Murder After Helping Wife Commit Suicide*, Reuters, Aug. 24, 1990.
207. 343 Mass. 19, 175 N.E.2d 387 (1961).

be criminally wanton or reckless." In *State v. Bier*,[208] the Montana Supreme Court upheld the defendant's conviction for negligent homicide based on his conduct in placing a loaded, cocked gun within the reach of his intoxicated and suicidal wife, who subsequently killed herself with the gun. The court stated that not only was this conduct the "cause in fact" of the death, it also foreseeably endangered the victim, thus giving rise to criminal liability.[209]

While there is still some debate over how much participation in the suicide is necessary to constitute aiding or abetting, in cases where the accused committed the actual act that caused the death of the deceased, the courts have unanimously declared the act to constitute murder rather than aiding or abetting a suicide.[210] In each case, the court determined that the accused's overt participation in the act caused the death of the victim; therefore, refusal by the trial court to allow jury instructions on the lesser offense of aiding suicide was proper.[211]

There have been no cases reported in which a physician was convicted for aiding, abetting, or assisting a suicide under either the common law or the existing statutes.[212] In a highly publicized incident in

---

208. 181 Mont. 27, 591 P.2d 1115 (1979).

209. *Id.* at 32-33, 591 P.2d at 1118.

210. People v. Matlock, 51 Cal. 2d 682, 336 P.2d 505 (1959); State v. Cobb, 229 Kan. 522, 625 P.2d 1133 (1981); State v. Fuller, 203 Neb. 233, 278 N.W.2d 756 (1979), *modified*, 281 N.W.2d 749 (1980).

211. *Matlock*, 51 Cal. 2d at 688, 336 P.2d at 511; *Cobb*, 229 Kan. at 527, 625 P.2d at 1136; *Fuller*, 203 Neb. at 239, 278 N.W.2d at 760.

212. D. MEYERS, *supra* note 94, § 7:12, at 133; Engelhardt & Malloy, *supra* note 96, at 1029. Over the past century, eleven doctors have been charged with murder in the death of a patient or family member. *The Hemlock Society*, 34 HEMLOCK Q. 6 (Jan. 1989) (updated by newsletter, Dec. 1990). The cases include: Dr. Harold Blazer in 1935 (acquitted of murdering 30-year-old daughter, a victim of spinal meningitis, with chloroform); Dr. Hermann N. Sanders in 1950 (acquitted of murdering terminally ill patient by lethal injection); Dr. Vincent Montemarano in 1972 (acquitted of murder in death of terminally ill patient by lethal injection); Drs. Robert Nedjil and Neil Barber in 1981 (murder charges arising out of the termination of ventilation and fluids to patient in "hopeless" coma dismissed on appeal); Dr. John Kraal in 1985 (committed suicide before charges could be filed after injecting lethal dose of insulin in chest of patient suffering from Alzheimer's disease and gangrene of the foot); Dr. Joseph Hassman in 1986 (found guilty of murder and sentenced to two year probation, fined $10,000, and ordered to perform community service for injecting patient suffering from Alzheimer's disease with lethal dose of Demerol at the family's request); Dr. Peter Rosier in 1987 (acquitted of murder in death of wife after injection of morphine—deceased actually died after being suffocated by stepfather without Rosier's knowledge); Dr. Donald Caraccio in 1989 (sentenced to five years probation and community service after pleading guilty to murder charges in death of comatose, terminally ill patient from lethal injection of potassium chloride); Dr. Richard Schaeffer in 1990 (arrested but not yet charged in death of patient caused by lethal injection while at home after suffering a stroke); and Dr. Jack Kevorkian in 1990 (murder charges stemming from use of "suicide machine" in death of Alzheimer's victim dismissed on grounds that aiding suicide was not criminal under Michigan

June of 1990, Dr. Jack Kevorkian of Ann Arbor, Michigan, used the "suicide machine" he invented to assist a woman suffering from Alzheimer's disease to commit suicide.[213] Dr. Kevorkian was charged with murder for his participation in the death,[214] a charge that was later dismissed by the trial judge after a determination that Michigan has no statute that makes aiding suicide a criminal act.[215] A temporary injunction, issued in November of 1990,[216] prohibiting the further use of the device was made permanent in February of 1991. The Kevorkian case has resulted in the proposal of legislation making the assisting of a suicide a felony in Michigan.[217]

A Death With Dignity Initiative, officially known as Initiative 119,[218] will be on the ballot in Washington which will amend the state's Natural Death Act to allow terminally ill patients to die with

---

law). *Id.* For a more complete discussion of Dr. Kevorkian's case, *see infra* notes 213-17 and accompanying text.

213. For a sample of the myriad articles concerning Dr. Kevorkian and his suicide machine, *see Suicide Doctor Might Disobey Court Order,* United Press International, Oct. 4, 1990; *Murder Trial Is Ordered for Man Who Helped Wife Commit Suicide,* N.Y. Times, Sep. 8, 1990, § 1, at 10; *Man to Stand Trial for Murder in Michigan Suicide Case,* Reuters, Sep. 7, 1990; Goldstein, *"Thanks for Life, Mere Life"; The Pursuit of Physical Perfection Is a Ritual of Faith in Science. It Leaves Us Unprepared for the Ultimate Life Experience,* L.A. Times, Sep. 1, 1990, pt. B, at 7; Borger, *The Odd Odyssey of "Dr. Death,"* U.S. News & World Report, Aug. 27, 1990, at 27; Botsford, *In America: With a Little Help From Dr. Death,* The Independent, Aug. 18, 1990, at 17; Byland, *Judge Threatens Injunction in Michigan Suicide-Machine Case,* Reuters, Aug. 17, 1990.

214. Quindlen, *Seeking a Sense of Control,* N.Y. Times, Dec. 9, 1990; *The Kevorkian Cure: Death,* N.Y. Times, Dec. 9, 1990.

215. Anderson, *Suicide Doctor Wins Dismissal,* 77 A.B.A. J. 22 (Feb. 1991). The judge agreed with the report by the medical examiner that the charge lacked probable cause under existing law. *Id.* The prosecuting attorney has announced that the decision will not be appealed. *Id.*

216. *Suicide Doctor Might Disobey Court Order,* United Press International, Oct. 4, 1990; *Man to Stand Trial for Murder in Michigan Suicide Case,* Reuters, Sep. 7, 1990; Byland, *supra* note 206. Dr. Kevorkian has expressed an interest in continuing to aid those persons wishing to end their lives. Borger, *supra* note 213, at 28.

217. Pluta, *Right-to-die Bill Clears Committee,* United Press International, Sep. 13, 1990. A right-to-die bill was approved by the Michigan Senate Human Resources and Senior Citizens Committee, and has been sent to the floor of the full Senate. *Id.* The measure would allow people to appoint an advocate for the purpose of making medical decisions should the person become incapacitated. *Id.* Both bills will remain on the Senate floor until the House acts on the proposed assisted suicide measure. Pluta, *Right-to-die Deal Waylaid by Politics,* United Press International, Sep. 25, 1990. Michigan's governor, James Blanchard, has expressed support of both bills, and has indicated that he will sign the right-to-die legislation if called upon to do so. *Id.*

218. Johnston, *Hemlock Society Notes Progress on Right to Die,* Seattle Times, Sep. 16, 1990.

the assistance of a physician without the threat of prosecution for murder.[219] The initiative is supported by the Washington Citizens for Death with Dignity organization and the Oregon-based Hemlock Society,[220] an organization that "supports the principle of a person who is terminal and suffering to end their life, and if necessary get help in doing so, ideally from a physician."[221] The initiative was modeled after a similar system that has been in use in Holland since 1980.[222] Other pro-euthanasia initiatives are being advanced in California, Florida and Oregon.[223] In addition, some states have enacted statutes granting immunity from criminal prosecution to counselors or persons, such as teachers or employees of educational services agencies, who attempt to prevent suicides.[224]

---

219. Figdor, *Initiative Seeks Law to Let Physicians Assist in Suicides; Health: The Measure Would Protect Doctors From Prosecution for Aiding in the Deaths of Terminally Ill Patients Who Want to Die*, L.A. Times, Sep. 16, 1990, pt. A, at 21. The law defines terminal condition, the prerequisite to action under the law, as one in which at least two doctors concur that the patient has six months or less to live or is in an irreversible coma. *Id. See also* Colen, *Washington State's Initiative 119 Would Allow Doctors to Act on Terminally Ill Patients' Requests for "Aid in Dying,"* Newsday, Jul. 31, 1990. The request for assistance must be in writing by the patient, and charges of first degree murder could be brought against anyone concealing a recision of the written request. *Id.* The initiative was originally introduced as a bill and subsequently expired in committee. Valid signatures from 150,001 eligible voters were required to place the initiative on the November 1991 ballot. WASHINGTON CITIZENS FOR DEATH WITH DIGNITY, NEWSLETTER ABOUT INITIATIVE 119. Sources report that more than 158,000 signatures had been collected before the end of 1990. Johnston, *supra* note 218.

220. Johnston, *supra* note 218.

221. *Q. and A., supra* note 130. The Hemlock Society, unlike other euthanasia societies in the United States, "works for the acceptance of both passive and active voluntary euthanasia." *Id.*

222. Rarick, *Regional News*, United Press International, Jul. 28, 1990.

223. *Id. See also* Harrison, *Man Helps Wife in Suicide, Now Faces Murder Charge; Mercy Death: Californians Thought Michigan Law Was Lenient. They Picked Wrong State at the Wrong Time*, L.A. Times, Sep. 8, 1990, pt. A, at 1. A bill has been ratified in Minnesota that permits a living will to be placed on the driver's license. HEMLOCK SOCIETY, COMMUNITIES ADOPT "DO NOT RESUSCITATE" ALERTS (adapted from articles appearing in San Bernadino Sun, Springfield Newsleader, and the Rochester Post-Bulletin). San Bernardino County, in California, allows persons close to death to wear wristbands advising paramedics of the desire to not be resuscitated. *Id.* The wearing of the wristband must be approved by a physician. *Id.* The city of Santa Cruz, California, has instituted a program that allows individuals, after consent by a physician, to designate on a form that is filed with the county their wish to not be resuscitated. HEMLOCK SOCIETY, SANTA CRUZ 911 OFFERS "CHOICE". When called to the scene of an emergency, medical personnel call to confirm the status of the individual, and may cease resuscitation efforts after verifying that a form is on file. *Id.*

224. TENN. CODE ANN. § 33-10-102 (1984); WIS. STAT. ANN. § 939.48 (West 1982). It is an affirmative defense to a civil action for damages for personal injuries or death that the plaintiff was attempting suicide if the damages relate solely to the attempt, unless the defendant caused the attempt in whole or in part by failure to comply with a legal standard. TEX. CIV. PRAC. & REM. CODE § 93.001 (Vernon Supp. 1991).

V. The Applicable State Interest

Beginning with the 1976 decision in *In re Quinlan*,[225] numerous courts, when faced with the decision of whether to cease life support or life sustaining medical treatment, have recognized the existence of four legitimate state interests. These interests include: 1) the preservation of life; 2) the preservation of the medical profession's ethical integrity; 3) the prevention of suicide; and 4) the protection of innocent third parties from unwanted intrusion.[226] The interests are not absolute, but must be balanced against the individual's constitutionally protected right to privacy or liberty. In *Cruzan v. Director, Missouri Dep't of Health*,[227] the most recent Supreme Court right-to-die case, the court recognized the state's interest in preventing suicide by stating that "[w]e do not think a State is required to remain neutral in the face of an informed and voluntary decision by a physically-able adult to [commit suicide]."[228] The Court recognized, however, that "[t]he choice between life and death is a deeply personal decision. . . ."[229] The dissent argued that "[c]hoices about death touch the core of liberty . . . [o]ur duty, and the concomitant freedom, to come to terms with the conditions of our own mortality are undoubtedly . . . 'ranked as fundamental' . . . and indeed are essential incidents of the unalienable rights to life and liberty. . . ."[230] The dissent acknowledged that laws against suicide evidence a belief that persons who attempt suicide have at least some interest in living, and would later appreciate intervention.[231] The dissent further declared that "[a] State that seeks to demonstrate its commitment to life may do so by aiding those who are actively struggling for life. . . ."[232] These statements appear to support the idea that suicide prevention is best accomplished by increasing the desire to live.

---

225. 70 N.J. 10, 355 A.2d 647, *cert. denied*, 429 U.S. 922 (1976).

226. Satz v. Perlmutter, 362 So. 2d 160, 162 (Fla. Dist. Ct. App. 1978), *aff'd*, 379 So. 2d 359 (Fla. 1980); Brophy v. New England Sinai Hosp., Inc., 398 Mass. 417, 431, 497 N.E.2d 626, 634 (1976); *In re* Torres, 357 N.W.2d 332, 339 (Minn. 1984); Cruzan v. Harmon, 760 S.W.2d 408, 419 (Mo. 1988), *aff'd*, 110 S. Ct. 2841 (1990); *In re* Farrell, 108 N.J. 335, 348-54, 529 A.2d 404, 410-13 (1987); *In re* Colyer, 99 Wash. 2d 114, 121, 660 P.2d 738, 743 (1983).

227. 110 S. Ct. 2841 (1990).

228. *Id.* at 2852.

229. *Id.*

230. *Id.* at 2885 (Stevens, J., dissenting).

231. *Id.* at 2887 (Stevens, J., dissenting).

232. 110 S. Ct. 2841, at 2892 (Stevens, J., dissenting).

VI. The Purpose of the Criminal Law and How it Relates to Suicide

It has been argued that the criminal law is not the proper forum in which to deal with the issue of suicide prevention.[233] This argument is supported by both logic and statistics. Most suicides are prompted not out of a desire to end life, but out of a desire to gamble with self-destruction.[234] It is unusual for the suicide attempt to be committed for the sole purpose of dying.[235] Modern psychiatrists view suicide attempts as symptoms of mental illness; therefore, they conclude that no rational basis exists for affixing criminal liability to the act.[236] There is also a prevailing attitude among the public that suicide arises out of mental illness rather than antisocial behavior.[237] To treat suicide as an act arising out of felonious intent, or as an act against society ignores this view.

The motives for committing suicide vary between age groups.[238] Illness and depression due to the loss of loved ones are more frequent causes of suicide among the elderly, while broken relationships result in more suicides among the young.[239] Changes in society, such as poor economic conditions, war, or disruptions in politics, tend to cause fluctuations in the suicide rates.[240] The suicide rate in the United States changed little between 1950 and 1964,[241] a period in which numerous studies concerning suicide were conducted, and has remained relatively stable since that time.[242] The age at which the greatest percentage of suicides occur is between fifty-five and sixty-four, and the greatest number of attempts are made by those between the ages of twenty-four and forty-four.[243]

---

233. *See Punishment, supra* note 86, at 468.

234. STENGEL, *supra* note 2, pt. xvii, at 87. This would seem to be supported by the fact that the majority of suicide attempts are unsuccessful. *Id.* at pt. xxiv. *See also, Criminal Aspects, supra* note 82, at 158 (attempts are eight times more common than successful suicides). A one to two percent suicide rate per year can be expected among those who had made previous unsuccessful attempts. HANDBOOK, *supra* note 2, at 153, 175.

235. STENGEL, *supra* note 2, pt. xxiv at 87.

236. *Punishment, supra* note 86, at 463.

237. *Criminal Aspects, supra* note 82, at 160.

238. STENGEL, *supra* note 2, at 47.

239. *Id.*

240. *Id.* at 48.

241. HANDBOOK, *supra* note 2, at 191.

242. NATIONAL CENTER FOR HEALTH STATISTICS, 1990 REPORT (1990).

243. STENGEL, *supra* note 2, at 91.

More women as compared to men attempt suicide, but more men are successful. Men tend to use more violent methods, and the methods used vary according to country of origin.[244] The rate is lower for married persons as compared to those who are single, divorced, or widowed.[245] There is conflicting evidence concerning the connection between social status and suicide rates.[246] Some psychoanalysts view suicide as "an act of self-perpetuation rather than of self-extinction, in which the individual denies the barrier separating life and death."[247] It is likely that the Church condemns suicide because it is viewed as taking away that which only God has the right to take away—life.[248]

The purposes of criminal law include protection of the public from antisocial behavior, removal of those antisocial members from society, rehabilitation, and primarily, deterrence of future antisocial behavior.[249] Protection of the public health is one of the most common reasons for using the state's police powers.[250] Punishment, in the form of incarceration of offenders, is incident to the goals of deterrence and prevention.[251] Merely private wrongs are not covered by the criminal law, and remedies for injuries from such acts must be found in other areas of the law, such as tort law.[252] There is no evidence showing that laws criminalizing certain behavior have any deterrent effect on such behavior, yet these laws remain an integral part of our society.[253] Therefore, it is likely that legislation is aimed at achieving goals of the criminal law other than the goal of deterrence.

In most areas of the criminal law, there has been movement away from the notion of using the criminal law to condemn sinful acts.[254] The protection of property and promotion of economic well-being has

---

244. HANDBOOK, *supra* note 2, at 151, 175.

245. *Id.* at 193. *See also* notes 21-77 and accompanying text.

246. HANDBOOK, *supra* note 2, at 100-05, 191-92. In the U.S., the mortality rate from suicide is highest among laborers, while in England, the professional and laborer groups have higher rates as compared to other occupations. *Id.* at 190.

247. STENGEL, *supra* note 2, at 53.

248. *Id.*

249. A. COHN & R. UDOLF, THE CRIMINAL JUSTICE SYSTEM AND ITS PSYCHOLOGY § 2, at 12 (1979); J. SIGLER, UNDERSTANDING CRIMINAL LAW 12-14 (1981).

250. Larremore, *supra* note 3, at 339.

251. SIGLER, *supra* note 249, at 24. *See also* May v. Pennell, 101 Me. 516, 64 A. 885, 887 (1906) ("[t]he end of punishment is the prevention of crime").

252. SIGLER, *supra* note 249, at 31.

253. *Id.* at 21. *See also* ZILBOORG, THE PSYCHOLOGY OF THE CRIMINAL ACT AND PUNISHMENT 27-33 (1954). In England, studies have shown that the laws against suicide and attempted suicide had absolutely no deterrent effect on either the persons convicted or anyone else. STENGEL, *supra* note 2, at 112.

254. SIGLER, *supra* note 249, at 35.

gained a position of relative importance in the criminal law.[255] This is evidenced by the reduction in the number of crimes requiring specific intent or including malice as an element.[256] The number of crimes have increased in the last century, possibly due to an unjustified dependence on the criminal law as a means of dealing with social problems.[257] The drafters of the Model Penal Code attempted to combat this trend by generally opposing criminal culpability in the absence of specific intent.[258]

One commentator has suggested that in light of the purpose of the criminal law, suicide should not be treated as either a mental illness or a crime, but rather, should be judged on a case by case basis.[259] The police power of the state should not extend to cases involving actual suicidal behavior,[260] because this behavior can be explained as a logical means to escape an unbearable or unwanted situation.[261]

VII. CONCLUSION

The passing of moral judgment on the act of suicide through the thinly veiled use of the criminal law is neither proper nor necessary.[262] Given the purpose of the criminal law and the inconsistencies among the states in the treatment of suicide, attempted suicide, and assisted suicide, action should be taken by the states to clear up these inconsistencies in order to retain the true objectives of the criminal law. The lack of evidence of a deterrent effect resulting from the criminalization of suicide, supports the idea that the criminal law is not equipped to deal with this area of abnormal behavior. In most cases, there is no danger to anyone but the person who is attempting suicide; therefore,

---

255. *Id.*

256. *Id.* at 37.

257. *Id.*

258. *Id.* at 283.

259. *Criminal Aspects, supra* note 82, at 160.

260. Actual suicidal behavior should be distinguished from alleged suicidal behavior in cases where there is another person involved in the act (for example, someone who allegedly merely rendered assistance). The latter should give rise to criminal liability for murder or manslaughter in the absence of compelling evidence that shows that the victim consented to or requested assistance. The existence or absence of a suicide note should not be determinative, because only a minority of people who commit suicide leave a note. STENGEL, *supra* note 2, at 43.

261. *Criminal Aspects, supra* note 82, at 160.

262. It is likely that the statutes condemning acts associated with suicide arise out of a legislative desire to promote the ends of the moral majority for largely political reasons; a position that is borne out by the historical condemnation of suicide at common law that arose only after the Church gained power in England.

there is no need to protect society from the act, and psychiatric treatment is the best method for dealing with the suicidal individual.[263] The states should recognize that there is a zone of privacy in which the right to commit suicide may be exercised without penalty.[264]

The right to seek assistance in the commission of a suicide should also be removed from the scope of the criminal law. Furthermore, the person who assists an act of suicide should not be held criminally liable for the resulting death if there is clear evidence that the death resulted from the suicide rather than a homicidal act by the alleged abettor. This is not to suggest that states should refrain from attempting to reduce the incidence of suicide, but rather, that they should use proactive rather than reactive legislation. Legislation should be enacted such as that proposed in Washington concerning assisted euthanasia, that requires the following of strict guidelines prior to receiving assistance in committing suicide. Also, additional guidelines could provide for mandatory counseling and medical treatment. If these legislative guidelines are met, no criminal liability should attach to the person assisting in the commission of a suicide. This type of legislation would likely result in the achievement of two distinct desirable ends—the provision of medical and psychological aid to those in need of such assistance, and the potential reduction in suicide rates. If assistance was given, however, without following specific guidelines, those actions could be deemed to constitute homicide within the existing criminal statutes. No special provisions concerning assisted suicide would be required.

The founder of the Hemlock Society has predicted that in the next decade, most states will have enacted legislation allowing physicians to render aid to terminally ill persons who wish to end their lives. If this is true, should not the statutes criminalizing other assistance for suicides be repealed? The removal of the act itself from the realm of the criminal law evidences an acknowledgment that suicide is not the proper subject for the exercise of police powers. Efforts to reduce the suicide rate are better spent if the focus is on removing the motivation for the act, rather than the means to accomplish it. In the absence of a motive or reason to commit suicide, there will be no need

---

263. *Punishment, supra* note 86, at 471. In England, the suicide rate decreased with the advent of community care rather than custodial care for patients at high risk of committing suicide. HANDBOOK, *supra* note 2, at 166-67. This supports the theory that involuntary incarceration by any means is not the way to reduce suicide rates.

264. *In re* Garrett, 547 A.2d 609, 611 (Del. Ch. 1988).

for statutes of this type. The states should institute mental health programs specifically organized to reduce suicide rates. By shedding light on an act traditionally viewed as dark and evil through the removal of criminal sanctions, the potential for the lowering of suicide rates in this country is increased.

ASSISTED SUICIDE

In most cases, society is willing to permit a terminally ill patient to commit suicide (passive voluntary euthanasia) by declining treatment. Further, although some might consider it deplorable, little can be done to prevent a person from committing suicide utilizing more active means. The issue becomes much more complex, however, when a person needs or requests help, either in the form of providing the means or asking someone to actually do the killing.

Robert Sedler ("Constitutional Challenges to Bans on 'Assisted Suicide': The View from Without and Within") is a law professor and advocate for the American Civil Liberties Union (ACLU). In 1994, the ACLU adopted a litigation strategy targeted at eliminating Michigan's ban on assisted suicide. In his article, Sedler puts the debate in a constitutional law context and argues that the principle of an individual's right to bodily integrity, as developed in the reproductive freedom cases, extends, at a minimum, to the right of a terminally ill patient to hasten an inevitable death through physician-prescribed medication. In response to slippery slope arguments,[1] Segler asserts that, far from opening the door to forced euthanasia, the principle of bodily integrity also preserves the individual's right to delay an inevitable death as long as possible. Further, under a constitutional balancing approach, the state, which has a recognized interest in preserving life, may intervene to prevent suicide by most non-terminally ill individuals.

Jennifer Zima ("Assisted Suicide: Society's Response to a Plea for Relief or a Simple Solution to the Cries of the Needy?"), on the other hand, is highly critical of any attempt to legalize assisted suicide. In Zima's view, arguments in favor of assisted suicide incorporate, overtly or implicitly, quality-of-life judgments. She argues that such arguments manifest social prejudice against the ill, the disabled, and the elderly. Further, she argues that doctors who must evaluate whether their patients are making informed and rational decisions to commit suicide often disregard the clinical depression suffered by seriously ill patients. Rather than offering the escape of suicide, Zima suggests that the medical and lay communities should address the legitimate fear of dependency and abandonment that creates the desire to end one's own life.

Leslie Bender ("A Feminist Analysis of Physician-Assisted Dying and Voluntary Active Euthanasia") provides a fresh perspective. Using the deconstructionalist tools of the critical legal studies movement, she argues that the terms and structure of the debate distorts the proper focus of the debate: the process of dying. Instead of focusing on treatment versus death and active versus passive euthanasia, Bender advocates an ethic of care paradigm, in which the physician acts to empower the dying person and "gives medical care" by responding to the dying person's needs during the dying process. In this paradigm, "medical care" is the most appropriate treatment for the dying person's particular situation and may include radical medical intervention, maintenance care, and assisted-dying.

Because assisted suicide leaves someone behind to face the authorities, right-to-die advocates support legislation that would protect those who assist a suicide from civil or criminal liability. Initiatives authorizing physician-assisted suicide narrowly failed in Washington in 1991 and California in 1992. Faye Girsh ("Physician Aid in Dying: A Proposed Law for California") is a member of the Hemlock Society and a former proponent of the California "Death with Dignity Act" (DWDA). The proposed act would permit physicians to assist terminally ill patients (defined as dying within six months) in committing suicide. Girsh defends the DWDA based on the fact that it narrowly defined the conditions under which assisted suicide would be permitted, even more narrowly than those under which an appointed surrogate could terminate care for an incompetent. She argues that assisted suicide is necessary for people with AIDS, cancer, or other terminal illnesses for which there is no treatment to be withheld and for those where terminating treatment will only result in a prolonged and difficult death. In such case, Girsh argues, the DWDA would permit such terminally ill individuals to choose a death that was "gentle, pain-free, certain, quick, inexpensive, and in the presence of loved ones."

David Llewellyn ("Licensed to Kill: The 'Death with Dignity' Initiative"), on the other hand, opposed the DWDA. In his polemic against the DWDA, Llewellyn argues that permitting physicians to assist their patients in committing suicide "would convert a license to practice medicine into a license to kill." He argues that the state of medical knowledge is not sufficient to accurately determine, except in the most extreme circumstances, when a person's illness is terminal and that the initiative would allow patients to choose suicide at a time when they are most likely to be suffering from depression brought about by their illness. Finally, he argues that permitting assisted suicide subverts respect for life and opens the door to euthanasia of the old, the infirm, and the unproductive.

Assisted suicide creates numerous legal and ethical problems for the living. In some ways assisted suicide is little more than an extension of the individual's right to choose to die. After all, why should a person lose that right merely because he is physically unable to perform the act? On the other hand, the "ethic of care" requires enormous flexibility from the attending physician, who one day is devoted to preserving the patient's life and the next is helping to end it. Further, it goes against our ingrained morality of "thou shalt not kill" and, no matter the circumstances, leaves the person who assisted the suicide with the feeling that he or she has killed. Perhaps, however, that feeling, more than anything else, is the greatest protection against the potential for abuse inherent in assisted suicide.

NOTES

1. Sedler is responding to arguments advanced by Yale Kamisar. An example of Kamisar's slippery slope argument can be found in Part 10.

Constitutional Challenges to Bans On "Assisted Suicide": The View From Without and Within

By ROBERT A. SEDLER*

Introduction

Michigan is the home state of "assisted suicide's" most visible practitioner, Dr. Jack Kevorkian. Although public opinion polls in Michigan show strong support for assisted suicide in certain circumstances, and for that matter, for Dr. Kevorkian himself, efforts to "stop Kevorkian" have long been a prominent feature of the Michigan legal and political scene. Kevorkian's assisted suicide activity has been strongly opposed by a number of legislators and prosecutors, and by the politically powerful Michigan Right to Life lobby.[1] During the 1992-93 session, a number of bills dealing with assisted suicide were introduced in the Michigan Legislature, ranging from permitting assisted suicide in certain circumstances[2] to completely prohibiting assisted suicide in all circumstances.[3] Faced with this politically-charged and highly controversial issue, the Michigan Legislature decided to do what legislatures often do in such a situation—appoint a blue ribbon commission to study the matter. The day before the agreed-upon bill establishing the study commission[4] was to be voted on in the Michigan House, however, Kevorkian performed another of his now familiar

---

* A.B., 1956; J.D., 1959, University of Pittsburgh. Professor of Law, Wayne State University. This Article is a substantially expanded version of an earlier article, Robert A. Sedler, *The Constitution and Hastening Inevitable Death*, HASTINGS CTR. REP., Sept.-Oct., 1993, at 20. Professor Sedler is an active constitutional litigator, predominently as a volunteer attorney for the American Civil Liberties Union. He is a member of the ACLU legal team challenging Michigan's assisted suicide law, with the primary responsibility for developing a substantive constitutional challenge to the law.

1. Gene Schabath & Robert Ourlian, *Kevorkian Opponents Want Aided-Suicide Ban Moved Up*, DET. NEWS, Feb. 16, 1993.

2. S. 211, 87th Leg., Reg. Sess. (Mich. 1993).

3. S. 32, 86th Leg., Reg. Sess. (Mich. 1991).

4. The study commission was directed to make recommendations to the legislature on the entire subject of "assisted suicide"—including whether or not "assisted suicide" should be made a criminal offense.

assisted suicides, which, as usual, received nationwide media coverage.[5] This renewed the legislative clamor: "Stop Kevorkian" and "Don't let Michigan become the Nation's suicide capitol." The study-commission bill was amended on the floor of the House to add a provision making assisted suicide a criminal offense. The amended bill was quickly passed by the House and the Senate and signed into law by the Governor.[6]

Michigan's ban on assisted suicide is sweeping in scope. Under the law, a person is guilty of "criminal assistance to suicide" if that person "has knowledge that another person intends to commit or attempt to commit suicide and . . . intentionally (a) [p]rovides the physical means by which the other person attempts or commits suicide [or] (b)[p]articipates in a physical act by which the other person attempts or commits suicide."[7] The only intent necessary for a violation of the law is the intent to "provide the physical means" or "participate in a physical act" with the "knowledge that another person intends to commit or attempt to commit suicide." *There need not be any intent that the other person should actually commit suicide.* So if a terminally ill person has told a spouse or friend, "I sometimes wish I could die," and the spouse or friend provides the glass of water that the terminally ill person uses to swallow a lethal dose of medication, the spouse or friend has violated the law. The furnishing of the "physical means" with the requisite knowledge that a person has threatened suicide is sufficient to subject the spouse or friend to up to four years' imprisonment.

The law does not make any exception for the terminally ill, and specifically defines assisted suicide to include the prescription of lethal medications by a physician to a terminally ill patient for the purpose of enabling the patient to use the medications to hasten inevitable death.[8] Thus, Michigan law prohibits a physician from prescribing medications to terminally ill patients in quantities that would empower the patients to use the medications to hasten inevitable death, and prohibits them from instructing patients how to make use of the medications for this purpose. In other words, in Michigan, a termi-

---

5. *Michigan Vote Declares Assisted Suicide a Felony*, WASH. POST, Nov. 25, 1992, at A2.

6. *See* MICH. COMP. LAWS § 752.1027 (1993).

7. *Id.* at § 752.1027(1).

8. The law states that it does not apply to "[a] licensed health care professional who administers, prescribes, or dispenses medications or procedures to relieve a person's pain or discomfort, even if the medication or procedure may hasten or increase the risk of death. . . ." *Id.* at § 752.1027(3).

nally ill person, no matter how excruciating that person's pain and suffering, will not be able to receive any assistance from a physician, family member, or friend, in implementing that person's decision to hasten inevitable death. For these and other reasons, the American Civil Liberties Union of Michigan has asserted a constitutional challenge to the state's ban on assisted suicide.

This Article's analysis of constitutional challenges to bans on assisted suicide comes "from without and within"—from the dual perspectives of the author's role as an academic commentator and as a constitutional litigator.[9] To the extent that the impartial and dispassionate perspective of a pure legal scholar is considered a virtue, this perspective is admittedly lacking. However, participation as an advocate can yield insights that detached scholarly observation cannot provide.

Initially, this Article will discuss the ACLU's substantive constitutional challenge to Michigan's ban on assisted suicide.[10] The basis of that challenge to the ban[11] is a limited one, specifically that the ban on assisted suicide is unconstitutional insofar as it prohibits terminally ill persons from making use of physician-prescribed medications to hasten inevitable death. The Article then engages the "slippery slope" argument, distinguishing between the application of a ban on assisted suicide to terminally ill persons and persons who have become so debilitated by illness that their life has become "unendurable," and other persons, who wish to end their life "for whatever reason."[12] This Article argues that, under applicable Supreme Court doctrine and precedent, a ban on assisted suicide is unconstitutional as applied to the terminally ill and to the physically debilitated persons who wish to end their "unendurable" life, but is constitutional in its completely hypothetical application to persons who wish to end their life "for whatever reason." In advancing this

---

9. The author has approached other legal questions in this manner. See Robert A. Sedler, *The Unconstitutionality of Campus Bans on "Racist Speech:" The View from Without and Within*, 53 U. PITT. L. REV. 631 (1992); Robert A. Sedler, *The Summary Contempt Power and the Constitution: The View from Without and Within*, 51 N.Y.U. L. REV. 34 (1976); Robert A. Sedler, *Metropolitan Desegregation in the Wake of Milliken: On Losing Big Battles and Winning Small Wars: The View Largely from Within*, 1975 WASH. U. L.Q. 535; Robert A. Sedler, *The Procedural Defense in Selective Service Prosecutions: The View from Without and Within*, 56 IOWA L. REV. 1121 (1971).

10. *See infra* notes 13-47 and accompanying text.

11. In addition to the substantive constitutional challenge and the challenge to the process by which the law was enacted, *see infra* notes 13-18 and accompanying text, the law has been challenged as being unconstitutionally vague and indefinite.

12. *See infra* notes 48-61 and accompanying text.

view, this Article develops the *"choice principle."* The concluding portion of the Article contends that the choice principle protects a person's decision to prolong life as well as to terminate it, and so imposes significant constitutional restraints on any governmental effort to "ration" the health care necessary to prolong the life of terminally ill persons or very old persons or to alleviate the condition of physically debilitated or disabled persons.

I.   The Constitutional Right of the Terminally Ill to Hasten Inevitable Death

The ACLU's substantive constitutional challenge to Michigan's ban on assisted suicide is based on the Fourteenth Amendment's due process guarantee of liberty. The ACLU and this Article argue that the Fourteenth Amendment protects the right of terminally ill patients to hasten their inevitable death, and that Michigan's ban on assisted suicide is unconstitutional as an undue burden on that right. In developing this constitutional challenge, this Article responds to the contention advanced by opponents of assisted suicide, such as Professor Yale Kamisar, that laws against assisted suicide are fully constitutional.[13] In so doing this Article frames the issue for the specific context of the ACLU constitutional challenge to Michigan's ban on assisted suicide. This is quite different from the way the opponents of assisted suicide have typically framed the issue.

A.   Properly Framing the Issue

A distinguished constitutional scholar has observed: "Once taken into our constitutional law system, the dialogue takes on a new seriousness. It is, therefore, critically important that we get the questions right and the answers right, because constitutional law is written in concrete and is not easily washed out by rain or tears."[14] The right question, as regards the ACLU challenge to Michigan's ban on assisted suicide, is not whether there is a constitutional right to assisted suicide or a constitutional right to die. Rather, the right question is about a terminally ill person's right to hasten inevitable death. The right question is whether an absolute ban on the use of physician-prescribed medications by a terminally ill person to hasten that person's inevitable death, *if and when the person chooses to do so*, is an undue

---

13. *See* Yale Kamisar, *Are Laws Against Assisted Suicide Unconstitutional?*, HASTINGS CTR. REP., May-June 1993, at 32.

14. Robert G. Dixon, Jr., Bakke: *A Constitutional Analysis*, 67 CAL. L. REV. 69, 70 (1979).

burden[15] on that person's due process liberty interest. Any undue burden here is a violation of the Fourteenth Amendment's Due Process Clause[16] and thus unconstitutional.

As in many constitutional cases, an understanding of the ACLU challenge to Michigan's assisted suicide ban must begin by looking at the people who are bringing the challenge and how the ban effects what they want to do. The ACLU did not bring the constitutional challenge to the law on behalf of Dr. Kevorkian,[17] on behalf of proponents of voluntary euthanasia, or on behalf of non-terminally ill persons who wish to terminate an unendurable existence. The principal plaintiffs in the case are both terminally ill cancer patients who want to have the *choice* to hasten their inevitable death by taking a lethal dose of physician-prescribed medications, and the physicians who want to prescribe medications so that their patients will have this choice. The physician plaintiffs do *not* want to give lethal injections to terminally ill patients, nor to perform voluntary euthanasia in any way whatsoever, and the patient plaintiffs do not want to have their lives ended in such a manner.

What the patient plaintiffs do want, and what the physician plaintiffs want to provide, is *patient empowerment* to choose to hasten inevitable death. The physician plaintiffs want to be permitted, when they consider it medically appropriate, to provide their patients with barbiturates, opiates, or other medications in sufficient quantities that the patients may, at the time of their own choosing, immediately terminate their lives by consuming a lethal dosage. In this respect, patient empowerment encompasses both pain control and the hastening of inevitable death. The patient takes the medications to relieve pain, but if the pain becomes so unbearable that the patient no longer wants to continue living with it, or if the patient simply does not want to go on living any longer, the patient can "take the whole bottle," so to speak, and bring the suffering to a merciful end.

Unlike Dr. Kevorkian's assisted suicides, and unlike voluntary euthanasia, patient empowerment means that physician intervention is not necessary at the time of death, and that there may not be direct physician involvement with the patient's death at all. There are no

---

15. *See* Planned Parenthood v. Casey, 112 S. Ct. 2791 (1992) (plurality opinion).

16. The 14th Amendment to the United States Constitution states in part: "No State shall make or enforce any law which shall abridge the privileges or immunities of citizens of the United States, nor shall any State deprive any person of life, liberty, or property, without due process of law; . . . ." U.S. Const. amend XIV, § 1.

17. By tacit mutual agreement the ACLU and Dr. Kevorkian have kept at some considerable distance from each other.

"suicide machines" or television cameras. There is no appointed time at which the physician comes to the patient's home or hospital room to administer a lethal injection. Everything is in the patient's control. Only the patient, or family members, friends, or the physician, if the patient so chooses, will know of the patient's decision before it is carried out. The only sign of death is the empty bottle. The patient herself has determined the *timing* of her inevitable death and her release from unbearable pain and suffering.

Once the right of terminally ill patients to hasten their inevitable death by the use of physician-prescribed medications is firmly established as a matter of constitutional law, much of the controversy over assisted suicide may dissipate by its own force. At the least, the controversy will no longer involve the terminally ill. Once it is understood by both physicians and patients that physicians are legally permitted to prescribe medications in such quantities as to empower the terminally ill patient to make the choice to hasten inevitable death, there will no longer be any need for Dr. Kevorkian and his suicide machine. And there may not even be a need for voluntary euthanasia. A terminally ill patient will be able to obtain the necessary quantity of lethal medications from the patient's physician, and if the particular physician refuses to prescribe them, the patient can simply find another physician. Consequently the controversy over assisted suicide, at least in regard to terminally ill patients, may well be superseded by the constitutional recognition of patient empowerment to hasten inevitable death.[18]

---

18. Derek Humphry, the founder and from 1980-1992, the Executive Director of the Hemlock Society, has defined "assisted suicide" as "[p]roviding the means by which a person can take his or her own life," such as a physician's supplying medications with the intention that a terminally ill person be able to use those medications to bring about that person's death, and "active voluntary euthanasia" as "[t]he action of one person directly helping another to die on request," such as "a physician agreeing to give a terminally ill person a lethal injection." DEREK HUMPHRY, LAWFUL EXIT: THE LIMITS OF FREEDOM FOR HELP IN DYING 12 (1993). Mr. Humphry argues that both "assisted suicide" and "active voluntary euthanasia" should be legally permitted, because some terminally ill persons will be unable to administer their own medications, and because many terminally ill persons prefer the intervention of a physician to bring about their death. *Id.* at 81-86. As a constitutional matter, a statute permitting the prescription, but not the administration of lethal dosages of medications would be constitutional unless it was empirically demonstrated that some number of terminally ill persons were unable to make effective use of the medications. If this was demonstrated, then the regulation would be unconstitutional as imposing an "undue burden" on the right of terminally ill persons to hasten their inevitable death. *See generally Casey*, 112 S. Ct. at 2791 (plurality opinion).

Professor Kamisar, who contends that a ban on assisted suicide should properly extend to the terminally ill,[19] is somewhat troubled by the narrow and specific nature of the ACLU's substantive constitutional challenge to Michigan's ban on assisted suicide. He says that the ACLU is engaging in "good advocacy" tactics when it "only assert[s] the rights of the *terminally ill* who may desire death by suicide."[20] As explained above, however, the ACLU challenge to Michigan's assisted suicide ban only involves the constitutionality of that ban as applied to terminally ill persons, because only terminally ill persons and physicians treating terminally ill persons are seeking to challenge the ban in this case. Moreover, the challenge is not to the law's general prohibition against assisted suicide—the plaintiffs in this case do not care about a ban on Dr. Kevorkian's suicide machine or a ban on physician-administered lethal injections—but only to the ban on physician-prescribed medications that would empower terminally ill persons to make the choice to hasten their inevitable death.

For this reason, the constitutional issue presented in the ACLU challenge is relatively narrow and quite specific. It is also the issue that Professor Kamisar and the other opponents of assisted suicide find the most troubling, because they have great difficulty in responding to the issue on the merits. They have a hard time justifying requiring terminally ill people to bear unbearable pain and suffering, and denying them the right to hasten their inevitable death. This is why they quickly change the subject and warn of the slippery slope that will follow if terminally ill people were empowered to use physician-prescribed medications to hasten their inevitable death.

The fact that the issue presented in the ACLU challenge to Michigan's ban on assisted suicide is so specific is not, as Professor Kamisar says, simply "good advocacy." Nor is it, as Professor Kamisar also asserts, "the technique of overcoming opposition to a desired goal by proceeding step by step."[21] Instead, it is the way that constitutional issues are supposed to be litigated in the American constitutional system. In the American constitutional system, constitutional law develops in a "line of growth," on a case-by-case, issue-by-issue basis. Indeed, a fundamental principle of constitutional adjudication is that, "constitutional issues . . . will not be determined . . . in broader terms than are required by the precise facts to which the ruling is to be ap-

---

19. Kamisar, *supra* note 13, at 36 ("There is no principled way to distinguish for constitutional purposes between the terminally ill and others who desire 'death by suicide.'").

20. *Id.*

21. *Id.*

plied."[22] The meaning of a constitutional provision develops incrementally, and that provision's line of growth strongly influences its application in particular cases.[23]

The line of growth of constitutional doctrine is clearly illustrated by the development of the constitutional protection of a woman's right to have an abortion. The protection of abortion is part of the constitutional protection afforded to the broader interest of reproductive freedom, which in turn is a part of the even broader liberty interest textually protected by the Fourteenth Amendment's Due Process Clause. The constitutional protection of reproductive freedom as a due process liberty interest traces back to a 1942 Supreme Court decision holding unconstitutional the discriminatory sterilization of convicted felons.[24] The concept of reproductive freedom as a fundamental right, first recognized by the Court in that case, was later invoked by the Court in 1965 to hold unconstitutional a ban on the use of contraceptives by married couples,[25] and then, in 1972, invoked to strike down a ban on access to contraceptives by unmarried persons.[26]

So when the Court in the celebrated and controversial 1973 case of *Roe v. Wade*[27] had to confront the constitutionality of anti-abortion laws, reproductive freedom had already been established as a fundamental right. The question before the Court in *Roe* was whether the state's interest in protecting potential human life from the moment of conception was "sufficiently compelling" to justify a prohibition on a pregnant woman's entitlement to a medical abortion.[28] The Court held that this interest was not sufficiently compelling until the stage of viability had been reached,[29] and so in effect held that a woman had a constitutionally protected right to a pre-viability abortion. In its 1992 decision of *Planned Parenthood v. Casey*,[30] the Court reaffirmed the essential holding of *Roe v. Wade*, but modified the decision somewhat by holding that the state could regulate the abortion procedure, even

---

22. See the Supreme Court's classic discussion of this point in Rescue Army v. Municipal Court, 331 U.S. 549, 569 (1947).

23. See the discussion in Robert A. Sedler, *The Legitimacy Debate in Constitutional Adjudication: An Assessment and a Different Perspective*, 44 OHIO ST. L.J. 93, 118-20 (1983). The concept of "line of growth" of constitutional doctrine is explained in Terrance Sandalow, *Constitutional Interpretation*, 79 MICH. L. REV. 1033, 1034 (1981).

24. Skinner v. Oklahoma, 316 U.S. 535, 541 (1942).

25. Griswold v. Connecticut, 381 U.S. 479, 485 (1965).

26. Eisenstadt v. Baird, 405 U.S. 438, 454-55 (1972).

27. 410 U.S. 113 (1973).

28. *Id.* at 154.

29. *Id.* at 163-64.

30. 112 S. Ct. 2791 (1992) (plurality opinion).

for the purpose of discouraging women from having an abortion, so long as the particular regulation did not impose an "undue burden" on the woman's decision whether or not to have an abortion.[31]

In light of the case-by-case, issue-by-issue development of constitutional doctrine, the ACLU's constitutional challenge to Michigan's assisted suicide ban thus does not involve a claimed right to assisted suicide or a claimed "right to die." It involves the specific question of whether the liberty protected by the Fourteenth Amendment's Due Process Clause embraces the right of a terminally ill person to choose to hasten inevitable death and, if so, whether Michigan's absolute ban on the use of physician-prescribed medications to hasten inevitable death is unconstitutional as an undue burden on that right. In actual constitutional litigation, that issue must be confronted directly with reference to applicable Supreme Court constitutional doctrine and precedents, and it cannot be avoided by "slippery slope" and "but what if" kinds of arguments. Although these arguments may be appropriate for academic or political discourse, they have no place in constitutional litigation, and cannot be relied on to avoid confronting the specific constitutional issue presented in the case before the court.

In contending that there is no constitutional right to assisted suicide, Professor Kamisar does not directly address the constitutionality of a ban against the use of physician-prescribed medications by terminally ill persons to hasten their inevitable death. Instead, he insists that for constitutional purposes, there is no principled way to distinguish between terminally ill persons seeking to hasten their inevitable death and anybody else desiring "death by suicide."[32] In the real world, of course, we have no difficulty identifying the terminally ill. They are patients who will die from a specific disease within a relatively short period of time. Their medical treatment is limited to alleviating their pain, and the only thing that is not certain is the precise time when their death will occur. They thus constitute a distinct and identifiable class of persons, clearly separate from all other persons

---

31. *Id.* at 2818-19. Applying the undue burden standard, the Court upheld a Pennsylvania law imposing a 24-hour waiting period before the woman could have the abortion and another requirement relating to physician-furnished information. *Id.* But the Court invalidated a requirement that a married woman's husband be notified of her intention to have an abortion. *Id.* at 2826-31. The Court concluded that a fear of violence by her husband when informed of her decision to have an abortion could discourage some small number of women from having an abortion. *Id.* Thus, the requirement imposed an undue burden on the woman's abortion decision, and so was unconstitutional. *Id.*

32. Kamisar, *supra* note 13, at 36.

who, to use Professor Kamisar's term, might seek death by suicide.[33] And for this reason, it is not only possible, but indeed quite proper, in the context of the ACLU challenge to Michigan's ban on assisted suicide, to limit the challenge to the unconstitutionality of the law insofar as it prohibits terminally ill persons from making the choice to hasten inevitable death by the use of physician-prescribed medications.

B. The Right to Hasten Inevitable Death

The first part of the substantive constitutional challenge to Michigan's assisted suicide law is that the liberty protected by the Fourteenth Amendment's Due Process Clause embraces the right of a terminally ill person to hasten inevitable death. The essence of the liberty protected by the Due Process Clause is personal autonomy. A person has the right to bodily integrity, to control of that person's own body, and to define that person's own existence. As the Supreme Court recently stated in *Casey*:

> It is a promise of the Constitution that there is a realm of personal liberty which the government may not enter . . . . It is settled now . . . that the Constitution places limits on a State's right to interfere with a person's most basic decisions about family and parenthood, as well as bodily integrity . . . . At the heart of liberty is the right to define one's own concept of existence, of meaning, of the universe, and of the mystery of human life. Beliefs about these matters could not define the attributes of personhood were they formed under compulsion of the State.[34]

---

33. It is appalling that the pejorative label "suicide" would be put on a terminally ill person's choice to hasten his or her inevitable death. In no meaningful sense of the term can a terminally ill person's choice to hasten his or her inevitable death by the use of physician-prescribed medications be labeled a suicide. The term suicide conjures up the image of a person jumping off a bridge or "blowing his brains out." The terminally ill person, who is facing death, and who seeks to have the choice to hasten inevitable death by the use of physician-prescribed medications, is not committing suicide by ending a life that otherwise is of indefinite duration. The life of the terminally ill person is coming to an end, and the question is whether the terminally ill person must undergo unbearable suffering until death comes naturally, or whether that person can end the unbearable suffering by the use of physician-prescribed medications.

Professor Kamisar does not say very much about the terminally ill, emphasizing instead that most people who commit suicide are not terminally ill. *Id.* at 38. He, along with most other opponents of assisted suicide, is rather uncomfortable when talking about the terminally ill. So Professor Kamisar quickly brushes them off when he says that there is no principled way to limit the purported right to commit suicide to the terminally ill. *Id.* at 36-37. The opponents of assisted suicide then start down the familiar "slippery slope," suggesting that once we start allowing terminally ill people to hasten their inevitable death, we are but a few steps away from putting all "old and sick people" on the modern equivalent of an "ice floe going out to sea" and ridding ourselves of the "inconvenience" of having to care for them. *Id.* at 39.

34. *Casey*, 112 S. Ct. at 2805-07 (plurality opinion) (footnotes omitted).

A person's entitlement to bodily integrity and control over that person's own body protects the person's right to refuse unwanted medical treatment, including the right of a competent adult person to make the personal decision to discontinue life-saving medical treatment.[35] It protects the right of a woman to have an abortion[36] and the right of men and women to use contraception in order to prevent pregnancy.[37] For the same reasons, a terminally ill person's right to control that person's own body must include the right to make decisions about the voluntary termination of that person's life. Terminally ill persons must have the right to make the "most basic decisions about . . . bodily integrity," "the right to define [their] own concept of existence" and "the attributes of [their] personhood," without the "compulsion of the [s]tate."[38] Thus, logically, they must have the right to decide whether to undergo unbearable suffering until death comes naturally, or to hasten their inevitable death by the use of physician-prescribed medications.

In arguing that any constitutional protection of a right to die does not include protection of a "right to assisted suicide," Professor Kamisar says that there is a difference between withholding or withdrawing life-sustaining medical treatment and affirmatively committing suicide.[39] This is true. But it is also irrelevant to resolving whether the right of terminally ill persons to hasten their inevitable death is a protected due process liberty interest and whether an absolute ban on the use of physician-prescribed medications for this purpose is an undue burden on the exercise of that right.

Professor Kamisar does not explicate any principled difference, *in constitutional terms*, between the right of a competent terminally ill person to hasten inevitable death by refusing life-sustaining medical treatment and the right of the same competent terminally ill person to hasten inevitable death using physician-prescribed medications. No

---

35. *See* Cruzan v. Director, Mo. Dep't of Health, 497 U.S. 261, 279 (1990) ("[W]e assume that the United States Constitution would grant a competent person a constitutionally protected right to refuse lifesaving hydration and nutrition."). In her separate opinion in *Cruzan*, Justice O'Connor fully developed the reasons why the right of a person to refuse life-saving medical treatment is encompassed within the liberty protected by the Fourteenth Amendment's Due Process Clause. ("[T]he liberty guaranteed by the Due Process Clause must protect, if it protects anything, an individual's deeply personal decision to reject medical treatment, including the artificial delivery of food and water."). *Id.* at 287-89 (O'Connor, J., concurring).

36. Roe v. Wade, 410 U.S. 113 (1973); *Casey*, 112 S. Ct. at 2791.

37. Griswold v. Connecticut, 381 U.S. 479 (1965).

38. *Casey*, 112 S. Ct. at 2805-07.

39. Kamisar, *supra* note 13, at 33-35.

principled difference can be found in the applicable constitutional doctrine, and Professor Kamisar does not suggest one. Just as the personal autonomy reflected in the constitutional right of reproductive freedom protects both the right of a woman to use contraception to prevent pregnancy from occurring and her right to have an abortion to terminate an unwanted pregnancy that has already occurred, the right of a terminally ill person to bodily integrity includes the right to hasten inevitable death, either by discontinuing life-saving medical treatment, or by taking a lethal dose of physician-prescribed medications.[40]

C. Constitutional Protection of the Right to Hasten Inevitable Death

As pointed out above, what is protected by the Fourteenth Amendment's Due Process Clause is liberty, and a number of specific individual interests are encompassed within this protection. It is true, as opponents of assisted suicide contend, that the Constitution does not specifically guarantee the right to commit suicide or the right to die. But it is equally true that the Constitution does not specifically guarantee the right to obtain an abortion, or to use contraception, or for that matter, to marry or to parent children. Rather, all of these specific individual interests are encompassed within the Due Process Clause's guarantee of liberty, and, under applicable constitutional doctrine and precedent, any governmental interference with these interests is subject to constitutional challenge and must be justified.

Under the Court's two-tier standard of review for due process and equal protection challenges, the degree of justification required for an interference with a specific individual interest depends on whether that interest is treated by the Court as constituting a "fundamental right."[41] If it is, then the exacting compelling governmental

---

40. For a further discussion of this point, see John A. Robertson, Cruzan *and the Constitutional Status of Nontreatment Decisions for Incompetent Patients*, 25 GA. L. REV. 1139, 1176-77 (1991) ("If the competent patient has a right to cause her death passively by refusing medical care, then her right to kill herself by active means should logically follow as should her right to have the assistance of others in pursuing that end. State prohibitions on suicide or assisted suicide may be viewed as imposing bodily burdens—by preventing their removal—just as forcing unwanted treatment on a competent person imposes bodily burdens. Suicide enables the patient to avoid the bodily burdens of severe illness and a life no longer worth living, just as the refusals of medical care do. This logic would also make consensual active euthanasia a constitutional right of a competent patient unable to cause her own death.").

41. Fundamental rights have been defined as those rights which are "so rooted in the traditions and conscience of our people as to be fundamental." Palko v. Connecticut, 302 U.S. 319, 325 (1937). See the discussion of fundamental rights in Roe v. Wade, 410 U.S. 113, 152-53 (1973).

interest standard applies instead of the less restrictive rational basis standard.[42] Looking to the precedents, particularly to *Roe v. Wade* and *Casey*, it would surely seem that the individual's interest in bodily integrity and in having the right to define one's own concept of existence that is reflected in the decision to hasten inevitable death qualifies as a fundamental right, so as to bring into play the compelling governmental interest standard of review.

If the Court were to apply the test from *Casey*, it should find that an absolute ban on the use of physician-prescribed medications imposes an undue burden on the right of a terminally ill person to hasten inevitable death. In *Casey*, the Supreme Court held that a state may not impose an undue burden on the exercise of a person's fundamental right to bodily integrity and control over that person's own body.[43] The Court held that a law imposes an undue burden on the exercise of a woman's right to have an abortion when it places a substantial obstacle in the path of a woman seeking an abortion of a nonviable fetus.[44] A ban on the use of physician-prescribed medications obviously places a substantial obstacle in the path of a terminally ill person seeking to hasten inevitable death. Indeed, a more extreme burden on the exercise of that right cannot be imagined, and for this reason, Michigan's ban on the use of physician-prescribed medications for this purpose is unconstitutional.[45]

The state cannot assert *any* valid interest in requiring a terminally ill person to undergo unbearable pain and suffering until death comes naturally. The interest typically asserted to justify a ban on assisted suicide is that of preserving life, or as Professor Kamisar puts it, in

---

42. The compelling government interest standard requires that when the government uses a classification based upon a fundamental right, it must show that the classification is necessary (narrowly tailored) to a compelling or overriding government interest. JOHN E. NOWACK & RONALD D. ROTUNDA, CONSTITUTIONAL LAW 579 (4th ed. 1991).

43. *Casey*, 112 S. Ct. at 2819 (plurality opinion).

44. *Id.* at 2804.

45. There is no question, of course, that the state, in the exercise of its power to impose reasonable regulations on the practice of medicine, could constitutionally regulate physician participation in assisting the voluntary termination of life. Such regulations would be constitutional so long as they did not impose an undue burden on the right of a competent terminally ill person to hastening inevitable death. For example, the state might limit physician participation in assisting the voluntary termination of life to practicing clinical physicians and/or to clinical physicians who have been directly involved in the care of the terminally ill patient. Such a regulation would assumedly be constitutional, because it would not prevent the competent terminally ill person from obtaining physician assistance in implementing his or her decision to hasten inevitable death. For an example of a proposed regulation of physician participation in the voluntary participation of life, see the model "Death with Dignity Act," in HUMPHRY, *supra* note 18, at 133-52 (1993).

preventing the disregard for life that he sees resulting from a "suicide-permissive" society.[46] But there can be no valid interest in preserving life when there is no life left to preserve. A ban on the use of physician-prescribed medications by a terminally ill person to hasten that person's inevitable death does not advance any conceivable interest in preserving life. Quite to the contrary, it does nothing more than force a terminally ill person to undergo continued unbearable suffering until death mercifully intervenes.

As stated at the outset, in constitutional litigation, it is "critically important that we get the questions right and the answers right."[47] The question presented in the ACLU challenge to Michigan's ban on assisted suicide is whether the absolute ban on the use of physician-prescribed medications by terminally ill persons to hasten their inevitable death is an undue burden on the liberty protected by the Fourteenth Amendment's Due Process Clause. The answer to this question, in terms of the constitutional doctrine and precedents applicable to the right of personal autonomy, should be resoundingly in the affirmative.

II. A Journey Down the "Slippery Slope"

This section of the Article joins Professor Kamisar and the other opponents of assisted suicide in a journey down the purported slippery slope of legalizing assisted suicide and considers constitutional challenges to a ban on assisted suicide that did not involve the terminally ill. As emphasized above, all the ACLU seeks is a holding that a ban on assisted suicide is unconstitutional as applied to use of physician-prescribed medications by terminally ill persons to hasten their inevitable death. The holding would be a relevant but not a controlling precedent in a future case involving the constitutionality of a law that prohibited suicide assistance to a person who was not terminally ill, or that prohibited suicide machines or physician euthanasia. Whether or not that precedent would be extended in future cases will be determined only if and when those cases arise. This Part, however, considers hypothetical future cases involving other applications of a ban against assisted suicide.

In arguing that the Constitution should not protect a right to assisted suicide, Professor Kamisar says that there is no principled way to distinguish for constitutional purposes between the terminally ill

---

46. Kamisar, *supra* note 13, at 39.
47. Dixon, *supra* note 14, at 70.

and others who desire "death by suicide."[48] He goes on to say that, in certain circumstances, life may be unendurable for one who is not terminally ill, and asks if that person should have the same right to assisted suicide that is being asserted for one who is terminally ill.[49] Professor Kamisar's observations are true in part, but only in part. The person who is not terminally ill but who desires what Professor Kamisar calls "death by suicide" must base his or her constitutional claim on the same Fourteenth Amendment liberty interest on which we have based the constitutional claim of the terminally ill person to hasten inevitable death by the use of physician-prescribed medications. And there can be no doubt that the Fourteenth Amendment's guarantee of liberty, as defined by the Court in *Casey*, would extend to a person's desire to end a life which has become unendurable.[50] For constitutional purposes, however, the situation of these persons is at least potentially different from the situation of persons who are terminally ill in regard to the justification that the state may be able to assert for its interference with their choice to end an unendurable life.

Consider a case involving a hypothetical state law that prohibits all assisted suicide except for the use of physician-prescribed medications by terminally ill persons to hasten inevitable death. This law is challenged first by a person who has become so debilitated by multiple sclerosis that the person is unable to move from his bed in a nursing home, requires constant nursing care, and cannot eat or perform bodily functions without the assistance of others. The person wants to end his life by consuming a quantity of lethal medications, which his physician is willing to prescribe for him. That person contends that the law is unconstitutional insofar as it prevents him from obtaining physician-prescribed medications so that he can end his unendurable life. There is no doubt that if this person's condition were such that he could be kept alive only by being put on a respirator, he could refuse to be put on the respirator or, if he had already been put on one, could insist on being removed from it. As has been discussed previously, a competent adult has the right to make the personal decision to discon-

---

48. Kamisar, *supra* note 13, at 36.

49. *Id.*

50. Again, to take the language from *Casey*, these persons have the right to make the "most basic decisions about . . . bodily integrity," the right to "define [their] own concept of existence" and "the attributes of their own personhood" without the "compulsion of the state." The right to choose whether to continue to live a life that has become unendurable or whether to bring that life to an end precisely because it has become unendurable is encompassed by these concepts. Planned Parenthood v. Casey, 112 S. Ct. 2791, 2805-07 (1992) (plurality opinion).

tinue life-saving medical treatment.[51] Professor Kamisar has said that there is a difference between the withholding or withdrawal of life-saving medical treatment and "affirmatively committing suicide."[52] As we have pointed out however, this difference is irrelevant as to whether the person's interest in ending a life that for that person has become unendurable is a protected liberty interest for due process purposes. But is it relevant in regard to the justification that the state can give for the interference with this person's liberty interest by denying him the use of physician-prescribed medications for this purpose?

Again, what is the justification that the state can assert in this situation? The claim of the multiple sclerosis victim that for him life has become unendurable, like the claim of the terminally ill person seeking to hasten inevitable death, is objectively reasonable. A rational person in the circumstances of the multiple sclerosis victim, like a rational person who is terminally ill, could indeed reasonably conclude that the continuation of life has become unendurable. So, it seems that the state would have a difficult time asserting the justification that it is trying to prevent an irrational person from committing an act that would cause his death. The state then would be forced to rely on the essential justification that it asserts to justify any ban on assisted suicide, that of "preserving life," or as Professor Kamisar puts it, in preventing a "suicide-permissive" society.[53]

In the case of the terminally ill person, this asserted preserving life justification is easily countered, as discussed, by noting that there can be no valid interest in preserving life when there is no life left to preserve. Here, there is life left to preserve. The person debilitated by multiple sclerosis may live for some additional years, and the state's interest in preserving life is admittedly advanced to some degree by keeping that person alive against his will.

The constitutional question then becomes whether this asserted interest in preserving life is of sufficient constitutional importance to outweigh the interest of the multiple sclerosis victim in ending a life that has become unendurable. The answer to this question requires constitutional balancing. The state's asserted preservation-of-life interest must be balanced against the resulting interference with the

---

51. *See supra* note 35 and accompanying text. For examples of such cases see, e.g., Bouvia v. Superior Court, 179 Cal. App. 3d 1127 (1986); State v. McAfee, 385 S.E.2d 651 (Ga. 1989); McKay v. Bergstedt, 801 P.2d 617 (Nev. 1990).

52. Kamisar, *supra* note 13, at 33-35.

53. *Id.* at 39.

personal autonomy of the person seeking to end an unendurable life. This justification is not likely to be found sufficient in the balancing equation. In *Roe v. Wade*,[54] for example, the Court held that the state's interest in protecting potential human life was not of sufficient constitutional importance to outweigh the interest of the pregnant woman in bodily integrity. Assuming that a person's right to end a life that has become unendurable would be treated by the Court as a fundamental right for due process purposes, then the *Roe v. Wade* precedent may loom large in the balancing equation. There, the right of the pregnant woman to control of her own body outweighed the state's interest in protecting the right to life of the fetus, notwithstanding that the great majority of pregnancies will end in a live birth. In the assisted suicide case there is not even any third party life that the state is seeking to protect. The state's asserted interest in the preservation of life turns out to be no more than a symbolic interest, which would seem to be of even less constitutional importance than the tangible preservation of life interest that was found insufficient in *Roe v. Wade*. And since the multiple sclerosis victim is helpless to bring about his own death, a ban on physician assistance to enable him to do so is obviously an undue burden on his right to end an unendurable life.

Once we get beyond the terminally ill and the physically debilitated, for whom life has become unendurable, do we need to proceed further down the "slippery slope?" It is difficult to posit a realistic constitutional challenge to a ban on assisted suicide brought by a person who is not terminally ill or physically debilitated. Nonetheless, for the sake of completeness, let us posit the following hypothetical case. Jones wants to kill himself, but does not own a gun. He prevails on his friend Smith, who does own a gun, to give him the gun and show him how to use it. Smith does so, Jones kills himself, and Smith is prosecuted for a violation of the state's ban on assisted suicide.[55] Smith asserts in defense that the prosecution against him for assisting Jones' suicide violates Jones' constitutional rights, and we may assume that Smith would be permitted to assert this defense.[56]

---

54. 410 U.S. 113, 163-64 (1973).

55. In State v. Bauer, 471 N.W.2d 363 (Minn. App. 1991), a 17-year-old defendant was convicted of aiding a suicide and fetal homicide, when his 18-year-old girlfriend, who was pregnant with his child, killed herself as part of a purported "suicide pact" between them. He furnished the gun that she used to kill herself, but claimed that he tried to talk her out of it and that she killed herself as he walked away.

56. *Cf.* Griswold v. Connecticut, 381 U.S. 479 (1965) (holding that a physician being tried as an accessory to a violation of the state's anti-contraceptive law for furnishing contraceptives to a married couple could assert the constitutional right of the married couple to use contraceptives).

Here the state's preservation-of-life justification is much more substantial than in the case of the terminally ill person or the multiple sclerosis victim for whom life has become unendurable. Here, the state's justification is tangible rather than symbolic, and involves the state's interest in protecting Smith against himself, so to speak. Contrary to Professor Kamisar's fears, we are not in danger of becoming a suicide-permissive society, and we do not believe that it is objectively rational for people to commit suicide. We will try to stop someone from jumping off a bridge or blowing his brains out. Someone who attempts suicide may be suffering from a form of mental illness at that time, so that the attempt at suicide is considered to be pathological and irrational.

It is well-settled that the state may, consistent with due process, impose restrictions on a person's freedom in order to prevent that person from doing something that the legislature considers harmful to that person's health or safety.[57] This principle—that the government has the power to protect us from ourselves—is relied upon to defeat due process challenges to a host of restrictions on individual freedom, such as substance abuse laws, cyclist helmet laws, and mandatory seat belt laws.[58] It is also relied on to justify the involuntary commitment of a person who is "a danger to [himself]."[59] Undoubtedly the courts would invoke this principle to sustain the constitutionally of a ban on assisted suicide as applied to persons who are not terminally ill or not so physically debilitated that it is objectively reasonable for them to find that their life has become unendurable.[60]

---

57. This principle is recognized in early cases sustaining against due process challenges the constitutionality of laws limiting the number of hours that an employee could work on the ground that the laws were necessary to protect employee health. *See, e.g.*, Bunting v. Oregon, 243 U.S. 426 (1917) (manufacturing); Muller v. Oregon, 208 U.S. 412 (1908) (hours of work for women); Holden v. Hardy, 169 U.S. 366 (1898) (underground mining).

58. As Professor Tribe has observed:

[T]here are few constitutional checks on the government's power to protect us from ourselves, whether by requiring the wearing of crash helmets and seat belts, or by banning the smoking of tobacco, the snorting of cocaine, or the recreational use of all-terrain vehicles. The intuition that one's safety is wholly one's own business is simply too far out of phase with the reality of our interdependent society to find any plausible expression in our constitutional order.

LAURENCE H. TRIBE, AMERICAN CONSTITUTIONAL LAW 1372-73 (2d ed. 1988).

59. *See, e.g.* Heller v. Doe, 113 S. Ct. 2637, 2644-47 (1993).

60. From a doctrinal standpoint, the courts might say that the right to commit suicide in this context is not a fundamental right, so that the rational basis standard of review applies. Or they may say that the state's interest in preventing a person from committing suicide in this context is "compelling." Either way, in this circumstance, they will sustain the constitutionality of the application of the ban against assisted suicide.

Essentially, under applicable constitutional doctrine and precedent, where it matters, bans on assisted suicide should be held to be unconstitutional. These bans matter for people who are terminally ill and for people who are so physically debilitated that for them life has become unendurable. It is these people who need the assistance of their physicians to prescribe lethal medications so that they can bring their lives to a merciful end. And it is to these people and the physicians who seek to assist them that current bans on assisted suicide are being directed.

Allowing these people to receive physician-prescribed medications to bring their lives to a merciful end will not result in a suicide-permissive society. Rather, it will allow them to have control over their own destiny, and, in the words of the *Casey* Court, to "define [their] own concept of existence, of meaning, of the universe, and of the mystery of human life."[61]

Concluding Note: The "Right to Go On Living"

Opponents of assisted suicide have argued one step further down the purported slippery slope. They have contended that once terminally ill people are allowed to hasten their inevitable deaths or physi-

---

In this connection, mention should be made of the rather bizarre case of Donaldson v. Lungren, 2 Cal. App. 4th 1614 (1992). This was a suit brought against the state attorney-general, asserting a broad constitutional challenge to the state's law against assisted suicide. One of the plaintiffs was suffering from an incurable brain disease, and he alleged that he wanted to commit suicide with the assistance of the other plaintiff, so that his body could be cryogenically preserved. It was his hope that sometime in the future, when a cure for his disease was found, his body may be brought back to life. He sought among other things, a "judicial declaration that he has a constitutional right to cryogenic suspension premortem with the assistance of others," an injunction against the prosecution of the other plaintiff for a violation of the assisted suicide law, and a court order to prevent the county coroner from examining his remains. *Id.* at 1618-19.

In rejecting this broad constitutional challenge to the assisted suicide law, the court emphasized that the state had a "legitimate competing interest in protecting society against abuses," which was "more significant than merely the abstract interest in preserving life no matter what the quality of that life is." *Id.* at 1622. The ban against assisted suicide, said the court, "protect[s] the lives of those who wish to live no matter what their circumstances," and "[t]he state's interest must prevail over the individual because of the difficulty, if not the impossibility, of evaluating the motives of the assister or determining the presence of undue influence." *Id.* at 1622-23. The court also noted that the ban would "discourage those who might encourage a suicide to advance personal motives," and that "suicide is an expression of mental illness." *Id.* at 1624.

As this case demonstrates, a broad constitutional challenge to a ban on assisted suicide cannot be sustained, since the state does have a valid interest in protecting people from themselves, particularly when they want to kill themselves so that their body can be frozen and they can come back to life sometime in the future.

61. Planned Parenthood v. Casey, 112 S. Ct. at 2791, 2807 (1992) (plurality opinion).

cally debilitated people to end their unendurable lives, we as a society are but a few steps away from putting all "old and sick people" on the modern equivalent of an "ice floe going out to sea" and ridding ourselves of the inconvenience of having to care for them.[62] From a constitutional standpoint, nothing could be further from the truth.

This Article has argued that the constitutional protection of personal autonomy embraces the right of terminally ill persons to hasten their inevitable deaths and the right of physically debilitated persons to end their unendurable lives. The constitutional protection of personal autonomy is even-handed. It means the right to choose between available alternatives. The same Constitution, for example, that protects the right of a woman to choose to have an abortion also protects her right to choose not to have an abortion. Thus, the state cannot compel a pregnant woman to have an abortion any more than it can prevent her from having one. By the same token, the Constitution that protects the right of a terminally ill person to choose to hasten inevitable death also protects that person's right to choose *not* to hasten inevitable death. The specter of government euthanasia that is at the end of Professor Kamisar's slippery slope would be constitutionally impermissible. More specifically, any governmental efforts to ration medical care would be subject to serious constitutional challenges precisely because they would interfere with the right of old and sick people, and of people who are terminally ill, to make the choice to go on with their lives.

At this point, there are no direct governmental efforts to ration medical care under governmentally sponsored programs of medical assistance, such as Medicare and Medicaid. But let us posit a health care system, such as that which might emerge from the Clinton health care proposal, in which there would be sufficient governmental involvement in the delivery of *all* health care so as to satisfy the state action requirement for constitutional purposes. Let us further suppose that in an effort to keep health care costs down, the government adopts regulations that eliminate costly life-prolonging treatments for terminally ill or very old persons, and that eliminate costly medical

---

62. Kamisar, *supra* note 13, at 39. Professor Kamisar asks:

In a climate in which suicide is the "rational" thing to do, or at least a "reasonable" option, will it become the unreasonable thing *not* to do? The noble thing *to* do? In a suicide-permissive society plagued by shortages of various kinds and a growing population of "nonproductive" people, how likely is it that an old or ill person will be encouraged to spare both herself and her family the agony of a slow decline, even though she would not have considered suicide on her own?

Id. (footnotes omitted).

treatments that would alleviate the condition of physically debilitated and disabled persons.

The justification of controlling medical costs or that "treatment won't do them any good anyway," will probably not be constitutionally sufficient to justify a denial of costly medical treatment that is necessary to support a terminally ill person's choice to continue living. Also, it will probably not be constitutionally sufficient to justify a denial of medical treatment that is necessary to prolong the life of very old persons, or that is necessary to alleviate the condition of physically debilitated or disabled persons.

The *choice principle*[63]—the constitutional guarantee of personal autonomy embodied in the Fourteenth Amendment's Due Process Clause—protects the right of terminally ill persons to hasten their inevitable death and the right of physically debilitated persons to end a life that for them has become unendurable. The same choice principle protects equally the right of the terminally ill to go on living. Once this is understood, it may be that the slippery slope will no longer be so frightening to opponents of assisted suicide, and that they will no longer be so fearful of a Constitution that protects the right to choose to go on living in the same manner as it protects the right to choose to die.

---

63. The choice principle relates to governmental interference with an individual's choice to make decisions about that person's own life. It does not refer to "choice" in a philosophical or psychological sense. People are subject to external pressures in all of the decisions that they make and it may be, as Professor Kamisar contends, *supra* note 13, at 39, that once a constitutional right to terminate life in some circumstances is recognized, the "old and sick" will come under pressure to end their lives. However, it cannot be a valid constitutional justification for a governmental interference with an individual's choice to make decisions about that individual's own life that some persons will be pressured when they are making that choice. It cannot be doubted that some women are pressured by their husbands, their boyfriends or their parents to have an abortion, and that in the absence of such pressure, they would make the choice to continue their pregnancies. This cannot be a constitutional justification for a prohibition on abortion. By the same token, the fact that some terminally ill persons may feel pressured to make the choice to hasten their inevitable death cannot constitutionally justify a prohibition on their right to make that choice. Of course, the government can adopt reasonable regulations to ensure that this choice, like any other choice, is voluntary and informed.

ASSISTED SUICIDE: SOCIETY'S RESPONSE TO A PLEA FOR RELIEF OR A SIMPLE SOLUTION TO THE CRIES OF THE NEEDY?

I. INTRODUCTION

On June 4, 1990, Janet Adkins, a 54 year old schoolteacher from Portland, Oregon killed herself.[1] Mrs. Adkins' death may be seen as tragic, but what made her suicide one of the most controversial acts of 1990 was the manner in which it was committed.[2] Mrs. Adkins' suicide was induced by Dr. Jack Kevorkian's[3] "suicide machine," a contraption the Michigan pathologist made which simultaneously drips saline solution, pain killer, and poison potassium chloride into the victim, causing death by heart stoppage.[4] Mrs. Adkins, suffering from the early stages of Alzheimer's Disease,[5] became the first person to use Dr. Kevorkian's machine. She traveled more than 2,000 miles to Michigan, where she was connected to his machine in the back of his Volkswagen bus in a public campground. She was dead within five minutes of arrival.[6]

This seemingly simple act fueled the debate between right-to-die

---

1. Nancy Gibbs, *Dr. Death's Suicide Machine; An Ailing Teacher's Last Decision Inflames the Euthanasia Debate*, TIME, June 18, 1990, at 69.

2. This was the first time a "suicide machine" was used to induce death. This machine was a "low-technology" homemade device, made by a retired doctor. *Id.*

3. Dr. Kevorkian is known as a "pugnacious maverick", recommending (among other things) a plan whereby doctors would render death row inmates unconscious and use their bodies for medical experiments. In recent years Dr. Kevorkian has fought hard for approval of assisted suicide. *Id.*

4. Dr. Kevorkian hooked up the machine to Mrs. Adkins by inserting the intravenous needle into her arm. This started the flow of the deadly saline solution. Mrs. Adkins, however, was the one who pushed the button which began the flow of pain killer and potassium chloride into her system. This is a key distinction. If Dr. Kevorkian had pushed the button, his act could be seen as murder, but since Mrs. Adkins pushed the button, her act may be deemed a suicide. Sydney H. Wazen et al., *The Physician's Responsibility Toward Hopelessly Ill Patients*, 320 NEW ENG. J. MED. 844, 848 (March 30, 1989).

5. Mrs. Adkins has been described as ". . .[a] strong lively woman who loved hang gliding and mountain climbing and playing her flute, she was not yet very sick" Gibbs, *supra* note 1, at 69. A week before her death, she had beaten her 32 year old son in a tennis match. *Id.* Her personal doctor for many years, Dr. Raskind, described his former patient as physically fit and in good spirits. Moreover, he said that her disease was in its early stages and that he did not consider Mrs. Adkins to be terminally ill. Isabel Wilkerson, *Prosecutors Seek to Ban Doctor's Suicide Device*, N.Y. TIMES, Jan. 5, 1991, at A6, col.5.

6. Mrs. Adkins' family knew what she was about to do when she left for Michigan. Her husband, Ronald, traveled with her to Michigan. He bought her a round trip ticket hoping that she would change her mind at the last minute. Gibbs, *supra* note 1, at 69.

activists and euthanasia opponents. For right-to-die activists, Janet Adkins became a symbol for all who attempt to face both a frightening illness and death with dignity.[7] To many euthanasia opponents, Dr. Kevorkian's actions amount to nothing short of murder.[8]

Dr. Kevorkian's act has forced us all to re-examine our views on death and the right to control its time and manner.[9] In our society, where the number of people over the age of 50 continues to grow, and modern technology is daily increasing life expectancies,[10] issues and decisions about death are of timely importance. This note will examine the issues raised by the Kevorkian case. To aid in understanding euthanasia, Part II will examine how the law, and more specifically the courts, view euthanasia and the distinctions the courts have made based on interpretations of the Constitution. Part III will show how Dr. Kevorkian's vision of allowing all individuals the right to die may unduly discriminate against the disabled, elderly, and abandoned. Part IV examines the doctor's role in the choice of when and how to die, and Parts V and VI discuss the role that sanctions must play in this choice. Part VI contains a specific proposal for the enactment of legislation to prevent the affirmative exercise of this choice.

---

7. *See infra* note 26 and accompanying text. Dr. Kevorkian believes that individuals should have the choice of when to terminate their lives. Dr. Kevorkian claims that American society is "in the dark ages" regarding suicide, and that he would like to see non-profit suicide clinics across America. Therefore, people like Janet Adkins could die using a more sophisticated version of the device he invented at one of his suicide clinics. Kathleen Byland, *American Suicide Attitudes In The "Dark Ages", Doctor Says*, Reuters Library Report, June 11, 1990, *available in* LEXIS, Nexis Library.

8. In December, 1990 Dr. Kevorkian was charged with first degree murder in Michigan for facilitating the suicide of Janet Adkins. *Arraigned*, TIME, Dec. 17, 1990, at 113. However, the criminal charges against Dr. Kevorkian were dropped shortly thereafter. According to Michigan District Judge Gerald McNally, the prosecution failed to prove that Dr. Kevorkian planned and carried out Adkins' death. *See infra* notes 107-11 and accompanying text for the result of Dr. Kevorkian's case.

9. Euthanasia has been thrust into the spotlight by the 1991 publication of Derek Humphry's *Final Exit: The Practicalities of Self-Deliverance and Assisted Suicide for the Dying*. Humphry is the President of the Hemlock Society, a euthanasia organization founded in 1980. Humphry believes that the time is right for a "responsible" suicide manual. Kathrine Ames et al, *Last Rights*, NEWSWEEK, August 26, 1991, at 40-41. (See *infra* note 26 for more on Derek Humphry and the Hemlock Society). Although FINAL EXIT proposes extreme measures, it does offer an alternative to the prospect of being kept alive by machines, a concern of many Americans. *Id.*

10. Americans over fifty make up 25.7% of the population, and they thus form a potent political force. By 2010, that group will make up over 34% of the population. This figure will rise to 39% by 2020. Andrew H. Malcolm, *What Medical Science Can't Seem to Learn: When to Call it Quits*, N.Y. TIMES, Dec. 23, 1990, at D6, col.1.

II. Euthanasia Under the Law

The courts have distinguished several categories of euthanasia;[11] the primary one being the distinction between active and passive euthanasia.[12] Active methods of euthanasia are those which hasten the natural process of death.[13] Passive methods of euthanasia are limited to the refusal to engage in life-prolonging medical activity.[14] While the courts have generally had little difficulty deferring to a competent adult choosing passive means of euthanasia, the law remains wary of active methods, even in voluntary cases.[15]

However, the courts have not stopped at the active/passive distinction. In the early common law cases, courts discussing the right to refuse medical treatment also distinguished between ordinary and extraordinary treatment.[16] In one early euthanasia case, the court held that a terminally

---

11. Courts have made a further distinction between voluntary and involuntary euthanasia. Courts and legislatures refuse to authorize withdrawal of treatment against the express wishes of the patient, and according to one author, ". . .there is little reason to anticipate that this will change in the foreseeable future." Donald L. Beschle, *Autonomous Decisionmaking and Social Choice: Examining the "Right to Die,"* 77 KY. L.J. 319, 330 (1988-89). However, many courts have allowed withdrawal of treatment where the patient's intentions were never explicitly expressed. (See *infra* notes 56-59 and accompanying text for the cases of Carrie Coons, Sydney Greenspan, and Mary O'Connor.) If provisions barring doctor-assisted suicide are removed, there is a danger that involuntary euthanasia will result. See *infra* notes 91-92 for analogous situations in the Netherlands and Nazi Germany.

12. The law has traditionally distinguished between acts and omissions in many contexts, including homicide. One who shoots another will generally be found guilty of homicide. If, however, a physician passed the scene of an accident without stopping to offer assistance, no crime has been committed. Thomas J. Marzen et al., *Suicide: A Constitutional Right?*, 24 DUQ. L. REV. 1, 10-11 (1985). A failure to rescue does not give rise to criminal liability, unless a special duty to rescue exists. Joel Feinberg, *The Moral and Legal Responsibility of the Bad Samaritan*, 3 CRIM. JUST. ETHICS 56, 57 (1984). Professors Prosser and Keeton explain the reason for the distinction:

The reason for the distinction may be said to lie in the fact that by "misfeasance" the defendant has created a new risk of harm to the plaintiff, while by "nonfeasance" he has at least made his situation no worse, and has merely failed to benefit him by interfering in his affairs. . . .

W. PAGE KEETON, THE LAW OF TORTS § 56 at 373-74 (5th ed. 1984).

13. Beschle, *supra* note 11, at 328.

14. *Id.*

15. For example, in Lane v. Candura, 376 N.E. 2d 1232 (Mass. App. Ct. 1978), a Massachusetts court found that a competent patient could refuse to submit to a leg amputation, even if it was not the "rational" thing to do. This right to choose passive euthanasia is not absolute: it can be overridden by a compelling state interest. However, in passive euthanasia cases courts have seldom overridden the patient's choice. Beschle, *supra* note 11, at 329.

16. The two have been described as follows:

Ordinary means are all medicines, treatments, and operations which offer a

ill patient in a comatose state could refuse extraordinary treatment when confronted with imminent death.[17] More recently, the "treatment" sought to be withdrawn is assisted feeding, specifically nutrition and hydration. In recent years, courts have reexamined the traditional view that food and water are not medical treatment, and thus cannot be withdrawn.[18] In *In re Conroy*,[19] the New Jersey Supreme Court held that since cutting off food and water is purely symbolic, it would no longer recognize the distinction between food and water and medical treatment.[20]

By abandoning the distinction between food and water and medical treatment, the New Jersey Supreme Court also abandoned the distinction between ordinary and extraordinary treatment.[21] The repudiation of this distinction signified a marked change in judicial standards for euthanasia.

---

reasonable hope of benefit and which can be obtained and used without excessive expense, pain, or other inconvenience. Extraordinary means are all medicines, treatments, and operations, which cannot be obtained or used without excessive expense, pain, or other inconvenience, or which, if used, would not offer a reasonable hope of benefit.
John A. Robertson, *Involuntary Euthanasia of Defective Newborns: A Legal Analysis*, 27 Stan. L. Rev. 213, 236 (1975).

17. *Eichner v. Dillon*, 426 N.Y.S.2d 517, 544-46 (App. Div. 1980), *modified sub nom*, 420 N.E.2d 64 (N.Y.), *cert. denied sub nom*, 454 U.S. 858 (1981). The case was consolidated on appeal with the related case of In re Storar, 433 N.Y.S.2d 388 (Sup. Ct.), *aff'd* 434 N.Y.S.2d 46 (App. Div. 1980), *rev'd* 420 N.E.2d 64 (N.Y.), *cert. denied*, 454 U.S. 878. *Storar* dealt with the ordinary/extraordinary distinction in the context of blood transfusions. If the treatment involved great expense or pain and offered no reasonable hope of benefit, the court did not view the patient's refusal of treatment as committing suicide. Succumbing to an inevitable death by avoiding nonbeneficial treatment was therefore outside the definition of suicide. However, if the treatment involved no excessive pain and a reasonable hope of benefit, then the patient's refusal of treatment could be seen as intending to cause his own death, which the court would not allow. Clarke D. Forsythe & Victor G. Rosenblum, *The Right to Assisted Suicide: Protection of Autonomy or an Open Door to Social Killing*, 6 Issues in L. & Med. 3, 8 (1990).

18. *See e.g.*, In re Conroy, 464 A.2d 303 (N.J. Super. Ct. App. Div. 1983), *rev'd*, 486 A.2d 1209 (N.J. 1985). *See also*, In re Gardner, 534 A.2d 947, 955-56 (Me. 1987) (Maine Supreme Court allowed withdrawal of food and fluids based on patient's prior statements); Brophy v. New England Sinai Hospital Inc., 497 N.E.2d 626, 638 (Mass. 1986) (Massachusetts Supreme Court allowed withdrawal of food and fluids from patient in persistent vegetative state, even though patient was not terminally ill or dying.)

19. 486 A.2d 1209 (N.J. 1985).

20. *Id.* at 1236. The "symbolism" of feeding Mrs. Conroy stemmed from the importance of that act in meeting the fundamental moral and legal obligations of society and medicine to disabled persons.

21. Even if food and water were medical treatment, they would be seen as ordinary, not extraordinary, treatment. Food and water neither induce undue expense or pain, nor do they offer a reasonable hope that the treatment will accomplish its intended result.
  In virtually all of the recent food and fluid cases, there is little or no evidence that providing food and fluids to the patient will impose a physical or psychological burden to the patient. And the expense of sustaining these patients in secondary

When a court utilized the ordinary/extraordinary distinction, it employed an objective standard to evaluate the benefits and burdens of treatment. In this way, the courts protected the sanctity of life — all stages of life were protected without regard to physical condition.[22] The rejection of the objective ordinary/extraordinary distinction, and the acceptance of living wills[23] and substitute judgments[24] means that the courts are now examining the patient's subjective desire for death by examining the quality of the patient's life.[25]

A growing number of euthanasia advocates[26] are fighting for greater

---

facilities is commensurate with sustaining competent, older patients at the same facilities.
Forsythe & Rosenblum, *supra* note 17, at 11.

22. By protecting the sanctity of life at all stages, the common law protected all patients, no matter how sick or vulnerable. The erosion of the traditional distinction between different forms of treatment means that the courts are not equally protecting all stages of life. Consequently, the more vulnerable members of our society are the ones who suffer. Forsythe & Rosenblum, *supra* note 17, at 11. *See infra* notes 46-61 and accompanying text for a complete discussion of this issue.

23. *See infra* note 37.

24. Substitute judgments arise when another person, usually a family member, doctor or judge, determines how and when an incompetent patient would choose to die. Forsythe & Rosenblum, *supra* note 17, at 18-19. Courts allow substitute judgments because an individual's subjective desires cannot be captured in a document, such as a living will. Some substitute judgments are unavoidable, i.e. when a patient has lost the cognitive ability to decide for him or herself. However, we should not delude ourselves into thinking that third parties are always able to discern what that individual patient would choose in those particular circumstances. For "[w]hen a judge, a relative or a guardian decides to terminate another's medical treatment, that person is the one making the choice." Beschle, *supra* note 11, at 360. Although the decisionmaker may make a good faith attempt to choose as the patient would have chosen, the patient's choice is essentially unknowable. *Id.*
This may be true even if the patient has made a prior decision through a document such as a living will. When a patient determines when and under what conditions his or her life should be maintained, they are acting as a "hypothetical" person. "[W]hen such a statement is made well in advance of an actual confrontation with death, the declarant is too far removed from the reality of the choice to be making a sufficiently informed decision." *Id.* Courts, however, have been slow to recognize these discrepancies in honoring substitute judgement decisions.

25. Quality of life arguments are rooted in a functional ethic which focuses on the "worth" of the individual. Worth is judged externally by what an individual can contribute to a society of which they are a member. Evaluating a life based on its quality will inevitably lead to extensions of the rationale as the cases get harder and death appears to be the most humane alternative. Robert A. Destro, *Quality-of-Life Ethics and Constitutional Jurisprudence: The Demise of Natural Protection Rights and Equal Protection for the Disabled and Incompetent*, 2 J. CONTEMP. HEALTH LAW AND POL'Y 71, 89 (1986).

26. The Hemlock Society is the foremost advocate of right to die legislation. According to Derek Humphry, founder of the organization, the Hemlock Society is the only organization in the United States presently campaigning to legalize assisted suicide. Ethan Rarick, UPI, Domestic News, July 23, 1990, *available in* LEXIS, Nexis Library, UPI file. The Hemlock Society was originally a small organization comprised mainly of elderly men

protection over the choice of death by calling for constitutional protection of a right to die.[27] Some courts have responded to these arguments. In *In re Quinlan*,[28] one of the foremost cases on the right to die, the New Jersey Supreme Court held that a comatose patient has a constitutionally protected privacy interest.[29] This privacy interest is not absolute, however, and can be outweighed by a countervailing state interest.[30] A California Court of Appeals judge[31] extended this right even further than the New

---

and women. However, its membership has recently skyrocketed to 33,500. This dramatic increase is largely attributable to the AIDS epidemic, and to the ever-increasing ability of technology to keep people alive. *Id.*

27. A constitutionally protected right to die would have to be found in the right to privacy first enunciated by the Supreme Court in Griswold v. Connecticut, 381 U.S. 479 (1965). In *Griswold*, the Court examined a state statute banning the use of contraception, and found that this statute violated the "zone of privacy created by several fundamental constitutional guarantees." *Id.* at 485. In Roe v. Wade, 410 U.S. 113 (1973), the Supreme Court broadened the right to privacy to include a woman's decision whether or not to terminate her pregnancy. Right to die advocates argue that this right is broad enough to encompass the right to die, but the Supreme Court has not agreed. *See infra* notes 33-36 and accompanying text for a discussion of the *Cruzan* case.

28. 70 N.J. 10, 355 A.2d 647, *cert. denied sub nom*, 429 U.S. 922 (1976). In *Quinlan*, the patient had lapsed into a coma of unknown origin. 10 N.J. at 23, 355 A.2d. at 653-54. After a year in a coma and on a respirator, her father, Joseph Quinlan, appealed to the New Jersey courts requesting termination of all extraordinary forms of medical treatment. *Id.* at 30, 355 A.2d at 657-58.

29. Joseph Quinlan based his petition on three claims: (1) an independent parental right to exercise freedom of religion, (2) protection against cruel and unusual punishment, and (3) the right of privacy. *Id.* at 35-42, 355 A.2d at 661-62. The court refused to recognize the first two claims, but accepted the assertion of the patient's right to privacy. *Id.* 38-42, 355 A.2d at 661-64.

30. *Id.* at 37-38, 355 A.2d at 664. Four recognized state interests include the preservation and sanctity of human life, maintenance of the ethical integrity of the medical profession, prevention of suicide, and protection of innocent third parties. *Id.* at 40-52, 355 A.2d at 663-70. The first interest may include the prolongation of life as well as the sanctity of life. Elizabeth Helene Adamson, Note, *The Right to Refuse Life Sustaining Medical Treatment and the Noncompetent, Nonterminally Ill Patient: An Analysis of Abridgement and Anarchy*, 17 PEP. L. REV. 461, 472-73 (1990). The second interest does not require the medical profession to provide medical treatment or intervention in every case. However, a physician should not intentionally cause death. Current Opinions of the Council on Ethical and Judicial Affairs of the American Medical Association — 1986. Withholding or Withdrawing Life-Prolonging Treatment. Chicago: American Medical Association, 1986, *cited in* Wazen et al., *supra* note 4, at 844. The state's interest in the prevention of suicide is not necessarily in conflict with the patient's right to refuse medical treatment. If death results from natural causes, the patient has merely allowed the process of death to continue unchecked. Adamson, *supra*, at 473-74. Finally, the state's interest in protecting third parties seeks mainly to safeguard minor children from emotional and financial harm. *Id.* at 475. *Cf.* Makay v. Bergstadt, 801 P.2d 617 (Nev. 1990) (discussing the state interests in detail).

31. Bouvia v. Superior Court, 225 Cal.Rptr. 297 (Cal. Ct. App. 1986). This case is discussed *infra* notes 50-55 and accompanying text. However, Justice Lynn Compton's concurring opinion contains the strongest judicial sanction of the right to die thus far. He

Jersey Supreme Court by holding that a competent, nonterminally ill patient has the "absolute right to effectuate that decision [i.e. decide to die]" as long as he or she has made a conscious and informed choice.[32]

These last words are startling because they imply an absolute right to privacy. This view has yet to receive United States Supreme Court approval. In *Cruzan v. Missouri Department of Health*,[33] the first right to die case heard by the Supreme Court, the Court held that the due process clause protects the liberty interest of a competent person to refuse unwanted medical treatment.[34] However, this liberty interest is not absolute and must be balanced against relevant state interests.[35] The Court held that Missouri's general interest in protection and preservation of human life justified the requirement that evidence of an incompetent's wishes to withdraw life-sustaining treatment be proved by clear and convincing evidence.[36]

The Supreme Court's rather conservative view on euthanasia comports with state attempts to codify their positions on euthanasia. At least

---

writes: "This state and the medical profession instead of frustrating her [the patient's] desire, should be attempting to relieve her suffering by permitting and in fact assisting her to die with ease and dignity." *Id.* at 307. He further hopes that this case ". . .will cause our society to deal realistically with the plight of those unfortunate individuals to whom death beckons as a welcome respite from suffering." *Id.* at 308.

32. *Id.* at 307.

33. 110 S.Ct. 2841 (1990). In *Cruzan*, the guardians of a patient in a persistent vegetative state brought a declaratory judgment action, seeking to terminate artificial nutrition and hydration. *Id.* at 2845. The state trial court authorized the termination on the basis that a person in Cruzan's condition has a fundamental right under the state and federal constitutions to refuse or direct the withdrawal of life support systems. *Id.* at 2846. The Missouri Supreme Court reversed, expressing doubt that either the state or federal constitutions contained such an expansive right to privacy. *Id.*

34. *Id.* at 2851. According to the Court, the principle that a competent person has a constitutionally protected liberty interest in refusing unwanted medical treatment is based on earlier court decisions. *See e.g.*, Washington v. Harper, 110 S.Ct. 1028, 1036, (1990), where the Court recognized that prisoners possess "a significant liberty interest in avoiding the unwanted administration of antipsychotic drugs under the Due Process clause of the Fourteenth Amendment." *Id.*

35. 110 S.Ct. at 2851-52. The petitioners in *Cruzan* argued that the incompetent person possesses the same right to refuse medical treatment as the competent person. The Supreme Court refused to expand this right so broadly, instead holding that where an incompetent person is the patient, the state can require clear and convincing evidence of the patient's intent. *Id. See supra* note 30 (discussing the recognized state interests).

36. According to the Supreme Court, in this context the state has a more particular interest at stake. Since "[t]he choice between life and death is a deeply personal decision of obvious and overwhelming finality," the state may justifiably require heightened evidentiary standards. *Id.* at 2852-53. Furthermore, the Supreme Court announced that the state may assert an "unqualified" interest in the preservation of human life. *Id.* at 2853. Thus the state need not make judgments about a particular patient's quality of life, but can equally protect all stages of life.

forty states have enacted living will statutes.[37] However, many of these statutes are very limited and have been narrowly construed.[38] Most of these statutes allow a terminally ill patient to authorize withdrawal of life-sustaining procedures.[39] Some of these statutes provide that such a withdrawal constitutes neither suicide nor homicide.[40] Ironically, many living will statutes do not contain this last provision, yet these same states have laws condemning assisted suicide.[41] A lack both of clarity and substantial guidance by the state legislatures has forced the courts to single-handedly develop the law governing euthanasia.

III. LEGALIZED SUICIDE'S EFFECT ON THE ELDERLY AND POOR

State statutes[42] and the *Cruzan*[43] decision would seem to indicate that the legalization of assisted suicide through a constitutionally protected right to die is unlikely. But for many of the more oppressed members of our society, the right to die is being protected by the courts in this country.[44]

---

37. *See* Peggy L. Collins, Note, *The Foundations of the Right to Die*, 90 W. VA. L. REV. 235 (1987) for a list of jurisdictions with living will statutes.

38. *Id.* at 258. Natural death acts apply only to incompetent patients in a terminal condition who would die regardless of life sustaining procedures and who, with the exceptions noted, have executed a living will when competent. *Id.*

39. "The living will expresses the desire of the patient that his or her dying not be prolonged by life-sustaining procedures. It directs the withholding or withdrawal of such procedures in the event that the declarant becomes incompetent . . . and in a terminal condition." *Id.* at 248. The legal procedures involved in these Natural Death Acts require that the document be in writing, signed by the declarant in the presence of two witnesses of legal age, and dated. All of these statutes also provide more lenient and informal procedures for the revocation of a living will. *Id.* at 249.

40. *Id.* at 252. Also, the acts afford immunity to health care providers who withdraw or withhold life-sustaining procedures. *Id.* at 250. However, many of the acts contain statements that reflect legislative concern that they not be extended further than contemplated. Many statutes contain provisions that condemn mercy killing or affirmative acts to end a human life. *Id.* at 252-53.

41. Forsythe & Rosenblum, *supra* note 17, at 12. The statutes in at least ten states expressly repudiate suicide and euthanasia. *Id.* However, many statutes do have provisions condemning affirmative acts of euthanasia/suicide. *See infra* notes 96-100 and accompanying text.

42. *See id.*

43. *See supra* notes 33-36 and accompanying text.

44. *See infra* notes 50-55 and accompanying text for the *Bouvia* case; *see infra* notes 57-59 and accompanying text for the cases of Sydney Greenspan and Mary O'Connor. There are numerous other examples in which the courts have allowed certain patients to withdraw life-sustaining equipment and/or food and water, even where the patient was not terminally ill or dying. *See e.g.*, In re Grant, 747 P.2d 445, *corrected* 757 P.2d 534 (Wash. 1988) (court allowed the withdrawal of assisted feeding from a patient with Batten's Disease, a neurological disorder), *vacated* 757 P.2d 534 (Wash. 1988) (changed vote of one justice); Delio v. Westchester County Medical Center, 516 N.Y.S.2d 677 (N.Y. App. Div.

Some celebrate this newfound right, but as judges continue to base euthanasia decisions on quality of life perceptions, the danger to the ill, disabled, and elderly grows. In examining the quality of life of an individual patient, the court may impose its own perception of the quality of life and decide that an individual's life is worthless to society. A subjective standard gives rise to fears that the patient's real wishes and needs will not be heard in the decision-making process. Due process demands that safeguards be placed on these decisions, lest the right to die become an "open door to social killing."[45]

Janet Adkins, an Alzheimer's sufferer who feared the horrifying death that lay ahead of her, killed herself because she did not wish to be a burden to her loved ones.[46] Had she gone to the courts requesting relief from her suffering through the aid of Dr. Kevorkian's machine, the courts would not have allowed it. Active methods of euthanasia are usually not permitted by the courts.[47] Mrs. Adkins shared feelings of abandonment, uselessness, and fright with other terminally ill, disabled or elderly people. Since society is unwilling to help them combat these fears, the unfortunate solution many seek is suicide. By ignoring the needs of these members of society, we are teaching the public that fear of dependence and frailty can reasonably be acted upon to end one's life.[48]

Since the quality of life standard was introduced in the courts, the decisions have become more prejudicial to society's oppressed.[49] The case of Elizabeth Bouvia, a highly publicized case in the California Court of Appeals which involved a bedridden quadriplegic woman who sought to end her life, is illustrative.[50] Although the trial judge rejected her petition

---

1987) (New York Supreme Court allowed assisted feeding to be withdrawn from Daniel Delio, an individual in a chronic vegetative state, but not terminally ill or dying).

45. Forsythe & Rosenblum, *supra* note 17, at 3.

46. *See supra* note 5 and accompanying text.

47. *See supra* notes 12-15 and accompanying text.

48. Forsythe & Rosenblum, *supra* note 17, at 22-23.

49. "The conclusion is now inescapable that the severely disabled have been singled out for lesser protection than the law would provide to 'normal' patients with a good prognosis for recovery." Destro, *supra* note 25, at 121. In one case, the trial court admitted that it had authorized the withdrawal of feeding from "[a] person who was otherwise healthy, who would be quite capable of leading a normal, active lifestyle which would include employment." *Brophy v. New England Sinai Hospital*, No. 85E009-G1, slip op. at 10 (Mass P. & Fam. Ct. Oct. 21, 1985) (finding of fact #55) *cited in* Destro, *supra* note 25, at 121-22. Cases like *Brophy* indicate that entitlement to equal protection under the law apparently hinges on whether an individual is "otherwise healthy", and not whether he or she is a "person." Destro, *supra* note 25, at 122.

50. Robert Lindsey, *Ruling is Upheld in Suicide Appeal*, N.Y. TIMES, Jan 20, 1984, at B4, col.3. Ms. Bouvia checked herself into the psychiatric unit of Riverside County Hospital. She subsequently announced her wish to end her life, and since she was physically

to withdraw her feeding tube, the Court of Appeals granted it.[51] The Court of Appeals said cryptically:

> Although alert, bright, sensitive, perhaps even brave and feisty, she must lie immobile, unable to exist except through the physical acts of others. Her mind and spirit may be free to take great flights but she herself is imprisoned and must lie physically helpless subject to the ignominy, embarrassment, humiliation and dehumanizing aspects created by her helplessness.[52]

In its opinion the Court of Appeals manifested the deep-seated social prejudice against the disabled held by much of society.[53] In this decision,

---

unable to do so on her own, enlisted the hospital for help. *Id.* When the hospital refused, she convinced the American Civil Liberties Union (ACLU) to help her force the hospital to comply with her wishes. *Id.*

51. Bouvia v. Superior Court, 224 Cal. Rptr. 297 (1986). The California Court of Appeals granted Ms. Bouvia the right to terminate her life. According to one critic, the court ". . .granted her a right to a judicially sanctioned, medically assisted suicide." Paul K. Longmore, *Elizabeth Bouvia, Assisted Suicide and Social Prejudice*, 3 ISSUES IN L. & MED. 141, 157 (1987).

52. *Bouvia*, 225 Cal. Rptr. at 305. In its opinion, the court emphasized only the physical disabilities of Ms. Bouvia's illness. The court discussed Ms. Bouvia's quadriplegia and cerebral palsy, which would cause her to remain bedridden for the rest of her life. *Id.* at 300. Although the *Bouvia* Court chastised the trial court for not considering a quality of life standards, in fact the *Bouvia* Court concentrated only on Ms. Bouvia's physical quality of life, not on her overall quality of life. On this ground, the court found her quality of life ". . .diminished to the point of hopelessness, uselessness, unenjoyability and frustration." *Id.* at 304.

53. There is a long history of social prejudice against the disabled. Prior to the 18th century, people with disabilities were regarded as "subhuman." *See* L. WOLFENSBERGER, THE ORIGIN AND NATURE OF OUR INSTITUTIONAL MODELS, 7-13 (1975), *cited in* Longmore, *supra* note 51, at 142 n.2. Later in the 19th and early 20th centuries, prejudice against the disabled took a different form — the mentally retarded and disabled were often blamed for social problems ranging from poverty to crime. *Id.* at 35-36. As a result, the disabled were segregated out of the mainstream of society. One Chicago ordinance prohibited "any person who is diseased, maimed, mutilated or in any way deformed so as to be an unsightly or disgusting object or improper person to be allowed in or on the public ways or other public places in this city, from exposing himself to public view." F. BOWE, HANDICAPPING AMERICA 186 (1978), *cited in* Longmore, *supra* note 51, at 144 n.18. Segregation was seldom enough for those who feared the disabled. State legislatures passed laws compelling the sterilization of many disabled people. The Supreme Court upheld a law approving the sterilization of mentally retarded persons confined to state institutions, reasoning that "three generations of imbeciles are enough." Buck v. Bell, 274 U.S. 200, 207 (1927).

Today, the discrimination against the disabled and mentally retarded has eased somewhat with the passage of federal laws prohibiting discrimination in federally funded programs. This legislation has ensured rights such as equal access to public places and transportation. Longmore, *supra* note 51, at 147-48. Furthermore, disability rights activists continue to lobby for legislation promoting equal access and opportunity. *Id.* at 148. However, prejudice against and fear of people who look and act differently still exists.

the court seems to equate social disability with social death. The court reached its decision despite the fact that this woman had graduated from college, was pursuing a master's degree, had been married, and planned on becoming a mother.[54] By allowing Ms. Bouvia to die, the court is essentially saying to her, "Your fear is valid. You are useless to society, and your desire not to be a burden on others is sufficient to justify your death."[55]

The elderly are not immune to this social prejudice.[56] Sidney

---

Moreover, hostility often exists towards those that require greater accommodation to meet their needs. The danger today is that these fears and prejudices will not be manifested openly, but will be ". . .masked by an avowed compassion, contempt cloaking itself in paternalism." *Id.* at 141.

54. By focusing on the physical side of Ms. Bouvia's disability, the court ignored the problems that forced Ms. Bouvia to seek suicide. Before she checked into the hospital to have her feeding tube withdrawn, Ms. Bouvia suffered a number of personal and professional setbacks. On a personal level, her brother drowned, she suffered a miscarriage, and she and her husband separated. Wayne Biddle and Margot Slade, *'Withdrawal' or Suicide?*, N.Y. TIMES, Dec. 11, 1983, at D7, col.5; Judith Cummings, *Plea by Patient for Starvation Barred by Court*, N.Y. TIMES, Dec. 17, 1983, at A8, col.1. Professionally, Ms. Bouvia was pursuing a Master's Degree at San Diego State University. She was denied the opportunity to perform the field work required for her degree at the hospital of her choice, and told that she could only work with other disabled people. Afraid that she could never achieve her career goals, she dropped out of school. M. Pabst Battin, *Ms. Bouvia Challenges Law, Medicine, and Morality*, 15 HEMLOCK QUARTERLY 4, 4 (1984).

If one examines the underlying facts of Ms. Bouvia's situation, it is clear that these personal setbacks were a contributing, if not primary, cause of her suicide request. The court's failure to take into account the circumstances surrounding her request is inexcusable. While cloaking its words in compassion, the California court is in essence denying Ms. Bouvia's worth as a person.

55. Many far-reaching implications can be drawn from the *Bouvia* case. As the disabled and the mentally retarded remain a target of covert prejudice, the right to die may evolve into a socially accepted "duty" to die. People with disabilities will be forced into "choosing" to end their lives; and unless courts look at the underlying facts of the situation, this "choice" might be upheld. Longmore, *supra* note 51, at 158-59. *See also, Quality of Life, supra* note 25, at 122-130.

56. *See infra* notes 57-59 and accompanying text for the cases of Sydney Greenspan and Mary O'Connor. The most dramatic case involving an elderly patient is the case of Carrie Coons. Coons was an 86 year old woman who suffered a stroke, and who remained in a persistent vegetative state for four and a half months. Nat Hentoff, *The Church, the Law, and the Advancing Armies of Death*, 33 CATH. LAW 1, 8 (1990). Mrs. Coons' family petitioned to have her feeding tube withdrawn. Judge Harris of the New York Supreme Court granted her request, claiming that Carrie Coons would have wanted this if she were here right now. In re Application of Gannon v. Albany Memorial Hospital (Coons), No. 0189-017460 (N.Y. Sup. Ct., Feb. 14, 1989). The judge ordered the feeding tube withdrawn within two weeks. When the hospital staff learned of the decision, they urged Carrie Coons to eat, and shortly thereafter she awoke from her persistent vegetative state. Hentoff, *supra*, at 9. Needless to say, the order was withdrawn soon afterwards. The lawyers and doctors credit the caring nursing staff for Mrs. Coons' recovery. *Id.* at 9. This case is evidence of both the imprecision of medical judgment, and of the dangers inherent in allocating a personal choice of life or death to family members.

Greenspan, whose case awaits decision before the Illinois Supreme Court, expressed little more than a fear of frailty and dependence while he was competent.[57] However, the Cook County Public Guardian sought to withdraw his assisted feeding.[58] Seventy-seven year old Mary O'Connor received authorization from the New York Supreme Court to have her assisted feeding withdrawn, although she was not in a persistent vegetative state, a coma, terminally ill, or dying. Her status as an elderly woman suffering from a mental disease was sufficient, according to the trial court, to endanger her life.[59]

Suicides among the elderly are increasing. According to Austrian authority Dr. Erwin Ringel, worldwide suicide rates among persons over sixty are "high and are steadily increasing."[60] He continues by asserting "if we look at the behaviour of many people toward the old and even toward the merely aging, we may begin to wonder just how sincere the wish of the community is to keep its older people alive."[61] By comparison, "in areas where the aged enjoy real esteem (as in certain Far Eastern countries), suicide among the old is actually a rare occurrence."[62]

Right-to-die advocates claim that their cause is based on individual autonomy; that the individual has the choice of when and how to end his or her life. This proposition, however, does not address the social choice

---

57. Mr. Greenspan was diagnosed as being in a chronic vegetative state without any hope of recovery. In re Estate of Greenspan, 558 N.E.2d 1194 (Ill. 1990). However, he was not terminally ill and there was no testimony that Greenspan ever commented on the use or withdrawal of assisted feeding. *Id.* at 1198.

58. Although Mr. Greenspan made no express statements on the use of assisted feeding, the Cook County Public Guardian wished to rely on other statements to withdraw the feeding tube. When visiting friends in a nursing home, Mr. Greenspan once commented that he would never wish to live that way. *Id.* Also, his wife testified that he would not wish to be a burden to society. *Id.*

59. Mary O'Connor was diagnosed as having "multi-infarct dementia," a condition involving impairment of an individual's cognitive abilities. Forsythe & Rosenblum, *supra* note 17, at 31. Her daughters petitioned the court to have her assisted feeding withdrawn, and although the two lower courts agreed with the daughters, the Court of Appeals reversed. *Westchester Cty. Medical Center ex rel Mary O'Conner*, 531 N.E.2d 607 (N.Y. 1988). Since the Court of Appeals believed that there had not been clear and convincing evidence that Mary O'Connor would have chosen to extract the feeding tube, the court reversed. *Id.*

60. Erwin Ringel, *Suicide Prevention and the Value of Human Life, cited in* Mary Rose Barrington, *Apologia for Suicide, in* SUICIDE: THE PHILOSOPHICAL ISSUES 90 (M. Pabst Battin & C. Mayo, eds. 1980) at 208. In a recent study, the Center for Disease Control (CDC) found that from 1980-86, the rate of suicide among people 65 and older increased 21% in the United States. *More Elderly Turn to Suicide*, Gannett, Sept. 16, 1991, *cited in* LEXIS, Nexis Library, Gannett file.

61. Ringel, *supra* note 60, at 90.

62. *Id.*

involved when judges base their decisions on quality of life standards. The legal decision of when to permit euthanasia is inevitably tied to the social question of when a life is not worth living and, therefore, not worth preserving.[63] Viewed in this light, euthanasia is repugnant to society because it threatens one of the most fundamental assumptions of our system: that all are equal in the eyes of the law.[64] The cases of Elizabeth Bouvia, Sidney Greenspan and Mary O'Connor, in which the courts found some forms of life unworthy of protection, threatens this principle.

There are certainly unresolved problems stemming from the right to die decisions. However, these decisions have advanced the idea that suicide is the solution to the needs of the disabled, elderly, and sick in our society. Suicide does not have to be the only answer. The need for doctor-assisted suicide is significantly reduced if the basic fears of the ill and elderly are addressed. According to Franne Whitney Nelson, the operator of a hospice program in Virginia Beach, "[p]eople have two basic fears: the fear of pain and the fear of abandonment. Help with those emotions and . . . [euthanasia] won't even be an issue."[65] It is too late for Janet Adkins, but it is not too late for the burgeoning numbers of elderly in our society. Helping the elderly and infirm face their fears of declining health and death is preferable to legally sanctioned suicide.

IV.   THE DOCTOR'S ROLE IN FACILITATING SUICIDE

One of the most hallowed canons of medical ethics is that doctors must not kill.[66] Yet courts, doctors and commentators on medical ethics have

---

63. Beschle, *supra* note 11; at 357, *citing* Richard Sherlock, *Liberalism, Public Policy and the Life Not Worth Living: Abraham Lincoln on Beneficient Euthanasia*, 26 AM. J. JURIS. 47 (1981).

64. *Id.* Sherlock claims that these highly difficult decisions are less troublesome if we think of them not as our decision, but instead as our response to the individual patient's choice.

65. *Hospice Director Says Death Doctors Not Needed*, UPI, Aug. 7, 1990, *available in* LEXIS, Nexis Library, UPI file. The purpose of Ms. Nelson's hospice program is to give the terminally ill a feeling of worth. *Id.* Ms. Nelson tries to ease both the physical and the emotional fears of these patients. In the words of one patient in the hospice program, "I'm not afraid of dying. . . . [W]hen you have people around you who care, it makes the road a lot easier." *Id. See also, Planning for Death*, WASHINGTON POST, June 25, 1991, at Z6, where the author contends that patients such as Mrs. Adkins might benefit from effective counseling and psychotherapy that could help the person appreciate the rich possibilities that exist in life, even when severe, progressive and disabling illness is present.

Doctors also agree with Ms. Nelson's care of the terminally ill. "If care is administered properly at the end of life, only the rare patient should be so distressed that he or she desires to commit suicide." Wazen et al., *supra* note 4, at 847.

66. Willard Gaylin et al., *Doctors Must Not Kill*, 259 JAMA 2139 (1988). As recently as 1986, the Judicial Counsel of the American Medical Association affirmed the

clung to the distinction between stopping useless treatment and actively taking steps to end a patient's life.[67] Today this distinction is arguably becoming less important as more people call for the legalization of doctor-assisted suicide. Nevertheless, a different set of problems results from allowing doctor-assisted suicide. Dr. Kevorkian's case highlights one of the problems that may arise: when a doctor advances the choice of death, the role of doctor as "healer" is diminished.

Dr. Kevorkian's decision to assist Janet Adkins' suicide rested on one dinner table conversation with her a few days before her death.[68] Some doctors argue that Alzheimer's disease rendered Janet Adkins incompetent to make this decision.[69] None, however, would argue that Dr. Kevorkian was qualified to make this decision. One critic stated, "[e]ven the staunchest proponents of physician-assisted suicide should be horrified at this case because there were no procedural protections."[70]

---

principle that a physician "should not intentionally cause death." *Id.* According to Gaylin, "[n]either legal tolerance nor the best bedside manner can ever make medical killing medically ethical." *Id.*

67. *Id.* For centuries, doctors have not been permitted to take such active steps to end a patient's life because ". . .killing on demand would erode patient trust and the moral basis of the profession." Lawrence K. Altman, M.D., *The Doctor's World*, N.Y. TIMES, June 12, 1990, at C3. However, there is anecdotal evidence which suggests that some doctors advise patients that they would die if they ingested a few more pills. Other doctors have admitted that they have administered extra morphine to terminally ill patients. *Id.*

68. *The Kevorkian Cure: Death*, N.Y. TIMES, Dec. 9, 1990, at D16. Two days after the dinner table conversation, Dr. Kevorkian traveled to a public campground where he hooked Mrs. Adkins up to his machine. He went to the campground because he could not obtain the consent of any other local establishment to permit the suicide on its premises.

69. Since Alzheimer's affects cognitive abilities, the onset of the disease may render the patient incompetent to make life or death decisions. A doctor "has to claim she [the patient] made her decision competently," observes Dr. Joanne Lynn, professor at George Washington University, "but the diagnosis of Alzheimer's is almost incompatible with that claim." Gibbs, *supra* note 1, at 69. Moreover, there is no simple test to reliably diagnose Alzheimer's disease. Doctors usually diagnose the disease by taking a detailed medical history and by identifying symptoms that are characteristic of the disease, i.e. memory loss, personality changes, confusion, and the inability to solve complex problems. Natalie Angler, *Diagnosis of Alzheimer's is No Matter of Certainty*, N.Y. TIMES, June 7, 1990, at D22. Physicians then try to rule out other causes for the symptoms, such as strokes, head trauma or brain tumors. When these competing explanations have been eliminated, doctors often settle on a diagnosis of probable Alzheimer's. Even with a positive diagnosis of Alzheimer's, the patient's condition worsens only gradually. As it is difficult to make a definitive diagnosis of Alzheimer's, it would be "precipitous", at best, for a patient diagnosed with Alzheimer's to commit suicide. *Id.*

70. Susan M. Wolf of the Hastings Center, Gibbs, *supra* note 1, at 69. Where procedural precautions have been followed, however, doctor-assisted suicide is more socially acceptable. In July, 1991, a Rochester, New York grand jury declined to indict Dr. Timothy Quill for prescribing barbiturates along with instructions for a lethal dose to a leukemia patient. Lisa W. Foderaro, *New York Will Not Discipline Doctor for His Role in Suicide*, N.Y. TIMES, Aug. 17, 1991, at A25. The New York Board for Professional

Proponents of death with dignity legislation are careful to include procedural safeguards in their proposed laws. Many of these statutes require that patients make a witnessed legal request in writing, and further require two independent doctors to confirm that the patient's condition is unbearable and irreversible.[71] In this case, Dr. Kevorkian ignored all procedural protections: he and the patient were barely acquainted, he was not a specialist,[72] and he ignored her family doctor's opinion that Mrs. Adkins had several years to live.[73] Furthermore, at the time Mrs. Adkins answered the advertisement he placed in a magazine, Dr. Kevorkian was actively searching for a "volunteer" to test his machine.[74] This apparent conflict of interest casts serious doubt on his ability to make decisions in the best interests of his patient.[75]

Moreover, difficulties may arise within the doctor-patient relationship that will prevent the doctor from accurately diagnosing the patient's

---

Medical Conduct, a three-member panel that functions as the disciplinary arm of the New York State Health Department, found no evidence of misconduct on the doctor's behalf. The Board emphasized that although it did not condone assisted suicide, Dr. Quill's longstanding relationship with his patient and his failure to directly participate in the taking of life distinguished this case from Dr. Kevorkian's. *Id.*

71. Gibbs, *supra* note 1, at 69.

72. Dr. Kevorkian and Mrs. Adkins met over one dinner table conversation. *See supra* note 68. Furthermore, Dr. Kevorkian was a retired pathologist and not an Alzheimer's specialist. *The Kevorkian Cure: Death, supra* note 68, at D16.

73. Dr. Raskind, Janet Adkins' personal physician, testified at the hearing before Circuit Judge Alice Gilbert on the motion to ban Dr. Kevorkian's machine from use in Michigan. *See infra* notes 107-08 and accompanying text. Dr. Raskind, a professor and vice chairman for research development at the University of Washington's Psychiatric and Behavioral Sciences Department, testified that although Janet Adkins was doomed to die, she could have lived another seven to ten years if she had not taken her own life. *Suicide Machine Victim Could Have Lived Another Decade,* UPI, Jan. 4, 1991, *available in* LEXIS, Nexis Library, UPI file. Furthermore, Dr. Raskind stated that "Adkins was not competent to make such an important decision and appeared to have trouble remembering certain things." *Id.* Raskind had received a phone call from Dr. Kevorkian in May, and Kevorkian told him he intended to use the machine on Mrs. Adkins in June. Dr. Raskind strongly discouraged Dr. Kevorkian from testing the machine on Adkins. *Id.*

74. After inventing his suicide machine in the fall of 1989, Dr. Kevorkian attempted to advertise it in a local medical journal. When the editors refused, he peddled his machine in local newspapers. As a result, Dr. Kevorkian found himself on the "Donahue" show. *Suicide Machine, supra* note 1, at 69.

75. *The Kevorkian Cure: Death, supra* note 68, at D22. Because Dr. Kevorkian sought a volunteer for his machine, his judgment was somewhat impaired. While doctors are supposed to act in the best interests of the patient, i.e. make objective decisions that will further the patient's welfare, Dr. Kevorkian's decision seems to be based at least partially on his own self-interest. Dr. Kevorkian wished to send a message to society, that suicide should be a viable alternative in the face of suffering. The facts of the Adkins case, coupled with his desire to test the machine, casts doubt on whether Dr. Kevorkian considered what was best for Janet Adkins.

problem. Diagnosis of Alzheimer's disease is both uncertain[76] and frightening, since the cause of the disease is unknown and there is no cure.[77] As a result, people diagnosed with incurable conditions like Alzheimer's Disease often become depressed or suicidal. According to researchers, the problem is that doctors do not recognize the warning signs of depression or confuse them with the signs of the disease.[78]

Research has shown that one-quarter to one-third of all Alzheimer's patients become clinically depressed at some point in the course of the illness.[79] If a doctor is allowed to advocate the choice of "rational suicide", then patients suffering from Alzheimer's or other incurable diseases could make this life or death decision while suffering from depression. Severe depression may so cloud a patient's thinking that he or she is incapable of making a clear decision;[80] yet if the doctor does not recognize the symptoms of depression, the patient may be permitted to opt for suicide.

"Two incorrect assumptions are often made about suicides that follow a physical illness. . . . One is that these individuals are free from mental disorders . . . [t]he second incorrect assumption is that the physical illness is the only basis for the suicide decision."[81] Individuals seeking suicide may wish to escape not only the debilitating effects of the disease, but the societal rejection that often accompanies illness or disability.[82] It is the

---

76. *See supra* note 69.

77. Alzheimer's Disease is a progressive neurological disorder that results in the gradual and irreversible destruction of brain tissue. About four million people are believed to suffer from Alzheimer's. Most of these people are over the age of 65. *See supra* note 69.

78. Miriam Shuchman, *Depression Hidden in Deadly Disease*, N.Y. TIMES, Nov. 15, 1990, at B17. Depression is often ignored in patients with terminal illnesses because many of the symptoms, such as loss of appetite and low energy, can be attributed to the illness, or are seen as a response to the diagnosis. *Id.* Also, according to these researchers, even if doctors recognize the signs of depression, they take a "fatalistic" view of the disease, and do nothing about them. *Id.*

79. *Id.* According to researchers, Alzheimer's patients are especially at risk for depression early in the disease, because they fear that they will become a burden to their families. The same risk of non-diagnosis of depression exists for other patients with terminal diseases. Recent studies show that 10-15% of cancer patients meet the criteria for clinical depression, however only 3-5% are treated with anti-depressant medication. *Id.* In 1990, the American Journal of Psychiatry performed the first controlled study of the treatment of depression among people with Alzheimer's. The study found that depressed Alzheimer's patients respond favorably to anti-depressant medication, as well as to alternative forms of treatment, such as increased social stimulation. *Id.*

80. *Id.* If a patient is adjudged incompetent, then doctors are, in many jurisdictions, "legally obligated to override the decision to die." *Id.* However, since many doctors are unaware of the patient's depressed condition or are unwilling to treat it, the depressed patient's wish may be fulfilled.

81. Marzen et al, *supra* note 12, at 132.

82. The authors claim that if societal rejection was replaced by societal care and acceptance, many people would not choose suicide. *Id.* The authors cite the case of Larry

doctor's responsibility to identify not only the patient's physical ailments, but their mental infirmities as well. To effectively treat the patient, knowledge of the patient is of paramount importance.[83] "The key is having a relationship with the patient, and being willing to treat what is treatable."[84] Treating the underlying pain, depression, or delirium may eliminate the patient's wish to die.[85]

Many doctors consider Dr. Kevorkian's actions a breach of the doctor-patient trust. However, other physicians believe that public attitudes toward dying patients have changed,[86] and that the general public may feel very differently about euthanasia than doctors do.[87] These doctors encourage the medical profession to be open to physician-assisted suicide.[88] But these commentators ignore the fact that this issue touches medicine "at its very moral center."[89] Since the Oath of Hippocrates, Western medicine has viewed the killing of patients as the most severe violation of its ethical code. If doctors are permitted to kill, they "will never again be worthy of trust and respect as healer and comforter and protector of life in all its frailty."[90] Nazi Germany[91] and the Netherlands[92] serve as examples

---

LeBlanc, a forty- four year old man with multiple sclerosis who attempted to take his life. A friend stopped him, and since then he has developed new relationships and interests that have given him more satisfaction with his life. *Id.* at 130-33. In a complete role reversal, he has sought to preserve the life of Elizabeth Bouvia, another severely disabled woman. *See supra* notes 50-55 and accompanying text.

83. Shuchman, *supra* note 78.

84. *Id.*, (quoting Dr. Donna Greenberg, a psychiatrist who treats cancer patients at Massachusetts General Hospital in Boston, Massachusetts).

85. *Id. See also* note 65 and accompanying text.

86. *The Physician's Responsibility*, *supra* note 4, at 844.

87. George D. Lundberg, M.D., *"It's Over Debbie" and the Euthanasia Debate*, 259 *JAMA* 2142, 2143 (1988). A recent Roper Poll shows that a majority of Americans support euthanasia and the right to die in certain instances. *Id.* The state of Washington had Initiative 119 on its ballot this past November, the nation's first proposal permitting doctor assisted suicide for the terminally ill. Jay Mathews, *'Death with Dignity' Issue Set for Washington Vote*, PHILA. INQUIRER, Feb. 17, 1991 at A30. Although the initiative failed by a 54%-46% margin, the state of California will have a similar initiative on the ballot this fall. Peter Steinfels, *Beliefs*, N.Y. TIMES, Nov. 9, 1991, at A11. California's initiative, however, promises to contain more procedural safeguards than those contained in the Washington initiative. These safeguards include a waiting period between the time a request is submitted to a physician and the patients' death, and a requirement that those patients requesting aid in dying inform their families of their intent. *Id.*

88. Lundberg, *supra* note 87, at 2143.

89. Gaylin et al., *supra* note 66, at 2139.

90. *Id.* at 2140.

91. In Nazi Germany, a massive euthanasia program was implemented against disabled Germans. Longmore, *supra* note 51, at 145. The managers of this euthanasia program claimed that persons "delivered by death" would be chosen through a series of examinations by two doctors. *Id.* In practice, however, this procedure was not followed, and the disabled were arbitrarily "condemned to death in droves." *Id.*

of the consequences which may arise when the protections against doctor-assisted suicide are removed. Doctors cannot be authorized to rid society of its "burdensome" members.

If doctor-assisted suicide is legalized, procedural safeguards to protect the patient may not be sufficient. The advent of doctor-assisted suicide changes the moral core of the medical profession. "For if medicine's power over life may be used equally to heal or to kill, the doctor is no more a moral professional, but rather a morally neutered technician."[93] The doctor that was once seen as the "last friend"[94] of the suffering patient may no longer be so viewed.

V. SANCTIONS FOR ASSISTED SUICIDE

Doctor-assisted suicide has not been accepted in this country. Since aiding suicide may unduly discriminate against the disabled, elderly, and abandoned,[95] sanctions are needed to discourage doctors and others from advocating this choice. The present law on assisted suicide is unclear in many states[96] and many judges and juries are reluctant to convict because they view the criminal penalties as too severe.[97] State legislatures must take a serious look at the sanctions mandated in euthanasia/assisted suicide cases to ensure a more coherent policy towards those accused of facilitating suicide.

Many states already have identified assisted suicide as a crime. A distinct minority of states have statutes that punish the aiding or causing of

---

92. The Netherlands is the only Western country where doctor-assisted suicide is permitted. That country has, sadly, produced "well-documented cases" of unwarranted killings by doctors. *See* Gaylin et al, *supra* note 66, at 2140, for foreign periodical treatment of this issue.

93. *Id.*

94. *See* Edward J. Grant & Clarke D. Forsythe, *The Plight of the Last Friend: Legal Issues for Physicians and Nurses in Providing Nutrition and Hydration*, 2 ISSUES IN L. & MED. 277 (1987).

95. *See supra* notes 42-65 and accompanying text.

96. Almost half of the states do not have laws prohibiting assisted suicide. Michigan is one of these states, and inasmuch as Michigan law is similar to law in other states, the ambiguity seems evident. In Michigan, under common law, one could be charged with assisting suicide. For the history of state prosecution of assisted suicide in Michigan, see People v. Campbell, 335 N.W.2d 27 (Mich. App. 1983). *See also Suicide Doctor Might Disobey Court Order*, UPI, Oct. 4, 1990 *available in* LEXIS, Nexis Library, UPI file. However, since this position has not been codified, the courts have refused to follow it. *Id.* Thus prosecutors must charge those who assist suicide with murder. Since the state laws are not uniform, a person like Dr. Kevorkian could "forum shop" for the state which imposes lighter sanctions against a defendant.

97. *See infra* notes 103-05 and accompanying text.

suicide as murder or manslaughter.[98] However, the majority of states that impose criminal liability for assisting suicide have established it as a separate offense.[99] The state's interest in preserving life supplies the underlying rationale for these statutes. Many state decisions, which have rejected applications by healthy persons to commit suicide, indicate that the state's interest in preserving life will override an individual's preference for death.[100]

Right to die activists criticize this state policy as "excessive paternalism" and as an invasion of a constitutionally protected right to die.[101] However, this argument ignores the fact that suicide is often a tragedy, greatly affecting the lives of the victim's loved ones. "At least when an individual is physically healthy, it seems morally wrong for a person to assist that individual's suicide, much less participate in it, and the states have acted to express their interest in preserving life by imposing criminal penalties for such behavior."[102]

Suicide assistance statutes are generally targeted at those who provide the means of suicide.[103] In the past ten years, however, in assisted suicide prosecutions, states have focused upon many defendants who claimed to be motivated by love and compassion. Most of these cases involved ailing suicide victims who were determined to end a painful existence.[104] Judges sympathetic to the plight of the defendants gave lenient sentences, even in cases where the statute imposed harsh sanctions.[105]

To date, no doctor has been successfully prosecuted for assisting a suicide.[106] Dr. Kevorkian was charged with first degree murder for the

---

98. *See e.g.*, ARIZ. REV. STAT. ANN. § 13-1103 (A)(3) (1989) ("A person commits manslaughter by. . .[i]ntentionally aiding another to commit suicide. . . .").

99. At present, twenty-six states have such statutes. *See, e.g.* CAL. PENAL CODE § 401 (West 1988).

100. Catherine D. Shaffer, Note, *Criminal Liability for Assisting Suicide*, 86 COLUM. L. REV. 348, 354 (1986). For the specific state interests involved, *see supra* note 30.

101. *Id.* Euthanasia activists consider the right to die to be an integral part of the constitutional right to privacy.

102. *Id.* For the argument that even where a person is not physically healthy, it may be morally wrong for the state to allow an assisted suicide, *see supra* notes 42-65 and accompanying text.

103. *Id.* at 360-61.

104. In a typical case, a retired man helped kill his cancer-stricken wife by giving her an overdose of sedatives and putting a plastic bag over her head. He confessed, and was only sentenced to a year of probation, community service, and psychiatric treatment. UPI, Sept. 11, 1984, *available in* LEXIS, Nexis Library, UPI file, *noted in* Shaffer, *supra*, note 100, at 360 n.79.

105. For example, the statute under which the defendant was convicted carried a minimum sentence of fifteen years imprisonment.

106. In California v. Barber, 195 Cal. Rptr. 484 (1983), two doctors who withdrew an unconscious patient's ventilator with family approval were prosecuted for first degree

facilitation of Janet Adkins' suicide. The District Court judge, however, dismissed the charge.[107] Calling suicide a "private and personal matter," the judge concluded that Dr. Kevorkian committed no crime under state law and that the question of the criminality of assisted suicide was an issue for the legislature and not the courts to decide.[108]

Within days of the dismissal, Governor-elect John Engler called for legislation outlawing assisted suicide.[109] The prosecutors in the Kevorkian case, though not appealing the District judge's decision, pursued a civil remedy which called for a permanent bar against the use of Dr. Kevorkian's machine in Michigan.[110] On February 5, 1991, Circuit Judge Alice Gilbert granted this injunction.[111]

Judge Gilbert's ruling foreclosed the use of Dr. Kevorkian's machine by others clamoring to use it.[112] In light of the prejudice many courts have manifested in deciding quality of life cases involving the disabled and elderly,[113] Judge Gilbert's awareness of the plight of society's unwanted should be applauded. Judge Gilbert's recognition of the dangers of using methods like Dr. Kevorkian's is an approach which should be followed by judges and lawmakers throughout the country.

---

murder. Because the doctors had not acted with malice in removing the tubes, their actions were not seen as unlawful and they were ultimately dismissed. *Id.* at 487.

107. *Judge Frees "Suicide Machine" Doctor*, UPI, Dec. 13, 1990, *available in* LEXIS, Nexis Library, UPI file.

108. *Id.*

109. Rick Pluta, *Engler Says He Would Sign Assisted-Suicide Ban*, UPI, Dec. 14, 1990, *available in* LEXIS, Nexis Library, UPI file.

110. Isabel Wilkerson, *Prosecutors Seek to Ban Doctor's Suicide Machine*, N.Y. TIMES, Jan. 5, 1991, at A6.

111. *Kevorkian's 'Death Machine' Permanently Barred From Michigan*, N.Y. TIMES, Feb. 5, 1991, at A12.

112. Sherry Miller, a 42 year-old woman from Roseville, Michigan, expressed a desire to use Dr. Kevorkian's suicide machine. *M.S. Victim Would Welcome Suicide Machine*, UPI, Jan. 9, 1991, *available in* LEXIS, Nexis Library, UPI File. On October 23, 1991, she got her wish when she died using Dr. Kevorkian's suicide machine. Miller, along with Marjorie Wantz, a Michigan woman suffering from a painful pelvic disorder, became the most recent victims of Dr. Kevorkian's controversial suicide machine when they died in late October at a lakeside cabin in Michigan. *Tale of Two Suicides*, U.S.A. TODAY, October 25, 1991, at A1. These deaths were subsequently labeled as homicides by Dr. L.J. Dragovic, the county medical examiner. *Two Suicides Assisted by 'Dr. Death' Ruled Homicides*, Gannett, Dec. 19, 1991, *available in* LEXIS, Nexis Library, Current File. As a result, the Oakland County Prosecutor has asked a grand jury to conduct a murder investigation of Dr. Kevorkian. *'Dr. Death' Could Face New Charges*, UPI, Dec. 19, 1991, *available in* LEXIS, Nexis Library, UPI File. Dr. Kevorkian's lawyer has instructed Kevorkian (and all other witnesses present on October 23, 1991, including Kevorkian's sister) not to cooperate with the grand jury probe. *'Dr. Death' Won't Cooperate With Grand Jury, Lawyer Says*, UPI, Jan. 6, 1992, *available in* LEXIS, Nexis Library, UPI file.

113. *See supra* notes 42-65 and accompanying text.

VI. Proposed Legislation

New legislation is needed to prevent the courts from fashioning ad hoc remedies to prevent actions like Dr. Kevorkian's. State statutes should contain provisions similar to those proposed below:

Model Statute:
Section (1) It shall be a crime for any person to affirmatively act to end another's life;
Section (2) Affirmative action occurs when an actor:

   (a) provides the means of the suicide, or
   (b) voluntarily participates in the suicide.

Withdrawal of extra-ordinary means of medical treatment shall not constitute an affirmative act for the purposes of this section. Extra-ordinary means are all medicines, treatments and operations which cannot be obtained or used without excessive pain, expense or other inconvenience, or which if used could not offer a reasonable hope of benefit.[114]
Section (3) The crime of assisted suicide shall be a felony in the second degree and shall bear a mandatory sentence of not less than one nor greater than four years.

This statute will serve a three-fold purpose: First, the statute will deter people from assisting suicide; second, the statute will ensure that those who do facilitate suicide will be prosecuted, convicted, and sentenced appropriately; and finally, the statute will represent a legislative policy decision that the solution to the problems of the elderly, ill, and disabled is not to rid society of them. With specific limits set by statute, courts will have little room to make subjective decisions based on the victim's quality of life. This legislation ensures that the values of dignity and life would be insulated from judicial interpretation, for "[h]uman dignity is protected by preserving a person's life, and protecting that person's well-being without regard to the physical or mental condition of the person."[115]

VII. Conclusion

At the present time, most courts use the subjective quality of life test as a basis for euthanasia decisions. There is an inherent danger in measuring human life qualitatively. Who can be certain that a life not worth living today may be worth living tomorrow? Moreover, a life worth preserving in the eyes of one judge may not be worth preserving in the eyes of another. The risk to a patient increases if doctors are allowed to advocate

---

114. Robertson, *supra* note 16, at 236.
115. Forsythe & Rosenblum, *supra* note 17, at 21.

suicide. The role of doctors in our society is to preserve life, not to end it. The courts have ignored the risks inherent in subjective decision-making, and the minimal guidance offered by state legislatures has not lessened the potential danger. The public debate over the Kevorkian case is evidence that the time is right for new legislation affirming society's role in protecting human life. Such legislation would send a powerful message to society — especially those potential victims of suicide. In reaffirming their worth, we would reaffirm the worth of all members of society who may one day confront the same feelings of helplessness, loneliness, and abandonment that the elderly and sick face today.

Jennifer A. Zima

A FEMINIST ANALYSIS OF PHYSICIAN-ASSISTED DYING AND VOLUNTARY ACTIVE EUTHANASIA

LESLIE BENDER*

Benjamin Franklin said the only certainties in life are death and taxes.[1] As medical technology has developed, our capacity to extend

---

* Professor of Law, Syracuse University College of Law. A version of this paper was originally presented as the Maynard Pirsig Distinguished Lecture, William Mitchell College of Law, in November 1991. I would like to thank the William Mitchell faculty and the law faculties at Syracuse and Cincinnati, the Syracuse Consortium on the Cultural Foundations of Medicine, the Ethics Committee of the Onondaga County Medical Society, the Legal Theory Workshop at the University of Maryland College of Law, and the community at St. Lawrence University for their helpful comments and feedback. My research assistant, Diane Van Epps, Class of 1993, provided invaluable editorial assistance, and Michele Gagnon, Class of 1993, did a wonderful job helping me with the preliminary research.

For my brother, Steven Bender, always caring and attentive to others' needs.

I have titled my essay "A Feminist Analysis of Physician-Assisted Dying and Voluntary Active Euthanasia." I would like to say a little bit about the title. I say "a" feminist analysis because there are many feminist analyses and perspectives, of which my arguments are only one. Feminisms are varied and multiple. Second, I call my work "feminist" because it is grounded in a rich body of writings and thinking in feminist ethics. Because many readers are unaware of the extensive writing and theorizing within feminism and from feminist premises about every kind of subject, they think feminist is a label meaning "political struggles for women's rights." Certainly feminist means that but it also means more.

Some themes in feminist ethics are challenges to the values and conceptions of human natures and human interactions that dominate our current discourses in law, medicine, and ethics. Some feminist theorizing emphasizes the need to value and focus on care, compassion, responsiveness, responsibility, conversation, and communication, as well as learning to listen closely to others and to pay attention to others' needs, regardless of their differences from our own. I write in that tradition.

Feminist ethics also challenges power structures and systemic biases in law and ethics that undervalue or disregard the perspectives and experiences of all women in differing ways and of men of subordinated statuses, whether subordinated by structures of race, class, sexual identity, some other identity-based classification, or some combination thereof. Feminism seeks to reconstruct our understandings and practices in ways that more closely respond to the needs of those people in their daily lives and, I would argue, deaths, or, as I prefer, dying processes. I am as strongly committed to these feminist analyses, although this particular essay, limited by space and time, does not begin to address them adequately.

I have included a bibliography at the end of this essay that collects some of the many writings on euthanasia and feminist ethics that inform ongoing discussions about this topic and bioethics in general—discussions that I hope this essay advances.

1. "But in this world nothing can be said to be certain, except death and taxes." Letter from Benjamin Franklin to Jean Baptiste Le Roy (Nov. 13, 1789), in 10 THE WRITINGS OF BENJAMIN FRANKLIN, at 68 (Albert H. Smyth ed., 1905).

human lives beyond what would be their natural deaths has been so astonishing that the keenness of Franklin's aphorism seems nearer to dying than many human bodies. Thus far, we have not mastered "suspended animation" or "immortality,"[2] but medical technicians and scientists have been able to create states of "living" or "undeath" that have not been known before. Lives continue, or are restored, despite hearts stopping, lungs collapsing, livers and kidneys failing, and neocortical brains ceasing to function. For what it is worth, we now can keep bodies "alive" without minds to control them and without any recognizable connection to the personhood or personality of the former owners. Even if science defies the certainty of death, Franklin can still get his due for having it right about taxes.

Regardless of humans' valiant efforts, death remains an unavoidable issue in all our lives. Science and medicine have, at best, learned to delay its inevitability and, at worst, have painfully distorted its processes. Death is seen as a single event, rather than as part of a process of dying. The medical, scientific, and technological segments of our society seem to be in a state of frenzied denial about the inescapable reality of death in everyone's life. Recently, a significant portion of the public has begun to back away from the compulsive drive to extend life at all costs.[3] They have seen its pain, its victims,

---

2. Some people have sought immortality through cryopreservation or cryonics. For example, Thomas Donaldson, along with Alcor, a cryonics organization, unsuccessfully petitioned California courts to permit Donaldson to have his head cryonically suspended before his death and to protect Alcor from prosecution for assisting suicide. *Donaldson v. Van de Kamp*, 4 Cal. Rptr. 2d 59 (Cal. Ct. App. 1992); *see* Miles Corwin, *Tumor Victim Loses Bid to Freeze Head Before Death*, L.A. TIMES, Sept. 15, 1990, at A28; Cynthia Gorney, *Cryonics and Suicide: Avoiding 'the Slippery Slope,'* WASH. POST, May 1, 1990, at D6. The cryonics movement began 30 years ago when Robert Ettinger published THE PROSPECT OF IMMORTALITY (1961). *See* Laura Wisniewski, *Cryonics Groups Pin Their Hopes on the Big Chill*, TORONTO STAR, May 5, 1991, at B6. The title of Ettinger's book indicates the objective of this movement. In 1990, there were already 13 complete bodies and 13 heads in cryonic suspension at three cryonics centers. *See* Maria Goodavage, *Man Pins His Hopes on a Frozen Future; De-Animated—Not Dead*, USA TODAY, Sept. 25, 1990, at 6A. Because it is very expensive to freeze a whole body (about $100,000-120,000), most participants choose to freeze only their heads (at a cost of $28,000-35,000) in liquid nitrogen at 320 degrees Fahrenheit below zero. They hope they can be thawed and cured in the future when there will be the technology to regenerate bodies from the head's remaining cell tissues or to attach other bodies. Corwin, *supra*.

3. *See* Patients Self-Determination Act, Omnibus Budget Reconciliation Act of 1990, § 1866(a)(1), 42 U.S.C.A. §1395cc(a)(1) (West 1992); Cruzan v. Missouri Dep't of Health, 110 S.Ct. 2841 (1990); Bouvia v. Superior Court, 225 Cal. Rptr. 297 (Cal. Ct. App. 1986); Bartling v. Superior Court, 209 Cal. Rptr 220 (Cal. Ct. App. 1984); *In re* Estate of Longeway, 549 N.E.2d 292 (Ill. 1989); *In re* Lawrance, 579 N.E.2d 32 (Ind. 1991); Care and Protection of Beth, 587 N.E.2d 1377 (Mass. 1992); Guardianship of Jane Doe, 583 N.E.2d 1263 (Mass. 1992); Brophy v. New Eng. Sinai Hosp., 497 N.E.2d 626 (Mass. 1986); *In re* Farrell, 529 A.2d 404 (N.J.

its indignity, and its costs. It is not that these people are Luddites who totally reject all medical technology; instead they want technology to be used responsibly and in accord with their needs and values. They are searching for alternative ways to die with dignity, in their homes or with their family and friends, and under circumstances over which they have more control. They are increasingly asking for their physicians to assist them in regaining control over their own dying.

This paper is an attempt to reorient discussions about legal responses to physicians who submit to their patients' pleas for help. I am limiting my discussion here to the "easy" case—to the person who is competent and has expressed her or his wish for physician assistance. Answers to more difficult questions such as those concerning incompetent patients and patients in persistent vegetative states must be reserved for another day. I believe, however, the model I suggest will better enable us to resolve the more difficult questions, but we cannot reach them until we more fully understand the easy case. Even within this simplified inquiry, there are many complex problems that I cannot address here. In choosing which arguments to present, I have focused primarily on offering an alternative feminist legal and ethical paradigm for resolving questions about physician assistance to patients requesting it at the end of life. I realize that switching to a feminist ethic of caring, as I propose, is only part of a feminist analysis. Time constraints have forced me to exclude questions about potential gender biases and gender dynamics within and flowing from application of my proposed model.[4] Although I am omitting these issues from my

---

1987); *In re* the Guardianship of L.W., 482 N.W.2d 60 (Wis. 1992); HASTINGS CENTER OF NEW YORK, GUIDELINES ON THE TERMINATION OF LIFE-SUSTAINING TREATMENT AND THE CARE OF THE DYING (1987); PRESIDENT'S COMMISSION FOR THE STUDY OF ETHICAL PROBLEMS IN MEDICINE AND BIOMEDICAL AND BEHAVIORAL RESEARCH, DECIDING TO FOREGO LIFE-SUSTAINING TREATMENT: A REPORT OF THE ETHICAL, MEDICAL, AND LEGAL ISSUES IN TREATMENT DECISIONS (1983); COUNCIL ON ETHICAL AND JUDICIAL AFFAIRS OF THE AMER. MEDICAL ASS'N, GUIDELINES FOR WITHHOLDING OR WITHDRAWING LIFE PROLONGING MEDICAL TREATMENT (1986); George P. Smith, *All's Well That Ends Well: Toward a Policy of Assisted Rational Suicide or Merely Enlightened Self-Determination?*, 22 U.C. DAVIS L. REV. 275, 329 n.392 (1989) (listing several Natural Death Acts); Allan Parachini, *The California Humane and Dignified Death Initiative* HASTING CENTER REP. Jan.-Feb. 1989, at 10-12 (special supp.).

4. I am particularly concerned about three aspects of the gender dynamics and power hierarchies that must be considered in analyzing dilemmas about decisions to end life. First, I am concerned that, thus far, only women have requested assisted death, or at least, the only publicized cases involve women. This may be because women are socialized differently from men and find it easier to ask for help. Additionally, or alternatively, women may find it more unbearable to make significant others suffer from watching their slow, debilitating death. Or women may feel uncomfortable being "cared for" because their socialization usually requires them to be caregivers. Second, there are severe race, gender, and class based biases in access to health care that must be accounted for in this analysis. Finally, women are primarily the caretakers of the ill and elderly in our society—as nurses, in families, and as health care aides. We also must examine how altering rules about physician assistance in dying affects the experiences, power, roles, and needs of these women.

discussion, I hope it does not minimize their importance, and that you realize this paper is only a small portion of a larger work in progress.

Two more introductory caveats: First, I am deeply committed to major systemic changes in the funding and delivery of health care in our nation. We need a national health care system to ensure no citizen is forced to make medical decisions based on the scarcity of funds or insurance. We also need to re-evaluate the commodification and dehumanization of medicine. The way that most medicine is now delivered, in ten minute segments, often from a series of different physicians or specialists without any sense of continuity for patients, permits few of us to develop relationships with our physicians. It is crucial that we move to a just health care system, although it is impossible without systemic changes in funding and delivery. With that in mind, accompanied by my fears that a revamped health care system is not in our immediate future, my proposal is premised on a continuation of our current system of funding and delivery. That I ask for changes in the system we use should not be understood as an acceptance of this model but as an attempt to work within it until it is changed. Hopefully, my proposals would better serve their ends in a restructured system.

Second, I do not mean to imply that shifting to the paradigm I propose will provide simple answers to all future questions; nor will it eliminate struggles and conflicts in coping with the intersections of dying, medicine, technology, and ethics. It may, however, enable us to deal more humanely, more cooperatively, and more supportively with dying persons, those who love them, and compassionate physicians.

Questions about physician-assisted suicide, active voluntary euthanasia, mercy-killing, or, as I would prefer to call it, "medical care at the end of life" or "medical care in the dying process" have increased over the recent past. Before I make arguments advocating changes in our understandings and legal treatments of this practice, I think it is useful to share with you a brief chronology of some of the most vivid stories shaping this debate in the medical, legal, and bioethical communities.

In March 1991, Dr. Timothy Quill, a Rochester, New York physician, published an impassioned article in the *New England Journal of Medicine*, detailing the decision-making process involved in the death of one of his patients.[5] Diane was a middle-aged business woman, mother, and wife, who was diagnosed as having acute myelomonocytic leukemia, a fatal disease. Dr. Quill advised Diane about available

---

5. Timothy Quill, *Death and Dignity: A Case of Individualized Decision Making*, 324 NEW. ENG. J. MED. 691-94 (1991).

treatment options and the course of her disease without treatment. After careful consideration of her options, Diane refused to undergo painful, drawn-out chemotherapy, which could have given her a twenty-five percent chance of remission. Dr. Quill reported being very troubled by his patient's decision, but he acknowledged the decision about treatment was hers to make. He had no doubt that she made it in an informed, rational manner with her husband and son.

Once she had decided to forego potential life-preserving treatment, she had to decide how to cope with the disease, her pain, and her inevitable, rapidly approaching death. Diane was advised about hospice and comfort care treatment. She asked Dr. Quill about help in dying. Because Dr. Quill was conflicted about determining his appropriate role in responding to this request, he recommended that Diane contact the local Hemlock Society to learn more. She did and later returned to Dr. Quill complaining of sleeping troubles and asking for a prescription. Knowing that this was part of a Hemlock Society "suicide," Dr. Quill questioned her about how she would use the drugs. He described the interaction as follows:

> In our discussion, it was apparent that she was having trouble sleeping, but it was also evident that the security of having enough barbiturates available to commit suicide when and if the time came would leave her secure enough to live fully and concentrate on the present. It was clear that she was not despondent and that in fact she was making deep, personal connections with her family and close friends. I made sure that she knew how to use the barbiturates for sleep, and also that she knew the amount needed to commit suicide. . . . [S]he promised to meet with me before taking her life, to ensure that all other avenues had been exhausted. I wrote the prescription with an uneasy feeling about the boundaries I was exploring—spiritual, legal, professional, and personal. Yet I also felt strongly that I was setting her free to get the most out of the time she had left, and to maintain her dignity and control on her own terms until her death.[6]

Three and one-half months later, Diane's condition had deteriorated, and she was left to choose between increasing pain and discomfort or sedation and dependence. Diane then called Dr. Quill and her friends to say goodbye. When she decided her life was over, she asked her husband and son to leave her alone for an hour, and she died peacefully on her couch at home. Dr. Quill called the medical examiner and reported her cause of death as "acute leukemia." By sharing Diane's story and his own angst in caring for her, Dr. Quill made a

---

6. *Id.* at 693.

heart-felt plea to the medical community for more dialogue about the appropriate roles of physicians in helping their patients achieve death with dignity.

Dr. Quill's plea to the medical community was quickly transferred to the legal community when a Rochester area District Attorney, Howard Relin, said he would attempt to prosecute Dr. Quill for assisting a suicide—a crime in New York. Initially, Relin's inability to identify "Diane" impeded prosecution, but an anonymous phone call gave him enough information to proceed.[7] The case against Dr. Quill was presented to a grand jury in July 1991, which, in its wisdom, refused to indict him.[8] Dr. Quill suffered the threat of criminal prosecution for over four months—not a pleasant experience for a doctor who conscientiously and compassionately cared for a dying patient.

Dr. Quill's story is just one of a number of stories about physician-assisted death and the legal system's response. Several physicians have been prosecuted over the years, and others have avoided prosecution by keeping their actions secret from the public and sometimes even from the families of the patients they helped die. Other physicians, like Dr. Quill, have sought publicity to raise the public's consciousness on the issue. In some ways, Dr. Quill's story was an antidote to powerful, contemporaneous media stories about Dr. Jack Kevorkian, a retired Michigan pathologist, who invented a "suicide machine" to enable dying patients to voluntarily end their lives once the suffering or loss of dignity accompanying their diseases became unbearable. In 1990, Dr. Kevorkian's actions captured the public and medical ethicists' attention when he permitted Janet Adkins, a fifty-four year old woman suffering from Alzheimer's disease, to use his machine to end her life.[9] The apparent publicity-seeking nature of Dr. Kevorkian and the strange conditions of Adkin's death—that is, the use of this jury-rigged machine in the back of a 1968 Volkswagen van—had skewed the debate about physician-assisted death. Dr. Kevorkian ultimately avoided criminal prosecution in December 1990 because Michigan did not have a law criminalizing the assistance of suicide, and his actions did not amount to murder since he did not cause her death.[10] He was subjected to a civil court order in early 1991 enjoining his further use

---

7. B.D. Colen, *On Death and Dying—MD Who Aided in Suicide Aims to Humanize Debate*, NEWSDAY, Aug. 11, 1991, at 3.

8. *Id.*

9. Kevorkian named his crude, jury-rigged contraption Thanatron, but his lawyer defense team suggested he rename it the "Mercy Machine" for trial. Ron Rosenbaum, *Angel of Death: The Trial of the Suicide Doctor*, VANITY FAIR May 1991, at 147. Kevorkian now refers to his machines as "mercytron." What is in a name? *See infra* note 21-27 and accompanying text.

10. *Case Against 'Dr. Death' Dropped After MI Judge Throws Out Charge*, 7 MED. ETHICS ADVISOR 13-16 (1991).

of his machine or one like it to aid someone else in committing suicide.[11] Last October, while he was still in the process of appealing that order, Dr. Kevorkian assisted two other women in ending their lives.[12] He is now being threatened with contempt proceedings for violating the injunction. His medical license was revoked on November 20, 1991, and on February 5, 1992, he was arrested after a grand jury returned two murder indictments and criminal charges for illegal delivery of a controlled substance against him.[13]

Nonetheless, in March 1991, when Dr. Quill's article was published, his presentation of the issues recaptured the public debate and returned it to a seemingly more medicalized model. Because I am a teacher of bioethics and law, these stories instantly seized my attention. They have also affected political and legislative processes. Washington citizens, through the initiative process, introduced a Death with Dignity proposal on their November 1991 ballot, which, had it passed, would have been the first in the country to explicitly permit physician aid-in-dying.[14] The measure failed by a small margin at the polls (fifty-four percent to forty-six percent), despite earlier polls that indicated a sure victory.[15] California citizens are currently attempting to get a slightly different referendum regarding physician-assisted death on the 1992 ballot—one providing for a waiting period and family notification.[16] Citizens in Oregon and Florida are pressing initiatives for 1994 and 1996, respectively.[17] Other states are also engaged in these debates.[18] Additionally, Derek Humphry, founder of the Hemlock So-

---

11. Judge Alice Gilbert of the Oakland County Circuit Court in Michigan, before whom one facet of Kevorkian's case was heard, described Dr. Kevorkian as having "a propensity for media exposure and seek[ing] recognition through bizarre behavior." *Kevorkian Told: Hands Off Machine!* 4 DOCTOR'S PEOPLE NEWSLETTER 2(1) (March 1991). His lawyers have appealed her decision to enjoin use of his machines and chastised the judge for her moralizing and "unprofessional attack" on Dr. Kevorkian. *Permanent Ban Against Assisted Suicide Appealed,* UPI, Feb. 22, 1991, *available in* LEXIS, Nexis Library, UPI File.

12. Isabel Wilkerson, *Opponents Weigh Action Against Doctor Who Aided Suicides,* N.Y. TIMES, Oct. 25, 1991, at A10; Eric Harrison, *"Dr. Death" Arrested in 2 Women's Suicides,* L.A. TIMES, Feb. 6, 1992, at A15.

13. *Kevorkian Chronology,* Gannett News Service, Feb. 5, 1992, *available in* LEXIS, Nexis Library, Gannett File. In May 1992, Kevorkian assisted Susan Willilams's death by giving her canned carbon monoxide. Al Koski, *'Dr. Death' Strikes Again,* UPI, May 16, 1992, *available in* LEXIS, Nexis Library, UPI File.

14. Washington Citizens for Death with Dignity led the movement for passage of Initiative 119, which provided for "aid in dying" as a right of terminally-ill, mentally competent patients. Joyce Price, *Ire Over Prosecution Helps 'Right-to-Die' Bill,* WASH. TIMES, May 13, 1991, at A4; Merle S. Goldberg, *The Right to be Right; Ethics Issues Grow in Number and Complexity,* WASH. TIMES, June 3, 1991, at M3.

15 Jane Gross, *The 1991 Election: Euthanasia; Voters Turn Down Mercy Killing Idea,* N.Y. TIMES, Nov. 7, 1991, at B16.

16. Janny Scott, *Suicide Aid Focus Turns to California,* L.A. TIMES, Nov. 7, 1991, at A3.

17. *Id.; see also supra* note 14.

18. Proposed measures in the United States are often compared to those in

ciety, a group organized around the right to die, recently published *Final Exit*, a book of explicit instructions on suicide methods directed toward the terminally ill.[19] The book has been a best seller since its release. Sales have been impeded only by a shortage of printed copies.

This brief summary of some recent stories about death and dying in our culture raises many questions for lawyers. How ought our legal system respond to these human experiences of dying, medicine, and technology? What role should law play in resolving these foundational ethical dilemmas? More particularly, as a lawyer and academician interested in bioethics, I want to examine how law ought to deal with physicians who assist their patients in ending their lives. Soon after Dr. Quill's story reached the press, I began my research on laws about suicide, assisting suicide, and homicide. I learned that no longer do any states have laws criminalizing suicide, and about half the states have laws making assisting or causing suicide a crime, but my questions about what the law ought to do and why remained unanswered. I then read ethicists, philosophers, physicians, and legal scholars' writings on euthanasia, suicide, and terminal illnesses. I can assure you there is more material out there about this area of inquiry than any one person could ever read in a lifetime.[20]

---

the Netherlands, where doctor assisted death, or voluntary active euthanasia, is excused, if strict guidelines are followed. In the Netherlands, the courts and medical societies have established guidelines for when active, voluntary euthanasia by physicians will be legally justified (that is, not subject to criminal prosecution). *See generally*, John Horgan, *Science and the Citizen: Death with Dignity*, 264 Sci. Am. 17 (1991). The Royal Dutch Pharmacists Association has published a ten-page pamphlet explaining the most sensible ways for physicians to offer their patients "death on request." Michael Specter, *Thousands of Dutch Choose Euthanasia's Gentle Ending; U.S. Physicians Debate Death on Request*, Wash. Post, Apr. 5, 1990, at A1. Doctors' death-assisting conduct is evaluated after the fact by local prosecutors who determine if the guidelines, which refer to things like repeated patient requests, medical consultations, and interminable suffering, were complied with, in which case no prosecution follows or a finding of not guilty will be entered. *See id.* When doctors fail to follow guidelines but death assistance is compassion motivated, a guilty verdict without punishment may result. *See id.* For a carefully detailed examination of the development of active voluntary euthanasia in the Netherlands, see Wainey, *infra* note 21 at 653-64. Many commentators have suggested that the United States follow a model similar to that in the Netherlands. *See, e.g.*, George Garbesi, *infra* note 21. It would be unfair, however, to represent the Dutch system as without serious dissent. Because of the tensions involved, Ineke Stinissens, a 47 year old woman who had been comatose for 15 years because of an overdose of anesthesia during childbirth, was forced to starve to death for 11 days after her feeding tubes were removed. Galina Vromen, *Patient's Starvation Death Intensifies Dutch Mercy-Killing Row*, The Reuter News Reports, Jan. 20, 1990, *available in* LEXIS, Nexis Library, Reuter File. Her husband spent years in court trying to get her nursing home to let her die, but when a court finally agreed to let her tubes be disconnected, it refused to order doctors at her convalescent home to end her life. *Id.* Issues of euthanasia are affecting political coalitions in the Netherlands.

19. Derek Humphry, Final Exit: Self-Deliverance and Assisted Suicide for the Dying (1991).

20. For a comprehensive compilation of resources, see Smith, *supra* note 3;

The more I read and thought, the more it seemed that my questions about the role of law in these situations could not be answered without a final determination about the meaning of life, the meaning of personhood, and the meaning of death. As I drifted in a sea of philosophical and spiritual inquiry, Dr. Quill and Diane's story kept calling me back. This was not a hypothetical problem or an abstract investigation. The legal system's treatment of this problem was affecting the resolution of these dilemmas in people's lives every day, whether I ever figured out the propriety of using a sanctity-of-life or quality-of-life analysis, whether I could discern under what circumstances suicide was ever morally justified, or whether a meaningful difference between "letting die" and "killing" existed. Questions about the legality of physician-assisted death concerned real people, immediate dilemmas, and intense suffering.

My critical feminist consciousness was aroused. Why were the debates framed in terms of abstract principles like autonomy, paternalism, and beneficence or revealed through abstract, hypothetical situations perched tenuously on slippery slopes—for instance, some theorists argue that if we let a doctor respond to a request by a terminally ill patient to die, this would lead to doctors killing disabled people or the elderly poor against their will. Why did the ethical or legal analyses seem to emphasize labeling actions as suicide, assisted suicide, euthanasia, murder, or refusing treatment rather than to emphasize examining the specific facts and contexts, discussing people's feelings and relationships, and responding to patients' needs? Why do we discuss informed consent and who should decide, without discussing caregiving, compassion, responding to needs, interpersonal relationships, dignity, empowerment, and love? And last, but not least, why are we always very careful to leave out the needs and interests of family, friends, and caregivers when we discuss a dying person, as if those subjects are taboo?

Feminist theories help me in my inquiries because they press me to question assumptions and labels and to eschew universal rules, abstractions, and generalizations that impede attention to contexts and lived experiences. Feminist theories promote the values of caring, responsibility, and responsiveness to needs absent in our current legal paradigm.

I. Power Of Naming

An elementary premise of feminist theories recognizes that defining or naming a problem is a political act.[21] When we call doctors' actions

---

Don V. Bailey, The Challenge of Euthanasia: An Annotated Bibliography on Euthanasia and Related Subjects (1990).
    21. One of the most difficult parts of discussing this issue is naming the

"aiding suicide," "euthanasia," or "killing," we prefigure the ensuing debate. These labels carry pejorative baggage. Suicide is often connected with notions of irrationality and wrongdoing, whether a spiritual or religious wrong or a mistake in judgment that ought to be corrected. When we think someone behaves nobly in consciously sacrificing her life, we do not label her act suicide. If someone throws himself before an oncoming car to prevent his child from being hit, we do not say he committed suicide. If a fire fighter dies putting out a fire, we do not label her act "suicide."

Freud committed suicide by asking his physician to end his suffering from cancer of the jaw.[22] Bruno Bettelheim committed suicide.[23]

---

subject area. The names used for this phenomenon are wide-ranging, and each label shapes the discussion in a particular way. Institute of Medical Ethics Working Party on the Ethics of Prolong Life and Assisting Death, *Viewpoint: Assisted Death*, 336 LANCET 610, 611 (Sept. 8, 1990) [hereinafter *Viewpoint: Assisted Death*]; *see also* MARTHA MINOW, MAKING ALL THE DIFFERENCE (1990) (discussing the power of naming and labeling and its effects on our thinking). Theorists of physician-assisted death have recognized the relevance of naming by using varieties of labels: Physician- or doctor-assisted death, *Viewpoint: Assisted Death*, *supra*; rational suicide, Stephen A. Newman, *Euthanasia: Orchestrating "The Last Syllable of . . . Time,"* 53 U. PITT. L. REV. 153, 161 (1991); euthanatic rational suicide, Shari O'Brien, *Facilitating Euthanatic, Rational Suicide: Help Me Go Gentle Into That Good Night*, 31 ST. LOUIS U. L.J. 655 (1987); assisted suicide, George C. Garbesi, *The Law of Assisted Suicide*, 3 ISSUES L. & MED. 93, 93-111 (1987), H. Tristram Engelhardt, Jr. & Michele Malloy, *Suicide and Assisting Suicide: A Critique of Legal Sanctions*, 36 SW. L.J. 1003 (1982), Victor G. Rosenblum & Clarke D. Forsythe, *The Right to Assisted Suicide: Protection of Autonomy or an Open Door to Social Killing?*, 6 ISSUES L. & MED. 3 (1990); mercy-killing, James S. Goodwin, *Mercy Killing: Mercy for Whom?*, 265 JAMA 326 (1991); perimortal initiatives, Count D. Gibson, *Perimortal Initiatives: Issues in Foregoing Life-Sustaining Treatment, Suicide, and Assisted Suicide*, 3 ISSUES L. & MED. 29 (1987); timing-of-death decisions, Sandra Segal Ikuta, *Dying at the Right Time: A Critical Legal Theory Approach to Timing-of-Death Issues*, 5 ISSUES L. & MED. 3, 3-66 (1989); life-shortening palliative care, Donald G. Casswell, *Rejecting Criminal Liability for Life-Shortening Palliative Care*, 6 J. CONTEMP. HEALTH L. & POL'Y 127 (1990); aid-in-dying, *Model Aid-in-Dying Act*, 75 IOWA L. REV. 125 (1989); enlightened self-determination, George P. Smith, II, *All's Well That Ends Well: Toward a Policy of Assisted Rational Suicide or Merely Enlightened Self-Determination?*, 22 U.C. DAVIS L. REV. 275 (1989); arranged or negotiated deaths, Catherine Shaffer, Note, *Criminal Liability for Assisting Suicide*, 86 COLUM. L. REV. 348, 369, 370 (1986); consciousness, Steven Goldberg, *The Changing Face of Death: Computers, Consciousness, and Nancy Cruzan*, 43 STAN. L. REV. 659 (1991); direct and indirect euthanasia, JOSEPH FLETCHER, HUMANHOOD: ESSAYS IN BIOMEDICAL ETHICS 149 (1979), Robert Barry & James Maher, *Indirectly Intended Life-Shortening Analgesia: Clarifying the Principles*, 6 ISSUES L. & MED. 117 (1990); active voluntary euthanasia, Helga Kuhse, *The Case for Active Voluntary Euthanasia*, 14 LAW, MED. AND HEALTH CARE 145 (1986), Deborah A. Wainey, Note, *Active Voluntary Euthanasia: The Ultimate Act of Care for the Dying*, 37 CLEV. ST. L. REV. 645 (1989); active euthanasia, Francis Molenda, *Active Euthanasia: Can It Be Justified?*, 24 TULSA L. REV. 165 (1988).

22. In 1939, Freud asked his doctor to inject him with sufficient drugs to kill him when he could no longer bear the suffering from incurable cancer of the jaw.

So did the eminent jurist, Judge Henry Friendly.[24] So, arguably, did Socrates.[25] Yet we rarely talk about rational suicide because the words seem incongruous. Many of our legal opinions are carefully crafted to distinguish between suicide and decisions to forego medical treatment. When a patient asks that a ventilator be withdrawn or refuses consent for chemotherapy, the law does not say that the patient is committing suicide. Jurists have recognized the need to distance these acts from that label. An act or decision is not inherently suicide. A social context is needed to understand the act, making suicide a social construct. At least for the time being, the social construction of that word imbues the event or act with a taint of illegitimacy. State laws making it criminal to aid a suicide are based on underlying assumptions that suicide is irrational or the aid represents a form of coercion. Therefore, if we label the doctor's conduct as "aiding suicide," we raise up those senses of wrongfulness, irrationality, or coercion, when they may, in fact, be totally absent from the event.

Likewise, the word "euthanasia," while originally meaning "good death,"[26] has also taken on images of coercion. Despite careful distinctions in law and ethics between voluntary and involuntary euthanasia, or between murder and euthanasia, mention of the word raises the specter of Nazi Germany in too many minds. The word is infused with imagery of forced exterminations and immoral medical practices. It almost seems that many contemporary physicians and bioethicists think euthanasia is a German word meaning gas chambers, lethal injections, and selective exterminations. Hence, discussing this problem as one of active voluntary euthanasia brings forth debates about slippery slopes and bad actors doing immoral acts.

The words "killing" or "kill" color the discussion even more negatively. Killing sounds criminal. To say it is "mercy killing" for a physician to give a patient a requested lethal dose to end her suffering is to invest the act with an air of criminality that the word "mercy" does not adequately temper. Words affect how we think and feel about acts, how we classify them, and how we treat them legally.

Understanding the politics of naming, as any feminist lawyer does, I prefer to discuss this "issue" as one about death, not suicide,

---

Victor Cohn, *An Assisted Suicide; Is it the First Step Toward Euthanasia?*, WASH. POST, June 12, 1990 (Health), at 27.

23. Celest Fremon, *Love & Death; In His Final Interview, Just Before His Suicide, Bruno Bettelheim Explained Why He Wanted to Die*, L.A. TIMES, Jan. 27, 1991 (Magazine), at 17.

24. *Henry Friendly; Judge Was "One of the Greatest,"* CHI. TRIB., Mar. 13, 1986, at C8.

25. *See, e.g.,* ROBERT CAMPBELL AND DIANE COLLINSON, ENDING LIVES 8-12 (1988).

26. The prefix "eu" means well or good and "thanatos" means death. WEBSTER'S NEW UNIVERSAL UNABRIDGED DICTIONARY 631 (2d ed. 1983).

euthanasia, or mercy-killing. Yet even death is inadequate because it seems to indicate one moment or event rather than an ongoing process. A better naming would be to say this is about "dignified dying," or about "timing of dying decisions," "end of life decisions," "care for dying people," "controlling our own dying process," or "life-completing decisions." Certainly we do not object to giving people control over the completion of their lives. Few, if any, would be morally offended by the provision of care for dying people.

There are other phrasings of these problems that subvert constructive conversations. I am troubled by use of the phrase "physician-assisted" or "doctor-assisted." By starting with the physicians or doctors, we center our attention on them, even though they ought not be the focus. By labeling the event "physician-assisted dying," we concentrate on the actions of the physician, almost making it sound as though the physician is a decision-maker, rather than orienting ourselves toward a discussion of the entire decision-making process and the dying person. And while I am seeking new labels, I would like to reject the word "patient." As the hospice movement has so aptly discerned, the word "patient" has come to connote passivity—someone acted upon.[27] It is objectifying and distancing. Certainly we can find a better word with more decision-making agency and more subjectivity.

II. FALSE DUALISMS

Feminist and post-structuralist theories have also criticized our tradition of viewing the world in dichotomies—seeing events as polar opposites; drawing lines that divide the world of concepts into twos.[28] It is not just our naming of things that is problematic but also our narrow bipolar classification schemes. I would like to highlight a few examples of how this has impeded our ability to work through problems of physician assistance to dying people. Dualistic thinking leads us to an either/or, self/other analysis instead of plural, multiple, variant, and contextualized analyses. While dividing all things into two groups, where some thing or event must fall in or out of the group, simplifies our tasks of classification, it papers over the ever-changing relationships and interconnections between categories and experiences and deludes us into believing the categories are fixed, natural, or inherent.

As technology has advanced, we have learned that our understanding of life and death as opposites and fixed categories is inadequate.

---

27. Hospice calls the people with whom they work clients instead of patients. Alice Lind, *Hospitals and Hospices: Feminist Decisions about Care for the Dying,* in HEALING TECHNOLOGY 263, 270 (Kathryn S. Ratcliff ed., 1989).
28. *See, e.g.,* Frances Olsen, *The Sex of Law, in* THE POLITICS OF LAW 453 (David Kairys ed., rev. ed., 1990).

Life and death seem more like interrelated processes on a continuum than clearly delineated and oppositional states. Although our culture holds fast to a view of science as distinct from faith, we continuously encounter difficulties differentiating science from spirituality, especially when we analyze birth and death issues. Nonetheless, our dominant cultural norms seem to privilege doctors' medical knowledge over others' knowledges in caring for dying people, as if death and dying were purely "scientific" or "medical" processes. Despite the ill-fitting nature of our bipolar categories, we continue to separate and favor science over spirit, body over soul, reason over emotion, and self over others. An ontology that examines relationships and interactions among concepts, actions, people, and institutions seems preferable to one fixated on delineating boundaries.

Another false dualism that dominates discussions about euthanasia in law and ethics is active/passive or act/omission. Whether we call something "active" or "passive," or "killing" or "letting die," it is a conclusion, not an inherent fact. Criminal laws and tort laws often distinguish between acts and omissions. If a doctor gives a patient a lethal injection, it is considered an affirmative act, resulting in a charge of active euthanasia or homicide. Yet, if a doctor withdraws a life-support system, whether a respirator or a feeding tube, that is "letting nature take its course," an "omission," or being "passive." Even though there is an "act" of detaching, it is not considered active. Even though the need to detach is related to the earlier "act" of attaching the person to life-prolonging machinery, it is considered merely passive or omissive to withdraw it. An original decision not to attach a patient to life-support, whether due to triage resource allocations or apparent futility, is also passive. There is no legal liability and, for most ethicists, no ethical liability. In each case, the patient dies in conjunction with a decision about her care that is effected by a physician. Yet when a person dies in conjunction with a decision to end her suffering from a terminal illness that is effected by a physician giving her a lethal injection or a prescription for a potentially deadly dose of medicine, the law seems to say it falls on the killing side of the dichotomy.

Once an appropriate decision to complete the life process and allow death to occur has been made, physicians, ethicists, and the legal system should seek out the most compassionate way to care for the dying person. It is unseemly for the legal system's analysis to turn on whether the physician's role was active or passive, or whether the conduct is more appropriately labeled killing or letting die. Many prominent theorists have argued against this distinction's relevance much better than I can.[29] They challenge legal and ethical paradigms

---

29. *See, e.g.*, James Rachels, *Active and Passive Euthanasia* in EUTHANASIA: THE MORAL ISSUES 45-51 (Robert M. Baird & Stuart E. Rosenbaum eds., 1989).

that evaluate physicians' conduct through an active/passive, act/omission lens.

Physicians are not immune from this dualistic approach to assessing active voluntary euthanasia. Many physicians measure appropriate conduct through a healing/killing dichotomy. Doctors say they are trained to heal, not kill, as if those terms covered the whole universe of actions, as if they are fittingly contrasted, and as if actions could clearly fall in one category or the other. I have heard doctors claim that the bright line between healing and killing is necessary to keep physicians principled and honorable. If the law permits a blurring of the line, they argue, doctors may prematurely end the lives of dying or obstreperous patients out of impatience or exhaustion from the heavy demands of caring for a desperately ill, dying patient, out of frustration or a sense of defeat at their lack of success in curing the patient, or even for economic reasons.

The law seems to use similar justifications for its active/passive or killing/letting die distinctions. These rationales are legitimate only if we agree with three underlying assumptions: 1) laws and ethical principles must be designed for the "bad actors"; 2) each line must be firmly set to prevent a precipitous decline down the proverbial slippery slope; and 3) truly bad actors are in fact deterred by laws. I am unpersuaded by each. Although there are, and always will be, a number of bad actors, most of us do not fall in that category. If we write our laws or set our standards to curtail the actions and improper motivations of a small contingent of people on the margin, we may disempower the majority of us in the center from acting on noble and virtuous impulses. Physician aid-in-dying exemplifies this critique.

To deter negligent, indifferent, malevolent, or lazy physicians from involuntarily terminating some patients' lives (or wrongfully persuading patients that death is their only option), we have to endure a rule that deters compassionate physicians from providing competent, suffering patients requested dignity, security, and control over their dying processes. Similarly, we prohibit family members from mercifully ending the suffering of loved ones or create high legal barriers to families making termination of life-support decisions for incompetent loved ones based on our fear of bad families. The social and ethical price of designing our laws and rules for the bad actors is significant suffering and indignity to innocent, humane people because of unnecessary restraints on their freedom to act out of care in a manner responsive to particularized circumstances of need.

Laws making doctor assistance illegal may deter caring physicians from acting. Few doctors want to be vulnerable to the whims of prosecutorial discretion, particularly if it is an election year, and even fewer want to risk the possibility of criminal prosecution or license revocation, although they are likely to prevail ultimately. Compassionate and caring doctors who want to comply with their patients' pleas will be deterred, unless we have laws clearly authorizing them to act and outlining conditions under which they will be free from prosecution.

Why are we so quick to constrain the power of most people's moral agency? Why do we presume that if we give physicians freedom to implement their patients' decisions about care at the end of dying, they will behave irresponsibly? As a society, we readily give physicians a great deal of responsibility to exercise their best judgments and skills in caring for patients. If we are willing to presume they are responsible enough under most situations to deal with matters of life and death, why would they suddenly be less responsible in helping to implement patients' decisions at life's end?

Moreover, I am not completely convinced that such laws or rules are very effective deterrents to the truly bad actors—the lazy or callous physicians or parsimonious families who are cruel to those in their care. Despite the existence of these rules, we still have bad actors who violate them. Clearly some in the small group of bad actors in the margin are never deterred by laws. For this reason, the class of people for whom we are calibrating our laws is reduced in size even further. Maybe we should reconsider whether the cost of pitching our laws to this relatively small number of people, at least in cases of aid-in-dying, is too great for the benefit we receive. If we respect the autonomy and dignity of dying people, we should make laws that create an environment where people can get the care they need from their physicians, rather than laws that merely deter a few dishonorable, bad physicians.

Our legal system loses its legitimacy when faced with questions of doctor-assisted death. Laws seem to make doctor-assisted death criminal, based on active/passive distinctions or notions of irrational suicide, and yet doctors are rarely prosecuted and even more rarely convicted.[30] The law says it is impermissible, but then winks at the conduct. Prosecutors often use their discretion not to prosecute, and juries use their discretion to dismiss acts of mercy.[31]

In one way, one could say that our legal system is responding appropriately. It is contextualizing our system of justice to fit the circumstances. To that extent, these verdicts or results excusing physician conduct are good. But there are other dynamics about which we need to be concerned. If the active/passive distinction is a correct ethical and legal analysis, then juries and prosecutors ought not subvert the law. If there is something fallacious or ill-fitting about the active/

---

30. For detailed reviews of earlier cases against physicians, see Wainey, *supra* note 21, at 668-70 (Drs. Sander, Montemarano, Kraai, Neidjil, Barber, Hassman, Rosier and Caraccio); DEREK HUMPHREY & ANN WICKETT, THE RIGHT TO DIE: UNDERSTANDING EUTHANASIA (1986) 42-45 (Dr. Sander), 103-04 (Dr. Montemarano), 140-42 (Dr. Kraai) (1986); *Eight Doctors On Euthanasia Charges*, HEMLOCK Q., Jan. 1989, at 6.

31. *Id.*

passive distinction, then we should find a better analysis for judging the legality and rightness of compassionate acts complying with patient requests to end their lives. More often than not, juries reject our present model because it does not reflect their experiences and understandings of justice. If, for the most part, our legal system is clandestinely applying an ethic of care in these cases, why not bring it out in the open? It would not be a radical shift because it represents the current practice, if not the language, of the legal system. To permit the laws to be overtly disrespected by judges, prosecutors, and juries impairs the legitimacy of our legal system.

If what we are talking about is physician participation in the care of dying people, it should not matter whether a physician helps by disconnecting machines, by giving an injection, or by giving a prescription. The appropriateness of the conduct should not turn on an artificial distinction between healing and killing. What should matter, and what we should be asking about, is whether a physician thoroughly discussed the medical aspects of the dying process and care options with the dying person, and whether there have been ongoing conversations about dying between the dying person and loved ones, caregivers, and medical providers. We then should ask whether the physician was "giving medical care" that responded to the dying person's needs, concerns, and values.

III.   A Caring Paradigm For Medical Ethics And Law

It is this notion of "giving needed medical care," informed by an ethic of care paradigm, that I want to explore for the rest of this paper. My feminist critique of medical ethics and legal practice regarding this issue is ultimately a critique of the paradigm we use. In part because of the language usage and dualism problems I discussed, but more because of our dominant, liberal paradigm premised on a society composed of autonomous individuals who interact with others by choice out of self-interest, we look for resolutions of problems about end-of-life medical care in an ethic of justice and rights. We construct abstract, generalized rules that are supposed to cover all situations for all time. Our current analysis prevents people from aiding others to die with dignity because we understand rights as barriers to interference by others, rather than as enabling conditions. Our ethical constructs grow out of elaborate conversations, which are deeply philosophical and richly argued, and yet we leave out the heart and soul of real people's concerns about dying. We leave out discussions about caring, empathy, love, compassion, relationships, and the dying person's needs and perspective. When applying our existing rules to the legality of physician assistance in the dying process, we may talk of "mercy seasoning justice," but I would prefer an understanding that speaks of "justice tempering care." We can change the substance of our normative discourse in medical ethics and law by moving to a care-based paradigm like the one I propose.

In addition to the absence of values like compassion and care, and the focus on rights as barriers between independent equal individuals, our current ethical paradigm is defective because it fails to account for the effects of changes in technology on analyzing issues of dying. Medical ethics, for instance, is ahistorical because it relies on ancient ethical codes, such as the Hippocratic Oath,[32] devised 2500 years ago in a a wholly different historical and social context in which our present medical technologies were unfathomable. Many medical ethicists and doctors follow these codes and declare that active killing of dying patients is wrong, regardless of the circumstances.

Modern society is characterized by a boundless quest for technological innovation to dominate nature and control life processes. Our drive for technological mastery of natural phenomena has often eclipsed our humanitarian and ecological concerns. In medicine, technology has been as wonderful as it has been alienating and destructive. Sometimes our strivings for medical and technological glory and for conquering death are so strong that we lose sight of the suffering we prolong and create.

Even where technology has succeeded in fending off death's assaults, it often distances us from the feelings and experiences of those who are dying. People seem less touchable, less human, and less real when connected to complicated medical equipment and tubing. They are often in intensive care or special hospital units, blocked off from visitors and all things familiar. Our technological revolution in medicine has usurped many people's opportunities to die with dignity at times or in manners of their own choosing, with their family or friends around, and in their homes.

Concepts of justice and rights should not be jettisoned when shifting to an alternative feminist analysis, but they should be used as correctives to an ethic of care when needed to make sure that power is not abused. A care- and responsibility-based ethic rests on assumptions that seem closer to the experiences of dying and death in people's lives than assumptions underlying a rights- or rule-based ethic, which arguably might be more appropriate in other settings. A care-based ethic arises out of perceptions of human beings as relational, interdependent, and supportive as opposed to our current rights-based ethic in which people are separate, autonomous, and equally empowered actors. A care-based ethic acknowledges that emotions are as important as reason in our lives, decision-making, and dying, and that preserving relationships with and enabling others is as important as having rights to protect us from others.[33]

---

32. L. Edelstein, *The Hippocratic Oath: Text, Translation and Interpretation*, 19 BULL. HIST. MED. 1164 (1943); *Hippocratic Oath*, in JUDITH AREEN, ET AL., LAW, SCIENCE AND MEDICINE 273 (1984); *see* Curley Bonds, *The Hippocratic Oath: A Basis for Modern Ethical Standards*, 264 JAMA 2311 (1990) (arguing that the ancient oath's fundamentals are still applicable today).

33. *See generally* CAROL GILLIGAN, IN A DIFFERENT VOICE (1982). Some

Feminist ethics derive from an alternative or richer conception of human nature—one that understands people as being motivated by love, friendship, responsibility, and caring rather than solely by self-interest and fear. A responsibility-based ethic, or an ethic of care, does not reject all the assumptions about human nature that undergird a rights-based ethic. Instead it contextualizes them, and at a minimum, it credits people in relationships with finer motivations and qualities. Although each ethic comes from different original premises about human nature, they are ultimately reconcilable if we can maintain an ongoing dialogue regarding both of them.[34]

Finding bridges from our current ethic's foundation in personal autonomy to a care-based ethic is critical to our making a successful shift. Autonomy, the power of an individual to control her own life and death, is as much a cornerstone of a care-based ethic as it is of modern medical ethics and legal practice.[35] The differences are in the sources and meanings of autonomy. In a care-based ethic, individual autonomy is a *process* nurtured in webs of relationships and responsibilities instead of a static condition pre-existing them.[36] Whereas the ideological basis of a rights-based ethic rests on an assumption of equally empowered, independent people, an ethic of care recognizes that many relationships contain dependencies between differently em-

---

additional works in feminist ethics on which I rely are NEL NODDINGS, CARING (1984); NEL NODDINGS, WOMEN AND EVIL 130-42 (1989); SARA RUDDICK, MATERNAL THINKING: TOWARD A POLITICS OF PEACE (1989); Annette C. Baier, *The Need For More Than Justice, in* SCIENCE, MORALITY & FEMINIST THEORY 41 (Marsha Hanen & Kai Nielsen eds., 1987) [hereinafter FEMINIST THEORY]; Lorraine Code, *Second Persons, in* FEMINIST THEORY 357; Ann Ferguson, *A Feminist Aspect Theory of the Self, in* FEMINIST THEORY 339; Marilyn Friedman, *Beyond Caring: The De-Moralization of Gender, in* FEMINIST THEORY 87; Virginia Held, *Non-Contractual Society: A Feminist View, in* FEMINIST THEORY 111; Alison Jaggar, *Feminist Ethics: Projects, Problems, Prospects, in* FEMINIST ETHICS 78 (Claudia Card ed., 1991); Carol S. Robb, *A Framework for Feminist Ethics, in* WOMEN'S CONSCIOUSNESS, WOMEN'S CONSCIENCE: A READER IN FEMINIST ETHICS 211 (Barbara Hilkert Andolsen et al. eds., 1985) [hereinafter WOMEN'S CONSCIOUSNESS]; Ruth L. Smith, *Feminism and the Moral Subject, in* WOMEN'S CONSCIOUSNESS 235; Joan C. Tronto, *Women and Caring: What Can Feminists Learn About Morality from Caring? in* GENDER/BODY/KNOWLEDGE: FEMINIST RECONSTRUCTIONS OF BEING AND KNOWING 172 (Alison M. Jaggar & Susan R. Bordo eds., 1989); Virginia Warren, *Feminist Directions in Medical Ethics,* 4 HYPATIA 73 (1989); Caroline Whitbeck, *A Different Reality: Feminist Ontology, in* BEYOND DOMINATION (Carol Gould ed., 1983); WHO CARES: THEORY, RESEARCH, AND EDUCATIONAL IMPLICATIONS OF THE ETHIC OF CARE (Mary M. Brabeck ed., 1989).

34. *See, e.g.,* Robin Dillon, *Care and Respect, in* EXPLORATIONS IN FEMINIST ETHICS: THEORY AND PRACTICE 69 (Eve Browning Cole & Susan Coutrap-McQuin eds., 1992).

35. *See, e.g.,* PRESIDENT'S COMM'N FOR THE STUDY OF ETHICAL PROBLEMS IN MEDICINE AND BIOMEDICAL AND BEHAVIORAL RESEARCH: DECIDING TO FOREGO LIFE-SUSTAINING TREATMENT 26-27, 44 (1983); TOM L. BEAUCHAMP & JAMES F. CHILDRESS, PRINCIPLES OF BIOMEDICAL ETHICS 67-119, 210 (3d ed., 1989).

36. *See, e.g.,* Smith, *supra* note 33, at 235.

powered people—parents and children, caregivers and mentally or physically impaired people, teachers and students, doctors and patients, and at times lovers and friends.[37] The autonomy of an ethic of care can be melded with the autonomy concerns in a rights-based medical ethic, if it is understood to mean self-governing moral agency, rather than independent or self-contained decision-making. Self-governing in an ethic of care does not mean governing alone by abstract reasoning and distant observations, but means choosing options with respect to responsibilities, relationships, conversations, and dialogues with others.

Autonomy, the premiere value in contemporary medical ethics, is transformed from a notion of independent decision-making to an interactive process of developing agency and empowerment through relationships, connections, and interdependencies. Caregiving becomes a means of empowering a cared-for person—of enhancing her autonomy. An ethic of care framework implores a caregiver to use his or her power, expertise, knowledge, and attention to respond and enable the cared-for person to communicate and meet her needs. If the empowerment to act as a moral agent or decision maker in one's own life is dependent upon the care or assistance of others, non-interference or failure to assist may be contrary to, rather than consistent with, autonomy.[38] In a care-based ethic, refusing care or assistance in particular contexts might be neglectful and unethical rather than obedient to abstract norms.

We need to reconceptualize the physician's role as medical caregiver in light of an ethic of care in the context of our contemporary society, which has pursued technology and science to its outer limits. If we define the physician's relationship to a dying person as "giving medical care" rather than as prolonging life or healing, we need to redefine "giving medical care" as responding to the dying person's needs during the dying process. Legal and ethical questions about appropriate medical practice should be about "how best to care for" the person in need. Sometimes dying people have needs for radical technological interventions, sometimes for maintenance care, sometimes for pain relief and comfort, sometimes for security and dignity, and sometimes for aid in their dying process. All of those may be appropriate ways for doctors to give medical care, but the ethical propriety of a particularized method of caring is context-specific.

Caring for dying people requires careful attention to their particularized needs. The caregivers must discover what those needs are by listening to the patient; conversing with her and those who know her

---

37. Baier, *supra* note 33, at 53-56; Marilyn Friedman, *Feminism and Modern Friendship: Dislocating the Community, in* EXPLORATIONS IN FEMINIST ETHICS. THEORY AND PRACTICE 89 (Eve Browning Cole & Susan Coultrap-McQuin eds., 1992); Held, *supra* note 33; RUDDICK, MATERNAL THINKING, *supra* note 33.

38. Baier, *supra* note 33.

best and are responsible for her care; and learning about her options, beliefs, and her concerns for her well-being and the well-being of others about whom she cares. Depending upon the person and the context, these needs may be met by empowering the dying person to act for herself—whether by refusing potentially life-extending treatments, by utilizing self-administered, pain relief pumps, or by giving a prescription for a potentially lethal dose of drugs as Dr. Quill did. There will be times under a care-based paradigm where the giving of medical care by a physician is the giving of treatment that completes the dying process rather than elongates it. If this medical care responds to a patient's request for assistance in dying with dignity—a request which has been made after ongoing conversations with family, friends, and caregivers that carefully considered all options—it is the ethical response of a physician to use her special knowledge and skills to help her patient implement this meaningful decision.

In shifting from a rule-based ethic to a care-based ethic we can also reclaim the dying process from a totally medicalized definition. By reclaiming it, rehumanizing it, and returning it to the person dying and the people with whom that person is interconnected, we can establish more agency, more responsibility, and more control over our own deaths. We can reclaim it as a process that centers on our bodies, but is about our lives, our roles, our relationships, and our connections.

Dying, particularly dying from illness or old age rather than from a sudden accident, is not a process involving only one person. Although the process focuses on the dying person's wants and needs, it is interactive, relational, and connected. It is social and communal. We show our love and care as a community when we act responsively and compassionately in accord with the dying person's needs. These are not abstract questions about isolated individuals. These are concrete processes in lives of interconnected people. Dying must be reconceived as the social, communal process it is. Decision-making about dying ought to grow out of ongoing conversations among interrelated people.

Participating in and responding to the dying person's experiences and needs is the caring response, the role of the physicians and health care workers, and the compassionate act. The doctor becomes one of a community of people involved in the process. She can share information, explain options, and implement treatment decisions made by patients with loved ones. The decision to end life ideally would be worked out collaboratively with multiple inputs, including the physician's, but it is not the physician's decision to make. The physician's role is to provide the requested medical care or to enable the patient to receive it.

Usually at this point, a doctor responds: "Why doctors? If you want people to aid others in ending their lives, why not let families do it or hire special people as executioners?" "We do not want the responsibility," say the doctors. "It is not our job." While I understand these arguments, I would respond to physicians that it is your job. Part of a doctor's medical expertise is caring for dying people. This model does not empower doctors to make the decisions for patients; they are asked only to help implement patients' decisions. We are not increasing their responsibility beyond what they undertook when they agreed to provide medical care for a patient. We are legally empowering them to use their medical training and expertise to care for someone dying in a manner that is most compatible with their expressed needs. If this is what they were licensed to do, why should they remove themselves?

Families and friends, while in closer relationships with the dying person to help decide about appropriate avenues of care consistent with that person's needs, lack the necessary medical expertise and access to means of easy pain relief, or quick "death with dignity," to perform direct acts of assistance in dying. Lay people often have to resort to violence and crude methodologies, like guns and strangulation, to end someone's life. Even if given access to the drugs, they are unfamiliar with their administration and dosages, with what to do if difficulties arise, and with mechanisms for determining their success.

In addition, I would be remiss if I did not acknowledge the added emotional torment to a dying person of having to ask a friend or family member to assist in her dying and the emotional strain that such assistance must place on the loved one asked. It seems to me that the doctor's slight removal from the inner web of relationships puts him or her in a better position to give the medical care that ends life, if that is what the patient needs. I emphasize again that even though the process of dying is not a medical process, the physical action of giving life-ending medical care is.

IV. CONCLUSION

The important change that results from applying a care-based paradigm is the understanding of requested life-ending treatment as one form of medical caregiving for dying patients. We can establish guidelines that assure that patients are clear and consistent in their request and that they have discussed their decisions with friends, family, and caregivers. The guidelines should not be an impediment to implementing a person's end-of-life option for medical assistance but a mechanism for preventing abuse. Under a care-based analysis, the option of physician assistance may give dying people the security, dignity, and control that Dr. Quill spoke of giving Diane. That would be empowering and consistent with autonomy.

In summary, my arguments are addressed toward cases like the one presented by Dr. Quill—terminally ill patients who request physician assistance to end their suffering during their dying process. At a minimum, the law and medical ethics must be able to respond appropriately to this easy case before it can tackle the more difficult ones. I have reserved for another day questions about terminally ill versus non-terminally ill patients and questions about physical versus psychic pain. I explicitly avoided cases of patients unable to communicate their desires. I would ultimately hope that my arguments will serve to enrich conversations about those patients as well. I also focused on the role of the physician rather than other health care providers, in particular nurses, who play a critical role in caring for dying patients. Time limitations prevent me from addressing issues of nurses' roles here.

The crux of my argument is that we ought to alter the paradigm and language of our discussion about physicians' roles in care for the dying. By utilizing a care-based ethic, we can better realize goals of patient autonomy and dignity while emphasizing values of care, compassion, and responsibility.

Our battles over physician-assisted death seem to be smokescreens for our unwillingness to accept the inevitability of death. Our denial of death and the strength of the medical model to resist it at all costs have led to heroics, to violent interventions, and to prohibitions against acting in furtherance of dying people's needs when those needs are to die. If we use feminist ethics to reconceive of death as a process of dying in particularized people's lives and we come to understand the role of medicine as caring for rather than prolonging life, where caring can include multiple ways of responding to dying peoples' needs, our legal system can make spaces in its laws to legitimize rather than punish or wink at that kind of compassionate, caring medical response.

PHYSICIAN AID IN DYING: A PROPOSED LAW FOR CALIFORNIA

by Faye J. Girsh*

"Dying is personal. And it is profound. For many, the thought of an ignoble end, steeped in decay, is abhorrent. A quiet, proud death, bodily integrity intact, is a matter of extreme consequence."[1]

On November 3 Californians will vote on the Death with Dignity Act[2] (DWDA) which would permit competent terminally ill adults to request and receive aid in dying from their doctors. The DWDA qualified for the ballot following the submission of 567,407 signatures, more than twice the number required. It is similar to Washington's Proposition 119 which garnered 46% of the vote in that state in 1991 but the DWDA has significant additional safeguards.

If this Act passes it will be the first law of its kind. Even in Holland, which has permitted physician aid-in-dying since 1983, it is permitted by judicial decree rather than by statute, i.e., doctors who carry it out are not prosecuted if judges certify that certain criteria are met.

Chances are good that the measure will be approved. Survey data from the 1990 Gallup California Health Care Poll and the 1990 California Roper Poll indicate over 70% support for the concept that a terminally ill person should be able to ask for help in dying.[3]

---

* Faye J. Girsh, Ed.D., is a clinical and forensic psychologist and jury consultant who has been in private practice in San Diego for 14 years. She received her doctorate from Harvard University and was on the faculty of the University of Chicago School of Medicine. Involved professionally in the evaluation of competence for Elizabeth Bouvia in 1983, she has continued her interest in the right to die and is founder and president of the Hemlock Society of San Diego and Secretary of the board of the National Hemlock Society.

1. *Cruzan v. Director, Missouri Department of Health*, 497 U.S. 261, 110 S. Ct. 2841, 2868 (1990) (Brennan, J., dissenting).

2. California Death with Dignity Act. Title 10.5, proposed to amend Division 3 of part 4 of the CAL. CIVIL CODE. The DWDA will appear on California ballots as Proposition 161.

3. Irene Wielawski, *Public Voices Anger Over Health Care*. L.A. TIMES, May 15, 1991, at A3.

333

California has traditionally been a pioneer in statutory and case law to protect and expand personal freedoms and, in particular, the right to die. In 1976 the California legislature was the first to pass a "Living Will" law, the California Natural Death Act.[4] Although seriously flawed until it was changed in 1991, it recognized the right of a competent terminally ill patient to refuse medical treatment and to execute a directive stating his or her wishes. In 1984 the California legislature again led the country by enacting the Durable Power of Attorney for Health Care Decisions Act[5] which gives a person the right to appoint a health care agent to act in his or her behalf in the event of incompetence. This is a broad law which does not require terminal illness for the agent to refuse or withdraw treatment. Despite the doomsayers who predicted dire consequences of such patient autonomy, no abuses have been reported of either law and most other states have followed suit.[6] In 1990 the *Cruzan* decision by the U.S. Supreme Court set forth the right of all Americans to refuse or terminate unwanted medical treatment including food and hydration, and to have it done by an authorized surrogate through an advance directive — rights that were already firmly in place in California.

The Death with Dignity Act (DWDA) would follow in the tradition of California's pioneering efforts in the right to die arena. This is what is proposed in the DWDA — written initially in 1987 by Los Angeles attorneys Robert Risley and Michael White and revised by them in 1991:

1. Only a competent adult may request — through a Voluntary Directive to Physicians — and receive physician aid-in-dying.

2. The person making the request must be terminally ill. Two independent physicians — one of whom is the attending physician — must certify, within reasonable medical certainty, that

---

4. CAL. HEALTH & SAFETY CODE § 7185 et seq. (West Supp. 1992).

5. CAL. CIVIL CODE § 2500 et seq. (West Supp. 1992).

6. At least twelve other states and the District of Columbia have durable power of attorney statutes expressly authorizing the appointment of proxies for making health care decisions. See Alaska Stat. Ann. §§ 13.26.335, 13.26.344(1) (Supp. 1989); D.C. Code § 21-2205 (1989); Idaho Code § 390-4505 (Supp. 1989); Ill. Rev. Stat., ch. 110 1/2, P904-1 to 804-12 (Supp. 1988); Kan. Stat. Ann. § 58-625 (Supp. 1989); Me. Rev. Stat. Ann., Tit. 18-A, § 5-501 (Supp. 1989); Nev. Rev. Stat. § 449.800 (Supp. 1989); Ohio Rev. Code Ann. § 1337.11 et seq. (Supp. 1989); Ore. Rev. Stat. § 127.510 (1989); Pa. Con. Stat. Ann., Tit. 20, § 5603(h) (Purdon Supp. 1989); R.I. Gen. Laws § 23-4.10-1 et seq. (1989); Tex. Rev. Civ. Stat. Ann. § 4590h-1 (Vernon Supp. 1990); Vt. Stat. Ann., Tit. 14, § 3451 et seq. (1989). All fifty states and the District of Columbia have general durable power of attorney statutes.

334

the patient has an irreversible and incurable condition which is likely to result in death within six months.

3.   If there is a question of competence, the physician may request a psychological or psychiatric evaluation, with the consent of the patient.

4.   The Directive may be revoked at any time, verbally or in writing, by the patient, without regard to his or her competency.

5.   The request must be an enduring one.

6.   The patient determines the time he or she is ready to receive aid-in-dying.

7.   The manner of death would be determined by the patient and the physician. The patient may request medication to take him or herself or may choose to have the medication injected.

8.   No physician, health care giver, or hospital is required to administer aid-in-dying.

9.   There are no penalties for failing to effectuate the Directive unless there is willful failure to transfer the patient if he or she has requested it.

10.   A hospital, physician, or health care personnel acting under a physician's orders is immune from civil or criminal liability.

11.   Aid-in-dying is not to be considered suicide. Life insurance would not be negated if a person died in accordance with the Act.

12.   No insurance company could require disclosure of the patient's wishes regarding aid-in-dying nor would any type of policy be affected by having or not having executed a Directive.

13.   No one may be pressured to make a decision to seek aid-in-dying because he or she is a financial or emotional burden. Coercion to execute a Directive is a misdemeanor; it would be a felony if death occurred as a result of such coercion.

14.   Causing aid-in-dying by forgery of a directive or withholding infomation about intent to revoke would be considered grounds for prosecution for unlawful homicide.

15.   Hospitals and health care providers who carry out aid-in-dying would report the number of cases, age of patient and type of illness annually to the State Department of Health Services; the patient's name would not be disclosed.

16.   Mercy killing is not authorized or condoned by this Act.

17.   The patient is encouraged to inform his or her family.

18.   The directive would be part of the patient's medical record.

19.   The directive would be signed by two unrelated witnesses who are not health care providers and who have no claim against the estate. If the patient is in a nursing home one witness must be an Ombudsman or Patient Advocate.

335

20.   The Act may be amended by two-thirds vote of each house of the legislature and the signature of the Governor.

Why do we need such a law? Under our current system a terminally ill person can only accelerate the dying process by refusing or withdrawing treatment or by committing suicide. Many people with AIDS, cancer or other terminal diseases do not have treatment that can be withheld or refused. Their choice is often between having to die a lingering, painful, and undignified death or using a violent, uncertain, lonely, possibly painful means of committing suicide if they choose to have their suffering over more quickly. Even those patients who do refuse treatment or have it withdrawn can often anticipate a prolonged and difficult death, e.g., refusal of dialysis, antibiotics, chemotherapy, or food and hydration.

For those people who want to know they have control at the end of life, who want to know they have the option to die at the time and in the manner of their choosing, and who want death to be gentle, pain-free, certain, quick, inexpensive, and in the presence of loved ones, one more option has to be in place — they should be able to ask for help in dying from a doctor. Without imposing this form of dying on those who find the suffering of death ennobling, those who are opposed on religious or moral principles, or those who choose to live their lives out to the very end, the DWDA provides a choice for those who might want another way. It is an insurance policy against unwanted suffering and loss of dignity of life's end.

The DWDA would be limited to a relatively small number of cases. It would not have protected Dr. Jack Kevorkian, for instance, who is currently being prosecuted in Michigan for assisting in the suicide of four women. They were not terminally ill, as the DWDA requires. It would be narrower than the practice in Holland where the main criterion is that the patient be in a condition of unbearable suffering, as defined by the patient and including psychological suffering although it is estimated that 80% of the patients in Holland who make this request do have terminal cancer. Although patients there must be competent, they may be minors.

The impetus for these changes in the law stems from the raising of public consciousness by some of the following events in the past two years:

* Janet Adkins getting help in dying from Jack Kevorkian because of her diagnosis and beginning symptoms of Alzheimer's disease;

* The unsuccessful prosecution of Bertram Harper, a 73 year old California man who helped his cancer-ridden wife of 18 years die in Michigan;
* The struggle of Nancy Cruzan's parents to remove the feeding tube from their 28 year old daughter who had been in a persistent vegetative state for seven years;
* The rise of Derek Humphry's *Final Exit* to the best seller list, its translation into the major languages of the world, and its subsequent banning in Australia and New Zealand;
* The courage of Dr. Timothy Quill who wrote and signed an article in the prestigious NEW ENGLAND JOURNAL OF MEDICINE[7] explaining why he gave his leukemia patient, Diane, a lethal dose of medication to help her die at her request;
* The Congressional passage of the PATIENT SELF-DETERMINATION ACT[8] which requires every medical care facility to tell patients on admission what their rights are to execute advance directives;
* The near win of Proposition 119 in the state of Washington;
* The TV movie of LAST WISH in which author Betty Rollin helps her spunky, cancer-ridden mother die at her request;
* The upcoming trial of Jack Kevorkian in Michigan which may result in still another jury nullification where the public says that it is not murder when a caring person helps a hopelessly ill person to die at their request;
* Legislation now introduced in five states — Oregon, Maine, Michigan, Iowa and New Hampshire — which would permit voluntary physician aid-in-dying for the terminally ill.

Opposition to the DWDA is expected from the Catholic hierarchy. However, rank and file Catholics are likely to support it based on several polls including the most recent data from the May issue of the *Journal of the American Medical Association (JAMA)* which indicated that, of the religious groups polled on the question of support for legalizing physician aid in ending the lives of patients with incurable diseases, Catholics were the most supportive with 72% agreement. By comparison, 68% of Jews and 59% of Protestants support legalized euthanasia.[9]

Although the medical hierarchy is officially opposed, an increasing number of physicians favor the concept. A 1990 article by

---

7. Timothy Quill, *Death and Dignity: A Case of Individualized Decision Making* 324 NEW ENG. J. MED. 691-694 (1991).

8. 42 U.S.C.A. § 1396A(w) (1991).

9. Robert J. Blandon, Ulrike S. Szalay, Richard A. Knox, *Should Physicians Aid Their Patients in Dying? The Public Perspective*, 267 JAMA 2658-2662 (1992).

337

12 distinguished physicians in the *New England Journal of Medicine* indicated support for the idea by ten of the authors.[10]

Atto: .eys are still working on it. The concept has been endorsed by the Beverly Hills Bar Association and the 1987 Conference of Delegates to the State Bar of California although it did not get the vote of the House of Delegates of the American Bar Association in 1992. The San Francisco Bar Association has recently endorsed the DWDA.[11]

Strong opposition is expected from right-to-life organizations which comprise a vocal but small proportion of the population. The basic thrust revolves around the sanctity of life — at any cost and contrary to the wishes of the person who is living that life. Their argument spuriously equates the voluntary choice of aid-in-dying with the compulsion to choose, and suggests that it is humane to allow someone to suffer but inhumane to grant their wish to put an end to the suffering. It imputes poor judgment to the medical profession and negates the potential benefits which choice would provide to many because of the rare possibility of abuse.

Let's begin with some definitions. The word "kill" is often used by opponents to describe the behavior of the physician who helps his or her patient die under conditions in which a request has been made and the patient is dying anyway. "Killing" means the deliberate causing of the death of another. We do not have a word which would add to that definition that the death is at the patient's request except the term Active Voluntary Euthanasia. In this context "killing" is to aid-in-dying as love-making is to rape.

In a recent issue of the *Hastings Center Report*, ethicist Dan Brock argues that some killings are ethically justified and that the act of a doctor allowing a patient to die at his or her request is not morally different from actually causing death.[12] He points out that wrongful killing denies the victim the chance to carry out his or her valued future plans. In the case of helping or allowing to die at the request of a terminally ill patient, the helper is hastening the death of an already dying person who does not want the future that the disease is creating. The protections of the DWDA further docu-

---

10. S.H. Wanzer, S.D. Federman, S.J. Adelstein, et. *The Physician's Responsibility Toward Hopelessly Ill Patient*, 320 NEW ENG. J. MED. 844-849 (1989).

11. Personal communication between author and Michael White, May 12, 1992.

12. Dan W. Brock, *Voluntary Active Euthanasia*, HASTINGS CENTER REPORT 10-22 (March-April 1992).

ment that the physician is acceding to a well thought-out, enduring, carefully documented and witnessed request.

There is also the word "suicide" which refers to a person taking his or her own life. There is no distinction made by opponents between emotional suicide — where a person may well change his or her mind as the influence of the emotional state wanes — and rational suicide in which the person would choose to live, absent the incurable, irreversible, terminal illness. The DWDA does not in any way promote emotional suicide. But rational suicide is often a chosen remedy for indignity and suffering which is reducing the quality of life to an unacceptable degree. It is not a choice between life and death, but between death and death.

The term "mercy killing" has generally been reserved for instances in which a doctor, good friend, or relative has taken upon himself or herself to end the life of someone suffering from a hopeless illness in which the person could not give consent or make a request. The shooting by Roswell Gilbert in Florida of his wife who had Alzheimer's disease was such a situation. The DWDA does not condone mercy killing because of the critical importance of the request of the patient.

In "assisted suicide" the person who dies is the primary agent of his or her death and is asking for help to accomplish it. This is illegal in most of this country (Michigan is an exception which is what will make Dr. Kevorkian's trial interesting.) Other examples, besides Kevorkian's four cases, are Betty Rollin's helping her mother die and Dr. Timothy Quill helping his patient, Diane, die.

The DWDA creates a new legal category, Physician Aid-in-Dying. This would include both physician assisted suicide (giving the patient medication to take him or herself) and active voluntary euthanasia (the physician administering the lethal dose at the patient's request.) In both cases the choice rests fully with the patient and the request is generated by someone who is dying.

There are objections by opponents to using the criterion of terminal illness — having six months or less to live, as verified by two independent physicians, and in the context of an irreversible and incurable illness. It is suggested that some patients may outlive their prognoses. Of course, occasional misdiagnoses are made but we still rely on our medical system to make treatment decisions assuming that most of the time they are right. The DWDA requires a second independent opinion which is often more than most people

339

get who consent to major surgery or debilitating treatments, or, who chose to end their lives by refusing treatment. For every rare story of someone outliving their prognoses, there are thousands of cases of people who do actually die in a span of time approximating their physician's approximation. This would include the 10% who leave hospice care after six months and may die a week or two later. In any case, there is no requirement that a person choose aid-in-dying the minute the prognosis is made. It is likely that such a choice would not be made until the disease has debilitated a person and severely compromised the quality of life. Now, people end their lives based on their doctor's word, how they feel, and what they see others go through with the same disease. But they do it with guns, plastic bags, drugs that may not work, and they do it alone because they do not want to jeopardize their loved ones or doctor by asking for help.

Besides, the criteria for ending life in the DWDA are stricter than those set forth in the laws we already have. A terminal condition is not required under the Durable Power of Attorney for Health Care Act for a surrogate decision maker to ask for removal or to refuse life support or any unwanted medical treatment. Similarly, a competent adult in any situation can refuse treatment and die whether they are terminal or not. These rights have been upheld for religious minorities over the years and are now the law of the land. Even the Catholic church has concurred. If an individual cannot make important decisions about the burden of living versus the benefits of ending life then who will make these decisions? It must be up to the individual to determine the criteria for his or her quality of life; no objective standard is possible.

There is the rare situation where a person awakes from a lengthy persistent vegetative state just before artificial feeding is discontinued. Again, there is confusion about existing law which clearly permits treatment to be removed if the patient's wishes are known or if someone is appointed to act in his or her behalf. This is not aid-in-dying and the patient is not terminal. It could happen if the agent provided by the Durable Power of Attorney has been authorized to withdraw treatment if such a condition were to occur. Or, if no agent were specified the Court could make the decision. If a person is concerned about such a possibility, he or she should specify that treatment should never be discontinued under any circumstances where there is the remotest chance that recovery may occur.

340

The case of Elizabeth Bouvia is often mentioned, noting that Ms. Bouvia chose to continue her life despite her earlier wish to not take food and hydration. She would not have been dead under the DWDA since her illness is not terminal. But, she would have died under California case law after 1986 which, thanks to her case, included food and hydration under treatment, a decision that was affirmed in *Cruzan*. Maybe we had better go back and rethink our definition of the right to refuse treatment. If people change their minds maybe patient autonomy is not a good idea and we should make decisions for them even if they are competent adults.[13] And, it should be noted, that competency is not an issue in discontinuing medical treatment. If competency is lost a surrogate can carry out the patient's wishes. Just as there are not restrictive and complex competency definitions, there are no stringent witnessing requirements to either the Living Will or the Durable Power of Attorney for Health Care, although DWDA opponents question these provisions for the DWDA.

Emotionally charged words are often used in the attack on physician aid-in-dying. Besides the repeated use of the word, "kill", there are phrases like, the "duty" of the doctor to act. Under this proposed law no doctor has the "duty" to issue any orders — it is the patient's choice and decision. The word "dehumanizing" is often associated with accelerating the end of life. What is dehumanizing to many is to lie in a hospital bed with tubes extruding from every orifice with no chance of recovery and with no resemblance to human life as that person would like to know it.

The inference is that people must choose between a caring, spiritual, "natural" death surrounded by loved ones or a cold, calculated, "barbaric" death by "suicide" which is plotted by the family and the doctor. This characterization is ludicrous! There may have been an era in which the family stood around granny's bed while she died of pneumonia in a few days. Now dying can be prolonged for weeks or months, often at incredible expense and degradation. Most people dread this option and envy the person who dies quickly and painlessly with all his or her faculties. With the DWDA a person can choose not to be a burden, not to see the funds

---

13. After examining Ms. Bouvia for competence (of which there was no doubt by the examiners and the Court) I inserted my comment about her choice and asked her to reconsider. She responded to this indignity by ending the interview and wheeling herself speedily out of the room. She was lucid and not depressed. How could someone else make this judgment for her?

341

earmarked for the children go to pay useless medical costs, or to be remembered as an active, self-reliant person. It is NOT a compulsion, it is an option.

The recent article reporting polling data in JAMA indicates that 47% of those who would consider alternatives to end their lives if they were terminally ill would do so because of fears of burdening their families. The authors report results from other national surveys showing that 60% of adults report being worried about becoming a financial burden on their children or other people as they grow older.[14] Not being a burden is an important consideration to people! Moreover, that person's death is more likely to occur surrounded by loved ones than the person hooked up in the hospital who recognizes no one or who sees the pain in the faces of loved ones who visit. One person's dignity may be another's humiliation — there must be a choice.

It is folly to suggest that, like the person who is contemplating emotional suicide, dying people can have meaning restored to their lives rather than allowing them to end their life. This assumes that death and terminal illness are reversible, that dignity can be restored when there is a loss of bladder and bowel control, when a person is dependent on machines or other people for every need, or when they cannot speak or have normal cognitive functioning. Most people fear loss of control at the end of their lives more than they do death itself. They are not concerned about "the total surrender of all moral standards"; they want choices and control of their own lives. The suggestion that society can respond to the problems of people facing a lingering death by learning to love, not learning to kill is a meaningless platitude. It was also enunciated by the claque of demonstrators around the hospital where Nancy Cruzan finally died, after seven years of cognitiveless existence. They said to her tortured parents that she should live so they could love her. It is an insult to the caring family of people who choose to die to suggest that they love that person less because they chose to end their lives earlier.

Even Hospice, the compassionate, humane alternative to a prolonged death with aggressive treatment, is not enough. At least 10% of pain cannot be remedied, many do not want the side effects

---

14. Cited in Blandon, et al, *supra* note 9, at 2660. Twenty percent said they would not want to live in pain if they were seriously ill, 19% said they would not want to live dependent on machines, and 12% said they would not want to go on living unable to perform most daily activities.

342

that accompany even effective pain relief, and hospice care cannot make the other indignities of dying go away. Ideally there could be hospice care which would also provide the option of aid-in-dying — they are not incompatible choices.

The provisions of the DWDA have been compared to what happened in Germany but this is simply a rewrite of history. There never was a law permitting the dying to ask for help; whatever Hitler called his murder and genocide it was certainly not done at the request of the dying person. What happened in Germany could happen here if voters were ever rash enough to vote into power a totalitarian government which could obliterate people's rights and take their lives. The DWDA is not the first step; denying choices, speaking half-truths, and allowing a religious minority to restrict the freedoms of the majority may be.

Opponents argue that there are reports of abuses of the Dutch system; these are simply hearsay. There may be a reluctance by Dutch doctors to report all cases since they do not have an actual law, like the DWDA, which governs physician aid-in-dying. That can be remedied by changing their practice but it is not troubling to the Dutch people. The provisions of the DWDA are clear and mandate reporting and penalties for abuse. The idea that the Dutch are fearful of involuntary euthanasia is not substantiated by objective investigation. What is alarming in this country is the increase in aid-in-dying by friends, relatives, and doctors with legal impunity. People write books and go on national TV describing what they've done but there is no prosecution or they are acquitted by juries who nullify the law. Jurors do not see these assisted suicides and mercy killings as something which should be illegal and can imagine themselves being in the same position. The DWDA should be enacted if for no other reason than to restore confidence in the laws we have and to monitor the process that is already occurring.

The slippery slope argument is often made. After this legislation passes, what is next. Will there be death on demand? It is difficult to know what people will want in 10 or 100 years; we would not have predicted in 1950 that the U.S. Supreme Court would have affirmed the right of every American, or their surrogate, to refuse unwanted medical treatment including food and hydration. Who would have known that 18 year olds of both sexes and every race could vote in 1992 when the first suffrage was granted only to white men with property. The dire predictions of the slippery slope cannot deter the enactment of a law with clearly defined limits. In fact,

343

opponents often wind up arguing for the law's expansion by pointing to the fact that non-terminal suffering people are excluded. Is that a reason not to have the law at all?

The pro-life position compares the right to an abortion with the right to die. There are interesting similarities and differences between the two, the most obvious being that no other life is involved in the request of the person who is dying. But, if the parallels are to be drawn, it should be noted that since abortion has been legal there have been no complaints of duress or coercion; women continue to trust their doctors; there is no need for a sophisticated test of competence; nor that there has become a "duty" to abort. What has happened is that abortion is legal and safe now. When the DWDA becomes law the botched, violent, lonely, secretive suicides of terminally ill people would be eliminated. People could die gently and certainly, holding the hand of a loved one. Furtive trips to doctors to get a lethal stash of medication would be unnecessary. Compassionate doctors, elderly spouses, children, and partners of people with AIDS would be spared the risk of court proceedings; and people would not have to have garbage bags tied around their heads at the time of death.

The endless trivial objections to the various provisions of the DWDA are red herrings for the basic objection: so-called "right to life" groups do not want the people of California to have a choice. Dying people will have dignity and autonomy only when they can legally choose how and when their lives will end.

Support for this idea comes from Justice Lynn Compton in the decision by the Court of Appeal in the Bouvia case:

> The right to die is an integral part of our right to control our own destinies so long as the rights of others are not affected. The right should in my opinion, include the ability to enlist assistance from others, including the medical profession, in making death as painless and quick as possible. . . . If there is ever a time when we ought to be able to get the "government off our backs" it is when we face death — either by choice or otherwise.[15]

---

15. Bouvia v. Superior Court, 179 Cal. App. 3d 1127, 1147, 1148 (1986) (Compton, J., concurring).

344

PERSPECTIVES

LICENSED TO KILL: THE "DEATH WITH DIGNITY" INITIATIVE

by David L. Llewellyn, Jr.*

The "Death With Dignity Act" initiative[1] would convert a license to practice medicine into a license to kill. The DWDA would authorize doctors to kill patients, at their request, when, in the doctors' judgment, they have a terminal condition and are expected to die naturally within six months or less.

This modest proposal for killing the people of California,[2] if adopted, undoubtedly will kill non-terminal people. In the name of false autonomy, the DWDA also will kill people who decide to take their lives under the effects of depression or despair, not thoughtful self-determination. The ideology of the DWDA—to encourage and assist (that is, to pressure) the old, infirm, or unproductive to take their own lives by assisted suicide—subverts respect for life and promotes the chilling pro-euthanasia ethics of Nazi Germany and contemporary Holland. The DWDA has been cleverly titled to mislead the public, since it contains no criteria requiring would-be suicides to be suffering any pain or indignity. Finally, the DWDA contains numerous legal flaws, both technical and substantive—such as its astonishing lack of any standards to determine the mental competence of a person considering assisted suicide, its arbitrary and unre-

---

* © David Llewellyn 1992. Mr. Llewellyn is a civil rights attorney and President of the Western Center for Law and Religious Freedom, a public interest law firm based in Sacramento, California.

1. The "Death With Dignity Act" (DWDA) initiative has qualified for submission to the voters of California as Proposition 161 on the ballot of the November 3, 1992, statewide election.

2. The DWDA sounds remarkably like Jonathan Swift's "A Modest Proposal For Preventing the Children of Poor People in Ireland from Being a Burden to Their Parents or Country; and for Making Them Beneficial to the Publick" which proposed to solve overpopulation by killing unwanted children and using them for food. Jonathan Swift, GULLIVER'S TRAVELS AND OTHER WRITINGS 488-496 (Modern Library 1958) (1729). This satirical proposition seemed outrageous then but may have lost its emotional impact on a state and nation which already legally kills unwanted children before birth and which has proposed, not satirically, to use their dead bodies (which, curiously, are otherwise argued to be not human but mere tissue) not for food but for medicine.

309

liable death-within-six-months definition of "terminal condition," and its ambiguously indefinite "enduring request" requirement—that make it a danger to itself and others.

CONSTITUTIONAL RIGHTS TO LIFE AND DEATH

Advocates of euthanasia and assisted suicide contend that the legal rights of the patient-victim outweigh the interests of the state, the people, in preserving life.

Euthanasia proponents assert rights of privacy and autonomy. These rights have been interpreted by the courts as encompassing a qualified "right to die." Specifically, people have constitutionally recognized rights to refuse medical treatment, even when the treatment is necessary to sustain life.[3] These rights are based upon the Fourteenth Amendment to the U.S. Constitution and, in California, on the right of privacy in Article 1, § 1, of the California Constitution.

Counterbalancing these rights are the interests of the community, the state, in promoting and protecting life and other important public values.

"Pertinent state interests include preserving human life, preventing suicide, protecting innocent third parties such as children, and maintaining the ethical integrity of the medical profession."[4]

Also, especially with respect to the right to die, "the state has a legitimate competing interest in protecting society against abuses."[5] With regard to assisted suicide, abuses include the presence of undue influence[6] and threats to the "sancity of life."[7]

When the question presented to the courts has been a right to die by the removal of artificial means of sustaining life, the interests of the individuals and the right to die have prevailed. When the question has turned away from the passive role of non-intervention

---

3. *Cruzan v. Director, Missouri Health Department* 497 U.S. —, 110 S. Ct. 2841 (1990); *Donaldson v. Van De Kamp* — Cal. App. 3d —, 4 Cal. Rptr. 2d 59 (1992); *People v. Adams* 216 Cal. App. 3d 1431, 265 Cal. Rptr. 568 (1990); *Conservatorship of Drabick* 200 Cal. App. 3d 185, 245 Cal. Rptr. 840 (1988); *Bouvia v. Superior Court* 179 Cal. App. 3d 186, 225 Cal. Rptr. 297 (1986); *Bartling v. Superior Court* 163 Cal. App. 3d 186, 209 Cal. Rptr. 220 (1984); *Barber v. Superior Court* 147 Cal. App. 3d 1006, 195 Cal. Rptr. 484 (1983).
4. *Donaldson v. Van De Kamp* — Cal. App. 3d —, 4 Cal. Rptr. 2d a59, 62 (1992).
5. *Id.* at 63.
6. *Id.* at 64. See infra.
7. *Id.* at 65.

310

to prevent inevitable death and faced active intervention to kill, the concerns of the people collectively and duty to preserve life have prevailed. These exists "no constitutional right to a state-assisted death."[8]

"No statute or judicial opinion countenances [a] decision to consent to be murdered or to commit suicide with the assistance of others."[9]

After rejecting arguments by euthanasia activists for constitutional rights to assisted suicide and immunity from criminal prosecution, the courts have concluded that "the legal and philosophical problems" involved are a "legislative matter."[10] Hence, the proponents of physician-assisted suicide now turn to the public forum and their proposed initiative legislation, the Death With Dignity Act.

THE DEATH WITH DIGNITY ACT

Many of the general policy arguments concerning the Death With Dignity Act initiative have been anticipated by a resolution propounded to the American Bar Association by the Beverly HIlls Bar Association (BHBA) in support of "voluntary aid in dying to terminally ill persons," a resultion which tracks in substance the provisions of the DWDA.[11] The BHBA contends for the resolution

---

8. *Id.* at 64.

9. *Id.* at 63, citing *Von Holden v. Chapman* 87 A.D.2d 66, 450 N.Y.S.2d 623, 627 (1982), which found an " 'essential dissimilarity' between right to decline medical treatment and any right to end one's life." *Id.*

10. *Id.* at 64.

11. Beverly Hills Bar Association Report to the House of Delegates Recommendation, RESOLVED, That the American Bar Association recommends that all jurisdictions provide by statute rules permitting voluntary aid in dying to terminally ill persons who request such aid in ending their own lives; and that such rules include at least the following safeguards:

   a. That such aid in dying end a life swiftly, painlessly, and with dignity.

   b. That such aid in dying be provided (1) only by trained and licensed medical doctors or physicians, and (2) without undue influence or duress by relatives, friends, or caretakers of the patient or physician.

   c. That a request for aid in dying is the expressed, unequivocal desire of the terminally ill person, after careful consideration, and that such request is known by the administering doctor or physician to be the wish of the terminally ill person.

   d. That any person, entity, or institution be permitted to decline to participate in assisting the terminally ill person to die for moral or ethical reasons.

   e. That aid in dying shall not constitute a homicide, nor assisting a suicide.

   f. That no doctor, physician, or person assisting such doctor or physician shall be subject to criminal, civil, or administrative liability for giving such aid in dying.

   g. That no person or entity assisting a terminally ill person to die shall be

311

on the grounds of enhancing patient autonomy, relief from intractable pain and legalizing the "merciful ending of a life."

This ABA resolution has elicited unanimous opposition from the Commission on Legal Problems of the Elderly. The Commission, which has strongly supported previous ABA resolutions favoring durable powers of attorney for health care and which supports the rights of patients to personal autonomy and to refuse medical intervention, opposes the assisted suicide resolution on numerous grounds. The Commission argues that (1) previous resolutions were ethically distinct from endorsing intentional termination of life; (2) there can be no "truly voluntary choice to terminate life" without "universal access to affordable health care"; (3) "[e]uthanasia is illegal throughout the civilized world," although in the Netherlands it is not prosecuted if certain conditions are met' (4) the Netherlands data indicate that 89-90% of deaths by euthanasia are not reported (and therefore not investigated); (5) over 1,000 people who died by euthanasia in the Netherlands in 1990 alone had not made clear and enduring requests according to a recent Dutch government repoprt; (6) criminal law based on intent to kill is the best demarcation line against sliding down "a 'slippery slope' to state-sanctioned death"; (7) " 'terminal' lacks any truly objective, operational definition"; (8) the competence standard is inadequate and raised the problem of arguable injustice to incompetent people who are suffering and cannot request aid to die (virtually inviting state intervention and nonconsensual death); (9) the concurrence of the physician is entirely subjective and standardless; (10) to a vulnerable person, such as an elderly person without adequate medical care or financial resources, the right to die may be perceived as a duty to die.[12]

An examination of the proposed Death With Dignity Act shows it likewise to be fatally flawed, both in concept and implementation.

---

permitted to charge more than a fee reasonably related to the services rendered.

h. That no policy of life or health insurance shall be denied, legally imparied, or invalidated, as a result of a request for aid in dying.

i. That there be adequate and appropriate sanctions for any person who interferes with a patient's rights pursuant to the statue.

8 ISSUES L. & MED. 115 (1992).

12. "Memorandum to American Bar Association," 8 ISSUES IN L. & MED. 117 (1992).

312

1. DWDA OVERKILL

The DWDA purports to authorize the killing only of "terminal" people.[13] If the Hemlock Society and the promoters of the DWDA have their way, however, non-terminal people also will be killed. People will be misled by their doctors' mistaken opinions about the prognosis of their diseases and about their apparently brief life expectancies, and they will authorize their doctors to kill them. No one will know, of course, that the doctors were wrong, because their patients will be dead. Indeed, the only doctors who can predict with certainty that their patients will die within the next six months—the standard of divination required of physicians under the DWDA[14]—are doctors who kill their patients.

When her physicians diagnosed Diana Schmidt's condition, they determined that her deadly polycystic liver disease meant that she would be in constant pain, and that she had just six months to live. If the DWDA had been the law when Diana received this grave prognosis, she could have replied, "Six months is not worth the pain. Just kill me now." with the help of her doctors she could have committed physician-assisted suicide.[15]

Why not? Her doctors knew Diana was going to die anyway, and this would avoid pain for her, expense for her family, or her insurer or the public health system, and would help to relieve overcrowding of hospitals and wasted time and effort by her doctors.

Unfortunately, Diana's condition was never cured or corrected. Fortunately, however, Diana received her deadly diagnosis before the DWDA could endow doctors with the godlike power to advise people when it would be appropriate to take their lives and with the devilish duty to execute dehumanizing orders to kill their patients.

Diana Schmidt, you see, outlived her doctors' death sentence. Pronounced terminal and told she would be dead in six months in 1981, she still lives today, eleven years later.[16]

---

13. " 'Qualified patient' means a mentally competent adult patient . . . who has been diagnosed . . . to be afflicted with a terminal condition. . . ." § 2525.2(h).

14. " 'Terminal condition' means an incurable or irreversible condition which will, in the opinion of two certifying physicians exercising reasonable medical judgment, result in death within six months or less." § 2525.2(j).

15. DWDA advocates object to the term "suicide." *See* § 2525.16 and Section 2 amending CAL. PENAL CODE § 401. But what else can we call it? *See infra.*

16. *Her liver is too big, checkbook too small,* SACRAMENTO UNION, April 21, 1992, at A2. The name of the patient has been replaced in this article by a pseudonym.

313

Diana might enjoy meeting Carrie Coons and sharing experiences. Carrie, then age 86, went into a coma in October 1988 and was diagnosed by her doctors as being in a "persistent vegetative state." Two weeks short of six months later, a New York judge entered an order, based upon the doctors' opinions, directing the removal of her gastrostomy tube, so that Carrie could be starved to death. Embarrassingly, however, just days before the order to kill her could be carried out, Carrie "awoke."[17]

Hospices report that approximately 10% of allegedly terminal patients admitted to die instead survive and are released, due both to unexpected remission of their conditions and misdiagnosis by their doctors.[18]

The DWDA will certainly kill people who would not otherwise die within six months. Unsuspecting, misinformed people will die, with legal sanction. Under the DWDA, contrary to the popular adage, "What you don't know can kill you."

2. SUBVERSION OF THE DIGNITY OF LIFE

Sympathetic people grieve with patients hospitalized in apparently hopeless conditions, whose lives seemingly are coming to an end. Friends and family gather around such people, to comfort them, to assist them in arranging their affairs, to provide spiritual aid, to appreciate their lives and to enjoy their final days together. Not to plot their deaths.

The DWDA does not waste sorrow or sympathy on such people. The DWDA in effect tells people facing death that it would be undignified to rely upon others for their care for the last half year of their lives, that they should feel embarrassed to impose upon their families and the limited medical resources of their community just to postpone their impending deaths, that reasonable people would

---

17. Since the court had been told that Carrie would not want to be kept alive by artificial means, her doctor dutifully told her about the court order to remove her feeding tube. She recoiled from the idea. "That's a very difficult decision to make," she said. "I never really thought of it in quite that way." The death order was quashed. *See*: Gannon v. Albany Memorial Hospital, No. 0189-017460 (N.Y. Sup. Ct. February 14, 1989; *'Hopeless' Hospital Patient, 86, Comes Out of Coma*, TIMES UNION (Albany, New York), April 12, 1989 at A1; *Right to Die Order Revoked as Patient in Coma Wakes*, NEW YORK TIMES, April 13, 1989 at B3; *Not a 'Hopeless Case' After All*, WASHINGTON POST, April 29, 1989 at A25—cited in Victor G. Rosenblum and Clark D. Forsythe, *The Right to Assisted Suicide: Protection of Autonomy or an Open Door to Social Killing?*, 6 ISSUES IN L. & MED. 3, 19 n.93 (1990).

18. D. Alan Shewmon, M.D., *Active Voluntary Euthanasia: A Needless Pandora's Box*, 3 ISSUES IN L. & MED. 219, 223 (1987).

314

rely upon the prognosis of their doctors and would spare others—family, friends, medical personnel, taxpayers, the public health system, insurance companies, people paying escalating insurance rates, hospital shareholders—the waste of time, money, equipment and medical expertise necessary to coddle their now-useless bodies for the sake of the meaningless last 180 days remaining to them, that to remain alive is mere selfish indulgence.

"Your life was acceptable," the DWDA implies, "so long as you were capable of taking care of yourself and were a productive member of society, but now . . . better to kill yourself."

"Your life is over. The days and hours between now and your natural death are superfluous. If you were really courageous, you would kill yourself. If you really cared about other people, you would kill yourself. Society has determined that a life like yours now is just a waste of time—your pointless time and our valuable time. As soon as you realize this, the law has authorized your doctors to kill you. This is what you should do, if you want to preserve the respect of those around you and your own personal dignity. If you doubt this, just ask your doctor, who will not only confirm the futility of your continued existence but will offer to kill you at your convenience, right now if you like."

The DWDA calls killing such people "dignified." In fact, it is barbaric evidence of the regression of American culture and values. Suicide cannot cure anything, for individuals or societies. If people's lives have lost meaning, the remedy is not to murder them, with or without their permission, but to restore the meaning to their lives. A society which abandons people who have given up on themselves has relinquished the right to call itself a society. Like armies that shoot their wounded, whatever cause or ideals they were fighting for have already been destroyed.

Every human being possesses inherent dignity. Whether human dignity is recognized as a divine endowment or a natural characteristic of humanity, every person has this dignity as an inalienable attribute. People have retained this human dignity despite harrowing experiences of war, prison camps, famine, plague, injury, deformity, disasters and personal loss. Death and deprivation cannot destroy this dignity.

What, then, is the source of the asserted indignity of death which the DWDA seeks to avoid? The loss of dignity which the

315

DWDA decries arises from the DWDA itself and from the moral and social values from which it is derived.

Although natural human dignity cannot be destroyed, people lose their awareness of this dignity, they lose their inner sense of self-respect, by violating accepted standards of morality or ethics and by receiving ridicule, cruelty or indifference from people upon whom they depend for physical or emotional support.

The DWDA denigrates the inborn sense of human dignity by encouraging people to violate their God-given and natural instincts for survival and their innate reverence for life by embracing suicide, for themselves and others. The DWDA further promotes the dehumanization of the ill and elderly by treating their lives with indifference, cruelty and ridicule, by proposing to them that their lives are not worth living, that they would be better off dead. To remedy the loss of community and individual self-worth, a loss aggravated by the philosophy behind the DWDA itself, the DWDA recommends a remedy of total surrender of all moral standards by legitimating suicide.

Placed in their best light, the advocates of the DWDA may be motivated by compassion, but it is compassion gone awry. To respond to elderly, injured and diseased people, facing the ends of their lives, by encouraging them to be killed cannot, in a sane world, be humane. What does physician-assisted suicide tell such patients except that their opinions of the meaninglessness of their lives are shared even by those responsible for their care and, indeed, by society as a whole?

Death is not the problem these people face, and advancing their deaths cannot resolve the flaw in our culture responsible for their true trauma. The indignity of their impending deaths comes not from death itself but from the loneliness and emptiness of the remainder of their lives, wounds inflicted upon our ill and elderly by the loss of community in our culture, wounds that would be exacerbated by the DWDA. We leave people alone to die. Their pain is not in their deaths but in their abandonment.

> No man is an island, entire of itself. Every man is a piece of the continent, a part of the main. . . . Any man's death diminishes me, because I am involved in mankind. And therefore never send to know for whom the bell tolls; it tolls for thee.[19]

19. John Donne, *Meditation VII, in* THE COMPLETE POETRY AND SELECTED PROSE OF JOHN DONNE, 440-441 (modernized text) (Random House, 1952).

316

The duty of society to respond with dignity to the problem of people facing lingering death is not to learn to kill but to learn to love.

3. DEATH AND INDIGNITY FOR ALL

The promise of death with dignity under the DWDA is belied by the actual experience in countries which have experimented with legalized euthanasia.

GERMANY. Even before the Nazi era, Germany had legalized euthanasia. Assisted suicide was advocated in a popular German book in the 1920's entitled *The Permission to Destroy Life Not Worth Living*.[20] This devaluation of human life led to Hitler's euthanasia orders of 1939 and, in turn, to mass extermination of physically, mentally, religiously or racially undesirable people and to the medical practice of killing patients with even minor physical problems, which continued to the end of the war.[21]

THE NETHERLANDS. In Holland the Dutch have had legalized euthanasia since 1981.[22] Dutch doctors kill approximately 2,300 adults each year by euthanasia, according to government reports, and, under government-approved regulations, the physicians are immune from liability.[23] People no longer need to be terminally ill to obtain doctor-assisted suicide in Holland. The courts have expanded legal death assistance to conditions such as multiple sclerosis and simple old age.[24] The Royal Dutch Medical Association recommends legalization of euthanasia for minors, without parental consent.[25] The practice of killing newborn infants (and disguising the cases as natural deaths) has become sufficiently common that the Dutch Pediatric Association is now seeking official guidelines for infanticide.[26]

Euthanasia has led to serious loss of public trust in the medical profession and to destruction of the fiduciary relationship between doctors and their patients. Legalization of euthanasia in Holland has led to deceptive practices by doctors, who reportedly declared

---

20. Shewmon, *supra*, note 8, at 227.

21. *Id.* at 228-229.

22. *Id.* at 226.

23. *Dutch Doctors Want Rules on Euthanasia for Newborns*, SACRAMENTO BEE, July 30, 1992, at A12.

24. Shewmon, *supra*, at 229.

25. *Id.*

26. *Sacramento Bee, supra* note 23.

317

false "natural" causes on death certificates to avoid legal investigations. Dutch doctors report that elderly patients have become reluctant to go to hospitals or to see physicians, for fear that they will be victimized by involuntary euthanasia and that their murders will be concealed by being falsely reported by doctors as occurring by natural causes.[27]

4. THE MYTH OF AUTONOMY

The DWDA purports to implement personal autonomy for terminally ill patients by permitting them to direct their own deaths. This alleged autonomy is illusory.

We all know from common experience that most people who fail in their attempts at suicide later look back at their suicidal episodes as aberrant behavior, not as an expression of true autonomy. People typically commit suicide when they are distressed or depressed, not when they are feeling fulfilled, flushed with urges of self-determination and eager to exercise their autonomy.

Feelings of distress or depression expand exponentially when people are hospitalized and suffering fear, pain, injury or disease, financial pressures, separation from family, loss of productivity, psychological dislocation, confinement to unfamiliar and foreboding surroundings, and subjection to the impersonal treatment characteristic of most medical care. Making an irreversible decision to die under such conditions does not bear the indicia of rational autonomy.

Even people who, because of their medical conditions, have contemplated suicide over a long period of time and who have expressed an "enduring request"[28] to be aided in killing themselves may, under future conditions, look back with relief that the death wishes made in their extended times of difficulty were not executed.

Elizabeth Bouvia is such a person. Ms. Bouvia suffers from cerebral palsy which has immobilized her, except for limited movement of her head and facial muscles and of the fingers on one hand. She went through an extended period of despair in which she

---

27. Allan Parachini, *The Netherlands Debates the Legal Limits of Euthanasia*, LOS ANGELES TIMES, July 15, 1987, at IV-1; Richard Fenigsen, *Involuntary Euthanasia in Holland*, WALL STREET JOURNAL, September 29, 1987 at 29—cited in Shewmon, *supra*, note 8, at 229-230.

28. The DWDA provides for a right to assisted suicide on the basis of an "enduring request," which is defined as "a request . . . expressed on more than one occasion." § 2525.2(i). *See infra*.

318

sought a court order releasing her from medical care so that she could be permitted to starve herself to death. After extensive legal efforts, eventually the California Court of Appeal granted her request.[29] Despite having gone to such determined efforts, however, she later changed her mind. She did not take her life.[30] Thus, the most noted California case on the right to die actually illustrates the transitory nature of the wish for suicide.

"Undue influence of others also taints claims to autonomy.

In the case of assisted suicides, however, the state has an important interest to ensure that people are not influenced to kill themselves. The state's interest must prevail over the individual because of the difficulty, if not the impossibility, of evaluating the motives of the assister or determining the presence of undue influence."[31]

"One reason for the existence of criminal sanctions for those who aid a suicide is to discourage those who might encourage a suicide to advance personal motives."[32]

5. SUICIDE AND PAIN

Arguments for the DWDA often turn to pain. The promoters of the DWDA initiative called themselves "Californians Against Human Suffering." But pain provides no argument for the DWDA. The argument goes too far and yet falls short.

First, the argument from pain proves too much. If pain justifies self-inflicted death, then the DWDA fails in its objective because it does not authorize doctors to obtain consent to kill all patients who are suffering severe and constant pain. The DWDA as presently written permits the killing only of people whose doctors expect them to die anyway within six months. All others the DWDA leaves to suffer years, lifetimes, of agony before they come

---

29. Bouvia v. Superior Court, 179 Cal. App. 3d 1127, 225 Cal. Rptr. 297 (1986).

30. One might speculate that the focused effort to gain the legal right to kill herself paradoxically helped to restore meaning to her life. I was present at the Bouvia trial, as associate counsel to her husband (whom she was then divorcing) who tried to intervene to save her life, and I heard her testify. Ironically, the trial court judge, who interacted with her personally, denied her a right to take her life, but the Court of Appeal, acting only on legal arguments and the cold, written record, determined that she had a right to have her nasogastric tube removed so that she could starve to death, based on their "respect" for her "mental and emotional feelings" and the "dehumanizing aspect of her condition." *Bouvia, Id.* at 1134. In the end, the trial court's assertedly heartless judgment proved to be compassionate and correct.

31. Donaldson v. Van De Kamp, *Id.* at 64.

32. *Id.* at 65; citing In Re Joseph G., *supra*, 34 Cal. 3d at 437.

319

within six months of their natural deaths, at which time they may be killed. Perhaps we should surmise that beyond "DWDA, Part I: The Six-Month Rule"[33] the producers of this killer law have in mind a horror sequel, "DWDA, Part II: Death on Demand."[34]

Legal demands for rights to assisted suicide in the absence of suffering and in advance of the six month pre-death period have already been advanced and rejected.[35]

Second, the argument from pain likewise proves too little. The DWDA contains no requirement that people who qualify to kill themselves be in pain. Our natural compassion for people enduring incurable physical torment is being manipulated by the champions of the DWDA to support a law justifying death in the absence of any pain or suffering whatsoever. If unbearable, intractable pain were the actual concern of the DWDA backers, the initiative would have been directed to authorize doctors, at the request of patients suffering excruciating pain, to administer pain-relieving medications or procedures sufficient to suppress the pain, even if the treatment risked the death of the patient.

> "No state interest is compromised by allowing [Plaintiff] to experience a dignified death rather than an excruciatingly painful life."[36]

But the presence of pain is irrelevant under the DWDA.

---

33. The six month term is adopted from the 1982 "Hemlock Manifesto" (defining "terminal illness" to mean that "the person is likely, in the judgment of two examining physicians, to die of that condition within six months"). 8 HEMLOCK QUARTERLY I.C.A. (1982), *reprinted in* Derek Humphrey, LET ME DIE BEFORE I WAKE 100-114 (3d ed. 1984)—cited and quoted in Shewmon, *supra*, note 8, at 223 n.16.

Six months is an arbitrary duration. Doctors of patients who want suicide will be tempted to shade their predictions into the six month range. Courts could easily decide that no principled distinction can be drawn between a six-month and a seven-month case and soon will find difficulty distinguishing a seven-month case from a seven-year case.

34. Writings of the euthanasia movement and the Hemlock Society have "progressed" beyond advocating death only for the terminally ill, to others: "incurable" people, such as people with Alzheimer's disease or osteoporosis; quadriplegics; people whose spouses or life partners have died. Shewmon, *supra*, note 8, at 224-225 and citations therein. Dr. Shewmon concludes that the Hemlock Society is moving toward "euthanasia on demand." This conclusion is supported by the legal rationale in the Bouvia case to permit death by starvation of an incurable but not terminal person.

35. Donaldson v. Van De Kamp, *Id.* at 61 (seeking assisted "premortem cryogenic suspension").

36. *Id.* at 63.

6. SUICIDE AND INDIGNITY

Just as the DWDA requires no pain for doctor-assisted suicide, neither does it require that a "qualifying" patient be facing any loss of dignity. Whether loss of dignity should justify suicide represents a point of moral, ethical, spiritual and political debate. But an initiative appealing to the electorate that people should rather be killed than suffer indignity ought at least to have as one of its requirements that the patient-victim have suffered loss of dignity sufficient to justify his or her death. One would assume that a law entitled the "Death With Dignity Act" would provide for killing people only as a last resort to prevent their loss of dignity. On the contrary, the DWDA makes no demand of any loss of dignity, however slight, as a prerequisite for legalized suicide. Anyone, no matter how revered and respected, no matter how cared for or comfortable, no matter how dignified, can order his or her suicide under the DWDA.

It appears that the focus of the DWDA is not as much a compassionate concern for individuals facing death as an ideological belief in the moral value (the "dignity") of committing suicide. The "Death With Dignity Act" seeks to do more than to decriminalize euthanasia. The DWDA seeks a legal declaration that some forms of suicide and homicide will henceforth be recognized by law and society as honorable, as dignified, ways to die.

7. LEGALIZED SUICIDE, HOMICIDE, EUTHANASIA

DWDA promoters dislike the terms "suicide" and "euthanasia." The DWDA peremptorily declares that killing oneself under its terms is not "suicide."[37] The so-called "aid-in-dying" section does, however, authorize suicide-like "self-administration" of death-inducing medication.[38]

Likewise, the DWDA declares that its provisions do not approve "mercy killing."[39]

What other terms could be used? Perhaps "putting to sleep," the euphemism we employ for killing animals—except that animals do not choose to kill themselves, as people would under the DWDA.

---

37. "Requesting and receiving aid-in-dying by a qualified patient in accordance with this title shall not, for any purpose, constitute a suicide." § 2525.16.

38. § 2525.2(k).

39. § 2525.23.

321

The argument of the DWDA promoters against the term "suicide" seems to be that doctors usually do the killing,[40] so the proper term would be "homicide." But the DWDA initiative also amends the criminal law to forbid calling it homicide.[41] We cannot call it "murder" because murder requires killing someone unlawfully[42] and the DWDA would make killing people legal. No, "suicide" or "assisted suicide" remain the most accurate terms to use for legal death under the DWDA.

Perhaps the solution to this legal language problem is to declare that a human being who doctors decide will die within six months is no longer a "person." If an unborn baby is legally only "potential life,"[43] it should be easy to decide that a dying adult is legally "potential non-life."

The Court of Appeal in *Bouvia* described the presence of a nasogastric feeding tube and the dependence of Ms. Bouvia upon others for her personal care as "dehumanizing."[44] Thus, a sentient, educated and articulate person suffering from quadriplegia was adjudged to be "dehumanized," less than human. Consider where that logic leads.

Society, then, in good conscience, could be able to terminate the adulthood of this once-human being the way we terminate a pregnancy, routinely. Consider the balance and symmetry—the genius—of the law, which would permit children to be killed legally in the first nine months of their lives, before natural birth, and also permit adults to be killed legally in the last six months of their lives, before natural death. Granted, it is easier to predict within six months the time of a child's birth than of an adult's death, but no law is perfect.[45]

The devious DWDA initiative attempts to change moral-based language by enacting a law that denies the obvious—a law which insists that people who kill themselves are not committing suicide

---

40. The California Natural Death Act expressly refuses to authorize doctors to participate in "assisted suicide" or to perform "any affirmative or deliberate act or omission to end life other than to permit the natural process of dying." CAL. HEALTH & SAFETY CODE § 7191.5(g).

41. DWDA, Sec. 2, amending CAL. PENAL CODE § 401.

42. CAL. PENAL CODE § 187.

43. Roe v. Wade, 410 U.S. 113 (1973).

44. Bouvia v. Superior Court 179 Cal. App. 3d at 1134, 225 Cal. Rptr. at 299.

45. Perhaps, as *Roe v. Wade* generated the abortion clinic industry, the DWDA may start a new growth business in death clinics. Or abortion clinics could handle adult terminations as a sideline.

322

and that doctors who take the lives of their patients are not performing euthanasia. These provisions illustrate the double-speak mind-set of the DWDA proponents, who evidently believe that their law has power not only to "dignify" suicide but even to define suicide and euthanasia out of existence.

8. "TERMINAL CONDITION"

One of the preconditions for physician-assisted suicide under the DWDA is that two doctors, "exercising reasonable medical judgment" must be of the opinion that the person has an "incurable or irreversible condition which will . . . result in death within six months or less."[46]

"Reasonable medical judgment" cannot reliably predict the deaths of individuals six months in advance. Virtually everyone has heard of someone still living who was told at sometime in the past that he or she had only six months to live. This mistake is so common as to have become a cliche. The California Natural Death Act[47] defines a "terminal condition" as one which will "result in death within a relatively short time."[48] In context of the Natural Death Act, "relatively short time" presumably refers to hours or days, not up to six months. Accurate medical judgment cannot extend that far.

The DWDA relies upon a false premise, that predicting the time of death for specific individuals—not statistical averages—with an accuracy of six months or less (but not more) is "reasonable." What percentage of accuracy is required for a physician's death predictions to be reasonable? Will we liken it to baseball, where a batter is outstanding when he connects for a hit three times out of ten at-bats? Or would it be reasonable for people to outlive their death estimates only 50% of the time, so that only one out of every two people who kill themselves under the DWDA will have taken their lives prematurely? Perhaps wrongfully killing only one person in ten would be acceptable.[49]

The DWDA takes no chances about second-guessing the doctors' word, no matter how inaccurate their "reasonable" death time

---

46. § 2524.24(j). *See* notes 19 and 20, *supra*.

47. CAL. HEALTH & SAFETY CODE § 7185 et seq. The Natural Death Act authorizes a terminal patient to refuse medical care that would sustain life artificially.

48. CAL. HEALTH & SAFETY CODE § 7186(j). *See also* § 7186.5(b).

49. *See* note 9, *supra*, and related text.

323

tables prove to be. Doctors, hospitals and medical personnel can claim immunity from civil, criminal and administrative liability.

9. "MENTAL COMPETENCE"

The mental competence of a person ordering his or her own death must be of intense concern. The "prevailing thought" in the law is that "suicide or attempted suicide is an expression of mental illness."[50]

How does the DWDA determine the mental competence of a person to demand "physician aid-in-dying"? The attending physician decides.[51] No special training or expertise is required of the attending physician to render this life-or-death opinion.

What form of examination of the mental state of this would-be suicide is required of the attending physician? No particular examination is required at all.

What set of medical criteria must the attending physician use to determine the patient's mental state? No medical criteria. The DWDA standard is entirely subjective and undefined. In fact, the DWDA focuses not on the patient but on the physician.

The DWDA asks only whether the "physician has a concern about the patient's competence."[52] A doctor's level of concern reflects a totally subjective judgment and will guarantee erratic and unpredictable results. A patient whose physician is a member of the Hemlock Society would get one standard, a patient whose physician is a right-to-life Roman Catholic would get another, and other patients would get some other "Doctor knows best" or "Every physician for himself" judgment based on the individual idiosyncrasies of their doctors.

This is suicide roulette, gambling patients' lives on the chance of a doctor's subjective feelings about patients' mental states. Even a criminal facing the death penalty would be entitled to an objective determination of the facts of the case and his mental competence beyond reasonable doubt.

"PSYCHIATRIC OR PSYCHOLOGICAL CONSULTATION." An especially quirky provision of the DWDA allows an attending physician concerned about a patient's competence to request a

---

50. Donaldson v. Van De Kamp, *Id.* at 64, citing the California Supreme Court in In re Joseph G., 34 Cal. 3d 429, 433-434, 194 Cal. Rptr. 163 (1983).
51. § 2525.13.
52. *Id.*

consultation with a psychiatrist or psychologist—but only if the patient consents![53] How many mentally unstable patients intent on suicide will consent to a psychological examination to prove their incompetence?

Quirkier still, the patient's consent to a competency consultation must be given by a "QUALIFIED patient."[54] A "qualified patient," by DWDA definition, means a "MENTALLY COMPETENT adult patient."[55] Hence, in order to give a valid consent to a competency consultation, the patient must be mentally competent. A mentally incompetent patient cannot consent to a competency consultation under the DWDA.

The competency consultation provisions of the DWDA are a sham. They can only be invoked when they are unnecessary, that is, when a competent patient consents to the competency examination. No patient who actually needs a competency examination can validly consent to one.

Thus, the attending physician is left to his or her own judgment, without professional training or consultation on the mental competence of people contemplating suicide, and with only his or her personal sense of "concern" to protect incompetent patients from consenting to their deaths.

10. "ENDURING REQUEST"

The DWDA contains a provision intended to reassure patients and their families that people will not opt for doctor-assisted suicide on the spur of the moment and then die before they have a chance to regret it. This is the requirement that an election to be killed by assisted suicide must represent an "enduring request."[56] This terminology is lethally ambiguous.

"Enduring" does not refer to the considered opinion of a lifetime. It does not require extended consideration. It does not even demand a persistent request or a request over an extended period of time; it means merely, "a request . . . expressed on more than one occasion."[57] An "occasion" is not defined in the law, so it may be possible for a patient to establish a purportedly "enduring request"

---

53. *Id.*
54. § 2525.13, emphasis added.
55. § 2525.2(h), emphasis added.
56. § 2525.7.
57. § 2525(i).

325

for suicide by expressing it twice within a single day, or perhaps a single hour, or any other undefined period. Even mere commercial transactions have longer mandatory "cooling off" periods for reconsideration.[58]

11. "VOLUNTARY DIRECTIVE TO PHYSICIANS"

People who want to be killed under the DWDA first indicate their intention by executing a form called a "Voluntary Directive To Physicians."[59] The law twice requires that the Directive be in substantially the form provided in the DWDA.[60] Discrepancies between the statutory form of the Directive and the text of the DWDA also raise problems of vagueness, ambiguity and substantial compliance. The form of Directive authorized by the DWDA is potentially misleading to patients and misstates some of the elements of the DWDA itself.

The Directive tells patients that aid-in-dying may be triggered by "a terminal condition OR ILLNESS." The DWDA says only a "condition."[61] Medical and legal distinctions between "illness" and "condition," if any, are not explained.

The Directive states that the right to die is triggered when the terminal condition or illness is "certified by two physicians, and they determine that my death will occur within six months or less." It then repeats, "When the terminal diagnosis is made and confirmed. . . ." This suggests to patients that their deaths within six months are virtually certain, and that the diagnosis, after being made by two physicians, will somehow be "confirmed." The DWDA itself requires only an opinion of two doctors, one of whom is the attending physician, "exercising reasonable medical judgment,"[62] without further confirmation. The Directive acknowledges that "I recognize that a physician's judgment is not always certain." This language suggests that a high percentage of the time a doctor's judgment about the time and inevitability of death within

---

58. *See* notes 17 and 18, *supra*, and related text. The California Natural Death Act, when originally adopted, contained a provision requiring a 14-day waiting period between the time when a person was first diagnosed as terminal and the execution of a Declaration under the Act which would authorize withdrawal of life-sustaining treatment. Former CAL. HEALTH & SAFETY CODE § 7191(d); Barber v. Superior Court, 147 Cal. App. 3d 1006, 1015, 195 Cal. Rptr. 484, 489.

59. § 2525.24.

60. §§ 2525.3, 2525.24.

61. § 2525.2(j), emphasis added.

62. *Id.*

326

six months is certain, whereas in fact the DWDA provides no standard whatsoever to gauge the accuracy of the judgment of death of a patient's doctors.

In the Directive, the patient urges the attending physician to administer aid-in-dying or to find a colleague who will. The Directive does not tell the patient that only the attending physician has legal authority to administer the patient's death under the DWDA or that an attending physician who refuses to undertake the patient's death has no legal duty to help find another attending physician to perform the task. If the patient finds another doctor on his or her own, the DWDA does provide for legal liability for an attending physician for willful failure to transfer the patient to another doctor of the patient's choosing.[63]

The Directive states that "Determining the time and place of my death shall be in my sole discretion." The DWDA makes no provision as to place, and the provision as to time relates only to the decision by the patient that the time has come to die.[64] The scheduling of the assisted suicide is not in the patient's sole discretion.

The Directive assures the patient that it can be revoked at any time. The Directive does not inform the patient that it can be revoked only in the manner prescribed by the DWDA.[65] The Directive does not inform the patient that a verbal revocation is effective only if communicated directly by the patient to the attending physician; nor that a written revocation must be signed and dated by the patient and must be recorded in the patient's medical record; nor that a revocation is effective only when it results in actual notice to the person who carries out the assisted suicide.[66]

The Directive states that informing the patient's family of the decision to invoke the DWDA is the sole responsibility of the patient. This suggests that doctors may have a duty of confidentiality not to disclose this decision to a patient's family, even if this goes against the doctor's medical judgment. Apart from the form Directive, the DWDA makes no such promise of confidentiality.

The Directive requires that it be dated. The DWDA does not contain a dating requirement when executing a Directive, but it does require dating when revoking one in writing.[67]

---

63. 2525.10.
64. 2525.7.
65. 2525.6.
66. 2525.5.
67. 2525.5(b).

327

The Directive provides for attaching additional pages to the form. Neither the Directive nor the DWDA makes any provision for the interpretation of these additional pages, for their legal effect, for their witnessing or other form of validation, or for their revocation. By comparison, the California "Durable Power of Attorney for Health Care"[68] expressly authorizes the attachment of additional pages and requires that the patient must date and sign each of the additional pages at the same time the power of attorney is dated and signed.

The responsibility of the witnesses to determine the identity of the person signing the Directive is said to be established by "satisfactory evidence," which is not defined. Leaving the identification of patients, who are otherwise unknown to the witnesses, to unspecified evidence renders the witness identification useless as an independent source of confirmation of the patient's action. Their signatures may mean nothing more than an orderly or clerical aide told them that the person signing is in fact the proper patient.

Witnesses to the execution of a California "Durable Power of Attorney for Health Care," by contrast, are legally required either to know the principal (the signer) personally or to "have the identity of the principal proven" to them "by convincing evidence."[69] "Satisfactory evidence," the DWDA standard, is subjective—whatever satisfies the witness. "Convincing evidence," the Durable Power of Attorney for Health Care standard, is objective, and the law explicitly limits legal evidence to specific forms (passport, drivers license, state or federal identification card) and requires that these forms must be current, must contain a photograph of the person, must have been signed by the person and must contain a serial number or other identifying number. "Other kinds of proof of identity are not allowed."[70]

The Directive makes inconsistent statements about what the two witnesses must observe. One clause of the "Statement of Witnesses" represents that the patient "signed or acknowledged this

---

68. CAL. CIVIL CODE § 2500. The "Durable Power of Attorney for Health Care" form permits a patient to appoint an agent to make health care decisions for the patient, in accordance with the provisions and instructions in the power of attorney, in the event of the patient's incapacity to make such decisions, including decisions that will result in the death of the patient.

69. *Id.*

70. *Id.* Curiously, the Natural Death act requires the witnesses to watch the Declarant sign but contains no requirement for witnesses to verify the identity of the Declarant. CAL. HEALTH & SAFETY CODE § 7186.5(b).

328

document," indicating that the Directive could be signed previously and merely acknowledged to the witnesses by the patient, but the next clause states that the patient "signed and acknowledged this Directive in my presence." Which is the law? DWDA §§ 2525.2(b) and 2525.3, concerning the witnesses, do not mention the requirement in either form.

The Directive requires the "Statement of Witnesses" to declare that the witnesses observe that the patient "appears to be of sound mind and under no duress, fraud, or undue influence." This declaration goes beyond the competence of untrained witnesses when observing briefly a person who is already affected by some medical condition (and perhaps medication), the effects of which the law does not require to be explained to the witnesses, and who may be acting under stress or depression. This momentary observation would appear to be especially ineffectual when the proceeding requires only the writing of a signature and does not require any verbal expression on the part of the patient. The standard that the patient "appears" competent to such witnesses is too low for a document which is going to authorize the taking of the patient's life.[71]

12.   MEDICAL STANDARDS AND IMMUNITY

The DWDA would set questionable medical standards that intrinsically interfere with the doctor-patient relationship. The DWDA would compel doctors to make estimates of life expectancy, to make such estimates within an accuracy of six months or less, and to communicate their estimates to their patients. Without these estimates and disclosure, doctors would be depriving their patients of the information necessary to exercise their rights under the DWDA.

The DWDA dubiously presumes that "reasonable medical standards" permit the making of such estimates. But whether or not standards exist for reliably estimating life expectancy within the DWDA parameters, the compulsory disclosure of such information

---

71. The "Durable Power of Attorney for Health Care" witness jurat uses the same langauge as the DWDA ("appears to be of sound mind and under no duress, fraud, or undue influence," CAL. CIVIL CODE § 2500.). The DWDA Declaration, however, is likely to be executed by a patient in contemplation of taking his or her own life in the immediate future, a circumstance that requires a higher standard than the Durable Power of Attorney, which may be executed well in advance of any need, by a person in good health. In any event, the standard for the witnesses to the Durable Power of Attorney has not been legally tested and may itself be insufficient to satisfy due process in light of its life or death consequences.

329

to all patients places an impermissible constraint upon the medical judgment of the treating physician. The incorporation of the "reasonable medical standards" language into the DWDA cannot save the statute from improper interference, because nondisclosure of a life expectancy prognosis to a patient, based upon the medical standards of the treating physician, would effectively eviscerate the statute altogether.

Doctors who comply with the formalities of the DWDA are promised immunity from liability for killing their patients.[72] The mere presence of so much exculpatory language should raise a warning flag that the DWDA involves substantial risk for doctors.

DWDA § 2525.9 says that it absolves from liability medical professionals who act in accordance with the DWDA. This promised immunity may prove illusory.

First, doctors may be prosecuted criminally or sued civilly on allegations that they failed to follow the DWDA. If a doctor fails to act "in accordance" with the DWDA, the immunity language of the DWDA will be nullified, and the doctor, hospital and support personnel will be subject to criminal prosecution for homicide or assisted suicide; to civil litigation for wrongful death, medical malpractice, breach of fiduciary duty and other causes of action; and to regulatory proceedings and penalties against medical licenses and hospital privileges.

Second, acting "in accordance" with the DWDA is deceptively risky for doctors. Medically, the DWDA requires doctors to conform to unspecified "reasonable" medical procedures, such as the determination of patients' mental competence to decide to kill themselves or precise prognostication of a patient's survival for six months or less.

Third, the DWDA[73] requires doctors also to make legal determinations: that the Directive is properly executed and witnessed (which would also involve a determination that it has not been revoked by any of the three prescribed methods of revocation, with their technical requirements[74]); that "all steps" (that is, every aspect of the entire procedure, not just all material or significant steps) follow the patient's desires, as declared not only in the Directive but also in the patient's personal conversations with the doctor; that the

---

72. §§ 2525.6, 2525.9, 2525.14.
73. § 2525.14.
74. § 2525.5.

330

knowledge of the doctor (for example, whether expressed concerns by the patient give rise to an oral revocation, or whether the medical records contain any reference that may be considered a revocation[75]) does not nullify the presumption of validity of the directive.[76]

When, for example, should a patient's statements in their personal discussions require a doctor to conclude that a new Directive be executed?

Fourth, the validity of the statutory immunity itself also may be questioned in light of constitutional guarantees protecting life[77] and prohibiting the taking of life without due process of law.[78] The DWDA presents serious due process problems, including authorizing the killing of people on the basis of questionable medical judgments that are historically and statistically certain to have a significant margin of error, thus permitting the killing of people who would not otherwise die within six months and absolving their killers. The immunity language of the DWDA may itself violate due process by attempting to make such legal concepts as good faith, reasonableness, assumption of the risk and contractual compliance into justifications for intentional killing.

AMENDMENT

The DWDA declares that it can "be amended only by statute passed by a two-thirds vote of each house of the legislature and signed by the Governor."[79] This provision is ambiguous. (1) The state Constitution provides that an initiative may be amended by any later statute if it is approved by the electorate.[80] The DWDA cannot nullify this constitutional provision. The provision that the DWDA can "only" be amended by the prescribed statutory means is inaccurate.

(2) If this Section of the DWDA is intended to require that a statute adopted pursuant to Article II, § 10(c) for submission to the voters must first be passed by a two-thirds vote of both the Assem-

---

75. *Id.*

76. § 2525.14.

77. CAL. CONST. art. I, § 1, and U.S. CONST. amend. IX, incorporating the Declaration of Independence, declare "inalienable" rights to life.

78. U.S. CONST. amends. V and XIV.

79. DWDA, Sec. 3.

80. CAL. CONST. art. II, § 10(c).

bly and the Senate, then the super-majority requirement is an invalid attempt to amend the Constitution.

(3) The amendment section may, perhaps, be interpreted (ignoring the word "only") as an alternative means to amend the statute, in addition to the constitutional process. If so, it may be valid, but it nevertheless raises severe obstacles to the adoption of any language to correct the vagueness, overbreadth and ambiguity of the Death With Dignity Act.

CONCLUSION

Existing law recognizes a right to reject medical treatment even when exercise of that right will result in death. People whose lives are being sustained artificially, or their appointed agents and conservators, may elect to forego medical intervention and may thereby choose death.[81] The Death With Dignity Act is unnecessary for these truly terminal people.

The DWDA targets an arbitrarily defined group of people and labels them "terminal" because they may die within six months, although some of them, unless killed by their doctors under the DWDA, doubtless will long outlive their dire predictions. The certainty of killing some non-terminal people represents a severe flaw in the DWDA.

Even if legislation of assisted suicide were a wise public policy, the DWDA contains dangerously complicated, vague, ambiguous and misleading language that would put in jeopardy any person who attempts to invoke it, whether patient or doctor.

But the DWDA should be rejected as a matter of public policy. Legalization of the killing of people before their natural deaths cheapens life and encourages societies to avoid their duty to learn to care for their own. Such death evokes not dignity but despair.

---

81. *See* Conservatorship of Drabick, 200 Cal. App. 3d 185, 245 Cal. Rptr. 840, 47 A.L.R.4th 1 (1988), and uniform decisions of the cases cited at 200 Cal. App. 3d 189; Barber v. Superior Court, 147 Cal. App. 3d 1006, 195 Cal. Rptr. 484 (1983); Bouvia v. Superior Court, 179 Cal. App. 3d 1127, 225 Cal. Rptr. 297 (1986); People v. Adams, 216 Cal. App. 3d 1431, 265 Cal. Rptr. 568 (1990).

LIVING WILLS

The law seems clear on one thing—competent and conscious adults, properly counseled, may refuse any medical treatment for any reason, even if that refusal will result in their own death. But what happens when that adult is not competent? Who decides then, and is there even a choice to be made? If society is willing to let a person choose to die rather than be treated, is it also willing to let someone else make that decision?

If a choice is to be made, who should decide? Doctors, of course, are the most knowledgeable about an incompetent patient's medical prognosis. Only in rare cases, however, does a doctor have intimate knowledge of the patient while competent. If that patient's wishes are to be the determining factor, doctors may not be in a position to discern them. Further, doctors are trained to preserve life and often view death as a defeat, one that, often, they are unwilling to concede. On the other hand, doctors are also aware of the costs of health care, of the limited resources available, and of the burdens on health care professionals of dealing with terminal patients.

Families face similarly contradictory pressures. On the one hand, they did know that patient and are, therefore, in the best position to carry out his wishes. On the other hand, they are subject to the emotional ties of a lifetime and may not be able to "kill" their loved one. Further, love may be expressed in different ways—both by honoring the patient's wishes (or what they believe those wishes would be) and by refusing to let go. This conflict may be played out both within individual members of the family and between family members, thus causing yet more emotional turmoil at an already difficult time.

The case studies in Part 7 and the court decisions in Part 9 highlight these problems. These problems, however, may be mitigated to a large degree if the now incompetent patient clearly and unmistakably expressed his wishes concerning treatment while he was competent or designated a particular person to make the decision in his stead. Written and legally enforceable instruments expressing such wishes are commonly referred to as "living wills" or "advance directives," while an appointment of a surrogate decision maker is referred to as a "durable power of attorney." The articles in this section discusses the strengths and weaknesses of these different mechanisms.

Many states have enacted "living will" or "advance directive" statutes. Luis Kutner ("Due Process of Euthanasia: The Living Will, A Proposal") was an early advocate of a "living will," a document signed by a competent adult stating his wishes concerning treatment in the event he later becomes incompetent. Significantly, Kutner, writing in 1969, limited the enforceability of the living wills to "passive euthanasia."

Despite the widespread approval of living wills, few people have executed one. Richard Vance ("Autonomy's Paradox: Death, Fear, and Advance Directives") argues that the concept of autonomy on which living wills is based carries with it a competing rejection of death as the end of the self. In times past, when society shared more of a consensus about core values and their application, living wills were unnecessary because individuals trusted that those who would make decisions for them shared their values. Our society, however, has become so fragmented that "the moralities that made trusting relationships in health care possible are attenuated at best, and are perhaps irretrievably lost." Thus, Vance argues, we must sign advance directives to require society to respect our values.

Living wills are powerful indications of an incompetent patient's wishes. David Peters ("Advance Medical Directives: The Case for the Durable Power of Attorney for Health Care") argues, however, that it is unlikely that a living will will be sufficiently precise to permit the treating physician to determine in every situation the specific course of treatment (or lack thereof) that the will's author would have wanted. Further, when the advance directive is ambiguous or an unforeseen condition arises, various members of the patient's family and friends may not agree on what the patient's wishes would have been. In such circumstances, the physician is likely to be in a worse position than if there was no living will at all. Thus, Peters suggests that, in lieu of or in addition to a living will, the individual, while competent, should sign a durable power of attorney appointing a specific individual whom he trusts and who knows him well to act in his stead and empower that person to make all necessary decisions. Thus, this individual can instruct the physician and consent or refuse to consent to treatment depending on the specific circumstances.

Similarly, Joanne Lynn ("Why I Don't Have a Living Will"), a medical practitioner, argues that a living will may actually thwart the true wishes of a patient under certain circumstances. Because a living will will not achieve some of the results that its author wishes and because the clumsiness of the commonly available form cannot predict the appropriate treatment in any circumstances, Lynn argues instead for a family-based system of determining medical care for the temporarily or permanently incompetent. As she notes from her experience with treating terminally ill and elderly patients, patients are often willing to trust that their loved ones will make a decision out of love, *even if it is not the decision that they might have made.*

Finally, no matter how detailed the living will or how durable the power of attorney, other interests may intrude on the decision-making process. Several states with living will statutes, for instance, provide that a woman's living will is invalid while she is pregnant. Molly Dyke-Dillon ("A Matter of Life and Death: Pregnancy Clauses in Living Will Statutes") explores constitutionality of these clauses as applied to terminally ill women. She argues that the trend of Supreme Court decisions and of lower court decisions recognizing fetal rights in some circumstances may indicate that such clauses would be enforced. She argues that such a result is improper and that the courts, rather than pitting the woman's interests against the fetus, should focus on the woman's decision-making autonomy.

COMMENTS

DUE PROCESS OF EUTHANASIA: THE LIVING WILL, A PROPOSAL

Luis Kutner†

"She asked me to do it," explained Robert Waskin, a young college student, after he had fatally shot his cancer-striken mother while she lay in her hospital room. The Grand Jury of Cook County, Illinois, dispassionately returned an indictment of murder in the first degree.[1] The story became headline news, and euthanasia became the subject of editorial comment on radio and television talk shows.

> After a trial of one week, Robert Waskin was freed by a jury that deliberated only forty minutes before determining that he was temporarily insane when he shot his mother three times. The jury further found that he was no longer insane. The foreman of the jury commented: 'He knew he shot his mother. That was not disputed, but the prosecution failed to show he was of sound mind when he did it.' Robert Waskin is quoted as he prepared to pick up the threads of a nearly shattered life: 'The moral issue of euthanasia . . . was not taken up at the trial, and it should have been faced squarely. Some day it will have to be.'[2]

This case illustrates a dilemma in the criminal law. The underlying values of our society and the Constitution assert the right to life. The protection of life is basic to any legal order. Indeed, as Thomas Hobbs affirmed, the protection of human life is the prime justification for the existence of a state and the accompanying legal machinery. However, when one individual observes another who is suffering from the pain of an incurable disease or a genetic deformation and, motivated by compassion, ends his life, the question arises as to whether he should be regarded as a murderer. One so acting takes the life of another, an act forbidden by law; but his actions are not motivated by malice or personal

---

†Chairman, World Habeas Corpus Committee, World Peace Through Law Center. Member of Illinois and Indiana Bars. The research assistance of Ernest Katin, Ph.D., is acknowledged.

1. Letter from Patrick A. Truite, State's Attorney's Office, Criminal Division, Cook County, Illinois. The State also charged that the defendant previously had tried to administer sleeping pills. Chicago Sun-Times, Aug. 18, 1967.

2. Chicago Daily News, Jan. 25, 1969.

profit, rather they are motivated by the very human desire to end suffering.

Mercy killing raises a myriad of philosophical and theological considerations. However, this paper wll confine itself to a consideration of the issue from the perspective of law and individual rights. This paper will first consider the present state of the law, examine proposed solutions, and suggest an approach to the problem.

THE PRESENT STATE OF THE LAW

The common law does not recognize motive as an element of homicide. If the proved facts establish that the defendant in fact did the killing wilfully, that is, with intent to kill, and as the result of premeditation and deliberation, there is murder in the first degree regardless of motive.[3] Motive is relevant evidence only to establish the degree of murder or homicide (premeditation).[4] Conceptually, if the elements of wilful premeditation exist, the perpetrator of the act stands equally condemned regardless of the fact that he may have acted from an impulse of mercy.[5]

The law in this area, however, cannot be confined to a consideration of statutory language and appellate court reports. An observation of what takes place at the trial level indicates that the law in practice deals differently with mercy killing than does the theory and letter of the law. "The Law In Action is as malleable as the Law On The Books is uncompromising."[6] There is a high incidence of failure to indict, acquittals, suspended sentences and reprieves where the killer had mercy as his motive.[7]

An illustration of one trial court's approach to mercy killing was

---

3. P.J.T. CALLAHAN & J. CALLAHAN, THE LAW OF MEDICINE 58-59 (1950) ; State v. Ehlers, 98 N.J.L. 236, 119 A. 15 (1922) ; Annot., 25 A.L.R. 1007 (1923).
The word 'euthanasia' has a Greek origin and is made up of two component parts, namely *eu* and *thanatos*. The best translation for *eu* is: easy, happy, pleasant, painless, while *thanatos* means death. The meaning of the word is therefore: an easy, painless death. To relieve the pains that precede death is the duty of every doctor and may truly be called one of the outstanding missions of the medical profession. This explains why this particular form of euthanasia is universally recognized and accepted.
Rud, *Euthanasia*, J. OF CLINICAL AND EXPERIMENTAL PSYCHOPATHOLOGY, Jan.-Mar. 1953, at 1.
4. *Id.*
5. For further examples, see State v. Ehlers, 98 N.J.L. 236, 119 A.15 (1922) ; People v. Roberts, 211 Mich. 187, 178 N.W. 690 (1920) ; People v. Kirby, 2 Park Crim. Rep. (N.Y.) 28 (1823) ; and Rex v. Simpson, 84 L.J.R. (n.s) 1893 (K.B. 1915).
6. See Kamisar, *Some Non-Religious Views Against Proposed "Mercy Killing" Legislation*, 42 MINN. L. REV. 969 (1958).
7. *Id.*, at 971 nn.11, 12, & 13.

furnished by *People v. Werner*,[8] involving a sixty-nine year old defendant who suffocated his wife, a hopelessly crippled, bedridden arthritic. In arraignment proceedings, the state waived the murder charge and permitted the defendant to enter a plea of guilty to a charge of manslaughter. The court then found the defendant guilty of this charge on his stipulated admission of the killing. After hearing the testimony of the defendant's children and pastor concerning his unfailing care and devotion during the deceased's two-year illness and reading a letter from her doctor attesting to her excruciating pain and mental despair, the court allowed the defendant to withdraw his plea and entertained a plea of not guilty and then found the defendant not guilty because under the circumstances the jury "would not be inclined to convict." Because there was no reason to be concerned about recidivism, the court withheld the "stigma" of a finding and judgment of guilty and allowed the defendant "to go home . . . and live out the rest of [his] life in as much as [he] can find it in [his] heart to have."

Despite the statutory provisions to the contrary, the court in this case based its decision on the defendant's motives. The procedure followed by the court was criticized as not having been authorized by statute.[9] Although the court had the discretion to permit the defendant to withdraw his plea of guilty, this discretion is limited to those particular instances where it appears that there is doubt as to the defendant's guilt, or that he has any defense at all worthy of consideration by a jury, or that the ends of justice will be served by submitting the case to a jury.[10] These criteria were absent in this case. Nevertheless, in view of the facts, the court's action accords with what may be regarded as a sense of justice. That juries, too, often disregard the dictates of the law on this point is well evidenced by the *Waskin*[11] case and by cases in other jurisdictions.[12]

---

8. Crim. No. 58-3636, Cook Co. Ct., Ill., Dec. 30, 1958, *reported in* Williams, *Euthanasia and Abortion*, 38 U. Colo. L. Rev. 178, 184 & n.15 (1966); and *noted in* 34 Notre Dame Law. 460 (1959).

9. 34 Notre Dame Law. 460 (1959).

10. People v. Throop, 359 Ill. 354, 194 N.E. 553 (1935); People v. Kleist, 311 Ill. 179, 142 N.E. 486 (1924).

11. For other examples of cases of juries superimposing their own beliefs upon the law, see Kamisar, *supra* note 6, at 1019, 1021; and N.Y. Times, May 9, 1939, at 48, col. 1; May 12, 1939, at 1, col. 6; Jan. 23, 1939, at 24; Oct. 2, 1939, at 1, col. 3; Oct. 3, 1938 at 34, col. 3; Oct. 19, 1938 at 46, col. 1.

12. The *Suzanne van de Put* case received international attention. This case involved the trial in Liege, Belgium, of a woman for the murder of her eight day old daughter, born deformed as a result of the use of thalidomide during pregnancy. The husband, mother, sister, and family doctor were arraigned as abettors. Popular sympathy in Belgium and elsewhere was with the defendants, who had acted from what they had imagined were unselfish motives. At the end of a six day trial, the jury acquitted all five defendants. The verdict was greeted with exultation throughout the city. N. St. John-Stevas, The Right to Life ch. 1 (1964); Oulahan, *Euthanasia: Should One*

Mercy Killing No Different from Other Killing

Clearly, although conceptually the law does not treat mercy killing differently from other cases involving the taking of human life, in practice an exception does exist. Prosecutors, judges and juries do approach a mercy killing case differently. Public opinion simply does not reflect the same revulsion against an act of mercy killing that it does towards other instances of murder. Therefore, society is not prone to inflict the same type of punishment. Although there may be opposition to mercy killing in principle, there is sympathy for the mercy killer. Significantly, in *People v. Roberts,*[13] one of the few cases where a mercy killer was convicted of first degree murder and sentenced to life imprisonment, the decision was rendered by a judge without a jury.

Invariably, because of the human interest element involved, a mercy killing case will receive wide press coverage and focus public attention. The tendency is for public sympathy to side with the defendant, as was illustrated in the *Suzanne van de Put* case.[14] In the *Waskin* case the presiding judge, the defendant's father and his lawyer received letters urging that mercy be shown.[15] Although objection may be made as to this treatment of mercy killers, it is necessary to separate what may be regarded as the "ought" from the "is." The judicial process as it "is," deals differently with mercy killers. The defendant may be not prosecuted, found innocent because of insanity, or found guilty of a lesser offense then murder and given a light sentence.

The Absence of Standards Governing Euthanasia

Thus, the law in regard to euthanasia leaves much to be desired. The absence of at least a semblance of objective determination places a gap within the legal system. The element of symmetry is lacking.[16] The accused in a mercy killing case must rely almost entirely on public sentimentality. Objective criteria are not operating. Conceivably, public sentiment may be misplaced, and a clever manipulator of public opinion could kill with evil motive and escape punishment by posing as a mercy killer. In such a situation, the victim is not assured protection. Moreover, the present state of the law, as it is evolving from judicial practice, may in effect be permitting mercy killing without adequate protection for the victim whose death may be unwarranted and uncanted. Clearly, the lack

---

Kill a Child in Mercy?, Life, Aug. 10, 1962, at 34-35: Gallahan, *Tragedy at Liege, van de Put's Thalidomide Baby*, Look, Mar. 12, 1963, at 72-74.

13. See note 8 *supra*.
14. See note 12 *supra*.
15. Chicago Sun-Times, Aug. 18, 1967, at 30.
16. K. Llewellyn, The Common Law Tradition (1962).

of definiteness in the present state of the law does not comport with notions of due process of law.

From another perspective, the current state of the law does not recognize the right of the victim to die if he so desires. He may be in a terminal state suffering from an incurable illness and literally forced to continue a life of pain and despair. Such a denial may well infringe upon an individual's right of privacy.

SUICIDE AND EUTHANASIA AIDING AND ABETTING

Related to euthanasia is the law on suicide. If an individual wishes to die and another assists him by providing him with the means for committing suicide, he may be guilty of murder.[17] In early common law suicide was regarded as a criminal offense. The punishment for one who committed suicide was interment in the highway with a stake driven through the body, and the forfeiture of lands, goods and chattels to the king. While sanctions against the body and property of the suicide have been removed, the attempt of a person in England to end his own life deliberately is still an attempt to commit a felony, though not an attempt to commit murder within the Offences against the Person Act of 1861.[18] Although the English common law on suicide was never fully accepted in the United States, in some jurisdictions, such as New York, suicide—though declared not to be a crime—is censured by statute as a "grave public wrong."[19] In at least one American jurisdiction, attempted suicide is still regarded as a misdemeanor.[20]

Today, immunity of suicide actually means immunity of attempted suicide with the law varying in different jurisdictions as to instigators, aiders and abettors. In jurisdictions where the distinction between accessory and principal is abolished, they are treated as principals in homicide.[21] Where punishment of accessories is predicated upon the criminal character of the act of the principal, the instigator, aider and abettor of suicide enjoy immunity, the act of the principal, not being a crime, as prevailing in Germany and France. Finally, some statutes specifically define instigating, aiding and abetting suicide as independent crimes, *sui generis*.

---

17. See, *e.g.*, People v. Roberts, 211 Mich. 187, 178 N.W. 690 (1920). The defendant husband was convicted of murder in the first degree. He had prepared a poison and had placed it within his wife's reach upon her request while she was confined to bed with arteriosclerosis.

18. N. ST. JOHN-STEVAS, *supra* note 12, ch. 4.

19. N.Y. PEN. LAW § 2301 (McKinney 1944).

20. Silvig, *Euthanasia: A Study in Comparative Criminal Law*, 103 U. PA. L. REV. 350, 371 (1954). The discussion is based on the material presented in this article.

21. N.Y. PEN. LAW §§ 2304, 2305 (McKinney 1944).

Generally, the law in the United States does not permit one to assist another to commit suicide regarless of motive or if done at the request of the suicide. Some jurisdictions, however, appear to distinguish situations where one has instigated or suggested to another that he commit suicide from where the idea came to the suicide originally.[22] The law does not generally appear to condone suicide. Adaptation is needed to account for situations where the assistance for the commission of suicide is given to one who freely requests such help.

PROPOSED SOLUTIONS

Glanville Wiliams, a recognized legal scholar who has long been an outspoken advocate of euthanasia, has urged that a statute be enacted to permit "voluntary" mercy killing.[24] As originally formulated, his proposal, which is supported by the euthanasia societies in Britain and the United States, envisions the establishment of a means to immunize relatives or physicians who would administer a means of ending life upon a patient who is suffering great pain from an incurable disease for which there is no cure or relief and which if fatal.

The English Society would require the eligible patient who is over twenty-one and suffering from a disease involving severe pain to forward a specially prescribed application—along with two medical certificates, one signed by the attending physician and the other by a specially qualified physician—to a specially appointed euthanasia referee who would satisfy himself by means of a personal interview with the patient and through other means that the conditions have been met and, if so satisfied, would issue a euthanasia permit.[25]

The American Society would have the eligible patient petition for euthansia in the presence of two witnesses. The petition would then be filed with the certificate of an attending physician in a court of appropriate jurisdiction. The court would then appoint a committee of three, of whom at least two would be physicians, who would forthwith examine the patient and such other persons as they deem advisable or as the court might direct. The committee would then within five days report to the court as to whether or not the petition should be granted. The American

---

22. Annot., 13 A.L.R. 1259 (1921).
23. Examples include J. FLETCHER, MORALS AND MEDICINE (1954) ; Fletcher, *The Patient's Right to Die*, HARPER'S, Oct., 1960; Fletcher, *Anti-Dysthanasia: The Problem of Prolonging Death*, published by the Euthanasia Society, 1962; Collins, *Should We Let Them Die?*, SAT. EVE. POST, May 26, 1962; Anonymous, *A New Way of Dying*, THE ATLANTIC, Jan. 1957.
24. G. L. WILLIAMS, THE SANCTITY OF LIFE AND THE CRIMINAL LAW (1957) ; and Kamisar, *supra* note 6.
25. Kamisar, *supra* note 6, at 982ff.

proposal was introduced unsuccessfully as a bill in the legislatures of Nebraska and New York.[26]

However, these proposals cover only "voluntary" euthanasia and do not cover the many instances of "involuntary" mercy killing, such as the *van de Put* case. Moreover, the procedure is too cumbersome and bureaucratic in that it brings the law into a sick room. Furthermore, the safeguards are inadequate. There is always the possibility of a mistaken diagnosis that the patient's condition is incurable.

A difficulty also exists in determining whether the consent of the patient is in fact freely given. A patient who has been subjected to drugs is unlikely to be in a rational state. He may well be subject to suggestion by those around him. Moreover, the study of psychology and psychoanalysis has indicated that all men have a suppressed urge for death, the death wish or *thanos*, which may emerge when an inidvidual is seriously ill. This melancholic impulse may temporarily manifest itself in a desire to end life and then later ebb. The ending of life is a final and irrevocable act which cannot be lightly permitted. The inherent risks involved in such a scheme render the proposal objectionable.

Williams, in urging "voluntary" euthanasia, argues for human freedom, the freedom to end one's life. He urges that the law cannot forbid conduct merely because it is undesirable, but only if the social order is adversely affected. In American law, the case might be made that to forbid "voluntary" euthanasia is an infringement of the constitutionally recognized right of privacy[27] as derived from either the fourth amendment, the ninth amendment, or the due process clauses of the fifth and fourteenth amendments. However, the right of privacy may be subordinated to other supervening legislative ends. In this instance, what is involved is society's concern for the security and preservation of human life. Because the authorization of voluntary euthanasia may result in instances in which individuals might be involuntarily deprived of their life, perhaps even with malice or for personal benefit, the state may be deemed justified in forbidding it.

The advocates of "voluntary" euthanasia appear to regard the promotion of their proposal as an entering wedge for the adoption of so-called mercy killing in other instances as well, such as for the elimination of the aged, the congenitally defective and others.[28] Williams reveals this fact when he writes:

---

26. *Id.*
27. Griswold v. Connecticut, 381 U.S. 479 (1965); Katin, *Griswold v. Connecticut: The Justices and the Uncommonly Silly Law*, 42 NOTRE DAME LAW. 680 (1967).
28. Kamisar, *supra* note 6.

Much of the literature discussing voluntary euthanasia has concerned the 'merciful release' of those who are painfully diseased. Yet this is only part of a wider problem of easing the passage of all those who are burdened with the ills frequently associated with old age.

. . . .

We should, in short, try to shake off the neurotic attitude towards death that has afflicted us for so long, and replace it with a realistic appreciation of death's biological function. To quote Dr. Slater . . . 'death plays a wholly favorable, indeed an essential, part in human economy. Without natural death, human societies and the human race itself would certainly be unable to thrive.' Perhaps when we realize this, we may come to realize at the same time that there is a point in the degeneration of our bodies when life loses its value, and we may then be prepared voluntarily to leave the scene to our successors.[29]

The experience of Nazi Germany illustrates the danger of the wedge problem. There euthanasia was expanded from the "voluntary" variety to the elimination of mentally ill and defective and then used as a rationale for genocide.[30] Indeed, the Nazi authorities had even contemplated the elimination of all cardiac cases. To cite the Nazi example is more than a mere paralogism, for implicit in the rationale behind the advocates of euthanasia is a subordination of the value of human life. Man is not considered an end of himself, but as subordinate to the advancement of other social purposes. When this philosophy becomes predominant, the nature of the social order is subordinate to radical change.

To meet the problem of dealing with the perpetrator of a mercy killing, reference has been made to other legal systems.[31] The German approach of providing the defense of necessity for preserving the community is unacceptable, as there should be neither exculpation nor reduction of sentence where death is administered for the benefit of any person or persons other than the suffering patient.[32] In Modern European codes, motive is considered relevant in classifying an offense. If the motive is the altruistic desire to comply with the victim's request to be killed, the homicide turns into the separate crime of "homicide upon request,"

---

29. Williams. *supra* note 8.
30. Kamisar, *supra* note 6; Alexander, *Medical Science under Dictatorship*, 241 NEW ENGLAND MEDICINE 39 (1949) ; Ivy, *Nazi War Crimes of a Medical Nature*, 139 J.A.M.A. 131 (1949) : Koessler, *Euthanasia in the Hadamar Sanitarium and International Law*, 43 J. CRIM. L. C. & P.S. 735 (1953).
31. Silvig, *supra* note 20.
32. *Id.*

punishable by imprisonment in terms of only a few years. The mercy killer is then provided with a more lenient treatment under statutory provisions rather than by resort to more devious means. Moreover, since special treatment is warranted by statute, there is more assurance of uniformity in the adjudication of euthanasia cases.

These concepts could be extended to American law to cover euthanasia. That the concept of motive is not totally alien to the Anglo-American legal system is illustrated by the provision in English law for the offense of infanticide, a modern felony created by statute in 1922 and modified in 1938. A woman who kills her child under the age of twelve months while her mind is disturbed from the effects of giving birth is held to be guilty of manslaughter rather than murder, thereby leaving the sentence to the discretion of the judge.[33]

Another facet of euthanasia involves the situation in which a doctor acts to prolong the life of a patient. The law recognizes a patient's right to consent to or to refuse treatment whether it be an injection or an operation.[34] The Illinois Supreme Court has refused to condone the authorization of blood transfusions to a competent adult who had stead-fastly asserted her religious beliefs against such a transfusion despite the fact that she was *in extremis*.[35] The attitude of the law is to recognize the inviolability of the human body. The patient's consent must be voluntary and informed.[36] These notions are buttressed by the constitutionally recognized right to privacy. Clearly, then, a patient may refuse treatment which would extend his life. Such a decision must rest with the patient.

However, when a patient is unconscious or is not in a position to give his consent, the law assumes a constructive consent to such treatment as will save his life.[37] The physician's authority to proceed with treatment is based upon the presumption that the patient would have consented to treatment necessary to protect his life of health if he had been able to do so. But the problem arises as to how far such constructive consent should extend.

A patient may be in a coma suffering from cancer or cerebral hemorrhage. The doctor acts to prolong his life by a series of operations and

---

33. N. St. John-Stevas, *supra* note 12.

34. Morse, *Legal Implications of Clinical Investigations*, 20 Vand. L. Rev. 747, 752 (1967).

35. *In re* Brooks' Estate, 32 Ill. 2d 361, 205 N.E.2d 435 (1965). A similar decision was reached by a New York court in Erickson v. Dilgard, 44 Misc. 2d 27, 252 N.Y.S.2d 705 (Sup. Ct. 1962). A different approach is taken with regard to a minor when the parent refuses permission for blood transfusion. Note, 41 Notre Dame Law. 722 (1966).

36. Morse, *supra* note 34.

37. *Id.*

intervenous treatment which continues interminably. The patient may be paralyzed or completely unresponsive to the world about him. The question arises as to how far the physician should go to preserve the patient's life. Catholic theologians have taken the position that the doctor is obliged to take all ordinary means but not extraordinary means.[38] Ordinary means include those medicines and treatment which can be used without causing unnecessary pain or expense. The distinction between ordinary and extraordinary means will vary with time, place, and circumstances. This position may be related to the legal obligation of exercising due care, with ordinary means taken to be coincident with exercise of due care. The standard should be that which is generally practiced.

Under German law a physician's failure to prolong artifically an expiring painful life by applying stimulants is not regarded as homicide.[39] A distinction is made, however, where the victim is not incurably ill. Although the criminality of inaction by a physician has not been decided by American courts, as in the German system of jurisprudence where there is a duty to act, deliberate nonfeasance with intent to cause death is, generally, punishable homicide.[40] The physician's dilemma is further complicated where the patient's immediate illness is not incurable but where a cure will leave him a permanent sufferer. American law apparently requires that life be prolonged in such situations. But inaction when motivated by the physician's desire not to prolong the patient's suffering, is clearly distinguishable from active mercy killing. The argument may be made that since the physician's duty to act is contractual and predicated upon the patient's consent, there being no basis in such instances for presumptive consent, nonfeasance should be unpunished even though active euthanasia remains punishable.[41]

An aspect of this issue came to a head in Britain when it was revealed that a government supported hospital had followed a practice of denying the use of a resuscitator to patients who were aged. A clamor of public protest arose, and the government ordered that such a policy should be reversed.[42] In the United States, such a policy could be regarded as a denial of equal protection for persons in an arbitrarily designated class. The aged would be singled out for denial of essential medical treatment. However, the suspicion lingers that a person of modest means who is brought to a hospital is given less intensive care than would be the case with the wealthy. Less concern may be given to the poverty stricken or the

---

38. N. St. John-Stevas, *supra* note 12, at 52.
39. Silvig, *supra* note 20.
40. *Id.*
41. *Id.*
42. N.Y. Times, Sept. 24, 1967.

derelict. On the other hand, a patient of considerable means—or whose relatives are wealthy—may receive special attention. There is the possibility that the physicians and the hospital have a vested interest in keeping the patient alive in order to receive extensive remuneration.

A related problem arises as to at what point should the patient be assumed to be regarded as dead. The suggested criterion has been the point where an electroencephalograph indicated that no electrical discharges are being emitted from the brain. Difficult issues arise as to the lengths to which the physician should go to maintain life in such a situation and the fact that such decisions must presently be made renders euthanasia a seemingly less radical proposal.

A SUGGESTED APPROACH AND CONCLUSIONS

This survey indicates that the law effecting euthanasia in practice differs from its conceptual basis in that, in practice, the judicial process treats a mercy killer differently from a murderer with malice. The criminal code is in need of adaptation to account for this situation. The suggested approach is to adopt the standard of motive as indicated by the codes of other legal systems. The punishment for an accused who killed at the request of the victim, where the victim was suffering from an incurable disease and was in great pain, would be milder than in other incidents of homicide. A somewhat harsher, but still mild punishment, would be inflicted upon the accused who killed where the victim did not request to be killed or was incapable of giving his rational consent, but was suffering from an apparent physical or mental affliction and there was no element of malice or personal gain. Such an approach would accord with notions of due process. It is submitted that to subject the accused to life imprisonment or execution would constitute excessively cruel and inhumane punishment in contravention to the eighth amendment of the Constitution.

Proposals to date to legalize voluntary euthanasia have been rejected as incapable of providing the necessary safeguards and as being too cumbersome in application. Moreover, such proposals appear to be an entering wedge which opens the door to possible mass euthanasia and genocide.

The law, however, does recognize that a patient has a right to refuse to be treated, even when he is *in extremis,* provided he is an adult and capable of giving consent. Compliance with the patient's wishes

---

43. N.Y. Times, Oct. 1, 1967; Miami Herald, Feb. 14, 1967.
44. "The House of Lords defeated a Bill that would have permitted voluntary euthanasia in Britain. Opponents said the Bill would allow 'suicide by proxy.'" [Associated Press Release, London: Chicago's American, Mar. 26, 1969, at 10, col 8].

in such circumstances is not the same as voluntary euthanasia. Where, however, the patient is incapable of giving consent, such as when he is in a coma, a constructive consent is presumed and the doctor is required to exercise reasonable care in applying ordinary means to preserve the patient's life. However, he is not allowed to resort to extraordinary care especially where the patient is not expected to recover from the comatose state.

The standard to be applied should reflect the state of the medical art, the condition of the patient and the wishes of the relatives. To assure that patients are not arbitrarily deprived of ordinary medical care and to determine the state where the point has been reached where the patient's life has been deemed to have ended, a special ombudsmen-type board should be established to review each case. Every person, regardless of age or economic circumstance, should be deemed to have a right to life and to the same intensive type of medical treatment which would accord with a standard of ordinary care. Extraordinary care would be given if requested by the relatives. The answer lies in the Rule of Law carefully processed by a judicial determination based upon the best available evidence that merciful termination of a human life shall be decreed.

THE LIVING WILL

The law provides that a patient may not be subjected to treatment without his consent. But when he is in a condition in which his consent cannot be expressed, the physician must assume that the patient wishes to be treated to preserve his life. His failure to act fully to keep the patient alive in a particular instance may lead to liability for negligence. But it may well be that a patient does not desire to be kept in a state of indefinite vegetated animation. How then can the individual patient retain the right of privacy over his body—the right to determine whether he should be permitted to die, to permit his body to be given to the undertaker?

The law clearly prohibits mercy killing, even if undertaken at the patient's request. Thus, the patient cannot request another to end his life. Such an action would subject the actor to prosecution for murder. But an individual does have the right to refuse to permit a doctor to treat him, even if such treatment would prolong his live. If a doctor should act contrary to his wishes, he would be subject to liability.

Where a patient undergoes surgery or other radical treatment, the surgeon or the hospital will require him to sign a legal statement indicating his consent to the treatment. The patient, however, while still retaining his mental faculties and the ability to convey his thoughts, could append to such a document a clause providing that, if his condition becomes incurable and his bodily state vegetative with no possibility that he could recover his complete faculties, his consent to further treatment would be terminated. The physician would then be precluded from prescribing further surgery, radiation, drugs or the running of resuscitating and other machinery, and the patient would be permitted to die by virtue of the physician's inaction.

The patient may not have had, however, the opportunity to give his consent at any point before treatment. He may have become the victim of a sudden accident or a stroke or coronary. Therefore, the suggested solution is that the individual, while fully in control of his faculties and his ability to express himself, indicate to what extent he would consent to treatment. The document indicating such consent may be referred to as "a *living will*," "a declaration determining the termination of life," "testament permitting death," "declaration for bodily autonomy," "declaration for ending treatment," "body trust," or other similar reference.

The document would provide that if the individual's bodily state becomes completely vegetative and it is certain that he cannot regain his mental and physical capacities, medical treatment shall cease. A Jehovah's Witness whose religious principles are opposed to blood transfusions could so provide in such a document. A Christian Scientist could, by virtue of such a document, indicate that he does not wish any medical treatment.

The document would be notarized and attested to by at least two witnesses who would affirm that the maker was of sound mind and acted of his own free will. The individual could carry the document on his person at all times, while his wife, his personal physician, a lawyer or confidant would have the original copy.

Each individual case would be referred to a hospital committee, board or a committee of physicians. A precedent for the functioning of such committees or boards already exists in many hospitals for determining whether an abortion is medically necessary. The committee or board would consider the circumstances under which the document was made in determinining the patient's intent and also make a determination as to whether the condition of the patient has indeed reached the point where he would no longer want any treatment.

The individual could at any time, before reaching the comatose state, revoke the document. Personal possession of the document would create a strong presumption that he regards it as still binding. Statements and actions subsequent to the writing of the document may indicate a contrary intent. If the physicians find that some doubt exists as to the patient's intent, they would give treatment pending the resolution of the matter. The document, if carried on the patient's person, should indicate what persons should be contacted if he reaches a comatose state. The physician would consult with them in making a determination.

A *living will* could only be made by a person who is capable of giving his consent to treatment. A person who is a minor, institutionalized, or adjudged incompetent could not make such a declaration. A guardian should not be permitted to make such a declaration on behalf of his ward nor a parent on behalf of his child. If an individual makes a *living will* and is subsequently adjudged incompetent, the *will* would be deemed to be revoked. However, this revocation would not apply where the state of incompetency resulted from the medical condition which was contemplated in making the declaration.

The *living will* is analogous to a revocable or conditional trust with the patient's body as the *res*, the patient as the beneficiary and grantor, and the doctor and hospital as the trustees. The doctor is given authority to act as the trustee of the patient's body by virtue of the patient's consent to treatment. He is obligated to exercise due care and is subject to liability for negligence. The patient is free at any time to revoke the trust. From another perspective, the patient in giving consent to treatment is limiting the authority the doctor and other medical persons may exercise over his body. The patient has the ultimate right to decide what is to be done with him and may not irrevocably confer authority on somebody else. The patient may not be compelled to undergo treatment contrary to his *will*. He should not be compelled to take certain drugs, receive innoculations or therapy or undergo surgery without his express assent. At any point he may stop treatment or he may change physicians.

One problem to be encountered by the *living will* concept is mental illness. An individual who becomes mentally ill has the same rights as any other patient. He may, by the *living will*, anticipate mental illness and limit his consent to treatment accordingly. If in the course of his mental illness he enters an incurable comatose state, treatment may cease. The problem, however, is that, on becoming mentally ill, the court may find him incompetent and appoint a guardian.

Could or should the guardian revoke the *living will* or is it deemed to have become revoked? Here the approach of the trust concept is suggested. The trust relationship between the doctor and the patient was created by the *living will* with the patient as grantor. It was the patient's intent, in creating the trust and drawing the trust document—the *living will*—to cover contingencies wherein he would be incapable of granting or withholding assent to treatment. Incompetency because of mental illness is precisely such a situation. Therefore, the *living will* remains in effect. The guardian may not nullify it. However, when the patient is mentally ill, he may still have instances when his mind is lucid. During such instances he may indicate to his guardian that he wishes the *will* revoked and the guardian could then act accordingly. He might also indicate this intent to the physician who would so inform the guardian and have the *will* revoked.

The *living will* may be used within another context affecting a mentally ill patient. In agreeing to be committed for treatment to a hospital, he could condition the kind of treatment to be given to him. By voluntarily committing himself he does not automatically confer upon the doctor the right to perform a lobotomy, insulin or electric shock therapy, to deny him the right to choose another doctor, to deny him the right to receive visitors or to enjoy other rights. The *living will* could provide that he be released from the hospital if he fails to receive any treatment or does not respond to therapy. If he is confined against his will, the *living will* could be used as a basis for invoking a writ of habeas corpus to effectuate his release.

The *living will* is limited in its initial creation to adult patients who are capable of exercising their will. It applies to those patients who have the right to decide whether they may receive treatment. It does not apply to a parent acting on behalf of his child. Thus, while an adult patient may refuse to undergo an operation or receive a blood transfusion which will save his life, a parent may not deprive a child of such treatment. Though the state recognizes the rights of parents in relation to their children, it acts *in loco parentis* to protect the rights of the children. But the state may not interfere to infringe upon the rights of a mature individual as to the disposition of his body; the law is required to protect the autonomy of the patient.

However, while a patient may determine the type of medical treatment he may receive, he may not use the *living will* as a means for directing a doctor or another individual to *act* affirmatively to terminate his life. He may not authorize the commission of euthanasia. The Law of Trusts recognizes that certain types of trusts for certain designated purposes may be contrary to public policy. Similarly, a *living will* authorizing mercy killing is contrary to public policy. In this instance, public policy considerations outweigh the apparent rights of the patient. The basic function of the law is to protect human life. Because of the possibility that, if mercy killing be permitted without judicial controls, an individual would be killed contrary to his will and the law now extant cannot permit legalized euthanasia. The right to life is basic and the possibility of some persons being murdered regardless of their *will* means that euthanasia may not be condoned. Therefore, as of now, a doctor cannot be directed to act affirmatively to terminate a patient's life. He may, however, be directed and exculpated to act passively by inaction.

However, the patient's *living will* adjudicated by a court and buttressed by medical and lay testimony and evidence, can create the affirmative inaction termination of a patient's life. This can be resorted to in instances where the hospital board on euthanasia may decline to assume the responsibility.

Autonomy's Paradox: Death, Fear, and Advance Directives

by Richard P. Vance*

I. INTRODUCTION

"The trouble with our times," noted Paul Valery, "is that the future is not what it used to be."[1] As it is with the *zeitgeist*, so it is with advance directives ("ADs"). ADs are declarations that one does not want particular kinds of medical treatment when one loses decision-making capacity.[2] These mechanisms have received increased attention since the first living

---

* Coordinator, Section on Medical Humanities, Office of Medical Education; Associate Professor, Department of Pathology, Wake Forest University Medical Center, Winston-Salem, North Carolina. Wake Forest University (B.A., 1976); University of Chicago Divinity School (M.A., 1979); Bowman Gray School of Medicine (M.D., 1981).

1. Valéry, in THE PORTABLE CURMUDGEON 105 (J. Winokur ed. 1987).
2. ADs can be both formal and informal. The most common formal forms of ADs are living wills and durable powers of attorney. For purposes of this Essay, I will refer to formal ADs, and more specifically to living wills. For the most comprehensive discussion, see ADVANCE DIRECTIVES IN MEDICINE (C. Hackler, R. Moseley & D. Vawter eds. 1989) [hereinafter ADVANCE DIRECTIVES]; *see also* R. WEIR, ABATING TREATMENT WITH CRITICALLY ILL PATIENTS (1989) [hereinafter ABATING TREATMENT]; R. WEIR, GUIDELINES ON THE TERMINATION OF LIFE-SUSTAINING TREATMENT AND THE CARE OF THE DYING (1987); PRESIDENT'S COMMISSION, DECIDING TO FOREGO LIFE-SUSTAINING TREATMENT (1983); Bok, *Personal Directions for Care at the End of Life*, 295 NEW ENG. J. MED. 367 (1976); Kutner, *Due Process of Euthanasia: The Living Will, A Proposal*, 44 IND. L.J. 539 (1969); Sullivan, *The Dying Person—His Plight and His Right*, 8 NEW ENG. L. REV. 197 (1973); Note, *The Living Will: The Right to Die with Dignity?*, 26 CASE W. RES. L. REV. 485 (1976); Note, *Living Wills—Need for Legal Recognition*, 78 W. VA. L. REV. 370 (1976); Rosoff, *Living Wills and Natural Death Acts*, in LEGAL AND ETHICAL ASPECTS OF TREATING CRITICALLY AND TERMINALLY ILL PATIENTS 186 (A. Doudera & J. Peters eds. 1982); J. ROBERTSON, THE RIGHT OF THE CRITICALLY ILL (1983); Finnel, *Death with Dignity: The Living Will*, 3 CRITICAL CARE MONITOR 2 (1983); Gilfix & Raffin, *Withholding or Withdrawing Extraordinary Life Support*, 141 W. J. MED. 387 (1984); BY NO EXTRAORDINARY MEANS: THE CHOICE TO FOREGO LIFE SUSTAINING FOOD AND WATER (J. Lynn ed. 1986); R. VEATCH, DEATH, DYING, AND THE BIOLOGICAL REVOLUTION (1976); G. GRISEZ & J. BOYLE, LIFE AND DEATH WITH LIBERTY AND JUSTICE: A CONTRIBUTION TO THE EUTHANASIA DEBATE (1979).

will statute was passed in 1976.[3] Even more interest has arisen in light of the United States Supreme Court decision in *Cruzan v. Director, Missouri Department of Health*.[4] Since many states may now legitimately require "clear and convincing evidence" before treatment withdrawal decisions are made, ADs are perceived by many as the most effective mechanism through which that standard may be met.

Given the extraordinary benefits ADs confer, why are living wills such a rarity? What is it about ADs that so troubles us that we seldom execute them? After all, with living will statutes in at least forty states, and durable power of attorney statutes in all fifty states (twenty-five of which cover health care decisions in some way), no more than ten percent of us sign living wills.[5] We like to argue that the stakes are very high if we do not have ADs. Indeed, the most common argument is that ADs may be the *only* method to ensure a peaceful and dignified death. Most of us would like to think the lack of interest in executing ADs is primarily due to inadequate education: if only more people, the argument goes, knew about and understood ADs, they would exercise their rights to self-determination. Yet, such an explanation is too simplistic in light of the voluminous publications on both ADs and death and dying. In fact, many people are *eager to talk about* living wills and ADs, often in great detail. Very few people, however, actually sign living wills. How are we to explain this disparity between the theoretically attractive and the practically desultory?

---

3. California Natural Death Act, 1976 Cal. Stat. 6478 (codified at Cal. Health & Safety Code §§ 7185-7195 (West 1976). For a comprehensive historical presentation, see also Weir, Abating Treatment, *supra* note 2; *see also* Sprung, *Changing Attitudes and Practices in Foregoing Life-Sustaining Treatment*, 263 J. A.M.A. 2211 (1990); Blake, *State Interests in Terminating Medical Treatment*, Hastings Center Rep., May-June 1989, at 5; Emanuel & Emanuel, *The Medical Directive: A New Comprehensive Advance Care Document*, 261 J. A.M.A. 3288 (1989); Emanuel, *Does the DNR Order Need Life-Sustaining Intervention? Time for Comprehensive Advance Directives*, 86 Am. J. Med. 87 (1989).

4. 110 S. Ct. 2841 (1990); *see also* Weir & Gostin, *Decisions to Abate Life-Sustaining Treatment for Nonautonomous Patients: Ethical Standards and Legal Liability for Physicians After Cruzan*, 264 J. A.M.A. 1846 (1990); Angel, *Prisoners of Technology: The Case of Nancy Cruzan*, 322 New Eng. J. Med. 1226 (1990); Lo, Rouse & Dornbrand, *Family Decision Making on Trial*, 322 New Eng. J. Med. 1228 (1990); Annas, *Nancy Cruzan and the Right to Die*, 323 New Eng. J. Med. 670 (1990); Annas, *Bioethicists' Statement on the U.S. Supreme Court's Cruzan Decision*, 323 New Eng. J. Med. 686 (1990).

5. *See* P. McCarrick, Living Wills and Durable Powers of Attorney: Advance Directive Legislation and Issues (National Reference Center for Bioethics Literature Scope Note 2 (1990)). Anderson, *Living Wills: Do Nurses and Physicians Have Them?*, 86 Am. J. Nursing 271 (1986).

Ethical arguments for ADs tend to be based on notions of autonomy.[6] Indeed, ADs reflect the fundamental value we attach to self-determination. Respect for autonomy leads both to the requirement for informed consent, and to the right to informed refusal of treatment. Because of autonomy, refusal of treatment can be based on value preferences that are not medical in nature. Even if the physician believes that the treatment is in the patient's best interest, the patient may refuse. Self-determination has become important in health care because modern therapeutic modalities can not only provide extraordinary benefits, but also can impose intense and futile suffering on dying patients. Hence ADs allow us to preserve a number of basic goods: sustain individual liberty interests in a pluralistic society; prevent unwanted or futile therapy; reduce anxiety about preserving the dignity of dying; reduce guilt among family members regarding treatment withdrawal; reduce the costs of medical care; and lower anxieties among physicians who treat for *defensive* purposes.[7]

Interestingly enough, most arguments against ADs do not criticize the concept of autonomy directly.[8] Instead, they substitute for autonomy such phrases as the "infinite value of human life," and object to any action that appears to sanction active euthanasia. Clearly, arguments for autonomy do not have to be antithetical to arguments defending the special value of human life. And arguments about the value of human life often reflect presuppositions that support the notion of self-determination. For this reason, neither side seeks to destroy or dismantle the other—only in an indirect way, to limit or to relativize their opponent.

The purpose of this Essay is to provide a different sort of critique of ADs, one that helps explain why ADs are so rare in our society. My argument also specifically criticizes autonomy without at the same time proposing a surrogate such as "the special value of human life." Instead, the argument will focus on a paradox in our advance declarations to ensure a dignified death. The paradox touches on the very nature of our desire to be autonomous, as well as on political intuitions that autonomy is essential for a healthy society. Indeed, the paradox appears precisely because autonomy and death are linked to one another in a very curious way—not just in philosophical debate, but also in our lived experience. The paradox is that the denial of death and denial of autonomy occur together. And in our society, almost all of us—patients and physicians alike—will do almost anything to avoid talking about *our own* deaths.[9]

---

6. Moskop, *Advance Directives in Medicine: Choosing Among the Alternatives*, in ADVANCE DIRECTIVES, *supra* note 2, at 9; *see also* ABATING TREATMENT, *supra* note 2.

7. ADVANCE DIRECTIVES, *supra* note 2, at 1-8.

8. For a useful summary, see ABATING TREATMENT, *supra* note 2.

9. I am aware of the changes in assessment of denial as a defense mechanism. Whereas earlier treatments focused on denial as always deleterious, more recent treatments are more

I propose to look first at two very different philosophical defenses of ADs. One position defends ADs on the basis of autonomy; the other attempts to provide an explicitly social ethics context for ADs. Both positions fail, for different reasons, to account for the phenomenon of death-denial so common in our culture. Social ethics arguments for ADs fail because individual self-determination remains our most fundamental moral intuition. Arguments for ADs using the concept of autonomy are also inadequate because they fail to explain our denial of death and the peculiar connection between *autonomy* and *death*. So very few of us use ADs because our primary moral language raises in profound ways our inarticulable fear of death. Indeed, death-denial is itself a symptom of an important problem rooted in the very concept of autonomy.

II. DEFENSE OF ADVANCE DIRECTIVES: AUTONOMY AND TRUST

A. Advance Directives as Exercise of Autonomy

Is autonomy a coherent concept? Some contemporary philosophers have argued that it is not. Alasdair MacIntyre has argued that substantive moral agency evaporated in the post-Enlightenment era when we began to understand ourselves via autonomy.[10] Indeed, autonomy strictly understood leads not to self-determination, but to psychotic madness.[11] Since the very phenomenon of language is rule-governed, our mental integrity depends upon not being autonomous in very important and extensive ways. For MacIntyre, autonomy is both morally deleterious and intellectually fatuous. In a different though no less critical way, pragmatists like Richard Rorty argue that the language of autonomy is nothing more than learned linguistic behavior.[12] To presume that autonomy names something ontologically real is to fall prey to a philosophical illusion. Even if we put aside criticisms by MacIntyre and Rorty, though, most of autonomy's defenders recognize that autonomy is not a straightforwardly simple concept.[13] Joel Feinberg has noted, for example, that autonomy

---

carefully nuanced. *See* Lazarus, *The Costs and Benefits of Denial*, in LIVING WITH CHILDHOOD CANCER 50 (J. Spinetta & P. Deasy-Spinetta eds. 1981); Youngner, *Advance Directives and the Denial of Death: Should the Conflict Be Resolved?* in ADVANCE DIRECTIVES, *supra* note 2, at 127. What has not heretofore been adequately examined with regard to advance directives, however, is the peculiar connection between the moral psychology of individual autonomy and our denial of death.

10. MacIntyre, *How Moral Agents Became Ghosts, or Why the History of Ethics Diverged from That of the Philosophy of the Mind*, 53 SYNTHESE 295 (1982).

11. MacIntyre, *Epistemological Crisis, Dramatic Narrative, and the Philosophy of Science*, in PARADIGMS AND REVOLUTIONS 54 (G. Gutting ed. 1980).

12. *See* R. RORTY, PHILOSOPHY AND THE MIRROR OF NATURE (1979).

13. For an excellent anthology of classic essays on autonomy, see THE INNER CITADEL (J. Christman ed. 1989).

really has four distinct but related meanings: the *capacity* to govern one-self; the *actual condition* of self-government; a *moral ideal*; and the *sovereign right* of self-governance.[14] Yet, John Christman argues that nothing in Feinberg's list makes impossible a coherent *core meaning* for autonomy.[15] Indeed, such a core idea is typically associated with the notion of self-government, as explicated by Harry Frankfurt and Gerald Dworkin. As Dworkin puts it:

> A person is autonomous if he identifies with his desires, goals, and values, and such identification is not influenced in ways which make the process of identification in some way alien to the individual. Spelling out the conditions of procedural independence involves distinguishing those ways of influencing people's reflective and critical faculties which subvert them from those which promote and improve them.[16]

Hence, authentic autonomy is present "when the agent accepts the desire, value, or preference as part of her larger set of desires, beliefs, and principles, whether or not this is done for good reasons."[17]

A full explication of the Frankfurt and Dworkin notion of autonomy, including their discussions about lower and higher order desires, is beyond the scope of the present Essay. Even more, there are significant criticisms of the theory that I will not discuss.[18] However, if we assume that autonomy is a coherent concept, we still need another distinction not apparent in the Frankfurt-Dworkin model because it has a direct bearing on ADs. The distinction was first outlined by Isaiah Berlin in a famous essay on the difference between positive and negative liberty.

> The first of these political senses of freedom or liberty . . ., which I shall call the "negative" sense, is involved in the answer to the question "What is the area within which the subject . . . is or should be left to do or be what he wants to do or be, without interference by other persons?" The second, which I shall call the positive sense, is involved in the answer to the question "What, or who, is the source of control or interference, that can determine someone to do, or be, one thing rather than another?"[19]

Positive liberty is the freedom to choose and define life's goals and values. Negative liberty is freedom from unwanted interference or coercion from

---

14. Feinberg, *Autonomy*, in THE INNER CITADEL, *supra* note 13, at 27-53.

15. Christman, *Introduction* to THE INNER CITADEL, *supra* note 13, at 3-21.

16. Dworkin, *The Concept of Autonomy*, in THE INNER CITADEL, *supra* note 13, at 61.

17. Christman, *Introduction* to THE INNER CITADEL, *supra* note 13, at 7.

18. It is fair to say, however, that apart from those who dismiss the whole notion of autonomy, most critics have found the theory insufficient or incomplete but not fundamentally wrong. *See* THE INNER CITADEL, *supra* note 13.

19. I. BERLIN, TWO CONCEPTS OF LIBERTY 6-7 (1958).

others. While both notions are important, Berlin notes that only the negative sense is appropriate for liberal democracies. D.A.J. Richards demonstrates that autonomy in this negative sense is most likely the primary one in our political history precisely because autonomy was intended to *replace* the republican notion of public virtue.[20] Autonomy, he argues, is "a constitutive normative ingredient of American democratic constitutionalism because it specifies the empirical and normative conditions for the value of self-government essential to the very legitimacy of this form of government."[21] Hence, by defining a sphere of individual autonomy the United States Constitution "preserves to persons a critical moral independence itself often critical of the claims of state power in the pursuit of personal and ethical ends to which legitimate state power must be accountable, not conversely."[22]

In the area of medical ethics, no one has articulated the notion of autonomy as negative liberty—the right not to be interfered with—better than H.T. Engelhardt. In his systematic work, *The Foundations of Bioethics*,[23] Engelhardt is fully aware of the recent challenges to notions of systematic, universal, rational ethics made by Alasdair MacIntyre.[24] Indeed, Engelhardt accepts nearly all of MacIntyre's hypotheses, even as he turns the argument on its head. Since we live in a culture with many diverse communities, Engelhardt argues, no one of those communities can claim moral priority over the others. Moreover, we can provide an ethic for such a culture only by describing the most general, universal, and abstract characteristics of morality. Engelhardt claims to have salvaged only a small part of the Enlightenment heritage, the "minimal grammar of morality," out of the rubble of MacIntyre's assault. Nevertheless, the remnant he rescues is nothing less than the central Enlightenment affirmations: Kant's formal limits on human knowledge and the moral preeminence of each individual's self-determination. Rather than leading to intractable dilemmas, Engelhardt argues that this secular pluralistic ethic provides the only "rational method" that can allow diverse communities of belief, even in the face of moral disagreements, to live together peacefully.

As a libertarian, Engelhardt makes a definition and defense of the concept of "person" the methodological center of his work: "Persons, not humans, are special."[25] Persons are self-conscious, rational, and autonomous. Since persons have these capacities, they are able to form "peacea-

---

20. Richards, *Autonomy in Law*, in The Inner Citadel, *supra* note 13, at 246.
21. *Id.*
22. *Id.* at 248.
23. H. Engelhardt, The Foundations of Bioethics (1986).
24. A. MacIntyre, After Virtue (2d ed. 1984).
25. H. Engelhardt, *supra* note 23, at 104.

ble secular communities" in which all persons are free to pursue their own definitions of the good life as long as they do not interfere with the "autonomy" of other persons. Autonomy, in Engelhardt's ethic, is not simply equated with the value of freedom—the capacity to choose or to act. Instead, it is a "respect for freedom," the necessary condition for the possibility of mutual respect, the necessary condition for morality. As a result, the fundamental moral limit of action, the formal barrier morality places on all of us, is to avoid force to which the innocent have not consented.

For this reason, Engelhardt argues that the moral value in ADs is not so much the right of self-expression as it is the moral right to be left alone:

> Because a generally justifiable and authoritative, concrete view of the good life is not available in a secular context, the right to use such directives is best justified in general secular terms on the basis of the limits of others' rights to intervene in the competent actions of free individuals, rather than on the basis of the limits of concrete obligations to provide or accept treatment.[26]

These limitations on actions are based on an underlying cultural need to control medical technology "to assure that it will serve human needs and values and not follow a momentum of its own."[27]

B. Advance Directives as Gesture Toward Trust

Although there are numerous problems with Engelhardt's systematic work, his explication of autonomy as a negative liberty is descriptively powerful and appeals to many of our most basic political instincts. For Engelhardt, autonomy of persons in this negative sense is a profoundly important resource precisely because it allows us to live in a tolerably peaceful, secular, pluralistic society. Yet, some criticisms have been levelled specifically at this sort of interpretation of ADs.[28]

In particular, Larry Churchill argues that the language of individual rights and autonomy distorts the basic meaning of ADs.[29] At the heart of his argument is the concern to rehabilitate a notion of trust in health care ethics. This is not surprising since Churchill's analysis of justice in health care attempts to revitalize Adam Smith's ethic of sympathy for contem-

---

26. Engelhardt, *Advance Directives and the Right to Be Left Alone*, in ADVANCE DIRECTIVES, *supra* note 2, at 142.

27. *Id.* at 149.

28. For more comprehensive responses to Engelhardt, see S. HAUERWAS, SUFFERING PRESENCE (1986); E. PELLEGRINO & D. THOMASMA, FOR THE PATIENT'S GOOD (1988).

29. Churchill, *Trust, Autonomy, and Advance Directives*, 28 J. RELIGION & HEALTH 175 (1989).

porary society.[30] Indeed, Churchill wants to replace language of individualism and rights with those moral sentiments that connect us to one another and provide the substantive interdependent connections we have with one another. Churchill argues that the moral sentiments, and in particular *sympathy*, are more fundamental in our moral experience than are our private *inner citadels* of autonomy.

Hence, Churchill answers the rhetorical question, "Why do people write advance directives?" by arguing that most people are motivated by fear. Although self-determination and autonomy are also important, they are subsidiary to the perception that we cannot trust that those who care for us will do so wisely and humanely. Autonomy, therefore, is still essential for Churchill, but only because of the prior problem of fear and mistrust. Autonomy is a "fall-back position" we reach only when our moral sentiments do not sustain our interdependence.[31]

Why is the language of autonomy inadequate in dealing with ADs? Churchill cites several reasons:

> The first is that focusing on autonomy will draw our attention away from the lived experience of advance directive writing. So to concentrate on autonomy . . . is like rearranging trunks in the attic while neglecting the living quarters below. Concentrating on autonomy will keep us away from the core of the moral action.
>
> My second complaint is that autonomy is an inadequate moral tool, at least in its contemporary, largely negative, usage. Probing for moral meaning with autonomy as our guide is like deep-sea fishing with a fly-rod. The tool is inadequate to the task, and the catch will be meager because the instrument allows little depth.[32]

The limitations of autonomy lead to additional problems. Indeed, Churchill points out:

> The autonomy and free-choice emphasis also has the unsavory characteristic of an easy affiliation with the concept of "medical consumerism." Under this model, doctors, nurses, and other health "professionals" become "providers," while "patients" become "consumers." Consumers are then expected to choose from the vast medical supermarket which items or procedures for life maintenance they "want" . . . . Under this consumer model, writing an advance directive is like ordering a Chinese meal ten years in advance, from a menu which is constantly changing and in a language you do not understand. But, of course, this goes too far, since people write advance directives not to *have* something, but to make sure they will *not have* something. So writing an advance directive

---

30. L. CHURCHILL, RATIONING HEALTH-CARE IN AMERICA (1987).
31. Churchill, *supra* note 29, at 180-83.
32. *Id.* at 178-79.

may be more like calling the maitre d' ten years ahead and insisting that when you come to dine you definitely do *not* want the mu shu pork and the Szechuan chicken.[33]

Autonomy distorts our moral experience by ignoring both the historical or narrative dimension of our lives, and the profound uncertainties, limits, and tragedies our histories embody.[34] Because we tend to equate distinctively human life with our *autonomous inner citadels*—"self-interested centers of rationality only incidentally marked by common sentiments or capacities for fellow feeling, such as benevolence, altruism, or trust"—we have truncated our understanding of the moral life.[35]

Autonomy, Churchill goes on to say, blunts our understanding of our lives as fundamentally social. It gradually forces us to see ourselves isolated from others, and others isolated from us. Because trust, not autonomy, is our most fundamental moral reality, Churchill argues, it is not a naive sentiment. Even though trust exists only in the presence of trustworthy people, it is not an emotion; it is, instead, "a *capacity* we have, to greater or lesser degrees, and like all moral capacities, it must be taught, practiced, and nourished if it is to thrive and flourish. The flaw of autonomy-oriented ethics is that it discourages the practice of this virtue."[36] Therefore, expressions of autonomy in ADs should be the occasion for professional and institutional responses that seek "to re-establish trust, first by acknowledging the legitimacy of such expressions, and second by using advance directives as occasions for continuing conversations that will rebuild trust."[37] Hence, health-care professionals should receive ADs not as conversation-stoppers, as *moral* or *legal trumps*, but as gestures to get the conversation started, to look more closely at the values and concerns underneath the patient's preferences. In so doing, the appropriate goal is to rediscover the deeper moral sentiments that really bind us to one another.

III. CRITIQUE OF ADVANCE DIRECTIVES: POLITICAL AND THANATOLOGICAL

Engelhardt and Churchill provide two poles from which positive arguments for ADs can be constructed. Although Churchill's position is as critical of Engelhardt's as Engelhardt's is of Churchill's, both scholars

---

33. *Id.* at 179 (emphasis in original).

34. The value and limits of narrative approaches have been discussed at length by Hauerwas and Pellegrino; *see also* H. BRODY, STORIES OF SICKNESS (1987); Churchill, *Advance Directives: Beyond Respect for Freedom, in* ADVANCE DIRECTIVES, *supra* note 2, at 171.

35. Churchill, *supra* note 29, at 179.

36. *Id.* at 180 (emphasis in original).

37. *Id.* at 182.

present compelling arguments for the value of ADs. In this sense they are mirror images of one another, bound by the dialectical relationship between thought and sentiment, right and virtue, procedure and substance, and individual and society. An adequate critique of ADs must address both Engelhardt and Churchill. What follows, then, is a two-part argument. In the first stage, I demonstrate why Churchill is wrong about the priority of trust over autonomy. Autonomy is not a second-order, fallback position; it is our primary language. Consequently, fragmentation and mistrust are far more deep-seated than Churchill perceives. Communitarian elements in the liberal tradition serve merely to sustain our self-interested, individualistic presuppositions. Therefore, liberal individualism cannot be reinterpreted to mean simply a semantical encrustation of autonomy language over a bed of communitarian sentiment.

The second stage of my argument shows why Engelhardt's negative liberty is far from helpful in promoting ADs. Churchill is generally right in his suspicions that fear is a major issue surrounding ADs. As long as autonomy remains a fundamental concept in our moral discourse, such that we understand ourselves and others in some primary or essential way as autonomous individuals, we have good reason not to trust each other—especially when it concerns an issue as troubling and fearful as our death. Neither Churchill nor Engelhardt, however, identify the peculiar connection between *autonomy* and *fear*—specifically the fear and denial of death. For this reason, they both fail to recognize that as long as autonomy remains our society's moral and legal *justification* of ADs, it is also the most definitive way to keep ADs from becoming used in a widespread manner.

A.   Trust is Gone: Fragmentation of the Public Sphere

Churchill's argument about the primacy of trust in the moral life rests upon the presupposition that our social or public lives are fundamentally intersubjective and interdependent. Therefore, he is making not just a psychological point, but a political and social one as well. However, such a thesis is not easily sustained in light of the history of what the *public* has become. Jurgen Habermas's *The Structural Transformation of the Public Sphere*[38] is still the most comprehensive historical and philosophical

---

38.   J. Habermas, The Structural Transformation of the Public Sphere (1989) [hereinafter Structural Transformation]. It is ironic, of course, to use Habermas as the source of the disintegration of the public sphere in light of his massive recent work on communicative action and discourse ethics. *See* 1 & 2 J. Habermas, The Theory of Communicative Action (1989); J. Habermas, Moral Consciousness and Communicative Action (1990). Unfortunately, Habermas has never returned to the historical issues he details so well in his earlier work on the public sphere. In order to uphold his later arguments, he will have to deal with significant historical issues he raises here.

analysis of this subject. Habermas points out, for example, that in the Middle Ages *public* could only be applied to the feudal lord, or to those symbols and persons who represented him.[39] The *public*, in any sense that we might recognize, did not exist. To be public (*publicare*) meant simply "to claim for the lord."[40] By the end of the Renaissance, however, public referred to the bourgeoisie who were able "to compel public authority to legitimate itself before [them]."[41] As Habermas put it, "The *publicum* developed into a public, the *subjectum* into the [reasoning] subject, the receiver of regulations from above into the ruling authorities' adversary."[42] In the constitutional democracies of the early nineteenth century, therefore, public had developed into the *source* of governmental legitimacy. The crucial goal of the public's opinion was to protect the citizenry from dominating governmental power—"to dissolve any kind of coercion into the compulsion of reason."[43]

Fundamental problems emerged, though, that quickly changed the nature of the public sphere. These problems were first noticed by nineteenth century liberal democratic political theorists who found that the public sphere seldom served the sort of critical function it should.[44] Instead, as John Stuart Mill noted, there is "in the world at large an increasing inclination to stretch unduly the powers of society over the individual . . . by the force of public opinion."[45] Public opinion evolved not into an expression of universal interest, but instead into an antidemocratic coercive power. Tolerance of individual expression was, as Mill saw it, threatened. As a consequence, *representative* expression of public opinion became vital. As J.S. Mill argued, "political questions [should] be decided by a direct or indirect appeal to views, formed after due consideration, of a relatively small number of persons specially educated for this task."[46] In other words, the coercive power of public opinion could only be controlled by a smaller, more refined, more educated, and reflective version of the public. In the nineteenth century, however, this

---

39. Interestingly, this is very similar to the origins of our notion of "good" in the Greek word *agathos*, which initially referred in a very specific way to the Homeric tribal chieftain. *See* A. MacIntyre, A Short History of Ethics (1968); A. MacIntyre, Whose Justice? Which Rationality? (1989).

40. Structural Transformation, *supra* note 38, at 6.

41. *Id.* at 25.

42. *Id.* at 26.

43. *Id.* at 133.

44. *Id.*

45. Mill, *On Liberty*, in 40 Great Books of the Western World 273 (M. Adler ed. 2d ed. 1990).

46. Mill, *On Liberty*, in 18 Collected Works 247 (J. Robson ed. 1984).

representative form of public debate also degenerated, but this time into special interest politics.[47] As Habermas notes:

> Group needs that could not expect to be satisfied by a self-regulating market tended to favor regulation by the state. The public sphere, which now had to deal with these demands, became an arena of competing interests . . . . Laws passed under the "pressure of the street" could hardly be understood any longer as embodying the reasonable consensus of publicly debating private persons. They corresponded more or less overtly to the compromise between competing private interests.[48]

The realm of public opinion thus became merely the arena for the conflict of *opinion*—privately interested opinion.

The disintegration of the public sphere has left us with little more than a chaotic confrontation between private-self and group interests. This is the reason Sheldon Wolin believes that, ironically:

> Pluralism has undercut the practice of political citizenship by replacing the idea of a civic person who continuously shares and participates in the common concerns of society with the idea of the special-interest-group member who emerges from that small circle to vote every few years but is otherwise preoccupied with private interests. Pluralism has also discredited the idea that, except for national defense, there are common values that, as a collectivity, we can develop and share. There are only common means we can use to further individual, group, organizational, and class ends.[49]

Therefore, "competing private interests" is what the "public sphere" has come to mean. This transformation of the public sphere is certainly no trivial problem, precisely because we no longer have the resources to make intelligible what *public* means *apart* from self-interest. We find it quite natural "to think that politics and public life is primarily the sphere of the negotiation and conflict of competing interests."[50] Our interdependence is reduced to voluntary public participations—a participation that only means interest groups have a chance to have their say.[51]

Of course, this is extraordinarily problematic in a democracy because it means we do not have a rational consensus through which citizens can trust one another to seek something other than their self-interest. It also

---

47. *See* Wolin, *The American Pluralist Conception of Politics*, in Ethics in Hard Times 217 (Caplan & Callahan eds. 1981).

48. Structural Transformation, *supra* note 38, at 132.

49. Wolin, *supra* note 47.

50. Bernstein, *The Meaning of Public Life*, in Religion and American Public Life 41 (R. Lovin ed. 1986).

51. Kemp, *Planning, Public Hearings, and the Politics of Discourse*, in Critical Theory and Public Life 177 (J. Forester ed. 1985).

means that the social coherence demanded for a tolerable social ethic is shredded.[52] This is the reason Habermas can speak so cogently about the "depolitization of the mass of the population."[53] Indeed,

> [t]he communicative network of a public made up of rationally debating private citizens has collapsed; the public opinion once emergent from it has partly decomposed into the informal opinions of private citizens without a public and partly become concentrated into formal opinions of publicistically effective institutions. Caught in the vortex of *publicity that is staged for show or manipulation* the public of nonorganized private people is laid claim to not by public communication but by the communication of publicly manifested opinion.[54]

Hence, the historical notion of *a public* in the modern democratic state—at least in so far as it serves a trustworthy resource free from the influence of particular interests—is little more than a fiction.[55]

With that recognition, *trust* in even as sophisticated a form as provided by Churchill, seems terribly inadequate. Churchill argued that the act of writing ADs expresses a fear that our dignity will be assaulted at a time we lack all control over it. The emphasis on autonomy, he notes, "is not so much mistaken" as it is misplaced. Instead, patients are trying to assert their vision of their own good because they don't trust health care professionals to protect it.[56]

Trust, though, can have several different meanings. It can mean, perhaps most simply, that we believe we will get what we expect. This is essentially an expectation of consistency. Yet, Churchill is talking about something more: we expect to be treated in a way *we would want or will want*. Such an expanded definition of trust is actually more appropriate to health care because of the uncertainties surrounding the circumstances of our dying. Indeed, Churchill's definition of trust means *even more* than what most of us attach to the notion of respect. Autonomy requires or obliges others to *respect* our wishes and our values. Yet, Churchill is saying that trust requires that others genuinely understand and care about our values and wishes and honor them even in the absence of autonomy. Of course, simply talking about being sensitive to the motivational experiences of others does not make it more likely that this sort of trust will arise. Trust, in the sense Churchill defends, is much more substantial than merely developing a social perspective on ethics. Trust requires the existence—the concrete existence—of a society that is really a commu-

---

52. J. HABERMAS, THEORY AND PRACTICE 255 (1973).
53. J. HABERMAS, TOWARD A RATIONAL SOCIETY 103-04 (1970).
54. STRUCTURAL TRANSFORMATION, *supra* note 38, at 247.
55. *Id.* at 244.
56. Churchill, *supra* note 29, at 182.

nity. The community must share *our* vision of the good life, not because *our* vision is a private autonomous one, but because *our* vision is *shared by* and *arises out* of the community as a whole. Trust, in this sense, is not a matter of essentially autonomous individuals *bonding* or *reconnecting* to one another because they fear that these very same people will degrade and abuse them otherwise. Trust, if it occurs at all, will only emerge out of a moral tradition and community that has a shared vision of the proper ends of human life.

The problem we face in our society, therefore, is *not* that we have lost contact with a deeper dimension of our ethical experience or our moral sentiments, or that we have failed to maintain a careful balance between trust and autonomy, virtue and obligation, the social and the personal. Our problem is that the dominant moral tradition—the tradition of autonomy (as self-governance) and individual rights—makes us see ourselves primarily as self-interested individuals who know better than anyone else what our good is, often to the exclusion of anyone else.

B.   *Autonomy, Fear, and Death*

Yet, if Engelhardt is correct, and the primary issue in ADs is preservation of autonomy at the end of life against the onslaught of modern medical technology, how do we explain the rarity of living wills? After all, the danger from overweening medical technology is not decreasing. Surely, then, an additional factor must be involved. Denial of death is a well-recognized phenomenon in our culture. Indeed, it has been commented upon repeatedly since the 1960s. "Call no man happy until he is dead" is Solon's well-known ancient aphorism. Such a sentiment made sense in the context of Ancient Greek culture, but not in ours. Happiness, in the most important ways we use that word means simply *not* to die. Consequently, our modern denial of death is far more clearly reflected in our behavior than in our theoretical discussions of ADs. Paul Ramsey had the right answer when he noted that we will never adequately deal with our fear of death by writing about it or speaking about it persistently.[57] Death is not a problem we can solve, he argued; instead it is destined to remain, in the modern world, an impenetrable mystery.

Interestingly, the French historian, Philippe Ariès, has argued that there is a connection between views of the self and attitudes toward death.[58] For this reason, the contrast between classical and modern notions of the self turns out to be extremely important in understanding

---

57.   Ramsey, *Death's Pedagogy*, 100 COMMONWEALTH 497-502 (1974).

58.   P. ARIÈS, WESTERN ATTITUDES TOWARD DEATH (1974) [hereinafter WESTERN ATTITUDES]; P. ARIÈS, THE HOURS OF OUR DEATH (1981) [hereinafter THE HOUR].

modern death. Alasdair MacIntyre has succinctly described the classical and modern views of the self:

> The self of the heroic [Homeric] age lacks precisely that characteristic . . . that some modern moral philosophers take to be an essential characteristic of human selfhood: the capacity to detach oneself from any particular standpoint or point of view, to step backwards, as it were, and view and judge that standpoint or point of view from the outside. In heroic society there is no "outside" except that of the stranger. A man who tried to withdraw himself from his given position in heroic society would be engaged in the enterprise of trying to make himself disappear.[59]

The individual in Homeric society knew who he or she was through

> his or her membership in a variety of social groups . . . . I am brother, cousin and grandson, member of this household, that village, this tribe. These are not characteristics that belong to human beings accidentally, to be stripped away in order to discover "the real me." They are part of my substance, defining partially at least and sometimes wholly my obligations and my duties . . . . To know oneself as such a social person is however not to occupy a static and fixed position. It is to find oneself placed at a certain point on a journey with set goals; to move through life is to make progress—or fail to make progress—toward a given end.[60]

Such a definition of the self is thoroughly social. Similarly, death in Homeric society was not a private event. Proper funerals were *public* rituals performed by the community and were essential for the healing of the community to take place.[61] As long as an acceptable ritual procedure was followed, death remained an expected, even if an evil, part of life. If there was a terror in death, it was not to be found in death itself. The primordial fear was the absence of a proper funeral—leaving the corpse like a dead animal to be devoured by dogs and birds.[62] Such an *antifuneral* was unspeakably horrible precisely because it prevented the community from healing itself through the proper rituals. Ariès calls the classical view of death "tamed death," not because this death failed to elicit grief, but because our modern view of death has become *untamed*.[63]

Modern death, what Freud called that "painful riddle,"[64] is not primarily the occasion for social mourning, but is instead a terrible existential mystery. One of our most enlightened thanatologists, Ernest Becker, has argued that the modern world's chief characteristic is the "terror of

---

59. A. MacIntyre, *supra* note 24, at 126.
00. *Id.* at 00–04.
61. J. Redfield, Nature and Culture in the Iliad (1975).
62. *Id.*
63. Western Attitudes, *supra* note 58; The Hour, *supra* note 58.
64. S. Freud, The Future of an Illusion (1964).

death."[65] Becker focused on "universality of the fear of death" in the modern world in order "to convey how all-consuming it is when we look it full in the face."[66] We spend most of our time, Becker argues, trying to deny that death exists. Indeed, we have pushed death out of public view and into the hospital where it can be *managed* and *controlled*, so that all of us (doctors, families, and society) can find a way to tolerate it. Even our funerals are designed to prevent death from forcing uncomfortable questions upon us.[67] Indeed we are so uncomfortable about the whole phenomenon of death that we use phrases like "resting" or "dreaming" to describe the deceased. They are "not to be disturbed" since they have "suffered enough." The embalmer's handiwork is judged to be good only when the corpse mimics the person sleeping. Modern funerals provide the tools to cover over death as quickly and painlessly as possible. Jessica Mitford's classic treatment in *The American Way of Death*[68] is still relevant. Her description of the funeral industry's success as *doctors of grief* testifies to our modern concern to make death *invisible*.

I mentioned earlier that the histories of the self and death in the West have parallel courses. If death has receded from public view, then the self has disappeared as well. The privatization of modern self means that it "has no *necessary* social content and no necessary social identity."[69] Our *autonomous self*, in the truest and deepest sense, "can assume any role or take any point of view, because it *is* in and for itself nothing."[70] There is, therefore, a terrible and empty *polarity* that exists between our modern understanding of death and our modern understanding of the self. The modern self has no other adequate way to understand itself except through its opposite—through its absence. Because death and life lack finite and concrete social meaning, they are very much like two elements in a single dichotomous variable—either one if alive or zero if dead. They are inextricably linked because neither one has any meaning without the other. Witness the painful and paradoxical reflections of Leon Kass upon learning of his mentor's death:

> I entered the room, thunderstruck. There he lay, peacefully, a frail figure in a large bed, half-smiling, as if in a pleasant dream. Dreaming, I would have thought had I not met the nurse. Moments later, I found myself on my knees at the foot of the bed, full of awe and horror. Over and over, I asked myself, "Where *is* he? Where did he go? Where is that mind, that learning and understanding, those unwritten books that no one will now

---

65. E. BECKER, THE DENIAL OF DEATH (1973).
66. *Id.*
67. WESTERN ATTITUDES, *supra* note 58.
68. J. MITFORD, THE AMERICAN WAY OF DEATH (1963).
69. A. MACINTYRE, *supra* note 24, at 32 (emphasis added).
70. *Id.* (emphasis in original).

write?" There he lay or seemed to lie, but lay not; there he was or seemed to be, but was not. The body, the still warm and undisfigured body, identical in looks to what I had seen the day before, mocked me . . . .[71]

By examining our autonomy existentially, as a lived experience, we find ourselves confronted, therefore, with a paradox that *most* people in our society simply do not want to face.

It is no accident that the kind of death we discuss least often, the death about which our moral discourse is most silent, is the sudden one. Notice that we don't hold conferences or give papers on the moral implications of sudden death. Such deaths are horrible, of course. Yet, they conform quite well to the conceptual polarity that the modern self and death display. However, autonomy as a moral and conceptual tool gives us terrible problems when trying to make sense of the slow and often agonizing slide from self-governance into senility and finally into death. Indeed, it becomes morally problematic how to distinguish between the permanently incompetent and the dead. Hence, we find the common phenomenon that people would rather be dead than dependent. Our moral language of autonomy encourages us to believe that being persistently dependent on others is a peculiar kind of moral failure.

In this critique of autonomy, I must not be misunderstood. I have no intention to defend paternalism. I am not saying simply trust the physician; far from it. Physicians often know as little about death as the rest of society, and often deny it more vigorously. I am arguing that even if we have no substantive alternative to our individualistic rhetoric, it is still crucial to recognize that autonomy provides a meager tool for understanding the profoundly complex phenomena we face in death and dying. Our primary moral language and our most important moral intuitions are wholly inadequate to guide our moral experience as finite beings who die. When we have no other resources than autonomy with which to understand our lives, moral discourse is desiccated at precisely the time we experience profound discomfort regarding our own deaths. It is no accident, therefore, that so many have shunned the issue of ADs, since so much of the discussion surrounding them has been pitched at the level of autonomy.

IV. CONCLUSION

So where does this leave us? *Where*, some might ask, are the analogues to the kind of community presented earlier—communities in which both the self and death have concrete social meaning? At one time in this

---

71. L. KASS, TOWARD A MORE NATURAL SCIENCE 279 (1985).

country, religious communities provided a context within which many people could understand their lives in terms other than autonomy. To some extent that is still true, especially for traditions like the Mennonites. But it certainly is no longer possible *in general* because so much of American religion now displays all the special interest divisions that characterize the rest of society—churches are separated much more fundamentally by social class and party politics than by theological differences.[72]

So where does that leave us? Alasdair MacIntyre several years ago suggested in a short article in the *Hastings Center Report*[73] that regulations are a substitute for morality. Similarly, I am saying that ADs are a *substitute*, perhaps a *necessary* substitute, for dying in a community that cherishes an honorable, or a faithful life. The terrible truth is that we need ADs, not because they are a gesture toward trust, or because profound moral resources like autonomy demand their presence, but because the moralities that made trusting relationships in health care possible are attenuated at best, and are perhaps irretrievably lost.

---

72. For a compelling analysis of this phenomenon, see R. WUTHNOW, THE RESTRUCTURING OF AMERICAN RELIGION: SOCIETY AND FAITH SINCE WORLD WAR II (1988).

73. MacIntyre, *Regulation: A Substitute for Morality*, HASTINGS CENTER REP., Feb. 1980, at 31-33.

The Journal of Legal Medicine, Volume 8, Number 3, 1987

ADVANCE MEDICAL DIRECTIVES

THE CASE FOR THE DURABLE POWER OF ATTORNEY FOR HEALTH CARE

David A. Peters, Ph.D.*

INTRODUCTION

Thirty-nine states have now enacted "natural death acts," also termed "right to die" or "death with dignity" laws.[1] These laws give statutory authority to a type of document long available and frequently utilized, but never accorded legislative recognition before the passage in California in 1976 of the first natural death act,[2] the so-called living will. In the context of this legislation, the document is called a "declaration" or "directive to phyicians."

The purpose of living wills is to permit previously competent adults to control the course of their medical treatment when they become incapacitated. In a typical living will, the declarant lists types of medical interventions which should be provided, withdrawn, or withheld under specific conditions. The form usually instructs health care providers to discontinue or refrain from starting certain types of life-sustaining procedures (e.g., artificial ventilation) when the declarant is incompetent and he or she is medically determined to have a terminal condition, so

---

* Associate Professor and Chair, Department of Philosophy, University of Wisconsin–River Falls, River Falls, Wisconsin. Address correspondence and reprint requests to Professor Peters at the Department of Philosophy, University of Wisconsin–River Falls, River Falls, WI 54022.

[1] The following states have enacted this type of legislation—Alabama, Alaska, Arizona, Arkansas, California, Colorado, Connecticut, Delaware, Florida, Georgia, Hawaii, Idaho, Illinois, Indiana, Iowa, Kansas, Louisiana, Maine, Maryland, Mississippi, Missouri, Montana, Nevada, New Hampshire, New Mexico, North Carolina, Oklahoma, Oregon, South Carolina, Tennessee, Texas, Utah, Vermont, Virginia, Washington, West Virginia, Wisconsin, Wyoming, and the District of Columbia. *Newsletter, New York Society for the Right to Die*, Mar. 30, 1987, at 1.

[2] CAL. HEALTH & SAFETY CODE §§7185-95 (West 1976).

that the procedures in question would only serve to prolong the patient's dying. Medical staff who in good faith comply with the directives of a living will are relieved of civil and criminal liability, according to the provision of all natural death acts.

Because great attention has been given by the media in recent years to living wills, most people are doubtless familiar with the concept. There is, however, an alternative but less well-known legal device for protecting a patient's right to control his or her medical treatment when incapacitated, namely, the durable power of attorney for health care (DPAHC). This mechanism, an extension of existing durable power of attorney statutes available in all 50 states (with the exception of the District of Columbia), permits a competent adult to appoint a proxy to make medical decisions in the event of incompetency. An adequately drafted DPAHC instrument is superior to the living will as a means for protecting the fundamental right of a once-competent but now incapacitated patient to control the course of his or her medical care.

In this article, it is asserted that there are no virtues possessed by living wills that are not also possessed by reflectively framed DPAHC forms. Moreover, the DPAHC has no disadvantages escaped by living wills. Finally, the DPAHC provides greater assurance that the patient's personal values and desires will control his or her medical treatment during incompetency than can be afforded by living wills.

It follows that greater public attention deserves to be given to the DPAHC. Model DPAHC forms with features like those recommended in Section IV should be made available in physicians' offices in the same manner that living will forms have been available in the past. Physicians should discuss the DPAHC with patients and encourage them to complete such an instrument. States not expressly recognizing the DPAHC as a legitimate extension of their existing durable power of attorney statutes can perform a valuable service for citizens by enacting such legislation. (Durable power of attorney statutes in California,[3] Colorado,[4] Pennsylvania,[5] and Rhode Island[6] explicitly permit attorneys-in-fact to make health care decisions for principals.)

Such legislation would remove the doubt which some legal analysts have about the validity of the DPAHC absent explicit statutory authoriza-

---

[3] CAL. CIV. CODE §§2412.5, 2430-44, 2500-08, 2510-13 (West. Supp. 1986).
[4] COLO. REV. STAT. §§15-14-501 (Supp. 1986).
[5] PA. STAT. ANN. tit. 20 §§5602(a)(9), 5603(h) (Purdon Supp. 1986).
[6] R.I. GEN. LAWS §§23-4.9-1-2 (1986).

tion. It could also establish numerous important safeguards protecting citizens using the instrument and health care providers complying with the directives of patient-appointed proxies. State legislation expressly certifying the use of the DPAHC is therefore highly desirable, although there is evidence that it is not absolutely necessary in states that already recognize the more conventional durable power of attorney. The DPAHC merits at least the level of publicity heretofore afforded living wills. This article is an effort toward evening the balance.

I. LIVING WILLS: LEGAL FOUNDATIONS

A. Legal Basis of Living Wills: The Right of Self-Determination

The common law of battery and trespass and the constitutional right of privacy provide the legal bases for the patient protection provided by living wills. In *Scholendorf v. Society of New York Hospitals*,[7] Justice Benjamin Cardozo declared concerning medical care: "Every human being of adult years has a right to determine what shall be done with his own body; and a surgeon who performs an operation without his patient's consent, commits an assault, for which he is liable in damages."[8]

Courts have interpreted the constitutional right of privacy as giving individuals first authority to control what is done to their own bodies.[9] Save for emergency situations,[10] physicans and others are not permitted to render medical treatment to any competent adult without that person's informed consent.[11] The right of privacy encompasses the right to refuse *any* medical intervention, including life-saving procedures.[12] Adults who have been competent at any time do not lose the legal right to control what is done to their bodies when they become mentally disabled and hence

---

[7] 211 N.Y. 125, 105 N.E. 92 (1914).

[8] 105 N.E. at 93. *See also In re* Storar, 52 N.Y.2d 363, 438 N.Y.S.2d 266, 420 N.E.2d 64, *cert. denied,* 454 U.S. 858 (1981); Cobbs v. Grant, 8 Cal. 3d 229, 502 P.2d 1, 104 Cal Rptr. 505 (1972).

[9] *In re* Quinlan, 70 N.J. 10, 355 A.2d 647, *cert. denied sub nom.* Garger v. New Jersey, 429 U.S. 922 (1976), *overruled in part, In re* Conroy, 98 N.J. 321, 486 A.2d 1209 (1985); Superintendent of Belchertown State School v. Saikewicz, 373 Mass. 728, 370 N.E.2d 417 (1977); Satz v. Perlmutter, 362 So. 2d 160 (Fla. Dist. Ct. App. 1978), *aff'd,* 379 So. 2d 359 (Fla. 1980).

[10] *See, e.g.,* Leach v. Shapiro, 13 Ohio App. 3d 393, 469 N.E.2d 1047 (1984).

[11] Scholendorf v. Society of New York Hospitals, 211 N.Y. 125, 105 N.E. 92 (1914); Cobbs v. Grant, 8 Cal. 3d 229, 502 P.2d 1, 104 Cal. Rptr. 505 (1972). *See also* W. PROSSER, THE LAW OF TORTS 161-64 (4th ed. 1971).

[12] *In re* Conroy, 98 N.J. 321, 486 A.2d 1209 (1985); Zebarth v. Swedish Hospital Medical Center, 18 Wash. 2d 12, 499 P.2d 1 (1967); Barber v. Superior Court, 147 Cal. App. 3d 1006, 195 Cal. Rptr. 484 (1983).

unable to directly exercise this right.[13] Living wills are designed to maximally extend a patient's right of self-determination into and through periods of incompetency.

B. Interpretive Standard for Living Wills: Substituted Judgment

Health care providers are expected to apply the legal standard of "substituted judgment" in interpreting the directives of living wills. This standard requires that those responsible for the declarant's medical care ask: what would the patient choose in this situation? Treatment is to be administered, withdrawn, or withheld in accord with the answer derived from this exercise.[14]

Two other legal standards for determining the proper response to an incompetent person's medical condition are thus inappropriate for interpreting the directives of a living will: the "best interest" standard and the "reasonable person" standard. According to the former, physicians are to do everything that will maximally benefit the patient, presumably without excessive burdens. According to the second standard, appropriate treatment is that treatment which a reasonable person in the patient's circumstances would choose if knowledgeable about the risks and benefits of alternative treatment modalities and the alternative of doing nothing at all. The reasonable person standard systematically removes from consideration possible or known idiosyncratic views and values of the particular incompetent patient for whom treatment decisions are being made.[15] The standard would seem to require empirical evidence concerning typical reactions of people under similar circumstances. Otherwise it runs the risk of collapsing into the privatized judgment of some individual, such as a physician, who asks not what this patient would choose, but "what I would want."[16]

---

[13] *In re* Quinlan, 70 N.J. 10, 355 A.2d 647, *cert. denied sub nom.* Garger v. New Jersey, 429 U.S. 922 (1976), *overruled in part, In re* Conroy, 98 N.J. 321, 486 A.2d 1209 (1985); Barber v. Superior Court, 147 Cal App. 3d 1006, 195 Cal. Rptr. 484 (1983); John F. Kennedy Memorial Hospital, Inc. v. Bludworth, 452 So. 2d 921 (Fla. 1984).

[14] Superintendent of Belchertown State School v. Saikewicz, 373 Mass. 728, 370 N.E.2d 417 (1977). *See also* Curreri, *Incompetent's Right to Choose Medical Treatment: Substituted Judgments and Protection of Personal Autonomy*, 33 MED. TRIAL TECH. Q. 1, 10-17 (1986). For a vigorous argument opposing the use of the substituted judgment standard by courts in determining whether life-supporting medical treatment should be withheld or withdrawn from incompetent patients see Weber, *Substituted Judgment Doctrine: A Critical Analysis*, 1 ISSUES IN L. & MED. 131 (1985).

[15] Buchanan, *The Limits of Proxy Decisionmaking for Incompetents*, 29 U.C.L.A. L. REV. 386, 396-97 (1981).

[16] Jackson & Youngner, *Patient Autonomy and "Death With Dignity,"* 301 NEW ENG. J. MED. 404, 408 (1979).

Substituted judgment is the correct standard to use in interpreting the directives of a living will because the right of self-determination which living wills are designed to protect is legally defined as "the right to make one's own choice, regardless of whether it agrees with what most reasonable people would want or is in one's best interest."[17] The right of self-determination is not an unqualified right, however. It stands in tension with numerous state interests to which courts on occasion give precedence: (1) the preservation of life;[18] (2) the protection of innocent third parties;[19] (3) safeguarding the public health;[20] and, (4) the prevention of suicide.[21] Robertson summarizes the conditions under which courts are likely to give precedence to these state interests in cases where a competent patient refuses medical treatment:

> When the person is not terminally ill, doctors will be more reluctant to honor the patient's refusal, and the courts are more likely to find the state's interests compelling. If the medical treatment necessary to keep the patient alive is not highly intrusive or painful, and the patient will be restored to a healthful condition, the courts are more likely to find that these [state] interests outweigh the patient's interest in self-determination.[22]

In general, however, courts tend to give preponderant weight to the right of self-determination when it conflicts with these state interests.[23]

How well do living wills extend and protect this fundamental right for once-competent patients who have become incapacitated? Poorly, in the author's view. After reviewing some of the patent disadvantages of

---

[17] *See* Buchanan, *supra* note 15, at 393. *See also* Superintendent of Belchertown State School v. Saikewicz, 373 Mass. 728, 370 N.E.2d 417 (1977); *In re* Estate of Brooks, 32 Ill. 2d 361, 205 N.E.2d 435 (1965).

[18] *In re* Caulk, 125 N.H. 226, 480 A.2d 93 (1984); Bouvia v. Superior Court 179 Cal. App. 3d 1127, 225 Cal. Rptr. 297, *review denied* (Cal. June 5, 1986); Brophy v. New England Sinai Hospital Inc., 398 Mass. 417, 497 N.E.2d 626 (1986); John F. Kennedy Memorial Hospital v. Heston, 58 N.J. 576, 279 A.2d 670 (1971); Application of President & Directors of Georgetown College, Inc., 118 U.S. App. D.C. 80, 331 F.2d 1000, *cert. denied*, 377 U.S. 978 (1964).

[19] United States v. George, 239 F. Supp. 752 (D. Conn. 1965); Raleigh-Fitkin-Paul Morgan Hospital v. Anderson, 42 N.J. 421, 201 A.2d 537, *cert. denied*, 377 U.S. 985 (1964).

[20] Jacobson v. Massachusetts, 197 U.S. 11 (1905).

[21] Bouvia v. Superior Court, 179 Cal. App. 3d 1127, 225 Cal. Rptr. 297 (1986), *review denied* (Cal. June 5, 1986); John F. Kennedy Memorial Hospital v. Heston, 58 N.J. 576, 279 A.2d 670 (1971).

[22] J. ROBERTSON, THE RIGHTS OF THE CRITICALLY ILL 34 (1983).

[23] Superintendent of Belchertown State School v. Saikewicz, 373 Mass. 728, 370 N.E.2d 417 (1977); *In re* Conroy, 98 N.J. 321, 486 A.2d 1209 (1985); Lane v. Candura, 6 Mass. App. 377, 376 N.E.2d 1232 (1978); *In re* Quackenbush, 156 N.J. Super. 282, 383 A.2d 785 (1978); Bartling v. Superior Court, 163 Cal. App. 3d 186, 209 Cal. Rptr. 220 (1984), 2 Civ. No. B017666 (Super. Ct. No. C500735) (Cal Ct. App. 2d Dist. Aug. 7, 1986) (attorney's fee decision), No. B015766 (Super. Ct. No. C500735) (Cal. Ct. App. 2d Dist. Aug. 25, 1986) (civil liability decision).

living wills, it becomes clear that it makes sense for anyone who is contemplating executing a living will to substitute for it a more effective but not necessarily more complicated legal instrument aimed at achieving the same autonomy-protecting goals as a living will, a Durable Power of Attorney for Health Care.

II. PRACTICAL DISADVANTAGES OF LIVING WILLS

A. The Unduly Narrow Scope of Living Wills

Most state natural death acts permit a person to direct, by means of the state approved living will form, the withdrawal or withholding of life-sustaining procedures in situations in which the declarant is incompetent and afflicted with a terminal condition. "Terminal condition" is variously defined in these statutes. For example, Arizona's "Medical Treatment Decision Act" defines a terminal condition as an "incurable or irreversible condition from which... death will occur without the use of life-sustaining procedures."[24] Delaware's "Death With Dignity Act" defines "terminal condition" as a condition from which there is no reasonable expectation of recovery and which, as a medical probability, will result in death regardless of whether artificial life-sustaining procedures are used.[25]

A practical problem posed by the terminal condition restriction is that there are non-terminal conditions which many or most people regard as pointless and undesirable, and thus unworthy of being treated with life-prolonging procedures, such as irreversible comas and persistent vegetative states.[26] Karen Quinlan remained in a persistent vegetative state for more than 10 years before dying on June 11, 1985. For a decade, her brain-stem, that part of the brain controlling important visceral functions

---

[24] ARIZ. REV. STAT. ANN. §§36-3201 (1986). For a discussion of the distinction between "incurable" and "irreversible" conditions and whether living wills should define "terminal condition" by reference to the conjunction or disjunction of these two terms see Marzen, The "Uniform Rights of the Terminally Ill Act": A Critical Analysis, 1 ISSUES IN L. & MED. 441, 460-65 (1986).

[25] DEL. CODE ANN. tit. 16 §2501 (1986). For a defense of the former, less restrictive formulation, see commentary to THE UNIFORM RIGHTS OF THE TERMINALLY ILL ACT, National Conference of Commissioners on Uniform State Laws (1985), in SOCIETY FOR THE RIGHT TO DIE, HANDBOOK OF 1985 LIVING WILL LAWS 35 (1986).

[26] Most Respondents Favor Ending Life Support, AM. MED. NEWS, Nov. 28, 1986, at 17. On the distinction between comas and persistent vegetative states see Hansotia, Persistent Vegetative States: Review and Report of Electrodiagnostic Studies in Eight Cases, 42 ARCHIVES OF NEUROLOGY 1048 (1985).

like heartbeat and respiration, functioned efficiently. But there is little scientific reason for believing that during this time Karen had any subjective experience of herself or of her surroundings.

Paul Hoffman, chairman of the American Hospital Association Advisory Committee on Bioethics, reported that, in April of 1986, 10,000 patients were hospitalized in persistent vegetative states in this country.[27] While these patients are not suffering (they sense nothing), their plight takes its toll on others—emotionally and financially. Besides causing anxiety and grief for their families and attending medical personnel, such patients are expensive to maintain. According to Hoffman, the average cost in 1986 for sustaining an individual in a persistent vegetative state was $125,000-$150,000 annually.[28] A living will adequate to protect the autonomy interests of most people would not limit its sphere of application to circumstances in which the declarant is incompetent and afflicted with an underlying terminal condition.

Moreover, living wills, limited by the terminal condition restriction, leave murky important questions concerning the legal validity of a person's prior oral statements opposing life-sustaining therapy in cases of irreversible incompetence absent an accompanying terminal condition. Can a physician rely on this evidence in making treatment/nontreatment decisions?

The probative weight attached by courts to prior oral directives of currently incompetent patients varies depending on the following considerations: (1) the nature of the circumstances in which the statements were uttered (were the circumstances casual or formal?); (2) the length of time between the onset of the mental impairment and the patient's declaration (might the patient's views have changed since then?); and, (3) how consistent the patient's prior oral request is with normal medical practice (inconsistency might be construed as evidence of the patient's incompetency at the time the directive was made). In general, the legal acceptability of an incapacitated patient's prior oral instructions concerning treatment in the event of incompetency increases the more formal the circumstances under which they are given, the more recent the declaration, and the more consistent the statement is with standard medical procedure.[29]

---

[27] *Increased Attention Sought on Bioethical Concerns*, AM. MED. NEWS, May 9, 1986, at 54.
[28] *Id.*
[29] Note, *Appointing an Agent to Make Medical Treatment Choices*, 84 COLUM. L. REV. 985, 996-98 (1984).

Advance written directives concerning one's medical care under medical disability, witnessed by persons who attest that the declarant was competent at the time of the document's execution, have the greatest initial authority in courts of law. Upon reflection, as we have said, most people would probably want the strongest legal assurance that their advance requests regarding the withdrawal or withholding of life-sustaining treatment will be honored if they are afflicted with a permanent neurological impairment like an irreversible coma or persistent vegetative state. Standard living will forms which speak only to the situation in which the declarant is incompetent and has a terminal condition are too narrow, therefore, to implement the broader protections most individuals actually desire. Most natural death acts permit individuals to vary the state-approved living will form—to amend it or construct a new one.[30] But even more broadly constructed documents are likely to be inadequate for reasons now to be considered.

B. Problems Interpreting Living Wills

One of the earliest and most widely used living will forms was developed by the Concern for Dying organization (formerly the Euthanasia Council). The document does not confine its scope to medical decisions made for incompetent terminal patients. Its central provisions read as follows:

> If a situation should arise in which there is no reasonable expectation of my recovery from physical or mental disability, I request that I be allowed to die and not be kept alive by artificial means or heroic measures. I do not fear death itself as much as the indignities of deterioration, dependence, and hopeless pain. I therefore ask that medications be mercifully administered to me to alleviate suffering, even though this may hasten the moment of death.[31]

The text contains references to numerous quality-of-life concepts: "recovery," "physical or mental disabilities," "deterioration," "dependence," "hopeless pain," etc. Sometimes it is difficult for those who must interpret these terms to determine whether the patient's existing or predicted health state is or will be an instance of a type addressed by a living will. Eisendrath and Jonsen describe the case of a 65-year-old woman who became incompetent from a stroke suffered while recuperating from surgery.[32] Prior to surgery she called to her physician's attention

---

[30] SOCIETY FOR THE RIGHT TO DIE, HANDBOOK OF 1985 LIVING WILL LAWS 28-32 (1986).

[31] CONCERN FOR DYING—AN EDUCATIONAL COUNCIL, A LIVING WILL (3d ed. 1978).

[32] Eisendrath & Jonsen, *The Living Will: Help or Hindrance?*, 249 J.A.M.A. 2054, 2055-58 (1983

a living will she had signed four years earlier (the Concern for Dying form). During the week following the stroke, she developed aspiration pneumonia. A tracheostomy was performed to control her ventilation. Her prognosis was uncertain. Some members of the medical team questioned the decision to continue acute care. They contended that, "if they persisted, the patient would end up trapped in a poorly functioning body, unable to even take her own life should she desire to do so. As a previously vigorous woman [the dissenting staff claimed], this is precisely what she did not want. . . . "[33] This patient, as it turned out, made a remarkable comeback after three weeks. She was discharged to a rehabilitation center a week later.

Eisendrath and Jonsen reflect on the early conflict between those physicians who pursued aggressive care for the patient and other staff members who objected to this response on the ground that it was contrary to the directives contained in the patient's living will. The first problem was the gross uncertainty about the level of functioning to which the patient might be restored under aggressive therapy. Given the highly indeterminate prognosis, attending physicians followed the rule: "When in doubt, favor life."

The second issue concerned the interpretation of the quality of life language contained in the patient's living will. What did the patient mean by the phrase "no reasonable expectation of my recovery from physical or mental disability"? What notion of "reasonable" did she have in mind? A 50 percent chance or better? If not, what? What level of disability would she accept as compatible with "recovery"? Eisendrath and Jonsen ask: "Had the patient meant by her recovery that she'd be able to play her usual round of golf or move around in a wheelchair?"[34]

A recent model living will published by the Society for the Right to Die seems to perpetuate the kinds of problems connected with the traditional Concern for Dying form. The key paragraph of the document reads as follows: "I direct that life-sustaining procedures be withheld or withdrawn if I have an illness, disease or injury, or experience extreme mental deterioration, such that there is no reasonable expectation of recovering or regaining a meaningful quality of life."[35] As Bok comments in another context: "[T]hose who take care of patients with [vaguely worded] living wills are often going to interpret the key words

---

[33] *Id.* at 2056.
[34] *Id.*
[35] Society for the Right to Die, The Physician and the Hopelessly Ill Patient 86 (1985).

according to what they already think it best to do. In this way they might at times do less than the patient might have wished, and at other times much more."[36]

Interpretive problems can be mitigated if more specific information is provided in the document itself concerning the types of treatment modalities, outcomes, risk-benefit ratios, etc., that the declarant regards as acceptable or unacceptable. Consider, for example, the following excerpt from a personally drafted living will:

> If intervention involves the loss either of a receiving sense or a form of communication with the rest of the world, I wish this to be considered in the following way: I would be willing to risk intervention which might involve my continuing to live blind alone *or* deaf alone, *or* incapable of movement of the lower half of my body. If further impairment were risked, I would be willing to live blind if I were able to hear and speak, or deaf if I were able to see and to write. In other words, I would want to be certain of being able to receive communications from others and of communicating with others in appropriately related ways.[37]

This kind of detailed information obviously is more useful to those seeking guidance from a living will than the unelaborated general terminology of the forms discussed above. It reduces the probability that the declarant's statements will be misinterpreted and thus better enables physicians to act in accord with the patient's true wishes. From the patient's perspective, such specificity increases the real power of the right of self-determination which living wills are principally designed to protect.

But specificity has practical limits. How omniscient can one be about the types of illnesses, injuries, and dysfunctions that might befall one in the future, the range of therapeutic options available at the time, and the risk-benefit ratios of each as related to one's medical profile? It is impossible to provide instructions concerning all such contingencies. Physicians obliged to abide by the standard of substituted judgment will in many cases still have to interpret the directives of a living will. When vagaries exist, whose proxy judgment for the patient is to be taken as authoritative?

It is customary to seek the advice of the patient's immediate family in such circumstances. The practice is based on the reasonable belief that family members are most familiar with the patient's value orientation and

---

[36] Bok, *Personal Directions for Care at the End of Life*, 295 NEW ENG. J. MED. 367, 368 (1976).
[37] Modell, *A "Will" to Live*, 290 NEW ENG. J. MED. 907, 908 (1974).

hence can comment most authoritatively on what the patient would choose in this circumstance if the patient were competent. While this is a defensible strategy, it still harbors numerous practical difficulties. Suppose family members, guided by the patient's statements in the living will, disagree among themselves about what the patient would want done in the present situation.[38] Or suppose the family holds to one interpretation of the document's instructions but the attending physician holds to another? Amidst this kind of disagreement among legitimate proxy voices for the patient, whose word is to be believed?

Other complicating scenarios are possible and are sometimes realized. Suppose an incompetent patient's wife and children agree that life-sustaining therapy should be withdrawn from the patient (in accord with his written or oral directions). Suppose further that the patient has a sister who has not seen him in 15 years. She arrives at the hospital and, ridden with guilt about her past relationship with her brother, insists that everything be done, i.e., that life-sustaining procedures be continued. Assume also that she has a dominating personality and intimidates the patient's immediate family into agreeing to continue treatment. Upon consulting the family, the physician finds a family consensus to continue treatment. Here again the question arises: is the patient's sister, who actually controls the course of the patient's care, the person whom the patient would have chosen to speak for him in the circumstance? Perhaps not. But how can this situation be prevented?

These problems could be resolved by a strategy which provides a consistent and more powerful extension of the right of self-determination which living wills are designed to further—a person's advance appointment of a proxy authorized to make medical decisions for him or her in the event he or she becomes incompetent. The "Directive to Physician" forms officially approved by natural death acts in nine states permit and encourage declarants to name individuals to serve as surrogate medical decisionmakers should they become incapacitated.[39] As the discussion in the next section will show, state-approved directives which provide for the appointment of a medical proxy recognize and employ the legal power called the "durable power of attorney for health care" even though they are called "living wills" rather than durable power of attorney instruments.

An effort will be made to show that it not only makes great practical sense for individuals to employ this power in extending personal control

---

[38] *See, e.g., In re* Nemser, 51 Misc. 2d 616, 273 N.Y.S. 2d 624 (Sup. Ct. 1966).

[39] SOCIETY FOR THE RIGHT TO DIE, *supra* note 30, at 28-32.

over their medical treatment while they are incompetent, but that it makes equally good sense to incorporate into the document establishing the medical agency certain explicit extensions of and limitations upon the proxy's liberties and responsibilities. Agent-appointing documents with these kinds of provisions are durable power of attorney for health care instruments in a model sense. The superior value of such "duly elaborated" DPAHC forms will be shown as compared with advance directives which exclude the designation of a medical agent, no matter how detailed the instructions may be in the latter documents.

III. THE DURABLE POWER OF ATTORNEY FOR HEALTH CARE—STRUCTURE, ADVANTAGES, AND RISKS

A. Nature and Function of the DPAHC

What is a DPAHC and how does it work? Three important concepts are involved in the instrument's title. It is a "power of attorney" which is "durable" and concerned with health care decisions.

Most people are familiar with the legal power called "power of attorney." In a power of attorney relationship, a party, A, authorizes another party, B, to act in A's stead when A is absent. B's decisions concerning those matters over which A gives B control (usually certain personal and property interests) carry the same legal weight as if A personally made these decisions. For example, A might empower B to disburse funds from A's bank account, sell securities or a land parcel for A, etc. A thus becomes the "principal" in this relationship and B is called the "attorney-in-fact," or, simply, A's "agent."

The standard power of attorney mechanism has an important restriction, however. Under legal rules governing the power of attorney, an agent is not permitted to conduct personal and property affairs for the principal if the latter becomes incapacitated and hence is unable to monitor, even in theory, the agent's actions.[40] This common law restriction on an agent's authority is designed to protect the principal from harmful actions performed by the agent when the principal is incompetent and unable to oversee the proxy's decisions.

This defensible limit on an agent's authority constitutes an important disadvantage of standard power of attorney relationships, however: the

---

[40] RESTATEMENT (SECOND) OF AGENCY §122 (1957); 24 C.J.S. *Agency* §§135-41.

agent's authority ceases at the very moment when the principal is incompetent and decisions concerning personal or property interests must still be made.[41]

The durable power of attorney is a power of attorney that survives the incapacity of the principal. It is typically used for the same purposes as the nondurable power of attorney, namely, for conducting a principal's personal or property affairs. All 50 states have adopted durable power of attorney statutes.[42] Recently, however, the device has been creatively extended to cover medical decisions made by an agent for an incapacitated principal. This novel extension of the power is technically called the durable power of attorney for *health care*. Four states—California, Colorado, Pennsylvania, and Rhode Island—explicitly recognize in their durable power of attorney statutes this expanded application of the power. It is important to determine, however, whether the scope of an agent's power under standard durable power of attorney legislation in the other 46 states—call these collectively "nonstatutory states"—is wide enough to include medical decisionmaking for an incapacitated principal.

In a careful 1984 study of durable power of attorney legislation in nonstatutory states, Fowler convincingly argued that there is no compelling historical or textual reason for holding that an agent's power under these laws cannot be legitimately extended through an appropriately drafted instrument to include the power to make medical decisions for an incompetent principal.[43]

Fowler points out that durable power of attorney statutes in most states are based on either the Model Special Power of Attorney for Small Property Interests Act (MSPA) of 1964, or the Uniform Probate Code (UPC) originally drafted in 1969.[44] Both of these documents were developed by the National Conference of Commissioners on Uniform State Laws (NCCUSL). Despite its title, the MSPA applies not just to property interests of a principal but to "personal" interests as well. The text of the Act says that the legal power of a proxy "may be restricted" or that an agent may be granted "complete authority to provide for the care of the principal's person and property."[45]

---

[41] E. COHEN, DURABLE POWER OF ATTORNEY: AN IMPORTANT ALTERNATIVE TO GUARDIANSHIP, CONSERVATORSHIP, OR TRUSTEESHIP 2 (1985).

[42] Rouse, *Questions and Answers: The Legal Aspects of Allowing to Die*, in SOCIETY FOR THE RIGHT TO DIE, THE PHYSICIAN AND THE HOPELESSLY ILL PATIENT 17 (1985).

[43] Note, *supra* note 29, at 1008-21.

[44] *Id.* at 1016-20.

[45] Model Special Power of Attorney Act §2, in 1964 PROC. NAT'L CONF. COM'N UNIF. STATE L. 276.

Fowler cites three reasons for believing that the language of the MSPA is broad enough to embrace the appointment of a medical agent. First, the Act specifically mentions "injury" and "disease" as causes of incompetency. Second, since medical care is understandably of special concern to an incompetent individual, it is reasonable to believe that the Commissioners intended medical care to be included within the sphere of those "personal interests" covered by the Act. Finally, the Act itself does not mention any specific applications of the durable power of attorney to personal matters. The range of application is open.[46]

The other standard model for state durable power of attorney statutes, the UPC, does not say anything about the types of interests which are within the scope of its durable power of attorney provisions. All it says is that any decisions made by a durable agent have the same legal force as if they were made by the principal. But, as Fowler points out, the durable power of attorney section of the UPC is aimed at giving to a durable agent those powers which a nondurable agent could exercise under pre-existing law. Under traditional civil law, a nondurable agent can act with respect to a wide range of the principal's interests, including personal interests.[47] Fowler argues that had the Commissioners intended to exclude personal interests from the class of interests which a durable agent could represent, the Commissioners could have expressly stated this in the UPC.

Moreover, Fowler points out, the NCCUSL promulgated the Model Health Care Consent Act in 1984. This Act specifically provides for the appointment of a medical agent. In commenting on the substance of this Act, the Commissioners state that this type of appointment can already be made in any state that has adopted an amendment to the UPC drafted by the Commissioners in 1979 called the Uniform Durable Power of Attorney Act. Fowler argues that since this amendment "simply parrots the relevant language contained in the original version of the UPC, the Commissioners appear to have endorsed, by transitivity, the position that health-care agents may also be appointed in all states that have adopted the original UPC or a close analogue."[48]

Fowler further observes that Colorado's power of attorney statute is based on the UPC and the text of that legislation expressly says that an agent's authority "includes by way of illustration but not limitation the

---

[46] Note, *supra* note 29, at 1017.
[47] *See* Note, *supra* note 29, at 1018 n.211.
[48] *Id.* at 1019.

power to consent or approve on behalf of the principal any medical or other professional care."[49] Thus, Fowler concludes, the appointment of a medical agent is a legitimate extension of state durable power of attorney statutes based on either the MSPA or the UPC.

Appointing an agent to make these kinds of decisions has numerous advantages over simply relying on directives contained in a living will. The following advantages, again, are cited by Fowler.

B. Advantages of the Durable Power of Attorney for Health Care

Since the agent has been personally picked by the principal, doubtless because the principal knows and trusts the person to make these important decisions, the probability is quite high that the agent's decisions will faithfully reflect the values and wishes of the principal better than anyone else who might be consulted.

The DPAHC also avoids the difficulty, inherent in living wills, of trying to provide instructions concerning treatment alternatives (or nontreatment) under the myriad of different medical conditions that might arise. An agent can, according to Fowler,

> ask questions, assess risks and costs, speak to friends and relatives of the patient, consider a variety of therapeutic options, seek the opinions of other physicians, evaluate the patient's condition and prospects for recovery—in short, engage in the same complex decision-making process that the patient himself would undertake if he were able.[50]

Moreover, an agent can "enforce the patient's treatment preferences, and ensure that they are not disregarded or forgotten by family members or physicians."[51] The DPAHC can also prevent critical decisions being made by a relative whom the principal considers untrustworthy and not fully in touch with and committed to advancing the principal's values and desires.

Physicians relying on health care directives of an incompetent patient's personally designated and legally recognized agent in all probability will be less vulnerable to legal reprisals or professional censure than if they rely on the informal consent of a relative. The DPAHC resolves uncertainty about who is authorized to consent for the incapacitated patient. It also resolves the problem of determining what should be done when relatives are in disagreement[52] or when the family disagrees

---

[49] COLO. REV. STAT. §15-14-501 (Supp. 1983).

[50] Note, *supra* note 29, at 1001.

[51] *Id.*

[52] Lo & Jonsen, *Clinical Decisions to Limit Treatment*, 93 ANNALS INT. MED. 764, 766 (1980).

with the physician(s). Providers will therefore have less need to resort to the courts when such disagreements arise, saving on legal costs for the hospital and for the patient's family. The patient also will be spared needless or useless intervention while the case is being litigated, and courts will doubtless not be called upon as often to resolve disputes between family members or between the family and health care staff concerning the proper response to an incompetent patient's medical condition.[53] Since an agent's decision is authoritative, physicians would not be required to obtain a consensus among family members concerning a patient's treatment (although this might still serve as an ideal). Beyond this, as Fowler says, "an agent, unlike a living will, gives doctors someone to talk to, someone who is empowered to make decisions," surmounting the problem of interpreting by guesswork the often vague terms of a living will.[54] Agency also "conforms more closely than a living will to the legal model of informed consent."[55] A final advantage of the DPAHC for physicians is that it solves substituted judgment problems for physicians meeting an acutely ill incompetent patient for the first time.

C. Some Worries About the DPAHC and Replies

1. Is the Scope of an Agent's Authority Under a DPAHC Dangerously Wide?

As stated earlier, the general rule is that an agent is empowered to do anything the principal is legally free to do. Can an agent thus order the withdrawal of artificial feeding and hydrating devices from an incompetent principal who has specifically requested in a DPAHC document that this be done under the circumstances now obtaining? This depends on whether legislation or case law in the jurisdiction where the DPAHC is in effect countenances the withdrawal or withholding of such devices at the request of competent patients,[56] or for incompetent patients by action or request of others.[57] The point is simply that an agent is never empowered

---

[53] Note, *supra* note 29, at 1004.

[54] *Id.* at 1005.

[55] *Id.*

[56] Bouvia v. Superior Court, 179 Cal. App. 1127, 225 Cal. Rptr. 297, *review denied* (Cal. June 5, 1986); *In re* Rodas, No. 86PR139 (Colo. Dist. Ct. Mesa County Jan. 22, 1987); *In re* Requena, No. P-326-86E (N.J. Super. Ct. Ch. Div. Sept. 24, 1986), *aff'd* No. A-442-86T5 (N.J. Super. Ct. App. Div. Oct. 6, 1986) (*per curiam*).

[57] *In re* Conroy, 98 N.J. 321, 486 A.2d 1209 (1985); Barber v. Superior Court, 147 Cal. App. 3d 1006, 195 Cal. Rptr. 484 (1983); Brophy v. New England Sinai Hospital, Inc., 398 Mass. 417, 497

to do anything illegal, irrespective of whether the principal requests such action in a DPAHC document.

In most jurisdictions, it is fairly safe to say that if a principal formally requested (in a DPAHC instrument) that he or she be given a lethal dose of drugs in the event of terminal illness, the agent would not be permitted to personally administer the drugs or order another individual to do so. The prospect may be more hopeful, however, for other types of controversial directives which a principal might include in a DPAHC document.

Suppose, for example, that a principal gave the following instructions in the DPAHC form:

> If I am blighted with Alzheimer's Disease or other severe neurological disease or similar condition in which there is no hope for me regaining a reasonable quality of life as discussed with my agent, I do not want to be maintained on antibiotics or artificial feeding or be put on a respirator.[58]

A court might rule that this directive is valid and should be implemented on the grounds accepted by the final courts of review in *Barber v. Superior Court*[59] and *Brophy v. New England Sinai Hospital, Inc.*[60] In the former case, the patient, Clarence Herbert, suffered brain damage and entered a vegetative state after a cardiopulmonary arrest following surgery to close an ileostomy. The vegetative state was judged likely to be permanent. Herbert's family prepared a written request calling for the cessation of all life-sustaining procedures. The attending physicians first removed Herbert from the respirator. Later they directed that artificial feeding and hydrating be stopped. The state of California brought criminal charges against the physicians. The California Court of Appeal, however, in a writ of prohibition, declared that murder and conspiracy charges could not be brought against the physicians.

Paul Brophy, age 45, suffered a brain hemorrhage as a result of an aneurysm. Following surgery, he lapsed into a persistent vegetative state that was judged to be irreversible. His wife requested that artificial feeding and hydration be stopped, stating that her husband would never approve this procedure under the circumstances. On appeal, the Mas-

---

N.E.2d 626 (1986); *In re* Bayer, No. 4131 (N.D. Burleigh County Ct. Feb. 5, 11, 1987); *In re* Jobes, 210 N.J. Super. 543, 510 A.2d 133 (Super. Ct. Ch. Div.), *review denied* (N.J. March 10, 1986). *Contra* Connecticut Death With Dignity Act, 1985 CONN. ACTS 85-606 (Reg. Sess.); Maine Living Wills Act, ME. REV. STAT. ANN. tit. 22, §2921(4).

[58] Personal communication with D. Robbins, Levine Institute on Aging, Detroit, MI (1985).
[59] 147 Cal. App. 3d 1006, 195 Cal. Rptr. 484 (1983).
[60] 398 Mass. 417, 497 N.E.2d 626 (1986).

sachusetts Supreme Court held that the substituted judgment of an incapacitated person in a persistent vegetative state to have artificial sustenance terminated must be honored. Since courts tend, as a rule, to give preponderant weight to a competent patient's personal decisions concerning health care, an advance directive containing a declaration like the one quoted above will carry great initial authority under judicial review. Individuals should therefore be encouraged and exhorted to include similar instructions in their DPAHC documents if they want to control the kinds of treatment they receive in similar situations.

2. Challenging the Correctness of an Agent's Decision

It might still be objected that a medical agent could make a decision for an incompetent principal that is inconsistent with the principal's desires or antithetical to the principal's best interests. The most appropriate initial reply to this objection is that those who make surrogate decisions for incapacitated patients by consulting these patients' living wills are liable to make the same errors of judgment. Such errors are probably less likely to occur, however, when the individual making the decision is someone who has been personally appointed by the principal.

The objection may hide a deeper question: can an agent's decision be challenged and even overridden? Obviously such a challenge may be posed in the context of litigation. It is important, however, to be clear about the nature of the burden that must be borne by those who contest a decision by a patient-appointed proxy. The question that must first be addressed may be put in two ways: Is the agent's decision consistent with the principal's known wishes? Would the patient make the same choice if competent? Suppose that in the DPAHC document the principal enumerates various medical circumstances that might develop, and offers specific instructions about treatment under these conditions. If the agent's decision is arguably consistent with these directives, the agent will or should be vindicated under judicial scrutiny.

But suppose the objector argues that the proxy's choice is contrary to the patient's best interests. This claim, even if well substantiated, evades the fundamental issue of patient choice which is at stake in the first phase of the inquiry. Hence it fails to meet the burden of proof required. The patient's exercise of the right of self-determination should be more compelling. On the other hand, if the incompetent patient has not given specific instructions in the DPAHC document pertaining to the present medical circumstance and if plausible alternative claims can be advanced about what the patient would have chosen under these conditions (by appeal to additional prior written or oral statements by the principal), then this type of challenge to an agent's decision would likely be upheld under judicial review. It must be understood, however, that only after determining that no conclusive answer can be given to the question of what the patient would have chosen under present conditions can the discussion properly shift to the quite different question of what is in the patient's best interests.

Even granting the legitimacy of the worries cited above concerning the use of the DPAHC, this device is still a more effective instrument for guaranteeing a patient's control over medical treatment during incompetency than the living will.

IV. CONSIDERATION OF TYPICAL DPAHC FORMS

This section offers suggestions for consideration in the development of DPAHC forms. The recommendations are based on numerous model documents published in the medical and legal literature. Being aware of the range of provisions that an instrument like this might contain can be of great assistance in fashioning documents that are informed, reflective, and personally suitable to patient wishes and concerns.

A. Standard Formalities

1. Document Title, Statement of Appointment, Statutory Justification

The title should identify the document's function. Specifically, it should be recited that the document establishes a durable power of attorney for health care decisions. The instrument's statutory basis, if any, should be cited, preferably early in the text, and the attorney-in-fact should be designated.

2. "Springing Power" Clause

For the conduct of some personal and property matters, a principal may appoint an agent to make decisions both while the principal is competent and in the event of incompetence. With health care decisions, however, the principal expects to make these decisions personally so long as he or she is able. The agent's authority will begin, then, at the moment when the principal becomes incapacitated. The point at which the agent's power becomes activated should therefore be stated in the document by a "springing power" clause like the following: "This power of attorney shall become effective upon the disability or incapacity of the principal.... "

3. *Signature by Principal, Witnesses, and Notary*

The principal must of course sign and date the document. A notary and at least two witnesses should sign the form attesting that the principal is of sound mind and under no duress, fraud, or undue influence at the time of executing the instrument. Credibility of the witnesses' attestations will be increased if at least one of them signs a declaration that he or she is unrelated to the principal by blood, marriage, or adoption, and not an heir to any portion of the principal's estate under an existing will or by operation of law. If the principal is a patient in a skilled care nursing facility, one of the witnesses should be a patient advocate or ombudsperson. For maximum self-protection, the principal should avoid selecting as witnesses the appointed agent, a health care provider or employee of a health care provider, or an employee of an inpatient facility where the principal may be hospitalized.[61]

A person executing a DPAHC instrument should deliver one copy of the document to the appointed agent and another to the principal's physician. A third copy should be kept in a readily available personal file. It would also be helpful for the person to carry in a wallet or purse a card indicating that a durable agency relationship exists and identifying the agent.

B. Substantive Provisions

1. *Endorsement of the Agent's Capacity to Knowledgeably Represent the Principal*

While it may be assumed that the person the principal selects as agent will be someone especially trusted by the principal, the principal's express affirmation in the DPAHC instrument itself of this level of confidence in the agent will establish the agent's authority to speak for the principal when the latter is incapacitated. The following example is suggested by Robbins:

> __(name of agent)__ is someone I trust with my life and accordingly someone who is aware of my innermost feelings and values surrounding my wishes. I appreciate (his/her) ability to weigh risks, alternatives, benefits, to explore and assess therapeutic options, and to engage in the same aggressive decision-

---

[61] Collins, *Breathing Life Into Wisconsin's "Living Will" Statute*, 58 WIS. BAR. BULL. 11, 13 (1985).

making that I would perform if I were competent and able. (His/her) decision is final and binding as if it were mine. No competing interests of family members or third parties shall interfere with or compromise (his/her) decision. We have discussed my wishes at length and discussed those situations which I might anticipate and I have given (him/her) guidance. For those decisions we have not discussed, I vest decision-making with (him/her) rather than in some other impartial third party including family members which might confuse or complicate decision-making.[62]

2. Statement of Powers Expressly Granted to Attorney-in-Fact and Limitations

A detailed specification of the scope of the agent's authority is appropriate and desirable. This may be done in a general and brief statement (example *a* below) or in a more detailed manner (example *b*):

(a) If I become incapable of giving informed consent for health care decisions, I hereby grant to my agent full power and authority to make health care decisions for me including the right to consent, refuse consent, or withdraw consent to any care, treatment, service, or procedure to maintain, diagnose or treat a physical or mental condition, and to consent to the release of medical information, subject to the statement of desires, special provisions, and limitations set out [below]....[63]

(b) As to decisions related to my health care, I hereby grant the following powers to my attorney-in-fact within the limits specified [below]:
  1. To authorize or withhold authorization for medical and surgical procedures.
  2. To authorize my admission to a medical, nursing, residential, or similar facility and to enter into agreements for my care.
  3. To arrange for my discharge, transfer from, or change in type of care provided.
  4. To arrange and pay for consultation, diagnosis or assessment as may be required for my proper care and treatment.
  5. To authorize participation in medical, nursing and social research, consistent with the limitations specified in paragraph (4) and such ethical guidelines as may appropriately govern such research....[64]

In an advance directive, no principal can provide detailed instructions concerning care under every conceivable medical circumstance. But this does not make specificity valueless. Supplying moderately detailed directives for a range of concrete situations of special importance to the

---

[62] Robbins, *supra* note 58.

[63] California Medical Association, San Francisco, *Durable Power of Attorney for Health Care* 3 (Form 1984).

[64] E. COHEN, *supra* note 41, at 15-16.

principal can greatly assist the agent (and other "consultants" of secondary authority) to make decisions for the incompetent patient/principal that are maximally in accord with the principal's wishes. At the very least, something should be said concerning circumstances for withdrawing or withholding life-sustaining procedures. One way to achieve this would be to include in the form an itemized list of statements, each of which gives instructions about a specific type of medical condition, e.g., persistent vegetative state, irreversible coma, etc.

Given the current controversy about the legality of withdrawing or withholding artificial feeding and hydrating devices, a principal who opposes the use of such procedures under certain conditions might wish to speak directly to this issue by specifically defining life-sustaining or life-prolonging treatment to include nourishment and hydration by any means.[65]

The principal should also consider whether there are any specific powers that are not to be vested in the agent and state these restrictions clearly in the document. For example, the principal may not wish to empower the agent to commit or place the principal in a mental health facility, to decide to submit the principal to convulsive treatment, psychosurgery, sterilization, abortion, etc.[66]

3. Standards for Determining Competency

Since the purpose of the DPAHC is to extend through incompetency the principal's right to decide matters pertaining to medical care, competency should be construed as the ability to give informed consent. A patient is presumed competent until incompetency is demonstrated.[67] Whether a person has this capacity is a question of fact.[68]

A directive like the following will ensure that the competency assessment is made according to valid professional standards:[69]

---

[65] See, e.g., Collin & Meyers, *Using a Durable Power of Attorney for the Authorization of Withdrawal of Medical Care*, 11 EST. PLAN. 282, 286 (1984). See also the Life-Prolonging Procedures Declaration form contained in Indiana's Living Wills & Life Prolonging Procedures Act, IND. CODE 16-18-11-12 (1985).

[66] See, e.g., California Medical Association, *supra* note 63, at 3.

[67] Bartling v. Superior Court, 163 Cal. App. 3d 186, 209 Cal. Rptr. 220 (1984), No. BO15766 (Super. Ct. No. C500735) (Cal. Ct. App. 2d Dist. Aug. 25, 1986) (civil liability decision).

[68] Grannum v. Berard, 422 P.2d 812 (Wash. 1967). For ingredients of this factual determination see 1 PRESIDENT'S COMMISSION FOR THE STUDY OF ETHICAL PROBLEMS IN MEDICINE AND BIO-MEDICAL RESEARCH, MAKING HEALTH CARE DECISIONS 55-62 (1983).

[69] E. COHEN, *supra* 41, at 18.

This durable power of attorney shall become effective upon my incapacity to carry on my affairs as determined upon certification that such is the case by (two physicians, one of whom shall be a forensic psychiatrist skilled in competency determinations), (a geriatric assessment team comprised of (a psychiatrist, a neurologist, a psychologist, and a social worker at a minimum)), (. . . as specified).

4. Appointment of Alternate Agents

A medical agent may not be able to speak on behalf of the incapacitated principal because the agent may have died, left the country, or otherwise be unavailable. It is advisable, therefore, that the principal designate, in the DPAHC document, one or two alternate agents who can substitute for the primary agent if the latter is unavailable.

5. Exculpatory Clause

To encourage health care providers to comply with the agent's directives, especially if the agent orders the withholding or withdrawing of life-sustaining therapy in accord with the principal's wishes, the principal should state that he or she releases health care providers from all liability if they follow the agent's instructions in good faith.

6. Personal Nomination of Guardian

A court appointed guardian has the legal power to revoke the authority of a durable agent appointed by an incapacitated individual who becomes the guardian's ward.[70] The guardian thereby assumes authority to make health care decisions for the incapacitated person. This transfer of authority carries the risk, however, that the guardian may not be as knowledgeable about or supportive of the incompetent person's values and directives (as expressed in the person's now abrogated DPAHC) as was the original attorney-in-fact. Hence, the guardian may make decisions for the incapacitated individual which are not as consistent with the latter's desires as those that would otherwise have been made by the now powerless agent.

To reduce the probability of this happening, the principal should, where permitted by law, include in the DPAHC form a declaration setting forth the name of the individual who the principal wishes to be appointed guardian in the event of an adjudication of incompetence or disability. The designated individual may be the attorney-in-fact appointed under the DPAHC.

[70] Note, *supra* note 29, at 1027.

7. Consent to Anatomical Gift

The DPAHC form is an ideal instrument for authorizing the posthumous donation of one's organs or tissues. Donor cards carried in a person's wallet or purse frequently get separated from a patient upon entering a hospital, especially under emergency conditions. (The wallet or purse is placed in a safe, for example.) If the patient dies in the hospital, the patient's effects may not be searched to locate a completed donor card. The patient's family or agent also may not be approached by hospital staff concerning the possibility of donation from the deceased. Including an organ donation section on the DPAHC form provides additional assurance that the patient's wishes to serve as a donor will be known by the appropriate parties (the agent especially, as well as the attending physician, organ procurement coordinators, etc.) and also actively pursued by the agent. Equally important, if a person does *not* wish to serve as a donor after death, the DPAHC form is again a strategic document for voicing this dissent.

8. Time Limitation and Power of Revocation

The close personal relationship between a principal and the appointed agent at the time a DPAHC is executed may not stand the test of time. The parties may have a falling out or the relationship may die for lack of contact and nurture. For these reasons it would be wise to place an initial time limit on the agency relationship, open to renewal, and state these conditions in the document itself.

The DPAHC instrument should also assert the principal's right to revoke, suspend, or terminate the agency relationship at any time by written or oral notice to the attorney-in-fact.

9. Directive to Initiate Legal Action Against Noncompliant Providers for Battery Against the Principal

In a compelling recent essay, Engelbert Schucking[71] describes the callous treatment he received from staff at a major hospital when he repeatedly ordered discontinuation of life-prolonging treatment for a prominent, then incapacitated authoress for whom he was the appointed durable medical agent. Schucking reports that he again and again presented the DPAHC document to these staffpersons. But his instructions were continually ignored or rebuffed. The supercilious and appall-

---

[71] Schucking, *Death at a New York Hospital*, 13 LAW, MED. & HEALTH CARE 261 (1985).

ing response of these medical professionals to Schucking's authority provides some reason for including in the DPAHC document a directive like the following, conveying to all readers the fully serious intent of the principal:

> If my attending physician refuses to honor the decisions of my agent concerning my medical care, I instruct my agent to direct the physician to transfer responsibility for my care to another qualified physician who will comply with my agent's decisions. If my agent's authority is thwarted, undermined, or not honored to its fullest extent by clinicians or institutions providing me care, I further instruct my agent to initiate action for battery against such providers.[72]

10. Declaration of Right to Revoke Agency, Even if Incompetent

A possible, though perhaps remote, state of affairs which a principal may want to guard against is that of being classified as mentally incompetent as the result of rejecting a course of action which, from the point of view of a family member, physician, or even the principal's appointed agent, is judged to be the only rational alternative.[73] The principal can be protected from such abuse by stipulating in the appointing document that the principal retains the right to revoke the agent's authority at any time—even by a communication made during a state of professionally declared incompetency.

11. Rejection of Authority of Specified other "Consultants"

At the time of executing a DPAHC, the principal may have good reason to believe that proxy medical decisions made by the appointed agent will be challenged by certain individuals whose authority the principal expressly rejects. If this is the case, the principal should explicitly state in the DPAHC document that input from these individuals should not be sought or given any weight by either the agent or a court of law. For example, a male homosexual estranged from his family and afflicted with AIDS may select a nonfamily member as his agent.[74] By including in the DPAHC form a provision forthrightly rejecting the authority of specified parties (besides the agent) who might naturally be

---

[72] Adapted from Robbins, *supra* note 58. *See also* Comment, *Damage Actions for Nonconsensual Life-Sustaining Medical Treatment*, 30 ST. LOUIS U.L.J. 895 (1986).

[73] *See, e.g.,* Erickson v. Dilgard, 44 Misc. 2d 27, 252 N.Y.S.2d 705 (1962); Lane v. Candura, 6 Mass. App. 377, 376 N.E.2d 1232 (1978); *In re* Brooks' Estate, 32 Ill. 2d 361, 205 N.E.2d 435 (1965).

[74] *See* Steinbrook, Lo, Moulton, Saika, Hollander, & Volberding, *Preferences of Homosexual Men With AIDS for Life-Sustaining Treatment,* 314 NEW ENG. J. MED. 457 (1986).

consulted (certain family members, for example), the principal can reduce the probability of undue meddling or legal challenge by these parties.[75]

C. The Continuing Need for Supportive Legislation

The preceding suggestions concerning provisions of a DPAHC form are offered to assist individuals who desire to execute such a document in states other than those which expressly recognize the DPAHC by statute. (These other states were earlier termed "nonstatutory states.") As clarified in section III(A), there is no compelling reason to believe that the conventional durable power of attorney mechanism recognized in nearly all states cannot be legitimately extended, by way of a specially constructed DPAHC form, to cover agent-made medical decisions for an incompetent principal. Many of the provisions and safeguards contained in the above suggestions are explicitly set forth in the California,[76] Colorado,[77] Pennsylvania,[78] and Rhode Island[79] statutes. Incorporating them into the body of a DPAHC form drafted in a nonstatutory state should give this form enhanced legal validity should it be subjected to judicial review in that state.

But this does not obviate the need for further enabling legislation in these jurisdictions. The most important advantage of such legislation is that it would remove uncertainty about the validity of this device in nonstatutory states. Statutory recognition of the DPAHC also would explicitly protect from civil or criminal liability medical staff who comply with an agent's directive to withhold or withdraw life-sustaining therapy from an incompetent principal as called for by the principal in the DPAHC form. Moreover, the best interests of principals who execute such instruments will be better served if various restrictions governing the construction of DPAHC documents are binding as a matter of law rather than simply being constraints which a principal is free to accept or reject in drafting such an instrument, e.g., limitations on who can serve as an agent or witness, prohibitions against euthanasia, and specific restrictions on an agent's authority, e.g., prohibiting the agent from subjecting the principal to psychosurgery, sterilization, etc.

---

[75] Support for this recommendation may be found in Collins v. Davis, 254 N.Y.S.2d 666 (1964), in which the court ruled that health care decisions by a competent adult may not be overruled by contrary wishes of the family.

[76] CAL. CIV. CODE §§2412-5, 2430-44, 2500-08, 2510-13 (West Supp. 1986).

[77] COLO. REV. STAT. §§15-14-501–502 (Supp. 1986).

[78] PA. STAT. ANN. tit. 20 §§5602(a)(9), 5603(h) (Purdon Supp. 1986).

[79] R.I. GEN. LAWS §§23-4.9-1–2 (1986).

CONCLUSION

Living will legislation has been enacted in nearly four-fifths of the states since 1976. While living wills are useful instruments for extending through incompetency a person's right to control the course of his or her medical treatment, they are plagued with numerous practical disadvantages. First, most state-approved living wills apply only in cases of terminal disease or injury. Yet, there are many nonterminal conditions that the majority of people regard as hopeless and not meriting medical treatment, e.g., irreversible comas, persistent vegetative states, and, generally, conditions in which the burdens of treatment outweigh its benefits from the patient's perspective. The scope of conventional living wills is therefore too narrow when compared with the range of protection most people actually desire to secure by executing advance medical directives.

Second, alternative forms of living wills not bound by the terminal condition restriction are not the most efficient means available for affording patients control of their medical treatment under incompetency. In a living will, a declarant cannot provide specific directives for every conceivable medical circumstance that might obtain in the event of incapacitation. The general instructions contained in these documents will therefore have to be interpreted by those responsible for the care of the incompetent declarant. When there is disagreement among members of the declarant's family concerning the course of action that is most consistent with the patient's instructions in the living will, or when there is a conflict of opinion on this matter between the patient's family and the attending physicians, the question arises as to who speaks authoritatively for the patient. The controversy may result in litigation with expenses to parties on both sides.

All of these problems with living wills can be significantly lessened by the use of an alternative device also designed to extend through incompetency a person's right to control the course of medical treatment, namely, the Durable Power of Attorney for Health Care (DPAHC). With this mechanism, an individual can designate a specific person to make health care decisions if the individual cannot personally decide about medical treatment because of mental disability. The appointment of such an agent makes it unambiguously clear who speaks authoritatively for the incapacitated person. An agent can engage in the same kind of reasoning about risks and benefits of alternative treatments (or no treatment) that the incapacitated principal would do if competent. Because the agent has been hand-picked by the principal, the agent's decision has the strongest claim to control the course of medical care for the incompetent patient. While an agent's decision is still open to legal challenge, those who contest it bear a strong burden to demonstrate that the agent's decision is not consistent with the patient-principal's own previously expressed values and desires.

In sum, the DPAHC possesses numerous significant advantages over living wills and represents the superior vehicle for extending and protecting a patient's right to control the course of medical treatment in the event of incompetency. While weighty arguments can be adduced for the claim that the DPAHC is a valid application of the standard durable power of attorney available in all 50 states, lingering uncertainties concerning its validity absent statutory authorization can and should be resolved in each state through legislation that expressly recognizes the legitimacy of this important and novel extension of the durable power of attorney mechanism.

Why I Don't Have a Living Will

Joanne Lynn

For a dozen years, my clinical practice has been largely with dying patients, my academic pursuits have focused on medical ethics, and my public service has been mostly at the interface of medicine and law. One would think that I would have "done the right thing" long ago and signed a living will. I have not. This essay is meant to illuminate my reasons. Some of my reasons may apply to others, and I will also mention some concerns that affect others but not me. However, I do not oppose the growth and development of advance directives. Rather, I hope to open the public and professional discussion of how to make decisions for incompetent adults in order to include more varieties of formal and informal advance directives and to force policy-makers to consider how to make decisions for incompetent adults who have no advance directives.

As a physician, I do use advance directives, both formal and informal, with many patients in all of my clinical settings. I have supported the Patient Self-Determination Act[1] and the distribution of living wills by Concern for Dying, and I have pushed for health care durable power of attorney legislation in my local jurisdictions. My endorsement of and enthusiasm for advance directives might well lead some to think that I am merely extraordinarily inefficient and imprudent in regard to my own affairs when they discover that I do not have a living will. While I may have these flaws of character, this particular behavior is not evidence for them.

I do not have a living will because I fear that the effects of having one would be worse, in my situation, than not having one. How could this be? A living will of the standard format attends to priorities that are not my own, addresses procedures rather than outcomes, and requires substantial interpretation without guaranteeing a reliable interpreter. Of course, a highly individualized formal advance directive might be able to escape these concerns, as is addressed below. First, however, I will consider the merits of a "standard" living will, such as is

available in stationery stores and through the mail.

On its face, a "living will" purports to instruct caregivers to provide no life-sustaining treatment if the person signing it ever were on the verge of dying, with or without treatment, and were unable to make decisions for himself or herself. On the one hand, this is hardly a surprising instruction. Some combination of short life, interminable personal suffering, and adverse effects upon others is enough that virtually all persons would prefer to have had the opportunity to avoid this outcome, even at the cost of an earlier death. I have seen enough suffering that I can readily list all manner of existences that would induce me to accept death rather than have medical treatment to extend life. Not just in my case but in most cases, the text of a living will in standard format rarely tells the physician anything that was not nearly as likely to be true without it. The fact that a person took the time and trouble to sign one and get it to the physician does imply something about that person's character and the seriousness with which he or she approaches these issues, but not much about the individual's preferences and priorities.

As a physician, I use the fact that a person presents a standard-format living will as an opportunity to explore what he or she really means to avoid, what is really feared and hoped for, and who would be trusted to make decisions. This use is exceedingly valuable, but requires no legal standing for the document and does not require that it be treated as the definitive statement of what should be done.

However, many persons believe that they accomplish some very different ends by signing a living will. They believe they keep themselves from ever ending up like Nancy Cruzan or Karen Quinlan, or like a family member who had a particularly gruesome end of life in an intensive care unit. That belief is wrong. The public use of the standard living will is largely premised on an implicit promise that the document cannot ensure. Stand-

101

ard form living wills *should* have virtually no impact upon the care of persistent vegetative state patients, persons receiving vigorous therapy for potentially reversible physiologic imbalance, or persons with no clearly progressive and irreversible course toward imminent death, for none of these people clearly meet the requirement of dying soon irrespective of treatment. When people feel, as they commonly seem to, that having signed a living will serves to ensure that they will avoid medical torment of all sorts, they are misconstruing the document.

Nevertheless, sometimes living wills do have an impact upon the care plan of all sorts of patients because physicians and other providers inattentively overgeneralize. All too commonly, someone who has a living will is assumed to have requested hospice-type care including a "Do not resuscitate" order, to prefer not to use intensive care, and to have refused curative treatments. This assumption can obviously shape the care plan without there being explicit confirmatory discussion with patient or surrogate. Thus, the living will can also lead to errors of undertreatment.

The standard form living will is thoroughly disappointing as a legal document. It does not reliably shape the care plan as intended and carries risks of affecting the care plan adversely. Unless it is used as a trigger for further communication, it has little justification. As a patient, I do not believe I will need to have that trigger.

The "standard-form" living will may be an unfair target for my critique, as there have been many efforts made to personalize and expand living wills,[2] especially by incorporating the designation of a proxy (which has conventionally been perceived as part of the durable power of attorney). While some of these are quite good, all entail some serious remaining difficulties that would preclude my using them and that should occasion some care in their use by others.

For example, a living will entails a construction of reality that identifies, at any one time, a group of persons who are "dying." The rest of us, in this conception, are not. Only if one is among the dying is the living will in effect. I cannot accept this construction of reality. Working with persons with advanced years, advanced cancer, and advanced AIDS has illuminated the hubris of this cultural view. Classifying some persons as "dying" does function to protect people, most of their lives, against recognizing that there is a death in store for each of us. The boundary between being merely mortal (like all humans) and being in the "dying" category is a boundary that people want desperately to find (and to find themselves in the "non-dying" group).

However, the schism simply does not exist. We all are dying. As the likely time of death comes closer, some issues tend to be more important, but there is no clear dividing line. Sometimes persons far from death are mainly concerned with comfort or spiritual concerns; sometimes persons facing death in the next few hours are still completing business deals. Pretending that there is a morally important demarcation between the merely mortal and the dying leads to harmful policies and practices generally. One stunning example is the societal support for hospice through Medicare which serves mostly relatively well-off cancer patients with homes, in contrast with the societal denial of adequate support for long term care for those who are severely disabled and alone.

Also, the way that living wills have generally come to be constructed has focused attention on the patient's status (dying soon no matter what is done) and the procedures to be forgone (those that are artificial and "only" serve to prolong dying, sometimes expressed as a list of medical procedures). These two attributes of the standard living will subtly distort good decision-making. Good decision-making rests primarily in pursuing the best possible future, from among those plans of care that can be effectuated, and with the "best possible" being defined from the patient's perspective to the extent possible. Nothing in this model needs to turn on the proximity to death or the nature of the procedure involved, except as these considerations shape the desirability of various future courses to the patient. Sometimes ventilators are morally required, but sometimes even changing the sheets is contraindicated. For someone to be asked to decide in advance whether he or she would want dialysis, ventilator, or feeding tubes, without knowing what using these procedures would yield, is incomprehensible.

In addition, the issues that have become conventional to deal with in extended-version living wills are but a frail reflection of the concerns that very sick patients actually express. In fact, some of their real concerns have almost completely lost a place in the discussion of any kind of formal advance directives. Many patients are concerned about the emotional, physical, and financial burdens that their prolonged existence might entail for family. So often one hears, with real sincerity, "I don't want to be a burden," and so often we fail to have the ability, within this culture, to acknowledge and explore that sentiment. Perhaps, if we all learned how to carry on the discussions, many persons would be found to be more concerned about the issues around imposing burdens on others than are concerned about the ignominy of persistent vegetative state or the torment of long-term ventilator use. Certainly, I would. However, this we do not talk about and we do not include in conventional advance directives.

Many people may also have a high preference for being able to choose a course of care that will never look foolish. Many persons seem to be more concerned to do the conventional thing, to be supported by friends and family as having "done his best," and never to have to feel that one bears much of the responsibility for the

102

outcomes that one must endure. For example, I accepted a widely-used protocol for the treatment of a family member's illness, even though I knew that there was no data to support using some of the particularly onerous components of the protocol. The reason was largely because refusing those components would leave me bearing the responsibility for any adverse outcome. Even a maximally creative living will is likely to have difficulty expressing this particular sentiment; the formal prose itself tends to make the author look silly.

A number of factors that are known to affect decision-making are not regularly given voice through living wills. How is a person to write a living will that would ask for his family to seek divine guidance in prayer, or to ensure that her death is as dramatic and public as the rest of her life has been? Certainly, doing so would be difficult with any form that I have seen. In fact, much of what people ordinarily take to be important in their other choices is shunned in the conventional living will and the process of writing it. There is little passion or pathos, only the clean, sterile, black and white of choices made and enforced. Perhaps that is not how some, or most, of us would choose to die, if all choices were available. I, for example, would hope that my family would be emotional about the choices to be made, not simply concerned with the application of my advance directives to my situation.

Although my personal concerns do not include the first of these, two special classes of patient refuse to be involved in living will negotiations because of a fundamental discord between their model of how life is to be lived and the decision-analysis model that informs advance directives discussions. A substantial number of patients simply find it incomprehensible or distasteful to imagine that their choices have an impact upon the length of life. Even if this counts as a denial of the facts of the situation, it still is cause for concern that there are a lot of people who refuse to "play the game" for what amounts to religious reasons. Such persons commonly state, "It's up to God." Surely they do not therefore gain the obligation to be tormented by modern medicine; but, at least under some legal conditions, that is their only option if they lose competence without giving advance directives limiting life-sustaining treatment.[3]

The other group who refuse to be involved in advance directives includes those who simply want to be able to live in the moment and to have a community and family that is trustworthy about making future choices. I personally have a great deal of sympathy with this claim. Why is it that the society wants individuals to get clear about their preferences and priorities and to express them in detail—only about life-sustaining medical treatment? Why can potential future patients not just trust that caregivers and family will make "about" the right choice? I prefer to believe that the "system" is caring and compassionate rather than that it is a cafeteria of services that can freely be chosen or forgone. One might well want to imagine that one's "circle of friends" would be affected by one's plight and motivated to ensure that the best possible choices were made. A survey of the competent residents of a nursing home that I served found that none of the residents' advance decisions (formal or informal) were known to all relevant caregivers and decision-makers, yet every resident was highly confident that the right choices would be made. Is this a less good state of affairs than if as many decisions as possible were made in advance and these choices were well-known and documented, but the system of care was feared by the clients? I think not. Of course, perhaps we can have trustworthy systems of care *and* formal advance directives; but, very likely, requiring formal advance directives before reasonable plans of care can be implemented for a variety of situations will prove an obstacle to a sense of trustworthiness.

I, and surely some other patients, prefer family choice *over* the opportunity to make our own choices in advance. The patient himself or herself may well judge the family's efforts less harshly than he or she would judge his or her own decisions made in advance or by the professional caregivers. I have had a number of seriously ill patients say that their next of kin will attend to some choice if it comes up. When challenged with the possibility that the next of kin might decide in a way that was not what the patient would have chosen, the patient would kindly calm my concern with the observation that such an error would not be very important. High[4] found that patients prefer family decision-making even if they have never discussed preferences with the family. Perhaps this is an important finding, one that should be enabled to find expression in advance directives if that is one mechanism that allows patients to express their views.

This is not the only way that the current focus on advance directives is troubling to a vigorous concept of family life. Families are those who grieve for the patient's suffering and death, who have a history of making decisions that account for the well-being of all concerned, and about whom the patient most likely would have had the most concern. Somehow to imagine that the society *could*, or *should* set up systems that remove the family from decision-making is almost outrageous. What if Nancy Cruzan had written a living will that stated that she wanted all treatment stopped if ever she were rendered unconscious for more than three days? Would the society really want caregivers to be obliged to stop treatment then, if her family vigorously objected?

Suppose that Justice Scalia, who wrote forcefully to encourage the requirement that life be sustained in the *Cruzan* case,[5] were afflicted with a terrible, lingering dying, relying upon all manner of medical torment to sustain life. Suppose also that his family claimed that they

103

359

knew better what he would have wanted than do those who interpret his public writings and that they want treatment stopped. Should this society really establish systems of care that require that the family's voice be silenced? Surely not. While they might have to discuss their views at some length, surely the voice of a loving family should be prominent.

The idea of family decision-making is further constrained by the common requirement in durable powers of attorney and proxy statutes that there be one solo decision-maker designated. For many families, making a unitary designation is contrary to the family's history of making conjoint decisions and imposes the possibility of generating an unnecessary discord, as someone must be granted disproportionate authority.

The question at this point might well be "Why do I use advance directives at all?" rather than "Why do I not have one?" I have found four good uses for formal advance directives. First, for anyone for whom a legally-sanctioned surrogate either does not exist or might be controversial (e.g., should it be the mother or the long-term mate of an AIDS patient), a durable power of attorney is quite valuable. Provided that the person has at least one other person willing and capable of serving as surrogate, having that person properly designated can ease a great deal of administrative and legal concerns. In Virginia and the District of Columbia for persons whose next-of-kin are appropriate surrogates, they are automatically granted the authority.[6] However, in many jurisdictions, even patients with close family would be well-served by having a durable power of attorney.

For a much smaller number of people, I use durable powers of attorney to document unusually specific preferences or unusual preferences. Thus, a person who never wants to be in a particular hospital again, or to have a particular treatment again, or to be treated for pain, might well benefit by carefully documenting this preference.

For another group of patients and families, anxieties are best laid to rest by generating a formal advance directive. The formal document might be more weighty and enduring than any one surrogate or caregiver. Also, the discussion about priorities and preferences might most naturally and easily be organized around the task of writing a formal advance directive.

For patients and families that would use a next-of-kin surrogate (which is legally authorized without additional formalities in my jurisdiction), who have fairly conventional preferences about the goals and burdens of advanced illness, and who are most comfortable with informal agreements, I do not encourage formal advance directives. These criteria fit my situation.

What should I do? Clearly, I could not use a living will in any of its standard formats. What I should do is to write a durable power of attorney naming my husband as surrogate (if I were to become incompetent outside of Virginia and the District of Columbia) and asking that all concerned defer to his judgment, however he comes to it, unless they feel that his decision amounts to abuse. Specifically, I would not want any judge or other person to overrule my family's choice on the basis of anything I have written or said about medical treatment (including anything else that I have said in this article!). I believe I have a trustworthy family and a supportive circle of friends. I would prefer to endure the outcome if they "err" in predicting my preferences, or even if they choose to ignore my preferences other than the preference for family decision-making, rather than to remove from them the opportunity and the burden of making the choices. I do not want anyone else presuming to impose what are taken to be my desires as expressed elsewhere upon that family.

Once signed and witnessed, that last paragraph can serve as my advance directive.

References

1. The Patient Self-Determination Act, Sections 4206, 4751, of the Omnibus Budget Reconciliation Act of 1990, P.L. 101-508 (Nov. 5, 1990).

2. President's Commission for the Study of Ethical Problems in Medicine and Biomedical and Behavioral Research, *Deciding to Forego Life-sustaining Treatment*, U.S.Government Printing Office, Washington, D.C., 1983; The Hastings Center, *Guidelines for the Termination of Treatment and the Care of the Dying*, Indiana University Press, Bloomington, IN, 1987; L.L. Emanuel, E.J. Emanuel, "The Medical Directive. A new comprehensive advance care document." *J.Am.Med.Asso.* 2989; 261:3288-93; L.J. Schneiderman, J.D. Arras, "Counseling Patients to Counsel Physicians on Future Care in the Event of Patient Incompetence." *Ann Intern. Med.* 1985; 102:693-8.; J.M. Gibson, National Values History Project. *Generations*

1990; XIV: 51-64; *Your Health Care Choices: A Guide to Preparing Advance Directives for Health Care Decisions in Arizona*, The Dorothy Garske Center and Arizona Health Decisions, 4250 East Camelback Road, Suite 185K, Phoenix, AZ 85018, October 1990.

3. *In re* O'Connor 72, N.Y.2d 517, 531 N.E.2d 607, 534 N.Y.S.2d 886 (1988); *Cruzan v Harmon*, 58 L.W. 4916, June 26, 1990; *In re* Christine Busalacchi, Missouri Court of Appeals No. 59582, March 5, 1991.

4. D.M. High, "All in the Family: Extended Autonomy and Expectations in Surrogate Health Care Decision-Making." *Gerontologist* 1988; 28 (Supplement) :46-52.

5. *Cruzan v Harmon*, 58 L.W. 4916, at 4924, 6-26-90 (Scalia, J, concurring).

6. Health Care Decisions Act of 1988, The District of Columbia, 35 DCR 8653, D.C.Code Ann. Chap. 21-2210; VA Code Sections 54.1-2981 to -2992 (1988 and Supp. 1990).

104

NOTES

A MATTER OF LIFE AND DEATH: PREGNANCY CLAUSES IN LIVING WILL STATUTES

INTRODUCTION

Recent advances in medical technology have given doctors control over the time and manner of death in ways never previously considered by their patients.[1] Today, a patient may find herself close to death in a sterilized hospital room full of life-sustaining[2] equipment. In these situations, questions arise as to whether such treatment prolongs life or simply extends the dying process, whether the prolonged "life" has dignity or purpose,[3] whether patients who wish to opt out of treatment[4] are committing suicide,[5] and whether those who take patients off treatment are committing murder.[6] These ethical problems are compounded further when the lives of a mother

---

[1] Examples of these advances include insulin, antibiotics, resuscitation, chemotherapy, organ transplantation, and kidney dialysis. *See* PRESIDENT'S COMMISSION FOR THE STUDY OF ETHICAL PROBLEMS IN MEDICINE AND BIOMEDICAL AND BEHAVIORAL RESEARCH, DECIDING TO FOREGO LIFE-SUSTAINING TREATMENT 1 (1983).

[2] A life-sustaining procedure or treatment means

any medical procedure or intervention which utilizes mechanical or other artificial means to sustain, restore, or supplant a vital function, which, when applied to a qualified patient, would serve only to artificially prolong the moment of death and where, in the judgment of the attending physician, death is imminent whether or not such procedures are utilized. 'Life-sustaining procedure' shall not include the administration of medication or the performance of any medical procedure deemed necessary to alleviate pain.

CAL. HEALTH AND SAFETY CODE § 7187 (West Supp. 1990). This definition is typical of those found in the living will statutes cited *infra* note 9. I will use the terms "life-support systems" and "life-sustaining procedures" interchangeably.

[3] *See* CAL. HEALTH AND SAFETY CODE § 7187 (West Supp. 1990). The California legislature explicitly found that prolonging life through the use of life-sustaining procedures may cause "loss of patient dignity and unnecessary pain and suffering." *Id.*

[4] In this situation, where the patient is already on a life-support system, any desire to be taken off would have to have been expressed before the incapacity.

[5] In our Judeo-Christian tradition, respect for human life demands that one not take another's or one's own life either by deliberate action or omission. Connery, *The Ethical Standards for Withholding/Withdrawing Nutrition and Hydration*, in 2 ISSUES IN LAW & MEDICINE 87 (1986). Recognizing this tradition, all of the statutes cited in note 9 *infra* contain provisions exempting patients and physicians from civil and/or criminal liability for acting in accordance with the statute.

[6] *See id.*

and her unborn child are at stake. This situation raises the additional question as to when life begins and ends.

Recently, some courts and legislatures have recognized that meaningful life may cease for persons who are utterly dependent upon medical technology.[7] In such circumstances, it may make little sense to keep a patient "alive" when she is terminally ill.[8] A majority of state legislatures have enacted living will statutes that permit a person to choose whether to forego or discontinue life-sustaining medical treatment.[9] These states include in an individual's right to privacy the right to refuse medical treatment.[10]

Conflicting interests arise, however, when a woman on a life-support system is pregnant. The patient's right to refuse treatment is juxtaposed with the fetus's alleged right to life. A number of states with living will statutes have determined that the right to refuse medical treatment, or the right to bodily integrity, carries less weight when the individual asserting the right is pregnant. These states have included pregnancy clauses in their living will statutes.[11] The clauses automatically invalidate the living will during the

---

[7] *See, e.g.,* cases cited *infra* note 51.

[8] The California legislature defines "terminal condition" as "an incurable condition caused by injury, disease, or illness, which, regardless of the application of life-sustaining procedures, would, within reasonable medical judgment, produce death, and where the application of life-sustaining procedures serve [sic] only to postpone the moment of death of the patient." CAL. HEALTH AND SAFETY CODE § 7187 (West Supp. 1990).

[9] *See* ALA. CODE § 22-8A-1 (1990); ALASKA STAT. § 18.12.010 (1989); ARIZ. REV. STAT. ANN. § 36-3201 (1989); ARK. STAT. ANN. § 20-17-201 (1990); CAL. HEALTH AND SAFETY CODE § 7185 (West Supp. 1990); COLO. REV. STAT. § 15-18-101 (1987); CONN. GEN. STAT. ANN. § 19a-570 (West Supp. 1990); DEL. CODE ANN. tit. 16, § 2501 (1983); D.C. CODE ANN. § 6-2421 (1989); FLA. STAT. ANN. § 765-01 (West 1986); GA. CODE ANN. § 31-32-1 (Supp. 1990); HAW. REV. STAT. § 327-D-1 (1988); IDAHO CODE § 39-4502 (Supp. 1990); ILL. ANN. STAT. ch. 110 1/2, para. 701 (Smith-Hurd Supp. 1990); IND. CODE ANN. § 16-8-11-1 (West Supp. 1990); IOWA CODE ANN. § 144A.1 (West 1989); KAN. STAT. ANN. § 65-28.101 (1985); LA. REV. STAT. ANN. § 40.1299.58.1 (West Supp. 1990); ME. REV. STAT. ANN. tit. 22, § 2921 (Supp. 1989); MD. HEALTH-GEN. CODE ANN. § 5-601 (Supp. 1990); MINN. STAT. ANN. § 145B.01 (West Supp. 1990); MISS. CODE ANN. § 41-41-101 (Supp. 1989); MO. ANN. STAT. § 459.010 (Vernon Supp. 1990); MONT. CODE ANN. § 50-9-101 (1989); NEV. REV. STAT. § 449.540 (1987); N.H. REV. STAT. ANN. § 137-H:1 (1989); N.M. STAT. ANN. § 24-7-1 (1986); N.C. GEN. STAT. § 90-320 (1985); OKLA. STAT. ANN. tit. 63, § 3101 (West Supp. 1990); OR. REV. STAT. § 127.605 (1989); S.C. CODE ANN. § 44-77-10 (Law. Co-op. Supp. 1989); TENN. CODE ANN. § 32-11-101 (Supp. 1990); UTAH CODE ANN. § 75-2-1101 (Supp. 1990); VT. STAT. ANN. tit. 18, § 5251 (1987); VA. CODE ANN. § 54.1-2981 (1988); WASH. REV. CODE § 70-122-010 (Supp. 1990); W. VA. CODE § 16-30-3 (1988); WIS. STAT. ANN. § 154.01 (West 1989); WYO. STAT. § 35-22-102 (1988).

[10] *See In re* Quinlan, 70 N.J. 10, 38-42, 355 A.2d 647, 662-64, *cert. denied,* 429 U.S. 922 (1976).

[11] Pregnancy clauses are included in all of the statutes cited *supra* note 9 except for the Louisiana, Maine, North Carolina, Oregon, Tennessee, Vermont, Washington, D.C., and Wyoming statutes.

course of the patient's pregnancy in order to protect the life of the fetus.[12] In effect, pregnancy clauses restrict what the states have otherwise deemed worthy of protection: the right to die a natural death.

This Note addresses the constitutionality of pregnancy clauses in light of emerging Supreme Court jurisprudence concerning fetal rights and the more established areas of privacy and abortion. The Note also examines state court decisions which seem willing to give greater weight to fetal rights than to the rights of the mother in cases where pregnant women have refused medical treatment.[13] Whether such decisions are constitutional depends upon the Supreme Court's interpretation of the conflict between fetal rights and privacy rights.[14]

Part I of this Note discusses living wills and elaborates upon the pregnancy clause issue. Part II explores the scope of the right to privacy, since determination of that scope will effectively decide the pregnancy clause question. In Part III, the Note considers the more specific right to abortion and closely examines *Roe v. Wade* and *Webster v. Reproductive Health Services.* Finally, Part IV addresses the state interest in the life of the fetus and concludes that the emerging trend in both abortion and fetal rights jurisprudence indicates that the current Supreme Court would not consider pregnancy clauses unconstitutional. In conclusion, the Note expresses concern regarding this trend which pits a woman against her fetus.

I. LIVING WILL STATUTES

Living wills authorize the withholding or withdrawal of life-support systems. Statutory authorization of living wills is a relatively recent way of allowing individuals to formalize their desire to refuse future medical care.[15] Currently, thirty-eight states and the District of Columbia have enacted living will statutes which grant competent adults the right to terminate medical treatment if they should become terminally ill.[16] The living will takes effect when the attending physician (some states require two physicians) deter-

---

[12] Typically, a pregnancy clause is included in the directive form which is found in the statute. (A directive is a written document executed according to formalities declaring the patient's wishes). California's pregnancy clause reads, "If I have been diagnosed as pregnant and that diagnosis is known to my physician, this directive shall have no force or effect during the course of my pregnancy." CAL. HEALTH AND SAFETY CODE § 7188 (West Supp. 1990).

[13] *See* cases cited *infra* note 130.

[14] *See* Roe v. Wade, 410 U.S. 113 (1973) (tracing the right to privacy to the Constitution and concluding that it is broad enough to encompass a woman's decision to terminate her pregnancy); Webster v. Reproductive Health Serv., 109 S. Ct. 3040 (1989).

[15] In 1976, California became the first state to enact a living will statute. *See* CAL. HEALTH AND SAFETY CODE § 7185-95 (West Supp. 1990). The California Natural Death Act is fairly typical of living will statutes. *See generally* D. MYERS, MEDICO-LEGAL IMPLICATIONS OF DEATH AND DYING 272-73 (1981).

[16] *See supra* note 9.

mines that the individual's condition is terminal. Generally, the individual can revoke the declaration at any time.[17]

The pregnancy clauses contained in many living will statutes reflect the state's concern for fetal life. States that have enacted pregnancy clauses have, in effect, determined that the state interest in protecting the fetus outweighs the patient's right to determine whether to forego medical treatment.

The typical pregnancy clause removes all force from the living will during the course of pregnancy. Only six states restrict the application of the pregnancy clause to cases in which the fetus is viable.[18] A majority of the states, however, make no distinction based on viability.[19] The Supreme Court's holding in *Roe v. Wade* that states may proscribe a woman's right to have an abortion only after viability,[20] has led some to argue that pregnancy clauses which interfere with a woman's right to have an abortion in order to protect a nonviable fetus are unconstitutional.[21]

The constitutional question arises when a terminally ill woman directs her

---

[17] *See, e.g.,* DEL. CODE ANN. tit. 16, § 2502 (1983) (stating that

[a]n individual, legally adult, who is competent and of sound mind, has the right to refuse medical or surgical treatment if such refusal is not contrary to existing public health laws. Such individual has the right to . . . [instruct] any physician . . . to cease or refrain from medical or surgical treatment should the declarant be in a terminal condition).

A typical statute begins by expressly recognizing a competent adult's right to refuse medical treatment, including life-prolonging treatment. Next, the statutes generally set forth the procedures necessary to make the declaration valid. As with testamentary wills, the declaration must be signed by two witnesses who are unrelated to the declarant and who do not stand to gain from the declarant's estate. Further, the witnesses may not be involved with the patient's medical treatment. *See* CAL. HEALTH & SAFETY CODE § 7188 (West Supp. 1990). Many of the statutes set forth forms in which the directive shall or should appear. *See, e.g., id.*

[18] *See* ALASKA STAT. § 18.12.040 (1989); ARIZ. REV. STAT. ANN. § 36-3205 (1989); ARK. STAT. ANN. § 20-17-206 (1990); COLO. REV. STAT. § 15-18-104 (1987); IOWA CODE ANN. § 144A.6 (West 1989); MONT. CODE ANN. § 50-9-202 (1989).

[19] The viability distinction is important in the abortion context. *See* Roe v. Wade, 410 U.S. 113, 163 (1973) (finding that the state interest in fetal life becomes compelling after viability). Viability may be defined as "[t]hat stage of fetal development when the life of the unborn child may be continued indefinitely outside the womb by natural or artificial life-supportive systems." BLACK'S LAW DICTIONARY 1404 (5th ed. 1979). Viability can occur as early as the 24th week of pregnancy. *Roe,* 410 U.S. at 160. *But see* City of Akron v. Center for Reproductive Health, Inc., 462 U.S. 416, 452-59 (1983) (O'Connor, J., dissenting) (pointing out that viability may occur sooner as medical science advances, thereby implying that the *Roe* framework is of little use).

[20] *Roe,* 410 U.S. at 163.

[21] *See* Note, *Pregnancy Clauses in Living Will Statutes,* 87 COLUM. L. REV. 1280 (1987) [hereinafter Note, *Pregnancy Clauses*]; Note, *A Time to be Born and A Time to Die: A Pregnant Woman's Right to Die with Dignity,* 20 IND. L. REV. 859 (1987) [hereinafter Note, *A Time to be Born*] (both Notes argue that, in light of *Roe,* any attempt to enforce a pregnancy clause prior to viability would be unconstitutional).

physician to discontinue her life-support treatment despite her pregnancy and contrary to the pregnancy clause in the state's living will statute.[22] Although this situation is rare, two state courts have considered the issue.[23] These opinions provide insight into the possible outcome of a federal case questioning the validity of pregnancy clauses.[24]

In *University Health Services v. Piazzi*,[25] the Georgia Superior Court implied that it would follow the state's pregnancy clause,[26] notwithstanding the objections of a patient's family. The court granted a hospital's petition to continue life-support procedures on a brain-dead pregnant woman.[27] No living will was involved in the case and the woman's wishes were unknown.[28] The patient's husband and family, however, requested that the life-maintenance systems be removed.[29] The court held that, according to Georgia law, the woman was dead and, therefore, had no protectable privacy interest.[30] The court also held that, because the legislature had already determined that a living will would be ineffective during the course of pregnancy, the woman's wishes regarding the maintenance systems were irrelevant.[31] While the constitutionality of the pregnancy provision was not before the Georgia court, the court's reliance upon the living will statute indicates that it might reject a claim that the pregnancy clause is unconstitutional.

In *DiNino v. State*,[32] the plaintiff executed a living will which differed from the model directive in two important respects. Washington's Natural Death Act[33] includes a provision which removes from the directive all "force or effect during the course of [a woman's] pregnancy."[34] DiNino's directive, however, added a sentence declaring the directive was a final expression of her "legal right to consent to termination of any pregnancy,"[35] and, indicating that the directive was to "still have full force and effect during the course

---

[22] *See* DiNino v. State, 102 Wash. 2d 327, 329, 684 P.2d 1297, 1299 (1984). The plaintiff in *DiNino* executed a living will which directed that it be given effect during the course of her pregnancy. The case was not decided on the merits.

[23] *Id.*; University Health Serv. v. Piazzi, No. CV86-RCCV-464 (Ga. Super. Ct. Aug. 4, 1986).

[24] While this Note involves a federal constitutional analysis upon which state court decisions have no precedential authority, these decisions do indicate an emerging trend in fetal rights which may affect the constitutional analysis.

[25] No. CV86-RCCV-464 (Ga. Super. Ct. Aug. 4, 1986).

[26] *See* GA. CODE ANN. § 31-32-3 (Supp. 1990) (the directive shall have "no force and effect during the course of [a woman's] pregnancy").

[27] *Piazzi*, No. CV86-RCCV-464.

[28] *Id.*

[29] *Id.*

[30] *Id.*

[31] *Id.*

[32] 102 Wash. 2d 327, 684 P.2d 1297 (1984).

[33] WASH. REV. CODE § 70-122-010 (Supp. 1990).

[34] *Id.* § 70-122-030.

[35] *DiNino*, 102 Wash. 2d at 329, 684 P.2d at 1299.

of [her] pregnancy."[36] DiNino and her physician sought a judgment declaring that her directive was valid and that no physician would be liable for obeying it.[37] The court found no justiciable controversy and failed to reach a decision on the merits. The state, however, in its brief and at oral argument, conceded that "an individual can draft a directive that contains a properly worded abortion provision, or in the alternative, simply delete the pregnancy provision of the model directive."[38] This concession undermines the state's objective in enacting the pregnancy provision. If the state has deemed the fetus worthy of protection, then ignoring the mandate of the statute vitiates the state's interest in fetal life and repudiates the rationale for the provision.[39] Once a state has included a pregnancy provision in its living will legislation, and assuming there is a valid constitutional argument for the state's pregnancy clause, the balance between the woman's privacy right and the fetal rights is struck in favor of the fetus. As a result, there is no justification for allowing the clause to be amended on an individual basis.[40]

II. THE RIGHT TO PRIVACY

The scope of the constitutional right to privacy will likely determine the constitutionality of pregnancy clauses. If the privacy right is broad enough to grant women complete autonomy regarding reproductive decisions, pregnancy clauses must fail as unconstitutional for attempting to restrict that autonomy. If, on the other hand, the right to privacy is limited to the extent that a pregnant woman must forfeit her decision-making power to the state, the clauses are constitutional. The cases which attempt to define the breadth of the right to privacy fall somewhere between these two extremes.[41]

---

[36] *Id.*

[37] *Id.*

[38] *Id.* at 331, 684 P.2d at 1300.

[39] *See supra* p. 870.

[40] If the pregnancy clause sets up only a rebuttable presumption, there would be an argument for avoiding the clause if the woman indicated her desire to maintain the living will's effect even during pregnancy. However, none of the statutes provide for this.

It is important to note that the outcome of this balance in favor of the fetus is different from that in *Roe* where the woman's right to privacy outweighed the state's interest in potential life before viability. Roe v. Wade, 410 U.S. 113, 162-63 (1973). The question contemplated by this Note is whether this balance is constitutional in light of existing privacy and abortion jurisprudence.

[41] *See* Griswold v. Connecticut, 381 U.S. 479 (1965) (including within the right to privacy a right to use contraceptives); *Roe,* 410 U.S. 113 (holding that a woman's qualified right to terminate her pregnancy is within the right to privacy); City of Akron v. Akron Center for Reproductive Health, 462 U.S. 416 (1983) (invalidating a statute that required abortions after the first trimester to be performed in a hospital because the result was an unnecessary economic burden on a woman's right to an abortion); Webster v. Reproductive Health Serv., 109 S. Ct. 3040 (1989) (holding that a statute restricting the use of public employees and facilities for abortions is not an unconstitutional burden on a woman's right to an abortion); *infra* text accompanying notes 86-114.

While the Constitution does not explicitly mention a right to privacy, such a right has been found among the penumbrae of guarantees enumerated in the Bill of Rights.[42] In *Griswold v. Connecticut,* the Supreme Court recognized the right to privacy in the realm of procreation and invalidated a state statute which prohibited a married couple's use of contraceptives.[43] Building on the idea of reproductive autonomy established in *Griswold,* Justice Brennan, writing for the majority in *Eisenstadt v. Baird,*[44] observed that "[i]f the right of privacy means anything, it is the right of the *individual,* married or single, to be free from unwarranted governmental intrusion into matters so fundamentally affecting a person as the decision whether to bear or beget a child."[45]

The Supreme Court extended the right to privacy to the abortion context in *Roe v. Wade.*[46] The Court found that a woman's right to privacy is broad enough to encompass the decision whether to terminate a pregnancy before the third trimester, when the state may intervene to protect the fetus.[47] Presumably, then, the privacy right covers a woman's decision on matters of childbearing during the first two trimesters of pregnancy. This interpretation of the right to privacy, however, may be more limited than it appears. For instance, the Court has yet to rule on other aspects of pregnancy, such as how a woman gives birth—by vaginal or caesarean delivery—or whether a court can order surgery against a woman's objections in order to save her unborn child.[48] Furthermore, the Court has yet to address the balance between a woman's right to privacy and protection of the fetus outside the abortion context, which leaves the constitutional status of pregnancy clauses even more unclear.[49]

A fundamental aspect of the right to privacy is the "freedom to care for one's health and person, [free] from bodily restraint or compulsion."[50] Some courts have held that the right to bodily integrity includes a right to die or

---

[42] *Griswold*, 381 U.S. at 484. The ninth amendment of the Constitution ensures that the government shall not infringe upon this unenumerated right. *Id.* The right to privacy also has roots in the first amendment, Stanley v. Georgia, 394 U.S. 557, 564 (1969) (right to private possession of obscene matter), the fourth amendment, Terry v. Ohio, 392 U.S. 1, 9 (1968) (right to walk down the street undisturbed), and the due process clause of the fourteenth amendment, Meyer v. Nebraska, 262 U.S. 390, 399 (1923) (right to teach one's children).

[43] *Griswold*, 381 U.S. at 481-86.

[44] 405 U.S. 438 (1972).

[45] *Id.* at 453 (emphasis in original).

[46] 410 U.S. 113 (1973).

[47] *Id.* at 164. A state may regulate abortions during the second trimester in order to protect the health of the mother. *Id.*

[48] *See, e.g.,* cases cited *infra* note 130.

[49] The Court has recently circumscribed the right to privacy to allow for more state intervention during the second trimester than *Roe* permits. Webster v. Reproductive Health Serv., 109 S. Ct. 3040, 3057 (1989). *See infra* text accompanying notes 86-114.

[50] Doe v. Bolton, 410 U.S. 179, 213 (1973) (Douglas, J., concurring).

refuse medical treatment.[51] State court analysis of the right to forego medical treatment usually parallels analysis of the privacy rights found in *Griswold* and *Roe*.[52] "Presumably [the] right [to privacy] is broad enough to encompass a patient's decision to decline medical treatment under certain circumstances, in much the same way as it is broad enough to encompass a woman's decision to terminate pregnancy under certain conditions."[53] In the living will context, the individual's right to privacy is juxtaposed against the state's interest in preserving the life of the patient. As the right to privacy is less than absolute,[54] the state may interfere with a person's right to refuse medical treatment when the state's interests become compelling.[55] In upholding living wills, courts have considered that life-support measures may prolong suffering while discontinuing them may allow a natural death.[56]

A recent Supreme Court decision, *Cruzan v. Director, Missouri Department of Health*,[57] suggests that living will statutes are constitutional. In *Cruzan*, the Court affirmed a decision by the Supreme Court of Missouri that required clear and convincing evidence of a patient's desire to end life-sustaining procedures before such a request would be honored.[58] Justice Brennan, writing for the dissent in *Cruzan*, noted that the Supreme Court of Missouri "did not specifically define what kind of evidence it would consider clear and convincing, but its general discussion suggests that only a living will or equivalently formal directive from the patient when competent would meet this standard."[59] By upholding the requirement of clear and convincing evidence of a patient's desire to end life-sustaining treatment, the Supreme Court impliedly approved of living will statutes.

---

[51] John F. Kennedy Memorial Hosp., Inc. v. Bludworth, 452 So. 2d 921, 924 (Fla. 1984) (holding that, in the case of a terminally ill person with a living will in effect, the guardian need not obtain court approval before terminating life-support systems); Superintendent of Belchertown State School v. Saikewicz, 373 Mass. 728, 739, 370 N.E.2d 417, 426 (1977) (recognizing the right of a person to refuse medical treatment, including life-support systems); *In re* Quinlan, 70 N.J. 10, 38-39, 355 A.2d 647, 662, *cert. denied*, 429 U.S. 922 (1976).

[52] *See Saikewicz*, 373 Mass. at 739, 370 N.E.2d at 424 ("As [the right to privacy] reaches out to protect the freedom of a woman to terminate pregnancy under certain conditions, so it encompasses the right of a patient to preserve his or her right to privacy against unwanted infringements of bodily integrity in appropriate circumstances."); *In re* Quinlan, 70 N.J. at 40, 355 A.2d at 663 (relying upon *Roe*, the court recognized a terminally ill woman's right to privacy and allowed the discontinuance of her artificial life support); Note, *Pregnancy Clauses, supra* note 21, at 1287-88.

[53] Note, *Pregnancy Clauses, supra* note 21, at 1288 (emphasis omitted) (quoting *In re* Quinlan, 70 N.J. at 40, 355 A.2d at 663).

[54] Roe v. Wade, 410 U.S. 113, 154-55 (1973).

[55] *See id.* at 155.

[56] *See* Saunders v. State, 129 Misc. 2d 45, 492 N.Y.S.2d 510 (1985).

[57] 110 S. Ct. 2841 (1990).

[58] *Id.* at 2854-55.

[59] *Id.* at 2874-75.

The living will situation is altered, however, when the patient is pregnant. In this case, the mother's right to terminate her pregnancy and the state's interest in potential life must also be considered. At issue is whether the state has a compelling interest in protecting the life of the fetus at the expense of refusing the mother's wish to die.

III. THE RIGHT TO TERMINATE A PREGNANCY

A. Roe v. Wade

Roe v. Wade sets forth the current framework regarding a woman's right to terminate a pregnancy. As this right is less than absolute, the state's interests become dominant at some point.[60] Only where state interests are compelling may the state promulgate regulations which limit the fundamental right.[61] In the discussion of *Roe* which follows, this Note intends to show that, while the analysis of fundamental rights versus compelling state interests applies to the inquiry regarding the constitutionality of pregnancy clauses, a narrow reading of the right to abortion indicates that the precise framework surrounding the right is inapposite to the living will situation.[62]

The Supreme Court based the right to have an abortion on the fourteenth amendment,[63] and established a framework for analyzing state abortion regulations. During the first trimester of pregnancy, because an abortion may be less hazardous than giving birth, the woman and her physician are free to determine whether or not to terminate the pregnancy without regulation by the state.[64] During the second trimester, the state's compelling interest in maternal health allows the state to adopt regulations seeking to promote safe abortions.[65] When the fetus becomes viable, usually during the third trimester, the state may prohibit abortions, except when necessary to protect the health of the mother.[66] While *Roe's* language is broad and its framework was intended for future application, the framework only addresses state regulation of abortions where maternal health plays a vital role. Nothing in the Court's opinion suggests that the Justices considered the situation involved in pregnancy clauses where maternal health is the least important concern. The decision in *Roe v. Wade,* therefore, does not necessarily imply that pregnancy clauses which affect nonviable fetuses are unconstitutional.

The Supreme Court refused to hold that the fetus is a person within the

---

[60] Roe v. Wade, 410 U.S. 113, 155 (1973).

[61] *Id.*

[62] The Court's recent curtailing of the right to abortion (and implicitly the right to privacy) indicates a reluctance to construe the right to abortion broadly. *See* Webster v. Reproductive Health Serv., 109 S. Ct. 3040, 3057 (1989); *infra* notes 86-114 and accompanying text.

[63] *Roe*, 410 U.S. at 153.

[64] *Id.* at 163-64.

[65] *Id. But see Webster*, 109 S. Ct. at 3057 (a plurality of the Court seems willing to permit further state regulation during the second trimester).

[66] *Roe*, 410 U.S. at 164.

meaning of the fourteenth amendment.[67] Even so, the Court recognized the interest in fetal life, but fell short of embracing the view that life begins only at live birth.[68] Justice Blackmun, writing for the majority in *Roe,* remarked that "[t]he pregnant woman cannot be isolated in her privacy. She carries an embryo and, later, a fetus. . . . The woman's privacy is no longer sole and any right of privacy she possesses must be measured accordingly."[69] The opinion takes into account the "important and legitimate interest in protecting the potentiality of human life,"[70] and emphasizes that this interest is present throughout pregnancy.[71] The question is, when does that concern become compelling so as to justify impinging upon the right to privacy?

In *Roe,* the Court found that the interest in the "potentiality of human life" did not become compelling until viability, at approximately the third trimester.[72] Once the Court recognized that the right to privacy included a right to have an abortion, considerations of maternal health and potential life governed the entire trimester framework.[73] But, the interest in maternal health is irrelevant in the pregnancy clause situation because the woman is beyond recovery. When maternal health is not at issue, the interest in the potential life of the fetus could become compelling at an earlier date, before viability.[74] The trimester approach addresses only the abortion context where the state must consider both an interest in maternal health and an interest in potential life. The trimester approach, therefore, may not apply

---

[67] *Id.* at 157-58. *But see Webster,* 109 S. Ct. at 3049 (holding that the preamble to Missouri Senate Committee Substitute for House Bill No. 1596, which sets forth "findings" by the legislature that "[t]he life of each human being begins at conception," imposes no substantive abortion restrictions and, therefore, the Court need not pass on its constitutionality).

[68] *Roe,* 410 U.S. at 160-64.

[69] *Id.* at 159.

[70] *Id.* at 162.

[71] *Id.* at 162-63. *But cf. Webster,* 109 S. Ct. at 3057 (apparently misreading *Roe,* Chief Justice Rehnquist states that the Court did not "see why the State's interest in protecting potential human life should come into existence only at the point of viability").

[72] *Roe,* 410 U.S. at 162-63. *But see Webster,* 109 S. Ct. at 3057 (describing the *Roe* framework as "rigid" and "indeterminate" and allowing the state to regulate abortions so as to protect potential human life during the second trimester).

[73] *Roe,* 410 U.S. at 162-65. The interests in maternal health and in potential life are state interests which the Court found to be compelling during the second and third trimesters, respectively. *Id.* at 164-65. Only when one of these interests becomes compelling can the state circumscribe the woman's right to privacy, which includes the right to have an abortion. *Id.* at 162-64.

[74] The willingness of at least a plurality of the Court to find the interest in potential life compelling before viability can be seen in the *Webster* decision, where the plurality flatly contradicts *Roe* and concludes that Missouri's interest in potential life is compelling at twenty weeks. *Webster,* 109 S. Ct. at 3055.

to the living will context and the *Roe* viability standard may not determine the constitutionality of pregnancy clauses.[75]

In the ordinary living will situation, where the terminal individual is not pregnant, the state's interests that conflict with the individual's privacy rights include the prevention of suicide, the preservation of the patient's life, the protection of third parties[76] and the protection of the ethical integrity of the medical profession.[77] When a woman with a living will is pregnant, the additional state concern is that of protecting the life of the fetus, while the individual has the additional right to terminate her pregnancy.

State courts that have upheld a patient's right to forego treatment[78] have concluded that the state's interests are weaker than the individual's right to privacy.[79] The state's interest in the preservation of life weakens as the individual's prognosis dims.[80] As a result, the issue in ordinary living will cases "is how long and at what cost the dying process should be prolonged."[81] If, however, the dying woman is pregnant, courts must consider the additional state interest of protecting a potential life. The addition of potential life to the equation may make the state's interests compelling earlier than when the only party involved is a terminally ill patient. This suggests that the Supreme Court may alter the *Roe* trimester approach in the pregnancy clause situation. Although the Supreme Court's position on living wills is uncertain, the Court has, at different times, given credence to each of the conflicting interests in the pregnancy clause situation. The Court has recognized an interest in the protection of fetal life,[82] but has also recently stated that "[t]he principle that a competent person has a constitutionally protected liberty interest in refusing unwanted medical treatment may be inferred from . . . prior decisions."[83] While the Court has held that a woman's right to decide whether to give birth is a fundamental aspect of her right to privacy, it is possible that state interests might override this right in order to protect a

---

[75] *But cf.* Note, *Pregnancy Clauses, supra* note 21, at 1292.

[76] For example, one court mentioned the effect on minor children of an adult's decision to refuse life-sustaining treatment. Superintendent of Belchertown State School v. Saikewicz, 373 Mass. 728, 742, 370 N.E.2d 417, 426 (1977); *see also In re* Jamaica Hosp., 128 Misc. 2d 1006, 1008, 491 N.Y.S.2d 898, 900 (1985) (mentioning the mother's responsibility to her living children in ordering a blood transfusion upon an unwilling mother so as to protect the life of the nonviable fetus).

[77] *Saikewicz*, 373 Mass. at 744-45, 370 N.E.2d at 426.

[78] *See* cases cited *supra* note 51.

[79] *See* John F. Kennedy Memorial Hosp., Inc. v. Bludworth, 452 So. 2d 921, 924 (Fla. 1984) (citing Satz v. Perlmutter, 362 So. 2d 160 (Fla. Dist. Ct. App. 1978)); *Saikewicz*, 373 Mass. at 741-45, 370 N.E.2d at 425-27.

[80] *Bludworth*, 452 So. 2d at 924.

[81] *Id.*

[82] Webster v. Reproductive Health Serv., 109 S. Ct. 3040, 3049-50 (1989); Roe v. Wade, 410 U.S. 113, 162 (1973).

[83] Cruzan v. Director, Missouri Dep't of Health, 110 S. Ct. 2841, 2851 (1990).

fetus when the woman is terminally ill.[84] "There is simply no intellectually honest way of getting around the fact that the interest in preserving the life of a fetus is significant."[85]

B.   Webster v. Reproductive Health Services

The most recent Supreme Court abortion case is *Webster v. Reproductive Health Services.*[86] Although the effect of *Webster* is still unclear, *Roe v. Wade*[87] remains good law for the present, leaving the above analysis intact. The future of *Roe* is uncertain, however, since at least four Justices appear willing to overturn the decision or, at a minimum, to circumscribe the right *Roe* discusses.[88]

The law at issue in *Webster* was a Missouri statute ("the Act") that requires a physician, prior to performing an abortion on a woman who is twenty or more weeks pregnant, to conduct tests to determine whether the fetus is viable, and "prohibits the use of public employees and facilities to perform or assist abortions not necessary to save the mother's life."[89] The first provision before the Court, a preamble, "contain[ed] 'findings' by the [Missouri] state legislature that '[t]he life of each human being begins at conception,' and that 'unborn children have protectable interests in life, health, and well-being.' "[90] The Act further mandated that the state laws be interpreted so as to provide unborn children with "all the rights, privileges, and immunities available to other persons, citizens, and residents" of Missouri subject to the Constitution and Supreme Court precedent.[91]

The Court found the preamble to be merely precatory and to impose no substantive limitations on abortions.[92] By doing this, the Court was able to permit the preamble to remain without considering its constitutionality.[93] The significance of this decision, in terms of the pregnancy clause situation, is that the Court appears willing to recognize the existence of fetal rights, at least outside the context of abortion.[94] Because a pregnancy clause in a liv-

---

[84] *See* L. TRIBE, AMERICAN CONSTITUTIONAL LAW § 15-10, at 1348-49 (2d ed. 1988); *supra* text accompanying notes 72-77.

[85] L. TRIBE, *supra* note 84, § 15-10, at 1348-49.

[86] 109 S. Ct. 3040 (1989).

[87] 410 U.S. 113 (1973).

[88] Chief Justice Rehnquist, writing for the plurality and joined by Justices White and Kennedy, placed the *Roe* framework in a category of Constitutional constructions that have "proved unsound in principle and unworkable in practice." *Webster*, 109 S. Ct. at 3056 (quoting Garcia v. San Antonio Metro. Transit Auth., 469 U.S. 528, 546 (1985)). Justice Scalia believed that the plurality implicitly overruled *Roe.* He added, though, that he would do so more explicitly. *Id.* at 3064 (Scalia, J., concurring).

[89] *Id.* at 3047.

[90] *Id.* (quoting Mo. REV. STAT. §§ 1.205.1(1)-(2) (1986)).

[91] Mo. REV. STAT. § 1.205.2 (1986).

[92] *Webster*, 109 S. Ct. at 3050.

[93] *Id.*

[94] *Id.* at 3049-50.

ing will falls outside the abortion context,[95] the current Court may find that the fetus of a pregnant woman with a living will has more important rights than the mother's right to privacy.

The most important part of the Act for the purposes of this analysis, and the section that gave the Court the most trouble, provided that:

> Before a physician performs an abortion on a woman he has reason to believe is carrying an unborn child of twenty or more weeks gestational age, the physician shall first determine if the unborn child is viable by using and exercising that degree of care, skill, and proficiency commonly exercised by the ordinarily skillful, careful, and prudent physician engaged in similar practice under the same or similar conditions. In making this determination of viability, the physician shall perform or cause to be performed such medical examinations and tests as are necessary to make a finding of the gestational age, weight, and lung maturity of the unborn child and shall enter such findings and determination of viability in the medical record of the mother.[96]

This section of the Act is the only one that the plurality construed as implicating *Roe*.[97] Here, the plurality suggested a dramatic reversal of its prior abortion decisions.

The Court found that the Eighth Circuit had plainly erred in construing the statute.[98] The Eighth Circuit read the section as requiring that, after twenty weeks, "doctors *must* perform tests to find gestational age, fetal weight and lung maturity."[99] Because such tests are unreliable at twenty weeks, costly at any stage of pregnancy, and, in some situations, may impose significant risks for the pregnant woman, the lower court invalidated the provision.[100] Chief Justice Rehnquist read the statute to require "only those tests that are useful to making subsidiary findings as to viability."[101] Under this reading of the statute, then, the first sentence qualifies the second.[102] The implication is that a physician would only be required to administer those tests that are necessary or useful to a determination of viability.[103]

According to the plurality, the viability-testing provision imposes an additional burden on second trimester abortions as a way of furthering the state's interest in potential human life.[104] *Roe*, however, stated that the state's

---

[95] *See supra* notes 72-77 and accompanying text.

[96] Mo. Rev. Stat. § 188.029 (1986).

[97] *Webster*, 109 S. Ct. at 3055-58.

[98] *Id.* at 3054-55.

[99] *Id.* at 3054 (emphasis in original) (quoting Reproductive Health Serv. v. Webster, 851 F.2d 1071, 1075 n.5 (8th Cir. 1988)).

[100] *Id.*

[101] *Id.* at 3054-55.

[102] *Id.*

[103] *Id.* at 3055 & n.13 (Rehnquist, J., dissenting) (Chief Justice Rehnquist looked to Black's Law Dictionary to give the word "necessary" the meaning "useful").

[104] *Id.* at 3057.

interest in potential life becomes compelling only at viability, or, in other words, around the third trimester of the pregnancy.[105] Because the right to terminate a pregnancy is fundamental,[106] a state can pursue its interest in potential life by regulating abortions only after viability.[107] Chief Justice Rehnquist discounted precedent when he treated the inconsistency between the case law and the Act as a fault of the case law.[108] Chief Justice Rehnquist, announcing the judgment of the Court, stated that

> the doubt cast upon the Missouri statute by these cases is not so much a flaw in the statute as it is a reflection of the fact that the rigid trimester analysis of the course of a pregnancy enunciated in *Roe* has resulted in subsequent cases like *Colautti* and *Akron* making constitutional law in this area a virtual Procrustean bed.[109]

Chief Justice Rehnquist's challenge to the *Roe* trimester approach was compounded by his observation that such a framework is "hardly consistent with the notion of a Constitution cast in general terms, as ours is, and usually speaking in general principles, as ours does."[110] Chief Justice Rehnquist further wrote that the plurality could not "see why the State's interest in protecting potential human life should come into existence only at the point of viability."[111]

The *Webster* opinion has broadened a state's opportunity to pass laws regulating abortion during the second trimester. States may conceivably justify such regulations as necessary to protect either the interest in maternal health, under *Roe,*[112] or the interest in potential life, under *Webster.*[113] The advent of this more permissive attitude toward protecting the fetus reflects

---

[105] Roe v. Wade, 410 U.S. 113, 160, 163 (1973).

[106] *Id.* at 152-53.

[107] *Id.* at 163.

[108] The Chief Justice failed to recognize his own inconsistency in advocating a strict and narrow reading of the Constitution while treating precedent in a dismissive and cavalier manner. Justice Blackmun noted that the testing provision, as construed by the plurality, does not conflict with *Roe* and its progeny, and Chief Justice Rehnquist, therefore, need not have challenged the trimester framework in order to uphold the provision. Webster v. Reproductive Health Serv., 109 S. Ct. 3040, 3070-71 (1989) ("[n]othing in *Roe,* or any of its progeny, holds that a State may not effectuate its compelling interest in the potential life of a viable fetus by seeking to ensure that no viable fetus is mistakenly aborted because of the inherent lack of precision in estimates of gestational age").

[109] *Id.* at 3056 (citing Colautti v. Franklin, 439 U.S. 379 (1979) (holding that requiring physicians to perform viability tests is an unconstitutional legislative intrusion on a matter of medical skill and judgment) and Akron v. Akron Center for Reproductive Health, Inc., 462 U.S. 379 (1979) (holding Ohio legislation regulating second trimester abortions unconstitutional)).

[110] *Id.*

[111] *Id.* at 3057.

[112] Roe v. Wade, 410 U.S. 113, 163 (1973).

[113] Webster v. Reproductive Health Serv., 109 S. Ct. 3040, 3057 (1989).

the plurality's willingness to uphold any law which furthers the state's interest in potential life.[114]

Because the current Court is apparently prepared to do away with the viability distinction in the abortion context, it probably would not hesitate to uphold a pregnancy clause which does not draw a line at viability. In the pregnancy clause situation, where the mother's interests are given less weight than in the abortion situation because of the mother's terminal illness, the plurality is even more likely to uphold a regulation that seeks to further the interest in potential life.

IV. THE INTEREST IN THE LIFE OF THE FETUS

The number of courts and legislatures that recognize a state's interest in the life of a fetus has been growing since the years immediately preceding *Roe v. Wade*.[115] As the interest in the fetus has taken on greater significance, state courts have diluted the rights of women in order to increase fetal rights.

The increasing recognition of fetal rights is illustrated by the transformation of tort law. Prior to 1946, nearly every jurisdiction denied recovery to children damaged *in utero* as a result of injury to the pregnant mother.[116] The controlling rationale was that the defendant owed no duty to a fetus, because a fetus could not be deemed a "person" in existence at the time of the injury.[117] Beginning in 1946, however, the ban against recovery was effectively reversed.[118] By 1967, every jurisdiction maintained a cause of action for a child injured *in utero* that was subsequently born alive.[119] This development has been so widespread that a few courts have held that a woman may be liable for her prenatal negligent conduct if it harms her subsequently born child.[120] By permitting recovery only to children subsequently born alive rather than permitting the fetus itself to recover, courts have recognized the existence of the fetus as something that may be injured

---

[114] In his dissent in *Webster*, Justice Blackmun recognized that the increasing interest in fetal protection, combined with the plurality's view that a regulation will be constitutional if it "permissibly furthers the State's interest in protecting potential human life," is a boon to the anti-abortion movement. *Id.* at 3076-77. Justice Blackmun emphasized the potential effect the plurality's opinion could have on the abortion right by noting that "every hindrance to a woman's ability to obtain an abortion must be 'permissible'. . . . A tax on abortions or a criminal prohibition would both satisfy the plurality's standard. So, for that matter, would a requirement that a pregnant woman memorize and recite today's plurality opinion before seeking an abortion." *Id.* at 3076.

[115] *See infra* notes 120-31.

[116] W. PROSSER & W. KEETON, PROSSER AND KEETON ON TORTS 367 (5th ed. 1984).

[117] *Id.*

[118] Bonbrest v. Kotz, 65 F. Supp. 138 (D.D.C. 1946), was the first case to hold that a viable fetus has a cause of action.

[119] W. PROSSER & W. KEETON, *supra* note 116, at 368.

[120] *See, e.g.*, Grodin v. Grodin, 102 Mich. App. 396, 401, 301 N.W.2d 869, 871 (1980) (holding that a woman may be liable for taking tetracycline while pregnant).

but have, as yet, failed to accord the fetus qua fetus any rights. In these actions, courts view the fetus as the potentiality of life, not life itself.

Criminal law has also witnessed an expansion of fetal rights. A number of states impose punishment for the crime of feticide.[121] The California legislature went a step further and included the killing of a fetus in its definition of murder.[122] In addition, the California Supreme Court recently ruled that a person can be sentenced to death for killing a fetus.[123] Finally, California child abuse statutes extend protection to the fetus.[124] In other jurisdictions, courts have ordered women to carry their pregnancies to term in jail or have seized custody of the fetuses so as to protect them from the mother's drug use.[125]

These statutes and judicial rulings represent a change in how a fetus is perceived. Traditionally, any protection granted the unborn was in recognition of potential life. Recent changes, however, grant rights to the fetus as something more than potential life. In some jurisdictions, the fetus is akin to an already-living entity, an entity that necessarily requires greater protection than that commonly afforded a potentiality.[126] From the *Roe* decision to the present, judges seem to have moved from speaking of the fetus as "potential life" to treating it as a child,[127] or as a patient in need of medical care.[128] In

---

[121] FLA. STAT. § 782.09 (1983); ILL. ANN. STAT. ch. 38, para. 9-1.2 (Smith-Hurd Supp. 1990); IND. CODE § 35-42-1-6 (1986); IOWA CODE § 707.7 (1985); MICH. COMP. LAWS § 750.323 (1979); S.D. CODIFIED LAWS ANN. § 22-17-6 (1988).

[122] "Murder is the unlawful killing of a human being, or a fetus, with malice aforethought." CAL. PENAL CODE § 187(a) (West Supp. 1990). The section does not apply if "[t]he act was solicited, aided, abetted, or consented to by the mother of the fetus." *Id.* § 187(b)(3).

[123] *See* People v. Bunyard, 45 Cal. 3d 1189, 756 P.2d 795, 249 Cal. Rptr. 71 (1988) (holding that the act of murdering a pregnant woman can qualify as multiple homicide, thus triggering the death penalty).

[124] CAL. PENAL CODE § 270 (West Supp. 1990) ("A child conceived but not yet born is to be deemed an existing person insofar as this section is concerned.").

[125] *See, e.g.,* Wash. Post, July 23, 1988, at 1, col. 5 (reporting order by a D.C. Superior Court judge that required a woman convicted of second degree theft to serve out the term of her pregnancy in jail); Note, *The Creation of Fetal Rights: Conflicts with Women's Constitutional Rights to Liberty, Privacy, and Equal Protection,* 95 YALE L.J. 599, 605 (1986).

[126] *See* MO. REV. STAT. §§ 1.205.1(1)-(2) (1986) (Missouri statute providing that life begins at conception and that fetuses have protectable interests); Special Project, *Legal Rights and Issues Surrounding Conception, Pregnancy, and Birth,* 39 VAND. L. REV. 597, 826-28 (1986) (discussing cases and legislation that define the fetus as a person, child or patient).

[127] *See* Jefferson v. Griffin Spalding County Hosp., 247 Ga. 86, 87, 274 S.E.2d 457, 459 (1981) (ordering woman to undergo cesarean section to protect the viable fetus).

[128] *See In re* Jamaica Hosp., 128 Misc. 2d 1006, 1008, 491 N.Y.S.2d 898, 900 (1985) (describing the fetus as a "human being, to whom the court stands in *parens patriae,* and whom the court has an obligation to protect," and appointing a doctor to "do all that . . . was necessary to save its life").

cases involving a mother's wish to die, such a shift may indicate a willingness by courts to give greater weight to the state's interest in protecting the fetus as a patient in its own right.[129]

A growing number of courts have found that protection of the fetus justifies the imposition of medical treatment upon an unwilling mother.[130] In the first of these cases, *Raleigh Fitkin-Paul Morgan Memorial Hospital v. Anderson,* [131] a woman in her thirty-second week of pregnancy was ordered to accept blood transfusions if they were necessary to save her and her unborn child. Unfortunately, the court's opinion does not describe the legal principles underlying the decision. The court merely mentions that the welfare of the mother and child are so "intertwined and inseparable that it would be impracticable to distinguish between them."[132] A similar situation confronted the Georgia Supreme Court in *Jefferson v. Griffin Spalding County Hospital.*[133] In that case, the court justified the infringement upon the woman's right to religious freedom[134] and bodily integrity because the life of the viable fetus was intertwined with the mother's, and because the court deemed it "necessary to give the child an opportunity to live."[135]

Most of the cases involving a pregnant woman's refusal of treatment rely on the viability distinction in striking a balance between the woman's rights and the rights of the fetus. The state courts have followed *Roe* in holding that any state encroachment upon the woman's right to privacy is justified only when the fetus is viable.[136] After the *Webster* decision, however, these courts may not hesitate to protect the interests of the fetus at an earlier date. Courts that protect fetal rights in cases where the mother refuses treatment would presumably do the same in the living will context. Courts may view pregnancy clauses as a necessary means to protect fetal interests rather than as an unconstitutional infringement upon a woman's right to privacy.

According to *Roe,* the state interest in potential life may not override a woman's right to have an abortion before the fetus is viable.[137] The *Roe* Court did not decide, however, whether the state interest in potential life

---

[129] *See* Note, *A Time to be Born, supra* note 21, at 867.

[130] *See In re* A.C., 533 A.2d 611, 617 (D.C. 1987) (affirming the lower court's order to a hospital to perform a cesarean section against the wishes of the mother to protect the interests of the viable fetus); *Jefferson,* 247 Ga. at 87, 274 S.E.2d at 459; Raleigh Fitkin-Paul Morgan Memorial Hosp. v. Anderson, 42 N.J. 421, 422, 201 A.2d 537, 538 (ordering the administration of blood transfusions to a pregnant woman), *cert. denied,* 377 U.S. 985 (1964).

[131] 42 N.J. at 422, 201 A.2d at 538.

[132] *Id.*

[133] 247 Ga. 86, 274 S.E.2d 457 (1981).

[134] In both *Jefferson* and *Anderson,* the women objected to blood transfusions on religious grounds.

[135] *Jefferson,* 247 Ga. at 87, 274 S.E.2d at 458.

[136] *See, e.g., In re* A.C., 533 A.2d 611, 616-17 (D.C. 1987); *Jefferson,* 247 Ga. at 87, 274 S.E.2d at 458.

[137] Roe v. Wade, 410 U.S. 113, 163 (1973).

before viability is sufficient to override a woman's decision to refuse medical treatment. The distinction is important, for when a woman is not exercising her right to have an abortion, arguably the *Roe* distinction does not apply.[138]

Only two courts have had to apply the balancing test to cases involving a nonviable fetus.[139] In both cases, the pregnant woman declined treatment necessary to save the fetus's life and a third party brought suit requesting the court to order the necessary medical procedure.[140] In *Taft v. Taft*,[141] the Massachusetts Supreme Judicial Court refused to order the requested surgery.[142] The woman was competent and clearly did not want the treatment.[143] Because her constitutional rights were established on the record while the state's rights were not,[144] the court refused to order the operation.[145] The court cautioned, though, that "in some situations, there [might be] justification for ordering a [woman] to submit to medical treatment in order to assist in carrying the child to term."[146]

In *In re Jamaica Hospital*,[147] the New York Supreme Court also weighed the conflicting rights of the parties but reached a different result than the *Taft* court. The judge wrote:

> While I recognize that the fetus in this case is not yet viable, and that the state's interest in protecting its life would be less than "compelling" in the context of the abortion cases, this is not such a case. In this case, the state has a highly significant interest in protecting the life of a mid-term fetus, which outweighs the patient's right to refuse a blood transfusion on religious grounds.[148]

The court found that the state had an obligation to the fetus as a human being "to whom the court stands in *parens patriae*, and whom the court has

---

[138] *See supra* notes 72-75 and accompanying text; *see also In re* Jamaica Hosp., 128 Misc. 2d 1006, 1008, 491 N.Y.S.2d 898, 900 (1985) (finding the state's interest in protecting a mid-term fetus outweighs the patient's right to refuse treatment despite the fact that, in an abortion case, the state's interest would not be compelling).

[139] *See* Taft v. Taft, 388 Mass. 331, 446 N.E.2d 395 (1983); *In re* Jamaica Hosp., 128 Misc. 2d 1006, 491 N.Y.S.2d 898 (1985).

[140] *Taft*, 388 Mass. 331, 446 N.E.2d 395; *In re* Jamaica Hosp., 128 Misc. 2d 1006, 491 N.Y.S.2d 898.

[141] 388 Mass. 331, 446 N.E.2d 395 (1983).

[142] *Id.* at 333, 446 N.E.2d at 397.

[143] *Id.* at 333-34, 446 N.E.2d at 396-97.

[144] The court found that the woman had a right to privacy and to her religious beliefs. The record, though, showed no findings as to the state's compelling interests which might justify curtailing the woman's constitutional rights. The record was devoid of any findings regarding the operation, the risks to mother and child, or whether the procedure was desirable or necessary to save one or both of the lives involved. *Id.* at 335, 446 N.E.2d at 397.

[145] *Id.*

[146] *Id.* at 334, 446 N.E.2d at 397.

[147] 128 Misc. 2d 1006, 491 N.Y.S.2d 898 (1985).

[148] *Id.* at 1008, 491 N.Y.S.2d at 900.

an obligation to protect."[149] Since the mother's constitutional rights were at stake, the court asserted that it would not interfere if she were the only one involved.[150] In this instance, however, the mother's life was "not the only one at stake" and the court found it necessary to consider the life of the unborn fetus as well.[151]

These cases are analogous to situations involving living will statutes that contain pregnancy clauses. In these situations, the woman refuses medical treatment that is necessary to save her unborn child. When the fetus is viable, the courts are willing to order the procedures, thus deeming the state's interest in the life of the fetus to be more important than the woman's privacy rights. When the fetus is not yet viable, the courts are less certain that the interest in protecting fetal life outweighs the woman's right to privacy. The *Roe* viability framework has restrained the courts from going further in the direction of protecting nonviable fetuses. The *Webster* decision, however, indicates that the Supreme Court may turn to a narrow construction of the right defined in *Roe* which would restrict the *Roe* framework to the traditional abortion context. The *Roe* framework only governs situations where a woman affirmatively seeks to destroy the fetus.

The hypothetical pregnancy clause case, however, concerns a woman's refusal of medical treatment which results in the woman's natural death and, as a *consequence* of her death, the ensuing natural death of the fetus. This situation is distinct from the considerations in *Roe* and the Supreme Court is unlikely to summarily expand the framework in *Roe* to encompass pregnancy clause cases. When confronted with the issue, the Supreme Court may find the cases discussed above that involve a woman's refusal of treatment more analogous to the problem posed by pregnancy clauses in living will statutes than the *Roe* and *Webster* cases.

The Court may also reason that pregnancy clauses are constitutional because refusal to terminate artificial support systems is only a temporary denial of the woman's wishes. Once the child has come to term, the state would have no interest beyond those already balanced in the ordinary living will situation, and would presumably allow the discontinuance of the medical treatment. The Supreme Court may find that a terminally ill pregnant woman's privacy interest is not seriously infringed, but is merely postponed in order to protect the fetus. In this manner, the Court may hold that the balance weighs in favor of fetal protection, at any stage of development, and against the mother's desire to discontinue her life-sustaining treatment.

CONCLUSION

The Supreme Court has only recently held that a competent individual

---

[149] *Id.*

[150] *Id.* at 1007, 491 N.Y.S.2d at 899.

[151] *Id.*

has a constitutional right to refuse medical treatment.[152] On the other hand, fetal rights have gained wider recognition and are broadening in scope. As a part of this trend, the Supreme Court, if faced with the issue, may find that pregnancy clauses in living will statutes are constitutional.

A word of caution is in order. The route that the Supreme Court and some legislatures are taking in expanding fetal rights and narrowing the right to privacy as defined in *Roe v. Wade* and other cases[153] is a dangerous one. When the state subordinates a pregnant woman's choice to the rights of her fetus, the state is viewing the woman and her fetus as two distinct entities with hostile interests.[154] By depriving a pregnant woman of her decision-making autonomy, the state creates an adversarial relationship between the woman and her fetus.[155] If *Roe v. Wade* is to survive the recent dilution of the right to privacy, it must be read as a case about a woman's right to choose,[156] rather than as a case which pits fetal rights and maternal rights against each other.[157] Ultimately, the issue surrounding fetal rights versus a woman's privacy rights boils down to a question of decision-making autonomy.[158]

If the Supreme Court were to include a woman's decision-making autonomy within the right to privacy, lower courts would be unable to interpret cases like *Roe* narrowly.[159] If this were the case, restrictive decisions like the recent *Webster* case would be avoided. Courts considering pregnancy clauses in living will statutes would hesitate to find them constitutional. Until the Supreme Court recognizes that a woman has an absolute right to

---

[152] Cruzan v. Director, Missouri Dep't of Health, 110 S. Ct. 2841, 2851 (1990).

[153] *See supra* notes 41-45 and accompanying text.

[154] *See* Note, *supra* note 125, at 613.

[155] *Id.*

[156] L. TRIBE, *supra* note 84, § 15-10, at 1352.

[157] In Justice Blackmun's opinion, the issue was never phrased in such confrontational terms, nor was it phrased in terms of women's autonomy or sexual equality. Justice Blackmun was concerned instead with the relationship between doctors and patients. *See id.* § 15-10, at 1353.

[158] *Id.* § 15-10, at 1352.

[159] *See id.* § 15-21, at 1422-23; *see also* Bowers v. Hardwick, 478 U.S. 186 (1986) (finding a Georgia statute that criminalized sodomy to be constitutional). The Supreme Court, when it framed the issue, asked "whether the federal Constitution confers a fundamental right upon homosexuals to engage in sodomy," instead of asking whether the state can regulate the private consensual sexual activities of two adults. *Id.* at 190. Decades of privacy precedents including Meyer v. Nebraska, 262 U.S. 390 (1923) (invalidating a law prohibiting public school teachers from teaching foreign languages), Skinner v. Oklahoma, 316 U.S. 535 (1942) (invalidating a statute providing for the sterilization of persons convicted at least twice of crimes involving "moral turpitude"), and Roe v. Wade, 410 U.S. 113 (1973), were dismissed as irrelevant because they were about rights of "family, marriage, or procreation," and not about rights concerning one's autonomy or intimate human associations. *Bowers,* 478 U.S. at 190-91.

choose what happens to her own body, we are stuck with the present situation which pits a woman against her fetus, even in intimate decisions concerning her own life and death.

MOLLY C. DYKE

SOME MORAL PERSPECTIVES

Most of the essays thus far have dealt with very concrete issues and pragmatic decision making. The authors in this section seek to go beyond to first principles and to examine broader societal concerns that are reflected in the death and the law debate. Each of them discusses the principle of autonomy and its limits.

To begin, Ronald Dworkin ("The Right to Death") engages in a sustained criticism of the intellectual bases of Chief Justice Rehnquist's majority opinion in *Cruzan*. He sharply criticizes Rehnquist's argument that the state has an independent interest in life that could require maintaining a permanently vegetative patient on life support even when doing so is not in her best interests. Further, Dworkin argues that no rational person has an interest in living that way. Therefore, rather than requiring Cruzan's family to demonstrate that Cruzan would have wished to terminate her medical care, the Court should have required the state to prove that she had personal or religious beliefs such that she would have exercised her autonomy to require continued care.

Paul Kurtz ("The Case for Euthanasia: A Humanistic Perspective") stakes out the philosophical underpinnings for Dworkin's critique. In his view, the principle of autonomy is among the core principles shared by almost every member of society. He argues that, in an open, pluralistic, and democratic society, the right of privacy inexorably leads to the principle of self-determination in the context of medical treatment. Self-determination, in turn, leads to the right of an informed competent adult suffering from a terminal illness to choose to end his life and, if necessary, to demand assistance in doing so.

Stanford Kadish ("Letting Patients Die: Legal and Moral Reflections") argues that the principle of autonomy should be tempered by the power of compassion. He argues that autonomy has its most persuasive and commanding effect for patients who, in full possession of the faculties and able to weigh the alternatives, choose to forgo treatment and to die. For incompetent patients, however, even those with advance directives or durable powers of attorney, he contends that competing interests, specifically the power of compassion, may argue against giving full effect to a patient's express or implied wishes about medical treatment. The paradigm case for his argument is the patient who becomes incompetent in circumstances that he earlier stated were unacceptable—such as senile dementia—but who nevertheless is able to enjoy the life that is now left to him. In such circumstances, Kadish indicates that the power of compassion may override the patient's earlier wishes concerning medical treatment, made in anticipation of but before experiencing his life as an incompetent.

Gerald Coleman ("Assisted Suicide: An Ethical Perspective") argues from within the Catholic tradition that no person is wholly autonomous. Life, he argues, is a gift from God, and any act or omission intended to hasten death is immoral and presumptuous. Further, it is possible for person to achieve goals, both secular and religious, that are "encompassing, profound and lasting and yet to be in a state of great suffering . . . Suffering and death, joined to the suffering and death of Jesus, represent not dissolution but growth, not punishment but fulfillment, not sadness but joy." In his view, all life is sacred and filled with dignity, and no man has the right to terminate it, even from the best of motives.

Ernle Young ("Assisting Suicide: An Ethical Perspective") argues from a different religious perspective that the principle of autonomy does, in fact, justify permitting suicide, but only when the individual is suffering from a terminal illness, advanced physical decrepitude, or unmitigatable pain. Even in such straits, the individual's friends and caregivers should do their best to help him to recover faith, hope, and love. If he persists in his decision, however, they should assent. They are not obligated, however, to assist unless they, in the exercise of their own autonomy, share in the individual's values, belief systems, and reasoned arguments. If they do so, Young argues that there is little moral difference between the various degrees of assistance.

Mary Johnson ("Voluntary Active Euthanasia: The Next Frontier?") addresses the societal pressures that may prevent the proper exercise of autonomy. Although there is a general legal consensus that competent adults may terminate medical care at will, she fears that mentally alert, physically disabled individuals choose to do so only because they are given no other acceptable option. Far from being a rational exercise of autonomous decision making, such individuals may terminate medical care and die due to pervasive societal pressure to do so. Johnson argues that many would choose otherwise if society provided them with the emotional and social support and the technological and financial assistance to live fulfilling lives. "The right to die," she argues, "is no meaningful right when there is no equally available option to live."

Yale Kamisar ("When Is There a Constitutional 'Right to Die?' When Is There No Constitutional 'Right to Live?'"), the dean of the slippery slope advocates, warns of similar problems from a different perspective. Kamisar suggests that we have already progressed far down the slippery slope past the positions advocated by early proponents of passive euthanasia. He suggests, in fact, that now that there is broad acceptance of passive euthanasia under the guise of the "right to die," there is little to prevent active euthanasia from gaining broad acceptance as well. He argues, however, that even more disturbing possibilities lie down the slippery slope, including decisions to terminate care for conscious but incompetent patients based not upon their own interests, however diminished, but upon the financial, social, and emotional interests of society and their families.

Autonomy is the linchpin of the right to die. In our social contract, whatever is not surrendered to the state is retained by the individual. We place a high premium on preserving life and thus any person's choice to terminate his or her life should be viewed with caution. Nevertheless, if that person's choice is voluntary and rational (i.e., the product of reasoned consideration), that choice should be honored.

THE NEW YORK REVIEW OF BOOKS

VOLUME XXXVIII, NUMBER 3   JANUARY 31, 1991

THE RIGHT TO DEATH

RONALD DWORKIN

1.

The tragedy of Nancy Cruzan's life is now part of American constitutional law. Before her automobile accident in 1983, she was an energetic twenty-four-year-old recently married woman. Her injuries deprived her brain of oxygen for fourteen minutes, and left her in what doctors describe as a permanent vegetative state. Only the lower part of her brain stem continued to function. She was unconscious and oblivious to the environment, though she had reflexive responses to sound and perhaps to painful stimuli. She was fed and hydrated through tubes implanted in her stomach, and other machines performed her other bodily functions. She was washed and turned regularly, but all of her limbs were contracted and her fingernails cut into her wrists.

For months after the accident her parents and her then husband pressed doctors to do everything possible to restore her to some kind of life. But when it became plain that she would remain in a vegetative state until she died, which might mean for thirty more years, her parents, who had become her legal guardians, asked the state hospital to remove the tubes and allow her to die at once. Since the hospital refused to do so without a court order, the parents petitioned a Missouri court, which appointed a guardian *ad litem* (a special guardian appointed to represent her in these proceedings) to offer arguments why it should not grant that order. After a hearing the court granted the order on the ground that it was in Cruzan's best interests to be permitted to die with some dignity now rather than to live on in an unconscious state.

The guardian *ad litem* felt it his duty to appeal the order to the Missouri supreme court, though he told that court that he did not disagree with the decision. But the supreme court reversed the lower court's decision: it held that Cruzan's legal guardians had no power to order feeding stopped without "clear and convincing" evidence that she herself had decided, when competent, not to be fed in her present circumstances. Though a friend had testified that Cruzan had said, in a conversation soon after the death of her grandmother, that she would not want to be kept alive if she could not really live, the supreme court held that this testimony was not adequate evidence of the necessary decision.

Cruzan's parents appealed to the United States Supreme Court: their lawyers argued that the Missouri decision violated her right not to be subjected to unwanted medical treatment. The Court had not previously ruled on the question how far states must respect that right. Last June 25, by a five-to-four vote, the Court refused to reverse the Missouri decision: it denied that Cruzan had a constitutional right that could be exercised by her parents in these circumstances.

The main opinion was written by Chief Justice Rehnquist, and was joined by Justices Kennedy and White. Many newspapers and comments on the case declared that, although the Court had refused the Cruzan family's request, it had nevertheless endorsed a general constitutional right of competent people to decide that they should not be kept alive through medical technology. *The New York Times*, for example, said that the Court had decided that "the Constitution protects a person's liberty to reject life-sustaining technology," and congratulated the Court for a "monumental example of law adjusting to life." *The Washington Post* headline read, "Court Rules Patient's Wishes Must Control 'Right to Die.'"

It is important to notice, however, that Rehnquist took care to say that he and the two justices who joined his opinion were not actually deciding that people have a right to die. He said they were assuming such a right only *hypothetically*, "for purposes of this case," and he emphasized that he thought it still an open question whether even a competent person's freedom to die with dignity could be overridden by a state's own constitutional right to keep people alive.[1] Although the logic of past cases would embrace a "liberty interest" of a competent person to refuse artifically delivered food and water, he said, "the dramatic consequences involved in refusal of such treatment would inform the inquiry as to whether the deprivations of that interest is constitutional."

Even if we do assume that people have a constitutional right to refuse to be kept alive if they become permanently vegetative, Rehnquist said, Missouri did not infringe that right. It only insisted that people must exercise the right for themselves, while still competent, and do so in a formal and unmistakable way, by executing a "living will," for example. The United States Constitution does not prohibit states from adopting strict evidentiary requirements of that sort, he said. The Constitution does not require Missouri to recognize what most people would think was very strong evidence of Cruzan's convictions, that is, her serious and apparently well-considered statements to a close friend soon after a relative's death.

Justices O'Connor and Scalia, though they agreed to uphold the Missouri supreme court's decision, filed separate concurring opinions. O'Connor made an important practical point: that instead of drafting a living will describing precisely what should not be done to keep them alive, many people would prefer to designate someone else—a relative or close friend—to make those decisions for them when the need arises.[2] She stated her own view that the Constitution gave people that right, and emphasized that the Court's decision against Cruzan's parents was not to the contrary, since Cruzan had made no formal designation.

Scalia's concurring opinion was of a very different character. He repeated his extraordinarily narrow view of constitutional rights: that the Constitution, properly interpreted, allows the states to do anything that it does not expressly forbid. Since, he said, the Constitution "says nothing" about people's right to control their own deaths, there is no question of any constitutional right of that sort, and state legislatures are free to make any decision they wish about what can be done to people to keep them technically alive. Scalia left little doubt about his own views of what a sensible state legislature would decide; he said that no reasonable person would wish to inhabit a body that was only technically alive. But, he said, the Constitution does not require state legislatures to be either reasonable or humane.

Justice Brennan dissented in an opinion joined by Justices Marshall and Blackmun. Brennan's opinion, one of the last he delivered before his retirement, was a valedictory address that made even plainer how much his humanity and intelligence will be missed. He pointed out the main fallacy in Rehnquist's opinion: it is inconsistent to assume that people have a constitutional right not to be given medical care contrary to their wishes, but yet for the state to be allowed to impose evidentiary rules that make it unlikely that an incompetent person's past wishes will actually be discovered. "Even someone with a resolute determination to avoid life-support under circumstances such as Nancy's," he said, "would still need to know that such things as living wills exist and how to execute one. . . . For many, the thought of an ignoble end, steeped in decay, is abhorrent. A quiet, proud death, bodily integrity intact, is a matter of extreme consequence."

Justice Stevens dissented separately. He criticized the majority for not having enough regard for Cruzan's best interests, and stressed the religious basis of Missouri's case. "[N]ot much may be said with confidence about death," he wrote, "unless it is said from faith, and that alone is reason enough to protect the freedom to conform choices about death in individual conscience."

Last August Cruzan's parents petitioned the lower court that had initially decided in their favor with what they called new evidence: three more friends of Cruzan had come forward prepared to testify that she had told them, too, that she would not want to live as a vegetable. Though this evidence was of the same character as that which the Missouri Supreme Court had earlier said was not sufficiently "clear and convincing," the state attorney general decided this time not to oppose the parents' petition. On December 14, the lower court granted the parents' petition. Within a few days feeding and hydration were stopped, and Cruzan was given medication to prevent pain. She died on December 26.

2.

When competent people refuse medical treatment that is necessary to save their lives, doctors and legal officials may face a dilemma. They have an ethical and legal obligation both to act in the patient's best interests and to respect his autonomy, his right to decide for himself what will be done with or to his body. These obligations may be in conflict, because a patient may refuse treatment the doctors think essential. Rehnquist introduced a third consideration into the constitutional issue. He contrasted the patient's autonomy not just with his or her own best interests but also the *state's* interest in "protecting and preserving life." In most cases when a competent person refuses lifesaving aid—for example, when he refuses an essential blood transfusion on religious grounds—there is no difference between what most people would regard as his best interests and the state's interest in keeping him alive, because it is assumed that it is in his best interests to live. But in some cases—when the patient is in great pain, for example, and cannot live very long even with treatment—then the state's supposed interest

389

in keeping him alive may conflict with his own best interests, not only as he but as most people would judge these.

If we accept that some state policy might be served by prolonging life even in such cases, then two constitutional issues are presented. Does a state have the constitutional power to impose life-saving treatment on a person against his will, that is, in defiance of his autonomy, when it believes that treatment is in his own best interests? Does it have the constitutional power to impose such treatment for his own purposes, even when it concedes that this is *against* his best interests, that is, in defiance of the normal rule that patients should not be given medical treatment that is bad for them?

The law of most American states seems settled that the autonomy of a competent patrient will be decisive in all such cases, and that doctors may not treat him against his will either for his sake or for the sake of some social interest in keeping him alive. The Supreme Court had never explicitly decided that the Constitution compels states to take that position, though in the present case, as I said, Rehnquist assumed hypothetically that it does.

In the case of people who are unconscious or otherwise incompetent, however, and who did not exercise their right of self-determination when they were able to do so, the distinction between their own best interests and the alleged interest of the state in keeping them alive is of great importance, as Rehnquist's opinion, carefully examined, makes clear. He offered two different, though not clearly distinct, arguments why Missouri has a right to tip the scales in favor of keeping comatose people alive by demanding "clear and convincing" evidence that they had decided they would rather die. His first argument

appealed to the best interests of incompetent people. He said that a rule requiring evidence of a formal declaration of a past decision to die, before life support can be terminated, benefits people who have become comatose because it protects them against guardians who abuse their trust, and because a decision not to terminate is always reversible if documented evidence of a formal past decision emerges later. His second argument is very different: it appeals not to the interests of comatose patients but to Missouri's supposed independent interests in keeping such patients alive. He said that a state has its own legitimate reasons for protecting and preserving life, which "no one can gainsay," and that Missouri is therefore entitled for its own sake to tip the evidentiary scales against termination.

He treats these as cumulative arguments: he thinks that taken together they justify Missouri's evidentiary rule. I shall consider them separately, however, because they raise very different issues, and because, though Rehnquist mentions the second only obliquely and in passing, it has important implications for other constitutional issues, including the abortion controversy, and so deserves separate study.

Rehnquist devotes most of his opinion to the first argument: that the Missouri rule is in the best interests of most of the thousands of people who live in a permanent vegetative state and did not sign living wills when they could. That seems implausible. Many people who are now in that position talked and acted in ways that make it very likely that they would have signed a living will had they anticipated their own accidents, as Nancy Cruzan did in conversations with her friends. The Missouri rule flouts rather than honors their autonomy.

Many others, at least in the opinions of their family and others who know them best, almost certainly would have decided that way if they had ever considered the matter. The Missouri rule denies them what they probably would have chosen. Why is so indiscriminate a rule necessary? Why would it not be better to allow lower courts to decide each case on the balance of probabilities, so that a court might decide that on the best evidence Nancy Cruzan would have chosen to die, as the initial Missouri court in fact did decide?

While Rehnquist concedes that Missouri's rigid rule may sometimes lead to a "mistake," he says that the Constitution does not require states to adopt procedures that work perfectly. But his arguments that the Missouri rule would even in general work to the benefit of incompetent people are question-begging: they reflect a presumption that it is normally in the best interests of permanently comatose people to live, so that they should be kept alive unless there is decisive evidence that they have actually decided to the contrary. It is true that in some situations a presumption of that kind is sensible. A state need not accept the judgment of devout Jehovah's Witnesses, for example, that it would be in the best interest of an unconscious relative not to have a blood transfusion that would bring him back to conscious life, even if the state would accept his own decision not to be treated were he conscious. But we think the presumption sensible in that case because we believe that life and health are fundamentally so important that no one should be allowed to reject them on behalf of someone else.

No such assumption is plausible when the life in question is only the insensate life of the permanently vegetative. That kind of life is not valuable to anyone. Some people, no doubt, would want to be kept alive indefinitely in such a state out of religious convictions: they might think that failing to prolong life as long as possible is insulting to God, for example. But even they do not think that it is in *their* interests to live on; most such people would hope, I think, for an early death in that situation, though one in which everything had been done to prolong life. They would regard an early death as an instance of God's mercy.

But Rehnquist is so far in the grip of the presumption that life is of great importance even to people in a vegetative state that he argues, at times, as if the Cruzan family's petition was a proceeding *against* their daughter. He says that the state is entitled to act as a "shield" for the incompetent, and he cites cases in which the Supreme Court required that government have "clear and convincing" evidence of fault before deporting someone, or depriving him of citizenship, or terminating his parental rights. In such cases constitutional law properly tips the scales against punitive action, because, as in an ordinary criminal trial, a mistake on one side, against the defendant, is much more serious than a mistake on the other. Cruzan's case is not an adversary proceeding, however. Her own parents are seeking relief on her *behalf*, and fairness argues for only one thing: the most accurate possible identification of what Nancy Cruzan's wishes were and where her interests now lie.

Some of Rehnquist's arguments depend not on the assumption that it is normally in the interests of a permanently comatose person to continue living, but on the equally implausible assumption that continued life in those circumstances is never against such a person's interests. This is the premise of his argument, for example, that it is better to keep a comatose patient alive than to allow her to die, even if the chances of recovery are infinitesimal, because the latter decision is irreversible. He assumes that someone in Nancy Cruzan's position suffers no disadvantage continuing to live, so that if there is only the barest conceivable possibility of some extraordinary medical discovery in the future, however remote that may seem now, it must be on balance in their interests to continue living as long as possible.

If the only things people worried about, or wanted to avoid, were pain and other unpleasant physical experiences, then of course they would be indifferent about whether, if they became permanently comatose, their bodies continued to live or not. But people care about many other things as well. They worry about their dignity and integrity, and about the view other people have of them, how they are conceived and remembered. Many of them are anxious that their relatives and friends not have to bear the burdens, whether emotional or financial, of keeping them alive. Many are appalled by the thought of resources being wasted on them that might be used for the benefit of other people, who have genuine, conscious lives to lead.

These various concerns explain the horror so many people feel at the idea of existing pointlessly for years as a vegetable. They think that a bare biological existence, with no intelligence or sensibility or sensation, is not a matter of indifference, but something bad for them, something that damages their lives considered as a whole. This was the view Nancy Cruzan expressed to her friend after her grandmother's death. Rehnquist seems depressingly insensitive to all these concerns. In any case his assumption—that people lose

nothing when permission to terminate their lives is refused—ignores them. A great many people, at least, believe the contrary: that a decision to keep them alive would cheat them forever of a chance to die with both dignity and consideration for others, and that to be deprived of that chance would be a great and irreversible loss.

Of course, given the devastating importance of the decision to terminate life support, a state may impose strenuous procedural constraints on any doctor's or guardian's decision to do so. The state may require them to show, for example, in an appropriate hearing before a judge or hospital committee or some other suitable body, and with appropriate medical support, that there is no genuine hope that the victim will ever become competent again. It may require guardians to show, moreover, that there is no persuasive reason to think the patient would have preferred to have life support continued. It may also adopt suitable precautions to insure that the decision is made by people solely concerned with the patient's wishes and interests; it may specify, for example, that the decision not be made by guardians who would gain financially by the patient's early death. Though these and other procedural constraints may somewhat increase the chance that a patient who would have wished to die is kept alive, they can plausibly be described as in the best interests of patients overall, or in the interests of protecting their autonomy.

The Cruzan family satisfied all such requirements, however. These is no evidence that Nancy Cruzan had any religious beliefs that would have led her to prefer mere biological life to death. On the contrary, the evidence of her serious conversations strongly suggested—to put it at its weakest—that she would vigorously oppose being kept alive. Since Missouri itself paid the full cost of her treatment, the family had no financial incentive to allow her to die. So the state's evidentiary procedures cannot reasonably be said to have been in Cruzan's best interests, or in the best interests of vegetative patients generally. If Missouri's rule is constitutional, it must be for some other reason.

3.

We must therefore turn to Rehnquist's second, much less developed, argument: that Missouri can impose evidentiary requirements, even if that is against Cruzan's interests and those of other permanently incompetent people, in order to protect its own interests in preserving life. He said that "societal" and "institutional" issues are at stake, as well as individual ones, that no one can "gainsay" Missouri's "interest in the protection and preservation of human life."

No doubt Missouri pressed this agreement, and perhaps Rehnquist adopted it, with an eye to the abortion controversy. In 1989's abortion case, *Webster v. Missouri Reproductive Services*, Missouri cited its own sovereign interest in preserving all human life as justification for refusing to allow abortions to be performed in state financed medical facilities. Even *Roe v. Wade*, the 1973 decision that established a woman's limited right to an abortion, acknowledged that a state has a legitimate concern with protecting the life of a fetus. Though Justice Blackmun said, in that case, that a state's right to protect a fetus is outweighed by a woman's right of privacy during the first two trimesters of pregnancy, he held that the state's right was sufficiently strong thereafter to allow a state to make most third-trimester abortions illegal. In the *Webster* decision, several justices said that the state's legitimate interest in protecting human life is more powerful than Blackmun recognized, and justifies more sweeping regulation of abortion than he allowed.

Nevertheless, in spite of the crucial part that the idea of a legitimate state interest in preserving all human life now plays in constitutional law, there has been remarkably little attention, either in Supreme Court opinions or in the legal literature, to the question of what that supposed interest is or why it is legitimate for a state to pursue it. It is particularly unclear how the supposed state interest bears on the questions that were at stake in the *Cruzan* case. Of course government is properly concerned with the welfare and well-being of its citizens, and it has the right, for that reason, to try to prevent them from being killed or put at risk of death from disease or accident. But the state's obvious and general concern with its citizen's well-being does not give it a reason to preserve someone's life when his or her welfare would be better served by being permitted to die in dignity. So the state interest that Rehnquist has in mind, as justifying Missouri's otherwise unreasonable evidentiary rule, must be a different, less familiar, one: it must supply a reason for forcing people to accept medical treatment when they or their guardians plausibly think they would be better off dead.

Scalia, in his concurring opinion, said that we must assume that states are constitutionally entitled to preserve people's lives, even against their own interests, because otherwise familiar laws making either suicide or aiding suicide a crime, which no one doubts are valid, would be unconstitutional. As I said, he disagreed with Rehnquist's hypothetical assumption that, at least, competent people have a constitutional right to refuse life-saving medical treatment. But Scalia's argument is doubly suspect.

First, his assumption that states have the constitutional power to prevent suicide in all circumstances is too broad and it is premature. It is true that both suicide and assisting suicide were crimes according to common law, and Scalia relied heavily on the views of William Blackstone, the famous and influential eighteenth-century legal commentator, who declared that it was a crime even for someone suffering a terminal illness and in terrible pain to take his own life. But there are many examples in constitutional history of contraints on liberty that were unquestioned for long periods of history but were then reexamined and found unconstitutional because lawyers and the public as a whole had developed a more sophisticated understanding of the underlying ethical and moral issues.[3] That is particularly likely when the historical support for the constraint has been mainly religious. It was long unquestioned that states have the power to outlaw contraception, for example, before the Supreme Court held otherwise in 1965 in *Griswold v. Connecticut.*

Longstanding practice is an even worse guide to constitutional law when technological change has created entirely new problems or exacerbated old ones. Doctors can now keep people alive in terminal illness for long periods that would have seemed incredible in the recent past, and their new abilities have made the position of people who would rather die than continue living in pain both more tragic and more common. So when the Supreme Court is next asked to rule on whether states can constitutionally forbid someone in that position from taking his own life, or can make it criminal for a doctor to assist him, even if the doctor takes every precaution to be sure that the person has freely decided to do so, the Court will face a very different situation from that in which the common law principles about suicide developed. It seems premature for Scalia simply to declare that the power of states to forbid suicide has no exceptions at all. Government is entitled to try to prevent people from killing themselves in many circumstances—in periods of severe but transient depression, for example. But it does not follow that it has the power to prolong the suffering of someone in terrible and pointless pain.

In any case, it is bizarre to classify as suicide someone's decision to reject treatment that would keep him alive but at a cost he and many other people think too great. Many people whose lives could be lengthened through severe amputations or incapacitating operations decide to die instead, and they are not thought to have taken their own lives for that reason. It seems plain that states have no constitutional power to direct doctors to perform such operations without the consent and against the wishes of the patient. People imagining themselves as permanently comatose are in the same position: their biological lives could then be prolonged only through medical treatment they would think degrading, and only in a form they would think worse than death. So it is a mistake, for that reason, to describe someone who signs a living will as committing hypothetical suicide. It seems a mistake for another reason as well. Even if Scalia were right, that a conscious and competent patient who refuses an amputation that would prolong his life should be treated as a suicide, it would still not follow that someone who decides to die if he were to become a permanent vegetable is in fact taking his own life, because it is at least a reasonable view that a permanently comatose person is, for all that matters, dead already.

4.

Scalia's argument is therefore a red herring, and in spite of Rehnquist's confident remark that no one can "gainsay" Missouri's interest in protecting and preserving life, we still lack an explanation of what that interest is and why it is proper for Missouri to pursue it. It might be said that keeping people alive, even when they would be better off dead, helps to protect the community's sense of the importance of life. I agree that society is better and more secure when its members share a sense that human life is sacred, and that no effort should be spared to save lives. People who lack that sense may themselves be more ready to kill, and will be less anxious to make sacrifices to protect the lives of others. That seems to me the most powerful available argument why states should be permitted to outlaw elective abortion of very late-stage fetuses, for example.[4] But it is extremely implausible that allowing a permanently comatose patient to die, after a solemn proceeding devoted only to her wishes and interests, will in any way erode a community's sense of the importance of life.

So a state cannot justify keeping comatose people alive on the instrumental ground that this is necessary to prevent murder or to encourage people to vote for famine relief. If Rehnquist is right that a state has a legitimate interest in preserving all human life, then this must be in virtue not of any instrumental argument but of the *intrinsic* value of such life, its importance for its own sake. Most people do believe that human life has intrinsic importance, and perhaps Rehnquist thinks it unnecessary either to clarify or to justify that idea.[5] It is unclear, however, that they accept the idea on any ground, or in any sense, that supports his case. For some people, for example, life has intrinsic value because it is a gift of God; they believe, as I said, that it is wrong not to struggle to prolong life, because this is an insult to Him, who alone should decide when life ends. But the Constitution does not allow states to justify policy on grounds of religious doctrine; some more secular account of the intrinsic value of life would be needed to support Rehnquist's second argument.

It will be helpful to distinguish two forms that a more secular version of the claim might take. The first supposes that a human life, in any form or circumstance, is a unique and valuable addition to the universe, so that the stock of value is needlessly diminished when any life is shorter than it might be. That does not seem a convincing view. Even if we think that a conscious, reflective, engaged human life is inherently valuable, we might well doubt that an insensate, vegetable life has any value at all.

The view that all forms of life are inherently valuable is also disqualified for a different reason. On that view we would have as much reason to bring new lives into being, increasing the population, as for prolonging lives already in progress. After all, people who think that great art is inherently valuable have the same reason for encouraging the production of more masterpieces as for preserving art that now exists. But most people who think life has intrinsic significance do not think that they therefore have any general duty to procreate or to encourage procreation. In any case, the Supreme Court's decision in *Griswold*, which is now accepted by almost everyone, holds that the states have no power to prohibit contraception.

People who think that life has intrinsic value or importance, but do not think that this fact offers any reason for increasing the population, understand life's value in a second and more conditional way. They mean, I think, that once a human life has begun it is terribly important that it go well, that it be a good rather than a bad life, a successful rather than a wasted one. Most people accept that human life has inherent importance in that sense. That explains why they try not just to make their lives pleasant but to give them worth and also why it seems a tragedy when people decide, late in life, that they can take neither pride nor satisfaction in the way they have lived.[6] Of course nothing in the idea that life has intrinsic importance in this second sense can justify a policy of keeping permanently comatose people alive. The worth of their lives—the character of the lives they have led—cannot be improved just by keeping the bodies they used to inhabit technically alive. On the contrary, that makes their lives worse, because it is a bad thing, for all the reasons I described earlier, to have one's body medicated, fed, and groomed, as an object of pointless and degrading solicitude, after one's mind is dead. Rehnquist's second argument is therefore a dramatic failure: Missouri's policy is not supported but condemned by the idea that human life is important for its own sake, on the only understanding of that idea that is available in our constitutional system.

5.

It is a relatively new question how the medical technology that now allows doctors to keep wholly incompetent people alive for decades should be used. Of course the Constitution leaves considerable latitude to the state legislatures in fixing detailed schemes for regulating how and what doctors and guardians decide. But the Constitution does limit a state's power in certain ways, as it must in order to protect the autonomy and the most fundamental interests of the patient.

In the *Cruzan* case the Supreme Court recognized, even if only hypothetically, an important part of that constitutional protection: that in principle a state has no right to keep a comatose patient alive against his previously expressed wish that he be allowed to die in the circumstances he has now reached. But the Court undercut the full value of that principle by allowing Missouri to impose an evidentiary rule that substantially decreases the chance a patient will receive only the treatment he or she would have wanted. Even worse, the justification the Chief Justice offered for the Court's decision put forward two principles that, unless they are soon rejected, will damage the rest of the law as it develops. It is therefore worth summarizing the argument I have made against these principles.

Rehnquist assumed that it is in the best interests of at least most people who become permanent vegetables to remain alive in that condition. But there is no way in which continued life can be good for such people, and several ways in which it might well be thought bad. He also assumed that a state can have its own legitimate reasons for keeping such people alive even when it concedes that this is against their best interests. But that judgment rests on a dangerous misunderstanding of the irresistible idea that human life has intrinsic moral significance. We do not honor that idea—on the contrary we insult it—when we waste resources in prolonging a bare, technical, insensate form of life.

More than just the right to die, or even the right to abortion, is at stake in these issues. In the next decades the question of why and how human life has intrinsic value is likely to be debated, by philosophers, lawyers, and the public, not just with respect to those issues but others as well, including genetic engineering, for example. Constitutional law will both encourage and reflect the debate, and though it is far too early to anticipate what form that law will take, Rehnquist's unreasoned opinion was a poor beginning.

NOTES

1. In fact five justices—Justice O'Connor and the four dissenters—did declare that people have that right. But one of the dissenters, Justice Brennan, has retired, and it is not known whether Justice Souter, who took his place, agrees.

2. On July 1, 1990, the New York state legislature enacted a law, the "health care proxy bill," that provides for such delegation. Governor Cuomo said that the *Cruzan* decision helped to break a logjam on the bill. See *The New York Times*, July 2, 1990.

3. The recent, well-publicized case of Janet Adkins, who killed herself using Dr. Jack Kevorkian's suicide machine in the back of his Volkswagen van, suggests the moral complexity of suicide provoked by illness, and the degree to which Americans are divided about the issues raised by such suicide. Adkins was fifty-three and in the relatively early stages of Alzheimer's disease. Her mental capacity had begun to diminish—she found tennis scoring and the foreign languages she used to speak too difficult, for example, though she had lost little physical capacity, and had recently beaten her thirty-three-year-old son at tennis. She was still alert and intelligent, and had retained her sense of humor. But she wanted to die before the irreversible disease worsened; the life she would soon lead, she said, "is not the way I wanted it at all . . ." She telephoned Kevorkian, whom she had seen on television discussing his device. They met in Michigan, chosen because assisting suicide is not a crime there, in a motel room where he taped a forty-minute conversation which recorded her competence and her wish to die. Two days later he inserted a needle into her vein as she lay in the back of his van, and told her which button to push for a lethal injection. Michigan prosecutors charged Kevorkian with murder, but the judge acquitted him after listening to the tape.

The case raises serious moral issues that the Cruzan case does not. Janet Adkins apparently had several years of meaningful life left, and Kevorkian's examination may not have been long or substantial enough to rule out the possibility that she was in a temporary depression from which she might recover while still competent. It is of interest that about half of the 250 doctors who wrote in response to a critical article in a medical journal approved of what Kevorkian did, while the rest disapproved.

4. See my article "The Great Abortion Case," in *The New York Review*, June 29, 1989.

5. I do not mean to deny that animal life might have intrinsic importance, too.

6. I do not mean that many people often reflect on their lives as a whole, or live according to some overall theory about what makes their lives good or bad. Most people define living well in much more concrete terms: living well means having a good job, a successful family life, warm friendships, and time and money for recreation or travel, for example. But I believe that people take pride as well as pleasure in these concrete achievements and experiences, and have a sense of failure as well as displeasure when a job goes wrong or a friendship sours. Very few of them, perhaps, except those for whom religion is important, self-consciously think of their lives as an opportunity that they may either waste or make into something worthwhile. But most people's attitudes toward successes and failures do seem to presuppose that

view of life's importance. Most of us think it is important that the lives of other people, as well as our own, be worthwhile: we think it is a central role of government to encourage people to make something of their lives rather than just survive, and to provide some of the institutions, including the schools, necessary for them to do so. These assumptions are premises of liberal education, and also of the limited paternalism involved in stopping people from using drugs or wasting their lives in other ways, and in trying to prevent or discourage people who are depressed or despondent from killing themselves when they could in fact lead lives worth living.

That human life has intrinsic value in this sense—that it is important that a life go well once it has begun—obviously has important though complex implications for the abortion issue. In a recent Holmes Lecture at Harvard Law School I explored these implications. I argued that the idea that life has intrinsic value in the sense I described does explain many of our attitudes about abortion, including the opinion many people have that abortion even in a early stage poses moral problems. It does not follow that abortion is always wrong; indeed it sometimes follows that abortion is morally recommended or required. I argued, moreover, that understanding our moral notions about abortion as flowing from respect for the inherent value of life reinforces the Supreme Court decision in *Roe v. Wade* that the state has no business coercing pregnant women to take a particular view about what the principle of respect for the inherent value of life requires.

Different Viewpoints

The Case for Euthanasia: A Humanistic Perspective

Paul Kurtz, Ph.D.*

I wish to present the moral case for voluntary beneficent euthanasia, both active and passive. I also wish to outline an ethical theory in defense of it. Secular humanists are often challenged for defending euthanasia, but I submit that there is a profound ethical justification for it. The theory that I want to defend is known as naturalism. It is grounded in human experience, and its principles and values are tested by their consequences. It is not subjective but has an objective basis. Included in this theory is an important neo-Kantian reference, for I think there are prima facie general ethical principles that have been established over a long period of time, and also certain basic, widely shared values. Central to my position, though not exclusively so, is situational ethics.

So, first, I presuppose a body of ethical data that we share no matter what our religious, ethnic, or ideological positions. I maintain that these ethical principles are the common heritage of humankind. They are transcultural, for we live today in a world community. And since we have an opportunity for interaction in the planetary society, these principles have meanings for all parts of the human family. They are found in both the religious and philosophical traditions. They are what I call the "common moral decencies," the principles that we teach our children, the basic moral truths. Most people today will agree about their ring of authenticity, though no doubt there are some exceptions. First are the principles connected with integrity: truthfulness, promise-keeping, sincerity, honesty. Second are the principles connected with trustworthiness: fidelity and dependability. Third are those connected to benevolence: compassion, good will, and nonmalfeasance. Fourth are those connected to fairness: gratitude, accountability, justice, tolerance, and cooperation. I've only enumerated these common moral decencies

*Professor emeritus of philosophy, State University of New York at Buffalo; Editor of *Free Inquiry* magazine, published by the Council for Democratic and Secular Humanism; B.A., New York University; M.A., Ph.D., Columbia University.

without a chance to defend them or state them with any exhaustive accounting, but I am assuming that these are the shared ground upon which we stand.[1]

Second, there are also basic values that we don't necessarily all share but that have emerged in democratic societies as the rules of the game. These values are also the values of humanistic culture. Humanism, as I interpret it, is not a recent invention but has a long history going back to the classical philosophers of ancient Greece and Rome. It emerges again in the Renaissance and with the democratic and scientific revolutions of the modern world. Among these key values—I can again only enumerate them in order to give you something of the framework of this ethical theory[2]—is the value of autonomy, namely, that freedom of choice of the individual is cherished. The good is to maximize the range of human choice and allow people to grow creatively and develop so they can make their own decisions about their lives. It involves individual responsibility as a basic value and an effort to nourish it.

It also involves the value of excellence. There is a long-standing debate in the history of Western philosophy about hedonism versus self-realizationism. I would defend a combined theory, basic to which is the notion that we want to achieve a life in which there are significance, meaning, and degrees of perfectibility that are humanly attainable. Excellence emerges with the cultivation of a creative life in which there is a fullness of being and a quality of life in which people can enjoy happiness and well-being. I have used the term *exuberance* to describe the highest reaches of happiness, a life overflowing with joy.[3]

Third, I also wish to refer to the notion of human rights. This is a recent development of the past three centuries, and it largely comes out of the democratic revolutions. It is not found, for example, in the religious or biblical tradition, and the struggle to gain recognition for human rights has been long and hard. I won't here catalog these rights fully because I think that the United Nations' Declaration and other declarations have stated them well.[4] They range from the right to life, which includes the security and protection of one's own person and the defense from external aggression, to the right to personal liberty, the right to equal protection of the law, and to other democratic rights. Among the human rights recognized today is the right to health care,

---

[1] For a fuller discussion of these and other ethical issues, see PAUL KURTZ, FORBIDDEN FRUIT: THE ETHICS OF HUMANISM 63-96 (1988).

[2] *Id.* at 97-128.

[3] PAUL KURTZ, EXUBERANCE 175-76 (1979).

[4] For a full list, see KURTZ, *supra* note 1, at 179-98.

and this right applies in a significant way to the questions that we are debating in medical ethics. The question of what to include under the rubric of human rights is a growing one. There are struggle, debate, and dialogue on a worldwide basis. There is a framework of human rights widely accepted by the world community, but there are also demands that new rights and claims against society be recognized and that individuals be protected.

My fourth point concerns how we ought to guide our behavior and decide what to do among competing principles, values, and rights—but this in the last analysis depends upon the situations that we find ourselves in. Human agents are constantly faced with moral dilemmas and with alternatives to choose from. Moral dilemmas in the most dramatic form involve the tragedies that we encounter in life. There are often insoluble problems that we confront, and often our choice is between the lesser of two evils or the conflict between two rights, each obligatory. The question in life often is not between the good and the bad, or the right and the wrong—that's easy. It's between two goods, both of which we cannot have, or two unmitigated evils, the lesser of which we must choose. How do we do this? Moral philosophers from Aristotle to John Dewey[5] have recognized that we have to deal with the concrete situation at hand. We need, for example, to take into account the facts of the case. We need to ask, What are the unique circumstances in this context? Exhaustive investigation of the particulars is essential to decisionmaking. A focus on the agent or agents involved in the decision process is required. Next we need to ask, What are the conditions that here prevail? This involves a causal investigation of how and why the facts are what they are. For example, in a case of terminal illness we ask, What is the disease or disorder, and why has it developed thus far, and what is the prognosis? Next we have to ask, What are our options, what are the alternatives that are viable, the means that can fulfill our ends? Intelligent inquiry may bring to light new ones. Last, we ask, What are the consequences of our decisions? What are the effects of our actions?

Now, our choice, I submit, is a balance of the competing claims and demands within the situation, the alternatives and the options. We have to weigh the facts, our prima facie duties, the consequences of our choices, the values that we cherish, and human rights. Thus, what is morally right or wrong is the product of a reflective choice within the situation. We can only decide after inquiry. Every case in one sense is unique. On the other hand, there are general principles and rules that

[5]*See* ARISTOTLE, NICOMACHEAN ETHICS (Martin Ostwald trans., 1962). I consider my ethical framework as essentially Aristotelian. Also of interest is JOHN DEWEY, THEORY OF VALUATION (1939).

are relevant. Which general principles and rules apply cannot be determined a priori, but only after deliberation. Let me reiterate the point that
I think there are general moral principles which guide us. We have to
constantly clarify these principles. But they are not, I submit, absolute.
There is a difference between a general and an absolute duty, and I am
arguing that our duties are general, not ultimate or final, given that they
may conflict. There is a difference between a prima facie ethical principle
that we ought to abide by and that we might have to waive in a situation,
and a de jure principle, which is always binding. The problem in life is
that our principles and values often clash, and *how* they apply depends
on reflective analysis within the situation.

Let us now turn to medical ethics and ask, What are the ethical
grounds of a humanistic defense of voluntary euthanasia? The first
premise is that we live in an open, democratic, and pluralistic society
where there are competing life stances, value systems, eupraxophies,
and religious faiths. Thus we have an obligation to listen to and be
tolerant of different ethical convictions.

Second, basic to our democratic value system, however, is the
importance of the right to privacy. This right is a newly gained prima
facie ethical principle—a new common moral decency. People were not
aware of its authenticity say two or three centuries ago. The right to
privacy is a human right: Society should respect the right of an individual to control his or her own personal life. The zones of privacy that
society should not intrude upon without good reason are a person's
body, possessions, beliefs, values, actions, and associations insofar as
these pertain to his or her own private sphere of interest and conduct.[6]
This is a general statement. The right to privacy follows from the value
we place on individual autonomy, i.e., freedom of choice and the recognition of the importance of voluntary choice and individual responsibility. How the right to privacy applies is something that has to be
debated in society because obviously this right is not unlimited, and
society has a right under certain conditions to restrict it, depending upon
considerations of the common good. Nonetheless, it stands as a *general*
principle. I disagree with those libertarians who want to make it an
absolute.

Third, the right to privacy implies that one should have control
over one's body, one's own nutrition and health, and the treatment of
one's illnesses. This entails a principle of self-determination in regard to
questions that emerge in the context of medical treatment.

Fourth, the kind of euthanasia that I am talking about clearly

---

[6]For a fuller discussion of the right to privacy, see KURTZ, *supra* note 1, at 199-230.

applies only to adults. Where do you draw the line? When does a person become an adult? Surely it is before the age of twenty-one; perhaps it even applies to late adolescence, but primarily to adults. It also applies to disabled persons, too, who are adults. I am excluding children or infants from this discussion. The movement for voluntary euthanasia obviously does not mean voluntary choice by a child or an infant. That is a separate and distinct issue that I can't treat here, though there are important moral questions that have emerged concerning infanticide and that have to be carefully discussed. But I am only focusing upon adults in this essay.

Fifth, voluntary euthanasia implies that the adults are competent, able to make choices, and rational. Now, what is the meaning of the concept of *rationality?* This is a key question. But we are talking about the decision of a coherent person that is the result of a reflective judgment, and not a product of a hasty decision based upon the immediacy of pain.

Sixth, euthanasia involves informed consent. The patient should be fully informed in any medical context as far as possible so that he or she is capable of understanding his or her condition and the options and the consequences of alternative treatments. I don't like the term *patient*, but I would prefer *active person* who is being treated and is involved in a decision of what to do. The term *patient* suggests a paternalistic approach, where others decide what to do for him, but the term *active person* suggests active participation by the person in his own health care.

Seventh, an essential part of the movement for voluntary euthanasia is the insistence that the choice to end one's life should follow from reflection made over a period of time. Therefore a living will becomes crucial. I think most of the states now recognize the validity of a living will. The decision to opt for euthanasia ought to follow from a long-standing intention of a person that under certain conditions he or she does not want to have his or her life prolonged and possibly wishes to hasten its termination.

Eighth, another salient point is that voluntary euthanasia applies *only* to dying persons, i.e., only to people with terminal illnesses or injuries that are terminal. It doesn't apply to everyone in all circumstances. In my view, you cannot apply euthanasia unless you have a case where the process of dying has already set in. Here, in the judgment of the dying person, the quality of life is so impaired and so undermined that the person decides that he or she does not want to go on living and suffering and, having weighed the options, decides to die.

Ninth, these considerations apply, of course, to *passive* euthanasia. It is difficult to understand how anyone could be opposed to passive euthanasia. I suppose that in the debate today, virtually everyone supports some form of passive euthanasia. What this means is that no extraordinary means should be used to keep a person who objects alive who would otherwise die.

Tenth, in my judgment it also should apply to *active* euthanasia. Here is the crux of the controversy today. What does active euthanasia mean? If a person is dying or has a terminal illness and if he or she wishes to have some assistance in hastening the end of his life, then you can raise the question of whether a pluralistic and democratic society, which allows options or choices, should allow that person's request to be fulfilled. This can be done either by increasing dosages of morphine or by removing feeding tubes and other life-sustaining systems. Where to draw the line between active and passive euthanasia is often difficult to say. But clearly at one end of the scale, active euthanasia means that if someone is already dying and pleads for help to die with peace and dignity, then we have a moral obligation—and perhaps a legal right—to acknowledge that voluntary choice.

As I see it, it would be better if all of these matters were kept private, within the family, and were left to individuals to decide for themselves in consultation with their physicians. Both passive and active euthanasia have been going on from time immemorial. The problem has been exacerbated recently because many people who normally would have died were, because of the power of modern science and technology, kept alive beyond the time that would have been possible in the past. It is the tremendous progress of modern science that has led to these moral problems. The real question is not whether we should let the person die but whether we should keep the person alive in one sense. In either case we are intervening in natural processes, as I think we can and should do. Nonetheless, it would be better if this were a private matter. But since there may be misuses and abuses, society has to be concerned that people's rights are not abused and that there are not violations of the right to live. Therefore there is a need for legal protections, which must be worked out by democratic means.

Eleventh, what about the obligations of others? We're talking about those individuals within our community who do not believe in euthanasia and are opposed to it. Some individuals believe that suffering has some spiritual merit and that suicide is a sin, and they are profoundly offended by any effort to terminate a life. Of course, euthanasia does not apply to them. That would be involuntary euthanasia, which I would strenuously oppose. All that voluntary euthanasia recognizes is that there are tens of millions of people who, after a deliberative process, have decided that they want to terminate their lives, actively or passively. The question is whether their rights should be recognized. From the standpoint of the bystander, what are the principles that should guide that person? Let me emphasize an earlier point that nothing that I have said is absolute. There are only general guidelines, and it may be that in certain cases you would want to override autonomy. One can think of moral dilemmas in which this may be the most meaningful option. I am prepared to admit that. But, if you decide to limit autonomy, you have to give a *good reason*. In other words, it seems to me that we have a prima facie obligation to recognize and respect the autonomy of those persons who, after a reflective decision, have opted for voluntary active euthanasia. If you are going to deny them that right, then you have to make a strong case. There may be some cases concerning disabled or handicapped persons where this may apply, where coercion from those around them has applied undue pressure, where the decision is not reflective, or where other pressing factors may pertain. Euthanasia has to be a freely chosen option on the part of the person.

From the standpoint of the bystander, it seems to me that there is still another ethical principle that is relevant, and that is the principle that Marvin Kohl has eloquently enunciated in his writings, the principle of beneficence.[7] This suggests that loving members of the family, relatives, friends, even doctors and lawyers who know the person have some sense of compassion and mercy. I think this is a deep, Christian principle of Christ's commandment to "love thy neighbour"[8] and to be merciful to those who suffer. Accordingly, if there is a plea from someone that you know to help him to die with dignity, then that entails a kind of prima facie moral duty. That is a very powerful moral obligation in human society and should be considered within the context of a moral dilemma that a person is facing.

Another moral principle that should be taken into consideration is nonmalfeasance. We ought not to harm those persons whom we love or those people whose care we're entrusted with. This means that we ought to be concerned primarily with what will benefit the person. It is not always to the benefit of the active patient to be kept alive at all costs. You may be doing good to the active patient to help him die and thus not harm him by prolonging his agony. In other words, if you keep someone alive against his will who might otherwise die with some dignity, you may be hurting him and are inflicting cruel and unnecessary harm on him. That is immoral. Here then is a double-edged prima facie principle of beneficence and of nonmalfeasance: and it has emerged as a "common moral decency."

[7]*See* MARVIN KOHL, BENEFICENT EUTHANASIA (1975); MARVIN KOHL, THE MORALITY OF KILLING (1974). For another defense of euthanasia by a humanist, see JOSEPH FLETCHER, HUMANHOOD 149-58 (1979).

[8]*Mark* 12:31.

There may be cases in which an individual opts for euthanasia, while his relatives or his community oppose his decision as unreasonable. In such a case you have an obligation to try to persuade that individual to act otherwise. If you have a person who insists that he does not want to be kept alive and you think that he is mistaken and that he hasn't examined all of his options, or that he is reacting emotionally, then you have a duty to try to persuade him that there is still some quality to life and that he ought not to exit so rapidly. And you ought to try to prevail. But if, in the last analysis, the active person who is suffering does not agree and insists that he still wants to die, then I submit that we ought to respect that demand for dignity. We need not ourselves wish to help that person to die, and if in our inner conscience we cannot, we should at least not prohibit or prevent him from dying, thus imposing our will upon him. In a clash of wills, it is the person himself who must voluntarily decide whether his life is still meaningful, or whether he wants to die gracefully and with as much dignity as he can muster.

Letting Patients Die: Legal and Moral Reflections

Sanford H. Kadish†

Fifty years of medical advances have profoundly challenged some of our most deeply held moral beliefs about life and death. Doctors and hospitals that once would have prolonged life now routinely discontinue life-sustaining treatment. Professor Kadish examines the legal and moral aspects of these decisions. Courts have justified discontinuing treatment on grounds of the patient's right to autonomy. While they have sought to confine their decisions to letting-die situations, the strategy creates an instability, since in principle the right of autonomy extends to choices of suicide, assisted suicide, and active euthanasia. Professor Kadish then considers advance directives and the doctrine courts use when there has been no advance directive, the doctrine of substituted judgment. He argues that advance directives lack the full moral force of contemporary choices and should yield to the current compassionate interests of the patient, as well as to the patient's choice to live even if less than fully competent. Finally, he concludes that courts have gone astray by invoking the principle of autonomy in substituted judgment situations, because autonomy cannot be at issue when the patient has made no choice. Instead, Professor Kadish favors a decision based on the best interests of the patient, taken to mean a decision in conformity with the values and commitments that guided the patient's competent life, and one regardful of the quality of the experiences of the present patient. He rejects a standard that would seek a decision designed to make the patient's life as a whole a better one in any objective sense.

Since World War II dramatic advances in the power of medicine to sustain life have led to profound changes in the types of illness from which people die. At one time pneumonia, influenza, and other communicable diseases were the most common causes of death.[1] Today chronic,

---

† Copyright Sanford H. Kadish, 1992, Morrison Professor of Law, Emeritus, Boalt Hall School of Law, University of California, Berkeley. B.S.S. 1942, City College of New York; LL.B. 1948, Columbia University School of Law; Juris Dr. (h.c.) 1983, University of Cologne. This essay was written as a contribution to a *Festschrift* for Professor Joel Feinberg: IN HARM'S WAY: ESSAYS IN HONOR OF JOEL FEINBERG (Jules Coleman et al. eds., forthcoming 1993)

I am indebted to Meir Dan-Cohen, Michael Flick, Mort Kadish, Yale Kamisar, Eric Rakowski, and Jeremy Waldron for their critical reading and helpful suggestions, and to Daniel Saunders for his faultless research assistance.

1. PRESIDENT'S COMM'N FOR THE STUDY OF ETHICAL PROBLEMS IN MEDICINE AND

degenerative diseases such as cancer, heart disease, and cerebrovascular disease have become predominant, accounting for approximately seventy percent of all deaths in the United States.[2] This in turn has shifted the locus of dying. Whereas at the turn of the century most patients died at home, today nearly eighty percent of deaths occur in hospitals. Patients with degenerative diseases can be kept biologically alive for long periods of time through the use of drugs and machines, though sensate and functional life has gone forever.[3] As a consequence, in the language of one court, "[q]uestions of fate have . . . become matters of choice raising profound 'moral, social, technological, philosophical, and legal questions . . . .' "[4] For example, does keeping people biologically alive in these circumstances make sense? Whose interests are served by sustaining a life so limited in scope? In what does the value of a life lie? What is the role of the patient's preferences in cases where he has made a competent current choice, where he has made an earlier choice, where he has made no choice? These questions, thrust upon us by advances in medical technology, raise doubts about the continued validity of some of our most deeply held moral beliefs about life and death.

Despite some paradoxes and inconsistencies (for example, in our attitudes toward war, capital punishment, and risk), preservation of human life is generally seen as a supreme good in our culture.[5] Intentionally taking a life, at least an innocent life, is among the worst wrongs a person can commit. It is everywhere a crime, punishable by the severest penalties known to the law. Every innocent person, no matter what the quality of his life, has a legal right that his life not be taken.[6] Moreover, so great a value is put on life that a person may not waive his right to life; killing does not become non-culpable because the victim consented.[7] For similar reasons, suicide and attempted suicide were crimes at common law,[8] and helping another kill himself is still a crime in many American states.[9] Finally, although the law does not generally criminalize failure to save another, a physician who intentionally fails to save a

---

BIOMEDICAL AND BEHAVIORAL RESEARCH, DECIDING TO FOREGO LIFE-SUSTAINING TREATMENT 16 (1983) [hereinafter PRESIDENT'S COMM'N].

2. ROBERT F. WEIR, ABATING TREATMENT WITH CRITICALLY ILL PATIENTS 10-12 (1989).

3. PRESIDENT'S COMM'N, *supra* note 1, at 17-18.

4. *In re* Farrell, 529 A.2d 404, 406 (N.J. 1987) (quoting *In re* Conroy, 486 A.2d 1209, 1220 (N.J. 1985)).

5. *See* SANFORD H. KADISH, BLAME AND PUNISHMENT 109-32 (1987).

6. This is subject to the possible exception of a necessity defense, where the taking of one life is the only way to avoid the death of several. There is moral authority for this defense, but its legal authority in cases of killing is doubtful. *Id.* at 123.

7. *See* GLANVILLE WILLIAMS, TEXTBOOK OF CRIMINAL LAW 579 (2d ed. 1983).

8. 4 WILLIAM BLACKSTONE, COMMENTARIES *189; *see also* Paul Marcus, *Suicide: Legal Aspects, in* 4 ENCYCLOPEDIA OF CRIME AND JUSTICE 1526-27 (Sanford H. Kadish ed., 1983).

9. *See* George P. Smith, II, *All's Well that Ends Well: Toward a Policy of Assisted Rational Suicide or Merely Enlightened Self-Determination?,* 22 U.C. DAVIS L. REV. 275, 290-91 & n.106 (1989).

patient's life when able to do so may be guilty of some form of culpable homicide. These norms constitute the moral tradition threatened by the remarkable power of medicine to prolong life. How can this moral tradition ever accommodate a deliberate decision not to use all available medical power to save a life?

Departures from the official pieties usually occur first in our practices and only later in our professions.[10] So it has been with the issue of life-sustaining treatment. Doctors and hospitals have long engaged in or tolerated practices that contravene the moral tradition I have just described.[11] For decades doctors and hospitals have accepted what is called negative euthanasia. "Every day . . . respirators are turned off, life-perpetuating intravenous infusions stopped, proposed surgery canceled, and drugs countermanded. So-called Code 90 stickers are put on many record-jackets, indicating 'Give no intensive care or resuscita-

---

10. Other examples of this lag time can be found in the development of no-fault divorce, which came well after the widespread nullification of strict divorce requirements, *see* MAX RHEINSTEIN, MARRIAGE STABILITY, DIVORCE, AND THE LAW 51-105 (1972); Lawrence M. Friedman, *Rights of Passage: Divorce Law in Historical Perspective,* 63 OR. L. REV. 649, 664-69 (1984); the legitimation of plea bargaining which followed decades of its widespread but officially denied practice, *see* Brady v. United States, 397 U.S. 742 (1970); MORTIMER R. KADISH & SANFORD H. KADISH, DISCRETION TO DISOBEY 83-85 (1973); and the toleration of abortion under certain circumstances before Roe v. Wade, 410 U.S. 113 (1973), *see* Herbert L. Packer & Ralph J. Gampell, *Therapeutic Abortion: A Problem in Law and Medicine,* 11 STAN. L. REV. 417 (1959). There are situations, of course, in which pronouncements of moral principles precede and influence the practices themselves. One thinks of the Supreme Court's extension of the Bill of Rights and of its civil rights decisions, particularly in the Warren era. But these are cases where the change is from the low ground of practice to the high ground of principle, not where the change is the other way around.

11. Despite statutes in over half the states making it criminal to help another commit suicide, several recent, widely publicized incidents of this kind have occurred. In one case a Rochester doctor described in the pages of the *New England Journal of Medicine* how he prescribed the barbiturates that a long-standing patient needed to kill herself following her refusal of treatment for a severe form of leukemia. Timothy E. Quill, *Death and Dignity: A Case of Individualized Decision Making,* 324 NEW ENG. J. MED. 691, 693 (1991); *see* Lawrence K. Altman, *Doctor Says He Gave Patient Drug to Help Her Commit Suicide,* N.Y. TIMES, Mar. 7, 1991, at A1. An upstate New York prosecutor sought an indictment against the doctor for feloniously assisting another to commit suicide. Criticism of the prosecution was widespread. The officers and members of the Council of the Society of General Internal Medicine wrote the District Attorney that Dr. Quill's actions "were consistent with the range of acceptable practice of compassionate physicians . . . ." Letter from Robert H. Fletcher, President, Society of General Internal Medicine, to Charles Siragusa, District Attorney, SGIM NEWS (Society of General Internal Medicine), Oct. 1991, at 5. Significantly, the grand jury declined to indict. Lawrence K. Altman, *Jury Declines to Indict a Doctor Who Said He Aided in a Suicide,* N.Y. TIMES, July 27, 1991, at A1.

Another recently publicized example is the case of Dr. Kevorkian. He connected an Alzheimer's victim to a suicide device he had made, and watched as she pushed a button to operate it and died. The victim had apparently traveled to Michigan in order to use the machine because Michigan law on assisting suicide was ambiguous, there being no statute explicitly making it criminal to help another commit suicide. Lisa Belkin, *Doctor Tells of First Death Using His Suicide Device,* N.Y. TIMES, June 6, 1990, at A1, B6.

Dr. Kevorkian has since used his machine on other patients who have enlisted his services, and the final chapter on his activities has yet to be written. The "Dr. Strangelove" character of his death-promotional activities, however, has drawn considerable negative reaction. *See* Rob Carson, *Washington's I-119,* HASTINGS CENTER REP., Mar.-Apr. 1992, at 7, 9.

tion.' "[12] And though medical killing on request (active euthanasia) is apparently not common, neither is it unknown in American hospitals.[13]

The public has come largely to accept these practices, principally through the impact of such dramatic and highly publicized cases as *In re Quinlan.*[14] In 1976, the New Jersey Supreme Court held that a parent of Karen Quinlan, a young woman in a permanent vegetative state, could authorize removal of a respirator that was keeping Karen biologically alive.[15] Since then, public opinion polls have revealed an impressive shift of opinion in just one generation from a majority opposed to "pulling the plug" on permanently comatose patients to a large majority—sometimes nearing 90%—in favor of such measures.[16] Opinion as to whether doctors should be permitted to actively kill incurable and comatose patients has also changed. In 1947, a majority disapproved.[17] Since then, majorities of up to 64% have favored such proposals.[18]

There appears to be even less dissent when the patient is not comatose and competently chooses to die. A recent national survey showed that 79% of adults support laws allowing terminally ill patients to refuse life-sustaining treatment or to order that it be stopped.[19] A recent California poll indicates that about 70% of Californians feel that the assisted suicide of seriously ill patients who wish to die should be legalized.[20] In Washington state, voters defeated a referendum proposing that doctors be permitted to kill terminally ill patients at their request by a

---

12. JOSEPH FLETCHER, HUMANHOOD: ESSAYS IN BIOMEDICAL ETHICS 149 (1979).

13. *See It's Over, Debbie,* 259 JAMA 272 (1988) (anonymous letter describing doctor-author's administration of lethal dosage of morphine to patient in great distress and dying of incurable ovarian cancer who asked that death be advanced). Over 150 letters commenting on this letter were received by the editor of the journal. We are told that of those from physicians, 80% were unfavorable, implying that many, perhaps up to 20%, were supportive. George D. Lundberg, *"It's Over, Debbie" and the Euthanasia Debate,* 259 JAMA 2142 (1988) (editorial describing response to letter).

14. 355 A.2d 647 (N.J.), *cert. denied,* 429 U.S. 922 (1976).

15. *Id.* at 671-72.

16. Marcia Coyle, *How Americans View High Court,* NAT'L L.J., Feb. 26, 1990, at 1, 36 (citing National Law Journal/Lexis poll finding 88% in favor of letting family decide whether to end life support); Andrew H. Malcolm, *A Judicial Sanction for Death by Assent,* N.Y. TIMES, June 28, 1987, § 4, at 26 (discussing a shift in public opinion polls to a two-thirds majority in favor of giving patients right to terminate treatment); Clay Richards & B.D. Colen, *Poll: Most Favor "Right to Die" Laws,* NEWSDAY, June 10, 1990, at 15 (citing Times Mirror Center poll finding 80% supporting right to terminate treatment). The rise of a book on how to commit suicide (Derek Humphry's *Final Exit*) to the top of the best-seller list further reveals the shift in public attitudes towards death and dying. *See* Katrine Ames, *Last Rights,* NEWSWEEK, Aug. 26, 1991, at 40.

17. *See* DEREK HUMPHRY & ANN WICKETT, THE RIGHT TO DIE 35-36 (1986).

18. Melinda Beck, *The Doctor's Suicide Van,* NEWSWEEK, June 18, 1990, at 46, 47 (citing recent Hemlock Society poll reporting 64% approval); Andrew H. Malcolm, *Giving Death a Hand: Rending Issue,* N.Y. TIMES, June 9, 1990, § 1, at 6 (citing N.Y. Times/CBS News Poll finding 53% approval).

19. Richards & Colen, *supra* note 16, at 15.

20. Lisa Belkin, *Doctors Debate Helping the Terminally Ill Die,* N.Y. TIMES, May 24, 1989, at A1, A25.

vote of 56% to 44%.[21] But a month earlier a poll showed that, of those likely to vote, 61% were in favor, 27% were opposed, and 12% were undecided.[22] The defeat of the referendum might have been a manifestation of the "cold feet" phenomenon that sometimes occurs when the voter enters the voting booth.[23] Despite this apparent setback, the marked increase in public acceptance of killing terminally ill patients, both in Washington and nationally, has been striking.

Equally striking are the changes in enacted laws. When Karen Quinlan became comatose in 1975, no state recognized a patient's right to set limits on life-prolonging medical efforts. Now, over forty states have passed "living will" statutes[24] giving effect to a person's choice of medical treatment in the event of incompetency.[25] Although these laws tend to be highly restrictive,[26] they nonetheless represent a radical departure from what could have been expected of a legislature a decade earlier. More significantly, many states have enacted statutes allowing a person to authorize an agent, in the event of the patient's incompetence, to make those health care decisions that the patient could have made if competent.[27]

---

21. Jane Gross, *Voters Turn Down Mercy Killing Idea*, N.Y. TIMES, Nov. 7, 1991, at B16.

22. Peter Steinfels, *Beliefs*, N.Y. TIMES, Nov. 9, 1991, at 11; *cf. Euthanasia Favored in Poll*, N.Y. TIMES, Nov. 4, 1991, at A16 (noting results of October 1991 national poll showing that "nearly two out of three Americans favor doctor-assisted suicide and euthanasia for terminally ill patients who request it").

23. The negative reaction to the exploits of Dr. Kevorkian and his suicide machine, to which wide publicity was given in the days before the vote, is thought by some to have been a contributing factor. For a review of the public debate preceding the vote, see Carson, *supra* note 11.

24. *Introduction* to REFUSAL OF TREATMENT LEGISLATION: A STATE BY STATE COMPILATION OF ENACTED AND MODEL STATUTES (Society for the Right to Die ed., 1991) [hereinafter REFUSAL OF TREATMENT LEGISLATION]. Living-will statutes had been introduced in state legislatures as early as 1906, but none was enacted until after the *Quinlan* decision. Part of the explanation is that the early proposals would have authorized active euthanasia, while the current crop of statutes excludes it. *See* 3 JOEL FEINBERG, THE MORAL LIMITS OF THE CRIMINAL LAW: HARM TO SELF 367-68 (1986). California passed the first living-will statute in 1976. *See* Natural Death Act, CAL. HEALTH & SAFETY CODE §§ 7185-7195 (West Supp. 1992).

25. REFUSAL OF TREATMENT LEGISLATION, *supra* note 24.

26. Typically, living-will statutes apply only to persons in permanent vegetative states, or where death is inevitable and imminent and the living will is executed after the person becomes terminally ill. They also typically exclude the withdrawal of artificial nutrition and hydration, as well as "affirmative euthanasia." *See, e.g.*, CAL. CIV. CODE §§ 2430-2444 (West Supp. 1992) (California's provision for durable power of attorney for health care). For a comprehensive review of state legislation, see generally REFUSAL OF TREATMENT LEGISLATION, *supra* note 24.

27. There have been a number of studies of judicial developments under these statutes. *See, e.g.*, MARK A. HALL & IRA M. ELLMAN, HEALTH CARE LAW AND ETHICS IN A NUTSHELL 283-88 (1990); *Developments in the Law—Medical Technology and the Law*, 103 HARV. L. REV. 1519, 1670-72 (1990) [hereinafter *Developments*]; Rebecca Dresser, *Life, Death, and Incompetent Patients: Conceptual Infirmities and Hidden Values in the Law*, 28 ARIZ. L. REV. 373 (1986); Linda C. Fentiman, *Privacy and Personhood Revisited: A New Framework for Substitute Decisionmaking for the Incompetent, Incurably Ill Adult*, 57 GEO. WASH. L. REV. 801, 818-40 (1989); Nancy K. Rhoden, *Litigating Life and Death*, 102 HARV. L. REV. 375, 375-437 (1989). The strength of public policy behind these laws is evident in the federal Patient Self-Determination Act, amending the Social Security Act, which seeks to assure wider publicity to state laws permitting patients to refuse

In light of this sea change in public, medical, and legislative judgments, it was inevitable that American courts would be called upon to respond. Since the 1975 watershed opinion in the *Quinlan* case, there have been many cases from the state and federal courts, with most decisions authorizing letting the patient die. These cases will figure prominently in this paper. Part I describes the courts' development of the right of autonomy, their use of it as the basis for changing the law, and the ways they sought to limit the scope of change portended by full application of that concept. Parts II and III deal with the problem of determining when patients may be left to die when the right of autonomy is not fully applicable, as in cases of advance directives, or not applicable at all, as in cases where the patient never made a choice during his competent life.

I

AUTONOMY AND THE COMPETENT PATIENT

The fulcrum on which the courts moved the law away from its tradiional hostility to forgoing treatment was the concept of consent. The requirement of consent goes back to the common law, which made it a battery to subject a person to any force to which he had not consented, including such force as might be involved in providing medical treatment.[28] In dealing with such issues as the constitutionality of laws prohibiting contraception and abortion, the United States Supreme Court gave new and powerful support to the common law concept of consent.[29] The Court developed a jurisprudence of autonomy (sometimes under the misleading label of privacy), finding in the Constitution a fundamental right of individuals to make choices with regard to their own bodies. The lesson of the new autonomy jurisprudence for refusals of medical treatment was plain, and the *Quinlan* case[30] was one of the first to draw it explicitly. In that case the New Jersey court found that just as the constitutional right of autonomy over one's body encompasses a woman's decision to have an abortion, so does it "encompass a patient's decision to decline medical treatment," at least under some circumstances.[31]

---

treatment. Omnibus Budget Reconciliation Act of 1990, Pub. L. No. 101-508, § 4751, 104 Stat. 1388, 1388-204 to -206. Among other things, it requires medical institutions receiving Medicare or Medicaid funds to provide all patients with written information on their rights under state law to refuse medical care, including information on advance directives. It also requires the Secretary of Health and Human Services to develop and distribute informational materials on these subjects.

28. *See* Schloendorff v. Society of N.Y. Hosp., 105 N.E. 92, 93 (N.Y. 1914) (Cardozo, J.) ("Every human being of adult years and sound mind has a right to determine what shall be done with his own body; and a surgeon who performs an operation without his patient's consent commits an assault . . . ."), *overruled on other grounds by* Bing v. Thunig, 143 N.E.2d 3 (N.Y. 1957).

29. *See* Roe v. Wade, 410 U.S. 113 (1973) (right to abortion); Eisenstadt v. Baird, 405 U.S. 438 (1972) (same); Griswold v. Connecticut, 381 U.S. 479 (1965) (right to access to contraception).

30. *In re* Quinlan, 355 A.2d 647 (N.J.), *cert. denied,* 429 U.S. 922 (1976).

31. *Id.* at 663.

Other courts soon followed the *Quinlan* lead.[32]

In *Cruzan v. Director, Missouri Department of Health,*[33] the United States Supreme Court, in an opinion by Chief Justice Rehnquist, went a good distance toward lending its authority to a constitutional right to refuse medical treatment. The case involved a Missouri statute requiring that before artificial nutrition and hydration could be withdrawn from a patient in a permanent vegetative state, it must be established by "clear and convincing" evidence that she had decided when competent not to be kept alive in these circumstances.[34] Although upholding the constitutionality of the Missouri standard, the opinion stated that the logic of the Court's prior opinions supported the existence of a patient's constitutionally protected interest in refusing life-sustaining medical treatment, including artificial nutrition and hydration.[35]

As the Court further noted in *Cruzan,* however, the existence of a constitutionally protected interest does not necessarily preclude state regulation, for a state might have sufficiently weighty interests to override that of the individual.[36] Indeed, state and lower federal courts have recognized four distinct state interests that weigh against the choice of a competent patient to decline treatment: 1) its interest in preserving life as such; 2) its interest in preventing suicide; 3) its interest in protecting the interests of innocent third parties; and 4) its interest in maintaining the ethical integrity of the medical profession.[37] Only the first two figure at all seriously in the decisions, however.[38] Though some courts have treated the interest in preserving life and the interest in preventing suicide separately,[39] they are obviously interrelated considerations.[40] It is noteworthy, however, that lower courts in virtually all cases have upheld

---

32. *See Developments, supra* note 27, at 1661-65. Since *Quinlan*, courts have upheld with substantial unanimity the right of competent patients (under state or federal law) to reject life-sustaining treatment, at least in cases of terminal disease. *Id.* at 1645. Some have affirmed this right where competent patients were suffering painful and incurable ailments; many have extended the right to include rejection of artificial nutrition and hydration. A review of the case law may be found in the materials cited *supra* note 27.

33. 110 S. Ct. 2841 (1990).

34. *Id.* at 2854.

35. *Id.* at 2852.

36. *Id.*

37. *See* Superintendent of Belchertown State Sch. v. Saikewicz, 370 N.E.2d 417, 425 (Mass. 1977); *In re* Conroy, 486 A.2d 1209, 1223 (N.J. 1985).

38. *See* Martha A. Matthews, Comment, *Suicidal Competence and the Patient's Right to Refuse Lifesaving Treatment,* 75 CALIF. L. REV. 707, 729-43 (1987). In the early Jehovah's Witness blood transfusion cases, however, some courts gave as a further reason for compelling life-saving transfusions the interests of the patient's minor children. *Id.* at 732-33.

39. *See, e.g.,* Bartling v. Superior Court, 209 Cal. Rptr. 220, 225 (Ct. App. 1984); Brophy v. New England Sinai Hosp., 497 N.E.2d 626, 635-38 (Mass. 1986).

40. *See Conroy,* 486 A.2d at 1224 ("This state interest in protecting people from direct and purposeful self-destruction is motivated by, if not encompassed within, the state's more basic interest in preserving life. Thus, it is questionable whether it is a distinct state interest worthy of independent consideration.").

the right of a patient to reject life-sustaining treatment as required by a constitutional right of autonomy, and as such outweighing these state interests.[41]

The problem that naturally arises concerning this right of autonomy is its extent. Does it come into play only in these medical contexts, or does it extend to all cases in which the person chooses to achieve his own death, including perhaps those in which he obtains the help of another to further his choice? Courts have declined to extend the right of autonomy to nonmedical contexts and have sought to avoid doing so by distinguishing medical letting-die situations from conventional suicide and consensual euthanasia. Since such an extension would profoundly unsettle existing mores and might raise formidable problems for the law in preventing exploitation and abuse, it is not hard to understand the courts' motivation. Still, putting prudential considerations aside for the moment, can these distinctions withstand principled analysis?

One ground on which courts have sought to distinguish letting-die situations from conventional suicide is that the latter requires affirmative life-taking actions. On this view a patient refusing to be attached to an apparatus necessary for his survival is not taking his life, but is simply letting nature take its course. Hence death is caused by the disease, not by the person himself,[42] nor by the physician who respects his wishes. How persuasive is this distinction? Perhaps there is some support for this approach in the legal principle that imposes no duty to act to prevent a prohibited harm except in specified circumstances. After all, the traditional formulation of the ban on suicide is cast in terms of action,[43] so it is arguable that one who seeks death through inaction would not fall within the ban.[44] Yet it would be odd if that were so. The traditional disinclination of Anglo-American courts to interpret prohibitions on

---

41. *See supra* note 32.

42. *See, e.g.,* Satz v. Perlmutter, 362 So. 2d 160, 162-63 (Fla. Dist. Ct. App. 1978), *aff'd on opinion below,* 379 So. 2d 359 (Fla. 1980); Superintendent of Belchertown State Sch. v. Saikewicz, 370 N.E.2d 417, 426 n.11 (Mass. 1977) ("[T]o the extent that the cause of death was from natural causes the patient did not set the death producing agent in motion . . . ."); *Conroy,* 486 A.2d at 1224 ("Refusing medical intervention merely allows the disease to take its natural course; if death were eventually to occur, it would be the result, primarily, of the underlying disease, and not the result of a self-inflicted injury."); *see also* Norman L. Cantor, *The Permanently Unconscious Patient, Non-Feeding and Euthanasia,* 15 AM. J.L. & MED. 381, 433 (1989) ("The assertion that rejection of life-saving medical treatment by competent patients constitutes suicide has been uniformly rejected— usually based on a distinction between letting nature take its course and initiating external death-causing agents.").

43. *See, e.g.,* 4 BLACKSTONE, *supra* note 8, at *189 ("A *felo de se* therefore is he that deliberately puts an end to his own existence . . . .").

44. Deliberately starving oneself to death tends to strike people as suicide, although legal authority for that view seems limited to cases approving the force-feeding of prisoners, a very special situation involving the state's interest in the administration of the criminal justice system. The cases cited by Justice Scalia in his concurring opinion in the *Cruzan* case are of this kind. *See* Cruzan v. Director, Mo. Dep't of Health, 110 S. Ct. 2841, 2861 (Scalia, J., concurring).

causing certain results as requiring action to prevent those results is based on the value of the freedom of the individual not to be constrained by the interests of others. That value is not at stake in the prohibition of suicide for two reasons: first, because the interests of others are not necessarily involved, and second, because the ban on suicidal actions already constitutes a major inroad upon the person's freedom, so that excluding cases of passive choice to die out of concern for that very freedom would be eccentric at best.

In any event, if we view the issue in terms of moral principle rather than legal doctrine and take the traditional anti-suicide position as a serious starting point, the distinction between intentionally killing oneself and intentionally submitting to an avoidable death is suspect. There is disagreement over the general moral significance of the distinction between doing and letting happen,[45] but the intuitive appeal of the distinction is less in some cases than in others, and its appeal seems particularly weak in cases of treatment refusal.[46]

Consider a patient who finds himself attached against his will to some life-sustaining apparatus he had earlier explicitly rejected. He removes it for the same reason he earlier rejected it—he prefers death to living attached to a machine—and dies moments later. Presumably this would constitute suicide, since he achieved his death by positive actions. But could we justifiably say that if the doctors had followed his instructions and he had died, this would not be suicide because his death would then not have been caused by the patient's actions? Or consider an analogous case: a paralyzed man, sitting on a beach threatened by an incoming tide, deliberately, in order to end his life, declines to allow a lifeguard to move him out of harm's way, and drowns in consequence. (To make the analogy closer, assume he took no action to place himself in danger from the tide—say, for example, he was initially placed there against his will.) Would it not be correct to see this as a suicide? Yet the person dying of a disease who chooses not to permit some medical intervention that would save him is in no different a situation.

We might have good reasons to think that in certain circumstances intentionally achieving one's death is justifiable, or that it is less blameworthy in some circumstances than in others. Moreover, we may for these reasons, or indeed for other reasons of a more practical and prudential character, want to call it something else. But as a matter of prin-

---

45. *See generally* JONATHAN GLOVER, CAUSING DEATH AND SAVING LIVES 92-112 (1977); Warren S. Quinn, *Actions, Intentions, and Consequences: The Doctrine of Doing and Allowing,* 98 PHIL. REV. 287 (1989).

46. *Accord Conroy,* 486 A.2d at 1233-34 (rejecting "the distinction that some have made between actively hastening death by terminating treatment and passively allowing a person to die of a disease as one of limited use in a legal analysis of such a decision-making situation"); PRESIDENT'S COMM'N, *supra* note 1, at 4, 65-72 (discussing problem of overreliance on act/omission distinction and difficulty of evaluating moral significance of acts and omissions causing death).

ciple, that a person achieves his goal by refusing necessary medical intervention hardly seems a better reason to treat his action differently than that a person achieves his goal by letting the tide come to him rather than going to it.[47]

Another approach some courts have taken is to define suicide to require a purpose to take one's own life, sometimes called a specific intent. Those who reject treatment, it is reasoned, do not want to die; indeed, as one court put it, "they may fervently wish to live, but to do so free of unwanted medical technology, surgery, or drugs, and without protracted suffering."[48] When they reject treatment, therefore, they are not committing suicide.[49] Recently Ronald Dworkin has lent his considerable authority to this position.[50] In the course of criticizing Justice Scalia's argument in *Cruzan* that the venerability of the tradition of state condemnation of suicide establishes the state's equal entitlement to regulate treatment refusal,[51] Dworkin asserts that it is "bizarre to classify as suicide someone's decision to reject treatment that would keep him alive but at a cost he and many other people think too great."[52] He appears to be making two points: the first, that death is achieved by failing to act, I have already discussed; the second, that the person's decision is not suicide because his intention is not to achieve his death as such, but to avoid a life whose burdens are not worth the living, is an argument I take to be equivalent to the specific intent argument.

A case may be made for the specific intent argument in this context along the following lines. The purpose of the classic suicide in inflicting a mortal injury on himself, in the sense of purpose as the "conscious

---

47.

It would not make much sense to say that one may not kill oneself by walking into the sea, but may sit on the beach until submerged by the incoming tide; or that one may not intentionally lock oneself into a cold storage locker, but may refrain from coming indoors when the temperature drops below freezing.

Cruzan, 110 S. Ct. at 2861 (Scalia, J., concurring).

48.   *Conroy*, 486 A.2d at 1224; *see also* Superintendent of Belchertown State Sch. v. Saikewicz, 370 N.E.2d 417, 426 n.11 (Mass. 1977) ("[I]n refusing treatment the patient may not have the specific intent to die.").

49.   *See, e.g., Conroy*, 486 A.2d at 1226 ("[R]ejecting her artificial means of feeding would not constitute attempted suicide, as the decision would probably be based on a wish to be free of medical intervention rather than a specific intent to die, and her death would result, if at all, from her underlying medical condition . . . ."). For a discussion of the cases and a criticism of the distinction, see Matthews, *supra* note 38, at 735-38.

50.   *See* Ronald Dworkin, *The Right to Death*, N.Y. REV. BOOKS, Jan. 31, 1991, at 14.

51.   *Cruzan*, 110 S. Ct. at 2859 (Scalia, J., concurring).

52.   Dworkin, *supra* note 50, at 17. He goes on to say:

Many people whose lives could be lengthened through severe amputations or incapacitating operations decide to die instead, and they are not thought to have taken their own lives for that reason. . . . People imagining themselves as permanently comatose are in the same position: their biological lives could then be prolonged only through medical treatment they would think degrading, and only in a form they would think worse than death. So it is a mistake, for that reason, to describe someone who signs a living will as committing hypothetical suicide.

Id.

object" of an action,[53] is to cause his own death. The same cannot be said of all cases where the person refuses treatment he knows is necessary to keep him alive. In some of these cases his mental state with respect to his death is more properly characterized as knowledge rather than purpose;[54] that is, although he knows that his conduct will result in his death, his conscious object is not to die, but to be free of the medical treatment. That his object is not to die may be seen by noticing that if, contrary to the prediction of his doctors, he recovered without the treatment, his purpose would not be frustrated. The same could not be said of the classic attempted suicide.

The trouble with this line of argument is that the distinction between purpose and knowledge in this context is without moral relevance. The cases where the refusal of treatment can be said not to reflect a specific intent to die are those in which the irremediable condition which makes living not worthwhile to the person is prospective rather than already existing. If it is in prospect, we are able to see his purpose as avoiding his affliction. But when the afflictive condition already exists, the ending of the person's afflicted life would presumably be seen as his purpose in refusing treatment. So, for example, if a patient refuses amputation of his gangrenous legs (because he doesn't want to live without them), his purpose is to avoid the amputation, not to die, so that his subsequent death would not be considered a suicide. He would have been pleased to live if his legs could have been saved. But if a person whose legs have already been amputated refuses medical treatment necessary for his recovery (again because he doesn't want to live without his legs), his purpose is to die, so that his subsequent death *would* be deemed a suicide. But except in the case where death is itself sought as an end (the insured who wants his beneficiary to recover on his life insurance, for example), all suicides are motivated by the desire to end experiencing something unbearable in that person's life. It is hard to see any point in treating choices to end one's life differently depending on whether the motivating condition is present or anticipated.

I suggest, therefore, that the efforts by courts to maintain the traditional authority of the state over suicide by distinguishing it from refusal of treatment do not withstand scrutiny. I do not mean to suggest that the law cannot justifiably make distinctions on pragmatic grounds; it frequently does so for all kinds of prudential considerations. I mean only to suggest that the distinctions under discussion cannot be defended *except* on pragmatic grounds.

Consider the basic argument courts and commentators make on

---

53. *See* MODEL PENAL CODE § 2.02(2)(a) (1985) (a person acts purposely with respect to a result of his conduct if "it is his conscious object to . . . cause such a result").

54. *See id.* § 2.02(2)(b) ("A person acts knowingly with respect to . . . a result of his conduct [if] he is aware that it is practically certain that his conduct will cause such a result.").

behalf of the right to refuse treatment. The argument is that the choice between medical treatment and death is so fundamental that it is protected against state control by a constitutional right of autonomy. That being the case, however, there is no principled basis for denying the same freedom of choice to those not dependent on medical treatment for survival. The failure of efforts to distinguish suicide from refusal of treatment is attributable not simply to usage and definition, but to the equivalence between the two. The moral case for autonomy extends to both if it extends to one.

It isn't hard to surmise why courts have drawn back from the conclusion that there is no difference between suicide and refusal of treatment. To accept it would be to acknowledge a radical break with the received tradition and open the door to positions the courts are not yet willing to adopt: for example, that the state may not act to prevent suicide (except perhaps temporarily to assure competent consent),[55] or to prevent a person from assisting another's suicide, or conceivably even to prevent one person from killing another who competently consents to being killed.[56] By "open the door" I do not mean that courts would be compelled by consistency to adopt these positions. There might well be compelling practical considerations for not doing so, such as fear of

---

[55]. *See* Matthews, *supra* note 38, at 754-57 (suggesting that state interest should be held to extend only to preventing irrational suicides and proposing a test for determining competence).

[56]. *Cf.* FEINBERG, *supra* note 24, at 374 (arguing that only possible justification for state to continue prohibiting euthanasia is a "pragmatic" fear of mistake or abuse); Alister Browne, *Assisted Suicide and Active Voluntary Euthanasia,* 2 CAN. J.L. & JURIS. 35 (1989). *But cf.* Phillipa Foot, *Commentary: Active Euthanasia with Parental Consent,* HASTINGS CENTER REP., Oct. 1979, at 20 (maintaining that it is easier to justify "passive" euthanasia than it is to justify "active" euthanasia). Occasionally one finds a judge making the argument. *See, e.g.,* Bouvia v. Superior Court, 225 Cal. Rptr. 297, 308 (Ct. App. 1986) (Compton, J., concurring). In *Bouvia,* the court authorized the removal of a nasogastric tube from a competent but permanently paralyzed young woman who preferred to starve herself to death rather than to continue living. The concurring judge criticized the majority for not admitting that

> [t]he right to die is an integral part of our right to control our own destinies so long as the rights of others are not affected. That right should, in my opinion, include the ability to enlist assistance from others, including the medical profession, in making death as painless and quick as possible.

Id. at 307.

It is interesting to note that almost 20 years ago, before the *Quinlan* case launched the current rethinking of the right to die, Professor Glanville Williams advocated that proponents of euthanasia adopt as an interim strategy the distinctions to be found in Catholic doctrine between killing and letting die and between ordinary and extraordinary treatment. Glanville Williams, *Euthanasia,* 41 MEDICO-LEGAL J. 14, 18 (1973). He observed:

> If this distinction between an act and an omission is thought to be artificial, its artificiality is imposed on us by our refusal to accord the same moral freedom for action as we do for inaction. Pending a change of thought, the concept of an omission is a useful way of freeing us from some of the consequences of overrigid moral attitudes.

Id. at 21.

For a fuller account of the story of the success of Professor Williams' proposal, see Yale Kamisar, *When Is There a Constitutional "Right to Die"? When Is There No Constitutional "Right to Live"?,* 25 GA. L. REV. 1203, 1214, *passim* (1991).

abuse and difficulties of administering controls to prevent such abuse.[57] I mean only that, by not distinguishing suicide and consensual euthanasia, the courts would by implication be endorsing these positions in principle. Yet this would be the greatest affront to the moral tradition. The courts, therefore, have chosen to improvise lines of distinction, even at the cost of some coherence. The distinctions permit results that courts regard as right in the medical context while giving at least the appearance of continuity with the established tradition and avoiding positions that may be either impractical or premature. As I have suggested, it is not unusual for common law courts to adopt lines of distinction out of unspoken considerations of strategy rather than of logic and principle. This is such a case.

Another way, besides distinguishing suicide, that courts have sought to confine the precedent of permitting patients to refuse life-sustaining treatment has been to stress the special circumstances of the particular case. Courts have emphasized that the patient was soon to die in any event,[58] or that he was in a permanently comatose condition,[59] or that the medical treatment was complicated and intrusive ("extraordinary").[60] The implication is that when the patient is not dying, but instead has some appreciable time to live, or when he is sensate, or when the treatment is not unusual and intrusive ("ordinary"), then the interests in preserving life as such and preventing suicide will prevail, and the patient will be compelled to submit to treatment.

It is hard to be sure whether the courts really mean this, or whether the qualifying language is meant as sugar-coating to make the medicine go down. If the former, then much of the talk of autonomy in the cases is window dressing. After all, if what makes it proper to forgo treatment is the patient's inviolable right to choose, his choice cannot be dependent on a court's willingness to let him have his way in some circumstances but not in others. Therefore, to the extent courts continue to insist that his choice *is* so dependent, they can no longer seriously defend permitting him to die on the ground that it is the patient's inviolable choice that

---

57. *See* FEINBERG, *supra* note 24, at 374; LAURENCE H. TRIBE, AMERICAN CONSTITUTIONAL LAW 1370-71 (2d ed. 1988). Recently, Professor Feinberg has challenged this pragmatic justification on the ground that it falsely assumes it is always a greater evil to let a patient die by mistake than to keep him alive by mistake. Joel Feinberg, *Overlooking the Merits of the Individual Case: An Unpromising Approach to the Right to Die,* 4 RATIO JURIS 131 (1991).

58. *See, e.g.,* Tune v. Walter Reed Army Hosp., 602 F. Supp. 1452, 1455-56 (D.D.C. 1985); Satz v. Perlmutter, 362 So. 2d 160, 162 (Fla. Dist. Ct. App. 1978), *aff'd on opinion below,* 379 So. 2d 359 (Fla. 1980).

59. *See, e.g., In re* Guardianship of Barry, 445 So. 2d 365, 371 (Fla. Dist. Ct. App. 1984); *In re* Peter, 529 A.2d 419, 424 (N.J. 1987); *In re* Quinlan, 355 A.2d 647, 663-64 (N.J.), *cert. denied,* 429 U.S. 922 (1976).

60. *See, e.g.,* Superintendent of Belchertown State Sch. v. Saikewicz, 370 N.E.2d 417, 423-24 (Mass. 1977) (extraordinary methods to prolong life not required); *Quinlan,* 355 A.2d at 667-68 (what is ordinary for curable patient may be extraordinary for terminal patient).

they are enforcing and not their own. I expect that, in the end, these qualifying limitations are not likely to survive as part of the jurisprudence of forgoing medical treatment.[61]

II
AUTONOMY AND THE INCOMPETENT PATIENT

The right of autonomy, then, is what ensures that a patient may refuse treatment. But autonomous choice requires a competent chooser. What of the many cases where the patient is not competent? The response of the courts has been to rest on the intriguing argument that since incompetency cannot diminish a person's rights, denial of an incompetent's choice would constitute unconstitutional discrimination on grounds of personal handicap.[62] At the outset, therefore, the cases of incompetents raise a formidable conceptual problem. How can the right of autonomy over one's own body have any application where the patient is incompetent to make a choice? Whatever rights an incompetent person may be said to possess, how can autonomous choice be one of them when incompetency means precisely the inability to exercise choice?[63]

The current state of law in the area can be briefly summarized.[64] If the incompetent patient, at some time when he was competent, exercised his right to refuse medical treatment under circumstances like those now presented (possibly, but not necessarily, by a formal "advance directive" in a living will), the courts have been willing in most situations to give effect to that choice. Courts have also given effect to choices by patients who, while competent, authorized another to make the choice in the event of his incompetence (by a so-called "durable power of attorney"). If, during competency, the patient did not execute an advance directive, appoint an agent, or indicate a choice in some other way (which is the usual case),[65] the courts have invoked the concept of "substituted judgment" (sometimes called "surrogate decision-making"). Under this

---

61. The extraordinary/ordinary distinction seems already defunct. *See, e.g., In re* Conroy, 486 A.2d 1209, 1234-36 (N.J. 1985) (decided nine years after *Quinlan* by same court, rejecting any distinction between ordinary and extraordinary treatment or between termination of artificial feedings and termination of other forms of life-sustaining medical treatment); PRESIDENT'S COMM'N, *supra* note 1, at 82-89 (criticizing distinction as hopelessly ambiguous). Professor Kamisar has concluded, "The extraordinary/ordinary means distinction has been widely criticized and is now widely rejected." Kamisar, *supra* note 56, at 1220.

62. *See, e.g., Saikewicz,* 370 N.E.2d at 428 (failing to grant "the same panoply of rights and choices" to competent and incompetent persons "downgrade[s] the status of the incompetent person by placing a lesser value on his intrinsic human worth and vitality").

63. For a definitive treatment of these issues, see generally ALLEN E. BUCHANAN & DAN W. BROCK, DECIDING FOR OTHERS (1989).

64. For a discussion of the cases, see references cited *supra* note 27.

65. The United States Senate's proposed Patient Self Determination Act of 1989, *supra* note 27, recites in its statement of purposes and findings that "[e]stimates identify that 9 percent of the adult competent population have signed a living will; much less than 9 percent have designated a durable power of attorney for health care." S. 1766, 101st Cong., 1st Sess. § 2(b)(5) (1989).

approach, the decider (the court, the family, or others—courts have disagreed on whether judicial intervention is necessary)[66] makes the choice
on behalf of the incompetent.

A.   Where the Patient Made a Competent Choice in the Past: Advance Directives

I will start with situations that seem to me to present the least difficulty, those where the patient has made an actual choice in the past. One
set of such cases occurs when the patient is in a vegetative state that is
known to be permanent. Lacking capacity now and forever for having
experiences of any kind or for making a different choice, there is no basis
for not respecting his earlier competent choice to die.

Cases at the other extreme, those in which the person remains competent, are also easy. If a competent patient decides to change his mind
for some reason—perhaps because of new medical treatments, or because
facing dying as a present reality is different from facing it as a future
possibility, or perhaps because he has simply mellowed with age—the
principle of autonomy requires, not just permits, that he may do so.
Assuming there is no question of the patient's competence (a problem I
will return to shortly),[67] the principle of autonomy requires the person's
latest choice to govern.

The hard case is presented when a patient, plainly incompetent
on traditional criteria, is still sentient. Consider this hypothetical.
Composer Then is a famous musician whose whole life centers around
music. She executes a durable power of attorney in favor of her son,
instructing him that if she becomes permanently unable to experience
music in any way, needs medical treatment to save her life, and is not
competent to exercise choice, then no medical treatment should be
administered to keep her alive. Assume that years later she is in precisely this condition, a victim of senile dementia, as well as of a life-
threatening but readily curable disease. Call her Composer Now.
Though disabled in the ways I have described and lacking competence as
traditionally conceived, she still has some awareness and has the capacity
for sensations. For example, suppose Composer Now smiles at the sight
of her grandchildren, she is apparently comforted by sitting in a garden
or by being attended and talked to, and she shows preferences in foods
and television programs. Moreover, she gives no sign of being uncom-

---

66. *Compare In re* Quinlan, 355 A.2d 647, 664 (N.J.) (decision by guardian and family), *cert.
denied*, 429 U.S. 922 (1976) *with Saikewicz*, 370 N.E.2d at 435 (judicial resolution required) *and In
re* Spring, 405 N.E.2d 115, 120-21 (Mass. 1980) (listing factors to be considered in determining
whether prior judicial approval is required).

67. *See infra* text accompanying notes 83-87; *see also* Michael R. Flick, *The Due Process of
Dying*, 79 CALIF. L. REV. 1121, 1142-43 (1991) (discussing Bartling v. Superior Court, 209 Cal.
Rptr. 220 (Ct. App. 1984), in which the patient vacillated between a desire to die and a desire to
live).

fortable, in pain, or unhappy. Finally, when asked if she prefers to be left to die, she becomes agitated and says no, though how much she understands is unclear. (Shortly I will also consider the hypothetical without this last circumstance.)

Should doctors be authorized or required not to treat the curable disease Composer Now has contracted because Composer Then would not have wanted her life to continue in these circumstances? Does vindication of Composer Then's autonomy require it? Or must Composer Then's earlier choice yield to Composer Now's present interest in continuing to experience the limited life available to her, as she now seems to want?[68]

Ronald Dworkin would apparently hold that Composer's right of autonomy requires that her earlier competent wish be respected:

> A competent person's right to autonomy requires that his past decisions, about how he is to be treated if he becomes demented, be respected even if they do not represent, and even if they contradict, the desires he has when we respect them, provided he did not change his mind while he was still in charge of his own life.[69]

As Dworkin emphasizes elsewhere, he reaches this conclusion even in the harder case where the demented person "insists on and pleads for" medical treatment.[70] He argues that autonomy is the right to govern one's life as a whole and not only part of it, so the right must extend throughout the life of the person—including the period of his incompetency, whether permanent or temporary (Dworkin calls this the "integrity" view of the person).[71] To fail to recognize the right of the person when competent to control his fate when incompetent violates what Dworkin calls the right of "precedent autonomy," whose point is to enable us "to lead our own lives rather than being led along them, so that each of us can be . . . what he has made himself."[72]

---

68. Various positions in an ongoing philosophical debate over the nature of the self carry implications for how these questions should be answered. Some philosophers hold psychological continuity essential for determining the boundaries of the self. *See* DEREK PARFIT, REASONS AND PERSONS 204-07 (1984); Donald Regan, *Paternalism, Freedom, Commitment, in* PATERNALISM 113, 126 (Rolfe Sartorius ed., 1983). On this view, Composer Now, totally lacking psychological continuity with Composer Then, would be a wholly different person for moral purposes and therefore should not be governed by Composer Then's choices. *See* Dresser, *supra* note 27, at 381. Others contest this theory of selfhood, instead stressing the moral importance of physical continuity. *See* Ronald Dworkin, *Autonomy and the Demented Self,* 64 MILBANK Q. 4 (Supp. 2 1986); Rhoden, *supra* note 27, at 410-19. I will not here pursue the issue in these terms. *See generally* Allen E. Buchanan, *Advance Directives and the Personal Identity Problem,* 17 PHIL. & PUB. AFF. 277 (1988).

69. Dworkin, *supra* note 68, at 13.

70. RONALD DWORKIN, U.S. CONGRESS, OFFICE OF TECHNOLOGY ASSESSMENT, PHILOSOPHICAL ISSUES CONCERNING THE RIGHTS OF PATIENTS SUFFERING PERMANENT DEMENTIA 49-50 (1987), *microformed on* Philosophical, Legal, and Social Aspects of Surrogate Decisionmaking for Elderly Individuals, CIS No. OTA J952-30 (Congressional Info. Serv.).

71. Dworkin, *supra* note 68, at 8-9.

72. *Id.* at 8.

I do not dispute that the right of autonomy extends to having one's earlier choices govern during periods of later incompetence—Ulysses' sailors would have been on solid moral ground in refusing to untie him as they passed the sirens, even if they could have heard his orders to do so. Nor do I hold that a person's right of autonomy may not be violated if he can never experience its violation, as is true of a person who will never regain his competence.[73] Rather I will argue two propositions: first, that in our Composer case (in contrast to Ulysses' case) precedent autonomy is not as compelling as an exercise of contemporary autonomy (a current choice) would be; second, that such moral force as precedent autonomy has is morally overridden by considerations of human compassion.[74]

Dworkin tells us that he asked a number of people what they would prefer if they were suffering from senile dementia. He reports that they expressed a preference to be left to die.[75] I think he would have gotten a much more mixed response if he had asked a different question—not what they would prefer for themselves if they were someone like Composer Now, but what they would do if they were responsible for deciding whether to treat Composer Now. A number of people to whom I have put both questions answer Dworkin's question the way he reports, but answer my question the opposite way. They themselves would prefer to be left to die rather than to hang on to a life so limited. They are not so ready, however, to inflict the same fate on another person on the basis of their own preference. But why not, if the patient indicated in her advance directive that that was her preference also? The reason, I suggest, is a well-founded lack of confidence in the force of the earlier directive not to treat.

Some discounting of the advance directive in the Composer case is warranted on two grounds. First, the fact that advance directives are executed as future hypotheticals deprives them of the full moral force of contemporary choices. Unforeseen changes, such as new medical treatments, may substantially alter the person's interests. Moreover, the effect of severe, life-imperilling illness may well produce a marked revision in the attitudes and values of the person.[76] Indeed, even absent such traumas, it is common for a person to reach very different conclusions depending on whether he is imagining a future hypothetical situation or confronting an immediate, real predicament. What people thought they would want often turns out to be very different from what they do

---

73. *See infra* text accompanying notes 114-15.

74. It is unclear whether Dworkin would agree. He recognizes that his conception of precedent autonomy has "austere consequences," but his discussion leaves uncertain whether he means by this that it might be morally correct to override autonomy in such cases, or that it would be understandably difficult for people to resist being humane. Dworkin, *supra* note 68, at 13.

75. DWORKIN, *supra* note 70, at 39, 46, 101.

76. Dresser, *supra* note 27, at 381.

want.[77] Finally, as Buchanan and Brock have pointed out, an advance decision to forgo life-preserving treatment is less likely than a contemporaneous choice to elicit protective and supportive responses from persons close to the patient; hence, this informal safeguard against hasty and ill-considered action is not usually present in the case of advance directives.[78] In view of these considerations, disregard of the advance directive would not constitute as deep an inroad into the autonomy principle as would disregard of a contemporaneous choice.

This conclusion, of course, rests on the premise that at least one major element in the rationale for respecting autonomy is that people are normally the best judges of their own interests—for the reasons just given, this rationale is less well-grounded in cases of decisions to die in future circumstances radically different from those experienced by the person at the time of decision. Dworkin rejects this rationale of autonomy, however, (the "evidentiary" view, he calls it)[79] in favor of the integrity view, which makes the decisive point of autonomy the right to govern the course of one's life, including one's incompetency, according to a "recognized and coherent scheme of value."[80] Certainly this is one of the virtues of autonomy, but as I argue below, it is unduly limiting to give it the paramount place that Dworkin gives it.[81]

The second ground for discounting the advance directive is simply that Composer Now has subsequently indicated that she prefers to live. Of course, this would be determinative if she were competent. The question is whether to disregard it because she is not. I do not think that we should. Competence is a matter of degree and depends upon the kinds of action at issue.[82] Impaired people have varying capacities to think, reason, and evaluate, and some actions will call for less of these capacities than will others. A person may lack competence to make a will, for example, but be perfectly competent to choose whether to watch television or go to the beach. It seems to me that an expression of a wish to live, even by a person incompetent for most other purposes, is entitled to

---

77. *See* Yale Kamisar, *Euthanasia Legislation: Some Non-Religious Objections,* 42 MINN. L. REV. 969, 989 (1958). This is one of the major arguments for not holding a surrogate mother to her agreement with the infertile couple who retained her. *See* MARTHA A. FIELD, SURROGATE MOTHERHOOD 69-70 (1988); Stacey Okun, *Ruling Hailed by Opponents of Surrogacy,* N.Y. TIMES, Feb. 4, 1988, at B7 (surrogates may change their minds because at time of contract they are unable to project their feelings at time of birth).

78. BUCHANAN & BROCK, *supra* note 63, at 106-07. For a critique of living wills as advancing a patient's competent wishes over later, incompetent interests, see John Robertson, *Second Thoughts on Living Wills,* HASTINGS CENTER REP., Nov.-Dec. 1991, at 6.

79. *See* Dworkin, *supra* note 68, at 7.

80. *Id.* at 9.

81. *See infra* text accompanying note 86.

82. *See* BUCHANAN & BROCK, *supra* note 63, at 60-65 (arguing that "competence is a *relational property* determined by a *variable standard,*" *id.* at 60).

carry weight, even if less than the full weight which a fully competent expression would command.

Why should we defer to a decision to continue living made by someone with the barest minimum of capacity for understanding and judgment? At bottom, I think the reason has to do with a general presumption favoring respect for a wish to live. At least two factors seem to be involved. First, there is the universality of the struggle to survive that we perceive in all living things, which makes it odd to justify disqualifying an expressed wish to live simply because of the person's cognitive limitations. Second, there is the seriousness and finality of what is at stake—the ending of a person's life. Buchanan and Brock have developed the case for taking into account the seriousness of the harmful consequences for the person in deciding whether he is competent.[83] I follow them here. Their approach is usually employed to justify overriding a person's choice to take a course that would greatly injure him or his interests (for example, a decision to refuse medical treatment necessary to sustain life). But I see no reason why it should not also justify complying with his choice to take a course that would avoid those serious and permanent consequences. Indeed, I am inclined to think that no person should be regarded as so incompetent that his expressed wish to live should be given no weight. I do not take issue with Professor Feinberg that greater harm may possibly be done to a person by sustaining his life than by allowing it to expire.[84] But I do not believe that this is the case where the patient, even though generally incompetent, is asking to be kept alive.

Dworkin, to the contrary, believes that "autonomy, on the integrity view of that right, must be a *general* judgment about [the person's] overall capacity to seek integrity and authenticity, not a specific, task-sensitive judgment."[85] In his view, an autonomous person must have "the capacity to see and evaluate particular decisions in the structured context of an overall life organized around a coherent conception of character and conviction."[86] This seems to me too restrictive a limitation on the right of autonomy, for it would jeopardize the right to autonomy of many ordinary people who, by virtue of qualities of temperament or character, appear to lack an ability to make choices on the basis of consistent life-organizing conceptions. I think, rather, that a major point of autonomy is to enhance the freedom to decide for oneself, whether one decides with authenticity and a sense of coherence or just on the basis of

---

83. *Id.* at 51. *But see* Mark R. Wicclair, *Patient Decision-Making Capacity and Risk,* 5 BIOETHICS 91, 104 (1991) (arguing that, although harmful consequences go to the necessity of deciding whether the patient is competent, they should not affect the standard used to determine competence).

84. *See* FEINBERG, *supra* note 24.

85. Dworkin, *supra* note 68, at 10.

86. *Id.*

immediate preferences and transient urges. An unwise, uninformed, and eccentric choice is still a choice. It may be that ideally, autonomy functions to permit people, to the extent they can, to make choices that create a coherent whole of their lives. But to deny a person his choices because he cannot choose in terms of a "structured context of an overall life organized around a coherent conception of character and conviction"[87] would deny choice to an unacceptably large segment of the population.

But while precedent autonomy (as Dworkin calls it) in our Composer's case falls short of the full moral force of contemporary autonomy, I have not argued that it has no force. What is there about the circumstances of Composer Now which warrants overriding the force it has? For me, and I expect for many, it is compassion for the human being before us, living her limited life in apparent contentment and evidencing no wish to end it. Letting her die when a cure is readily at hand requires a certain distancing of ourselves from our human impulses, the suppression of a fundamental human empathy for another.

The choice to allow Composer Now to die is supported because earlier, when in full possession of her faculties, she stated that such a life for her would not be worth living. I do not mean to suggest that this is of slight moment. As I said, it has moral significance. But it does not have determinative significance. Without going so far as to regard Composer Now as a different person from Composer Then, I believe it is plain that there has occurred a great transformation in her capacities and perspectives. If we deny her the treatment that would save her, the harm we do is immediate and palpable—we end a life of sharply limited but still contented experiences, in stark violation of our humane sensibilities. If we grant her the treatment we also do harm, but the harm we do is remote and intangible—we violate an exercise of precedent autonomy which is so far separated and distant from her present circumstances that its entitlement to govern is severely compromised.

In the last analysis judgment turns on how much weight to give to the compassionate appeal of the person before us, as compared to the value of autonomy as a right to govern one's life according to a coherent normative structure. There is no algorithm for choosing. Still, those who choose, as I do, to give human compassion the greater weight have to confront whether the choice is a reflective, rational judgment or a reflexive, visceral response that should be the servant, not the master, of our judgment. This raises the great question of the foundation of our moral judgments, which is quite beyond me. I offer just these passing observations.

First, if the ultimate value of autonomy is its intrinsic value, then one may without embarrassment make the equivalent claim for compas-

---

87. *Id.*

sion. Second, insofar as the ultimate value of autonomy lies elsewhere—for example, in its being an essential ingredient of the good life, as Joseph Raz has argued[88]—it is relevant to observe that the sentiment of compassion for a fellow human being also serves a larger value, namely that it is an essential element in the very phenomenon of moral motivation and therefore of civilized society. Reflection, analysis, and theory contribute importantly to our understanding of the phenomenon of moral experiences, but it is the direct human experience itself that is the ultimate source of any vital morality.[89]

Third, compassion is not another word for personal squeamishness of the person making the decision. If it were, it would have the status of just one more competing interest of another person, comparable to the interest of a relative in being relieved of the financial and psychological burdens attendant to the patient's continued life. But it is not just another's competing interest; it rises to the level of a moral concern. This is because morality has a dimension that has to do with the person doing the action as well as with the person being acted upon. The patient's right of autonomy is a moral concern of the latter kind; the actor's motivation stemming from the impulse of human compassion is a moral concern of the former kind. The well-known phenomenon of agent-centered restrictions on actions[90]—moral restraints that make it wrong for an agent to do an action that would produce the best available outcome overall (including the fewest actions of that same kind by others)—would not raise the profound problems for moral theory that it does were it not that morality has these separate dimensions.

One final comment on the Composer hypothetical is in order. I have been addressing it on the assumption that Composer expressed a desire to be kept alive—an assumption that makes it harder to justify letting her die. I have done so to allow me to consider Dworkin's argument, which accepts the challenge of this harder case. It is apparent, however, that the argument from compassion I have made applies as well

---

88. JOSEPH RAZ, THE MORALITY OF FREEDOM 415 (1986).

89. *Cf.* Mary Warnock, *The Artificial Family, in* MORAL DILEMMAS IN MODERN MEDICINE 138, 154 (Michael Lockwood ed., 1985):

> I disagree entirely with those philosophers who would claim . . . that feelings alone cannot amount to a moral view, and that morality has to be a matter of reason. . . . Indeed the whole notion of reason, on the one hand, and feeling or sentiment, on the other, essentially opposed to each other, seems to me to be a mistake—a hangover from an eighteenth-century way of looking at things. I don't see why a moral view cannot both be grounded in feelings and at the same time (in some suitably broad sense) be rational, or at any rate not irrational.

See also the discussion of the distinction between the cognitive sense or concept of justice ("*Rechtsbewusstein*") and its emotional component ("*Rechtsgefühl*") in Wolfgang Fikentscher, *The Sense of Justice and the Concept of Cultural Justice: Views from Law and Anthropology,* 34 AM. BEHAVIORAL SCIENTIST 314, 316 (1991).

90. *See* THOMAS NAGEL, THE VIEW FROM NOWHERE 164-88 (1986); SAMUEL SCHEFFLER, THE REJECTION OF CONSEQUENTIALISM 80-114 (1982).

to a modified Composer hypothetical in which it is not possible for her to express a wish one way or the other. That she expresses a wish to live adds the appeal of autonomy to the appeal of compassion (as well as contributing to it), but I believe the appeal of compassion is enough without it.

B.   Where the Patient Never Chose: Substituted Judgment

I turn now to what are called "substituted judgment" cases, those in which a person now incompetent never exercised a choice when competent. As I have indicated, the courts try to deal with incompetents the same way they deal with competents, namely by seeking to determine the person's choice. But how do you find a choice when none has been made? Courts have responded by looking for what the patient *would* have chosen: What would this patient choose if he were competent to appraise his situation, including his medical condition and prognosis, as well as his present and future incompetency?[91]

This standard is puzzling because it implies that we are to ask what the permanently incompetent person would now choose if he were competent to choose and aware of his incompetency, as if this would tell us what an incompetent would choose. But it cannot be known what an incompetent person would choose precisely because he cannot choose. We can try to imagine that he is temporarily competent and making a choice that takes into account his anticipated incompetency. But this is a very different thing. Like an advance directive, it would be the choice of a competent patient anticipating, but not actually experiencing, his life as an incompetent; the choice, in short, of the person as he was, not as he now is, because he is now incapable of choosing.[92] This is, I think, all that courts can mean by the usual statement of the substituted-judgment standard.

This distinction may seem like a cavil, but it serves to avoid the kind of error a Massachusetts court made in considering whether to forgo medical treatment for an elderly incompetent person who had been incompetent his entire life. The court stated:

> In short, the decision in cases such as this should be that which would be made by the incompetent person, if that person were competent, but taking into account the present and future incompetency of the individual as one of the factors which would necessarily enter into the decision-making process of the competent person.[93]

---

91. For discussion and criticism of the substituted-judgment standard, see BUCHANAN & BROCK, *supra* note 63, at 112-17; PRESIDENT'S COMM'N, *supra* note 1, at 132; *Developments, supra* note 27, at 1646-51.

92. *Cf.* Louise Harmon, *Falling off the Vine: Legal Fictions and the Doctrine of Substituted Judgment,* 100 YALE L.J. 1, 58 (1990) (discussing substituted judgment as developed in 19th century England to govern expenditures of lunatics' income).

93. Superintendent of Belchertown State Sch. v. Saikewicz, 370 N.E.2d 417, 431 (Mass. 1977).

The trouble with this approach is that it requires finding something which isn't there to be found, since the patient was never competent to make a choice.[94]

Another question raised by the substituted-judgment standard, even interpreted as I have argued it should be interpreted, is this: To what extent is it required by the patient's right of self-determination? In the Composer hypothetical, I considered that question in connection with advance choices generally, and concluded that while the right of autonomy was indeed involved (because the patient exercised choice at some time in the past), the advance choice might in some circumstances lack the full moral force of a contemporaneous choice. The substituted-judgment standard entails the same difficulty since the evidence of what the patient would have chosen is in the patient's past. But this standard has an additional difficulty; namely, that it is invoked where there has been no choice by the patient at all, either in the past or now. Courts applying this standard search for evidence of the patient's past life in order to determine how he would have chosen. But whatever the justification for this standard may be (I shall argue it is best understood as part of a best-interests assessment), it cannot be based on the autonomy principle. In these cases we cannot say that the patient has the right that his choice be respected, because he has made none.

The reason for this lies in the distinction between evidence of what a patient would choose and an actual choice.[95] The right of autonomy is the right to have your own choices respected, not to have someone else make the choice he believes you would (or should) have made. The right protects your act of choosing. When someone else makes the choice, even if he chooses as he thinks you would, he is making the choice, not you. Since you made no actual choice, if he chose to disregard evidence of what you would have chosen, he would not be violating your autonomous right to choose.

Why should an actual choice be that crucial? Aren't there many cases in which the past life of the patient allows us to conclude with reasonable assurance that, if competent, he would have chosen a certain way? Surely this is so. The reason this is nonetheless not equivalent to an actual choice turns on a view of what an exercise of will entails. The

---

The Massachusetts court continues to adhere to this analysis. *See* Guardianship of Jane Doe, 583 N.E.2d 1263 (Mass. 1992).

94. *See* PRESIDENT'S COMM'N, *supra* note 1, at 133; TRIBE, *supra* note 57, at 1369 (noting that attempting to effectuate "patient's subjective wishes reaches almost "Alice in Wonderland proportions"); Daniel Wikler, *Patient Interests: Clinical Implications of Philosophical Distinctions,* 36 J. AM. GERIATRIC SOC'Y 951, 956 (1988).

95. In support of this distinction, see BUCHANAN & BROCK, *supra* note 63, at 116 (evidence of individual's preference does not carry same moral weight as individual's deliberate choice); Dworkin, *supra* note 68, at 13-14 (appeal to precedent autonomy requires an actual choice by patient in past); Rhoden, *supra* note 27, at 389 (right to autonomy is not violated absent actual choice).

view I am taking is that the will of a person stands apart from his character and dispositions; it is not one among other characteristics that, summed up, go to make the person what he is. Everything the person is and was may point to him doing X in some particular circumstance. But he is free to do not-X, and may do so, no matter how out of character it seems. The phenomenon of weakness of the will illustrates this point. Even when a person acknowledges that, from the standpoint of every relevant criterion he accepts he should do X, he may still choose not to do X. Just as a baseball game, in a notable aphorism, is "not over till it's over," so a choice is not made till it's made.[96]

Of course, it will sometimes be difficult to distinguish between an actual decision made in the past—and thus subject to autonomy considerations—and evidence of conduct pointing to what the patient would have decided. A written advance directive would be a clear case of the former. But the patient may have decided in less formal ways, such as by orally revealing his decision to others. By contrast, examples of the latter would be the patient's general reflections on the subject of dying, positions he had taken in discussion with friends, religious commitments that would suggest one position or another, and so on. These may give us clues to what his decision would be had he made one, but they are not decisions. There may be difficulties in applying this distinction, but that does not undermine the distinction in principle.

It does not follow from this distinction that evidence of the patient's preferences has no relevance. It plays a role in assessing his best interests, as I will argue. I only want to claim that cases of presumed preference are not morally equivalent to cases of actual choice, express or implied. This point is important because it allows us to see that, while in cases of contemporaneous choices (and, though to a lesser degree, in cases of advance choices as well) respect for autonomy requires doing as the patient directed, this is not so in substituted-judgment cases. Here, the deciding agent is obliged to make its own choice, the values and preferences of the patient in his competent state serving as guide to a best-interests judgment. Recall Composer Now and Composer Then. In order to make the case for treatment I had to justify compromising Composer Then's right of autonomy. Absent her directive not to treat, however, I would not have had to face that issue, because her autonomy would not have been involved.

The point has further import. So long as the ultimate issue is narrowly thought of as one of substituted judgment—that is, what the patient would choose if he could—there is some logic to courts insisting on a demonstration of that fact with a high degree of evidentiary certi-

---

96. There is a political dimension to this view of autonomy: it defeats an attempted justification of unconsented-to authoritative actions based on the view that those affected *would* consent and therefore may be taken to have done so.

tude. This was the narrow issue in the *Cruzan* case, in which the Supreme Court upheld the Missouri law requiring "clear and convincing proof" that the patient would choose to terminate treatment.[97] Viewing the task more broadly, however, as involving a construction from all the circumstances of what treatment decision comports best with the life and character of the patient and therefore furthers his best interests, changes the focus of inquiry. It puts the issue of proof in a more appropriate and realistic framework: not "Unless it is demonstrated with a high level of certainty what the patient would have chosen, treatment must continue," but rather, "From the evidence that is available, including the character and attitudes of the patient, what decision—to continue or terminate treatment—will serve his best interests?"[98]

III
Best Interests

The English courts of equity developed the best-interests standard to govern expenditures from the estates of incompetent persons.[99] But the standard has proved to be highly controversial in cases of incompetents who require medical treatment to stay alive.[100] There is concern over the appropriateness of the standard to determine whether a person should live or die and over how the concept should be interpreted and applied.

A fundamental objection arises from what is implicit in the standard, at least when understood apart from the setting of the patient's inferred preferences: that in certain circumstances the quality of a person's life may be so low that it is not worth living. This stands in stark opposition to the tradition that human life is always valuable. It is one thing for courts to defer to the patient's choice to die. This has proved difficult enough for some courts, as we saw, but at least the decision requires no judgment by the court or some other agent that the patient's life is no longer worth living—only that this is the choice of the patient whose life it is. It is quite different when the best-interests standard is applied independently of the patient's inferred preferences, because this requires the deciding authority itself—the court or some other agent—to make the substantive judgment of whether what is left of the patient's life is worth the candle.

One concern animating this objection is that assessing the quality of the patient's life requires a judgment of its social worth. As one court put it, it is improper "to authorize decision-making based on assessments of the personal worth or social utility of another's life, or the value of

---

97. Cruzan v. Director, Mo. Dep't of Health, 110 S. Ct. 2841, 2846-55 (1990).
98. Nancy Rhoden has made a similar point. *See* Rhoden, *supra* note 27, at 390.
99. The history of the doctrine is told in Harmon, *supra* note 92, at 16-55.
100. *See Developments, supra* note 27, at 1651-53.

that life to others" because to do so creates "an intolerable risk for socially isolated and defenseless people suffering from physical or mental handicaps."[101] Yet this concern seems misplaced, for there is nothing in the nature or history of the standard that requires judgments of the patient's worth to society generally or to particular others. Applied to the decision whether to treat, the accepted understanding of the best-interests standard is that it seeks to assess what would be best for the patient, not for his family, others, or the community as a whole.[102]

Even so, courts have found that judging whether a patient's future life is not worth living is a troubling decision for anyone to make. First, what makes a life not worth living anyway? Loss of the patient's cognitive powers, his ability to function independently, his ability to interact with others, his dependence on constant medical intervention? How much ability to sense and take comfort from experiences is required before we can say his life is not worth living? At bottom, the difficulty is that we have no way to make confident judgments about how far cognitive and physical deterioration must go before life ceases to be worth living, because the value judgments implicit in such a conclusion are in sharp contention in our society.[103] Second, there is the challenge of "don[ning] the mental mantle of the incompetent,"[104] understanding and judging his experiences as he lives and feels them, rather than from the biased perspective of a normally healthy person with unimpaired faculties. Finally, courts are often troubled by the specter of the slippery slope—the fear that once the precedent is established that a person may be left to die because someone judges his life not satisfying enough to be worth living, there will be nothing, or at least less, to stand in the way of that judgment being made of socially, mentally, and physically handicapped people on the margins of society.[105]

Courts have tried in various ways to allay these concerns. The efforts of the New Jersey Supreme Court in *Conroy,*[106] a case that attracted wide attention, are particularly instructive. In an effort to defeat the slippery slope, the court established the requirement of severe

---

101. *In re* Conroy, 486 A.2d 1209, 1232-33 (N.J. 1985).

102. *See* Suzanne Levant, Case Comment, *Natural Death: An Alternative in New Jersey,* 73 Geo. L.J. 1331, 1337 (1985) (arguing that decisions should be made solely from patient's perspective).

103. *See* Tribe, *supra* note 57, at 1369.

104. Superintendent of Belchertown State Sch. v. Saikewicz, 370 N.E.2d 417, 431 (Mass. 1977) (quoting *In re* Carson, 241 N.Y.S.2d 288, 289 (Sup. Ct. 1962)).

105. *See Conroy,* 486 A.2d at 1233 ("More wide-ranging powers to make decisions about other people's lives . . . would create an intolerable risk for socially isolated and defenseless people suffering from physical or mental handicaps."); Cruzan v. Harmon, 760 S.W.2d 408, 420 (Mo. 1988) ("Were quality of life at issue, persons with all manner of handicaps might find the state seeking to terminate their lives."), *aff'd sub nom.* Cruzan v. Director, Mo. Dep't of Health, 497 U.S. 261 (1990); *see also Saikewicz,* 370 N.E.2d at 432 (court bridled at suggestion that quality of life available to retarded person should be considered).

106. *Conroy,* 486 A.2d at 1232.

irremediable pain and suffering as a condition for any assessment of the quality of the person's life.[107] But medicine's considerable success in finding ways to suppress pain has largely eliminated pain as a reason for letting a person die (in contrast to the impaired quality of life which pain suppression can entail).[108] Pain is one, but hardly the only, circumstance that might make a patient's life so burdensome that his best interests lie in extending it no further. Hence, requiring the presence of pain excludes other situations in which quality-of-life considerations may call for terminating treatment.[109]

Two other, more felicitous moves by the court to avoid the worst dangers of quality-of-life judgments were first, to preclude judgments based on the social utility of the patient's life or on its value to others,[110] and second, of more direct relevance to my argument, to require that enough be known about the patient to make a reasonable inference as to his likely preferences before a judgment of his best interests is permissible.[111] This constitutes a helpful reorientation of the substituted-judgment standard. It properly identifies the reason for consulting the patient's inferred preferences: not because it serves his autonomy, but because it furthers his best interests, on the view that making a treatment decision truest to the kind of person he was informs a best-interests judgment. Of course, if there were evidence that he made an actual choice when competent to reject treatment in the circumstances presented, his right of autonomy would require doing as he chose unless some powerful consideration required doing otherwise (as in the case of Composer Now). However, we are here considering cases where evidence of such a choice is insufficient, but where there is evidence of the kind of person he was. How should this evidence be appraised in making a best-interest judgment?

Certainly evidence of the values that guided the patient's competent life (what Ronald Dworkin calls his "evaluative interests"[112])—his character, how he led his life, his attitude toward medical treatment, what it was about life that he thought made it worthwhile, how much it mattered

---

107. *Id.* The court held that treatment may be forgone when the pain reaches the point "that the net burdens of [the patient's] prolonged life markedly outweighs any physical pleasure, emotional enjoyment, or intellectual satisfaction that the patient may still be able to derive from life." *Id.*

108. PRESIDENT'S COMM'N, *supra* note 1, at 19, 50-51. However, there are a variety of social and institutional restraints—for example, inadequate medical education in pain management and fears of addiction—that hinder the use of available knowledge. *See* Kathleen M. Foley, *The Relationship of Pain and Symptom Management to Patient Requests for Assisted Suicide,* J. PAIN & SYMPTOM MGMT. 289 (1991).

109. It is instructive that even the dissenting justice in *Conroy,* while rejecting the requirement of pain, thought it necessary to require that the patient be facing imminent death, be incurable, in a comatose state, and suffering the loss of at least one major bodily organ or system. *Id.* at 1244, 1249 (Handler, J., dissenting).

110. *Conroy,* 486 A.2d at 1232-33.

111. *Id.* at 1231-32.

112. DWORKIN, *supra* note 70, at 32.

to him that he was burdening others, how sensitive he was to considerations of privacy and personal dignity—bears directly on a best-interests judgment. But there is another kind of consideration that needs consulting as well; namely, the patient's present experiences or lack of them (what Dworkin calls his "experiential interests"[113]). These include the patient's medical prognosis, the extent of his suffering, the degree of his mental and physical impairment, and the kind of experiences he would be capable of if he survived. The question then becomes whether, on the basis of both kinds of evidence, we can conclude that a decision to forgo treatment would be consonant with the kind of life he led and the kind of person he was, as well as with the kind of person he is now. If so, we can conclude that it is in his best interests to deny treatment.

Some regard evidence of the first kind—evaluative interests—as irrelevant, on the ground that one can have no interest in what is not and can never be experienced; under this view, only experiential interests count in cases of serious and permanent mental disability.[114] This argument has an attractively down-to-earth appeal, but as Joel Feinberg and others have shown, denying that a person's interests may be harmed when he does not and can never experience the harm takes too narrow a view of an interest.[115] Consider posthumous harms. There is a natural sense in which the interests of a person who is no longer alive may be harmed. Such harm occurs when that which he deeply cherished and to which he devoted his life suffers destruction, when his valued reputation as a person of honor and distinction is destroyed by malicious lies, or when significant promises he exacted to be performed after his death are foresworn. For like reasons, the evaluative interests of a living person

---

113. *Id.*

114. *See, e.g.,* Dresser, *supra* note 27, at 389:

Legal decision-makers have accepted the dubious notion that what was vitally important to incompetent patients when they were competent remains vitally important to them in their incompetent states. But incompetent patients differ from competent patients in material ways that invalidate this notion. Incompetent patients are incapable of appreciating the values and preferences they once held dear. As a consequence, standards attempting to honor those values and preferences fail to advance the incompetent patient's present welfare.

See also John A. Robertson, *Cruzan and the Constitutional Status of Nontreatment Decisions for Incompetent Patients,* 25 GA. L. REV. 1139, 1158-62 (1991).

115. FEINBERG, *supra* note 24, at 83-95 (1984) (arguing that people have interests that survive their death); *see also Conroy,* 486 A.2d at 1229:

The right of an adult who . . . was once competent, to determine the course of her medical treatment remains intact even when she is no longer able to assert that right or to appreciate its effectuation. As one commentator has noted:

Even if the patient becomes too insensate to appreciate the honoring of his or her choice, self-determination is important. After all, law respects testamentary dispositions even if the testator never views his gift being bestowed.

. . . .

Any other view would permit obliteration of an incompetent's panoply of rights merely because the patient could no longer sense the violation of those rights.

(citations omitted).

(his sensibilities, his concerns for his own dignity and for not burdening others, his prized self-determination) may be harmed by how we deal with him after he has permanently lost capacity to be aware that these harms are being done to him. The Composer hypothetical would not have been so difficult were it not that Composer's interest in having her right of autonomy respected continued even though she could not (and could never) experience it. It is important to stress that this approach to ascertaining best interests offers some protection against the feared precedent of permitting someone else's judgment of the quality of a patient's life to determine whether the patient should be permitted to die. It does so because it makes the patient's own value structure controlling of whether it is consistent with the patient's best interests to forego treatment.

Ronald Dworkin, to the contrary, has proposed that except in cases where the patient has made a competent choice for treatment sufficient to invoke his right of autonomy (Dworkin agrees that evidence of preferences short of such choice are insufficient to invoke this right,)[116] the standard of evaluation of the worth of the patient's continued life (his evaluative interests) should be objective rather than subjective. In other words, the standard should not be necessarily what the patient himself would regard as in his best interests, but what *is* in his best interests, period. Referring to patients with permanent and severe dementia, he concludes that:

> a fiduciary should take over a person's responsibility to make his life as good a life as it can be when that person is no longer capable of this himself . . . . [I]t follows that the right to beneficence includes the right not to be given life-prolonging treatment when seriously and permanently demented.[117]

This follows for Dworkin because a permanently and seriously demented person's life can contain nothing that would make his life better. Lacking a "sense of personality and agency," his experiences could not be rewarding.[118] And lacking "continuity of project and fulfillment," they could not be regarded as achievements.[119] On the other hand, a demented life can contain experiences that make the life of which it is a part worse—experiences of anxiety and pain, for example.

---

116. Dworkin, *supra* note 68, at 13-14 (stating that right depends on evidence of "an actual past decision contemplating the circumstances the patient is now in"). Despite this formulation, Dworkin apparently believes it would be sufficient to invoke the right of autonomy if "we have good reason to think he would have made that request [to be kept alive] if he had thought it necessary." DWORKIN, *supra* note 70, at 50. Of course there does come a point where the inference of a choice from an expressed preference is so strong that it counts as a choice. There is room for disagreement on precisely when this point is reached. I understand Dworkin to mean that his test should be applied in all cases where the inferred preference is not that strong.

117. DWORKIN, *supra* note 70, at 48-49.

118. *Id.* at 47.

119. *Id.*

What I have given of Dworkin's argument for an objective best-interests judgment is the barest outline, which fails to convey its subtlety and complexity, but it is enough to allow me to say why I find it troubling. First, a basic premise of Dworkin's argument is that it is in the best interests of a patient that a decision makes of the patient's life as a whole as good a thing as it can be, one marked by a sensitivity to values of privacy and dignity, by respect for and deference to the interests of others, and so on. This evokes his theory of adjudication as interpretation, requiring the judge to make of the law as good a thing as it can be.[120] But there is an important difference, for I doubt that a person's life is made better by decisions that are not rooted in him as a person. If a person during the course of his competent life has been indifferent to matters of respect for his person and for the interests of others, it does not seem to me that it serves to make his whole life a better one that in the end someone has made decisions for him which manifest these virtues. They are, after all, imposed on him and hardly do him credit.

Moral luck plays some role in the living of a good life,[121] and on that basis an argument can be made that the patient's good fortune in being permitted to die after suffering serious and permanent dementia makes his whole life, on balance, a better one than it would be if he were kept alive. But this seems unconvincing. Luck may be a factor in permitting a person to lead a good life, but to say that his life is made a better one because a good thing luckily happened to him after he had finished leading his life yields too much to the authority of fortune. It is a bit like flowers on a grave: they make lots of things better, but scarcely the life of the person beneath them. Consider the example of being a burden to others, often given as one among a set of reasons for declining treatment: it is a virtue for a person to permit himself to die to save burdening others, and he makes his whole life a better one for doing so. But it hardly makes his life a better one that a third party decides to sacrifice it for the benefit of others.

My second reason for demurring to Dworkin's conclusion is practical: it invites the danger that many courts and commentators have seen in best-interests standards—the danger that those making the decision cannot be relied on to keep separate what is objectively best and what is best for them. It is often in the interest of those around the demented patient that he be permitted to die—he is a psychological burden to them, the ministrations required for his bodily functions often offend their sensibilities, he requires the use of valuable resources, and the positive qualities of his limited life seem slight compared to the negative influence on the lives of others. We may insist that it is in his best interest that he be allowed to die, but when that decision is one that serves the

---

120. *See* RONALD DWORKIN, LAW'S EMPIRE 225 (1986).
121. *See* THOMAS NAGEL, MORTAL QUESTIONS 24-38 (1979).

interests of others (who often are the ones making the decision) there is the ever-present danger that it is their interests, not his, that are motivating the decision.

Another problem with Dworkin's position is that it is, most uncharacteristically for him, paternalistic, at least in the sense that it makes the final act in a person's life turn on the normative standards of others rather than on those of the person himself. Dworkin accepts that a demented person's earlier competent choice for treatment must prevail even if it is against what Dworkin would regard as his best evaluative interests, considered from an objective perspective. But there are plainly going to be cases where the person's life has left evidence consistent with a preference for continued treatment, although he made no actual or implied choice to which his right of autonomy would require deferring. It seems to me that we should want to say that such a person has an interest, that it is in *his* best interests, that the decision accord with his own values and preferences as best we can discern them. I agree that it would not violate his right to autonomy to disregard his inferred preferences (since he made no choice). Nonetheless, it would be inconsistent with his interest in having the end of his life governed by the kind of choices he made to govern his competent earlier life, and therefore, in this sense, paternalistic.

Nonetheless, there are situations where Dworkin's analysis has a strong appeal. These are the cases where we can make no reliable judgment based on the person's past values and commitments, either because the evidence is totally indeterminate or because he never was competent. Here it is not possible to tailor the choice to the character of the person. In this situation a decision that can be supported as better on impersonal, objective grounds is obviously preferable to a decision that cannot be so supported.

My final concern, which I suggested earlier in a related context, is that Dworkin's position unduly discounts the experiential interests of a demented person—the satisfactions that can come from sensory experiences and comforting feelings that do not require higher-order mentation. To paraphrase Bentham, the question is not whether demented people can reason, nor whether they can talk, but whether they can feel.[122]

IV

CONCLUSION

I conclude with a restatement of some of the positions I have tried to defend.

---

122. In deploring the tormenting of animals, Bentham wrote: "[T]he question is not, Can they *reason*? nor, Can they *talk*? but, Can they *suffer*." JEREMY BENTHAM, AN INTRODUCTION TO THE PRINCIPLES OF MORALS AND LEGISLATION 283 n.b (J.H. Burns & H.L.A. Hart eds., 1970).

A constitutional right of autonomy has provided the foundation for judicial treatment of decisions to let patients die. In principle this right extends to suicide and assisted suicide, although the extension could be resisted on plausible prudential grounds. The courts, however, have sought to distinguish suicide from cases of letting patients die on such grounds as the doing/allowing and purpose/knowledge distinctions, which have failed to carry the burden put on them.

The principle of autonomy controls the decision whether to let a patient die when there is a competent contemporary choice. In all other cases, it becomes just one of several factors to consider.

For reasons I suggested in connection with the Composer hypothetical, an advance competent choice has force, but not the conclusive moral force of a contemporary choice and not so much force as to preclude consideration of the possibly conflicting experiential interests of the patient.

Where the patient never made a choice during his competency, the right of autonomy is not implicated at all, contrary to what courts assume under the substituted-judgment standard when they seek to discover what the patient would have chosen. What we think he would have chosen is not what he chose. A judgment based on a search of the patient's competent life for his preferences, values, and commitments is appropriate not because it is required by his autonomy right but because it is in his best interests.

The patient's interests include his experiential interests—the quality of his future life if kept alive—as well as his evaluative ones, and if it is *his* best interests that are to be furthered, any judgment upon them must be made with reference to the values and commitments by which the patient chose to lead his life. For reasons I have tried to suggest, this subjective approach to determining his best interests is preferable to an objective one, which would seek to make his life as a whole a better one in terms of some objective criteria of the good life, but not those of the patient whose life we are deciding.

Different Viewpoints

Assisted Suicide: An Ethical Perspective

Gerald D. Coleman, S.S., Ph.D.*

State of the Question

In his celebrated book *A Private Choice*,[1] John T. Noonan, Jr. creatively and credibly demonstrates that, although abortion is a public issue, it has been legalized as a private act. Noonan carefully demonstrates, in other words, that, in the United States, by declaration of the Supreme Court, the description of abortion has been interpreted as a "private choice," as though the abortion decision was without social underpinnings and consequences.

This same "logic" is presently being employed in another area of ethical concern: the question of euthanasia or assisted suicide. In the massive literature on the question of assisted suicide,[2] one can detect at least three clear "logics" which reduce the question of euthanasia to "a private choice."

First, some literature on this question demonstrates an appeal to individual freedom. The radical appeal to individual freedom is of

---

*Full Professor of Moral and Pastoral Theology, St. Patrick's Seminary, Menlo Park, CA; B.A., St. Patrick's College, 1964; M. Div., St. Patrick's Seminary, 1968; M.A., University of San Francisco, 1970; Ph.D., Institute of Christian Thought, University of St. Michael's College, Toronto, Canada, 1974.

[1]J. NOONAN, A PRIVATE CHOICE (1979).

[2]SUICIDE, THE PHILOSOPHICAL ISSUES (M. Battin & D. Mayo eds. 1980); EUTHANASIA AND THE RIGHT TO DEATH: THE CASE FOR VOLUNTARY EUTHANASIA (A. Downing ed. 1971); J. GLOVER, CAUSING DEATH AND SAVING LIVES (1977); DEATH, DYING AND EUTHANASIA (D. Horan & D. Mall eds. 1980); M. KOHL, BENEFICIENT EUTHANASIA (1975); M. KOHL, THE MORALITY OF KILLING: SANCTITY OF LIFE, ABORTION AND EUTHANASIA (1974); P. SIMMONS, BIRTH AND DEATH: BIOETHICAL DECISION MAKING (1983); SUICIDE AND EUTHANASIA: THE RIGHTS OF PERSONHOOD (S. Wallace & A. Eser eds. 1981); ETHICAL ISSUES IN DEATH AND DYING (R. Weir ed. 1977).

special consequence when considered against the general Aristotelian and Thomistic background of Western ethical thinking.

Saint Thomas Aquinas proposed what might be called "the principle of *per-seity*."[3] Aquinas proposed that a law must be determined by what usually occurs per se, not by what sometimes happens per accidens. Aquinas argued that ". . . natural or moral rectitude in human actions is not determined according to what happens *per accidens* in one individual but according to what results for the whole species."[4] Aquinas' position argues that human reason indicates that certain actions are generally harmful to people; therefore, the natural law, insofar as it is itself ordered to the common good and exists to prevent a common danger, prohibits certain human acts. This prohibition by the natural law allows for no exceptions to be made on one's own private authority or individual discretion, even if it is certain that the harm which the law seeks to prevent will not occur in a specific case at hand. In other words, the common good is not to be jeopardized by private discretion, individual exception-making, or self-exemption from the law.

Clearly, then, arguments favoring euthanasia on the grounds of "individual freedom" run in the face of this traditional moral principle in Western ethical discourse.

A particular example in this line of thinking is found with those who argue that euthanasia would actually reduce the suffering and despair of elderly and debilitated patients. The "right to die," in this regard, appeals to radical individual freedom. Advocates of this position often endorse the individual "right to die" as "rational" suicide.[5]

What one often forgets in this argument, however, is that, if the freedom to kill oneself to end suffering or debilitation is the core issue, then logically this freedom cannot be granted only to the terminally ill. Some teenagers and others face equal or greater suffering in various circumstances and may wish the freedom to end their lives. When a "how-to" suicide manual for the terminally ill was published in France in 1982, its first reported use was by several depressed young men who were perfectly healthy.

If euthanasia advocates are serious about restricting their approach to certain groups of severely debilitated people, the fact that only this group is given its "freedom" will indicate, as a matter of fact,

---

[3]V. GENOVESI, IN PURSUIT OF LOVE: CATHOLIC MORALITY AND HUMAN SEXUALITY 169-70 (1987).

[4]*Id*. at 169.

[5]Doerflinger, *Euthanasia Gaining Ground*, in RESPECT LIFE PROGRAM 20 (1986).

that the real issue is a social judgment that some lives are objectively worthless.

It is clear, therefore, that a social movement has arisen, supported by a number of philosophers and legal commentators, that regards suicide as neither tragic nor wrong, but as a basic human right.[6]

From an ethical point of view, many advocates for "rational suicide" argue that some suicides are virtuous, and that the law ought not prohibit what is ethically good. Such arguments almost always ground themselves in an absolute respect for individual autonomy, or on a claim that the benefits of discouraging undesirable suicides are outweighed by the evils of coercion and the social burdens created by laws and policies opposing suicide. Suicide supporters, who maintain that some suicides are ethical, usually claim that death can be a benefit to the individual who commits suicide and that suicide can sometimes benefit others by relieving them of the burden of supporting an individual who has lost the desire or ability to continue living a full life. Common to all aspects of these ethical arguments is a vigorous assault on the assumption, traditionally accepted by law and society, that all human lives are essentially and equally valuable. Instead, the "quality of life," rather than the "sanctity of life," is considered the focus of inquiry. It is claimed, then, that when one's own life lacks sufficient quality or diminishes the quality of others' lives, suicide is the best ethical solution and the law should not, under such circumstances, hinder those who would assist these persons in committing suicide.

The ethical claim most frequently and strongly asserted by such proponents is clearly rooted in the principle of personal autonomy. What is clear in this ethical position is the assertion that, if one sustains an autonomy-based right to suicide, then one's motives for exercising this right are not within the scope of proper inquiry, any more than one's motives for attending a particular church would be.

Secondly, some of the literature on the question of assisted suicide appeals not so much to a principle of radical individual autonomy or freedom, but rather to a more personalistic principle that each person sustains a right to "die with dignity." The "logic" of this ethical approach is based on the claim that, since a competent patient has the right to refuse any and all treatment, then every individual also possesses a right to determine the way in which he or she will die, i.e., the right to die with dignity. For example, if a decision to refuse treat-

---

[6]*See* Marzen, O'Dowd, Crone & Balch, *Suicide: A Constitutional Right?*, 24 Duq. L. Rev. 1 (1985).

ment will result in a slow and painful death or if there is no specific treatment whose refusal will lead to death, then "death with dignity" requires further action and an additional actor: someone who will effectuate that dignified death.[7]

Advocates of this position usually argue that, if society is willing to let a person die by means of treatment refusal, then society is lacking in charity and compassion if it deprives a person of an easy (or easier) death.

In this regard, we should not forget that, some years ago, many critics of the position that a person has a right to refuse treatments that seemingly only prolong the dying process argued that such an ethical position was only the beginning of "a slippery slope." These critics argued that the "slide" would start with voluntary passive euthanasia: first, competent patients would be allowed to refuse life-saving treatment; subsequently, it would be incompetent patients whose refusal would be voiced by others; then it would be patients who had never been competent (babies and the mentally retarded). After that, it would move on to active euthanasia: competent patients would be the first to receive these benefits, and then the slide would continue for others who were not in a position to make their own choices. A good example of this "slide" is James Rachels' book *The End of Life*,[8] in which he argues that, if it is morally permissible to withdraw a respirator leading to a patient's death, it is morally permissible to directly cause the patient's death by active means.[9] Rachels acknowledges that there is a significant psychological difference between the two and, because of that, one may prefer the one to the other; however, a psychological difference does not translate for Rachels into a moral difference.

Thirdly, literature on the question of assisted suicide also advocates a position which appeals to an ethical attitude which maintains that, when the purpose of life is no longer attainable, then suicide is a moral option. In this approach to the question of euthanasia, certain presuppositions are in evidence:

1. An individual's life belongs to that individual to dispose of entirely as he or she wishes

2. The dignity that attaches to personhood by reason of the freedom to make moral choices demands also the freedom to take one's own life

---

[7] *See A Misguided Enthusiasm for Euthanasia*, Ethical Currents, Feb. 1987, at 1-2, 6.
[8] J. RACHAELS, THE END OF LIFE: EUTHANASIA AND MORALITY (1986).
[9] *Id.*

3. There is such a thing as a life not worth living, whether by reason of distress, illness, physical or mental handicaps, or even sheer despair for whatever reason

4. What is sacred or supreme in value is the "human dignity" that resides in one's own rational capacity to choose and control life and death[10]

This position likewise argues that, since "euthanasia" has lost its meaning as a merely descriptive term for a "happy and good death," a new term has been invented, namely "benemortasia." An ethic of benemortasia values compassion and freedom, appealing basically to the moral point that at times the purpose of human life is simply no longer attainable.

In his books *Death By Choice* and *The Moral Choice*, Daniel C. Maguire advances this argument by indicating that terminating a life under certain circumstances may be good so long as a greater good than physical life is being served.[11] For example, he regards such goods as personal integrity, human dignity, and the freedom of self-determination to be proportionate to the good of physical life. This position challenges the "absolute" and "exceptionalist" character of the principle, "thou shalt not kill."

Maguire regards that principle of "no direct killing of innocent life" to be valid "most of the time," but recognizes that in the specific circumstances of patient's moral situation, the principle may not apply and would have to yield to the principle of achieving a good death, when clearly one finds the purpose of human life no longer attainable.

It is important to note in this argument, however, that Maguire and others are not condoning a passion for euthanasia. Maguire argues that:

> There should be no passion for euthanasia. Indeed we should work for the conditions which make it less and less indicated. To say this, however, does not close the door to moral mercy killing any more than favoring the conditions of peace makes one into an absolute pacifist.[12]

In this school of thought, then, the generally accepted principle against the direct termination of life always counts in one's moral evaluation but does not always win. Values such as personal dignity, free-

---

[10]*See, e.g.,* A. DYCK, ON HUMAN CARE: AN INTRODUCTION TO ETHICS (1977); Dyck, *Beneficient Euthanasia and Benemortasia: Alternative Views of Mercy,* in BENEFICIENT EUTHANASIA 117 (M. Kohl ed. 1975).

[11]D. MAGUIRE, DEATH BY CHOICE (1974); D. MAGUIRE, THE MORAL CHOICE (1978).

[12]Maguire, *Death and the Moral Domain,* ST. LUKE'S J. THEO. 216 (June 1977).

dom of self-determination, or an excessive burden of expense are values which are proportionate to maintaining physical life, and are to be preferred in some instances. Therefore, euthanasia can sometimes be a legitimate moral choice.

In concluding this section on the "State of the Question," it is clear that, in the literature on the question of assisted suicide, one can detect at least three major positions:

1. That which appeals to radical individual freedom and autonomy

2. That which appeals to the right to die with dignity

3. That which appeals to the principle that physical life is not an absolute when the quality of life is no longer attainable

What should be concluded from this brief analysis is that present concerns about "beneficent euthanasia" are not motivated by some evil ethical intent, but are rather guided by compassion and an overall regard for social justice and the rights of every human person. Western philosophical and medical traditions surely advocate a pivotal role for human kindness. Cicero taught that our first duty is to help most where help is most needed.[13] Advocates of beneficent euthanasia thus translate "kindness" as a praise-worthy and virtuous moral attitude in allowing a person to have "a good death." This ethic of benemortasia is actually based on an *obligation* to act kindly.

Goethe wrote: "When the *taedium vitae* attacks a man it can only be regretted, not censured." Life-weariness clearly leads many persons to the act of suicide, an act which the Western philosophical and moral tradition has generally deemed ethically illicit for several reasons:

1. Suicide is a crime against society

2. Suicide is cowardly

3. Suicide is a violation of one's duty to God

4. Suicide is unnatural

5. Suicide is an assault to human dignity

6. Suicide is cruel in that it inflicts pain upon one's family and friends[14]

---

[13]THE BASIC WORKS OF CICERO (M. Hazas ed. 1951).
[14]Hook, *The Ethics of Suicide*, in BENEFICIENT EUTHANASIA 57 (M. Kohl ed. 1975).

Such reasonings have not *de facto* erased the reality of suicide. It is estimated that over twenty-five thousand people now commit suicide in the United States each year, and that over two hundred thousand attempted. The total number of reported suicides in this country has increased slightly since 1970 with the annual rate averaging twelve suicides per population of one hundred thousand. Statistics clearly demonstrate that the ranks of those who attempt suicide are disproportionately filled with marginal members of society: the aged, the poor, the ill, or the disabled; and with those who are isolated and lacking in personal and social support: the single or recently bereaved, the alienated, and the unhelped young.[15] The increasing interest in legalized euthanasia is an attempt to address these glaring and sad statistics.

A Moral Perspective

In its *Pastoral Constitution on the Church in the Modern World (Gaudium et Spes)*, the Second Vatican Council taught that euthanasia is "opposed to life itself" and "violates the integrity of the human person."[16] This *Pastoral Constitution* teaches that whatever is opposed to life, such as euthanasia, is indeed an "infamy" and consequently a crime against humanity. This ethical affirmation has found subsequent repetition in important and pivotal documentation in the Roman Catholic Church.

In 1980 for example the Congregation for the Doctrine of the Faith issued the *Declaration on Euthanasia*. This *Declaration* confirms and elaborates the teaching of the Second Vatican Council. It explains that human life is a gift from God over which humans have stewardship but not absolute dominion. Since life is the basis and necessary condition for all other human goods, its destruction is an especially grievous violation of the moral law, whether the victim consents or not.[17]

Particularly important is the *Declaration's* definition of euthanasia as "an action or an omission which of itself or by intention causes death, in order that all suffering may in this way be eliminated."[18] The *Declaration* thus affirms the teaching of Catholic theology that a deliberate effort to hasten someone's death is wrong whether achieved by gunshot or starvation. Morally what is important is that one intends

---

[15]Marzen, *supra* note 6, at 1.

[16]W. Abbott, The Documents of Vatican II 226 (1966).

[17]*Declaration on Euthanasia*, in Official Catholic teachings: Update 1980 180.

[18]*Id.* at 183.

the person's death, either as an end in itself, or as a means to another end, such as ending the person's suffering.

In 1984, the National Conference of Catholic Bishops of the United States of America issued *Guidelines for Legislation on Life-Sustaining Treatment.*[19] These *Guidelines* strongly assert that life is to be "celebrated" as a gift of the loving God and the life of every human person must be respected because all life is made in the image and likeness of God. These *Guidelines* support the "distinctive approach" of Catholic theology to the question of life and death as it emphasizes that the Catholic tradition not only condemns direct attacks on innocent life, but *also* promotes a general view of life as a sacred trust over which we can claim stewardship but not absolute dominion.[20]

> These *Guidelines* thus: Reaffirm public policies against homocide and assisted suicide. Medical treatment legislation may clarify procedures for discontinuing treatment which only secures a precarious and burdensome prolongation of life for the terminally ill patient, but should not condone or authorize any deliberate act or omission designed to cause a patient's death.[21]

Another example of this "distinctive approach" can be found in the front-page editorial of 25 January 1987 in *L'Osservatore Romano* entitled "With Regard to Euthanasia." This editorial was concerned with the Conference of Medical Associations of the European Community's recommendation of 15 January 1987 that "medicine needs in every circumstance to constantly respect the life, moral autonomy and free choice of the patient." The editorial criticizes the ambiguity of this statement for seemingly allowing a patient alone to judge what preserves human dignity. The editorial points out that physicians must always defend the exclusive dominion of God over human life and a sick person may never consent to terminate his or her life.

This same moral affirmation is found in the 1987 *Instruction On Respect For Human Life In Its Origin And On The Dignity of Procreation* of the Congregation for the Doctrine of the Faith.[22] This 1987 *Instruction* teaches:

> From the moment of conception, the life of every human being is to be respected in an absolute way because man is the only creature on earth that God has 'wished for himself' and the

---

[19]National Conference of Catholic Bishops, Guidelines for Legislation on Life-Sustaining Treatment 526 (1984).

[20]*Id.* at 526-27.

[21]*Id.* at 528.

[22]J. Ratzinger, Instruction on Respect for Human Life in its Origin and on the Dignity of Procreation: Replies to Certain Questions of the Day (1987).

spiritual soul of each man is 'immediately created' by God; his whole being bears the image of the Creator. Human life is sacred because from its beginning it involves 'the creative action of God' and it remains forever in a special relationship with the Creator, who is its sole end. God alone is the Lord of life from its beginning until its end: no one can, in any circumstance, claim for himself the right to destroy directly an innocent human being.[23]

In reading these documents, it is important to notice that the net is cast widely in terms of the audience. This teaching about the dignity of individual life appeals, as the *Declaration On Euthanasia* points out, to Christians, other believers, and people of goodwill. It is hoped, then, that the "distinctive approach" of Roman Catholic teaching on the questions of life and death appeals to Christians in that it speaks about the meaning of life and death from a Christological perspective; to other believers it appeals to the dignity of the human person; and to people of goodwill it appeals to human rights.

From a moral point of view, then, the teaching of the Roman Catholic Church regarding human life sustains a clear "bias for life." One would submit that this "bias for life" should inform all our decisions in every critical matter regarding life and death. This "bias" is *de facto* the foundation of the Judeo-Christian worldview as well as the motivating force which undergirds medical research and practice. It flows, for most people, from a theistic belief. However, as already mentioned, it has been and can be affirmed by those whose views of reality do not include the existence of God.

The "bias for life" requires that all individuals should direct their efforts toward the sustaining of life where it exists.

As indicated in the introductory remarks of this article, those who advocate the possibility of euthanasia generally do so out of concern for those who, for whatever reason, face deep and anguished suffering.

In light of this understandably human concern, it is critical to realize that it *is* possible for persons to achieve goals that are encompassing, profound, and lasting and yet be in a state of great suffering. It is essential to appreciate the fact that true human happiness cannot be measured merely by pleasure, comfort, or freedom from anxiety, tension, and guilt. Normally, pleasure, comfort, and peace are the consequences and the signs of the achievement of authentic human goals and the fulfillment of the true human needs, and hence they are good and desirable, but they are secondary signs and not the proof or

---

[23]*Id.* at 5.

measure of real human achievement. In other words, we must not measure good and bad merely in terms of pleasure and pain.

The Christian faith looks upon suffering and death in two different ways. On the one hand, death is evil because it is the result of sin. On the other hand, it is a liberating and grace-filled experience, if the proper motivation is present. These two views are not contradictory; rather they are complimentary. Suffering and death, joined to the suffering and death of Jesus, represent not dissolution but growth, not punishment but fulfillment, not sadness but joy. God allows suffering and death to enable us to live with Christ now and forever. This principle, supremely exemplified in the Cross of Christ, is rooted in the basic human need to preserve life, since people suffer only in order to achieve a renewed, purified, and enriched life.[24]

It is important to appreciate, then, that suffering is not an absolute human evil. Although suffering is truly an ontological evil to be alleviated whenever possible, it is not of itself a moral evil nor without supernatural and human benefits. Some will certainly scoff at this view, but the Christian tradition holds that great good can come out of suffering when this is joined to the suffering of Jesus. This teaching does not imply a masochistic desire for pain, nor does it stand in the way of medical progress. Suffering, therefore, can be an authentic means of spiritual growth.

It is legitimate to conclude that a "speciality of the house" for all Christian churches should be to provide authentic healing whenever suffering is present. Suffering as a means of spiritual growth is not destroyed if pain-killing drugs are used to assist the suffering person. For example, the *Ethical and Religious Directives for Catholic Health Facilities* of the United States' Catholic Bishops teaches: "It is not euthanasia to give a dying person sedatives and analgesics for the alleviation of pain, when such measure is judged necessary, even though they may deprive the patient of the use of reason, or shorten his life."[25]

What is clear is that a patient is to be helped to complete his or her life with the maximum of peace and composure. Suffering, in other words, needs not be a wasteland but can be a vital time in one's life, a period of reconciling one's self to life and to death and for attaining interior peace.

Our suffering is *human* suffering; it has meaning and thus can be transcended. Suffering can be made redemptive through the sufferer's creative spirit. Pope John Paul II expresses this same vision:

---

[24]B. Ashley & K. O'Rourke, Health Care Ethics: A Theological Perspective (1978).

[25]Ethical and Religious Directives for Catholic Health Facilities 7 (1971).

"Suffering has a special value in the eyes of the Church. It is something good, before which the Church bows down in reverence with all the depth of her faith in the redemption."[26] Moreover, we make a sincere gift of self when we reach out to relieve suffering. As John Paul II affirms, "Christ has taught man to do good by His suffering and to do good to those who suffer.... No institution can by itself replace the human heart, human compassion, human love or human initiative, when it is a question of dealing with the sufferings of another."[27]

Ethical Conclusions

Although human suffering in its multiple dimensions is a factor of life which causes great pain and human anguish, it must not be used as a reason for justifying the direct taking of human life. From an ethical point of view, therefore, there is no justification for euthanasia, even when placed in the category of benemortasia. This conclusion is based on the principle integral to the Catholic moral tradition of the sanctity of all life which concludes that every person's life must be reverenced because of its personal dignity and value. This "sanctity of life" principle is based on a variety of Christian doctrines, such as creation and redemption, the immortality of the soul, and a religious understanding of the human person. God must always be understood as the Creator and Sustainer of life. Norman St. John-Stevas situates this principle well: "The value of human life for the Christian in the first century A.D., as today, rested not on its development of the superior sentience but on the unique character of the union of body and soul, both destined for eternal life. The right to life thus has a philosophical foundation.... Respect for the lives of *others* because of their eternal destiny is the essence of the Christian teaching."[28]

Paul Ramsey makes the important point that the sanctity of life is not a function of the worth any human person attributes to life, but that its primary value lies in the relation of life to God: "One grasps the religious outlook upon the sanctity of human life only if he sees that this life is asserted to be *surrounded* by sanctity that need not be in a man; that the most dignity a man ever possesses is a dignity that is alien to him.... A man's dignity is an overflow from God's dealing with him, and not primarily an anticipation of anything he will ever be by himself alone."[29] Therefore, life is always a guaranteed value or

---

[26]Pope John Paul, II, *On the Christian Meaning of Human Suffering*, L'Osservatore Romano, Feb. 20, 1984, at 1-8.

[27]*Id* at 8, col. 1-2.

[28]N. St. John-Stevas, The Right to Life 12 (1963).

[29]Ramsey, *The Morality of Abortion,*, in Life or Death: Ethics and Options 71 (D. H. Laggy ed. 1968).

dignity because the only way life truly exists is in "covenant" or in relationship to God.

This grounding of the sanctity of life in religious convictions also has its equivalency in nonreligious groundings. The sociologist, Edward Shils, asks, "Is human life really sacred?" and responds, "I answer that it is, self-evidentally. Its sacredness is the most primordial of experiences."[30] Shils thus contends: "The chief feature of the protoreligious, 'natural metaphysic' is the affirmation that life is sacred. It is believed to be sacred not because it is a manifestation of a transcendent Creator from whom life comes.... [Rather] the idea of sacredness is generated by the primordial experience of being alive, of experiencing the elemental sensation of vitality and the elemental fear of its extinction."[31]

What matters critically in the euthanasia discussion, therefore, is the acceptance or nonacceptance of the sanctity of life as a general principle. The sanctity of life principle must engender an attitude which fosters a strong bias in favor of human life and encourages us to act in ways consistent with this bias.

Central to both Catholic and Protestant theology on this question is the conviction that God is Lord of Life and Death. This conviction is another way of affirming that the ultimate value and sanctity of human life comes from God. This conviction implies that no one can ever claim total mastery over one's own or another's life. In other words, life is God's loan to us: not only because life is grounded in God, but also because God has given us life as a value to be held in trust and to be used according to his will. Saint Thomas Aquinas thus taught: "That a person has dominion over himself is because he is endowed with free choice. Thanks to that free choice a man is at liberty to dispose of himself with respect to those things in this life which are subject to his freedom. But the passage from this life to a happier one is not one of those things, for one's passage from this life is subject to the will and power of God."[32]

---

[30]Shils, The Sanctity of Life, in LIFE OR DEATH: ETHICS AND OPTIONS 18-19 (D. H. Laggy ed 1968).

[31]Id. at 12.

[32]Not every author agrees, of course, with this interpretation of "Dominion." For example, Richard Westley equates Creator and the creature more unequivocally than traditional authors. On the basis of an incarnational faith, Westley claims that the Divine and Human are so wedded to one another as to eliminate any talk of Divine and Human prerogatives. For Westley, the mystery of the incarnation tells us that God has chosen to make Divine work our own. Since God lives in us, whatever belongs to Divine Dominion also belongs to us. Westley thus challenges absolute sovereignty and limited stewardship by exploring the meaning of life as a "gift" from

Human persons, then, have only a right to the use of human life, not to dominion over human life. What makes killing forbidden is that it usurps a divine prerogative and violates divine rights. When this conclusion is reached, moreover, the patient is never left alone. Advocacy of euthanasia does, in fact, leave the patient alone.[33] Every person is a locus of meaning and value. It matters, therefore, how a person dies. Those who advocate euthanasia or benemortasia actually allow a suffering person to die alone. Advocacy of assisted suicide is advocacy of defeat: a giving up on human life as sacred and filled with dignity.[34]

In his painting, "The Creation of Man," Marc Chagall paints at the bottom of the image an angel holding the limp body of Adam. At the top of the painting one finds some extraordinarily interesting symbols: the eight-branch candelabra of the Jewish faith, the scroll of the Law, the ladder, presumably Jacob's ladder, and the swirling sun from the story of Elijah in the Old Testament. On the other side of the sun, there appears certain symbols from the Christian faith: Jesus crucified, a fish, which is the symbol of the Eucharist, and the Tables of the Law. On the side there is a crowd of faces looking down on this whole event. Those faces look like a cheering crowd at a football game, presumably a crowd who are the children of Adam, all of us. The painting promises that, in a moment, the breath of God will enliven that limp figure, and it will come to life. And the first things that it will see are the cheering and smiling faces of all the children that will flow from this human being and all the symbols that our civilization has used to raise the great question of the meaning of life. The angel holding that body is true life support because that body will come to life, and know joy and know meaning and know sharing of fellowship in one's family and in one's culture.

Euthanasia and benemortasia are ethical postures which give up on "life support." Again and again, writers point out that it is not death itself but the dying process that frightens individuals. People want to make sure that they will not be sentenced to intractable pain and suffering. The appeal for release is certainly understandable, but killing the patient, even when done with the kindest of motives, is not the moral way to address the problem. There should be no passion for euthanasia or benemortasia.

God. As Westley sees it, if life is given as a gift, then it is subject to our freedom and to speak of stewardship is out of place in this context. *See* R. Westley, Morality and Its Beyond (1984).

[33]Fletcher, *The "Right" to Life and the "Right" to Die*, in Beneficient Euthanasia 44 (M. Kohl ed. 1975).

[34]R. Gula, What are They Saying About Euthanasia (1986).

Assisting Suicide: An Ethical Perspective

Ernlé W. D. Young, Ph.D.*

Although the primary intent of this article is to provide an ethical perspective on assisting *those who are terminally ill* to end their own lives, it will be helpful to begin the analysis by reflecting on suicide in general.

One of the advantages of a principled approach to ethics, whether deontological or rule utilitarian,[1] is that one does not have to reinvent the wheel each time one confronts a moral dilemma or faces a moral decision. Principles, serving as guiding norms, express the distillation of human moral wisdom. They suggest what, *prima facie*, one ought or ought not to do in a given situation. What one actually does, or does not do, or which among competing principles one chooses to protect, will, of course, depend on the facts of the case and, at least if one subscribes to the theory of W. D. Ross, a consequentialist calculation about which principle, above all others, will serve to maximize utility.[2]

---

*Chaplaincy Service, Stanford University Hospital; B.A., Rhodes University, Grahamstown, South Africa; Master of Divinity, Rhodes University, 1964; Ph.D., Southern Methodist University, 1971.

[1] The word "deontological" derives from the greek word *deon*, which means "duty" or "it is required." A deontological approach to ethics insists that, *a priori*, certain things are required of us, e.g., being truthful, and keeping promises. Conversely, a "rule-utilitarian" ethic is a system in which the "principle of utility" (deference to what will promote maximal general good, *see, e.g.*, Mill, *Utilitarianism*, in UTILITARIANISM, LIBERTY, AND REPRESENTATIVE GOVERNMENT, SELECTIONS FROM AUGUST COMTE AND POSITIVISM (H. B. Acton ed. 1972)) is used to determine the rules that will be used to guide proper conduct. *See generally* BEAUCHAMP & CHILDRESS, PRINCIPLES OF BIOMEDICAL ETHICS ch. 2 (2d ed. 1983), which also constitutes a good example of the conbination of two approaches. *Id.* at x, chs. 3-6.

[2] Whereas, in rule-utilitarianism, the principle of utility is employed to fashion the rules themselves as well as to apply them. *See* Beauchamp & Childress, *supra* note 1, at 25-26, 30-32. W. D. Ross uses a consequentialist calculus to determine which deon-

With respect to the issue of suicide, in general, two moral principles are always potentially in conflict. On the one hand, there is the principle of autonomy, from the Greek words *autos* (self) and *nomos* (law). This principle holds that, so far as is possible and consistent with the welfare of others, persons ought to be respected as and encouraged to be self-determining moral agents. Immanuel Kant (a rule deontologist) argued in his *Groundwork of the Metaphysic of Morals* that persons should always be treated as autonomous ends and never merely as means to the ends of others.[3] John Stuart Mill (one of the fathers of rule-utilitarianism) speaks of the individuality of action and thought in his celebrated treatise, *On Liberty.*[4] What Mill means by individuality is similar to what Kant denotes by the term autonomy. In our time, the consumer movement has stressed the importance of the autonomy of the consumer (whether of medical services or of other goods.[5] From the perspective of the principle of autonomy, the wish of someone to choose death rather than life ought to be respected, *providing that sound evidence shows that the person concerned is mentally competent and rational* (and that, therefore, the decision is in fact substantially autonomous). In the case of the mentally competent and rational person, suicide may be regarded as the ultimate expression of autonomy. Such an individual expresses the will to be self-determining, not only in matters of life, but also in the manner and timing of death. So long as acting on the basis of this principle does not harm others, it would be consistent with Mill's individuality of action and thought.

On the other hand, there is the principle of beneficence. Beneficence imposes on us a duty to benefit others, when in a position to do so. This principle is deeply embedded in the history of medicine

---

tological principle to apply in a particular situation where different principles compete for primacy. W. D. Ross, Foundations of Ethics 175-191 (1939).

[3]I. Kant, Groundwork of the Metaphysic of Morals 95-96 (trans. H. J. Paton 1964).

[4]J. S. Mill, On Liberty (introd. R. Kirk 1955), but *see* especially ch. III.

[5]In the 1970's, a host of books was published encouraging medical consumer assertiveness on the basis of the principle of autonomy. *See, e.g.,* A. S. Freese, Managing Your Doctor: How to Get the Best Possible Care (1975); G. J. Annas, The Right of Hospital Patients: The Basic Civil Liberties Guide to a Hospital Patient's Rights (1975); A. Levin, Talk Back to Your Doctor: How to Demand (and Recognize) High Quality Health Care (1975); S. E. Sagov & A. Brodsky, The Active Patient's Guide to Better Medical Care (1976); The Boston Women's Health Book Collective, Our Bodies, Ourselves (1976). It is also interesting to note that "The Patient's Bill of Rights," 42 C.F.R. §§405.1121, 442.311, assumed currency during the seventies.

and the medical ethical tradition. The Hippocratic corpus enjoins the physician not only to avoid inflicting harm on patients, but positively to benefit them.[6] Beneficence readily lends itself to paternalistic behavior. In the ethical literature, paternalism refers "to practices that restrict the liberty of individuals, without their consent, where the justification for such actions is either the prevention of some harm they will do to themselves or the prodution of some benefit for them they would not otherwise secure."[7]

In the normal course of events, it would be almost instinctive for the physician to act paternalistically and beneficently to attempt to save the life of someone who had tried to kill herself. In so deciding, the physician would be making the assumption that the suicidal person was not, at the time, mentally competent and rational. This, in turn, reflects a value judgment: no one "in his right mind" would want to kill himself; to want to kill oneself, one must be, in this conception, mentally off-balance or emotionally unhinged—at least temporarily. That the majority within our society subscribe to this value judgment sanctions the automatic paternalistic application of the principle of beneficence. For example, whenever someone is brought into an emergency room as the result of an overdose of some type of medication, such a person is presumed to have been mentally incompetent and irrational at the time the overdose was taken. The principle of beneficence, paternalistically applied (as is bound to be the case in an emergent situation), therefore requires that the stomach be pumped out, that the drug used be identified, and that immediate measures be taken to counter the effects of the drug—including, if necessary, cardiopulmonary resuscitation, ventilatory support, renal dialysis, and other intensive care interventions.

The principle of autonomy, therefore, is constantly in tension with the principle of beneficence. The wish to respect other people as self-determining moral agents (so long as their actions are not infringing upon the liberties of others or causing others harm, and so long as they are mentally competent and rational) is inherently opposed to the duty, negatively, to prevent harm from coming to them, or, positively, to benefit them. Death is valued negatively in our culture (with some few exceptions, presently to be considered); life is valued posi-

---

[6]For a fuller discussion of the principles of autonomy and beneficence, *see* Beauchamp & Childress, *supra* note 1, ch. 3 and 5, respectively, and also I. ENGLEHARDT, THE FOUNDATIONS OF BIOETHICS 66-87 (1986).

[7]Beauchamp, *Paternalism*, in ENCYCLOPEDIA OF BIOETHICS 1194-201 (W. I. Reich ed. 1978).

tively. Averting harm, then, is equated with preventing someone else from dying, and benefiting another is synonymous with intervening to enable that person to live.

In the absence of an underlying terminal and painful disease process, the principle of beneficence ought *prima facie* to take precedence over the principle of autonomy in responding to suicidal attempts or desires. When the suicidal person does have an underlying terminal and painful medical condition, or is in an advanced state of decrepitude, and is mentally competent and rational, however, the principle of autonomy ought *prima facie* to be ranked in priority over the principle of beneficence.

The first position hinges on the value judgment, shared by most people in our society, that, in the absence of some major misfortune, medical or otherwise, and on balance, life is preferable to death. Obviously, this is a value judgment not endorsed by everybody. Of serious concern to many of us are the data, beginning to be accumulated, which indicate the alienation of significant numbers of young people from this shared value.[8]

Two verses from a poem written by a seventeen-year old boy from an affluent home a year ago exemplify this alienation:

> Inside my head is pounding
> Been hurting me for weeks
> I've got to find salvation
> I've got to find some peace.
>
> I just now realized
> I have new decisions to make
> What building shall I jump from
> What pills should I take?

Despite being scholarly, athletic, musical, handsome, and in other ways gifted, Todd, a year after writing these lines, leaped to his death from a high-rise building on the campus where he was a student. He was one of the approximately six thousand who succeeded in killing themselves out of the estimated four hundred thousand young people who attempt suicide each year.[9] The recent spate of group

---

[8]The 1980 edition of the STATISTICAL ABSTRACT OF THE UNITED STATES reveals that suicide ranks among the top five causes of death for white males aged 10-55, and is the *second-ranked cause of death for all males aged 15-24*. Nearly 30,000 Americans a year choose to end their own lives; many experts believe that the official statistics grossly understate the actual number of suicides, perhaps by half.

[9]1984 figures.

teenage suicides and attempted suicides indicates how profoundly foreign to many of our young people are the values of their elders on the issue of suicide.

Values and value judgments, which enter decisively into the ethical decisions we make, whether consciously or unconsciously, are correlated closely with deeply-held metaphysical beliefs. Those who, standing within the Judeo-Christian tradition, affirm life (with all its problems and difficulties) to be a good gift from the hand of God, will be prone to value life above death, even in the worst of times. Those who, less directly connected to any religious tradition, nevertheless, affirm an evolutionary and optimistic worldview (e.g., the American dream), will also tend, on the whole and except under extreme stress, to value life above death. In both instances, value judgments are being made. The young, standing in the shadow of nuclear proliferation and annihilation, are understandably less easily able to believe that good will always and automatically triumph over evil, that the light will invariably drive back the darkness. With the belief and value systems of previous generations no longer credible to them, it should not surprise us that a disturbingly high number of young people will not automatically value life above death—even in the absence of profound personal affliction.

Nevertheless, those who, on balance, value life more than death constitute a majority within society. This majority, therefore, would endorse the primacy of beneficence over autonomy when someone is threatening or attempting to commit suicide—so long as there is no known underlying terminal disease process, increasing physical decrepitude, or unmitigable pain. The presumption (on the basis of the value judgment) is that this person's autonomy had been compromised (either by extrinsic or intrinsic factors) and that the threatened or attempted suicide was therefore not a truly autonomous act. The intention of intervening would be not only to prevent the death of the suicidal person but also to provide him with such appropriate therapy, counseling, or support as would serve eventually to remove the impediments to substantial autonomy that prevent him from affirming the goodness of life. A further assumption is that, if the intervention is effective (in both senses), the suicidal person would later provide *retrospective consent* to what was done to prevent death and to remove the obstacles to autonomy. It is anticipated that looking back, once the crisis is passed, the person who was previously suicidal will be glad and grateful that action was taken, on the basis of paternalistic beneficence, to avert death. That there is often empirical evidence, *ex post facto*, to indicate that these presumptions were, in fact, correct, further strengthens the bias in favor of subordinating autonomy to beneficence in the circumstance we are discussing.[10]

However, a majority in our society is also beginning to recognize that, when a person is afflicted with an underlying terminal condition, or is in a state of advanced physical decrepitude, or is in unmitigable pain, a distinction must be drawn between *extending life* (with all that makes life rich and full) and *merely prolonging an inevitable process of dying*. On the basis of this distinction, there may be a point beyond which life is no longer necessarily to be valued above death. In fact, the opposite may be the case—especially when the person is experiencing pain that cannot be alleviated. Now, *prima facie*, the principle of autonomy may in good conscience be ranked above the principle of beneficence—so long as the person concerned is mentally competent and rational, and so long as all possible steps have been taken to minimize the ensuing harm to others.[11]

This leads to the following conclusion: if (a) a person is either terminally ill or irreversibly decrepit in terms of physical functioning; (b) and is in unmitigable pain—whether physical or psychological, or both; (c) and is obviously mentally competent and rational; and (d) has attempted to mitigate the harmful effects—especially predictable feelings of guilt—of her action on those who will survive her, then it is morally licit to rank the principle of autonomy above the principle of beneficence in evaluating one's duty to respond to that person's suicidal attempts or desires. This means that the suicidal intent may now be perceived simply as the final expression of autonomy, deserving to be respected as such without any attempt to prevent it by paternalistically beneficent intervention.

However, at this juncture, a theological caveat may be in order. From a theological perspective, suicide may be regarded as a predictable response to the breakdown of *faith* (the ability to affirm the essential meaningfulness of human existence, especially in the face of pain), *hope* (being able to look at the future with confidence and cour-

---

[10]"Generally, persons who use the most-lethal methods in their suicide attempts and are unsuccessful have a lower risk of future suicide attempts than do those who use the less-lethal methods. In other words, the person who survives a self-inflicted gunshot wound is less likely to try suicide again than someone who unsuccessfully used a plastic bag." L. A. deSpelder & A. L. Strickland, The Last Dance: Encountering Death and Dying 364 (1983).

[11]It is only recently that a concerted effort has been made to substantiate the negative psychological, sociological, and physical effects of suicide on survivors. *See* Welu, *Pathological Bereavement: A Plan for its Prevention*, in Bereavement: Its Psychosocial Aspects 139 (B. Schoenberg ed. 1975).

age, especially in circumstances of present distress), and *love* (the ability to affirm the self and to receive from and give to others a similar affirmation). When terminal illness and the pain associated with it are experienced as essentially *meaningless*, when the future is perceived as holding nothing but further affliction and debilitation and there *no longer appear to be grounds for confidence and courage with respect to what is yet to be,* and when it seems that significant others *no longer care nor want to be cared for,* then the wish to choose death above life is eminently reasonable and understandable. "Why does anyone commit suicide?" ask Kastenbaum and Aisenberg.[12] Their response focuses merely on the first of the three theological ingredients we have identified (which they deem sufficient): "[M]ost generally, because life has no meaning."[13]

Nevertheless, before simply giving "permission" to someone who is terminally ill and in intractable pain to translate the suicidal desire into the deed, it is first of all necessary, from a theological perspective, for the caregiver to attempt to help that person discover or recover faith, hope, and love. In other words, one's primary obligation, theologically understood, is to endeavor to enable the terminally ill and suicidal person to find or regain a sense of the meaningfulness of all human experience—pain included. It is to attempt to facilitate in that person the capacity to look to the future with confidence and courage, especially if his vision can be extended beyond the horizons of time to the limitless vistas of eternity. And it is to try to instill in him the conviction that he is essentially lovable— no matter how his outward appearance may be changing, even deteriorating, from day to day, making it more and more difficult for him to love himself—and, therefore, capable of loving and being loved.

Such an attempt may or may not involve the use of religious figures and religious language. Spirituality is a category of human exprience broader and more universal than religion, yet including it. It is possible to speak of faith, hope, and love in either religious or secular language. Whether religious or secular symbols are employed will depend on the belief and value system of the suicidal person— again, because of the principle of autonomy. To attempt to impose one's own particular religious beliefs or values on others—for whatever good intentions—betrays a lack of respect for their autonomy and may even violate it.

---

[12]R. Kastenbaum & R. Aisenberg, The Psychology of Death 251 (1972).
[13]*Id.*

Only after the attempt has been made, seriously and strenuously, to enable the dying person to find or regain faith, hope, and love, and has failed, is it morally permissible to acquiesce in her wish to choose death rather than life. Only then is it morally licit to allow her to express her autonomy in this ultimate way rather than intervening with beneficently paternalistic motivation to frustrate it.

However, it is one thing to acquiesce; it is another to assist. Acquiescing in a terminally ill person's desire to end his life may be morally appropriate, especially where the conditions outlined above have been satisfied. Can the same be said of assisting? This is the issue to be taken up.

The first question to be raised is: Is there a moral difference between saying to someone who wishes to commit suicide, "I'll not stop you" and "I'll help you"? In saying "I'll not stop you," one may be expressing respect for a state of mind, a belief system, or an intention to act in a certain way, which may, in the circumstances, seem to be appropriate for the person concerned. For one to say "I'll help you," on the other hand, would require a much higher level of personal assent to the state of mind, the belief system, or the intention to act being evidenced. There is a difference between respect and assent. One may respect the views of Jehovah's Witnesses and of Marxists, but not assent to them. One may or may not assent to the suicidal desire being expressed which, for reasons already given, one may respect. If one cannot assent to the suicidal ideation, even though one may respect it, there is no moral obligation to go beyond saying, "I'll not stop you," to "I'll help you." If one can assent to the suicidal wish, and all the reasons for it that the person concerned might adduce, then, as expressive of his own autonomy, one may choose to say, "I'll help you."

The crucial point is that were one to say, "I'll help you," one would be acting autonomously and out of generosity, not because of a perceived moral obligation or duty. One of the principal reasons for choosing to help a suicidal person in the circumstances we are considering is compassion. However, acting on the basis of the principle of beneficence would require of the person assisting a stronger conviction that, in this particular situation, death would actually be a benefit, than acting on the basis of the principle of autonomy. It also presumes that there is a "right" to help which carries with it a concomitant duty. Beneficence requires help as a duty; autonomy allows assistance as a freely-offered gift. There is no duty to help someone who wishes to die to accomplish her death, since there is no corresponding "right" to be helped to die. However, assistance may freely be proffered as an act of generosity and compassion—in circumstances where one not only respects, but also assents to, the suicidal intention being expressed.

There are various factors which may lead one to go on to assent to views which, on other grounds, one might already respect. One would be the quality of the relationship with the person who now wishes to end her life. Another would be the degree to which one shares that person's values, belief systems, and reasoned arguments for wanting to end his life. Yet another would be the inability of the person wishing to die to accomplish his own death without assistance. A fourth would be the capacity of the person being asked for assistance to provide it. Where the relationship between potential helper and helpee is extremely close, where there is a high degree of assent to the values, beliefs, and arguments being expressed by the person contemplating suicide, where the person rationally wanting to die cannot possibly accomplish this without assistance (the case of the person with end-stage multiple sclerosis comes to mind), and where there are ways in which the potential helper can in fact help, then, while there may be no *duty* to assist, it would be difficult to argue that it would be *immoral* autonomously to choose to help.

Tristram Englehardt goes further. He argues in support of the right of individuals to commit suicide, and then concludes: "Insofar as individuals possess this right for themselves, they should have as well the right to be aided by others."[14] This seems to me not necessarily to follow and to go too far. The language of "rights" in this context implies corresponding duties. There is no duty to help someone to die, although, as has already been stated, one may voluntarily choose to provide assistance as a freely-offered act of kindness.

The motivation of the potential helper is crucial. Where the motive for offering help is indeed to benefit the person wishing to die, this is morally acceptable. But where the motive is selfish, as in an attempt to inherit the estate of the person wishing to die, this obviously would cast an altogether different light on the assistance being contemplated. Because motivation cannot be assessed before the fact, helping another person to die should never be given legal sanction.

This brings us to the final issue: the nature of the assistance that might be given, were one to be morally convinced of the appropriateness of helping someone who, on grounds discussed above, wanted to commit suicide but was unable to accomplish this act. Various pos-

---

[14]Englehardt, *supra* note 6, at 306.

sible types of assistance come to mind, ranging from seemingly innocent to far more incriminating. The options would include:

(a) Encouragement. Removing obstacles in the way of the person wishing to end their life, for example, by reassuring them that they will not be judged and damned by God; or suggesting that, if the roles were reversed, one would probably be contemplating suicide oneself.

(b) Information, of the sort provided by the "Hemlock Society" or "Exit"[15] about how to accomplish one's own death in the least traumatic and most effective manner.

(c) Provisions or procurement of the necessary means when the suicidal person is and would otherwise be without such means.

(d) Helping to administer the means to be employed, e.g., mixing the lethal dose and holding it to the lips of the person wishing to die, or holding the gun to the suicidal person's head and placing his finger on the trigger.

(e) Actually killing the person wishing to die, at their request, for example, by smothering, shooting, or poisoning. The line between assisted suicide of this kind and voluntary "mercy killing" is blurred. It is difficult to discern a moral difference between them.

As was suggested earlier, the spectrum of possibilities, outlined above, includes relatively innocuous forms of assistance, at the one end, and, at the other, the serious matter of taking the life of another human being. Each option might be considered moral, so long as the person wishing to die meets the criteria previously discussed, and so long as the motivation of the person providing assistance is solely that of wanting to benefit the dying person. How far along the spectrum, the helper will be willing to go, will depend on the factors previously mentioned: the quality of the relationship; the degree to which the beliefs, values, and arguments for wanting to die of the person seeking help are persuasive to the person in a position to help; the degree of inability of the suicidal person to accomplish the desired death; and

---

[15]The Hemlock Society was founded in 1980. It supports the options of active voluntary euthanasia for the terminally ill and assisted suicide. *See* D. HUMPHRY, LET ME DIE BEFORE I WAKE (3d ed. 1984). "Exit" is the British equivalent of the Hemlock Society.

the capacity—emotionally as well as practical—of the person being asked for help to provide it.

What is obvious is that the consequences of helping become much more serious as one moves from (a) through (e). Providing the sorts of assistance suggested in (d) and (e) could result in the helper being required to face civil or criminal charges. However, the helper who deeply loves the person wishing to die, shares his beliefs and values and is persuaded by his reasons for wanting to die, and is in a position to help—both emotionally and practically—may be willing to risk the adverse consequences and go as far as (d) or (e) where the person wishing to die is entirely incapable of accomplishing his own death. Were one so to act, this would be an act of compassion and courage of the highest order.

In conclusion, some legal implications must be drawn out from the argument that has been made, with a few recommendations to follow. We have outlined a range of possible responses to people who, for whatever reason, no longer regard life as a benefit and choose, rationally and competently, to act autonomously and commit suicide. In the case of those not afflicted with an underlying terminal illness, nor in a state of advanced decrepitude, the *prima facie* presumption is that their competency is in some way impaired or compromised and that, therefore, the principle of beneficence ought to take priority over the principle of autonomy. If, later, it is established that, with full rationality and competency, death was still being valued above life, and every possible effort has been made to enable the suicidal person to view life differently, as a benefit rather than as a detriment, and had failed, then, reluctantly, on the basis of the principle of autonomy, one would be required to acquiesce in the decision to die. It follows, *ipso facto*, that, if such suicidal attempts were unsuccessful, the persons concerned should not be subject to criminal charges.

Even more insistently, one must object to criminal charges being brought against those who unsuccessfully had tried to end their own lives in circumstances of terminal illness or advanced decrepitude and unmitigable pain, where every effort had been made to minimize for the survivors the untoward consequences of the act.

The more difficult question is what legal consequences, if any, ought to be born by those who assist people in the above category. For the reasons set out below, my own convictions are that encouragement or the provision of information ought not to be subject to legal penalties, that helping someone to accomplish his own death or actually to kill him (at his request) ought to be subject to legal penalties of a special lesser kind, and that procuring for someone who wishes to die the means necessary to accomplish it falls into an ambiguous category.

Encouraging or providing information to someone who wishes to die, in the circumstances we have asserted to be morally licit, represents a fairly modest step from acquiescence to assent and is consistent with it. Both are forms of assistance which affirm the autonomy of the person wishing to die. It would be hypocritical to argue that, while autonomy ought to be respected, acts which affirm or enhance autonomy ought to be subject to criminal charges. However, directly to assist the person to die or actually to kill her, even at her own request, are far more serious actions, susceptible to more serious kinds of abuse (for example, by those whose motivation is self interest rather than altruism). Because it is usually possible to be certain about motivation only *after-the-fact*, such actions should be subject to close legal scrutiny. This would require civil or criminal charges being brought against those so assisting or killing. However, in those cases where the motivation was demonstrably altruistic, the *penalties* ought to be light or nonexistent. To subject persons found guilty of killing for reasons of compassion to the same penalties as those found guilty of first- or second-degree murder seems excessive, unjust, and unwarranted.

This leaves the "ambiguous" category of those who procure for someone who wishes to end their own life, in the circumstances we are describing, the means that one is unable to obtain for oneself. Here, it seems that the "criminality," if any, of the assistance given should depend on a case by case assessment of what help was actually afforded. A physician who appropriately prescribes sleeping pills for a terminally ill patient ought not to be subject to criminal charges should the patient swallow all the pills at once, rather than two at a time, in order to end their life. On the other hand, a physician who inappropriately prescribes a medication whose sole effect is to cause death ought to be subject to civil or criminal charges. Again, should the motivation subsequently be proven to be compassion, the penalties should be light or nonexistent. Unless legal penalties are possible, even in cases where it was appropriate to help someone to die, the door could easily be opened to the inappropriate shortening of others' lives.

This leads to this article's final recommendations. Any remaining laws treating suicide as a criminal offense ought to be struck down. Laws forbidding the provision of assistance to someone wishing to die ought to be struck down, where the assistance is merely that of offering encouragement or providing information. And laws forbidding the provision of other kinds of assistance to someone wanting to die as in (c), (d), and (e), above ought to remain in place, but the penalties ought to be light or nonexistent in cases where it is clearly established that the motivation of the helper was not at all sinister, but unambiguously reflected compassion and altruism.[16]

---

[16]From a tangled history in which it was often deemed a crime against the sovereign or state, and a sin against God—with the victim's body buried ignominiously or his estate forfeited to the crown as punishment—suicide in American law is expressly regarded a crime now in only two states: Alabama and South Carolina. Several jurisprudential considerations seem to have propelled the decriminalization here: the futility of branding criminal an act which, by its very definition, permanently places the perpetrator beyond the chastening grasp of the state, the unfairness of punishing a suicide victim's survivors by disseising them of the suicide's estate, and the pointlessness, if not the unconscionability, of risking further brutalization of the suicide victim's survivors by subjecting his corpse to ignominy.

It is thus accurate to say, as matters of both legal and actual fact, that suicide is not punished criminally anywhere in the United States. Moral revulsion toward suicide, and convictions that on some level it is tragic—however unpreventable actually or unpunishable legally—survive in the form of strong judicial and legislative condemnations of the act. Attempted suicide is also not punished criminally anywhere in the U.S., preference being given to the view that people who try to kill themselves need medical help, not chastisement.

On the other hand, helping someone commit suicide is, by and large, still a crime in nearly every state in the nation. A large number of states has even passed legislation expressly criminalizing the act of aiding or abetting suicide. Yet even in the absence of such statutes, some courts have held guilty of murder persons who aid in suicide by providing the means of death.

For general background on, as well as specific state-by-state analysis of, laws regarding suicide, attempted suicide and assisting suicide, *see* Marzen, O'Down, Crone & Balch, *Suicide: A Constitutional Right?*, 24 Duq. L. Rev. 1, 17-100, 148-242 (1985).

Voluntary Active Euthansia: The Next Frontier?

Mary Johnson*

I am not a legal expert on voluntary active euthanasia; I approach the subject as a journalist. I have watched the media report stories about individuals with severe disabilities who come into the public eye because of a wish that their lives be ended, and have talked to people with disabilities who are angry about these issues—and sometimes angry with each other. I've published their thoughts about assisted suicide in the pages of *The Disability Rag*, a periodical published for the disability community. I have seen some authors who have disabilities gain a wider audience, e.g., Dr. Paul Longmore, Bill Bolte, and Dianne Piastro. This article will focus on and confine itself to the cases of mentally alert people with physical disabilities who have sought court or other help in ending their lives, giving examples of how the courts and the media have shaped the public's understanding of what is happening, and, perhaps more important, have identified what the public wants to believe about such cases.

If I believed that such mentally alert, physically disabled people truly wanted to end their lives for reasons similar to those given by nondisabled people who seek an end to life, this article would take a different perspective. But I believe that, in a significant number of cases, such mentally alert, physically disabled people are being subtly or not so subtly pressured, by doctors, family, media, and societal mores in general, to end their lives. It is this pressure that distinguishes the particular form of euthanasia that I will discuss.

None of these cases has been referred to in the media as voluntary active euthanasia but are usually referred to as treatment refusal or assisted suicide. Typically, court rulings are at pains to point out that they are not suicides; they are typically classified as "termination of treatment." However, this seems a gloss at best, certainly a distinction without merit. Such safe terms seem to be selected to assuage a guilt that society wishes not to confront.

It appears that people with disabilities are viewed in this society as

*Editor, The Advocado Press; Editor, *The Disability Rag*; A.B., Spalding University, 1970.

an expendable group—perhaps the only remaining expendable group—a group that we can verbally suggest ways of expending without incurring much opprobrium. In an era of tight resources, it seems, such encouragement of expendable people to seek an end to lives of "unbearable pain" may be considered acceptable social policy, viewed in the light of beneficient "euthanasia."

The "right to die" is not something I question in this article, as I believe that is a right which must remain available to the individual in a free society. The question is not one of right but of equality. It seems all too likely that the high moral ground of "right to die" has been appropriated as a cover for what appears to be occurring with an increasing number of mentally alert, but physically disabled, people. It is not the protection of a freely chosen right but the encouragement, perhaps by coercion, to exercise that "right" as the *only* option and the denial of life-sustaining options such as technology, medical treatment, pain relief, personal assistance, and access. Almost no mentally alert, physically disabled person who seeks assistance in dying receives the routine suicide prevention counseling made available to nondisabled people who seek help to terminate their lives. It is this consistent lack of assistance in exploring options other than choosing death that strongly suggests that death is the only option approved by society in more and more cases. This constitutes approval of voluntary active euthanasia for persons who are mentally alert, but physically disabled.

Voluntary Active Euthansia of Mentally Alert, Physically Disabled People

In the Press

Physically disabled but mentally alert people who seek court permission to end their lives have in the last decade provided fodder for high drama in the press. Reporters covering the cases of David Rivlin in Detroit, Larry McAfee in Georgia, and Kenneth Bergstedt in Las Vegas have followed the lead of reporters who wrote about Elizabeth Bouvia in the early 1980s, providing readers with stories that mix pity, sympathy, and hyperbole in a combination seemingly designed to jerk tears from readers rather than shed light on this extremely complicated situation, which almost always appears to be the result not of disability so much as factors such as lack of services to provide a meaningful quality of life.[1]

---

[1] *See* Margot Dougherty & Sandra Rubin Tessler, *For Quadriplegic David Rivlin, Life on a Respirator Wasn't Worth Living*, PEOPLE MAG., Aug. 7, 1979, at 56; Jeff German, *Right-to-Die Case Teaches Lessons About Life*, LAS VEGAS SUN, May 30, 1990, at C9; *A Misunderstood Case*, DISABILITY RAG, Feb.-Mar. 1984, at 9.

People magazine reporters Margot Dougherty and Sandra Rubin Tessler wrote of David Rivlin: "Nothing could tune out the sound that symbolized his ultimate imprisonment: the incessant whir of a respirator" and referred to him as someone "from whom true life had been taken."[2]

There was similar media reaction to the case of Elizabeth Bouvia in 1983. Harlan Hahn told *The Disability Rag*, regarding Bouvia: "When you try to talk to a nondisabled reporter and explain what's really going on in this case, it becomes clear that most of them don't begin to understand what you're trying to say."[3]

Of Kenneth Bergstedt, *Las Vegas Sun* reporter Jeff German wrote: "Though it's hard to conceive of someone wanting to give up on life, I sense the Bergstedts are making the right choice . . . . And frankly, we can't possibly understand the pain and sorrow the Bergstedts are going through."[4]

Ethicists, columnists, editorial writers, and news analysts have had much to say about such things as withdrawing food and hydration from comatose people, as occasioned by the *Cruzan* case.[5] They have written repeatedly about termination of life for older people kept alive on respirators. And there has been much written promoting the use of living wills to refuse life-sustaining medical treatment and care.

However, I have not yet found a single national columnist, analyst, ethicist, or editorial writer venturing commentary on the cases of mentally alert, physically disabled people seeking court permission for assistance in ending their lives. What little commentary has been published has been conducted by members of the disability community. Paul Longmore, Bill Bolte, Dianne Piastro—all have had op-ed articles published on the subject.[6]

Bolte has written that "an assumption . . . often held by people who have never had a severe disability . . . is that people by nature would rather die than have a life-altering disability, and that anyone who helps us die is therefore a hero rather than a criminal."[7]

No responses to these op-ed articles written by the disability community have appeared. There are no responding letters to the editor,

---

[2]Dougherty & Tessler, *supra* note 1, at 56.

[3]*A Misunderstood Case*, *supra* note 1, at 10.

[4]German, *supra* note 1, at C9.

[5]*See* Cruzan v. Director, Mo. Dep't of Health, 497 U.S. 261 (1990).

[6]*See* Paul K. Longmore, *The Shameful Treatment of Larry McAfee*, ATLANTA J.-CONST., Sept. 10, 1989, at B1; Bill Bolte, *Forget Suicide Machines, Give Disabled Right to Live*, ATLANTA J.-CONST., Dec. 9, 1990, at G1; Dianne B. Piastro, *Making It Easier for Quadriplegics to Live, Not Die*, DETROIT NEWS, Jan. 31, 1990, at C2.

[7]Bolte, *supra* note 6, at G1.

no commentary by columnists such as Ellen Goodman, Cal Thomas, Charles Krauthammer (himself disabled). It is as though the issue of severely physically disabled but mentally alert individuals seeking suicide exists simply in a vacuum.

In light of the extensive commentary by such columnists over cases such as *Cruzan*[8] and *Busalacchi*,[9,10] the lack of commentary about voluntary active euthanasia of mentally alert, physically disabled individuals must, it seems, have some significance: we do not want to discuss it as a nation.

In the Courts

Georgia Superior Court Judge Edward H. Johnson, who ruled that the state could not stop Larry McAfee from using a device he had created to commit suicide, said, "I think Larry [McAfee] loves life as much as any human being who's ever lived, and that's why he's seeking the relief he's seeking. . . . Mr. McAfee is not committing suicide, nor is he attempting to commit suicide." To keep McAfee on a ventilator "would not prolong his life but instead would prolong his death."[11]

In the Kenneth Bergstedt case,[12] District Judge Donald Mosley, in ruling that Bergstedt would not be commiting suicide, told the court that Bergstedt "suffers from physical and emotional pain because of his quadriplegia . . . [and] enjoys no pleasures from life, and has not enjoyed such pleasures from life for many years."[13]

These comments refer to cases of individuals who are nonelderly, severely disabled, but mentally alert. Therefore, they must be distinguished from older individuals or individuals who are incompetent. This is the public landscape of cases of voluntary active euthansia.

Before attempting to predict the future course of voluntary active euthansia, it is necessary to outline what I see as the critical issues that come into play when the desire for suicide arises.

The Desire for Suicide: Critical Considerations

On the Part of the Disabled Person Contemplating Suicide

Personal Context. As disability activist Julie Reiskin and others point

---

[8]*Cruzan*, 497 U.S. 261.

[9]*In re* Busalacchi, No. 93677 (Mo. Findings of Fact made Nov. 29, 1991).

[10]Marcia Angell, *The Right to Die in Dignity*, NEWSWEEK, July 23, 1990, at 9; Ellen Goodman, *The Death of Nancy Cruzan Leaves a Legacy*, TOLEDO BLADE, Jan. 1, 1991, at 11.

[11]Duane Riner, *Action Would Not Be Suicide, Johnson Rules, Fighting Tears*, ATLANTA J.-CONST., Sept. 7, 1989, at A1, A7 (quoting Judge Johnson).

[12]McKay v. Bergstedt, 801 P.2d 617 (Nev. 1990).

[13]*Judge Ok's Man's "Death with Dignity,"* LAS VEGAS SUN, June 23, 1990, at A1.

out, many forms of disability bring with them conditions and sensations that are difficult to bear. Among the ones most often mentioned are the existence of pain and fatigue.[14]

Others mentioned are mental/physical frustration at an inability to control one's body, the frustration of incontinence, of uncontrollable body odors, of the inability to have one's body respond to one's mind—conditions particularly emotionally difficult for people used to being physically adept or active who find they can no longer control or use a body in the way they have done for decades. These conditions, by all accounts, are harder to bear for people who were once nondisabled than for people born with the disability, hardest of all perhaps for physically athletic people who encounter such disabilities later in life. When individuals encounter these conditions, the fear, sadness, depression, anger, frustration, and panic that accompany the experience can lead them to seek the final way to reassert control: ending the pain, inabilities, depressions, by ending one's life.

But when one begins to closely examine any of these personal reasons, it becomes clear almost immediately that intertwined with the concrete, physical condition is a mix of what we can call social conditions, whose presence are affecting the person's ability to cope with the physical conditions.

The experience of pain may be considered the most personal, unalterable of conditions. People in constant pain, we think, must certainly have a life more difficult to bear than people not in constant pain. But what is pain? Is it physically caused by the condition itself—the message being sent to the brain by nerve endings ravaged by cancerous cells, for example—or is it intensified by a person's emotional state? It is known that a body's own endorphins can be called upon to lessen pain; biofeedback techniques draw on this. In some countries, individuals who would otherwise be in chronic pain are allowed heroin and live relatively pain-free lives.

So even the existence of pain has its social/political component. When a person is in pain, not always but not infrequently, that situation exists because of political and social decisions to not provide pain-killing or pain-dulling drugs.

As with pain, so with many of the accompaniments of disability. When closely examined, the "suffering" any disabled individual experiences may be seen to be at least partially a function of how the physical condition is responded to by social factors—those factors out-

---

[14]Julie Reiskin, *Suicide: Political or Personal?* DISABILITY RAG, Mar.-Apr. 1991, at 19.

side the physical body that are already existent in society either through the capacities of human social systems or by already existing technology.

As Julie Reiskin, who has grappled with this very problem in deciding on whether to seek suicide herself, puts it: "While all the access in the world can't stop my fatigue, I would be less fatigued if I could work part-time and collect enough benefits to maintain the lifestyle I want—the lifestyle I have when I work full-time. All the attendant services in the world cannot for me make up for the loss of independence. And knowing how few attendant service options there really are today does little to allay my fear of the future."[15]

There is very little that cannot be done with existing technology and social know-how to improve the life of a mentally alert, physically disabled person. But it is not routinely done. On the contrary, it seems to be socially accepted that it routinely can't be done. This attitude, it seems, is what creates the climate in which voluntary active euthansia can develop. And that is the society in which we now live.

It is at this juncture of the personal and the social—the physical sensation of loss and the lack of personal technology for free and complete movement; the experience of physical pain and the refusal to grant adequate chemical pain relief; the physical lack of control and the refusal to provide technological, robotic, and personal assistance—that things get confused.

Much if not most of what a person who becomes disabled feels about her condition, her life, is formed from attitudes acquired as a member of our society. We in society term "unbearable suffering" the very existence of persons with severe physical disability (not seeking to make distinctions among the specific functional differences between people like Bergstedt, McAfee, and Bouvia). Most right-thinking people feel sympathy for people with "unbearable suffering" and never think to examine what might be the components of this "unbearable suffering" (or whether, even, it might have components that can be alleviated through social change). *We believe that, in any remotely similar situation, we would want to end our own lives.* And we project these beliefs of ours onto mentally alert, physically disabled people. We also project onto them our belief that they must surely want to end their suffering—which to us can only mean seeking death—for we have no understanding that things like technological assistance or change in social arrangements could in any way alleviate any aspect of this "unbearable suffering." There is no question in our minds as to why such a person is experiencing what we regard as "unbearable suffering": we assume it to be a sine qua non of

---

[15]*Id.* at 22.

the life of the mentally alert, physically disabled person. And we without question assume that the only solution is death. Therefore, we view assistance in helping such people end their lives as an act of kindness and mercy. Because society inaccurately views most mentally alert, physically disabled people's lives as indistinguishable in their "unbearable suffering," society believes that voluntary active euthanasia is perhaps tragic, but on the whole a good, when applied to mentally alert, physically disabled people.

The Social Context. What does society think about disability that makes it consider death a preferable option? Society holds two attitudes toward disability, attitudes that work in tandem. One attitude defines a "real person" as one who can walk, talk, think clearly, control things, see, hear, act in a physical way, do things for oneself. In the past, societies have held other beliefs about what constitutes the essentialness of a human being: in Western society, it used to be something called "the soul." The essentialness of humanity focused on immanence and transcendence. Thus, the thing to be feared most was that which hurt the soul. Society focused on the moral life; sin, heaven, and hell were preoccupations.

Modern Western society sees the essential worth of a person in primarily physical terms, however. Though as a society we've never actually admitted we've dropped the earlier view, in effect we have; this is exhibited by the second attitude we hold toward disability: that people who can't do anything physically are obviously living "a fate worse than death," a "living death." One Los Angeles journalist, almost as if proving that modern society sees a functioning body as the essence of "humanness," much as former times saw the soul, calls comatose or brain-damaged people "lost souls."[16]

Such references in the popular press are almost always in reference to comatose or severely brain-injured individuals. There has been little commentary in the popular press about severely physically disabled but mentally alert people, save for articles written by members of the disability community itself.

An exception was the opinion piece by reporter Jeff German, who had covered the court case of Kenneth Bergstedt. German wrote, "Those who haven't met Kenneth might find it difficult to imagine why he wants to give up on life. Those who have met him [referring to himself] have no trouble understanding." German referred to Bergstedt's life as "21 years of hell."[17]

[16]Eileen Winters, *The Endless Grief of a Living Death*, L.A. TIMES, Aug. 12, 1990, at E1, E7.

[17]Jeff German, *High Court Too Cautious in Bergstedt Case*, LAS VEGAS SUN, July 19, 1990, at 3E.

A person's prior beliefs shape the emotions one brings to actual experiences. Thus, if a person has been told all his life that blacks are violent and Jews are money-grubbers, when he for the first time meets a black or Jewish person, he may behave as though that black or Jewish person really is violent or money-grubbing. Though these kinds of prejudices have today been revealed as nonsensical and wrong, no such expose has ever occurred regarding disability. On the contrary, disability activists who try to insist that their disabilities in themselves do not make their lives miserable are thought to be at worst out of touch with reality and at best in some sort of denial. In short, they are not believed.

When a formerly nondisabled person becomes disabled, much of what is brought to the personal experience is emotional baggage from the incipient prejudice against life with a disability that we as a society have been taught and which we internalize, unquestioned. It is a form of hate—hate now turned inward.

Large as this looms within a disabled person, who experiences self-loathing for one's now disabled body, along with fear, disgust, and depression, it is almost inconsequential compared to the other problems encountered as a result of the presence of disability. These problems are the result of the lack of services and the lack of a way to access needed, existent technology due to either cost or the unavailability of engineers to customize the technology, or both. Such technology, including computerized movement and communication aids, are not provided to any disabled person routinely. For the most part, such technology remains completely unavailable to all severely disabled people—except those rare individuals who have both vast amounts of money to pay for technology and services and the skill and know-how (or access to the skill and know-how of competent others) to seek out what are still little-talked-about and mostly unknown services, devices, and robotics.

Both the personal and the social context in which a disabled person finds herself propels the individual to a desire to end life. Everything is incredibly, almost insurmountably difficult when you are a disabled person today, and unrelenting in that difficulty, too. There are no time-outs during which you can rest from the struggle for services and access, no moment when, even for a short time, you can have everything you need and don't have to fight or beg for it. Ironically, many desperate and deluded disabled people sooner or later (aided by family or doctors) tell themselves that life in a nursing home will provide needed technology and services. Then they get there and learn different—but then it's too late.

The vast majority of the "ten thousand things" that make disability existence so difficult are the result of social constructs, social practices, and policies.

Some aren't, however. Other factors that influence an individual's desire for suicide include: To what extent does the person hold the belief that one's "humanness" is essentially, for want of a better term, the soul? A person who believes the essence of her life (that which makes her a person, valuable, and unique from others) is her own individuality, her own soul, her own immanence (more than and over and above her athletic prowess, her skill as a good dancer, her ability to play golf or the piano or tennis) will be less likely to feel that her "essence" has been destroyed by disability than someone who believes that to be human is to be an essentially physical, mobile entity, able to hop in the car, run around, look good physically to others, be sexually appealing (as society defines it), dance, play handball, and exercise. Today, more people hold the latter definition of "humanness" than hold the former. To most people, the latter is what they think of when the term "quality of life" pops up. For such people, disability may very well seem "a fate worse than death." Though one can contend that it is the disability that ruins such a person's life, it is just as fair to contend that it's the person's particular belief in what constitutes the essence of human life that causes the problem, making him decide that he "no longer has any kind of life," as Robert Bergstedt said about his son, Kenneth.[18]

Many oppressed individuals who have met with suffering and deprivation have gained emotional strength because of a belief that things would get better and drew from a group strength that ultimately resulted in their believing that they as individuals exerted influence as members of their particular minority or culture. Blacks have felt black power, have experienced African-American culture and pride; they have learned to say "black is beautiful." With the gay rights movement has come pride also; people who were once ashamed of their sexual orientation are now "coming out of the closet."

The disabled person seeking suicide seems to have no ability to see herself as valuable with the disability, to believe she is in any way desired or held in esteem.

Taking pride in oneself as a disabled person and feeling oneself part of a comforting "disability culture" is all but unknown among people with disabilities. Isolated and taught to avoid others with disabilities lest one act "more handicapped," seeking to avoid drawing attention to disability, most people who have disabilities have no knowledge of or any way to tap into the emotionally strengthening qualities of a disability community. It's reported that in a number of suicide attempts by dis-

---

[18]Telephone Interview with Robert Bergstedt, father of Kenneth Bergstedt (Aug. 5, 1990).

abled people, they consciously shut out the disability community's presence.[19]

Elizabeth Bouvia, who sought court permission for hospital assistance in starving herself, said in a statement: "I am aware that many disabled people volunteered to come to Riverside [Hospital] and talk to me about my decision, and about other options. While I appreciate those offers, . . . I now simply wish to be left alone."[20]

A journalist who reported on David Rivlin's last days said, "Hundreds of [disabled] people tried to help him but he closed them off."[21]

Though disabled people had tried to reach Kenneth Bergstedt prior to his death last fall, he did not want to be in contact with disabled people, according to his father, Robert Bergstedt.[22]

One cannot rate too highly the beneficial effect of a sense of belonging, of knowlege that "I am not alone, there are others who feel as I do, and we are doing something to make our lives better." Except for a few in tiny enclaves of disability activists here and there whose presence is simply unknown in the larger society, the idea of disability pride and disability culture is ludicrous. This "disability pride" is not the same as a "disabled person's group." Such groups rarely offer emotional solace or strength. More often than not, they exist to help disabled people learn how to "not act disabled."

Nor do suicidal disabled people believe things can get better. McAfee did not believe his life would ever be better than it had been.[23] McAfee was one of those essentially physical people, used to hunting, fishing, riding motorbikes. For someone like him, the essence of humanness was physical. Therefore, being unable to move was in a real sense a living death. Nor did he have any reason to believe he could ever have services to again let him live in his home and get about. He had no access to technology.

Because of the publicity he engendered, however, he acquired many needed services; he also became a convenient symbol newly organized disability activists in Georgia could use to fight to get the state to give McAfee and others like him attendant services in their homes,

---

[19]*See* Elizabeth Bouvia, *I Am Fully Aware . . .* , DISABILITY RAG, Feb.-Mar. 1984, at 5; Mary Johnson, *Drab Curtains—Or How the Press Didn't Cover the Issues That Led to David Rivlin's Suicide*, DISABILITY RAG, Sept.-Oct. 1989, at 23 [hereinafter Johnson, *Drab Curtains*]; Mary Johnson, *Unanswered Questions*, DISABILITY RAG, Sept.-Oct. 1990, at 16 [hereinafter Johnson, *Unanswered Questions*].

[20]Bouvia, *supra* note 19, at 5.

[21]Johnson, *Drab Curtains*, *supra* note 19, at 24.

[22]Johnson, *Unanswered Questions*, *supra* note 19, at 23.

[23]*See* State v. McAfee, 385 S.E.2d 651 (Ga. 1989).

not institutions. So some things McAfee believed would never change did, in fact, change for him. As a result, he no longer wanted to end his life.

Dr. Paul Longmore, who's spoken and written frequently on this issue, asks: "When will we get it through our heads that people don't make these choices [to seek suicide] because of their disabilities but because of their oppression?"[24]

Because of public policy, too often when a disabled person seeks suicide because of the belief that things will not change, they in fact do not change; the disabled person is correct in his assessment.

Some who seek public sanction for their suicides may be trying a desperate ploy to get attention, hoping from that attention to be given the technology and services that they need to live the kind of regular life they long to live again.

Psychologists see suicide as an attempt at control, a way to exercise some futile power over events the individual feels otherwise powerless to affect. With physically disabled, mentally alert, nonelderly people seeking suicide, society also plays a role.

On the Part of Society

When a nondisabled, "perfectly healthy" (as we say) person attempts suicide, effort is made to prevent the suicide. Life is better than death for that person, thinks society; the person's desire for death is considered a misjudgment.

Even if a person is "mentally ill," and in that sense a "disabled" person—but physically nondisabled—effort is made to prevent the suicide. Counseling is sought. The person is considered "potentially" normal—someone who can be normal once again—once the irrational reasons leading him to suicide can be sorted out and worked through.[25]

But when the disability is physical and cannot be cured easily, society's belief changes. Such people are considered "terminally" ill or disabled even if their condition is such that they might live a normal life span—the "terminal" being thirty or more years off—even if their disability, such as multiple sclerosis, is one that others are living with successfully.

The existence of physical inability seems to society worse than death. Death is seen as the better option. The concurrence of family, of doctors, and of the courts that death is the better option constitutes a not-so-subtle pressure on the disabled person to end his/her life. This

---

[24]Johnson, *Unanswered Questions, supra* note 19, at 25.
[25]Elissa Ely, *So Long 4 Ever*, BOSTON GLOBE, July 1, 1990.

can be considered in itself a kind of active euthanasia—the "voluntariness" is coerced. Whether the disabled person does the actual removing of the respirator tube or is "assisted" to do it seems to make little difference.

Courts generally regard the issue of physically disabled, mentally alert people seeking suicide as a "right to die" issue—the right to regulate one's medical care (the respirator being the "medical care"). But this is a false assessment of the situation. Death from their disabilities was not imminent for Bouvia, Bergstedt, Rivlin, or McAfee; they were not "terminally ill." They had an irreversible condition, but that condition itself was not coursing them toward their deaths. Nor had they lived full and long lives, approaching the normal time of people to die, as is the case of older people who experience a succession of end-of-life conditions that disable them.

But they did have a specific set of conditions that society fears. Peter A. Singer, M.D., believes the fear on the part of nondisabled people is of being "hooked to a machine at the end";[26] the real problem is that most nondisabled people make little distinction between that image and the very different situations of people like Kenneth Bergstedt, Larry McAfee, or Elizabeth Bouvia. All nondisabled people really see is that such people lack ability to physically control their own bodies. They are dependent on society for services and technology. They do not have enough money to finance these things themselves. This set of conditions makes their presence threatening to society. They overwhelm society.

We are all fearful of being in such a condition ourselves, and we are equally afraid of having to personally care for or provide resources so that such an individual can get technological, personal, or robotic assistance.

When such individuals ask to die, they solve for society a problem that it very much wants solved. In doing away with themselves, they ensure we don't have to feel guilty any more for failing to fight for the policy changes that would give them adequate services (or, failing that, have to provide the services ourselves as their friends, lovers, or family). And, by doing away with themselves, they also begin to create role models for other disabled people to do the same thing. And perhaps that's just fine with most of us in society. It's an easy solution that we as a society don't have to participate in or take responsibility for. It's the disabled person's own decision. The fact that the courts are moving to

---

[26]This quote is from a presentation by Dr. Singer at the Current Controversies in the Right to Live, the Right to Die III conference, Mayflower Hotel, Washington, D.C., April 13, 1991. *See also* Peter A. Singer, *Euthanasia—A Critique*, 322 NEW ENG. J. MED. 1881 (1990).

define it just in these terms of individual right is a sign that we, as society, want desperately to be let off the hook.

Though there is no official, open encouragement yet of suicide sought by nonelderly, mentally alert, physically disabled people, those who actively seek suicide are tacitly encouraged by family, lovers, and physicians who simply agree that they understand and sympathize with the disabled person when he expresses suicidal feelings. A more active encouragement occurs when offers to help are made, such as when Robert Bergstedt did so for his son. And of course doctors provide medicines that, on overdose, can kill, with full knowledge that this is what the person intends. The March 7, 1991, issue of the *New England Journal of Medicine* carried Dr. Timothy E. Quill's description of how he did just that.[27] The article has been met with respect. Quill has been said to have "significantly advanced the debates over doctor-assisted suicide."[28]

Kevorkian's and Quill's actions are not escalations of type but degree. They seem to be seeking—and tacitly gaining—an approval that our society is as yet too nervous to publicly convey.

Though no media commentary has publicly lauded mentally alert, physically disabled people who choose suicide, either with help or alone, the overtone of approval resonates. In a news story researched to describe efforts by the disability rights movement to move funding away from nursing homes to in-home care, *New York Times* reporter Gina Kolata became "fascinated" with the idea that there were "lots and lots" of disabled people who wanted to kill themselves.[29]

Her excitement at this discovery led her to develop a January 31 article that focused only peripherally on the need for in-home attendant services, giving most of its attention to how disabled people were coming to the logical conclusion to end their lives. "Staff members at rehabilitation hospitals say that the vast majority of suicides of disabled people occur far from the public eye. Although most patients [sic] choose to live, doctors say, more and more are becoming aware that it is also their right to die."[30] One wonders how long it will be until disabled people will begin to be aware that it is also their responsibility to die.

The article's tone was one of understanding and sympathy for such

---

[27]Timothy E. Quill, *Death and Dignity: A Case of Individualized Decision Making*, 324 NEW ENG. J. MED. 691 (1991).

[28]Lawrence K. Altman, *More Physicians Broach Forbidden Subject of Euthanasia*, N.Y. TIMES, Mar. 12, 1991, at C3.

[29]Telephone Interview with N.Y. *Times* reporter Gina Kolata (Dec. 1990).

[30]Gina Kolata, *Saving Life Is Not Enough, the Disabled Demand Rights and Choices*, N.Y. TIMES, Jan. 31, 1991, at B7.

actions; no quotes of horror were recorded. Though the disability spokesperson the reporter talked to expressed such a horror, the article took a more "reasoned" tone.

This seems the closest the media has come to admitting that it sees nothing particularly wrong with voluntary active euthanasia when it comes to mentally alert, physically disabled people. University of Michigan law professor Yale Kamisar writes in the *Detroit News* that "the distinction between 'letting die' and active euthanasia is quite thin . . . . After all, if a person has a 'right to die,' why doesn't she have the right to choose what *she regards* as the most 'humane' or 'dignified' way to do so?"[31]

As a society, we're set up for and understand that cure is the only solution to the problems faced by someone with a disability. Modern society is not interested in providing low-end services that allow physically disabled, mentally alert people to remain in control of their lives and continue to lead relatively typical lives and experience normal life-styles. Voluntary active euthanasia offers society a fairly simple way out of that dilemma.

As a result, voluntary assisted suicide is becoming "the thing to do."

The Future of Assisted Suicide among Mentally Alert, Physically Disabled People: Influencing Factors

There are both internal and external pressures brought to bear on mentally alert, physically disabled people to seek an end to their lives. Some are caused by the disability itself, but far more are exerted by society and its attitudes.

The two sides of this issue have been presented as being, on the one hand, the individual's right to make his own decision and the right to do so privately without state interference versus, on the other hand, the state's "compelling interest in life."

However, the division may more clearly be seen as being between those who simply don't want to have to "bother with" disabled people—coming up with the money for and/or actually providing the low-end services for severely disabled people (getting the technology in place, removing architectural barriers, and all that work!) versus those who think society ought to come up with these services and provide the technology, no matter how much the cost, because it's the right thing to do—and because, in the end, we will all benefit from it, since any of us

---

[31]Yale Kamisar, *Where to Draw the Line on Right to Die?* DETROIT NEWS, July 22, 1990, at 3B (emphasis in original).

has the potential to need such services and technology. The issue is really about providing services, technology, and access, about mainstreaming, and ceasing to discriminate. How will this issue likely evolve in the future?

Current Laws

Despite the passage of the Americans with Disabilities Act (ADA),[32] it doesn't seem that we as a society want to actually accord disabled people rights and access. Much of the new law is symbolic, offering little in the way of strong protections that were not already in place in state or local laws. It is a compromise law; businesses, though forbidden to discriminate, don't have to do anything to ensure accommodation that poses an "undue hardship."[33] Even public accommodations can ignore access requirements if they deem access to not be "readily achievable."[34]

The Fair Housing Amendments Act (FHAA),[35] passed in 1988, requires that new apartments be "adaptable" to tenants with disabilities.[36] Yet to date, builders have successfuly avoided having to build a single adaptable unit—petitioning the government to extend deadlines and write guidelines that allow such things as sunken living rooms and fail to require even that all bathrooms in a unit be accessible.

In such a climate, in which disability rights is not taken seriously, it's fair to believe that our nation has opted silently for the continuance of active voluntary euthanasia when it concerns mentally alert, severely physically disabled, nonelderly people.

Society's Willingness to Change Policy and Provide Service

There's no public understanding yet that lack of services (caused ultimately by discrimination) in large part drives people with disabilities to seek death. Instead, we cling to the belief that it's the horror of the uncured disability alone—something we as a society can offer no help for—that causes a person to seek an end to life.

People who are seeking assistance with suicide seem to be giving society a bright idea of a way to get out of having to provide services. If we just keep quiet about it and let the immutable forces of social conditioning and fear of disability do their work, more and more people

---

[32]Americans with Disabilities Act of 1990 §§ 1-514, 42 U.S.C.A. §§ 12101-12213 (West Supp. 1991).

[33]42 U.S.C.A. § 12112(b)(5)(A).

[34]42 U.S.C.A. §§ 12182(b)(2)(A)(iv)-(v).

[35]Fair Housing Amendments Act of 1988 §§ 800-815, 42 U.S.C. §§ 3601-3631 (1988).

[36] 42 U.S.C. § 3604(f)(3)(c)(iii).

with disabilities will seek suicide voluntarily (and eventually those who don't can be pressured). And if disabled people routinely end their own lives, society will be off the hook with having to provide services and access.

The issue is between what we are willing to commit to as a nation in order to change the lives of people with disabilities and how far we are willing to go to have disabled people end their lives.

We cannot change disabled people's lives totally. Not everything can change. It is naive to believe that if all people with disabilities had access to all the goods and services and technology they could ever need, all the robotic arms, voice synthesizers, and robotic attendants, none would seek suicide. Many seemingly happy, well-adjusted, financially secure people seek to commit suicide. Yet it is an equally specious belief that the availability of goods and services would not tip the balance in very many suicidal disabled people's lives. Of course it would.

That we as a nation choose not to provide the technology and services says, in effect, that we have chosen the option of allowing disabled people to commit suicide, rather than the option of our providing them technology and services.

There's a saying in the peace and justice movement: "If you want peace, work for justice." In the same sense, those who want people with disabilities to stop seeking suicide must work for real equality for them in society. We do not have real equality now, and the ADA will not bring it soon. It is important to expose the injustice in the lack of services and technology, and to seek more exposure of these issues.

Understanding on the Part of the Courts

Though the "right to die" may indeed be a right worth seeking and preserving, it is important that this right not exist in a vacuum. Courts do not seem to perceive the ramifications of this right at the present time. The right to die is no meaningful right when there is no equally available option to live, particularly when it is eminently within society's power to provide that option, and the know-how exists to do so. That society chooses, through its policies and practices, not to provide that option is an issue the courts do not seem as yet to have grasped.

No court yet has exhibited any glimmer of understanding of the relationship between lack of services and the desire for suicide; no court ordered a Kenneth Bergstedt while he was alive to be provided an attendant, his own apartment, or a van. So far, courts have only ordered that disabled people be allowed to kill themselves, justified by the right to refuse or discontinue medical treatment.

Other Factors

There will be no change until there are enough people with disabilities who espouse a disability pride and culture that can be seen by isolated people with disabilities, who can find a way to join and thus draw strength from it. This is a very long way off, if indeed it can ever happen in such a society as we now inhabit.

It will be another twenty to forty years until such understanding has any chance of gaining hold—and then only if disability activists continue to petition and educate the court—and if the court is ever willing to begin to listen and understand—and if disability culture can take hold in the court of public opinion.

All this will have to happen as a prerequisite for the laws now on the books, such as the ADA and FHAA, the Voting Accessibility Act,[37] and others, to begin to be enforced to the extent that they would make any meaningful difference in the lives of ordinary people with disabilities.

There would have to be a national attendant services program, with billions of dollars, one which actually allowed people with disabilities to hire their own attendants and run their own lives again.

Then, all this in place, perhaps we as a society would begin to see that people with disabilities can indeed have full and decent lives—and we would then be just as appalled when a person with disabilities seeks suicide as we are now when a nondisabled person does.

That time is at least a half century away. In the meantime, if the tide against assisted suicide is not turned by some understanding of the underlying issues (which I doubt very much is going to occur), then assisted suicide—rather than rights, services, and technology—will prevail.

---

[37]Voting Accessibility for the Elderly and Handicapped Act §§ 1-9, 42 U.S.C. § 1973ee (1988).

WHEN IS THERE A CONSTITUTIONAL "RIGHT TO DIE"? WHEN IS THERE *NO* CONSTITUTIONAL "RIGHT TO LIVE"?*

*Yale Kamisar***

When I am invited to participate in conferences on the "right to die," I suspect that the organizers of such gatherings expect me to fill what might be called the " 'slippery slope' slot" on the program or, more generally, to articulate the "conservative" position on this controversial matter.

These expectations are hardly surprising. The "right to die" is a euphemism for what almost everybody used to call a form of euthanasia—"passive" or "negative" or "indirect" euthanasia—and some thirty years ago, in the course of raising various objections to proposed euthanasia legislation, I advanced the "thin edge of the wedge" or the "slippery slope" argument with some zest.[1] This roused the ire of the renowned British legal commentator, Glanville Williams, perhaps the leading proponent of euthanasia to be found in academia at the time. Williams disparaged the argument as the "trump card of the traditionalist," one, he asserted, that was used in nineteenth-century England "to resist almost every social and economic change."[2]

---

* With some modification and amplification, these are the remarks I delivered at a conference on *Cruzan* and the "right to die" held at the University of Georgia Law School on October 8, 1990. The first Section consists of some general comments on the "right to die" and related matters; the second Section is a response to Professor John A. Robertson's Sibley Lecture, the centerpiece of the Georgia conference. *See infra* note 27 (citing Robertson's Sibley Lecture Paper, Cruzan *and the Constitutional Status of Nontreatment Decisions for Incompetent Patients*, 25 GA. L. REV. 1139 (1991)). Although footnoted and revised for publication, the structure and contents of this Paper continue to reflect the occasion and the forum for which it was written.

** Henry K. Ransom Professor of Law, University of Michigan. A.B., New York University, 1950; LL.B., Columbia University, 1954.

[1] *See* Kamisar, *Some Non-Religious Views Against Proposed "Mercy-Killing" Legislation*, 42 MINN. L. REV. 969, 1030-41 (1958). This article has been cited for the proposition that "slippery slope arguments have been employed to argue against [*inter alia*] all forms of euthanasia." Schauer, *Slippery Slopes*, 99 HARV. L. REV. 361, 363 n.16 (1985).

[2] Williams, *"Mercy-Killing" Legislation—A Rejoinder*, 43 MINN. L. REV. 1, 9-10 (1958). *See also* G. WILLIAMS, THE SANCTITY OF LIFE AND THE CRIMINAL LAW, 315 (1957). A decade

I. "Liberals," "Conservatives" and Slippery Slope Arguments

In light of the fact that proponents of various forms of euthanasia view themselves as the "liberals" in this debate, I find their disdain for the "slippery slope" argument a bit odd. For in other settings, "liberals" have been most adept at making this very argument. One might even say that, depending upon the circumstances, the argument has been the "trump card" of the "liberal" as much as it has been that of the "traditionalist." At the very least, it is a "card" that liberals have often played.

In a recent article on "slippery slope arguments," Professor Frederick Schauer pointed out that "these arguments appear commonly in discussions about freedom of speech."[3] He continued:

> The warning is frequently heard that permitting one restriction on communication, a restriction not by itself troubling and perhaps even desirable, will increase the likelihood that other, increasingly invidious restrictions will follow. The *Skokie* controversy provides one of the most notorious modern examples of this type of argument in freedom of speech debates. The argument there was not that freedom of speech in theory *ought* to protect the Nazis, but rather that denying free speech protection to Nazis was likely to start us down a slippery slope, at the bottom of which would be the denial of protection even to those who should, in theory, be protected.[4]

These arguments are perhaps even more prominent in criminal procedure cases. In this area we are admonished that "[t]he progress is too easy from police action unscrutinized by judicial au-

---

later, when both my article and Professor Williams' rejoinder were reprinted in a collection of essays on the subject, the Earl of Listowel, a voluntary euthanasia proponent who wrote the foreword to the collection, expressed his distaste for the "thin edge of the wedge" argument in the euthanasia debate.

[3] Schauer, *supra* note 1, at 363.

[4] *Id.* (footnotes omitted; emphasis in original). *See also* J. Feinberg, Offense to Others 92-93 (1985) (concluding that "the true motivation behind much of the A.C.L.U. opposition to legal action against Nazis" is the concern that "if the swastika and burning crosses are banned today on good grounds, relatively innocuous symbols may be banned tomorrow on not so good grounds"—"the 'falling dominoes argument,' or the 'foot in the door argument,' or the empirical (or political) form of the 'slippery slope argument.' ").

thorization to the police state"[5] and that "what seems fair enough against a squalid huckster of bad liquor may take on a very different face, if used by a government determined to suppress political opposition under the guise of sedition."[6] Indeed, perhaps the most grandiloquent statement of the "slippery slope" argument ever made, and surely the most famous one, appears in *Boyd v. United States*,[7] the landmark search-and-seizure case that paved the way for the fourth amendment exclusionary rule. On that occasion, when told by the prosecution that compelling defendants to turn an invoice over to the government was a trivial matter unworthy of the Court's attention because it lacked "many of the aggravating incidents of actual search and seizure,"[8] Justice Bradley responded for the majority:

> It may be that it is the obnoxious thing in its mildest and least repulsive form; but illegitimate and unconstitutional practices get their first footing in that way, namely, by silent approaches and slight deviations from legal modes of procedure . . . . [The Courts'] motto should be *obsta principiis*.[9]

Obsta principiis? For those of us whose Latin is rusty, Wayne LaFave, our leading authority on search and seizure, has provided a rough translation: "Resist the opening wedge! Hold that line!"[10]

II. Have We *Seen* the Slippery Slope? A Look Back at Glanville Williams' "Modest Proposals" and a Look Ahead

All this is a long-winded way of saying that I shall not disappoint the organizers of this conference. As many good liberals have

---

[5] United States v. Rabinowitz, 339 U.S. 56, 82 (1950) (Frankfurter, J., dissenting).

[6] United States v. Kirschenblatt, 16 F.2d 202, 203 (2d Cir. 1926) (L. Hand, J.).

[7] 116 U.S. 616 (1886).

[8] *Id.* at 635.

[9] *Id.* This passage, or at least significant portions of it, has appeared in more than thirty subsequent cases, but, unfortunately, more often in the dissents of such "liberals" as Justices Brennan and Marshall, than in majority or plurality opinions. *See* LaFave, *The Forgotten Motto of Obsta Principiis in Fourth Amendment Jurisprudence*, 28 ARIZ. L. REV. 291, 294-95 & n.21 (1986).

[10] LaFave, *supra* note 9, at 294. "It is high time," concludes Professor LaFave, that, in the search and seizure field at least, the present Court "reaffirm the stirring words of Justice Bradley . . . and recall just why it is that the motto *obsta principiis* makes such eminently good sense." *Id.* at 310.

done in other settings, I shall make the "slippery slope" argument in the euthanasia context. But I shall not be content with that. I think I can do better. .Three eventful decades have passed since Glanville Williams' highly influential book,[11] one that may be said to have launched the modern era of the euthanasia movement,[12] first evoked my interest in the general subject.[13] In that time, I think I can show, we have *moved down* the slippery slope a considerable distance; we have *seen* the slippery slope.

On rereading Williams' 1957 book recently, I was struck by the fact that with the passage of years most of the restrictions or conditions he prescribed for euthanasia have faded away.

One provision of Williams' proposed statute would have permitted a physician, in what he considered an appropriate case, "*to accelerate* by any merciful means" the patient's death.[14] Another provision would have allowed the physician "*to refrain* from taking steps to prolong the patient's life by medical means."[15] Williams did not, as some do today,[16] shrink from use of the "E" word. He regarded, and called, *both* courses of action "euthanasia."

Despite his uninhibited use of a term that was once a "nice" word (easy, painless death), but somewhere along the way became a "dirty" one, Professor Williams' proposals seem rather modest

---

[11] G. WILLIAMS, *supra* note 2.

[12] Although organizations sprang up in England and the United States in the 1930s that dramatized the plight of those suffering a painful and degrading illness and advocated the "right" to obtain a "release" from such a condition, "[f]or the next two decades, the issue remained dormant as a matter of law and public policy." R. SHERLOCK, PRESERVING LIFE: PUBLIC POLICY AND THE LIFE NOT WORTH LIVING 120 (1987). "The appearance of Glanville Williams' provocative book . . . and rejoinders to it . . . broke the silence forcefully." *Id. See also* G. GRISEZ & J. BOYLE, LIFE AND DEATH WITH LIBERTY AND JUSTICE 157-58 (1979); Beschle, *Autonomous Decisionmaking and Social Choice: Examining the "Right to Die,"* 77 KY. L.J. 319, 323-24 (1988-89).

[13] In large measure, my 1958 article, *supra* note 2, was an "essay review" of Williams' chapter on euthanasia.

[14] G. WILLIAMS, *supra* note 2, at 345 (emphasis added).

[15] *Id.* (emphasis added).

[16] *See, e.g.,* THE NEW YORK STATE TASK FORCE ON LIFE AND THE LAW, LIFE-SUSTAINING TREATMENT: MAKING DECISIONS AND APPOINTING A HEALTH CARE AGENT 40 (1987) [hereinafter NEW YORK STATE TASK FORCE]:

> Some authors distinguish between "active" or "positive" euthanasia and "passive" or "negative" euthanasia . . . . For the sake of clarity, the Task Force prefers to avoid the active-passive terminology and speak simply of "euthanasia" defined as measures to bring about the patient's death, as distinct from the "withholding or withdrawal of life-sustaining treatment."

when compared to those being advanced today. After completing his chapter on suicide, Williams began his chapter on euthanasia as follows:

> Whatever opinion may be taken on the general subject of suicide, it has long seemed to some people that euthanasia, the merciful extinction of life, is morally permissible and indeed mandatory where it is performed upon [1] a dying patient [2] with his consent and [3] is the only way of relieving his suffering. According to this view, which will be accepted in the present chapter, a man is entitled to demand the release of death from *hopeless and helpless pain*, and a physician who gives this release is entitled to moral and legal absolution for his act.[17]

A. Relieving the Patient's Suffering

Until recently, it could be said that "[m]ercy for the suffering patient has been the primary reason given by those [favoring] . . . a limited form of euthanasia."[18] But that can no longer be said—as evidenced by the two landmark "right to die" cases of our time: *In re Quinlan*[19] and *Cruzan v. Director, Missouri Department of Health*.[20] There was no evidence that either Karen Ann Quinlan or Nancy Beth Cruzan was suffering any pain. (It is plain, of course, that *their families* did suffer considerable pain.)

I realize that there is not universal agreement on this point. But the *amicus* brief of the American Academy of Neurology in support of Nancy Cruzan's "right to die" stated (one is tempted to say, conceded) that "PVS [persistent vegetative state] patients are permanently unconscious and devoid of thought, emotion, and sensation."[21] This reflected the position adopted a year and a half earlier by the Executive Board of the Academy of Neurology.[22]

---

[17] G. WILLIAMS, *supra* note 2, at 311 (bracketed numbers and emphasis added).

[18] Bok, *Euthanasia and the Care of the Dying*, in THE DILEMMAS OF EUTHANASIA 2 (1975).

[19] 70 N.J. 10, 355 A.2d 647 (1976).

[20] 110 S. Ct. 2841 (1990).

[21] Brief of *Amicus Curiae*, American Academy of Neurology, in support of the petition at 3, *Cruzan* (No. 88-1503) [hereinafter Brief of American Academy of Neurology].

[22] *Id.* app. A at 2a ("Persistent vegetative state patients do not have the capacity to experience pain or suffering . . . . [P]atients who are permanently and completely unconscious cannot experience these symptoms."). *See also* Council on Scientific Affairs and Council on Ethical and Judicial Affairs, American Medical Association, *Persistent Vegetative State*

B.   The Request or Consent of the Patient

Another one of Glanville Williams' limiting factors or conditions was *the consent* or *request* of the patient. Shortly before the *Quinlan* case, "the most important" safeguard, contained in various proposals to legalize euthanasia, was said to be "[t]he requirement that the patient should have *requested or consented expressly* to the act of euthanasia."[23] About the same time, one of the ablest proponents of voluntary euthanasia rejected "the most serious argument" against such a proposal—"that it would eventually lead to involuntary euthanasia"—on the ground that "[s]o long as careful attention is paid to the capacity of a person to request euthanasia, there is a large gap between voluntary euthanasia and involuntary elimination of social misfits."[24]

Although the *Quinlan* case was widely reported and discussed as a "right to die" case, Karen Ann Quinlan lacked the capacity to request anything. She did not (and in her condition, of course, could not) consent to her death or ask anyone to let her die. Nor had she made a living will or executed any other directive requesting that she be allowed to die without medical intervention. Indeed—although this feature of the case went largely unreported—both the trial court and the Supreme Court of New Jersey agreed that Karen's previous conversations with friends on this general subject were so "remote and impersonal" as to lack "significant probative weight."[25]

Nancy Cruzan's views, when still a vibrant person, on whether and when life-sustaining treatment should be withdrawn is a matter of some dispute.[26] But as Professor Robertson noted earlier,

---

and the Decision to Withdraw or Withhold Life Support, 263 J. A.M.A. 426, 428 (Jan. 19, 1990) ("Pain cannot be experienced by brains that no longer retain the neural apparatus for suffering.").

[23] Bok, *supra* note 18, at 4.

[24] Cantor, *A Patient's Decision to Decline Life-Saving Medical Treatment: Bodily Integrity Versus the Preservation of Life*, 26 RUTGERS L. REV. 228, 261 (1973).

[25] *In re* Quinlan, 70 N.J. 10, 51, 355 A.2d 647, 664 (1976).

[26] At least they were at the time the Supreme Court decided the case. Two months later, Nancy's parents asked the state probate court for a second hearing. At this new hearing, three of Nancy's former co-workers recalled conversations in which she said she never would want to live "like a vegetable" on medical machines. *See* N.Y. Times, Nov. 2, 1990, §A, at 14, col. 3. Since the State of Missouri withdrew from the case and Nancy's court-appointed guardian sought to disconnect the feeding tube, *see* N.Y. Times, Dec. 7, 1990, §A, at 24, col. 1, all remaining parties agreed that artificial nutrition and hydration should cease. A week

"there was no claim that [when] competent she had issued a written directive against treatment if she became incompetent."[27] Nor was there any claim that she had appointed a surrogate to make life-and-death decisions for her in the event she became incompetent. In some conversations with friends, Nancy indicated that "if sick or injured she would not wish to continue her life unless she could live at least halfway normally,"[28] but these conversations "did not deal in terms with withdrawal of medical treatment or of hydration and nutrition."[29]

Different people will assign different weight to Nancy's conversations with her friends. But whatever one makes of these conversations, I think it fair to say that they fall well short of the unequivocal consent or explicit request that yesteryear's proponents of voluntary euthanasia had in mind.

C. *A "Dying" or "Terminally Ill" Patient*

Recall another limitation on Glanville Williams' euthanasia proposal—that the patient be "dying" or "terminally ill." There is a good deal of confusion on this point. Many people would say—indeed, did say—that at the time of the litigation both Nancy and Karen *were* "dying" or "terminally ill." I think not—not as these terms have usually been defined.

Of course, if you favor refusing or withdrawing life-sustaining treatment, it is *good advocacy* to characterize the patient as "dying" or "terminally ill." Then, when you remove or withhold the life support you may say that you are not terminating a life, but only preventing the "drawing out of the natural death process."

Not "drawing out" or "prolonging" death has a nice ring to it, but it is a spongy, seductive term. Glanville Williams once observed, somewhat bitterly, I think it fair to say, that the statement

---

later, the probate judge ruled that there was "clear evidence" that the "intent" of Nancy, "if mentally able, would be to terminate her nutrition and hydration" and that there was "no evidence of substance" to the contrary. He then authorized the cessation of nutrition and hydration. *See* N.Y. Times, Dec. 15, 1990, §1, at 1, col 2. Twelve days later, and nearly eight years after she had lost consciousness and a feeding tube had first been implanted in her stomach, Nancy Cruzan died.

[27] Robertson, *Cruzan and the Constitutional Status of Nontreatment Decisions for Incompetent Patients*, 25 GA. L. REV. 1139 (1991) [hereinafter Robertson, *Cruzan and Nontreatment Decisions*].

[28] Cruzan v. Director, Missouri Dep't of Health, 110 S. Ct. 2841, 2846 (1990).

[29] *Id.* at 2847.

that a doctor must "prolong life" but need not "prolong death" "has become a cliché in orthodox medical circles, where it is apparently thought to solve the whole problem of euthanasia."[30] I think Professor Williams' unhappiness with this "formula," one might say "escape," is justified. In any event, this "escape" was not available either in the *Quinlan* or the *Cruzan* case.

When, during the oral argument in the Supreme Court of New Jersey, the Quinlan family's lawyer maintained that the respirator was serving no purpose "except to thwart the death process" and that the respirator was causing Karen "to debilitate to the point where she will ultimately die,"[31] one of the state justices pressed him on this point. The Quinlan family's lawyer then agreed that Karen's condition had "reached . . . a plateau" and that there had been "no further debilitation . . . for some time."[32]

Karen Ann Quinlan probably could have been kept alive for many years if her respirator had not been removed. Indeed, as many of you know, she stayed alive for nine years *after* the respirator was disconnected.

The view that all that was at stake was whether to drag out or cut short the "dying process" is even harder to sustain in the *Cruzan* case. As the state supreme court, adopting many of the trial court's findings, described Nancy's condition: "She is not dead. She is not terminally ill. Medical experts testified that she could live another thirty years."[33]

In general, living-will statutes provide that the directive only becomes operative after its maker has become "terminally ill." As many states, including Missouri, define this term, it means a condition that will shortly result in death *regardless* of the utilization of available medical treatment.[34]

---

[30] G. WILLIAMS, *supra* note 2, at 337.

[31] 2 IN THE MATTER OF KAREN QUINLAN: THE COMPLETE BRIEFS, ORAL ARGUMENTS AND OPINION IN THE NEW JERSEY SUPREME COURT 225 (1976).

[32] *Id.* at 226.

[33] Cruzan v. Harmon, 760 S.W.2d 408, 411 (Mo. 1988). *See also* Brief of American Academy of Neurology, *supra* note 21, app. A at 2a:

> Patients in a persistent vegetative state may continue to survive for a prolonged period of time . . . as long as the artificial provision of nutrition and fluids is continued. These patients are not "terminally ill."

[34] *See, e.g.*, Cantor, *The Permanently Unconscious Patient, Non-Feeding and Euthanasia*, 15 AM. J.L. & MED. 381, 405-06 (1989); Francis, *The Evanescence of Living Wills*, 14 J. CONTEMP. LAW 27, 35-38 (1988); Gelfand, *Living Will Statutes: The First Decade*, 1987

Because a "terminal illness" or "terminal condition" requirement greatly restricts the impact of living-will legislation,[35] several states have recently adopted provisions defining a "terminal" condition as one that would cause death in *the absence* of medical intervention.[36] This strikes me as going too far in the other direction. *A great many* illnesses would be "terminal" *without* medical treatment. Would anyone say that a pneumonia patient is in a "terminal" condition or that her death is "imminent" because she would die (assuming she would) *if* antibiotics were not available? I think most would respond: But antibiotics *are* available.

There *are* reasons to loosen or to wiggle out of the "dying" or "terminally ill" requirement.[37] But there are *also* reasons to take the requirement seriously. If death is unpreventable—if the best medical treatment available can only postpone death for a short time—the interest in preserving life seems much weaker. Moreover, if life support is terminated in such a situation, it makes some sense to say that the underlying condition "caused" the death or that discontinuing life support *merely permits* death to occur or *only prevents* the "drawing out" of the death process. *Whether or not* life-sustaining procedures are utilized, the patient is going to die in a short time anyhow. When a patient, though, can be kept alive for many years it is much harder to avoid the conclusion that the removal of life support, rather than the patient's un-

---

Wisc. L. Rev. 737, 741-42. A number of state courts, however, have rejected the terminal illness restriction, at least for those patients in a persistent vegetative state, and some states have defined the term to mean only that the patient be "incurable" or that her condition be "hopeless." *See* Gelfand, *supra*, at 741-47. Moreover, a few state courts have, in effect, held their state's terminal condition requirement unconstitutional. *See id.*

[35] As noted in Alexander, *Death by Directive*, 28 Santa Clara L. Rev. 67, 95 (1988), although the California "natural death act," the first living will statute enacted, "was drafted with Karen Quinlan's case in mind, Ms. Quinlan would not have benefited from the Act since her death was not imminent." One reason for this state of affairs may be that the attorney and the spokesperson for the Quinlan family depicted Karen as "terminally ill" or "dying," *see supra* note 31 and accompanying text, and much of the media described her the same way.

As noted in Beschle, *supra* note 12, at 335 n.72, "the most commonly used definition of terminal illness" is still the one found in the California statute. That statute defines the term as "an incurable condition . . . which, regardless of the application of life-sustaining procedures, would, within reasonable medical judgment, produce death, and where the application of life-sustaining procedures serves only to postpone the moment of death . . . ." Cal. Health & Safety Code § 7187(f) (West Supp. 1988).

[36] *See* Cantor, *supra* note 34, at 406 & n.81.

[37] *See id.* at 398-410.

derlying illness, brought about the patient's death. Furthermore, to say that a person who can be kept alive for many years should have her life support disconnected because she is "better off dead" or "might as well be dead"—and at bottom, I think, that is the principal argument for terminating the life-sustaining treatment in cases like *Quinlan* and *Cruzan*—is to grapple with "the hopelessly elusive question of a life not worth living."[38]

Whether, even if we try to combat an illness with every method known to doctors, death is unpreventable and imminent are medical judgments. Whether a person is "better off dead" is not a medical judgment; rather, it is a moral-legal-societal question, and a fundamental one at that.

Although Professor Robertson does not consider the significance of the "terminal illness 'limitation' " in his current paper, a decade and a half ago he did. On that occasion he distinguished the case of terminating lifesaving treatment for the defective infant, who, if treated, can usually live for a substantial period of time, from "the cases of terminal illness."[39] I fail to see why the comments Robertson made then about the defective newborn do not apply as well to the elderly patient who is severely debilitated but *not* terminally ill:

> The terminally ill patient will soon die with or without the [lifesaving] procedure. Thus, treatment merely prolongs dying. The defective infant, on the other hand, if treated, can normally live for significant periods. Unless the quality of his life affects its values, a judgment for which there is no legal precedent, the likelihood that treatment means life should justify the procedure.[40]

---

[38] R. SHERLOCK, *supra* note 12, at 137. Continues Professor Sherlock: "Moving beyond [the terminally ill patient, as that term has usually been defined] to include the chronically ill, the debilitated, and the comatose will inevitably entail insoluble problems setting forth a proper rule or the abdication of any prohibition of suicide or assisting in suicide when the individual or the family concludes that life is not worth it." *Id.*

[39] Robertson, *Involuntary Euthanasia of Defective Newborns: A Legal Analysis*, 27 STAN. L. REV. 213, 237 (1975) [hereinafter Robertson, *Involuntary Euthanasia*].

[40] *Id.*

D. Did the Cruzan Court Attach Any Significance to the Fact that Nancy was Neither "Dying" Nor "Terminally Ill"?

There may be a number of things wrong with the Missouri Supreme Court opinion in *Cruzan*, but I think it was right about one thing: To disregard the fact that a person is neither "dying" nor "terminally ill" and to focus on her "profoundly diminished capacity . . . and [the] near certainty that that condition will not change leads inevitably to quality of life considerations."[41]

The Missouri Supreme Court gave a good deal of weight to the fact that Nancy was neither "dying" nor "terminally ill."[42] At the outset of its opinion the Court stated that the "issue presented" was whether "nutrition and hydration [may] be withheld from an incompetent ward in a persistent vegetative state, who is neither dead . . . nor terminally ill."[43] And the court mentioned or discussed the fact that Nancy was not "terminally ill" five more times in its opinion.[44]

So far as I can tell, however, the United States Supreme Court failed to attach any significance whatever to the fact that Nancy Cruzan was *not* dying or terminally ill. In his majority opinion, the Chief Justice mentioned this aspect of Nancy's condition only once—in a footnote quoting from the state supreme court's detailed description of Nancy's medical condition.[45] In discussing the problems raised by the case, Chief Justice Rehnquist spoke only of judicial proceedings "seeking to terminate an incompetent individual's life-sustaining treatment"[46] or "seek[ing] to discontinue nutrition and hydration of a person diagnosed to be in a persistent

---

[41] Cruzan v. Harmon, 760 S.W.2d 408, 422 (Mo. 1988), *aff'd sub nom.* Cruzan v. Director, Missouri Dep't of Health, 110 S. Ct. 2841 (1990). Added the Missouri court: "The argument made here, that Nancy will not recover, is but a thinly veiled statement that her life in its present form is not worth living." *Id.*

[42] The Missouri living-will statute provides that lifesaving support could be terminated "where . . . . death will occur within a short time whether or not" such measures are utilized and provided further that a "terminal condition" is "an incurable or irreversible condition which . . . is such that death will occur within a short time regardless of the application of medical procedures." *See id.* at 420 (quoting Mo. Ann. Stat. § 459.010(3) & (6) (Vernon 1991)).

[43] *Id.* at 410.

[44] *See id.* at 411, 412, 419, 422, 424.

[45] *Cruzan*, 110 S. Ct. at 2845 n.1.

[46] *Id.* at 2854.

vegetative state."[47]

At no point in her concurring opinion did Justice O'Connor attribute any significance to the fact that Nancy Cruzan was not "terminally ill." Indeed, she never mentioned this factor. Moreover, at one point Justice O'Connor observed that "[a] seriously ill *or* dying patient whose wishes are not honored may feel a captive of the machinery required for life-sustaining measures . . . ."[48]

Dissenting Justice Brennan did observe that if kept on the feeding tube Nancy Cruzan might live for another thirty years.[49] In context, however, it is clear that Brennan considered this feature of the case another reason for *terminating* the lifesaving treatment, *not* a reason for continuing it.

The Supreme Court is likely to make plain in a future case what I think is implicit in *Cruzan*: As a matter of constitutional law there is no distinction between a patient (such as Nancy Cruzan) whose condition has "stabilized" or is not "terminal" (as that term is commonly defined) and a "dying" or "terminally ill" patient, that is, one facing an *unpreventable* and imminent death. To put it another way, if a patient otherwise "qualifies" for the "right to die" (for example, there is clear and convincing evidence of her wish to die under the circumstances), that right can probably no more be denied solely for the reason that the patient is neither "dying" nor "terminally ill" than it can be denied solely on the ground that the life support involved is a feeding tube rather than a respirator.

III.   "A TOEHOLD FOR EUTHANASIA PRINCIPLES IS PROVIDED BY
THE PRACTICE OF LETTING DIE"

As I have indicated, the proposals Glanville Williams made some thirty years ago for legalizing euthanasia seem rather modest when compared with those being advanced today. But I have passed over one feature of Professor Williams' proposals that may strike many

---

[47] *Id.*

[48] *Id.* at 2856. (O'Connor, J., concurring) (emphasis added).

[49] Despite Nancy's previous expression of her wish to forgo medical treatment under such circumstances as these, wrote Justice Brennan, "the Missouri Supreme Court, alone among state courts deciding such a question, has determined that an irreversibly vegetative patient will remain a passive prisoner of medical technology—for Nancy, perhaps for the next 30 years." *Cruzan*, 110 S. Ct. at 2863-64 (Brennan, J., dissenting).

(or, at least at one time struck many) as quite bold.[50] As had most proponents of euthanasia up to that time, Williams advocated *active* euthanasia.[51]

When Williams returned to the subject a decade and a half later, however, he realized that advocacy of *active* euthanasia had been a mistake—a mistake, I think it fair to say, in strategy, not in principle. Addressing the British Medico-Legal Society, he observed that "the case for voluntary euthanasia seems to have made little impression upon doctors generally."[52] He then considered, against "this background of medical rectitude or rigidity,"[53] "the extent to which the euthanasia movement is likely to make headway in the immediate future":[54]

> A toehold for euthanasia principles is provided by the practice of letting die, or what is now called passive euthanasia. The Roman Catholic Church has for over twenty years accepted that whereas the physician may never kill his patient by positive act, there is a limit to the extent to which he is required to fight for the life of a dying patient. At some point he may refrain from what Pope Puis XII . . . called "advanced techniques" as opposed to "conventional medical treatment." . . . The more common phrases used to express the distinction are "extraordinary measures" as opposed to "ordinary measures."[55]
>
>   . . . .
>
> If this distinction between an act and an omission is thought to be artificial, its artificiality is imposed on us

---

[50] *See* J. FEINBERG, HARM TO SELF (1986). Commenting on various bills to legalize voluntary euthanasia that were introduced in American state legislatures from 1906 to 1974 and similar proposals debated in the House of Lords in 1936, 1950 and 1969, Professor Feinberg notes that "[e]ither no distinction was made between active and passive euthanasia, or the definition of euthanasia clearly included taking active steps to end the suffering patient's life." *Id.* at 367.

[51] *See supra* text accompanying note 14.

[52] Williams, *Euthanasia*, 41 MEDICO-LEGAL J. 14 (1973). Williams also commented that "all the efforts of the euthanasia lobby to change the legal position [with respect to active voluntary euthanasia] have met with complete rejection by the medical profession at large." *Id.* at 16.

[53] *Id.* at 18.

[54] *Id.*

[55] *Id.*

by our refusal to accord the same moral freedom for action as we do for inaction. Pending a change of thought, the concept of an omission is a useful way of freeing us from some of the consequences of overrigid moral attitudes.[56]

The practice of "letting die" did indeed provide euthanasia principles with a "toehold"—and generated an inspired battle cry—the "right to die" or the right to die "naturally."

I share the view that the "right to die" "allows and encourages us to believe that when society makes significant and painfully difficult decisions about life and death, we are making no decision at all, but merely deferring to individual autonomy."[57] But I cannot deny that the "right to die" is a most appealing and seductive slogan. As my colleague Carl Schneider has observed, "when we think about a social problem, we in America today tend to think about it in terms of rights, a mode of thinking we find accessible, convenient and comfortable."[58] But, "defining an interest as a right makes accommodation seem to be the breaching of a right or the defining away of a right and thus, a moral and political wrong."[59]

Although Glanville Williams is not among them, many who support the "right to die" say they are strongly opposed to active euthanasia. I must say I do not find the arguments made by proponents of this distinction convincing. Least persuasive of all, I think, are the arguments that lifting the ban against active euthanasia would be to "embrace the assumption that one human being has the power of life over another"[60] (the withholding or withdrawal of life-sustaining treatment embraces the same assumption) and that maintaining the prohibition against active euthanasia "prevents the grave potential for abuse inherent in any law that sanctions the taking of human life"[61] (passive euthanasia, at the very least, presents the same potential for abuse).

Indeed, I venture to say that a law that sanctions the "taking of

---

[56] *Id.* at 21.

[57] Beschle, *supra* note 12, at 322.

[58] Schneider, *Rights Discourse and Neonatal Euthanasia*, 76 CALIF. L. REV. 151, 154 (1988).

[59] *Id.* at 172.

[60] NEW YORK STATE TASK FORCE REPORT, *supra* note 16, at 42.

[61] *Id.*

human life" indirectly or negatively rather than directly or positively contains much more potential for abuse. Because of the repugnance surrounding active euthanasia—because it is what might be called "straightforward" or "out in the open" euthanasia—I think it may be forcefully argued that it is *less likely* to be abused than other less readily identifiable forms of euthanasia.

Many a Down's syndrome baby has been "allowed to die" by not removing an intestinal blockage or otherwise performing relatively simple surgery.[62] Very few would have died if death were by lethal injection—if parents and physician could not deny what they were doing—if they had to accept the responsibility (or should one say "guilt") for "killing" rather than "letting die."

Glanville Williams was not enamored of the distinction between an "act" that would end life and an "omission" that would do so. Nor did he deny the "artificiality" of the distinction. But, as I read his remarks, he found the distinction serviceable (I am sure he would say beneficial) because it afforded the physician (and the patient's family) much more room to maneuver than would be possible if one had to proceed by lethal injection—and it gave the rest of us, or most of the rest of us, less cause for alarm. As subsequent events have made plain, "the concept of an omission," of withholding or withdrawing life-sustaining treatment, was a pragmatic and most effective way to free euthanasia proponents from the law on the books—and the official morality—against euthanasia (what Williams called "the consequences of overrigid moral attitudes"). But more leeway to decide life-and-death questions and to implement these decisions—and more freedom to evade the ban against euthanasia—means more potential for abuse, not less.

Although she did so unwittingly, of course, recently a strong proponent of the "right to die," Susan Wolf, confirmed the point I have been trying to make (or so it seems to me). Ms. Wolf made a

---

[62] Perhaps the best-known example is the "Hopkins baby," the 1971 Johns Hopkins case involving a Down's syndrome baby born with duodenal atresia, an intestinal blockage. To have fed the child by mouth in this condition would have killed him. The intestinal block could have been removed by relatively easy surgery, but the parents (who rejected the child upon learning of his condition) refused to permit the operation. The physician in charge acquiesced in their decision. The baby was put in a dark corner of the nursery where after fifteen days he became dehydrated enough to die a "natural" death. See Gustafson, *Mongolism, Parental Desires, and the Right to Life,* 16 PERSPECTIVES IN BIOL. & MED. 529, 529-30 (1973).

strong plea for maintaining the prohibition against active euthanasia because if the ban is removed "[t]he courts and prosecutors will
rush in"; "[o]ur own ambivalence toward the dying will surge forward";[63] and "if euthanasia were an accepted option limited to the
few," this would likely "exert pressure similarly to confine the
right to refuse treatment."[64] According to Ms. Wolf, among the
"major benefits" the legal prohibition against active euthanasia has
had "for the development of tolerable law and practice for the termination of treatment" are:

> First, that prohibition has to a large extent allowed the
> law to stay out of the way. Judges generally have en-
> couraged those involved in termination of treatment de-
> cisions to steer clear of the courts; legal authorities have
> almost always determined these bedside treatment deci-
> sions are not the province of the criminal law; and the
> states for the most part have avoided requiring a great
> deal of formality and paperwork. Thus, there has been an
> overall toleration of relatively informal, nonlegalistic
> processes and a trust in the commitment of physicians to
> do no harm.
>
> Second, maintenance of the prohibition has allowed a
> properly expansive reading by the courts of the right to
> refuse life-sustaining treatment. The courts have recog-
> nized this right for nonterminal patients, including those
> whose treatment is relatively simple and unburdensome.
> Dealing with active euthanasia, the courts might have
> been far more reluctant to reach the nonterminal, less
> burdened patient. Even the right of incompetents might
> have been threatened.[65]

Ms. Wolf then spelled out why legalizing active euthanasia
would inhibit the expansion of what she calls "termination of
treatment" and what I call "passive euthanasia":

> Proponents of euthanasia frequently advocate restrict-
> ing the category of those eligible; the recited require-

---

[63] Wolf, *Holding the Line On Euthanasia*, HASTINGS CENTER REP., Jan.-Feb. 1989 (Special Supp.), at 13.
[64] *Id.* at 14.
[65] *Id.* at 13.

ments often include competence, terminality, and intractable pain. In contrast, the courts in the termination of treatment cases have gradually recognized that the category of those who can refuse life-sustaining treatment, or have it refused on their behalf, is very broad. . . .

Would vindication of the right to refuse treatment have extended so far if there were a right to euthanasia limited to a narrow set of patients? Theoretically the two groups might be differently delimited, yet this would generate substantial tension. . . .

[The] inclination to restrict the category of those who can refuse life-sustaining treatment has generally been beaten back in the courts. But against the background of a restricted right to euthanasia, the inclination might well have prevailed.[66]

IV.   Should we Distinguish Between the Feeding Tube and Other Forms of Life Support? Between "Artificial Feeding" and "Natural" Feeding?

As indicated by the quotation from his address to the British Medico-Legal Society, Glanville Williams not only turned to a distinction that had its origin in Roman Catholic tradition, that between "killing" and "letting die," but alluded to another distinction that had it origins in the same tradition, that between "extraordinary" (or "heroic") and "ordinary" medical treatment.[67] What treatment *is* "extraordinary"? It soon became clear that little, if anything, turned on the *type* of medical treatment *in the abstract* but much, if not everything, turned on the condition of a given patient. As the *Quinlan* court observed: "[O]ne would have to think that the use of the same respirator or like support could be considered 'ordinary' in the context of the possibly curable patient but 'extraordinary' in the context of . . . an irreversibly doomed patient."[68]

As the *Quinlan* court suggested, "extraordinary" medical treatment came to mean, or the term was used widely to mean, medical

---

[66] *Id.* at 14.
[67] *See supra* text accompanying note 55.
[68] *In re* Quinlan, 70 N.J. 10, 48, 355 A.2d 647, 668 (1976).

treatment that was undesirable or inappropriate under the circumstances. But *why* was the treatment inappropriate under the circumstances? Because a determination had been made—without regard to the type of life-sustaining treatment involved—that there was no point in keeping the patient alive under the circumstances. Thus, as a presidential commission on the subject noted, the view "that [life-sustaining] treatment is extraordinary is more of an expression of the conclusion than a justification for it."[69]

The extraordinary/ordinary means distinction has been widely criticized and is now widely rejected.[70] I agree that the terms are so spongy and unilluminating and were used so loosely and inconsistently that there is little to be said for retaining them. But in their time, I think, these terms did more than generate confusion.[71] I think they provided reassurance—reassurance that only certain kinds of lifesaving measures could be, and would be, terminated; that disconnecting an unconscious patient's respirator in some vague way only constituted a "slight deviation" from our official morality; that if, as some contended and others wondered, we were making quality of life judgments or engaging in passive euthanasia it was "the . . . thing in its mildest . . . form."[72]

Yes, the time has come to say good riddance to the extraordinary/ordinary means doctrine. But over the years these terms have done their work. Their very vagueness seduced not a few—and, if I may say so, greased the slippery slope.

A. *The Respirator vs. the Feeding Tube*

As we all know, Karen Ann Quinlan's parents sought, and eventually obtained, permission to remove their comatose daughter from the respirator. But it is worth recalling that, probably be-

---

[69] PRESIDENT'S COMMISSION FOR THE STUDY OF ETHICAL PROBLEMS IN MEDICINE AND BIOMEDICAL AND BEHAVIORAL RESEARCH, DECIDING TO FOREGO LIFE-SUSTAINING TREATMENT 88 (1983) [hereinafter PRESIDENT'S COMMISSION].

[70] *See, e.g., id* at 82-89; A. MEISEL, THE RIGHT TO DIE §4.6 (1989); P. RAMSEY, ETHICS AT THE EDGES OF LIFE 153-60 (1978); R. VEATCH, DEATH, DYING, AND THE BIOLOGICAL REVOLUTION 105-14 (1976); Lynn & Childress, *Must Patients Always Be Given Food and Water?*, in BY NO EXTRAORDINARY MEANS 47, 53-55 (J. Lynn ed. 1989) (expanded edition).

[71] *Cf.* Brock, *Forgoing Life-Sustaining Food and Water: Is It Killing?*, in BY NO EXTRAORDINARY MEANS, *supra* note 70, at 117, 130 ("[T]he labeling of treatments as ordinary and extraordinary adds nothing to the analysis—except confusion.").

[72] *Cf. supra* text accompanying note 9 (citing Boyd v. United States, 116 U.S. 616, 635 (1885)).

cause they viewed feeding as "natural" or "basic" or "ordinary" care, Karen's parents did not request permission to remove the feeding tube that was to keep their daughter alive for another nine years. Indeed, Karen's father voiced surprise when asked when he wanted the feeding tube disconnected, replying, "Oh, no, that is her nourishment."[73] Nor did Karen's parents object when, some months after the case was decided, the director of the nursing home where Karen had been moved told them: "I can't see pulling out a feeding tube . . . because that is not a nice way to die, starving and wasting away over a period of weeks."[74]

If the Quinlans had sought permission to remove Karen's feeding tube, they probably would have been rebuffed—even if they could have shown by clear and convincing evidence that this was their daughter's wish. For as recently as the early 1980s the idea that fluids and nutriment might be withdrawn from a comatose patient

> was a notion that would have been repudiated, if not condemned, by most health professionals. They would have regarded such an idea as morally and psychologically objectionable, legally problematic, and medically wrong. The notion would have gone "against the stream" of medical standards of care.[75]

But the views of health professionals have changed—and the law has moved—very quickly in the decade and a half since the *Quinlan* case was decided.

In 1983, a presidential commission found "no particular treatments—including such 'ordinary' hospital interventions as parenteral nutrition or hydration . . . to be universally warranted"[76] and maintained that "[t]he sensitivities of the family and of care giving

---

[73] P. RAMSEY, *supra* note 70, at 270.

[74] J. QUINLAN & J. QUINLAN, KAREN ANN: THE QUINLANS TELL THEIR STORY 310 (1977).

[75] Siegler & Weisbard, *Against the Emerging Stream: Should Fluids and Nutritional Support Be Discontinued?*, 145 ARCHIVES OF INTERNAL MED. 129 (1985); *see also* Bleich, *Providing Nutrition and Hydration for Terminally Ill Patients*, 2 ISSUES IN L. & MED. 117, 127 (1986) ("At least until recent years, there would have been virtual unanimity among ethicists that withdrawal of nutrition and oxygen could not be sanctioned."); Sprung, *Changing Attitudes and Practices in Forgoing Life-Sustaining Treatments*, 263 J. A.M.A. 2211, 2212-13 (April 25, 1990) ("[T]he removal of such life-sustaining treatments as intravenous fluids and nutrition was considered a gross deviation from legal and ethical standards just 7 years ago.").

[76] PRESIDENT'S COMMISSION, *supra* note 69, at 90.

professionals" should determine whether or not permanently unconscious patients should be provided artificial feeding.[77] In 1986, the American Medical Association Council of Ethical and Judicial Affairs took the position that withholding or withdrawing artificially or technologically supplied nutrition or hydration should be evaluated according to the same standards applicable to other kinds of life-sustaining measures.[78]

The following year a Hastings Center taskforce on death and dying reached the same conclusion.[79] The same year, a New York State task force on life and the law also rejected any distinction between artificial nutrition and hydration and other forms of life-support,[80] finding the "symbolic importance" of providing nutrition and hydration outweighed by other considerations.[81]

It is fairly clear that what might be called the "bioethics establishment" no longer sees any need to "draw the line" short of terminating artificial nutrition and hydration. Nevertheless, on the eve of the *Cruzan* case, the issue was still a matter of considerable dispute. A goodly number of respected commentators argued that the distinction should be preserved for various reasons: (1) nutrition and hydration are basic care, not medical treatment; (2) providing such care is an important symbol of our human relatedness and commitment to care; (3) denial of such care poses a serious threat to the doctor-patient relationship; and (4) permitting withdrawal of nutrition and hydration undermines the psychological distinction between "killing" and "letting die."[82]

---

[77] *Id.* at 190.

[78] AMERICAN MED. ASS'N, CURRENT OPINIONS OF THE COUNCIL ON ETHICS AND JUDICIAL AFFAIRS § 2.18 (1986).

[79] THE HASTINGS CENTER, GUIDELINES ON THE TERMINATION OF LIFE-SUSTAINING TREATMENT AND THE CARE OF THE DYING 57-62 (1987).

[80] NEW YORK STATE TASK FORCE, *supra* note 16, at 36-40.

[81] *Id.* at 39.

[82] See generally the contributions of Robert Barry, David Bleich, John Connery, Dennis Horan and Gilbert Meilaender to ISSUES IN L. & MED. (Sept. 1987). See also the summary of the arguments that have been made for preserving the distinction in NEW YORK STATE TASK FORCE, *supra* note 16, at 37-38.

In 1987, ten experts in ethics, law and medicine prepared a statement against the withdrawal of "artificially provided" food and water for people suffering even the severest disabilities. See May, Barry, Griese, Grisez, Johnstone, Marzen, McHugh, Meilaender, Siegler & Smith, *Feeding and Hydrating the Permanently Unconscious and Other Vulnerable Persons*, 3 ISSUES IN L. & MED. 203, 211 (1987) ("It is not morally right, nor ought it to be legally permissible, to withhold or withdraw nutrition and hydration provided by artificial

Moreover, "nearly half" of the forty states that have adopted living-will statutes (including Missouri) "specifically exclude artificial nutrition and hydration from the category of life-sustaining treatment [that may be] refused."[83] I realize that some state courts have taken the position that such legislation does not foreclose the development of judicial doctrine allowing cessation of such medical procedures.[84] Nevertheless, if, as the Supreme Court recently informed us, "the pattern of enacted laws" is "the primary and most reliable indication" of national consensus,[85] the reluctance of many state legislatures to permit the termination of artificial feeding, even where the patient has executed a living will, would seem to pose a formidable obstacle to a constitutionally protected "right to die" in cases like *Cruzan.*

But Chief Justice Rehnquist, who wrote the majority opinion in *Cruzan,* drew no distinction between the feeding tube and other lifesaving measures.[86] And concurring Justice O'Connor explicitly

---

means to the permanently unconscious or other categories of seriously debilitated but nonterminal persons."). A hundred prominent persons from various disciplines and different religious traditions signed the statement. *See id.* at 212-17

[83] Francis, *The Evanescence of Living Wills,* 14 J. CONTEMP. L. 27, 33-34 (1988). *See also* Zinberg, *Decisions for the Dying: An Empirical Study of Physicians' Responses to Advance Directives,* 13 VT. L. REV. 445, 458-590 (1989) (twenty states specifically forbid termination of artificial nutrition and hydration pursuant to a directive).

[84] *See* Cantor, *supra* note 34, at 389.

[85] *See* Stanford v. Kentucky, 109 S. Ct. 2969, 2977 (1989). *See also id.* at 2975 (" '[F]irst' among the 'objective indicia that reflect the public attitude toward a given sanction' are statutes passed by society's elected representatives.").

[86] In describing post-*Quinlan* developments in the state courts, the Chief Justice observed—without any expression of approval or disapproval—that the New Jersey Supreme Court had "rejected certain categorical distinctions that had been drawn in prior refusal-of-treatment cases," such as the distinction "between treatment by artificial feeding versus other forms of life-sustaining medical procedures." Cruzan v. Director, Missouri Dep't of Health, 110 S. Ct. 2841, 2849 (1990). He also noted, again without comment, that recently the Illinois Supreme Court had "adopted the 'consensus opinion [that] treats artificial nutrition and hydration as medical treatment.' " *Id.* at 2850.

The best reading of the Chief Justice's opinion, I think, is that with one possible exception, the distinction between artificial feeding and other kinds of lifesaving measures is a distinction without a constitutional difference. The one possible exception may be evidence of the incompetent patient's wishes. Some people may be willing to remove a respirator or other forms of life support when they are in a certain medical condition, but balk at discontinuing artificial food and water. To put it somewhat differently, some people may have the respirator in mind, but not the feeding tube, when they say they do not want to live "as a vegetable" if and when they become permanently unconscious. Thus, some state courts are likely to require more specific evidence of the patient's wishes, and the Supreme Court is likely to give them more leeway in this regard when the particular form of life support at

rejected any such distinction. As she saw it, the artificial provision of nutrition and hydration implicated the same liberty interests as did other medical interventions—"the liberty guaranteed by the Due Process Clause must protect, if it protects anything, an individual's deeply personal decision to reject medical treatment, including the artificial delivery of food and water."[87] It was almost as if Justice O'Connor were responding to another Justice's argument to the contrary. So far as I can tell, however, *no* member of the Court argued to the contrary.

B. *"Artificial" Feeding vs. "Natural" Feeding*

What next? Not *all* patients in an "irreversible chronic vegetative state," as the court described Mildred Rasmussen's condition,[88] lose their swallowing reflex.[89] In *Rasmussen*, the public fiduciary sought appointment as guardian for the purpose of removing the patient's nasogastric tube. Before the intermediate appellate court could render its decision, the patient died "from complications following pneumonia."[90] In the course of its discussion of the case, the state supreme court noted, without further comment:

> For some reason, Rasmussen's physician removed the nasogastric tube after the petition for guardianship was filed and was surprised to learn that Rasmussen could

---

issue is artificially delivered food and water. In deciding that the Supreme Court of Missouri did not commit constitutional error in concluding that "clear and convincing" evidence of Nancy's wishes was lacking, the Chief Justice noted that the testimony as to Nancy's conversations about not wanting to live as a "vegetable" "did not deal in terms of withdrawal of medical treatment or of hydration and nutrition." *Id.* at 2847.

[87] *Id.* at 2857 (O'Connor, J., concurring).

[88] Rasmussen v. Fleming, 154 Ariz. 207, 218, 741 P.2d 674, 685 (1987). Rasmussen's physician testified that for two years she had been "in a chronic vegetative state from which she had a zero probability of returning to a higher level of functioning." *Id.* at 212-13, 741 P.2d at 679-80. According to a court-appointed neurologist, she "existed in a profound vegetative state from which she would never recover." *Id.* at 213, 741 P.2d at 680.

[89] "[I]t is sometimes possible (if inconvenient) to feed patients in [sic] persistent vegetative state with a spoon since their swallowing reflex persists." Wikler, *Not Dead, Not Dying? Ethical Categories and Persistent Vegetative State*, Hastings Center Rep., Feb.-Mar. 1988, at 41, 44. But feeding a PVS patient by hand "usually requires an enormous amount of time and effort by health care professionals and families." Cranford, *The Persistent Vegetative State: The Medical Reality (Getting the Facts Straight)*, Hastings Center Rep., Feb.-Mar. 1988, at 27, 31.

[90] 154 Ariz. at 213, 741 P.2d at 680. The court nevertheless retained the matter for decision because the issues presented were so important. *Id.*

swallow food on her own. The nursing staff, however, still had to place the food into [her] mouth. The record does not indicate whether the tube was ever reinserted.[91]

Although the *Rasmussen* courts did not address this issue, in the years ahead cases are bound to arise where the courts will be asked to authorize the discontinuance of "natural" feeding. How will they decide this question?

Although some commentators have forcefully argued to the contrary,[92] a plausible case—not a few physicians and ethicists would say an overwhelming case—can be made for the proposition that, unlike "manual feeding" or "regular feeding," "the administration of artificial nutrition has a distinctly medical cast."[93] After all, "[e]ven installation of a simple intravenous tube requires medical expertise"[94] and "[a] gastrostomy tube (as was used to provide food and water to Nancy Cruzan) or jejunostomy tube must be surgically implanted into the stomach or small intestine."[95] Thus, it would be no great feat to draw a legally significant line between artificial or technologically supplied nutrition and say, spoon feeding—or, more generally, between life-sustaining measures that are "medical" in character and those that are not.[96]

---

[91] *Id.* at 212 n.1, 741 P.2d at 679 n.1.

[92] *See supra* note 82 (citing *Issues in Law and Medicine* and New York State Task Force).

[93] Cantor, *supra* note 34, at 384.

[94] *Id.*

[95] Cruzan v. Director, Missouri Dep't of Health, 110 S. Ct. 2841, 2857 (O'Connor, J., concurring).

[96] This, it seems, is where many physicians and ethicists would draw the line today. *See, e.g.,* Ellman, Cruzan v. Harmon *and the Dangerous Claim that Others Can Exercise an Incapacitated Patient's Right to Die,* 29 JURIMETRICS J.L. SCI. & TECH. 389, 391 (1989):

> To [most bioethicists], and to the American Medical Association, the key difference is not between medical care on one hand and food and water on the other; it is between anything technologically supplied—nutrition, air or medicine—and the simple provision of food and water. The Missouri Supreme Court effectively treats the gastronomy tube like the dinner tray, while most authorities treat it like a respirator.

Adds Professor Ellman: "Because presenting food and water to a patient capable of eating and drinking can never be too burdensome, its denial can never be justified." *Id.* at 392. But some will argue that feeding a PVS patient by hand is extremely burdensome. *See, e.g., supra* note 89 (quoting Ronald Cranford). Moreover, what does it mean to say that a patient is "capable of eating and drinking"? Some are bound to draw a distinction between patients able to *feed themselves* and those able to swallow food on their own, but unable to place the food in their mouths on their own.

I think many courts, perhaps most, will draw such a line—at first. But what of the long run?

I very much doubt that the courts, and physicians' groups and ethicists, will "hold the line."[97] There is, to be sure, an important psychological and symbolic distinction between discontinuing artificial feeding and terminating what might be called natural feeding. The trouble is that not very long ago the same important distinction was thought to exist between turning off a respirator and removing a feeding tube. Yet the " 'right to die' movement" was powerful enough to override that once-formidable distinction in the space of a single decade.

"[T]he history of our activities and beliefs concerning the ethics of death and dying," it has been well said, "is a history of lost distinctions of former significance."[98] What reason is there to think that that history has come to an end? What reason is there to doubt that in the not-too-distant future the distinction between artificial and natural feeding will become still another "lost distinction of former significance"?

Why, it will be asked, should we dwell on "the details" of the method of feeding? People, we will be reminded, have rights and liberties, *not* spoons or bottles—no more than do respirators or gastrostomy tubes. The focus, we will be told, should be on the patient's condition, not her particular feeding mechanism.[99]

As I have already noted, at the time the *Quinlan* case arose, any attempt to remove Karen's feeding tube would have met strong resistance. But if Karen could have been fed "naturally," any attempt to terminate such feeding would have met overwhelming resistance. Indeed, I seriously doubt that anyone at that time would have had the audacity to ask a court to permit cessation of such feeding.

---

[97] One way to deal with this problem, and others raised by patients in a persistent vegetative state, is to "adjust[] our thinking about death," to "change[] the focus from biological to psychological processes," and to expand the definition of "death" to include "permanent loss of sentience." Wikler, *supra* note 89, at 44-45. If this change in definition were adopted, "cessation of treatment would not ever require an invocation of the patient's wishes." *Id.* at 44. If this definition were adopted, one might add, cessation of treatment would be permitted even in the face of the PVS patient's previously expressed wishes *to the contrary. See generally infra* text accompanying notes 118-20.

[98] Mayo, *Constitutionalizing the "Right to Die,"* 49 MD. L. REV. 103, 144 (1990).

[99] *Cf.* G. ANNAS, *Do Feeding Tubes Have More Rights than Patients?*, in JUDGING MEDICINE 302, 308 (1988).

However, what we cannot do—perhaps cannot even think about doing—in one step we are often able to do in two or three. Professor Schneider has called this "a psychological aspect of slippery slopes: they work partly by domesticating one idea [say, disconnecting the respirator] and thus making its nearest neighbor down the slope seem less extreme and unthinkable."[100]

Putting aside psychology, emotion and symbolism, the distinction between artificial and manual feeding *does* seem rather thin. After all, if one believes that a person suffering the plight of Nancy Cruzan or Mildred Rasmussen is "better off dead" (and it is plain that a great many people do), why keep her alive for many months, or even years, simply because she can be spoon fed?

The trouble (at least the trouble for me) is that putting aside psychology, emotion and symbolism, the distinction between "letting die" and active euthanasia seems quite thin, too. After all, if a person would be "better off dead" and she has a "right to die," or a "liberty interest" in not being kept alive in a permanently unconscious or barely conscious state, why does she not have the right or the liberty to choose what *she regards* (or her loved ones are convinced she would regard) as the most "humane" or "dignified" way to die?

V. When Is There A "Right to Die"? When Is There *No* "Right to Live"? Professor Robertson's Views on Both Questions

I concur in much that Professor Robertson had to say at this conference about the Supreme Court's decision in the *Cruzan* case. I agree that, whether or not one believes Missouri's vitalist posture toward Nancy Cruzan can be justified as a matter of ethics and policy (and Professor Robertson makes plain his belief that it cannot), "the Supreme Court's decision upholding this posture was correct as a matter of constitutional law."[101]

---

[100] Schneider, *supra* note 58, at 168. *See also* Burt, *Authorizing Death for Anomalous Newborns*, in Genetics and the Law 435, 440 (A. Milunsky & G. Annas eds. 1976).

[101] Robertson, *Cruzan and Nontreatment Decisions*, *supra* note 27, at 1156. *See also* Baron, *On Taking Substituted Judgment Seriously*, Hastings Center Rep., Sept.-Oct. 1990, at 7 ("I am a long-time advocate of patient's rights in general and the right to die in particular, but . . . [the *Cruzan*] Court, in my opinion, did not have legal authority to do what the Cruzans asked of it.").

As Professor Robertson observes:

> If [Nancy Cruzan] had no interest in further living . . .
> it does not necessarily follow that she also had an inter-
> est in dying. If allowing her to die cannot harm her . . .
> she cannot be harmed by further maintenance either.
> Nancy Cruzan simply had no further interests in being
> treated or not being treated. . . .
>   . . . How valid are the concerns about the indignity and
> humiliation which result from being sustained artificially
> which animate the dissenting opinions of Justices Bren-
> nan and Stevens? . . .
>   . . . [B]ecause [a permanently unconscious patient like
> Nancy Cruzan is] not capable of feeling the indignity or
> humiliation which may result from artificial treatment,
> these concerns do not show that gastrostomy feeding
> harmed Nancy Cruzan.[102]

Moreover,

> [A] state requirement for treatment of an incompetent
> patient would violate a right to refuse treatment by ad-
> vance directive only if the person, when competent, had
> in fact directed that treatment not occur. Inferences or
> guesses that the patient would have issued such a direc-
> tive if she had thought of it are not equivalent to making
> a directive.
>   . . . .
>   The majority's conclusion that the state may legiti-
> mately require a high degree of certainty that a prior di-
> rective against treatment has been made is neither irra-
> tional nor unjustifiably obstructive of such choices. If
> there is a right to refuse medical care in advance, state
> requirements to ensure that the right has in fact been ex-
> ercised serve legitimate state interests in protecting life
> and in preventing erroneous determinations about what
> the patient had chosen when she was competent.[103]

I also share Professor Robertson's view that the Court properly

---

[102] Robertson, Cruzan *and Nontreatment Decisions, supra* note 27, at 1158-59.
[103] *Id.* at 1163-64.

rejected the Cruzans' back-up argument that, even in the absence of substantial proof that their decision reflected the wishes of their daughter, they had an independent right to decide Nancy's fate as part of a fundamental right of "family autonomy" or "family privacy." *As a matter of constitutional law*, family autonomy has never embraced the right to terminate a close family member's life support and its sphere should not be expanded to include it.[104] As Professor Ira Mark Ellman put it on the eve of *Cruzan*:

> [A]ny constitutional rule protecting each individual's right to make her own medical decisions emerges from a principle of self-determination—or autonomy—and can therefore protect only an individual's right to make decisions about her own treatment. A guardian's or family member's judgment is not entitled to the special deference arising from the autonomy principle, for it is a judgment that one person makes about another, not a judgment that the patient makes about herself.
>
> . . . Since the autonomy principle is foundational to any constitutional claim that individuals may decide for themselves whether to accept or refuse life-sustaining treatment, the constitutional claim fails in [the *Cruzan*] case. The family's claim to decide cannot be piggybacked on Nancy's autonomy.[105]

I agree too, that the *Cruzan* majority's use of the term "liberty interest" rather than a "constitutional right of privacy"[106] is "a significant move in the Court's ongoing debate about the derivation of unwritten rights from the open-textured clauses of the Constitution"[107] and that this move is not merely "symbolic" but one that "could substantially affect the standard of scrutiny that state restrictions on treatment refusals must meet."[108]

---

[104] *See id.* at 1170-71.

[105] Ellman, *supra* note 96, at 395. *See also* Ellman, *Can Others Exercise An Incapacitated Patient's Right to Die?*, HASTINGS CENTER REP., Jan.-Feb. 1990, at 47-48.

[106] "Although many state courts have held that a right to refuse treatment is encompassed by a generalized constitutional right of privacy," noted the Court, "we have never so held. We believe this issue is more properly analyzed in terms of a Fourteenth Amendment liberty interest." 110 S. Ct. at 2852 n.7.

[107] Robertson, Cruzan *and Nontreatment Decisions*, *supra* note 27, at 1174.

[108] *Id.* Continues Robertson:

> By avoiding "fundamental right" language, the Court may implicitly allow

Finally, I agree that "*Cruzan* is hardly a decisive defeat for a constitutional 'right to die.' "[109] Indeed, as pointed out earlier, I believe that, although they did not achieve the result they desired in *Cruzan*, "right to die" proponents secured two significant victories: The Court seems to have rejected, or at least indicated that it would reject, any distinction (a) between the feeding tube and other forms of life support and (b) between "dying" or "terminally ill" patients and those whose conditions have stabilized and could be kept alive for many years.[110]

I part company with Professor Robertson, however, when he leaves the *Cruzan* case, when his focus shifts from the constitutional limitations on states, such as Missouri, which take a "vitalist" position to the constitutional restraints, if any, on those jurisdictions which adopt "nonvitalist" policies.[111]

A. Constitutional Restraints, If Any, on "Nonvitalist" State Policies

What about the incompetent but conscious patient—one who has "some interest in treatment" because that treatment is not harmful and provides "some additional, conscious life"? According to Robertson, if the additional life "is of very marginal quality," a state is free to conclude that "human life in such a diminished state need not be maintained if there are significant costs involved" (for example, if the burdens to "family, taxpayers or others" are great).[112] Indeed, Robertson goes so far as to say that "*[o]nly* where the interests in further living are *very clear and substantial* should the state be prevented from withholding

---

states to restrict this "liberty interest" upon a lesser showing of need than it would require if that interest were characterized as a fundamental right, thereby requiring the state to meet the rigorous standard of scrutiny traditionally applied to violations of fundamental rights.

Id.

[109] *Id.* at 1145 n.19.

[110] *See supra* text accompanying notes 41-49 & 86-87.

[111] "From the vitalist perspective, all human life is viewed as worthy of protection regardless of its quality or functional ability." Robertson, Cruzan *and Nontreatment Decisions, supra* note 27, at 1140. Nonvitalists "accept quality of life judgments"; they regard human life as worth protecting "only if that life meets certain minimal standards of functional ability." *Id.* at 1141.

[112] *Id.* at 1195.

treatment."[113]

The state has even more leeway to adopt nonvitalist policies, Professor Robertson tells us, when dealing with permanently unconscious patients.[114] "Such policies could take the form of allowing family or proxy to decide about treatment *on any basis, including their own interest*; in having state or private insurers withhold payment for maintenance of such patients; or adopting a cognitive death definition of brain death."[115]

Robertson asks, but does not directly answer, whether permanently unconscious patients are "persons" under the Constitution.[116] A reasonable approach, he tells us, is to say that "they are legal persons but lack interests that need protection from state nonvitalist positions."[117] Then, as I see it, they are *not* "legal persons" after all or *might as well not be called* legal persons.

I do not think Professor Robertson would disagree. At one point he observes that if a state wanted to define PVS patients or other permanently unconscious persons as "dead" it is "difficult to see" what would prevent it from doing so.[118]

What does it mean to say that defining a permanently unconscious patient as "dead" is "within state power"?[119] It means, I take it, that a hospital could *require* the termination of a PVS patient's life support over the objection of every close family member and could do so even though, when still a vibrant person, the patient explicitly and emphatically stated in writing that if she ever

---

[113] *Id.* at 1196 (emphasis added).

[114] In describing PVS patients and others who are permanently unconscious, Professor Roberston, as do many commentators, uses the terms "irreversibly comatose," "permanently comatose" or, sometimes, simply "comatose." *See id.* at 1196-99. However, according to Ronald Cranford, a leading authority on the PVS patient and a neurologist who was a consultant to the Cruzan family, PVS patients are unconscious, but not comatose, as many believe; "permanent unconsciousness" is the best term to describe them. *See* Cranford, *supra* note 89, at 28. Therefore, except when quoting Professor Robertson directly, I shall refer to PVS patients as "permanently unconscious" patients.

[115] Robertson, Cruzan *and Nontreatment Decisions, supra* note 27, at 1197 (emphasis added).

[116] *Id.*

[117] *Id.*

[118] *See id.* at 1199 ("Whatever the policy arguments against [taking the] position [that cortical death is death for all purposes], it is difficult to see that it would be unconstitutional.").

[119] "[A] definitional approach to the irreversibly comatose," observes Robertson, "would be within state power despite strong policy reasons against adopting such a position." *Id.* (footnote omitted).

became permanently unconscious she wanted to be kept alive. Dead is dead. Moreover, why bother about turning off respirators or removing feeding tubes? Why not simply administer a lethal injection? Dead is dead.

Nor is that all. Professor Robertson himself notes that if a state expands the definition of "brain death" to include the PVS patient, as he is fairly confident a state could do, "[as] a corollary," such a patient "could be used as a source of organs or as a subject of experimentation."[120] Again, dead is dead.

Does anyone really believe that if a number of states expanded their definition of "death" to include permanently unconscious patients, that would be the end of it? Does anybody really doubt that ten or twenty years down the road the definition would be expanded *again*? The next time around, the definition of "death" would, at the least, embrace elderly, incompetent patients who, though in extreme states of disability, are conscious—people such as Claire Conroy[121] or Mary O'Connor,[122] people who could be described as "minimally responsive" or "barely conscious."[123]

Unless and until the definition of "death" is expanded, a state may adopt what Robertson calls a "loose substituted judgment" test[124] or it may utilize what he variously calls a "best interests" or "patient's current interests" or "current best interests" test.[125] The latter test is not based, as is the substituted judgment test, on "what the patient would have chosen if she were competent."[126] Rather, Robertson tells us (*some* of the time), it focuses on "what

---

[120] *Id.* at 1199 n.203.

[121] See *In re* Conroy, 98 N.J. 321, 486 A.2d 1209 (1985).

[122] See *In re* Westchester County Medical Center, 72 N.Y.2d 517, 531 N.E.2d 607, 534 N.Y.S.2d 886 (1988).

[123] In an article Professor Robertson wrote recently with Professor Dresser, the authors take the position that conscious patients "cannot reasonably be said to have any continued interest in living" when their "level of awareness is so minimal" that they are "unable to appreciate being alive" and state further that "incompetent patients with minimal 'relational capacity,' such as Nancy Cruzan, Claire Conroy or Mary O'Connor, lack significant interests in having their lives maintained." Dresser & Robertson, *Quality of Life and Non-Treatment Decisions for Incompetent Patients: A Critique of the Orthodox Approach*, 17 Law, Med. & Health Care 234, 240 (1989).

[124] *See* Robertson, *Cruzan and Nontreatment Decisions*, *supra* note 27, at 1190-94. Robertson calls the test the *loose* substituted judgment approach because "[n]o requirement of actual evidence of past wishes is needed." *Id.* at 1192.

[125] *See id.* at 1194-95.

[126] *See id.* at 1192.

serves this patient's interests in her current situation of illness and permanent incompetency."[127]

As I hope to show in the next segment of this Paper, the "patient's current interests" test, an approach that Robertson favors, is misnamed, or at least misleading. In practice, I venture to say, it will not consider *the patient's* present circumstances as much as it will take into account the totality of the circumstances (especially the family's). In practice, I think, it will not turn on the "best interests" of the patient as often as it will turn on the "best interests" *of the family*—or *of society* generally. As Robertson recognizes elsewhere, one applying the "best interests" test, as he explains that test, will inevitably grapple with "quality of life assessments and the conflicts they pose with other interests."[128]

In the paper he presented at this conference, one might say, Professor Robertson only addressed the question whether a state is *constitutionally free* to adopt the "best interests" approach he describes. But Robertson leaves no doubt that he considers this test a better one than the more traditional substituted judgment approach.[129] And in a recent article he co-authored with Professor Rebecca Dresser, one that treats the best interests test more extensively than he did at this conference, Robertson makes it even clearer that he considers such an approach not merely constitutionally permissible, but good public policy.[130]

B. Robertson's "Best Interests" Test vs. A "Loose Substituted Judgment" Approach. How would Robertson's "Best Interests" Test Work?

As already indicated, I have considerable difficulty understanding what Professor Robertson means by a "best interests" test or

---

[127] *Id.* at 1194.

[128] *See* Dresser & Robertson, *supra* note 123, at 242: "The comparative advantage of the current interests test is that quality of life assessments and the conflicts they pose with other interests are faced openly, rather than in the guise of family or proxy decision of what the patient would choose if competent." If Robertson deems it desirable to face quality of life assessments and the conflicts they pose *with other interests* openly and honestly, he might consider changing the name of the test.

[129] *See* Robertson, *Cruzan and Nontreatment Decisions, supra* note 27, at 1194-96, 1201-02. Indeed, at two points Professor Robertson suggests that the "best interests" test is not only constitutionally permissible, but may be constitutionally required. *See id.* at 1195, 1201.

[130] *See* Dresser & Robertson, *supra* note 123, *passim.*

just how it would work. Sometimes he tells us that the test will focus only on the patient's present condition and will serve only *her* interests from *her* perspective. At other times, however, he seems to say something quite different.

Putting aside these inconsistencies for the moment, I cannot help wondering why, considering the other things he has to say about permanently unconscious and minimally conscious patients, Robertson would be attracted to a best interests *of the patient* test.

He emphasizes repeatedly that permanently unconscious patients "ha[ve] no further interests in being treated or not being treated."[131] Indeed, "they lack the mental substrate essential to the possession of interests."[132] Moreover, he has indicated elsewhere that conscious patients "cannot reasonably be said to have any continued interest in living"—and presumably no interest in dying either—if their "level of awareness is so minimal that [they are] unable to appreciate being alive."[133]

One might argue that maintaining the life of a permanently unconscious or minimally conscious patient is, or may be, a violation of that person's bodily integrity or dignity. But Robertson would disagree. Concerns about indignity and humiliation "cannot matter" to such a patient, he tells us, because she "lacks awareness of her situation and its impact on her family."[134] "The real offense" is *not* to the patient, who is incapable of feeling the indignity or humiliation that may result from medical intervention, but "to competent observers, *whose own concepts* of what constitutes dignified and respectful medical treatment for seriously compromised human beings have been violated."[135]

One might also argue that maintaining the existence of a permanently unconscious or minimally conscious person violates that person's *previous* values and interests. Again, however, Robertson would disagree. As he sees it, with the possible exception of the

---

[131] Robertson, Cruzan *and Nontreatment Decisions, supra* note 27, at 1158.

[132] *Id.* at 1157. *See also id.* at 1161-62 ("When the patient is irreversibly comatose . . . neither treatment nor its absence serves her interests because the patient lacks the mental capacity to have any interests whatsoever.").

[133] *See supra* note 123 (quoting Dresser & Robertson article).

[134] Robertson, Cruzan *and Nontreatment Decisions, supra* note 27, at 1159 (footnote omitted). *See also id.* at 1189.

[135] Dresser & Robertson, *supra* note 123, at 238 (emphasis added).

relatively rare case where a person has issued an explicit advance directive concerning medical conditions that have come to exist, "the patient's previous values and interests are no longer relevant to her because her situation has changed so drastically."[136] Indeed, a "key point" of his paper is that "respect for incompetent persons requires focusing on their present interests and welfare, not on the interests and values they had when they were competent."[137]

Where does this take us? If (a) only in the unusual case will the incompetent, severely debilitated patient have made an advance directive concerning future medical conditions; (b) in the usual case, where an explicit advance directive is lacking, the patient's previous values and interests are "no longer relevant" and thus not to be considered; (c) permanently unconscious or minimally conscious patients have *no* interest in living *or* in dying; and (d) such patients are incapable of feeling any of the indignity or humiliation that *others* may feel when they view them, in many cases what, if anything, will be accomplished by focusing on the *patient's* interests from *her* perspective?

The "best interests of the patient" test, unlike the substituted judgment approach, asserts Robertson, "has the great virtue of asking the right question because it recognizes that the decision affects the incompetent patient as she now is, not as she previously was."[138] It strikes me, however, that in many cases (at least if the test is taken seriously and applied strictly) Robertson's approach will have a great shortcoming—it will ask an *unanswerable* question.

Robertson tells us (some of the time) that his "best interests" test focuses on "the present interests of the incompetent patient, viewed from *her* current perspective"[139] and that it addresses "what serves *this* patient's interests in her current situation of illness and permanent incompetency."[140] But won't many incompetent, severely debilitated patients lack *any* interests? Won't many be unable to view anything from *their* perspective?

Robertson also tells us that his test "aims to protect the inter-

---

[136] Robertson, Cruzan *and Nontreatment Decisions, supra* note 27, at 1191. *See also* Dresser & Robertson, *supra* note 123, at 236.

[137] Robertson, Cruzan *and Nontreatment Decisions, supra* note 27, at 1201.

[138] *Id.* at 1144.

[139] *Id.* at 1194 (emphasis added).

[140] *Id.* (emphasis added).

ests of the present incompetent patient, rather than to serve *other* interests"[141] and that if this test is applied the decision "will be driven by respect for the patient, *rather than for other interests*."[142] But if, as Robertson tells us, many incompetent, debilitated persons have no interests to speak of, or no significant ones, won't a decisionmaker who rigorously applies this test often hit a blank wall? Isn't the decisionmaker likely to—indeed, bound to—look *beyond* the best interests of the patient from the *patient's* perspective? Isn't it almost inevitable that the decisionmaker will take into account *other* interests?

As Robertson's discussion proceeds, it becomes clear, I think, that this is so. "The most difficult policy questions will arise," he points out,

> in situations involving conscious, incompetent patients who have some slight interest in further treatment but where treatment would be burdensome for the patient's family, taxpayers or others. The advantage of loose substituted judgment is that it permits nontreatment to occur without confronting this conflict. On the other hand, *if a best interests test is followed, the conflict will inevitably arise.*[143]

Why, if we apply a best interests *of the patient* test strictly, will a conflict arise? Why should there *be* a "conflict"? If further treatment does serve *this* patient's interest, albeit slightly—and Robertson tells us that it does—why should it matter that maintaining her existence would burden "family, taxpayers or others"? Why shouldn't *the only thing that matters* be that the patient *does have* "some slight interest in further treatment"?

After all, there is always the possibility, however remote, that (a) a misdiagnosis has occurred or (b) a remarkable recovery may take place or (c) a miracle "cure" will be discovered.[144] *From the per-*

---

[141] *Id.* at 1195 (emphasis added).

[142] *Id.* (emphasis added).

[143] *Id.* at 1195-96 (emphasis added, footnote omitted).

[144] *Cf.* Cantor, *supra* note 34, at 413. Professor Cantor notes that, if a permanently unconscious patient "senses no detriment in an indefinite limbo, it is not so clear that his or her material best interests dictate removal of life-support." *Id.* Moreover, the best interests of the permanently unconscious patient, "as customarily measured in terms of physical and emotional benefits and burdens to the patient, are not determinable." *Id.* at 436.

spective of the patient, from the vantage point of *her* own net best interests, this is *not* a difficult case, let alone the most difficult one. It is, or ought to be, an easy case. If it is not, then we are not applying a best interests *of the patient* test.

Further evidence that we are not doing so when we apply Professor Robertson's test is provided, I think, by the 1989 article he co-authored with Professor Dresser. In that article the authors leave little doubt that what they call "the incompetent patient's current interests" test[145] is not strictly *a patient's* current interests test:

> An alternative approach [to the substituted judgment test] that is more likely . . . to give factors external to patient welfare their proper role is to ask whether treatment actually serves the incompetent patient's existing interests. If treatment cannot succeed in supplying patients with an acceptable quality of life, then external considerations should be permitted to affect the decision. *If treatment would serve patient interests but would impose heavy burdens on family or society, the conflict can be faced openly.*[146]

I do not deny that it is better to face a conflict openly rather than to deal with it covertly. Again, however, once it is stipulated, as it is, that "treatment would serve patient interests," why—under an "incompetent patient's current interests" test—should *there be* any "conflict" between the patient's interests and the "heavy burdens" her existence imposes "on family or society"? Why should "factors external to patient welfare" play *any* role—why should these "external considerations" be permitted to influence the life-or-death decision—if treatment does not assure an "acceptable quality of life"? Acceptable *to whom*? If the patient

---

Although he would favor termination of life support in many, or all, of the same cases that Professor Robertson would, Professor Cantor "prefers to call the applicable legal standard 'preservation of human dignity,' rather than 'best interests' of the patient." *Id.* However, Professor Robertson would not agree. *See supra* text accompanying notes 134-35. According to him, concerns about the indignity and humiliation which may result from medical treatment "cannot matter to the comatose patient, who lacks awareness of her situation and its impact on her family." Robertson, *Cruzan and Nontreatment Decisions, supra* note 27, at 1159.

[145] *See* Dresser & Robertson, *supra* note 123, at 240.

[146] *Id.* (emphasis added).

"obtains negligible benefits from life"[147] and experiences no pain and suffering, why would her continued existence be unacceptable *to her*?

Although I have serious problems with Professor Robertson's "best interests" approach, I have no affection for the "loose substituted judgment" test—one that he subjects to much-deserved criticism.[148] As other commentators have pointed out, ascertaining what a person would have decided if she miraculously became competent and aware of her present plight "is a quixotic enterprise in the absence of clearcut prior expressions by the patient,"[149] an enterprise that often "serves to mask the extent to which the decision is being made by another."[150]

The trouble is that much of Professor Robertson's criticism of this approach applies to his "best interests" test as well. Robertson complains that the substituted judgment test "ignores the patient's current interests,"[151] but according to him many severely debilitated patients have no interests or no significant ones to consider. Moreover, as the Dresser and Robertson article makes plain, even under Robertson's "best interests" test, "external considerations" may override a patient's net best interests. In practice, I fear, these "external considerations" will often play a decisive role.

A "substituted judgment" approach, observes Robertson and his co-author, "has a strong allure."[152] But so does a "best interests of the patient" test. Who can be *against* such a test? *Each* test carries a cosmetic label. Robertson's "best interests of the patient" test may mask the extent to which the decision serves interests *other than* the patient's every bit as much as the substituted judg-

---

[147] *In re* Conroy, 98 N.J. 321, 486 A.2d 1209 (1985) permits the termination of life-sustaining treatment, absent any explicit treatment directive or other clear evidence of an incompetent patient's past preferences, if the patient experiences pain so great that continued treatment would be "inhumane." Elsewhere in their article, Professors Dresser and Robertson criticize *Conroy* for articulating the benefit-burden analysis too narrowly, for the case "fails to include such factors as lack of awareness and relational capacity. Thus, it does not authorize nontreatment [the death] of permanently unconscious or barely conscious patients *who obtain negligible benefits from life*, but experience no pain and suffering." Dresser & Robertson, *supra* note 123, at 241 (emphasis added).

[148] *See* Robertson, Cruzan *and Nontreatment Decisions*, *supra* note 27, at 1142-44, 1190-94.

[149] Cantor, *supra* note 34, at 412.

[150] Beschle, *supra* note 12, at 364.

[151] Robertson, Cruzan *and Nontreatment Decisions*, *supra* note 27, at 1191.

[152] Dresser & Robertson, *supra* note 123, at 235.

ment approach may mask the extent to which the decisionmaker is exercising his own judgment, not trying to ascertain the patient's.

One reason the substituted judgment test is so attractive, we are told, is that "it recognizes a central role for family discretion in treatment decisions for incompetent patients."[153] The same can be said, however, for the "best interests of the patient" approach. "Close scrutiny of the family's assessment" of what the patient would choose if competent or what the patient in fact once said, Professors Dresser and Robertson point out, "is frequently omitted, thus giving [family members] ultimate discretion to decide the matter."[154] I agree. But I fail to see why the family's assessment of the patient's best interests will receive any closer scrutiny if, as will often be the case, physicians and family members will agree that the patient's quality of life is not "acceptable" or that the patient's state of existence is not "a sufficient good to justify further treatment."[155]

Under *either* test, I think, the likelihood is the same: In almost all cases in which the attending physician concurs in the family decision, neither family members nor physicians will have to justify their choice, nor will the decision be reviewed by a disinterested party.[156]

Under the "loose substituted judgment" test, protests Robertson, the family "is asked to decide what the patient would have chosen if she were competent but is given no guidance in choosing among the several meanings that that capacious phrase might have."[157] But under his "best interests" test "external considerations" come into play whenever treatment cannot provide patients with "an acceptable quality of life"—and that is a capacious phrase if I ever saw one. Moreover, assessing best interests "requires observers to evaluate from the incompetent patient's perspective indications of [her] subjective state, and ultimately, to judge whether this state of existence is *a sufficient good* to justify further treatment of the patient."[158]

When it comes to capacious questions, it is hard to top whether

---

[153] *Id.*

[154] *Id.*

[155] *See infra* text accompanying note 158.

[156] *Cf.* Robertson, *Involuntary Euthanasia, supra* note 38, at 268.

[157] Robertson, *Cruzan and Nontreatment Decisions, supra* note 27, at 1192.

[158] Dresser & Robertson, *supra* note 123, at 240 (emphasis added).

one's state of existence is "a sufficient good." That strikes me as *the ultimate* capacious phrase. If it has a rival, it is whether a patient has an "acceptable quality of life."

VI. Some Final Thoughts

Now that I have come to the end of my remarks, I realize that I have given the *Cruzan* case rather short shrift.[159] One reason is that Professor Robertson's analysis of *Cruzan* was so thoughtful, careful and thorough (I like to believe I would have said that even if I did not agree with him so much) that it left me very little to say about the case.

Another reason is that Professor Robertson took a long, hard look at the other side of the coin: When does a person have a constitutional "right to *live*"? A great deal of attention has been paid to the constitutional limitations on states, such as Missouri, that take a "vitalist" position. Robertson, though, addresses a question that has rarely been asked: What constitutional restraints, if any, are there on states that want to adopt "*non*vitalist" policies? I must confess that I had not thought about *this* issue very much until I read Robertson's paper. The more I think about it, however, the more I realize how difficult this issue is and the more I wonder why, until now, it has been so neglected.

This conference has been billed as "*Cruzan* and the 'Right to Die.'" But Professor Robertson gave all of us who attended the conference a big bonus. He made some very trenchant and provocative remarks (they certainly provoked me) about the constitutional "right to live" and when people have no such constitutional right, a topic I think few of us thought much about until today.

I have little doubt that Professor Robertson's comments will stimulate others in the field and generate a good deal of literature on the subject. And when others do take pen in hand they will have to read and reread Professor Robertson's paper. That will be the place to begin.

Because so little has been written or said about when one has no constitutional "right to live," it is easy to criticize *anyone* who is brave enough to wrestle with it. If I had taken the lead in discuss-

---

[159] For a long series of comments on the meaning and scope of *Cruzan*, see W. Lockhart, Y. Kamisar, J. Choper & S. Shiffrin, Constitutional Law: Cases—Comments—Questions 558-65 (7th ed. 1991).

ing this issue rather than merely commenting on Robertson's views, I am not sure what I would have done. I do know that if I had given the Sibley Lecture and Professor Robertson had *followed me* to the podium, I would have caught heavy fire.

I do have one tentative view on the "right to live." I am uncomfortable with a best interests test as well as a substantial judgment approach. I am also uneasy about reexamining, revising and gradually expanding the definition of "death." But if I *had to* choose, if I had to make a "choice of evils," I think I would select the "definitional" approach toward "death," however discomfiting that approach would be. Redefining and expanding the definition of "death" would, as I suggested earlier, pose "slippery slope" problems and it would be a disagreeable task, indeed an abhorrent one. Abhorrence, however, may be a virtue in this case. The very wrenchingness of the enterprise and the very awesomeness of the assignment (it would be hard to escape responsibility this time) would increase the likelihood that the process would move slowly and cautiously.

If a life-or-death judgment must be made, there is something to be said for "a collective social judgment, rather than idiosyncratic choices of parents and committees, as to when social costs outweigh individual benefits."[160] Professor Robertson said that a decade and a half ago when he wrote a much-acclaimed article on the involuntary euthanasia of defective newborns. (He was not reticent about using the "E" word in those days).

If a life-or-death judgment must be made, "it is essential that the circumstances in which nontreatment may be said to be in a patient's best interests be specified beforehand by an authoritative body, and that procedures which assure that a particular case falls within such criteria be followed."[161] Robertson said that, too.

As for granting parents and physicians ultimate discretion to decide these matters, "a central element of procedural justice is impartial decisionmaking after full consideration of relevant information. Yet, neither parents nor physicians are impartial or disinterested; both have a strong personal interest in the outcome of their decision."[162] Once again, Professor Robertson said that fif-

---

[160] Robertson, *Involuntary Euthanasia, supra* note 39, at 266.

[161] *Id.* at 255 n.221.

[162] *Id.* at 263 (footnote omitted).

teen years ago.

As for designating a committee to decide whether to terminate treatment, such an approach "risks losing society's pervasive symbolic commitment to the value of individual life, as well as embarking on the slippery path of rational-utility assessments of public worth."[163] "[E]mbarking on the slippery path"? This time those are Robertson's words, not mine.

I think one who reads Robertson's 1975 article in its entirety will conclude that in those days he balked at adopting *any* test for terminating life-sustaining treatment. "Comparisons of relative worth among persons, or between persons and other interests," he said then, "raise moral and methodological issues that make any argument that relies on such comparisons extremely vulnerable."[164] "Unless the quality of a [defective newborn's] life affects its value, a judgment for which there is no legal precedent," he also said then, "the likelihood that treatment means life should justify [the medical] procedure."[165]

It appears that in the last decade and a half Professor Robertson, along with quite a few others, has (if I may use that term one last time) moved a considerable distance down the slippery slope.

---

[163] *Id.* at 265 (footnote omitted).

[164] *Id.* at 252.

[165] *Id.* at 237 (footnote omitted). One may argue that different considerations govern the termination of treatment for newborns and for the elderly, but Robertson only drew a distinction between defective newborns and "terminally ill" elderly patients, those who "will soon die with or without the [medical] procedure." *Id.* As discussed at length earlier, neither Karen Quinlan nor Nancy Cruzan were "terminally ill" as that term is usually defined and as Robertson defined it. *See supra* Section II.D.